MAKING AGREEMENTS IN MEDIEVAL CATALONIA

This study examines the role of written agreements in eleventh- and twelfth-century Catalonia, and how they determined the social and political order.

By tracing the fate of these agreements – or *convenientiae* – from their first appearance to the late twelfth century, it is possible to demonstrate the remarkable stability of the fluid structures that they engendered in what is generally thought of as "feudal society." The opportunity presented by these records to examine the process of documentary change reveals the true nature and pace of the "transformation of the year 1000." Analysis of the *convenientia* as an instrument of power and its interaction with oral practices contributes to a deeper understanding of the role of the written word in medieval societies. Finally, a broad historiographical context establishes the significance of this study of Catalonia for a more general appreciation of the medieval Mediterranean world. The book thus raises in a forceful way many of the questions most intensely debated by historians of medieval Europe.

ADAM J. KOSTO is Assistant Professor of History, Columbia University.

Cambridge Studies in Medieval Life and Thought
Fourth Series

General Editor:
D. E. LUSCOMBE
Leverhulme Personal Research Professor of Medieval History, University of Sheffield

Advisory Editors:
CHRISTINE CARPENTER
Reader in Medieval English History, University of Cambridge, and Fellow of New Hall

ROSAMOND McKITTERICK
*Professor of Medieval History, University of Cambridge,
and Fellow of Newnham College*

The series Cambridge Studies in Medieval Life and Thought was inaugurated by G. G. Coulton in 1921; Professor D. E. Luscombe now acts as General Editor of the Fourth Series, with Dr. Christine Carpenter and Professor Rosamond McKitterick as Advisory Editors. The series brings together outstanding work by medieval scholars over a wide range of human endeavour extending from political economy to the history of ideas.

For a list of titles in the series, see end of book.

MAKING AGREEMENTS IN MEDIEVAL CATALONIA

Power, order, and the written word, 1000–1200

ADAM J. KOSTO

CAMBRIDGE
UNIVERSITY PRESS

PUBLISHED BY THE PRESS SYNDICATE OF THE UNIVERSITY OF CAMBRIDGE
The Pitt Building, Trumpington Street, Cambridge, United Kingdom

CAMBRIDGE UNIVERSITY PRESS
The Edinburgh Building, Cambridge CB2 2RU, UK
40 West 20th Street, New York, NY 10011-4211, USA
10 Stamford Road, Oakleigh, VIC 3166, Australia
Ruiz de Alarcón 13, 28014 Madrid, Spain
Dock House, The Waterfront, Cape Town 8001, South Africa

http://www.cambridge.org

First published 2001

Printed in the United Kingdom at the University Press, Cambridge

Typeface Monotype Bembo 11/12pt   *System* QuarkXPress™ [SE]

A catalogue record for this book is available from the British Library

Library of Congress cataloguing in publication data

Kosto, Adam J.
Making agreements in medieval Catalonia: power, order, and the written word, 1000–1200
p.   cm. – (Cambridge studies in medieval life and thought; 4th ser.)
Includes bibliographical references and indexes.
ISBN 0 521 79239 8
1. Power (Social sciences) – Spain – Catalonia – History – To 1500.   2. Juristic
acts – Spain – Catalonia – History – To 1500.   3. Oaths – Spain – Catalonia – History – To
1500.   4. Feudalism – Spain – Catalonia – History.   I. Title.   II. Series.

HN590.C36 K67 2001
303.3 – dc21   00-062162

ISBN 0 521 79239 8 hardback

CONTENTS

Contents

FIGURES

TABLES

ACKNOWLEDGMENTS

After many hours alone putting the finishing touches on this study, it is heartening to recall the help I have received from the many individuals who have made this anything but a solitary endeavor. First, the archivists, who kindly granted access and aid to this *nord-americà*: Josep Baucells i Reig (Arxiu Capitular de Barcelona); Reis Fontanals (Biblioteca de Catalunya); Benigne Marquès i Sala (Arxiu Capitular d'Urgell); Josep Maria Marquès i Planagumà (Arxiu Diocesà de Girona); Jaume Riera and Alberto Torra (Arxiu de la Corona d'Aragó); Gabriel Roura i Güibas (Arxiu Capitular de Girona); Marc Taxonera i Comas (Arxiu de l'Abadia de Montserrat); and at the wonderful archive of Vic, Mossèn Miquel S. Gros i Pujol, Ramon Ordeig i Mata, and Rafel Ginebra i Molins. It is with a deep respect for their labors that I offer to them and their staffs, as well as to those at other archives I have consulted, my thanks. Many colleagues on both sides of the Atlantic helped me in various ways, large and small: Agustí Altisent, Rick Barton, Robert Berkhofer, Pierre Bonnassie, Philippe Buc, Montserrat Cabré i Pairet, Fred Cheyette, Marjorie Chibnall, Alan Cooper, Philip Daileader, Robin Fleming, Paul Freedman, Patrick Geary, Matthew Innes, Elka Klein, Geoffrey Koziol, Ramon Martí Castelló, Bruce O'Brien, Susan Reynolds, Josep Maria Salrach, and Nicholas Vincent. Nat Taylor and Jeff Bowman have been particularly generous in sharing with me the fruits of their own labors on our common research interest, as has Pere Benito i Monclús, who has in addition been a good friend and invaluable *cicerone* on each of my visits to his country. Martin Aurell and Michel Zimmermann read parts of the manuscript and offered helpful criticisms. I am alone responsible, of course, for those errors that certainly remain.

This study began as a dissertation, the research for which was funded in part by a Jacob K. Javits Fellowship from the US Department of Education and a Frederick Sheldon Traveling Fellowship from Harvard University. Michael McCormick and Charles Donahue offered valuable criticisms of this study in its earlier form. The transformation from thesis to book started in Seattle, where Bob and Robin Stacey kindly welcomed a wandering scholar; it ended in New York, where David Armitage, Carmela Franklin, Martha Howell, Joel Kaye, Robert Somerville, and others have provided an ideal scholarly community in which to work. It has been my distinct privilege to have as a colleague at Columbia over the past three years Caroline Bynum; she has been a constant source of encouragement and inspiration. Rosamond McKitterick, who was there on the first day of my graduate training, has now reemerged ten years later as a most patient and helpful editor. My greatest scholarly debt is to Thomas Bisson, who introduced me to the riches of the Catalan archives, let me find my own way, and then guided this project to completion with gifts of good humor, wise counsel, access to his library, and the friendship of his family.

For the love, support, and occasional editorial comments of my parents I am truly grateful. Andrea Troxel patiently endured my travels, sat by my side while I wrote, and read every word along the way. These are just some of the expressions of her love that have enabled me to come this far.

AJK
New York
1 April 2000

As this book went to press, two works appeared that provide editions of and commentary on many of the previously unpublished eleventh-century documents cited in the present study: José Enrique Ruiz-Domènec, *Ricard Guillem: Un sogno per Barcellona*, Medioevo mediterraneo 1 (Naples, 1999); Gaspar Feliu et al., eds., *Els pergamins de l'Arxiu Comtal de Barcelona de Ramon Borrell a Ramon Berenguer I*, 3 vols., Col·lecció diplomataris 18–20 (Barcelona, 1999). The latter includes important essays on the chronology, typology, and diplomatics of eleventh-century Catalan archival records.

NOTE ON CITATIONS, DATES, AND NAMES

Citation of sources: (1) Whenever possible, I have cited in the notes the original documents that I have consulted rather than printed editions. While this practice may prove inconvenient for scholars using a particular edition, many of these documents are (or will be) edited or registered in more than one place, and an original offers the only unique reference. Originals for which a printed edition or register entry exists are designated with an asterisk (★) and listed in the Table of Published Documents (below, p. 295). (2) In transcriptions from originals, I have generally followed Robert-Henri Bautier, "Normalisation internationale des méthodes de publication des documents latins du Moyen Âge (2ᵉ édition)," *Bulletin philologique et historique (jusqu'à 1610) du Comité des travaux historiques et scientifiques: Année 1976* (1978), 9–54. In transcriptions from printed sources, however, I have followed strictly the practice of the various editors. This has resulted in some apparent inconsistencies, especially concerning the treatment of the consonantal u (which I transcribe as v), -ti-/-ci-, and numerals. I have employed "*sic*" only rarely; given the poor quality of some published editions and the peculiarities of the Latin of the original documents themselves, it should be understood for all transcriptions. (3) For frequently cited published sources (those listed in Abbreviations II, below, p. xvi), I refer to document rather than page numbers, unless otherwise noted. (4) Alternate published sources are listed in [brackets] following the main citation.

Dates: For Catalan documents in the period 1001–1180, I follow the dating system proposed by Anscari M. Mundó, by which the regnal year for all French kings changes on 24 June ("La datació de documents pel rei Robert [996–1031] a Catalunya," *Anuario de estudios medievales* 4 [1967], 13–34; "El concili de Tarragona de 1180: Dels anys dels reis francs als de l'Encarnació," *Analecta sacra Tarraconensia* 67:1 [1994], xxiii–xliii). While in occasional cases this system cannot be correct, I have found many more in which it obviously is, and thus I have adopted it as a general rule. This explains the occasional variation of one year of my dates from those given in the printed sources. For dating up to 1000, I have followed *ACondal*, pp. 44–80 (and table), although see now *DBarcelona*, pp. 42–55, 144–55. After 1180 (until 1351), dating from the Annunciation (25 March), "Florentine style," is the norm.

Names: With the exception of "Catalonia" itself, place names are given in modern Catalan forms for locations within historical Catalonia, including Valènica and Rosselló (Roussillon); for identifications, I have relied on Joan Coromines, ed., *Onomasticon Cataloniae*, 8 vols. (Barcelona, 1989–97) and *Catalunya romànica*, 27 vols. (Barcelona, 1984–98). Outside the region, I have followed local usage (Marseille, not Marsella) or common English forms (Rome, not Roma). Despite drawbacks, I have also followed modern local usage with respect to personal names: thus Alfons I, count of Barcelona, Alfonso VIII, king of Castile, and Alphonse-Jourdain, count of Toulouse. Where no obvious modern equivalent exists, the name is given in *italics* as it appears in the source; common Latin versions are given in the Index of Names (below, p. 346). Publication by modern authors under both Catalan and Castilian versions of their names, as well as the relatively recent standardization of Catalan orthography, prevents absolute bibliographical consistency; I have adopted a single form for each author.

ABBREVIATIONS

I. ARCHIVAL SOURCES

(Unless otherwise noted, archival abbreviations refer to the main series of *pergamins*.)

AAM	Montserrat, Arxiu de l'Abadia de Montserrat
ACA	Barcelona, Arxiu de la Corona d'Aragó
ACB	Barcelona, Arxiu de la Santa Església Catedral Basílica de Barcelona
ACG	Girona, Arxiu Capitular de Girona
ACU	La Seu d'Urgell, Arxiu Capitular d'Urgell
ACV	Vic (AEV), Arxiu Capitular de Vic (calaix/document)
ADG	Girona, Arxiu Diocesà de Girona
ADPO	Perpignan, Archives départementales des Pyrénées-Orientales
AEV	Vic, Arxiu Episcopal de Vic
ALI	ACA, Cancelleria reial, Pergamins Alfons I
AME	Vic (AEV), Arxiu de la Mensa Episcopal (llibre/document)
ap.	apèndix (within ACA series)
BC	Biblioteca de Catalunya
BRI	ACA, Cancelleria reial, Pergamins Berenguer Ramon I
BRII	ACA, Cancelleria reial, Pergamins Berenguer Ramon II
Extra.	ACA, Cancelleria reial, Pergamins Extrainventari
extra.	extrainventari (within ACA series)
LA	ACB, Libri antiquitatum (volume:document)
MEV	Vic (AEV), Museu Episcopal de Vic
OM	ACA, Ordes militars (Gran Priorat de Sant Joan de Jerusalem)
OR	ACA, Ordes religiosos (Monacals)
PEI	ACA, Cancelleria reial, Pergamins Pere I
RBI	ACA, Cancelleria reial, Pergamins Ramon Berenguer I
RBII	ACA, Cancelleria reial, Pergamins Ramon Berenguer II

List of abbreviations

RBIII	ACA, Cancelleria reial, Pergamins Ramon Berenguer III
RBIV	ACA, Cancelleria reial, Pergamins Ramon Berenguer IV
RBorrell	ACA, Cancelleria reial, Pergamins Ramon Borrell
sd	sense data (within ACA series)

II. PUBLISHED DOCUMENTS

ACondal Frederic Udina i Martorell, ed., *El archivo condal de Barcelona: Estudio crítico de sus fondos* (Barcelona, 1951)

Alfonso II Ana Isabel Sánchez Casabón, ed., *Alfonso II Rey de Aragón, Conde de Barcelona y Marqués de Provenza. Documentos (1162–1196)* (Zaragoza, 1995)

CCM Josep Maria Marquès i Planagumà, ed., *Cartoral, dit de Carlemany, del bisbe de Girona (s. IX–XIV)*, 2 vols. (Barcelona, 1993)

CDSG Ramon Martí Castelló, ed., *Col·lecció diplomàtica de la seu de Girona (817–1100)* (Barcelona, 1997)

CPF José Maria Font Rius, ed., *Cartas de población y franquicia de Cataluña*, 2 vols. in 3 parts (Barcelona, 1969–83)

CSCV José Rius Serra, ed., *Cartulario de "Sant Cugat" del Vallés*, 3 vols. (Barcelona, 1945–47)

CTavernoles Josefina Soler García, ed., "El cartulario de Tavernoles," *Boletín de la Sociedad castellonense de cultura* 36 (1960), 196–216, 248–79; 37 (1961), 65–80, 149–206; 38 (1962), 110–26, 218–38, 319–46, 428–42

DACU Cebrià Baraut, ed., "Els documents . . . l'Arxiu Capitular de La Seu d'Urgell," *Urgellia* 2 (1979), 7–145; 3 (1980), 7–166; 4 (1981), 7–186; 5 (1982), 7–158; 6 (1983), 7–243; 7 (1984–85), 7–218; 8 (1986–87), 7–149; 9 (1988–89), 7–312, 403–570 (index); 10 (1990–91), 7–349, 473–625 (index); 11 (1992–93), 7–160

DBarcelona Àngel Fàbrega i Grau, ed., *Diplomatari de la Catedral de Barcelona: Documents dels anys 844–1260*, 1 vol. to date (Barcelona, 1995–)

DI Próspero de Bofarull y Mascaró et al., eds., *Colección de documentos inéditos del Archivo general de la Corona de Aragón*, 50 vols. to date (Barcelona, 1847–)

DOliba Eduard Junyent i Subirà, ed., *Diplomatari i escrits literaris de l'abat i bisbe Oliba* (Barcelona, 1992)

DPoblet Agustí Altisent, ed., *Diplomatari de Santa Maria de Poblet*, 1 vol. to date (Barcelona, 1993–)

DTavèrnoles Cebrià Baraut, ed., "Diplomatari del monestir de Sant

	Sadurní de Tavèrnoles (segles IX–XIII)," *Urgellia* 12 (1994–95), 7–414
DVic	Eduard Junyent i Subirà, ed., *Diplomatari de la Catedral de Vic, segles IX–X* (Vic, 1980–96)
Eixalada-Cuixà	Ramon d'Abadal i de Vinyals, "Com neix i com creix un gran monestir pirinenc abans de l'any mil: Eixalada-Cuixà," *Analecta Montserratensia* 8 (1954–55), 125–337
FA	Thomas N. Bisson, ed., *Fiscal Accounts of Catalonia under the Early Count-Kings (1151–1213)*, 2 vols. (Berkeley, 1984)
Gerri	Ignasi M. Puig i Ferreté, *El monestir de Santa Maria de Gerri (segles XI–XV)*, 2 vols. (Barcelona, 1991)
HGL	Claude de Vic and Joseph Vaissette, *Histoire générale de Languedoc...*, new ed. (Privat), 16 vols. (Toulouse, 1872–1904)
LBSC	Frederic Udina i Martorell, ed., *El "Llibre Blanch" de Santas Creus (Cartulario del siglo XII)* (Barcelona, 1947)
LFM	Francisco Miquel Rosell, ed., *Liber feudorum maior: Cartulario real que se conserva en el Archivo de la Corona de Aragón*, 2 vols. (Barcelona, 1945[–47])
MH	Pierre de Marca, *Marca Hispanica, sive limes Hispanicus . . .* (Paris, 1688; repr. Barcelona, 1998)
NH	Francisco Monsalvatge y Fossas, *Noticias históricas*, 26 vols. (Olot, 1889–1919)
Òdena	María del Carmen Álvarez Márquez, ed., *La baronia de la Conca d'Òdena* (Barcelona, 1990)
Pallars i Ribagorça	Ramon d'Abadal i de Vinyals, ed., *Els comtats de Pallars i Ribagorça*, 2 parts (Barcelona, 1955)
Remences	Miquel Golobardes Vila, *Els remences dins el quadre de la pagesia catalana fins el segle XV*, 2 vols. (Peralada, 1970–73)
Santa Anna	Jesús Alturo i Perucho, ed., *L'arxiu antic de Santa Anna de Barcelona del 942 al 1200 (Aproximació històrico-lingüística)*, 3 vols. (Barcelona, 1985)
STCA	Antoni M. Udina i Abelló, *La successió testada a la Catalunya altomedieval* (Barcelona, 1984)
VL	Jaime Villanueva, *Viage literario a las iglesias de España*, 22 vols. (Madrid, 1803–52)

III. OTHER PUBLISHED SOURCES

Abadal, *L'abat Oliba*	Ramon d'Abadal i de Vinyals, *L'abat Oliba, bisbe de Vic, i la seva època*, 3rd ed. (Barcelona, 1962)
AM	*Annales du Midi*

List of abbreviations

Aurell, *Les noces du comte*   Martin Aurell, *Les noces du comte: Mariage et pouvoir en Catalogne (785–1213)* (Paris, 1995)

Benet, *Gurb-Queralt*   Albert Benet i Clarà, *La família Gurb-Queralt (956–1276)* (Sallent, 1993)

Benito-Kosto-Taylor, "Approaches"   Pere Benito i Monclús, Adam J. Kosto, and Nathaniel L. Taylor, "Three Typological Approaches to Catalonian Archival Evidence, 10–12 Centuries," *Anuario de estudios medievales* 26 (1996), 43–88

Bensch, *Barcelona*   Stephen P. Bensch, *Barcelona and its Rulers, 1096–1291* (Cambridge, 1995)

Bisson, *Medieval Crown*   Thomas N. Bisson, *The Medieval Crown of Aragon: A Short History* (Oxford, 1986)

Bofarull, *Los condes*   Próspero de Bofarull y Mascaró, *Los condes de Barcelona vindicados . . .*, 2 vols. (Barcelona, 1836; repr. 1988)

Bonnassie, *La Catalogne*   Pierre Bonnassie, *La Catalogne du milieu du Xe à la fin du XIe siècle: Croissance et mutations d'une société*, 2 vols. (Toulouse, 1975–76)

Bowman, "Law"   Jeffrey A. Bowman, "Law, Conflict, and Community around the Year 1000: The Settlement of Disputes in the Province of Narbonne, 985–1060" (Ph.D. diss., Yale University, 1997)

Catalunya i França   Xavier Barral i Altet et al., eds., *Catalunya i França meridional a l'entorn de l'any mil / La Catalogne et la France méridionale autour de l'an mil* (Barcelona, 1991)

Cheyette, "Sale"   Fredric L. Cheyette, "The 'Sale' of Carcassonne to the Counts of Barcelona (1067–1070) and the Rise of the Trencavels," *Speculum* 63 (1988), 826–64

CSMLT   Cambridge Studies in Medieval Life and Thought

La formació i expansió   Jaume Portella i Comas, ed., *La formació i expansió del feudalisme català* (Girona, [1986])

Freedman, *Origins*   Paul H. Freedman, *The Origins of Peasant Servitude in Medieval Catalonia* (Cambridge, 1991)

Freedman, *Vic*   Paul H. Freedman, *The Diocese of Vic: Tradition and Regeneration in Medieval Catalonia* (New Brunswick, N.J., 1983)

GMLC   M. Bassols de Climent et al., eds., *Glossarium mediae latinitatis Cataloniae*, 1 vol. to date (Barcelona, 1960–)

J-L   Philipp Jaffé, ed., *Regesta pontificum Romanorum . . .*, 2nd ed., 2 vols. (Leipzig, 1885–88; repr. Graz, 1956)

Kosto, "Agreements"   Adam J. Kosto, "Making and Keeping Agreements in Medieval Catalonia, 1000–1200" (Ph.D. diss., Harvard University, 1996)

Liber iudiciorum   Karl Zeumer, ed., "Liber iudiciorum sive Lex Visigothorum," in Zeumer, ed., *Leges Visigothorum*, MGH Legum sectio I (Hanover, 1902; repr. 1973), 33–456

List of abbreviations

Medieval France	Thomas N. Bisson, *Medieval France and Her Pyrenean Neighbours* (London, 1989)
MGH	Monumenta Germaniae historica
Ourliac, "La *convenientia*"	Paul Ourliac, "La *convenientia*," in Ourliac, *Études d'histoire du droit médiéval* (Paris, 1979), 243–52
Ruiz-Domènec, *L'estructura feudal*	José Enrique Ruiz-Domènec, *L'estructura feudal: Sistema de parentiu i teoria de l'aliança en la societat catalana (c. 980–c. 1220)* (Barcelona, 1985)
Shideler, *Montcadas*	John C. Shideler, *A Medieval Catalan Noble Family: The Montcadas, 1000–1230* (Berkeley, 1983)
Sobrequés, *Els grans comtes*	Santiago Sobrequés, *Els grans comtes de Barcelona*, 4th ed. (Barcelona, 1985)
Symposium internacional	*Symposium internacional sobre els orígens de Catalunya (segles VIII–XI)*, 2 vols. (Barcelona, 1991–92)
Us.	Joan Bastardas i Parera, ed., *Usatges de Barcelona: El codi a mitjan segle XII . . .*, 2nd ed. (Barcelona, 1991)

xix

The Catalan counties, *c.* 1000

INTRODUCTION

On 6 July 985, the armies of the Cordoban dictator al-Manṣūr breached the walls of Barcelona and sacked the city. The Arabic chroniclers give the impression that this was just another successful raid, and there is no reason to believe that al-Manṣūr thought any differently. It was, after all, his twenty-third campaign in just nine years.[1] From the perspective of Barcelona, however, the event was of capital importance, not only because of its effect on the city itself, but for its impact on the imagination of her inhabitants. An early and strong historiographical tradition sees in the events of 985 a formative step in the creation of a Catalan national identity. After the Carolingian reconquest of Barcelona in 801, Charlemagne organized the region between the Conflent and the Ebro River into the Spanish March. Over the course of the ninth and tenth centuries, Barcelona came to predominate over the other counties in the region. While the counts remained loyal to the faltering Carolingian house, they began to operate in an ever more independent fashion. The last Frankish military expeditions into the area took place in the 820s; Guifré I "the Hairy" of Barcelona (878–97) was the last count to be appointed by a Frankish king, Guifré II of Besalú (941–57) the last to swear fidelity. Following al-Manṣūr's attack, Borrell II of Barcelona, reversing his earlier policy, appealed to the Frankish court for aid. By 988, when an offer of assistance in return for renewed promises of fidelity finally arrived, Borrell had lost interest. The Catalan counties went their own way; 985 was the last straw.[2]

[1] Manuel Sánchez Martínez, "La expedición de Al-Manṣūr contra Barcelona en el 985 según las fuentes árabes," in *Catalunya i França*, 293–301; Luis Molina, ed., "Las campañas de Almanzor a la luz de un nuevo texto," *Al-Qantara* 2 (1981), 249–50. Muḥammad ibn Abī ʿĀmir, or al-Manṣūr, was from 978 to 991 the *hadjib*, or chancellor, to the powerless caliph Hišām II (976–1009, 1010–13). He turned the title over to his son ʿAbd al-Malik, though he continued to rule until his death in 1002. ʿAbd al-Malik, in turn, ruled in the name of Hišām until his own death in 1008.

[2] Bisson, *Medieval Crown*, 19–23; Josep Maria Salrach, *El procés de formació nacional de Catalunya (segles VIII–IX)*, 2 vols. (Barcelona, 1978); Ramon d'Abadal i de Vinyals, *Els primers comtes catalans*, Història de Catalunya, Biografies catalanes, 1, [3rd ed.] (Barcelona, [1980]); Paul H. Freedman, "Symbolic Implications of the Events of 985–988," in *Symposium internacional*, 1:117–29, and works cited there. In 1988, the autonomous government of Catalonia held millennial commemorations.

We may discount parts of this tradition as court propaganda, but it is harder to ignore a document from within two years of the event that attests to its immediate impact:

In the year of the Lord 986, the thirty-first year of Lothar's rule, on the kalends of July, a Wednesday [1 July 985], Barcelona was besieged by the Saracens and, with God's leave, and with our sins hindering [the defense of the city], it was captured by them in the same month, on the sixth, and all of the inhabitants of the city – and those of its county, who had entered the city on the order of the lord-count Borrell, for the purpose of guarding and defending it – all died or were taken captive; and all of their property was destroyed, whatever they had assembled there . . .[3]

Though recovery was in fact relatively rapid – Borrell II's son led a raid on Córdoba in 1010 – in the closing years of the tenth century Barcelona remained an abandoned frontier outpost of a fragmenting Carolingian empire. The principal city of the region lay in ruins, and Catalonia did not as yet exist.

On 12 September 1213, Borrell II's direct descendant Pere I suffered another defeat, losing his life in the battle of Muret while leading forces against Simon de Montfort and the knights of the Albigensian Crusade. But by now the count of Barcelona was no longer just one of many in a loosely organized frontier region; he had become the ruler of a confederation of counties that had for a century been called Catalonia. Furthermore, this confederation had been united since 1137 with the realm of Aragón: the count was also a king. Pere's ancestors had long pursued interests north of the Pyrenees and had played a major role, alongside the kings of Castile, in the *Reconquista*. The political community had recently begun the process of organizing the assemblies known as the Corts. And the city that lay in ruins in 985 was now a Mediterranean commercial capital of the greatest importance. Much had changed in two and one-quarter centuries.[4]

This dramatic growth of the power of the count of Barcelona, the influence of his region, and the importance of his city in the eleventh and twelfth centuries rested on fundamental changes in Catalan society. These changes were in the first instance economic: Catalonia took part in the general expansion of the European economy in this period, and

---

[3] *DBarcelona* 172: "Annus Domini DCCCCLXXXVI, imperante Leuthario XXXI anno, die kalendas iulii, IIII feria, a sarracenis obsessa est Barchinona et, permittente Deo, impediente peccata nostra, capta est ab eis in eadem mense, II nonas, et ibidem mortui uel capti sunt omnes habitantibus de eadem ciuitate uel de eiusdem comitatu, qui ibidem introierant per iussionem de dompno Borrello comite, ad custodiendum uel defendendum eam; et ibidem periit omnem substanciam eorum, quicquid ibidem congregauerant . . ." See also Michel Zimmermann, "La prise de Barcelone par Al-Mansûr et la naissance de l'historiographie catalane," *Annales de Bretagne et des pays de l'Ouest* 87 (1980), 194–201. [4] Bisson, *Medieval Crown*, 23–57.

its location on the sea and on a frontier gave it a particular advantage.[5] More important, however, was the ability of Catalonia to capitalize on its new prosperity. This required a restructuring of the social order to allow the ruling classes to transform prosperity into power. The history of power and social order in the eleventh and twelfth centuries is likewise a European, rather than a particularly Catalan problem.[6] That history is best examined in different ways in different regions, by taking advantage of the peculiar characteristics of the available evidence. What Catalonia offers for evidence is a wealth of archival records. This material can often seem lifeless, especially because the documentary riches of the region are not matched by a similar abundance of narrative sources. Nevertheless, certain highly descriptive records can compensate for the absence of narrative accounts, allowing studies to move beyond the presentation of patterns without context. For questions of power and social order in this period, one subset of these records is particularly rich: the written agreements known as *convenientiae*.

The phrase "Hec est convenientia . . ." ("This is the agreement . . .") opens hundreds of documents from the eleventh and twelfth centuries preserved in the archives of Catalonia. The substance of the documents and the status of the persons they concern vary widely: agreements detailing the terms of tenure of a castle from a count, or of a simple plot of land from a monastery; peace treaties between great lords, or settlements between brothers concerning division of an inheritance; promises to be faithful, or grants of right of first refusal of purchase of a property. Despite this variety, or perhaps because of it, *convenientiae* determined a social and political order.

This study developed from the detailed examination of approximately 1,000 of these *convenientiae*. The documents themselves prompted a first series of questions. When did the *convenientia* first appear in the Catalan counties? What were its sources? What were the reasons for its appearance and the rhythms of its diffusion? How did the various types of agreements to which scribes applied the label *convenientia* develop, and how and why did the distinctions among these various types gradually dissolve amidst a breakdown in formulae? The answers to these questions form an interesting story in themselves. They provide a window on the inner workings of scribal culture and a case study of semantic and diplomatic development and change. Such a study, however, would be incomplete; these narrower questions about documentary typology and language

---

[5] Robert Fossier, *Enfance de l'Europe, X^e–XIIe siècles: Aspects économiques et sociaux*, 2nd ed., 2 vols., Nouvelle Clio 17, 17bis (Paris, 1989), 2:615–799.

[6] E.g., Thomas N. Bisson, ed., *Cultures of Power: Lordship, Status, and Process in Twelfth-Century Europe* (Philadelphia, 1995).

must serve only as a foundation for a broader examination of the changing associations of individuals and communities over time. Thus a second series of questions focuses not on the documents themselves, but on the legal, social, political, and economic structures for which they provide detailed evidence. What explains the appearance, development, and spread of the institutions and relationships described in these agreements? How did these structures persist over time? How did they change? How did they operate within various segments of society? How may they be seen as providing the bases of social and political order? These are the larger historical problems that justify the close scrutiny of the *convenientiae*. This second story, however, is inseparable from the first, for in reconstructing the history of a society, it is essential to understand the nature of the evidence that was generated by and, in turn, helped to shape that society.

CATALONIA AND ITS NEIGHBORS

Regional studies run the risk of isolating an area under consideration from its wider context. This observation is particularly true for studies of late- and post-Carolingian Europe, where regions, rather than nation-states and empires, are increasingly seen as the proper units of analysis. The muses of regional historiography in the twentieth century always saw the method as a means to an end, however, and if regional studies are to prove useful, they must remain conscious of what lies beyond.[7] By accidents of geography and politics, Catalonia's context in this era was particularly complex.[8] Histories of the region point to a turn away from the Carolingian dynasty toward Rome and Córdoba as the principal development of the period. The appearance of the Venetian doge-turned-saint, Pietro Uresol, and his companion Romuald at Sant Miquel de Cuixà in the 970s; Gerbert d'Aurillac's contemporary residence at Santa Maria de Ripoll; embassies to Córdoba in 950, 956, 961x66, 971, and 974; meetings of Catalan counts with the Ottonian emperors at Rome: these are all indicators of Catalonia's "opening up to the world."[9] The travels of Sunyer, monk of Cuixà (950), and then of Bishop Guisad of Urgell, Abbot Arnulf of Ripoll, and Count Sunifred of Cerdanya (951) to the papal court marked an important opening on a different front, and the relationship between Catalonia and the papacy became a crucial

---

[7] E.g., Marc Bloch, "Pour une histoire comparée des sociétés européennes," *Revue de synthèse historique* 46 (1928), 45–47; Georges Duby, *La société aux XIe et XIIe siècles dans la région mâconnaise*, 2nd ed. (Paris, 1971; repr. 1988), 7.

[8] For a concise survey of physical and human geography, see Freedman, *Origins*, 20–25.

[9] Bonnassie, *La Catalogne*, 1:325–61; Abadal i de Vinyals, *Els primers comtes*, 305–38.

factor not only in the religious history of the region, but also in its political development.[10] While valid, this approach views the Catalan counties as a peripheral region, dependent on distant power centers.[11] The relations between the counties and their immediate neighbors, both across the Pyrenees and on the Iberian Peninsula, were in fact much more significant for the fate of the region.

The establishment of the Spanish March assimilated the Catalan counties into the Carolingian empire. Connections to the North were not new, as Visigothic rule had straddled the Pyrenees, and the Catalan counties shared with their neighbors in Septimania a traditional adherence to Visigothic law. From a Parisian perspective, they remained technically a part of the West Frankish and then French kingdom until 1258, when Louis IX abandoned his claims to the counties of Barcelona, Urgell, Besalú, Rosselló, Empúries, Cerdanya, Conflent, Girona, and Osona in the Treaty of Corbeil.[12] From Barcelona, as suggested above, the situation looked rather different; Capetian rights were long moribund, if not extinguished, by the millennium. If juridically independent, however, the Catalan counties remained nevertheless a part of the late- and post-Carolingian world, more closely attached to that milieu than to their Iberian neighbors. The notarial habits of Catalan scribes provide an apt symbol of the region's position. Despite the de facto political break from the Carolingian and Capetian dynasties, dating clauses refer to the regnal years of French kings until 1180; scribes in the rest of the peninsula, including Aragón after the union, employed the Spanish Era.[13]

---

[10] Paul Kehr, *Das Papsttum und der katalanische Prinzipat bis zur Vereinigung mit Aragon*, Abhandlungen der preussischen Akademie der Wissenschaften, Jahrgang 1926, Philosophisch-historische Klasse, no. 1 (Berlin, 1926); Thomas Deswarte, "Rome et la spécificité catalane. La papauté et ses relations avec la Catalogne et Narbonne (850–1030)," *Revue historique* 294 (1995), 3–43.

[11] Julia M. H. Smith, *Province and Empire: Brittany and the Carolingians*, CSMLT, 4th ser., 18 (Cambridge, 1992), and Smith, "*Fines imperii*: The Marches," in Rosamond McKitterick, ed., *The New Cambridge Medieval History*, vol. 2, *c. 700–c. 900* (Cambridge, 1995), 169–89, are particularly insightful on this issue.

[12] Alexandre Teulet et al., eds., *Layettes du Trésor des chartes*, 5 vols. (Paris, 1863–1909), no. 4411 (3:405–8). France reacquired Rosselló and part of Cerdanya through the Treaty of the Pyrenees (a. 1659); see Peter Sahlins, *Boundaries: The Making of France and Spain in the Pyrenees* (Berkeley, 1989), 25–60. The president of France, as the political "heir" of the count of Foix, maintains a foothold in the Pyrenees as joint head of state, alongside the bishop of Urgell, of the Principality of Andorra. The sovereignty of Foix/France and Urgell, rooted in treaties of 1278 and 1288 (the *Pariatges*), was extinguished only with the adoption of the Andorran constitution of 4 May 1993 and a trilateral treaty of 3 June 1993. See Jorri Duursma, *Fragmentation and the International Relations of Micro-States: Self-Determination and Statehood*, Cambridge Studies in International and Comparative Law 2 (Cambridge, 1996), 316–73.

[13] Anscari M. Mundó, "El concili de Tarragona de 1180: Dels anys dels reis francs als de l'Encarnació," *Analecta sacra Tarraconensia* 67:1 (1994), xxiii–xliii; Alvaro d'Ors, *La era hispánica*, Mundo antiguo 1 (Pamplona, 1962), 8 n. 5. The allegiance implied here is more cultural than political. Cf. Heinrich Fichtenau, "'Politische' Datierungen des frühen Mittelalters," in Herwig

The northern orientation of the Catalan counties is evident, too, in palaeography; while Aragonese documents maintain strong Visigothic influence, the *escritura condal* of tenth- and eleventh-century Catalan documents is a purer caroline minuscule.[14] Catalonia also followed a particular path in linguistic development, both in terms of the vernacular and Latin. As Roger Wright observes, "For practical purposes it can be regarded as a part of the Frankish and European area," meaning that in contrast to the rest of the Iberian Peninsula, Romance and Latin became distinct well before 1100.[15]

The ecclesiastical history of the region explains these palaeographical, linguistic, and notarial traditions. After the fall of the Romano-Visigothic metropolitan see of Tarragona in 714, and despite premature attempts at its restoration, the dioceses of the Catalan counties – Barcelona, Urgell, Vic, and Girona – became subject to the jurisdiction of the archbishop of Narbonne; these ties only became stronger with the notorious purchase of that office by the count of Cerdanya for his ten-year-old son sometime before 1019.[16] Administrative and cultural links were thus to the Carolingian church, rather than to the remnants of its Visigothic counterpart; while the western Pyrenean kingdoms resisted Benedictine monasticism and Roman liturgy until the late eleventh century,[17] these took root in Catalonia from the ninth century. Although Cluny lacked direct jurisdiction in the region, leading abbots established monastic con-

footnote 13 (*cont.*)

    Wolfram and Anton Scharer, eds., *Intitulatio*, 3 vols., Mitteilungen des Instituts für österreichische Geschichtsforschung, Ergänzungsband 21, 24, 29 (Graz, 1967–88), 2:453–548; Michael Borgolte, *Geschichte der Grafschaften Alemanniens in fränkischer Zeit*, Vorträge und Forschungen, Sonderband 31 (Sigmaringen, 1984), 29–77; Jean Dufour, "Obédience respective des Carolingiens et des Capétiens (fin Xe siècle–début XIe siècle)," in *Catalunya i França*, 21–44; Michel Zimmermann, "La datation des documents catalans du IXe au XIIe siècle: Un itinéraire politique," *AM* 93 (1981), 345–75.

[14] Zacarías García Villada, *Paleografía española . . .*, 2 vols., Publicaciones de la Revista de filología española 6 (Madrid, 1923), 1:243–57.

[15] Roger Wright, *Late Latin and Early Romance in Spain and Carolingian France*, ARCA Classical and Medieval Texts, Papers and Monographs 8 (Liverpool, 1982), 146–50; and below, pp. 152–56.

[16] Élisabeth Magnou-Nortier, *La société laïque et l'Église dans la province ecclésiastique de Narbonne (zone cispyrénéenne) de la fin du VIIIe à la fin du XIe siècle*, Publications de l'Université de Toulouse–Le Mirail, ser. A, 20 (Toulouse, 1974), 463–65; *HGL* 5:251. Independent bishops appear in the western counties of Pallars and Ribagorça from 888, and in 956 the archbishop of Narbonne recognized an independent diocese at Roda. Roda was destroyed in 1006; it was restored in 1068 under the protection of the king of Aragón. See Ramon d'Abadal i de Vinyals, "Origen i procés de consolidació de la seu ribagorçana de Roda," trans. Gaspar Feliu i Montfort, in Abadal i de Vinyals, *Dels Visigots als Catalans*, ed. Jaume Sobrequés i Callicó, 3rd ed., 2 vols., Col·lecció estudis i documents 13–14 (Barcelona, 1986), 2:57–139; Bisson, *Medieval Crown*, 14.

[17] The cultural impact is explored in Bernard F. Reilly, ed., *Santiago, Saint-Denis, and Saint Peter: The Reception of the Roman Liturgy in León-Castile in 1080* (New York, 1985); for Aragón, see Bisson, *Medieval Crown*, 13–14.

federations along the Burgundian model that included monasteries on both sides of the Pyrenees.[18] The marriage practices of the Catalan comital families confirm these northern leanings. The families all descended from Bello, a count of Carcassonne under Charlemagne, and after a brief period of endogamy, they looked back across the Pyrenees for marriage partners. Between 930 and 1080, twenty-two of thirty Catalan countesses came from outside the region, mostly from Languedoc, Auvergne, La Marche, Provence, and Burgundy; marriage alliances with the Christian kingdoms of the peninsula, while they did occur, were rare.[19]

Catalonia's strongest ties were to the North, but it also looked to the South. The relationships between the counties and peninsular Islamic powers passed rapidly through five distinct stages.[20] From the establishment of the frontier in 801 to the mid-tenth century, contact was limited to the occasional visit and the slightly more frequent raid; the polities of interest for the Catalan counties in this period were not so much the central powers in the South as the independent and occasionally rebellious governors of the northern marches, such as the Banū Qasīm of Zaragoza. The establishment of the caliphate under 'Abd al-Raḥmān III (912–61) eliminated these buffer areas, and from 950, the counts of Barcelona established direct diplomatic, economic, and cultural contacts with Córdoba. The dictatorships of al-Manṣūr (978–1002) and his son, 'Abd al-Malik (1002–8), ruptured whatever political ties had developed; Catalan sources report devastating raids in 985, 1000–1001, and 1003. From *c.* 1010, the political dynamic changed once again, with the dissolution of the caliphate into the *taifa* realms. The Catalan counties entered into and broke alliances with various Islamic and Christian factions in the subsequent years; their closest ties were with the coastal kingdoms of Málaga and Dénia and the adjacent polities of Zaragoza, Huesca, Lleida, and Tortosa. While this fluid situation continued into the late eleventh century – the Cid ruled in València until 1099, for example – from *c.* 1060 Castilian policy, papal intervention, the conquest of Toledo (1085), and the Almoravid response transformed the peninsular world once again; in the twelfth century, Catalonia was increasingly part of a united Christian front in the *Reconquista*. Despite these vicissitudes, throughout much of this period Catalonia's southern frontier remained very stable: Carolingian

[18] Anscari M. Mundó, "Moissac, Cluny et les mouvements monastiques de l'Est des Pyrénées du Xe au XIIe siècle," *AM* 75 (1963), 551–70.

[19] Aurell, *Les noces du comte*, 38–64.

[20] Bonnassie, *La Catalogne*, 1:340–59; Abadal i de Vinyals, *Els primers comtes*, 183–208, 327–44; José María Lacarra, "Aspectos económicos de la sumisión de los reinos de taifas (1010–1102)," in *Homenaje a Jaime Vicens Vives*, 2 vols. (Barcelona, 1965–67), 1:255–77.

forces withdrew from Tarragona in 809; the city was definitively restored only in the first decades of the twelfth century.[21] Another constant in Catalonia's relationship with the South, at least from 950, was economic contact. Mercenary wages, ransoms, piracy, and the regime of tribute payments (*parias*) kept money and goods flowing even during times of conflict; Islamic gold fueled Catalonia's first economic takeoff.

With the exception of the often independent western counties of Urgell, Pallars, and Ribagorça,[22] Catalonia's involvement in Iberian politics before the twelfth century was almost entirely defined by these relationships with the Islamic South. The progress of the *Reconquista* created closer ties between Catalonia and the Christian kingdoms, but only slowly; such contacts leave few traces before the twelfth century. Alliances, whether military or matrimonial, were few and far between.[23] Religious contacts operated solely through the occasional pilgrimage or pious bequest to Santiago de Compostela; Catalan bishops rarely met or even corresponded with their peninsular counterparts.[24] Castilian fabrics listed in the inventory of a Catalan baron attest to economic contacts, but these, too, were limited; Catalonia's trading interests looked north, south, and east. Most importantly, the counts of Barcelona resisted submission to potential hegemons, whether Sancho III Garcés of Navarre (1000–1035), Alfonso VI of León-Castile (1065–1109), or his grandson Alfonso VII (1126–57).[25] This independence allowed for Catalonia's less consistently belligerent stance toward her *taifa* neighbors. Counts and barons of the western regions were the first to be drawn into Aragonese and Castilian adventures from the 1060s.[26] Berenguer Ramon II of Barcelona followed, joining Aragón, Navarre, and the *taifa* states of Lleida and Tortosa in attacking the Zaragoza of the Cid in 1082. The marriage of the future Ramon Berenguer IV of Barcelona (1131–62) to Petronilla of Aragón sealed not only the formation of the Catalano-Aragonese confederation, but also Catalonia's deeper involvement in peninsular politics. Ramon Berenguer IV's collaboration with Alfonso VII in expeditions against Murcia (1144) and the conquest of Almería (1147), followed by his own capture of the remaining Islamic outposts of Tortosa (1148), Lleida (1149), and Fraga (1149), signaled the end of

[21] Lawrence J. McCrank, "Restoration and Reconquest in Medieval Catalonia: The Church and Principality of Tarragona, 971–1177" (Ph.D. diss., University of Virginia, 1974).

[22] *Pallars i Ribagorça*, pp. 71–224; Ferran Valls i Taberner, "Els orígens dels comtats de Pallars i Ribagorça," *Estudis universitaris catalans* 9 (1915–16), 1–101; Fernando Galtier Martí, *Ribagorza, condado independiente: Desde los origines hasta 1025* (Zaragoza, 1981).

[23] Bonnassie, *La Catalogne*, 1:135; Aurell, *Les noces du comte*, 61–64.

[24] Bonnassie, *La Catalogne*, 1:332–34; Nathaniel L. Taylor, "The Will and Society in Medieval Catalonia and Languedoc, 800–1200" (Ph.D. diss., Harvard University, 1995), 328 (Figure 5.1).

[25] Bonnassie, *La Catalogne*, 2:707, 795–96, 839–47.

[26] Bonnassie, *La Catalogne*, 2:665 n. 61, 789, 864–65.

an era. From then on, frequent treaties and squabbles with the Christian kingdoms marked Catalonia as a full partner in the *Reconquista*.[27] Further expansion in southern France in the twelfth century brought Catalonia into contact with such distant powers as England, the German empire, Italian city-states, and even Byzantium.[28] The most important influences on Catalonia, however, were always closer at hand. Administrative ties to Septimania and the strength of Carolingian traditions have encouraged the study of Catalonia as an extension of the empire, rather than as one of the Christian kingdoms of the peninsula.[29] Still, the region was not simply an appendix to Languedoc. The separate linguistic developments of Catalan and Occitan provide one proof; the distinct relationships between the papacy and the Catalan counties, on the one hand, and the other dioceses of the province of Narbonne, on the other, show this as well.[30] Furthermore, Catalonia shared the pressures and opportunities of the frontier with the Christian kingdoms in a way that it could not with lands north of the Pyrenees. Institutions, such as the archaic social structures of mountain enclaves, and movements, such as the repopulation of the plains below, are better understood in an Iberian context.[31] Thus Catalonia falls between two well-defined historical (and historiographical) frameworks. A third – the Mediterranean world – is rapidly establishing itself as an alternative model. All three must be kept in mind in following the region's internal development.

FEUDALISM IN ELEVENTH- AND TWELFTH-CENTURY CATALONIA

The aspect of that internal development studied here is the changing role of written agreements in Catalan society in the eleventh and twelfth centuries. This is not in the first instance a study of feudalism in Catalonia.

---

[27] Andrea Büschgens, *Die politischen Verträge Alfons' VIII. von Kastilien (1158–1214) mit Aragón-Katalonien und Navarra: Diplomatische Strategien und Konfliktlösung im mittelalterlichen Spanien*, Europäische Hochschulschriften, Reihe 3, Geschichte und ihre Hilfswissenschaften, 678 (Frankfurt am Main, 1995).

[28] Ernest Marcos Hierro, *Die byzantinisch-katalanischen Beziehungen im 12. und 13. Jahrhundert unter besonderer Berücksichtigung der Chronik Jakobs I. von Katalonien-Aragon*, Miscellanea Byzantina Monacensia 37 (Munich, 1996), esp. 57–76, offers a survey of Catalano-Aragonese involvement in "international" politics in the second half of the twelfth century.

[29] In addition to Roger Wright's observation above, n. 15, see Roger Collins, *Early Medieval Spain: Unity in Diversity, 400–1000*, 2nd ed. (New York, 1995), 263: "Catalonia . . . was patently distinguishable from the rest of the peninsula." He rightly goes on to note, however, that "this should not obscure the fact that it was one amongst several parts of a greater whole." Cf. Jean Dunbabin, *France in the Making, 843–1180* (Oxford, 1985), 78.

[30] Antoni M. Badia i Margarit, *La formació de la llengua catalana: Assaig d'interpretació històrica*, 2nd ed. (Barcelona, 1981); Deswarte, "Rome et la spécificité catalane."

[31] Bonnassie, *La Catalogne*, 1:77–78, 129.

Yet the subject matter and particularly the sources of this study implicate it in two heated controversies over the topic. The first of these is the debate concerning the "transformation of the year 1000" (*mutation de l'an mil*) or the "feudal revolution." This model stems primarily from the studies of Georges Duby. Duby's earliest work demonstrated the persistence in Burgundy until the year 1000 of a system of justice based on a Carolingian public order. Between 1000 and 1030, this jurisdiction collapsed, giving way to the private exercise of formerly public powers. In his landmark *thèse* on the Mâconnais (1953), Duby showed that additional changes occurred around the year 1000: the end of ancient slavery, the proliferation of castles and oppressive regimes of lordship, the rise of a knightly class, the suppression of a once free peasantry, and the reorganization of aristocratic families into lineages. Duby's initial findings have been confirmed and extended, with minor chronological variations, in a number of important French regional studies.[32] Challenging this model of rapid and radical change, proponents of continuity argue that "mutationism" exaggerates the notion of public order before the year 1000 and the extent of the violence after that date. The distinction between a monolithic ancient slavery and an equally monolithic free peasantry before the millennium oversimplifies a highly complex situation. Likewise, the idea of the rise of the knightly class is spurious. Too much of the argument rests on reading changes in language as evidence for changes in institutions, and changes in the nature of documentation as evidence for changes in society.[33] The *convenientia* has attracted the attention of partisans of both sides of the debate. Pierre Bonnassie described the *convenientia* as one of the three elements with which counts and princes throughout southern Europe reconstituted public authority after the millennial crisis.[34] On the other hand, Dominique Barthélemy,

[32] Georges Duby, "Recherches sur l'évolution des institutions judiciaires pendant le Xe et le XIe siècle dans le sud de la Bourgogne," *Le Moyen Âge* 52 (1946), 149–94; 53 (1947), 15–38; Duby, *La société aux XIe et XIIe siècles*. A synthesis and bibliography may be found in Jean-Pierre Poly and Eric Bournazel, *La mutation féodale: X^e–XIIe siècle*, 2nd ed., Nouvelle Clio 16 (Paris, 1991).

[33] Dominique Barthélemy, *La mutation de l'an mil a-t-elle eu lieu?: Servage et chevalerie dans la France des Xe et XIe siècles* (Paris, 1997); Barthélemy, *La société dans le comté de Vendôme de l'an mil au XIVe siècle* (Paris, 1993). This rather spirited debate may be followed in the pages of the *Revue historique de droit français et étranger* (Jean-Pierre Poly and Eric Bournazel, "Que faut-il préférer au 'mutationnisme'? ou le problème du changement social," 72 [1994], 401–12; Dominique Barthélemy, "Encore le débat sur l'an mil!" 73 [1995], 349–60; Jean-Pierre Poly and Eric Bournazel, "Post scriptum," 73 [1995], 361–62) and *Past & Present* (Thomas N. Bisson, "The 'Feudal Revolution,'" 142 [1994], 6–42; Dominique Barthélemy, Stephen D. White, Timothy Reuter, Chris Wickham, and Thomas N. Bisson, "Debate: The 'Feudal Revolution,'" 152 [1996], 196–223; 155 [1997], 177–225).

[34] The other two were vassalic engagement and the fief: Pierre Bonnassie, "Du Rhône à la Galice: Genèse et modalités du régime féodal," in *Structures féodales et féodalisme dans l'Occident méditerranéen (X^e–XIIIe siècles): Bilan et perspectives de recherches: École française de Rome, 10–13 octobre 1978*, Colloques internationaux du Centre national de la recherche scientifique 588 (Paris, 1980), 37–38.

whose study of the Vendômois is the strongest statement to date against Duby's model, has written, "That the 'private' convention, in apparent rupture with the law, flourished in the eleventh century is, to my mind, a purely documentary fact." His statement drew a rather pointed response from the other side: "this is to fly in the face of the evidence."[35] A study of the *convenientia*, therefore, necessarily contributes to the debate over the year 1000.

Bonnassie's masterly study of tenth- and eleventh-century Catalonia apparently established the region as the strongest example of the mutationist model, as even opponents of that model acknowledge. Bonnassie posited the continuity of public order, based on traditions of comital authority and Visigothic law, up to *c.* 1020; slavery persisted, as well, while the free population comprised an independent peasantry and nobles who recognized the count as their leader. The latter were bound to the count by fidelity (not vassalage or homage), which was a natural obligation, rather than one formed by agreement; the fief (*fevum*) existed only as a grant of public lands or revenues in return for service. For Bonnassie, around the year 1000, there was nothing feudal about Catalonia. From the late tenth century, economic growth, based on increased agricultural production, but encouraged, as well, by an influx of Islamic gold, generated a scramble for profits, with aristocratic lineages fighting each other, groups of peasants, and the counts for control. It is in these years of crisis (1020–60) that there appeared private armed clienteles (*milites*), remunerated with private fiefs, and bound to their superiors by homage and oaths of fidelity. This same period witnessed the enserfment of the once free peasantry, now laboring under the impositions of rapacious lords (*seigneurie banale*). Comital justice collapsed and was replaced by private pacts between lineages (*convenientiae*). From 1060, Ramon Berenguer I of Barcelona recovered, reestablishing comital authority, but he did so by using the elements that had developed among the aristocracy in the period of crisis. The count now granted fiefs, accepted homage and oaths of fidelity, and entered into pacts. In doing so, he abandoned the peasantry, his responsibility under the old order, to the whims of the aristocracy. As Bonnassie concluded, "by 1100, Catalonia has the appearance of a fully feudal society."[36]

A quarter century of research has inevitably revised portions of this picture. Josep Maria Salrach has studied how the establishment of the new "feudal order" of the eleventh century was preceded by and linked to the gradual breakdown of the "ancient order" over the course of the

---

[35] Dominique Barthélemy, "La mutation féodale a-t-elle eu lieu? (Note critique)," *Annales: Économies, sociétés, civilisations* 47 (1992), 773; Bisson, "The 'Feudal Revolution,'" 41.

[36] Bonnassie, *La Catalogne*; summarized in Bonnassie, "Du Rhône à la Galice," 19–23 (quotation at 23).

ninth and tenth centuries. Gaspar Feliu has challenged a number of aspects of Bonnassie's model of the socioeconomic order of Catalonia in the tenth century, especially with respect to the personal status of the peasantry and the role of independent farmers in the process of agricultural expansion. Jeffrey Bowman argues for elements of continuity in disputing practice of the tenth and eleventh centuries. Martin Aurell's periodization of the marriage practices of the Catalan counts posits breaks at 930 and 1080, ignoring the *an mil*. Working in the other direction, Paul Freedman shows that Bonnassie's period of crisis is only a "point of origin" for the enserfment of the peasantry, a process he describes as occurring in distinct stages over the course of the eleventh to fourteenth centuries. Stephen Bensch highlights an economic decline in the period 1090–1140, demonstrating that the eleventh century was not the key period in the commercial and urban development of Barcelona.[37] This research, while not denying the fact of significant change, extends its chronological framework; a new order did replace an old one, but not overnight.

This more nuanced position is less dramatic, but it is certainly a better reflection of reality. The more we learn about the tenth and earlier centuries throughout Europe — and not simply in France, which has been the focus of the debate — the more it is clear that there were elements of continuity, whether of court cultures, literacy, or modes of dispute settlement. On the other hand, there is ample evidence for significant change in the early eleventh century, whether in self- and group perception, the proliferation of violent lordship, or responses to that violence such as the Peace of God.[38] The ideas of mutation, revolution, transformation, adjustment, and persistence reasonably apply to certain developments in certain regions in certain decades of the tenth and eleventh centuries. In other words, the changes during this period, while widespread, were neither monolithic nor unidirectional. General interpretations of the period must attempt to address that heterogeneity and embrace the fundamental complexities of medieval societies. The debate over the year 1000 — and it is a worthwhile one — will best be served by

---

[37] Gaspar Feliu i Montfort, "Societat i economia," in *Symposium internacional*, 1:81–115; Josep Maria Salrach, "Entre l'estat antic i el feudal. Mutacions socials i dinàmica polìtico-militar a l'Occident carolingi i als comtats catalans," in *Symposium internacional*, 1:191–252; Bowman, "Law"; Aurell, *Les noces du comte*; Freedman, *Origins*; Bensch, *Barcelona*.

[38] C. Stephen Jaeger, *The Origins of Courtliness: Civilizing Trends and the Formation of Courtly Ideals, 939–1210* (Philadelphia, 1985); Rosamond McKitterick, ed., *The Uses of Literacy in Early Medieval Europe* (Cambridge, 1990); Wendy Davies and Paul Fouracre, eds., *The Settlement of Disputes in Early Medieval Europe* (Cambridge, 1986); Patrick J. Geary, *Phantoms of Remembrance: Memory and Oblivion at the End of the First Millennium* (Princeton, 1994), esp. 178; Thomas Head and Richard Landes, eds., *The Peace of God: Social Violence and Religious Response in France around the Year 1000* (Ithaca, 1992); Bisson, "The 'Feudal Revolution.'"

research that transcends its current polarized state. This study is conceived with that ultimate goal in mind.

In the face of this complexity, studies of the tenth to twelfth centuries must be careful in using the language of change and continuity in order to avoid assimilation into one of those opposed and potentially totalizing constructs. Much of this study focuses on transformations in structures of power, particularly comital power. Here there is no question that there was change. Crisis is not too strong a characterization of the internal political developments of the house of Barcelona in the mid-eleventh century. Ramon Borrell died in 1017, leaving a minor heir, Berenguer Ramon I; no fewer than five major political disputes erupted in the period 1018–23. Berenguer Ramon's own death in 1035 inaugurated another minority, that of Ramon Berenguer I; within a decade of his accession, rebels were lobbing missiles from the clock tower of the cathedral against the comital palace, barons were deserting the comital host, and a frontier lord was attempting to carve out a county of his own from the territory of Barcelona. The turmoil lasted until 1058. This crisis of comital power was not limited to Barcelona, though comital troubles in Pallars and Cerdanya began later and lasted longer.

These internal political crises did not, however, reflect or lead to a wholesale collapse of the social order. In contemporary *external* political developments, to consider just one aspect of the region's history, Berenguer Ramon I's reign witnessed victories and advances on the frontier, and the regime of *parias* that provided Ramon Berenguer I with the funds to solve his internal problems began with his assaults on Lleida and Zaragoza around 1045.[39] The problems of the counts did, of course, have consequences for their ability to exercise power and dispense justice, and those problems in turn had ramifications beyond the comital court and host. Those ramifications must be understood, however, in terms of more gradual changes in the nature of justice and comital power that had been occurring from before the millennium, changes that fit uncomfortably with the abrupt terminology of crisis. The interaction of scribal culture with these changes makes the *convenientia* an illuminating source, but its appearance corresponds to these developments – both crisis and more gradual change – in a more complex fashion than has been suggested. Extracting the *convenientia* from the master narrative of millennial mutation makes possible a more complex reading of Catalonia's history.

Intertwined with this debate over periodization is another, even more intricate discussion of various concepts of feudalism, both as a set of institutions regulating relationships between lords and men, and as a broader

---

[39] Sobrequés, *Els grans comtes*, 27–28, 62–64.

set of social and economic structures characteristic of medieval Europe.[40] The debate has progressed on three fronts. First, some have attacked the utility of the "historical construct" of feudalism, arguing that vassalage and the fief as they are discussed by modern historians have little relationship to medieval realities. Modern notions of these institutions, as well as ideas about their historical development, are based on an academic law that was not an organic outgrowth of earlier medieval customs.[41] Few would deny the artificiality of feudalism or its status as a generalization; opinions differ widely on the damage done by reference to the model. The present study, dealing as it does in specifics and in building rather than imposing models, can afford to sidestep the purely semantic aspects of this question.

A second polemic addresses notions of public order, especially as opposed to private exercise of power, and the transition from one situation to the other.[42] Here too, modern constructs are in question. The modern statist public/private distinction in early medieval Europe is an anachronism, but ideas of legitimacy, openness, accessibility, law, and their opposites are not. Still, in most cases, these notions seem hopelessly intertwined. What does it mean to suggest that former agents of public authority began to act in a private capacity when there is no change in their behavior? Is a bishop from a family of counts presiding over a tribunal that decides in favor of one of his relatives acting as a public or a private figure?[43] What about a king donating land to a monastery in return for prayers for his soul? Even in such situations, however, the terms "public" and "private" serve to highlight aspects of a composite whole; no one has yet developed a suitable alternative language with which these ideas might be expressed. Here, too, avoiding totalizing frameworks is helpful. A principal problem with the debate over the *mutation de l'an mil* is the assumption that public is equivalent to order, while private is equivalent to violence and chaos.[44] If this were in fact the case, it would be impossible for the *convenientia* (seen as private) to contribute to order (seen as public). But this is precisely what it did.

[40] Francophone scholars distinguish *féodalité* from *féodalisme*.

[41] Elizabeth A. R. Brown, "The Tyranny of a Construct: Feudalism and Historians of Medieval Europe," *American Historical Review* 79 (1974), 1063–88; Susan Reynolds, *Fiefs and Vassals: The Medieval Evidence Reinterpreted* (Oxford, 1994).

[42] See the works cited above, n. 33, and Fredric L. Cheyette, "The Invention of the State," in Bede Karl Lackner and Kenneth Roy Philp, eds., *Essays on Medieval Civilization*, The Walter Prescott Webb Memorial Lectures 12 (Austin, 1978), 143–78. Matthew Innes offers a particularly useful discussion of the issue in *State and Society in the Early Middle Ages: The Middle Rhine Valley, 400–1000*, CSMLT, 4th ser., 47 (Cambridge, 2000), 254–59.

[43] Adam J. Kosto, "Oliba, Peacemaker," in Imma Ollich i Castanyer, ed., *Actes del Congrés internacional Gerbert d'Orlhac i el seu temps: Catalunya i Europa a la fi del 1r mil·lenni: Vic-Ripoll, 10–13 de novembre de 1999*, Documents 31 (Vic, 1999), 135–49.   [44] Bowman, "Law," 349–60.

Third, there is the debate about the nature of "Mediterranean feudalism." The dominant models of feudalism, enshrined in the classic works of Marc Bloch and François-Louis Ganshof, were developed on the basis of evidence from the lands between the Loire and the Rhine; when institutions did not appear in the same forms in evidence from the southern lands, the feudalisms of this latter region were labeled incomplete or "skin deep," pale imitations of their northern analogues. More recent research has examined Mediterranean social structures on their own terms and has identified a rather vital and distinctive set of institutions, leading some to claim that it is the northern model that must now be viewed as incomplete.[45] Others argue for a widespread survival of Roman traditions in the South, delaying the appearance of any type of Mediterranean feudalism until well into the twelfth century. Among the latter, Élisabeth Magnou-Nortier stands out for her descriptions of completely nonfeudal Occitania, a vision that stands in stark contrast to Bonnassie's fully feudal Catalonia of *c.* 1100.[46] The agenda for this line of research is suggested by recent trends in urban historiography, where a new focus on Mediterranean towns is recasting older models based on the northern European experience.[47] An examination of the evidence for the "classical model" of feudalism, informed by a deeper awareness of southern phenomena, will lead to a fuller understanding of social structures and institutions throughout Europe.

Just as the *convenientia* is central to the debate over mutationism, it must also play a leading role in these discussions of feudalism, for the topics addressed by many of these written agreements are precisely those with which much historical scholarship on feudalism has concerned itself: mutual bonds of subordination and dependence, homage, fidelity, jurisdiction, and contracts of military service. Descriptions of feudo-vassalic

---

[45] Pierre Toubert, "Les féodalités méditerranéennes: Un problème d'histoire comparée," in *Structures féodales*, 1–13, and the other studies collected in that volume; *Les structures sociales de l'Aquitaine, du Languedoc et de l'Espagne au premier âge féodal: Toulouse 28–31 mars 1968* (Paris, 1969); Josep Maria Salrach, "Les féodalités méridionales: Des Alpes à la Galice," in Eric Bournazel and Jean-Pierre Poly, eds., *Les féodalités* (Paris, 1998), 313–88; A. Malpica and T. Quesada, eds., *Los orígenes del feudalismo en el mundo mediterráneo*, 2nd ed. (Granada, 1998). The nature of Iberian feudalism has been the subject of its own vigorous polemic; see, e.g., Abilio Barbero and Marcelo Vigil, *La formación del feudalismo en la Península Ibérica*, 2nd ed. (Barcelona, 1979).

[46] Magnou-Nortier, *La société laïque*; Magnou-Nortier, "La terre, la rente et le pouvoir dans les pays de Languedoc pendant le haut Moyen Âge," *Francia* 9 (1981), 79–115; 10 (1982), 21–66; 12 (1984), 53–118.

[47] Bensch, *Barcelona*, 6–12; Philip Daileader, *True Citizens: Violence, Memory, and Identity in the Medieval Community of Perpignan, 1162–1397*, The Medieval Mediterranean 25 (Leiden, 2000); Martin Aurell, "La chevalerie urbaine en Occitanie (fin Xᵉ–début XIIIᵉ siècle)," in *Les élites urbaines au Moyen Âge: XXVIIᵉ Congrès de la S.H.M.E.S. (Rome, mai 1996)*, Collection de l'École française de Rome 238, Publications de la Sorbonne, Série histoire ancienne et médiévale, 46 (Rome and Paris, 1997), 71–118.

institutions, especially in this early period, have generally been reconstructed from narrative texts, law codes, and phrases taken from scattered charter evidence. In the case of the Catalan *convenientia*, on the other hand, the historian can work with hundreds of documents from a small area that reveal the details of these arrangements as nowhere else. Origins, lines of development, and microregional peculiarities become clear. A detailed understanding of how these agreements functioned in a society in which the relationships they record were so well documented and widespread will shed further light on the evidence for similar ties in regions where the context is less abundantly clear.

THE SOURCES

The wealth of charter evidence from Catalonia is now well known to medieval historians. Common estimates of the holdings of Catalan archives claim approximately 5,000 individual records from the tenth century and 10,000 from the eleventh. No one has hazarded a guess at the figure for the twelfth century, though a survey found documents from that period in half of the 173 archives polled.[48] Aside from their volume, the Catalan holdings are distinguished by two facts. The first is the number of records preserved as single-sheet originals. Several important ecclesiastical cartularies survive, most notably those of the cathedral chapters of Barcelona and Urgell, and the monastery of Sant Cugat del Vallès, but the abundant survival of documents outside cartularies allows for the correction of some of the bias inherent in those compilations.[49] The second – and more crucial for the purposes of this study – is the number of nonecclesiastical records. The "Cancelleria" series of the Archive of the Crown of Aragón (ACA) contains an impressive run of documents of the counts of Barcelona, but it also includes independent "archives" incorporated over the years, such as documents of the counts of Urgell and Pallars Jussà, as well as a number of family collections. The comital cartulary, the *Liber feudorum maior* (*LFM*), is of singular importance. The ecclesiastical archives, too, contain many nonecclesiastical documents, such as records of previous sales handed over to an institution at the time of a donation of property.

---

[48] Pere Puig i Ustrell, *Els pergamins documentals: Naturalesa, tractament arxivístic i contingut diplomàtic*, Col·lecció normativa arxivística 3 (Barcelona, 1995), 155–57. For what follows, see Bonnassie, *La Catalogne*, 1:22–32. Accurate estimates of holdings are notoriously difficult to calculate because of archivists' tendencies toward exaggeration on the one hand, and nonresponse to surveys on the other.

[49] LA; ACU, Liber dotaliorum ecclesie Urgellensis (see DACU); *CSCV*. The question of why so many originals were preserved requires study; elsewhere in Europe, originals were destroyed or discarded after the compilation of cartularies (Geary, *Phantoms of Remembrance*, 82).

This wealth of evidence for the functioning of the lay world permits partial correction of the distorted picture offered elsewhere by purely ecclesiastical evidence. Furthermore, this lay evidence counters criticisms that certain feudo-vassalic institutions are known solely from ecclesiastical documentation.[50]

While working with charters is in some ways less treacherous than basing history on contemporary historical accounts, it presents its own problems. Most of the documents adhere to standard laconic formulae of donation, sale, exchange, and pledge, with the only variation found in the names of the actors, the location of the property, and the amount of money involved. These are ideal for investigations of economic cycles, the formation of domains, and onomastic patterns, but satisfying social history relies either on deviations from the formulae or on other types of evidence. The latter is not a possibility, as the historian of Catalonia can turn to only a handful of terse annals, regnal lists, *vitae*, mortuary rolls, letters, and commemorative verses, a half-legendary dynastic history, and a highly problematic law code.[51] Unlike most other contemporary acts, however, *convenientiae* do not adhere strictly to formulae. Their often highly descriptive texts can compensate for the absence of narrative accounts; when combined with similarly informative documents, such as records of judgment and testaments, it is possible to reconstruct the course of events.

This study departs from much earlier work on Catalonia in its historiographical approach. First, it crosses a traditional chronological boundary. The development, diffusion, and decline of the *convenientia* as an important element in Catalan society is a phenomenon of the eleventh *and* twelfth centuries. Studies of these two centuries together are surprisingly rare; this analysis of the *convenientia* therefore reveals elements of continuity and change that have been overlooked. Second, this study is transregional, cutting across geographical and archival boundaries. When Ramon de Caldes undertook in the late twelfth century the project of reorganizing the archives of Barcelona, he found the documents "in ordinatione confussa."[52] Ramon's successors as archivists at the comital court and elsewhere have been attempting to sort out that confusion for eight centuries. Their decisions over the years have had an impact on the nature of Catalan historiography.[53] One consequence has been the edition of documents in collections reflecting their modern distribution. Editions organized by person or office are rare, while those organized

---

[50] Reynolds, *Fiefs and Vassals*, 62–64.
[51] Thomas N. Bisson, "Unheroed Pasts: History and Commemoration in South Frankland before the Albigensian Crusades," *Speculum* 65 (1990), 281–308; *DOliba*, pp. 301–432.
[52] *LFM* prologue.   [53] Benito-Kosto-Taylor, "Approaches," 44–46.

around a particular place or institution often overlook relevant documents not found in the principal archive. Research projects mirror this phenomenon; they tend to be local, based on documents of many types found primarily in a single archive. The documents on which the present study is based were gathered in the course of a search, more or less systematic according to circumstances, of the pre-1200 holdings of the major repositories in Catalonia. The total number of *convenientiae* is approximately 1,000.[54] The largest number are housed in the ACA, principally in the series "Cancelleria" and the *LFM*, but also in many of the less prominent divisions of that archive. The other major sources of documents are the cathedral archives of Urgell, Vic, and Barcelona, and the archives of the Abbey of Santa Maria de Montserrat and the Biblioteca de Catalunya. For the period 1050–1200, *convenientiae* form roughly 10 percent of the "Cancelleria" series; in other collections the figure is closer to 5 percent. Given the variety of documentary forms, 5–10 percent is a substantial proportion for one type.

Finally, this study stands apart in that is based on the extended examination of a single type of document, rather than of an institution or an individual. There is some precedent for this methodology, although it is usually found in introductions to editions of documents, rather than historical analyses based on the documents. This approach poses a problem: notwithstanding the fact that Catalan scribal practice presents a ready-made typology of documents ("hec est convenientia"; "hec est carta donationis"; "hec est vinditio"), the *convenientia* is a difficult type to define. From a purely formal standpoint, *convenientiae* overlap with other types of acts, particularly oaths of fidelity. Furthermore, documents that begin with the phrase "hec est convenientia" concern a wide range of topics, while some of these same topics are addressed by documents that do not begin with that phrase. Thus I have attempted to consider as wide as possible a range of written agreements, whether or not scribes chose to label them *convenientiae*. In addition, transactions and relationships in eleventh- and twelfth-century Catalonia often involved several documents. A *convenientia* might be associated with a separate written oath and a separate charter of donation. In focusing on a single type of document, closely associated documents may be missed, both in the initial stages of gathering evidence, and in the later stages of analysis. Again, in discussing particular events and situations, I have attempted to adduce as many relevant documents as possible, whatever the diplomatic type. In general, however, the *convenientia* holds center stage. A study based on a single type

---

[54] Other series consulted include the Baluze and Doat collections at the Bibliothèque nationale (Paris), Série J of the Archives nationales (Paris), the holdings of the ADPO, and the Alart manuscripts at the Bibliothèque municipale in Perpignan.

of document can only present a partial picture of a society. Yet knowledge of the history of a type of document is an essential preliminary to a proper understanding of its value as evidence. To achieve the latter, we must ask the right questions of the selected documentation. In the case of the *convenientia*, these are questions concerning social structures built around networks of individual agreements.

HISTORIOGRAPHY OF THE *CONVENIENTIA*

For many years, the institution and indeed the term *convenientia* only attracted the attention of German and Italian legal historians. Their efforts focused on several related questions: Was the *convenientia* a purely Lombard institution, or did it have links to Roman practice? Was it a consensual or formal contract? What relationship did it have to the *stantia* and *wadiatio*? The conclusions of this earliest scholarship rested on the few mentions of these institutions in the Lombard law codes and their later commentaries. Francesco Calasso, in contrast, turned to Lombard charters for answers. He concluded that the *convenientia* was a purely consensual contract that gradually forced out the formal elements of Lombard contractual practice. He argued that this would have been perfectly in line with Church doctrine and even with what Justinian wanted to accomplish in the sixth century, but could not.[55]

Calasso's study was limited to Italian sources. With the exception of the authors of manuals of diplomatics,[56] historians of regions outside Italy hardly seemed to notice the *convenientia* – until Paul Ourliac. Ourliac succinctly presented the problems and questions – and provided some answers and images – upon which later scholars have constantly drawn. After acknowledging the previous scholarship on the Lombard *convenientia*, he presented the following ideas. The force of the *convenientia* was independent of a written document, oath, or other formal element; its essence was the "accord de volonté." Yet it was not a simple consensual contract; it encompassed notions not to be found in either Roman or Germanic practice. Its terms often involved future generations, creating links between lineages and eventually developing into custom. These terms were often unequal, making the *convenientia* at once a promise and

---

[55] Francesco Calasso, *La "convenientia": Contributo alla storia del contratto in Italia durante l'alto medio evo*, Biblioteca della Rivista di storia del diritto italiano 9 (Bologna, 1932); previous scholarship summarized at 9–18.

[56] Alain de Boüard, *Manuel de diplomatique française et pontificale*, vol. 2, *L'acte privé* (Paris, 1948), 97 n. 1; Arthur Giry, *Manuel de diplomatique*, new ed. (Paris, 1925), 466 n. 1; Harry Bresslau, *Handbuch der Urkundenlehre für Deutschland und Italien*, 2nd ed., 2 vols. (Leipzig, 1912–31), 1:62 n. 2; Cesare Paoli, *Diplomatica*, new ed., ed. G. C. Bascapè, Manuali di filologia e storia, 1st ser., 1 (Florence, 1942; repr. 1969), 53.

an order. Ourliac noted a change from *c.* 950, when the term *convenientia* referred to entire documents, to 1050, when it began to indicate individual clauses. Its use was increasingly limited to the upper levels of society, for only nobles could seal an agreement with *foi* alone. Its geographic distribution was not consistent: some regions in the South lacked *convenientiae*, while they could be found in some northern documentation. In the end, however, Ourliac's vision was that of a legal historian. Filling the gap between the final disintegration of Carolingian public order and the reintroduction of Roman concepts – a period, in his words, "devoid of all law" – *convenientiae* served to create and impose *legal* rules, if only for the upper reaches of society. The principal function of the *convenientia* was to establish a *droit des grands*.[57]

The work of Ourliac guaranteed that studies of the tenth to twelfth centuries would take notice of the *convenientia* when and where it occurred. Researchers were not content, however, to accept his formulations, and their work has revealed the wide range of issues implicated in the study of the *convenientia*. The most significant extensions and revisions have come from scholars of Mediterranean Europe, especially Pierre Bonnassie and Élisabeth Magnou-Nortier. Bonnassie first undertook a detailed analysis of a subset of *convenientiae* in eleventh-century Catalonia: those agreements that established "feudal" ties.[58] He created a tripartite typology of feudal conventions and established a chronology, fitting the convention into his vision of the overall shape of Catalan history. Bonnassie later refined these notions,[59] clarifying the relation between homage and *convenientia* and placing the *convenientia* in the context of European practices:

Understood in this sense, the *convenientia*, which takes place before homage and before the oath, appears as the principal element of any feudo-vassalic contract. Or, more exactly, it constitutes in itself that contract. Such pacts, duly negotiated between parties, must have existed everywhere: the originality of southern regions is only to have given them – very often if not always – a written form.[60]

---

57 Ourliac, "La *convenientia*." See also his comments during the Discussion of Pierre Bonnassie, "Les conventions féodales dans la Catalogne du XIe siècle," *AM* 80 (1968), 529–50, at *AM* 80 (1968), 555–56; Ourliac, "Troubadours et juristes," *Cahiers de civilisation médiévale* 8 (1965), 166–67; Ourliac, "La tradition romaine dans les actes toulousains des Xe et XIe siècles," *Revue historique de droit français et étranger* 60 (1982), 579 n. 5; and Paul Ourliac and Jehan de Malafosse, *Histoire du droit privé*, 2nd ed., 2 vols. (Paris, 1969–71), 1:80–81.

58 Bonnassie, "Les conventions."

59 Bonnassie, *La Catalogne*, 2:566–69, 736–39. For the Catalan *convenientia*, see also Ruiz-Domènec, *L'estructura feudal*, 79–96, and Thomas N. Bisson, "Feudalism in Twelfth-Century Catalonia," in *Medieval France*, 154–55. José Mas Martinez, "Las conveniencias condales de Ramon Berenguer I, 1040–1076" (tesi de llicenciatura, Universitat Autònoma de Barcelona, 1983), which I consulted only briefly, is based primarily on published material.

60 Bonnassie, *La Catalogne*, 2:737.

Bonnassie's findings, based primarily on the "feudal convention" and on eleventh-century evidence, are now regularly incorporated into studies of the history of Catalonia.

Magnou-Nortier, approaching the history of southern French society via lexicographical studies, has encountered *convenientiae* in several different institutional contexts. They played a role in the power struggles between the count of Toulouse and the *moyenne aristocratie* in the eleventh century and contributed to the rise and stabilization of courts of arbitration. But these uses of *convenientiae* by the lay aristocracy were less crucial, in her analysis, than their use by the Church; she has linked the *convenientia* to the Peace of God movement and attacks on "bad customs" (*malae consuetudines*).[61] Combining these several threads with her studies on the Merovingian and Carolingian periods,[62] Magnou-Nortier used the *convenientia* to illustrate a cultural divide between North and South. Thus northern relationships were based on *foi*, while southern ones were based on *convenientiae*; the *vasselage* of Roland on the one hand, and Marie de Ventadour's attack on the image of lover-as-servant on the other, serve as symbols of two different worlds.[63] Geoffrey Koziol similarly contrasts a northern culture based on hierarchy and supplication with a more pluralistic southern community held together by pacts.[64] The world depicted in the *Conventum* between William V of Aquitaine and Hugh of Lusignan (*c.* 1022x28) corresponds well to this model. While in formal terms this enigmatic document differs substantially from the Catalan

---

[61] Magnou-Nortier, *La société laïque*, 165, 190, 193; Magnou-Nortier, "Fidélité et féodalité méridionales d'après les serments de fidélité (Xᵉ–début XIIᵉ siècle)," *AM* 80 (1968), 461–64, and her comments during the Discussion of that paper, *AM* 80 (1968), 478; Magnou-Nortier, "Les mauvaises coutumes en Auvergne, Bourgogne méridionale, Languedoc et Provence au XIᵉ siècle: Un moyen d'analyse sociale," in *Structures féodales*, 142–43, 148–51, 161. See also Hideyuki Katsura, "Serments, hommages et fiefs dans la seigneurie des Guilhem de Montpellier (fin XIᵉ–début XIIIᵉ siècle)," *AM* 104 (1992), 153–61; Christian Lauranson-Rosaz, "Les mauvaises coutumes d'Auvergne (fin Xᵉ–XIᵉ siècle)," *AM* 102 (1990), 579.

[62] Élisabeth Magnou-Nortier, *Foi et fidélité: Recherches sur l'évolution des liens personnels chez les Francs du VIIᵉ au IXᵉ siècle*, Publications de l'Université de Toulouse–Le Mirail, ser. A, 28 (Toulouse, 1976). Aside from her studies, the only work to focus on the social dimensions of the early medieval *convenientia* has been Patrick J. Geary, "Extra-judicial Means of Conflict Resolution," in *La giustizia nell'alto medioevo (secoli V–VIII)*, 2 vols., Settimane di studio del Centro italiano di studi sull'alto medioevo 42 (Spoleto, 1995), 1:575–85.

[63] Élisabeth Magnou-Nortier, "La foi et les *convenientiae*: Enquête lexicographique et interprétation sociale," in Danielle Buschinger, ed., *Littérature et société au Moyen Âge: Actes du colloque des 5 et 6 mai 1978* ([Amiens], 1978), 249–62. See also her article in *Lexikon des Mittelalters*, 10 vols. (Munich, 1977–99), s.v. *convenientia*. Ourliac ("Troubadours et juristes," 284–85) found the culture of the *convenientia* expressed in troubadour lyric; cf. Fredric L. Cheyette, "Women, Poets, and Politics in Occitania," in Theodore Evergates, ed., *Aristocratic Women in Medieval France* (Philadelphia, 1999), 138–77.

[64] Geoffrey Koziol, *Begging Pardon and Favor: Ritual and Political Order in Early Medieval France* (Ithaca, 1992), 16.

convenientia, the relationships and conflicts it describes are very similar to those examined in the pages that follow.[65]

Many other studies touch on the subject of *convenientiae* without offering detailed treatments. In León and Castile, the history of the *convenientia* is tied to that of the "pledge-homage" (*pleito-homenaje*), the use of vassalic homage to reinforce a sworn promise to fulfill a commitment.[66] *Convenientiae* from tenth-century Provence defined agreements between landowners and tenants; later they determined the division of inheritances, the terms of castle-guard, the formation of alliances, and the details of other types of agreements.[67] In Latium, the *convenientia*'s primary function was to record the vassalic contract, though it also served to conclude judicial proceedings.[68] Additional studies have shown that *convenientiae* appear not only on the shores of the Mediterranean, but throughout the Midi and in unquestionably northern areas such as Coucy and the Beauvaisis.[69]

---

[65] Jane Martindale, "An Introduction to the *Conventum inter Guillelmum Aquitanorum comitem et Hugonem Chiliarchum*, 1969," in Martindale, *Status, Authority and Regional Power: Aquitaine and France, 9th to 12th Centuries* (Aldershot, 1997), VIIa; Martindale, ed., "*Conventum inter Guillelmum Aquitanorum comitem et Hugonem Chiliarchum*," in Martindale, *Status*, VIIb; George T. Beech, Yves Chauvin, and Georges Pon, eds., *Le Conventum (vers 1030): Un précurseur aquitain des premières épopées*, Publications romanes et françaises 212 (Geneva, 1995) provides a new edition. See also Jane Martindale, "Dispute, Settlement and Orality in the *Conventum inter Guillelmum Aquitanorum comitem et Hugonem Chiliarchum*: A Postscript to the Edition of 1969," in Martindale, *Status*, VIII (pp. 1–36); George T. Beech, "The Lord/Dependant (Vassal) Relationship: A Case Study from Aquitaine *c.* 1030," *Journal of Medieval History* 24 (1998), 1–30. While I do not accept Beech's general conclusions concerning the nature of the text, I agree that it is not a *convenientia* (Beech, Chauvin, and Pon, eds., *Le Conventum*, 16–21). The term does, however, appear in the text (Martindale, ed., "*Conventum*," 544; Beech, Chauvin, and Pon, eds., *Le Conventum*, 128, line 111), and the chronological coincidence with the earliest Catalan *convenientiae* is very striking.

[66] Hilda Grassotti, *Las instituciones feudo-vasalláticas en León y Castilla*, 2 vols., Pubblicazioni del Centro italiano di studi sull'alto medioevo 4 (Spoleto, 1969), 1:216–60; Grassotti, ed., "Homenaje de García Ramírez a Alfonso VII: Dos documentos inéditos," *Cuadernos de historia de España* 37–38 (1963), 318–29; Grassotti, ed., "Sobre una concesión de Alfonso VII a la iglesia salmantina," *Cuadernos de historia de España* 49–50 (1969), 339–46; Grassotti, ed., "Una 'convenientia' prestimonial entre un arzobispo y el emperador," *Cuadernos de historia de España* 51–52 (1970), 6, 15–18.

[67] Jean-Pierre Poly, *La Provence et la société féodale (879–1166): Contribution à l'étude des structures dites féodales dans le Midi* (Paris, 1976), 105–11, 146–53, 164–67, 207–9, 346–51. See also Stephen Weinberger, "Cours judiciaires, justice et responsabilité sociale dans la Provence médiévale: IXᵉ–XIᵉ siècle," *Revue historique* 267 (1982), 283–84; Weinberger, "Les conflits entre clercs et laïcs dans la Provence du XIᵉ siècle," *AM* 92 (1980), 269–79; Paul Amargier, "Un épisode de justice à la Cadière (Var) à la fin du Xᵉ siècle," *Provence historique* 28 (1978), 302.

[68] Pierre Toubert, *Les structures du Latium médiéval: Le Latium méridional et la Sabine du IXᵉ siècle à la fin du XIIᵉ siècle*, 2 vols., Bibliothèque des Écoles françaises d'Athènes et de Rome 221 (Rome, 1973), 2:1141–42, 1196 n. 2, 1251, 1303 n. 2. See now François Bougard, *La justice dans le royaume d'Italie de la fin du VIIIᵉ siècle au début du XIᵉ siècle*, Bibliothèque des Écoles françaises d'Athènes et de Rome 291 (Rome, 1995), 75–76, 343–46.

[69] Michel Rouche, "Les survivances antiques dans trois cartulaires du Sud-Ouest de la France aux Xᵉ et XIᵉ siècles," *Cahiers de civilisation médiévale* 23 (1980), 95–96; Constance Hoffman Berman, *Medieval Agriculture, the Southern French Countryside, and the Early Cistercians: A Study of Forty-Three Monasteries*, Transactions of the American Philosophical Society 76:5 (Philadelphia, 1986), 94–95,

Introduction

The *convenientia*, then, as a term and as an idea, covers wide semantic and geographical ranges. The work of Bonnassie and Ourliac represents a recognized orthodoxy, which is starting to work its way into textbooks and syntheses.[70] Nevertheless, previous scholarship has recognized and examined only partial facets of what appears to be a widespread social phenomenon. The interrelationship of the various meanings of *convenientia* and the import of regional differences remain poorly understood. The notion of the *convenientia* as a characteristic element of southern European society can only be advanced if its various aspects can be integrated. What holds together the ideas of contract, "feudo-vassalic relations," and dispute settlement? The findings of the various regional studies on the Midi need to be subjected to a synthesis, and additional work is required on the *convenientia* in the rest of the Iberian Peninsula. Furthermore, a clearer understanding is needed of the relationship between this documentation and prevailing social realities across Europe. Rereading northern European records in the light of southern material – an ironic reversal – is a particularly exciting possibility in this regard. The *conventiones* that appear during the "anarchy" of the reign of Stephen of England (1135–54), for example, offer striking parallels to the *convenientiae* in Catalonia under Ramon Berenguer I.[71] This is the work of the future; the aims of the present study are more modest.

This study addresses only a part of the history of the *convenientia*. Geographically, the focus is on Catalonia, or to be more accurate, the counties subject to the counts of Barcelona, some of which eventually became Catalonia – an ever changing set of lands. For the eleventh

107–14. See also André Debord, *La société laïque dans les pays de la Charente Xe–XIIe s.* (Paris, 1984), 257–58, 380, 397; Christian Lauranson-Rosaz, *L'Auvergne et ses marges (Velay, Gévaudan) du VIIIe au XIe siècle: La fin du monde antique?* (Le Puy-en-Velay, 1987), 358–65; Olivier Guillot, *Le comte d'Anjou et son entourage au XIe siècle*, 2 vols. (Paris, 1972), 1:289–90; Dominique Barthélemy, *Les deux âges de la seigneurie banale: Pouvoir et société dans la terre des sires de Coucy (milieu XIe–milieu XIIIe siècle)*, Publications de la Sorbonne, Série histoire ancienne et médiévale, 12 (Paris, 1984), 51–52; Olivier Guyotjeannin, "Recherches sur le développement de la seigneurie épiscopale au nord du royaume de France (Xème–début XIIIème s.): Les exemples de Beauvais et Noyon," 2 vols. (thèse de 3e cycle, Paris IV, 1981), 1:100 and n. 115. The published version of this thesis does not include the texts of the documents: Guyotjeannin, *Episcopus et comes: Affirmation et déclin de la seigneurie épiscopale au nord du royaume de France (Beauvais-Noyon, Xe–début XIIIe siècle)*, Mémoires et documents publiés par la Société de l'École des chartes 30 (Geneva, 1987), 26–27.

[70] E.g., Robert Boutruche, *Seigneurie et féodalité*, vol. 2, *L'apogée (XIe–XIIIe siècles)* (Paris, 1970), 313 n. 1; Fossier, *Enfance de l'Europe*, 1:444–45, 455–58, 464; Elizabeth M. Hallam, *Capetian France, 987–1328* (London, 1980), 55–56, 60; Poly and Bournazel, *La mutation féodale*, 146.

[71] Edmund King, "Dispute Settlement in Anglo-Norman England," *Anglo-Norman Studies* 14 (1991), 115–30; David Crouch, "A Norman 'conventio' and Bonds of Lordship in the Middle Ages," in George Garnett and John Hudson, eds., *Law and Government in Medieval England and Normandy: Essays in Honour of Sir James Holt* (Cambridge, 1994), 299–324; Charles Coulson, "The French Matrix of the Castle-Provisions of the Chester-Leicester *conventio*," *Anglo-Norman Studies* 17 (1994), 65–86.

century, the eastern counties of Old Catalonia provide almost all of the evidence; for the twelfth century, more materials are available from the reconquered lands to the west and from the trans-Pyrenean possessions to the north. A more intensive study of these regions is certainly possible, but here they play only a secondary role. The chronological limits of this investigation – 1000–1200 – are similarly flexible. The earliest surviving document with the form "hec est convenientia" dates from *c.* 1021, but understanding the context of this "first" *convenientia* requires an examination of the tenth-century Catalan evidence. At the other end of this time span, there is no "last" *convenientia* to mark an end to the period. The structures described shade into a new system in the course of the late twelfth century, a transition that has not been examined as fully as the earlier one. Despite this indistinct beginning and end, it is clear that these two centuries witnessed the development, diffusion, and decline of the *convenientia* as an important element in Catalan society.

This study is presented in six chapters. The first analyzes the emergence in early-eleventh-century Catalonia of the written agreement known as the *convenientia*, addressing head on the issue of the relationship between documentary change and social realities. By tracing the *development* of written agreements, rather than simply their appearance, it is possible to present a more sophisticated model of the connections between words written on parchment and the institutions that inspired those words. The next two chapters offer a synchronic presentation of the variety of written agreements and the structures they defined, with a focus on the agreements of Ramon Berenguer I of Barcelona. Chapter 2 examines the various types of *convenientiae*, explores what unifies them, and shows how collective analysis of these agreements illuminates the institutional structures of eleventh- and twelfth-century Catalonia. Chapter 3 considers the various means by which parties, having made these agreements, endeavored to keep them. This first half of the study thus analyses crucial aspects of medieval social, institutional, and legal history, as well as scribal practice, within the specific context of the documentary evidence from Catalonia.

Chapters 4 and 5 are more diachronic, and more explicitly concerned with the political history of Catalonia and neighboring regions. The focus here is on the changing role of written agreements, particularly agreements for castle tenure, for it is in that context that continuities and developments are most apparent. Chapter 4 details the establishment of structures of power in eleventh-century Catalonia, focusing on the diffusion of networks of castle holding and the use of the *convenientia*, first by the counts of the region and the lay aristocracy, and then by the four principal Catalan dioceses and three well-documented monasteries.

Chapter 5 chronicles the fortunes of these agreements, and networks of agreements, in the twelfth century in both lay and ecclesiastical milieux. Chapter 6 places the *convenientia* in a wider context by examining the relationship between writing and power in medieval Catalonia.

The interaction of power and the written word is an aspect of the wider debate on medieval literacy.[72] It has often been studied where it is most apparent: in the case of literate administration. This is, in part, because much of the relevant evidence was produced by governments, or by local lords whose activities occasionally resemble governance. But administration is only one piece of a larger puzzle. While the writing offices of eleventh- and twelfth-century Catalonia were bureaucratic organs only in a loose sense, especially in the earlier period and outside the comital court, the documents that they produced were at all times closely linked to the exercise of power. This is as true of an intrafamily agreement as it is of a contract for castle-guard. Furthermore, these documents were not simple byproducts of the exercise of power; they were integral elements of its conception, construction, and application. Thus we need to look at archival sources not simply for their content, but also for their own highly complex role in the societies that produced them. This certainly complicates the task of reading the sources, but at the same time it increases their value as evidence. This approach to the history of the eleventh and twelfth centuries in the medieval West can and should be applied beyond such a small, if archivally rich, region as Catalonia. But Catalonia has proved to be a particularly productive laboratory for the examination of medieval societies. It is thus a promising place to start.

---

[72] Hans-Werner Goetz, *Moderne Mediävistik: Stand und Perspektiven der Mittelalterforschung* (Darmstadt, 1999), 339–65, offers a useful survey of recent scholarship on medieval literacy and related issues. On literacy and power in particular, see Janet L. Nelson, "Literacy in Carolingian Government," in McKitterick, ed., *The Uses of Literacy*, 258–96, and Alan K. Bowman and Greg Woolf, eds., *Literacy and Power in the Ancient World* (Cambridge, 1994).

Chapter 1

THE FIRST *CONVENIENTIA*:
SOCIAL AND DOCUMENTARY CHANGE
AROUND THE YEAR 1000

Around the year 1021, the young counts of Barcelona and Urgell, Berenguer Ramon I and Ermengol II, met, held negotiations, and concluded an agreement. They made promises to each other concerning the granting and holding of castles, oaths of fidelity, guarantees, and procedures for the resolution of conflicts. The record of this agreement is the earliest surviving *convenientia* from the Catalan counties.[1] The complexity of the document suggests that it was not the first such agreement of its kind, nor the first to be written down. This very complexity and the prominence of the participants, however, make the agreement a useful symbol of a social and documentary transformation in the region. It provides a touchstone for an examination of the context in which the *convenientia* emerged, an examination that demonstrates the links between changes in documents and changes in institutions.

The exemplar of this first surviving *convenientia*, which appears to be an original, is striking both for its size and its length: at 2,500 words it is among the longest eleventh-century records in the comital archive. It is the form and substance of the agreement, however, that are most worthy of attention. While most charters from this period serve principally to record the actions of one party to a transaction (e.g., "I sell to you . . ."; "I grant to you . . ."), this document indicates in a balanced fashion the acts and responsibilities of *both* parties. The agreement has three main

---

[1] BRI extra. 2001★. For earlier commentaries: Sobrequés, *Els grans comtes*, 27; Michel Zimmermann, ed., *Les sociétés méridionales autour de l'an mil: Répertoire des sources et documents commentés* (Paris, 1992), 175–86. LA 4:437★, dated 977x78 and beginning "Hec est convenientia," is almost certainly a forgery (below, p. 181). *Remences* 3 is also highly suspect. The dating clause begins "Facta est hec convenientia," but the document is dated "anno Incarnationis Domini 971," two centuries before widespread adoption of dating by the incarnation year, and mentions as a witness the "Dapifer de Moncada" well before the earliest certain notices of either a seneschal or a Montcada (Shideler, *Montcadas*, 11; Antoni Pladevall i Font, "Els senescals dels comtes de Barcelona durant el segle XI," *Anuario de estudios medievales* 3 [1966], 115–16).

sections. The first describes the undertakings of Ermengol, the second the undertakings of Berenguer, and the third the procedures for the settlement of disputes.

The opening lines of the agreement reveal that Ermengol is to be the commended man of Berenguer, is to swear fidelity to him, grant him aid against all men except the viscount of Osona and his brother, and not defy a request to provide aid. Complicated details of his guarantees for the agreement form most of what follows. Ermengol offers four sureties to Berenguer "that he will remain in his homage and fidelity."[2] These individuals are to act as sureties until Ermengol holds in a solid (*solidus*) manner the five castles of Montmagastre, Alòs, Rubió, Malagastre, and Artesa, strategically located on the Segre River at the frontier with the *taifa* realm of Lleida. At that point Ermengol is to grant those castles and their holders to Berenguer as pledges. These new pledges, however, are not replacements for the four original sureties, for these four individuals are also sureties for this second part of the agreement: if Ermengol does not grant the castles in pledge to Berenguer within fifty days of having them solidly, the sureties have thirty days to hand themselves and their lands over to Berenguer. Furthermore, if he does hand over the castles in pledge, the four are still to act as sureties that he will remain in Berenguer's homage and fidelity.

The agreement then addresses, in equal detail, questions of succession. If Ermengol dies without an heir, the holders of the five castles have fifty days to transfer control of the castles to Berenguer, or to Berenguer's son, if Berenguer is dead. If there is an heir, he has 100 days to become the man of Berenguer, or of his son; if he fails to or does not wish to perform this homage, the holders of the castles are, likewise, to transfer control of them to the count of Barcelona. Similarly, if Berenguer dies while Ermengol is still alive, Ermengol is to become the commended man of Berenguer's son within 100 days of his father's death, making the same oaths and offering the same guarantees, in return for the same grants, with the same consequences for failure to do so. The next clauses record broader agreements concerning succession. If Ermengol dies without an heir, the whole county of Urgell shall revert to the count of Barcelona as an alod. If he dies leaving a minor heir, the county and its land are to be under the tutelage of the count of Barcelona. This first section of the agreement ends with a default clause, which sets a sixty-day period for emendation before the various pledges and sureties incur.

---

[2] "ut in sua fidelitate stet et hominatico." In what follows a "surety" is personal surety and a "pledge" is real surety. In the text, a single term is used (*pignus*). See below, pp. 124–33.

Berenguer's half of the agreement has the same basic structure (under-takings, guarantees, succession, default), but while in Ermengol's half the guarantees predominate, in Berenguer's half it is the undertakings. He swears not to injure Ermengol's person or his property and promises aid against all men and women except the viscount of Osona. He then prom-ises to grant back to Ermengol in fief (*per fevum*) the five castles, as well as the rights to and revenues of the diocese of Barcelona, the coastal castle of Eramprunyà, the viscounty of Barcelona, and the comital estates (*honores*) held by three individuals. The holders of those *honores*, as well as the viscount and the bishop, are to be the men of Ermengol, to accept their lands as fiefs from him, and to swear fidelity to him, reserving their fidelity, however, to the count of Barcelona. After a clause splitting the rights of election and investiture to the see of Barcelona, the agreement lists additional lands to be given to the count of Urgell, lands *not* described as granted in fief: a comital demesne near Eramprunyà, one-half of the count's present and future possessions in the county of Osona, and certain lands in the county of Girona after their recovery from the count-ess Ermessenda. Berenguer also promises to commend to Ermengol either the viscount of Girona with his lands or the viscount's son, Arbert Amat.[3] The next section concerns a promise of a payment of 5,000 *solidi* of Islamic silver or 100 ounces of gold, for which Berenguer offers the famous sword Tizona as a pledge.[4] If he does not grant the sword, he must follow a payment schedule, for which he offers his rights in Montmagastre and Alòs in pledge.

Berenguer then presents his guarantees for keeping the agreement; like Ermengol, he names four men with their comital *honores* (the three indi-viduals whose lands had been granted, as well as Mir Geribert, a power-ful frontier lord), and adds his rights in the five castles. The same terms are granted: fifty days for emendation of default and thirty days there-after for the sureties to perform. The clauses dealing with succession are repeated, mutatis mutandis. If Ermengol dies, Berenguer is to grant the same fief and swear the same oaths to his heir. If Berenguer dies with a minor heir, Ermengol is to hold the county of Barcelona in tutelage. The default clause is identical to the one added to Ermengol's half of the text.

The final section establishes procedures for the settlement of disputes arising from disagreements concerning the guarantees: a judicial duel, performed within sixty days of the initial complaint of either of the

---

[3] Jaume Coll i Castanyer, "Els vescomtes de Girona," *Annals de l'Institut d'estudis gironins* 30 (1988–89), 50, which proposes a different date for this document.

[4] Cf. Ramón Menéndez Pidal, ed., *Poema de mio Cid*, 6th ed., Clásicos castellanos 24 (Madrid, 1951), lines 2426, 2575, 2727, 3153, 3175, 3189, 3201, 3555, 3643. The Cid may have acquired this sword in 1090 as part of the ransom of Berenguer Ramon II (Sobrequés, *Els grans comtes*, 118).

parties to the agreement. The duel is to be performed by novice knights, ones "who have never done battle with a club and shield."[5] The agreement details the possible combinations of the disputants (among Ermengol, Berenguer, their heirs, and the bailiffs of underage heirs). The loser of the battle loses his pledges and sureties, while the winner's pledges and sureties are considered to be released. The effect of the outcome of this dispute on the agreement as a whole is not specified.

A proper analysis of the substance of this *convenientia* rests on an understanding of its historical context. On the surface, the agreement appears very unbalanced. Ermengol's obligations are limited to becoming the commended man of Berenguer and swearing fidelity and aid to him. In return, he receives an equivalent promise of aid and an oath lacking a promise of fidelity, but he also gains extensive grants in fief – including rights in the diocese and viscounty of Barcelona – and a payment of 100 ounces of gold. This apparent imbalance suggests that, in fact, the commendation was seen as highly significant, at least by the count of Barcelona. In retrospect, it appears as an early step in the reestablishment of the supremacy of the count of Barcelona over his neighbors, but this was probably not in the mind of Berenguer when he entered into this agreement. Such a heavy investment in what could only be long-term results from a count in a relatively weak position is unlikely. This first *convenientia* must have been directed at more immediate goals and concerns.

Two major political situations dominated this period. The first was the renewal of attacks on the western frontier. The text of the agreement shows that Ermengol II was not yet in possession of the five castles named.[6] The few indications for activity on this portion of the frontier in the early years of the reign of Berenguer Ramon I, however, point to Christian control of the lands.[7] Thus while the *convenientia* assumes that the castles will be held by Ermengol "solidly" in the near future, an offensive alliance against Lleida would not seem to be the prime motivation for the agreement. It does not describe such an alliance, nor does it raise the spectre of the *pagani* to whom Catalan scribes freely referred. It was not, then, problems of the frontier that motivated this pact, but a second political situation: the internal power struggle between Berenguer Ramon and his mother, the countess Ermessenda.

When did Berenguer Ramon leave the tutelage of his mother and begin to govern independently? This is partly an irrelevant question: Ermessenda participated in acts of governance throughout her son's

---

[5] "qui umquam non fecissent batala cum fuste et scuto."
[6] "usque Ermengaudus iamdictus habeat solidos . . . Et tunc quando predictus Ermengaudus habuerit hoc totum solidum."   [7] Below, n. 10.

reign, so the precise date of Berenguer's majority is not very important. There was, however, a serious dispute between mother and son, resolved with the intervention of the bishop of Girona in 1022. The document recording Ermessenda's pledges for the resultant agreement is the only explicit evidence for the dispute.[8] Nevertheless, an examination of the patterns of subscription of documents by the countess and her son in the years leading up to the resolution reveals traces of the conflict; this method suggests that the height of the conflict fell between the autumn of 1020 and the summer of 1022. Since Berenguer never acted independently before the autumn of 1020, the *convenientia* should be from after that date.[9] It may thus represent an alliance between the two counts against the countess in the conflict of 1020–22.

Two aspects of the agreement point to an anti-Ermessenda alliance. The first of these is the disposition of the castles. As noted above, these were in all probability under Christian control. A grant to the monastery of Sant Sadurní de Tavèrnoles mentions renders to the masters of the castles, and these would not have been Islamic masters. That does not mean, however, that they were necessarily men loyal to Ermengol II. The counts of Barcelona led the campaign to recover this region and would have installed their own men at these sites, even if the conquests were nominally in the territory of the count of Urgell. The counts of Barcelona maintained an active interest in the area, as the grant to Tavèrnoles and another to Sant Miquel de Montmagastre confirm.[10] These also show that the bishop of Urgell recognized the superior influence of the counts of Barcelona in his diocese. This orientation toward Barcelona may have been a result of a tutorial relationship between the counts of Barcelona and the count of Urgell. Ermengol II of Urgell is thought to have been under the supervision of his uncle, Ramon Borrell of Barcelona, at the time of the latter's death in 1017, though there is no direct evidence for this.[11] Whether or not Ermengol was still under tutelage in the early 1020s, he, like Berenguer, would have

---

[8] BRI 46*.

[9] See Kosto, "Agreements," 144–48. Cf. Sobrequés, *Els grans comtes*, 25–26; Bofarull, *Los condes*, 1:230–38; Antoni Rovira i Virgili, *Història nacional de Catalunya*, 7 vols. (Barcelona, 1922–34), 3:475–77.

[10] DTavèrnoles 43 [CTavernoles 17] (a. 1017); BC 4139 (a. 1019?). For the latter, see Pedro Sanahuja, "Arnau Mir de Tost, caudillo de la Reconquista en tierras de Lérida," *Ilerda* 2:1 (1944), 9–11.

[11] Historians claim that Ramon Borrell acted as tutor for his nephew Ermengol II of Urgell, and that this arrangement was set forth in the testament of Ermengol I (DACU 300), but this is not the case. A document of 1024 in which Ermessenda and Berenguer Ramon appear alongside Ermengol has been adduced as evidence that the count of Urgell was at that point only fourteen years old, but it is subscribed only by the count and reads "Haec omnia recognoscens me abere legtimos mee etatis .xiiii.^{cim} annos *et amplius integerrime* (i.e., 'and then some'; emphasis added) reddo atque dono" (DACU 390). See Bofarull, *Los condes*, 1:235; Rovira i Virgili, *Història*, 3:578; Sobrequés, *Els grans comtes*, 9–10.

felt himself to be in the shadow of Ermessenda. Once of age, he would have needed to gain the allegiance of Ermessenda's men in the castles on his frontier that were the subject of the agreement, or replace these men with his own, in order to have them "solidly."

The description in the *convenientia* of the lands in Girona also suggests that this agreement created an alliance directed against Ermessenda. Berenguer promises to Ermengol a grant "when he (i.e., Berenguer) has the county of Girona 'solidly' from the control (*potestas*) of the countess Ermessenda."[12] The eventual settlement of the dispute between Ermessenda and her son in 1022 did not deprive the countess of her interests in Girona, which continued to be her base of operations throughout the subsequent turbulent decades; the castles that made up the pledge for that agreement were in the counties of Osona and Barcelona, not Girona. Unless Berenguer was counting on her imminent death, the only hope he could have of gaining the county of Girona from his mother was to prevail by force or in negotiation. An alliance with his cousin – or rather, the political subordination of his cousin, despite the high cost – would place significant pressure on the countess.[13]

Such a reconstruction of the political context of this first *convenientia* must remain on the level of hypothesis; the *convenientia* itself offers more certain evidence for the procedures and language involved in the formation of agreements. The maturity of the vocabulary of the *convenientia* is particularly striking. Ermengol promises to become the commended man of Berenguer, by his own hands (*homo comendatus manibus propriis*). Later he is said to have commended himself to the count (*se comendare*), and Berenguer promises to commend (*comendare*) the viscount of Girona to the count of Urgell. Ermengol gives guarantees that he will remain in the homage (*hominaticum*) of Berenguer. Similarly, the parties understand a complex system of oaths. Ermengol swears fidelity (*iurare fidelitatem*) to Berenguer, and the bishop and viscount of Barcelona, among others, are to swear fidelity to Ermengol, but reserve their fidelity (*salva fidelitate*) to Berenguer. Not all oaths are alike, however. Berenguer does not swear fidelity to Ermengol, but his life, limbs, county, fief (*fevum*), alods, and castles, as well as aid (*adiutorium*). "Not to injure" and "to provide" are to be understood in this oath; fidelity is not. The sureties also swear oaths, but again not of fidelity. They confirm by oath (*per sacramentum confirmare*) that they will perform their duties, or swear (*iurare*) to carry out specific acts. There is even a recognized age at which an oath may

---

[12] "quando habuerit . . . Gerundensem comitatum solidum de potestate Ermessindis comitisse."

[13] The fact that in the reciprocal tutorial arrangement the age of majority for heirs is set at twenty does not seem consistent with the interpretation offered here. Berenguer himself would not reach this age until 1024 or 1025, though his cousin may already have done so.

be made.[14] Both of the comital oaths are called *sacramentum*, but the content is understood to be different. Distinctions are also present in the terminology of fiefs: the castles are granted *per fevum*, while additional lands in Girona are simply granted. Fiefs are described as received *per manum* and as accepted from a lord. The clauses describing the latter relationships imply a close connection between being the man (*homo*) of an individual, receiving lands from his hand, and swearing fidelity to him.

The timetables that give structure to the *convenientia* are even more complex than the tenurial and interpersonal relationships. The parties are given time periods within which to act: Ermengol has 50 days after obtaining the castles to exchange them for his other guarantees, 60 days to amend a violation of the agreement, and 100 days after Berenguer's death to renew his fidelity to his son. Berenguer agrees to similar schedules. The personal and real guarantees for the overall performance of the agreement, for the granting of other guarantees, and for several subsections of the agreement are also structured around these terms, with waiting periods of thirty or fifty days for sureties to hand over castles. The ultimate arbitration mechanism, the judicial duel, is to take place within sixty days.

Some material in this agreement appears entirely new: it offers among the earliest appearances in Catalonia – and Europe – of *hominaticum* and *homo comendatus manibus propriis*.[15] But this novelty must be seen in the context of the well-developed character and consistency of the language. Such a complex and well-formed document is unlikely to have had no antecedents. Fortunately, the richness of the Catalan archives allows the historian to identify those antecedents and to follow the development of the individual elements that come together in this first *convenientia*. In doing so, we can uncover the *process* of documentary change, rather than simply noting the fact of change. This approach makes it possible to reach surer judgments about the connection between changes in the form of the written record and changes in society.

THE DOCUMENTARY CONTEXT

Because the term *convenientia* does appear in early medieval documentation from across Europe, before examining the narrower context of Catalan scribal practice in the tenth and eleventh centuries, we must address the possibility of institutional or formal continuity.[16]

---

[14] "quando fuerit ipsius aetatis quo possit sacramentum facere."

[15] Bonnassie, *La Catalogne*, 2:569, who cites also *CSCV* 479 – another dispute settlement – and BRI 36*, both dated 1020.

[16] For the following, see Adam J. Kosto, "The *convenientia* in the Early Middle Ages," *Mediaeval Studies* 60 (1998), 1–54.

Convenientia exhibits a rather wide semantic range in the early medieval sources. Classical and postclassical Latin writers used the word, derived from the verb *convenire* ("to come together"), in a general sense to mean "understanding," "concord," "harmony," or "coherence." It is found with this meaning in its sole appearance in the *Corpus iuris civilis*. *Convenientia* also served as a technical term, most commonly in rhetorical and scientific texts.[17] In the works of the late antique and early medieval periods, however, it appears more and more frequently with the sense of "an agreement," such as a legal agreement between two individuals on a particular matter.[18] Isidore of Seville, for example, in the book of his *Etymologies* devoted to legal terminology, writes: "A purchase and sale is an exchange of things and a contract arising from an agreement (*convenientia*)."[19] Although this legal sense quickly became more widespread, the general sense remained common, and it is often difficult to tell which meaning a scribe intended the word to convey. The problem is complicated by the orthographic and possibly semantic conflation of three different Latin words: *convenire*, *conivere*, and *cohibere*. Furthermore, even when clearly referring to an agreement, *convenientia* coexisted with many other terms signifying agreement (*conventus*, *pax/pactum/pactio*, *amicitia*, *placitum*, *foedus*, *finis*, *concordia* . . .), and it is rarely clear if these words had distinct technical meanings. Finally, it is often difficult to determine if the term *convenientia* refers to a document, or simply to the agreement itself, independent of the document. Careful attention to the usage of regions, eras, and even individual authors and scribes is essential.

Despite these difficulties, the early medieval sources provide ample evidence of the widespread use of the term *convenientia*, and even of the existence of a document – a diplomatic form – with that name. What was the function of the *convenientia*, considered not just as a document, but also as a legal institution? In Frankish sources, and especially in private charters from Bavaria, Rhaetia, and Italy, it appears most frequently in the context of promises, conditional grants, and the

---

[17] *Thesaurus linguae latinae* (Leipzig, 1900–), s.v. *convenientia*, 1; Albert Blaise, *Dictionnaire latin-français des auteurs chrétiens* (Turnhout, 1954), s.v. *conuenientia*, 1, 3; Paul Krueger, ed., *Corpus iuris civilis*, vol. 2, *Codex Iustinianus*, 11th ed. (Berlin, 1954), C. 1, 12, 6, 10.

[18] *Thesaurus linguae latinae*, s.v. *convenientia*, 2; Charles du Fresne, sieur du Cange, *Glossarium mediae et infimae latinitatis*, ed. Léopold Favre, 10 vols. (Niort, 1883–87), s.v. *convenientia*, 1. Here, *convenientia* is simply a Late Latin and Vulgar Latin doublet of *conventio*. See Yakov Malkiel, *Development of the Latin Suffixes -antia and -entia in the Romance Languages, with Special Regard to Ibero-Romance*, University of California Publications in Linguistics 1:4 (Berkeley, 1945), 43–50; Francesco Calasso, *La "convenientia": contributo alla storia del contratto in Italia durante l'alto medio evo*, Biblioteca della Rivista di storia del diritto italiano 9 (Bologna, 1932), 45.

[19] Isidore of Seville, *Etymologiarum sive originum libri XX*, ed. W. M. Lindsay, 2 vols. (Oxford, 1911), V.24.23 (lines 4–5): "Emtio et venditio est rerum commutatio atque contractus ex convenientia veniens."

settlement of disputes – precisely the types of documents in which the language of the *convenientia* emerged in eleventh-century Catalonia. The evidence would seem to suggest, therefore, that Catalan scribes of the eleventh century simply adopted an early medieval term, form, and institution. Visigothic evidence that would confirm such a hypothesis is unfortunately lacking.

The only firm evidence that the *convenientia* as a type of agreement was known in the Visigothic kingdom is a novel of Egica (687–702) that prescribes penalties for those who, after having brought a dispute before the king, proceed then to "settle out of court." The law refers to this extrajudicial settlement first as a *finis convenientie* and then simply as a *convenientia*.[20] The *Liber iudiciorum* continued to be cited in Catalonia regularly into the eleventh century, and therefore this text might have directly influenced later scribes in their construction of the *convenientia*. Unfortunately, detailed studies of citations of Visigothic law in charters of the ninth to twelfth centuries have not uncovered a single citation of this text, despite references to other laws of Book II, Title 2.[21] Neither the so-called *Formulae Visigothicae* nor a tenth-century formulary from the Catalan monastery of Santa Maria de Ripoll contain any mention of the term.[22] Likewise, the few surviving Visigothic charters offer no confirmation of the *convenientia* in the Iberian Peninsula in the fifth to eighth centuries.[23]

The closest thing to proof for the continuity of the *convenientia* is the second constitution *De Hispanis* of the Carolingian emperor Louis the Pious, issued in the form of a diploma in 816 in response to two complaints of refugees from the Islamic invasion of the Iberian Peninsula who had settled north of the Pyrenees. The second of these complaints was that *Hispani* were being ejected from lands by those to whom they had commended themselves, after they had improved those lands. Louis ordered that they and their descendants be allowed to keep the lands on the same terms that they had originally accepted ("sub quali convenientia atque

---

[20] Liber iudiciorum, II.2.10 (pp. 87–88); Yolanda García López, *Estudios críticos y literarios de la "Lex Wisigothorum,"* Memorias del Seminario de historia antigua 5 (Alcalá de Henares, 1996), 393–409. The term appears three other times in the code: II.1.28 (pp. 75–76), meaning "appropriate"; XII.3.21 (pp. 450–51), as an alternate reading for *conhibentia*, meaning "permission"; II.5.17 (pp. 116–17), meaning "method."; cf. *convenire* at V.4.5 (p. 219).

[21] Aquilino Iglesia Ferreirós, "La creación del derecho en Cataluña," *Anuario de historia del derecho español* 47 (1977), 401; Michel Zimmermann, "L'usage du droit wisigothique en Catalogne du IXᵉ au XIIᵉ siècle: Approches d'une signification culturelle," *Mélanges de la Casa de Velázquez* 9 (1973), 251–52; Walther Kienast, *Studien über die französischen Volkstämme des Frühmittelalters,* Pariser historische Studien 7 (Stuttgart, 1968), 169 (n. 43).

[22] Karl Zeumer, ed., "Formulae Visigothicae," in Zeumer, ed., *Formulae Merowingici et Karolini aevi,* MGH Legum sectio V (Hanover, 1886; repr. 1963), 572–95; Michel Zimmermann, ed., "Un formulaire du Xᵉᵐᵉ siècle conservé à Ripoll," *Faventia* 4:2 (1982), 25–86.

[23] Ángel Canellas López, *Diplomática hispano-visigoda,* Publicaciones de la Institución "Fernando el Católico" 730 (Zaragoza, 1979).

conditione acceperunt").[24] Here *convenientia* is used in reference to conditional grants of lands. This edict was supposed to have been issued in the Catalan counties, but it remains a single ambiguous reference 200 years before the next appearance of the term in documents from the region. It is no proof.

There are three possible explanations for the appearance of the *convenientia* in the Catalan counties in the first decades of the eleventh century. First, Catalan scribes may have invented the *convenientia* independently: they created a similar solution for a similar problem. Second, the language and form may have been introduced from neighboring lands, such as Languedoc.[25] Third, the earlier existence of the *convenientia* in the region may be hidden from view by a dearth of sources and a rigid adherence to formula in those that have survived. A definitive solution of the problem is not possible, though a striking correspondence in language and form supports an argument for continuity. Even if the Catalan *convenientia* was purely a product of the creativity of Catalan scribes, their creativity was fueled by elements in a notably persistent early medieval notarial culture.

Conditions

While the sole surviving version of the second constitution of Louis the Pious for the *Hispani* is too far removed from the original to support

---

[24] Ramon d'Abadal i de Vinyals, ed., *Els diplomes carolingis a Catalunya*, vol. 2 of *Catalunya carolíngia*, 2 parts, Memòries de la Secció històrico-arqueològica 2 (Barcelona, 1926–52), 2:420–21; Alfred Boretius and Victor Krause, eds., *Capitularia regum Francorum*, 2 vols., MGH Legum sectio II, 1–2 (Hanover, 1883–97; repr. 1960), no. 133 (1:263–64 at 264 line 6).

[25] After a mention in a diploma of Carloman for the cathedral of Narbonne in 884 (Félix Grat et al., eds., *Recueil des actes de Louis II le Bègue, Louis III et Carloman II, rois de France [877–884]* [Paris, 1978], no. 73 [p. 189, line 14]), the term *convenientia* reappears in Languedocian charters only from the mid-tenth century: an exchange of lands in Nîmes in 956 (Paris, Archives nationales, J. 307 [Toulouse IV], 48*); an oath by the recipient of a guardianship over lands of the monastery of Sainte-Marie de Camon in 959 (Denis de Sainte-Marthe and Barthélemy Hauréau, eds., *Gallia christiana in provincias ecclesiasticas distributa*, 16 vols. [Paris, 1715–1865], vol. 13, Instrumenta, Mirepoix, no. 2 [cols. 226–27]; Élisabeth Magnou-Nortier and Anne-Marie Magnou, eds., *Recueil des chartes de l'abbaye de La Grasse*, vol. 1, *779–1119*, Collection de documents inédits sur l'histoire de France, Section d'histoire médiévale et de philologie, Série in-8°, 24 [Paris, 1996], no. 76 [pp. 125–27]); the testament of Raimond II, count of Rouergue, in *c.* 961 (*HGL* 5:111). The term, with varying orthography, also appears from the tenth century in texts from Aragón; it seems to arrive in the kingdoms of Castile and León only from the late eleventh century (although see below, n. 138). See Antonio Ubieto Arteta, ed., *Cartulario de San Juan de la Peña*, 2 vols., Textos medievales 6, 9 (Valencia, 1962–63), nos. 13 (1:45–47, a. 905x25, *comenenza/couenienza*), 31 (1:91–93, s. 10, *pagina convenientia*); Roger Collins, "Visigothic Law and Regional Custom in Disputes in Early Medieval Spain," in Wendy Davies and Paul Fouracre, eds., *The Settlement of Disputes in Early Medieval Europe* (Cambridge, 1986), 98–99 and app. 18 (pp. 255–56), Jaca, a. 958 (*cominenza*). For León-Castile, see Hilda Grassotti, ed., "Sobre una concesión de Alfonso VII a la iglesia salmantina," *Cuadernos de historia de España* 49–50 (1969), 339–46 and documents cited there; Grassotti, ed., "Una 'convenientia' prestimonial entre un arzobispo y el emperador," *Cuadernos de historia de España* 51–52 (1970), 15–18.

any firm conclusions about sub-Pyrenean vocabulary,[26] it does indicate the context for many of the earliest appearances of the vocabulary of the *convenientia* in this region: the condition. Tenth- and early-eleventh-century scribes used a variety of different phrases to introduce conditional clauses in documents, all of which meant essentially "with the condition that": "in tale videlicet racione," "in tale pactum, ut," "in tali deliberacione," "in tale capcione," "sub tali taxacione et tenore ut," "in eo modo, ut," or simply "ut."[27] Another variation, employed in the Catalan counties with increasing regularity in the tenth century, used a term closely related etymologically to *convenientia*: *conventus*. This word usually appeared in the phrases "in tale conventu, ut" or "in tale pactum et conventum, ut."[28] These conditional constructions are found most commonly in three types of documents: grants of land (usually, though not always, in the form of donations), testaments, and pledges.

Scribes of the late tenth century who attempted to record conditional grants of land have left a confusing body of documents; the result of attempts to classify these documents has been equally confused. Modern treatises on the topic of medieval tenure of land describe various types of precarial grants (*precaria data, oblata,* or *remuneratoria*), donations (*post obitum, reservato usufructu, ad plantandum*), emphyteutic tenures, and agrarian contracts, all of which overlap in form and content. This confusion is inevitable, as it is an accurate reflection of a documentation that uses Roman legal terms and Frankish and Visigothic formulae without regard for the consistency or context that would provide clues to the thought processes of its creators.[29] The parties to these agreements imposed a bewildering variety of conditions on their transactions, and the scribes wrote them down. "Tali conventu ut" is not the only phrase to introduce conditions in grants of land; among the *precaria oblata* of the cartulary of Sant Cugat del Vallès, for example, "in tale videlicet racione" predominates.[30] Nor is the use of *conventus* limited to a particular type of condition. The most common are reservations for the life of the donor of the usufruct of

---

[26] Similarly, the testament of Raimond II of Rouergue (*HGL* 5:111), which includes a grant to Sant Feliu de Girona.   [27] DACU 65, 104; *DVic* 176; *ACondal* 9; *CSCV* 84, 246, 539.

[28] *CSCV* 48, 79; *DBarcelona* 11, 101.

[29] Eduardo de Hinojosa, *El régimen señorial y la cuestión agraria en Cataluña durante la Edad Media* (Madrid, 1905), esp. 61–74; Francesch Carreras y Candi, *Notes sobre los origens de la enfiteusis en lo territori de Barcelona* (Barcelona, 1910); Roger Grand, *Le contrat de complant depuis les origines jusqu'à nos jours* (Paris, 1917), esp. 21–42. None of these focuses on the period of interest here. Raimundo Noguera de Guzmán, "El precario y la 'precaria' (Notas para la historia de la enfiteusis)," *Estudios históricos y documentos de los archivos de protocolos* 2 (1950), 151–274, is of more immediate interest. See also *CSCV*, 1:xxxiv–xxxv, and Pierre Bonnassie, ed., "Un contrat agraire inédit du monastère de Sant Cugat (28 août 1040)," *Anuario de estudios medievales* 3 (1966), 441–50.

[30] Noguera de Guzmán, "El precario," 221 n. 230.

the donated property.[31] Other conditions extend the usufruct to the lives of one or more additional individuals, or to the donor's descendants.[32] These reservations frequently include promises of yearly renders, especially when the beneficiary is an ecclesiastical institution,[33] but conditions of this sort are found in transactions between individuals, as well.[34]

Conditions are also common in testaments of this period, as in their Visigothic and Roman antecedents. Here, too, scribes used a wide range of phrases to introduce these clauses, only a small number are introduced by *conventus*, and the use of this construction is not limited to one type of condition.[35] The most common conditions echo those found in the grants, specifying the terms on which land is to be held, for example, "in service" ("in servicio"), for life, or against a portion of the harvest (*tasca*).[36] Some conditions name a specific member of an institutional beneficiary to enjoy the use of the grant. Others prescribe the performance of a specific task.[37] The object of a conditional disposition introduced by the term *conventus* is not always land: Bernat I of Besalú (988–1020) left the episcopacy of Besalú to his second son, Enric, on condition that he be twenty-five years of age, have entered orders, and that the see be held from his elder brother.[38] Testamentary conditions were carried over into the documents, usually donations, executing the will of a testator.[39]

The third type of document that commonly contains a conditional phrase is the pledge, or *carta (sub)impignorationis*.[40] Comparatively few pledges have survived (and very few for the late tenth and early eleventh

---

[31] *DVic* 245: "in tale conventum quod nos tenemus ab omdem integritatem."

[32] *DVic* 613 ("in tale conventu ut dum ego supranominato Salla vixero teneam et possideam ipsum suprascriptum alodem sine ulla inquietatione de ullumque ominem, et post obitum meum remaneat in potestate de Otto levita ut ille hoc teneat et possideat . . . et post obitum suprascripto Otto levita ille cui suprascripto Otto levita in potestate relinquerit"); DACU 222; CSCV 275.

[33] *ACondal* 121 ("Donamus nos iamdicti hec omnia in eadem pactum vel placitum et tale conventum ut dum ego Trassemirus vivo teneam et possideam et faciam inde servicium per singulos annos"); Eixalada-Cuixà 81, 96; *DVic* 440; *DOliba* 39.

[34] *DVic* 339 (*donatio* against a yearly payment to donor and his heirs), 426 (life grant, reverting to donor on death of recipient).

[35] *STCA*, pp. 128–30. See, e.g., ACV 6/843★, which uses "tale conventu ut," "tale videlicet racione ut," and "tale videlicet racione vel conventu ut."

[36] ACV 6/180★; *DVic* 635 [*STCA* 55]; DACU 370 [*STCA* 128]; Eixalada-Cuixà 92; *NH* 11:69.

[37] DACU 370 [*STCA* 128] ("teneat Seniofredus presbiter nepus meus"); ACV 6/843★ ("teneant clericos qui altare decantat Sancti Petri"), 6/1249★ ("ipsi clerici pro meis delictis exorare non pigeant"), 9/i/103★ ("donet ad domum Sancti Petri sedis Vico solidos CCCtos"), 6/180★ ("redime\re/ faciant filios meos").

[38] BRI 36★. Bernat had appealed to the pope for the creation of this ephemeral diocese in 1012x17. Thomas Deswarte, "Rome et la spécificité catalane. La papauté et ses relations avec la Catalogne et Narbonne (850–1030)," *Revue historique* 294 (1995), 12, 20.   [39] *DVic* 611.

[40] Aquilino Iglesia Ferreirós, *La prenda contractual: Desde sus orígenes hasta la recepción del Derecho Común*, Las garantías reales en el derecho histórico español 1:1, Monografías de la Universidad de Santiago de Compostela 38 (Santiago de Compostela, 1977), esp. 113–250 for this period (not limited to Catalonia); Bonnassie, *La Catalogne*, 1:399–409.

centuries); once a pledge was redeemed or forfeited, the original document would have been canceled in some fashion or destroyed. The earliest *impignorationes* date from only 972 and 973, and the archives contain fewer than a dozen from before the millennium. The existence of other pledges is attested through indirect means, such as mentions in testaments, sales of forfeited pledges, and judgments of forfeit, but these do not use the conditional clauses of interest here.[41] Such a clause is included, however, in the formula for a pledge found in the formulary of Santa Maria de Ripoll, datable to the period 960x80: "I pledge to you the said vineyard and transfer to you proprietary right on the condition that ('in tali uidelicet pacto') you hold it in your power and cultivate it."[42] None of the earliest surviving documents follows this formula exactly. Some introduce the conditions with a negative hypothetical: "if ('quod si') I am unable to redeem to you that *mancusus* on the next feast of Saint Michael . . ."[43] Others, like the formulary, use a conditional phrase, but replace its "tali videlicet pacto" with "in ea/tale videlicet racione ut," "in tale capcione ut," or "in tale conventum ut/quod."[44]

These uses of conditional phrases provide the immediate background for two of the earliest appearances of the term *convenientia* in the Catalan counties. The first is in a record of a judgment dated 1011 from Sant Sadurní de Tavèrnoles. It describes the source of the dispute as an improperly executed exchange: "he drew up a charter of exchange for them, on the condition that ('in tali convenientia, ut') after his death and the death of his wife Berenguera, the lands that they had exchanged should remain to one of their sons whom they chose." Here *convenientia* is used in precisely the same manner as *conventus* is in earlier documents. In fact, in the

---

[41] Eixalada-Cuixà 100 (a. 976, sale of a forfeited pledge); *CSCV* 139 (a. 981, testament); *CSCV* 437, with AAM, Sant Cugat del Vallès 66★ (a. 1011, *querimonia* and judgment). OR, Sant Llorenç del Munt 62★, an inventory of lands and *cartae* of 1011, cites "cartas viiii inpignorationis quod teneo."

[42] Zimmermann, ed., "Un formulaire," 79 [*CSCV*, 1:xxxvi]: "Inpignoro tibi iamdicta uinea et in tuo iure eam trado *in tali uidelicet pacto* ut eam teneas in tua potestate et exfructuare eam facias" (emphasis added).

[43] *DVic* 610 (a. 997): "*quod si* ad festa sancti Michaelis archangeli in isto anno veniente proxima ventura non possum tibi ipsum manchoso persolvere" (emphasis added). Cf. *DBarcelona* 125 (a. 978x79); *DVic* 497 (a. 982); RBorrell 78★ (a. 1005); BRI 41★ (a. 1022).

[44] "Racione/ratione": *DVic* 419 (a. 972); *CSCV* 102 (a. 973); *DVic* 550 (a. 990); Pere Puig i Ustrell, ed., *El monestir de Sant Llorenç del Munt sobre Terrassa: Diplomatari dels segles X i XI*, 3 vols., Col·lecció diplomataris 8–10 (Barcelona, 1995), no. 164 (2:844–45, a. 1017); BRI 41bis★ (a. 1022); *Santa Anna* 28 (a. 1028). "Capcione/captione": *DBarcelona* 231 (a. 992); Puig i Ustrell, ed., *Sant Llorenç*, no. 82 (2:738–39, a. 995); OR, Sant Cugat del Vallès 92★ (a. 1002). "Conventum": OR, Sant Benet de Bages 85 (a. 1010); ACV 6/192 (a. 1018); DACU 385 (a. 1024); Joaquim Miret i Sans, ed., "Los noms personals y geogràfichs de la encontrada d'Organyà en los segles Xè y XIè," *Boletín de la Real academia de buenas letras de Barcelona* 8 (1915–16), no. 76 (p. 439). If the date given by Miret i Sans for this last document is correct (929), this would be the earliest pledge and the earliest use of the phrase "tale conventum quod," but the document is probably from the 980s. See Kosto, "Agreements," 90 n. 33.

revised exchange, the text of which is included in the judgment, the condition is introduced with the phrase "in tale videlicet racione et conventu."[45] The second occurrence also appears in the context of a dispute in a cartulary from the northwestern regions, that of the monastery of Santa Maria de Gerri. Around 1018, Jofre Maier de Mur quitclaimed a disputed property to the monastery and received it back as a life grant: "I have accepted it on the condition that ('in tali convenientia accepi eam ut') I should hold it during my lifetime, and after my death it should remain freely and fully to the said monastery without any reservation."[46] Despite these two examples, the use of the term *convenientia* in conditional phrases of this type remained quite rare until later in the eleventh century.[47] The immediate future of the term was as a designation for a document or variety of agreement; its origins in this sense are to be found elsewhere, in the abstract use of terms normally used to introduce conditions.

Scribes in the ninth and tenth centuries referred to documents or to transactions recorded by documents with a circumscribed typological vocabulary: *vinditio* (sale), *donatio* (grant), *recognitio* (acknowledgment), *exvacuatio* (quitclaim), *concambio* (exchange), *pignoratio* (pledge), or most frequently simply *carta*. On a few occasions, however, they departed from this model by employing a term normally found in a conditional phrase. The first step was to use such terms outside conditional phrases. A testament from Vic dated 953 contains an example of this transition: it refers back to an earlier condition, which had been introduced by the phrase "in ea videlice ratione ut," with the phrase "with the abovementioned condition" ("in tale conventum quod supra insertum est").[48] Outside the conditional phrase, *conventus* was free to develop into the name for a type of agreement. A charter of sale, also from Vic, refers to "the agreement that was between us" ("ipsum conventum cot inter nos fuit"), which in turn seems to refer to an earlier agrarian contract, a type of conditional grant. Here *conventus* indicates not a single condition of an agreement, but an entire conditional agreement.[49]

---

[45] DTavèrnoles 41 [CTavernoles 16]: "karta illis comutacionis abebat facta *in tali convenientia, ut* post mortem suam et de uxoris sue Berengera ad unum de filiis illorum quem illi eligere voluissent, remansissent ipsos eschamios quod abebant inter se factos" (emphasis added).

[46] *Gerri* 4: "*in tali convenientia* accepi eam ut tenerem in vitam meam et post mortem meam libera et solida remaneat predicto cenobio sine ullo retinimento" (emphasis added). For the date, see Kosto, "Agreements," 92 n. 35.

[47] The possibility must be allowed that these two instances are a result of scribal errors in the twelfth-century cartularies. Other early citations: LA 2:410 (a. 1038); AAM, Sant Benet de Bages 139 (a. 1067).   [48] ACV 6/1249*.

[49] *DVic* 30 (a. 900). Cf. ACV 9/ii/16* (a. 1015: "hunc pactum scripture stabilitatis"); *CSCV* 130 (a. 978x79: "advenit michi per chartam conventatam . . . ego illi cartam conventatam feci"). *NH* 11:168 (a. 977), which ends "Facta est concordia," is probably a forgery or an interpolation (*CDSG* 114). See also below, n. 55.

At the same time, a new word entered the scribal vocabulary: *conventio*. Its earliest appearance is in a document recording the restitution of two churches to the monastery of Sant Esteve de Banyoles by Serf de Déu (Servus Dei), bishop of Girona, in 889. The grant was made on the condition that ("ea videlicet ratione ut") the monks render two measures of wine or grain to the see each year. The text refers back to this condition with the warning that they should not dare to violate "the abovementioned agreement" ("supradictam autem conventionem"). Nearly a century later (995), in the record of sale of the castle of Carcolze by Sal·la, bishop of Urgell, the bishop recounted how he had demanded repeatedly of Borrell II, count of Barcelona (947–92), that he fulfill the agreement for which he had offered Carcolze in pledge: "Time and again I granted additional deadlines for him to redeem what he had handed over to me in the agreement ('hoc convencione')."[50] In each case, the term is used abstractly, not in a conditional phrase but in reference to a particular agreement. The term is also found, used in this abstract sense, in a letter from Oliba, bishop of Vic, to the monks of Santa Maria de Ripoll, dated 1020x23. It refers to an agreement (*conventio*) that the bishop had arranged among the counts Guillem I of Besalú, Guifré II of Cerdanya, and Hug I of Empúries.[51]

In the course of the tenth century, *conventio* and other conditional terms used abstractly began to substitute for the more common typological designations (*donatio*, *venditio*, etc.), especially at the end of documents, in the dating clauses and subscriptions. The documents to which they were applied contain, not surprisingly, conditions of the type often introduced by these terms. The earliest example is a settlement charter, which represents well the origins of the subset of *convenientiae* that record conditional grants. In 954x55, Guitard granted lands at Fontanet (Piera) to a group of fifteen men in return for a fifth of the produce of the vineyards and the *tasca* due from the remainder of the lands. In addition, the men and their successors owed Guitard and his successors standard service and were required to construct a tower; they could only sell the land to others who would do the same. The guarantee clauses of both Guitard and the settlers refer to "supra(dicta) *conventione*." The dating clause begins "Facto *pacto* et *conventione*." Guitard's subscription reads "Sig(*signum*)num Witardus qui hanc *pactum* feci." The subscriptions of the settlers are followed by the phrase "Nos simul in unum qui hanc *con-*

---

[50] *MH* 49 [*NH* 11:42; reg. *CDSG* 21]; DACU 239: "Iterum atque iterum dedi ei alios placitos atque alios ut *hoc convencione* de supradicta omnia quod michi tradidit redimere fecisset" (emphasis added). These documents are known only from early modern copies.

[51] *DOliba*, Textos literaris I, 15. On this agreement, see Abadal, *L'abat Oliba*, 215–22. In *DOliba*, Textos literaris I, 16, Oliba used the phrase "convenientia pacis."

ventione et *pactum* fecimus." Finally, the subscription of the scribe reads "Gisimara qui hanc *pactum* scripsi." It is clear from the closing formulae of this document that the scribe, at least, conceived of the document he had written as something other than the standard charter of grant (*carta donationis*), even if he was still at a loss as to what exactly to call it.[52] A grant for life in 1016 of the parish of Sant Jaume de Frontanyà, to be held in service of the see of Urgell against a yearly payment, with many conditions concerning penalties for wrongs done to the bishop, has a similar closing formula ("Acta est hec convencio vel pacto . . . hanc scriptura convencio rogatus scripsi"), but begins with an opening formula that in a slightly different form became dominant: "Hic est conventio vel pacto inter . . ."[53]

Three documents from the *Libri antiquitatum*, the cartulary of the cathedral of Barcelona, offer what are perhaps the earliest appearances of terms that appear close to the orthography – *convenientia* – that would became canonical. There are, however, textual problems with each of them. The term *convencia* appears in two documents from the 960s. Unfortunately, the originals have not survived, and it is therefore impossible to determine if this is a scribal error for either *convencio* or *convenientia*.[54] The texts record two agrarian contracts made three years apart by Mir Llop to Guifré and his wife Orundina of lands in Premià. Mir provided the lands, on which Guifré and his wife were expected to plant grapevines. For a term of years (eight in the case of the first grant, five in the case of the second), Mir and Guifré would divide equally the produce of the land, except for one plot (*fructus*) that was Guifré's alone as insurance against bad harvests. At the end of the term, the vineyard would be divided equally, and Guifré would receive his half as an alod, along with a charter proving his rights (*carta legitima*). A penalty of 10 *solidi* would be applied in case of violation by either party. Many grants of this type also include a clause establishing a right of first refusal, which ensured the donor's continued control of the land. The scribes of these charters, or of the cartulary, garbled the clauses that seem to address this issue. The vocabulary applied to these documents is inconsistent. Each of the grants is made "ad complantandum vinea (*or* vinea complantandum) per precaria." In the dating clause of the first, *precaria* refers to the document as a whole, but Guifré and Orundina's portion of the guarantee

---

[52] *CPF* 5 [Antoni Bach, ed., *Col·lecció diplomàtica del monestir de Santa Maria de Solsona: El Penedès i altres llocs del comtat de Barcelona (segles X–XV)*, Col·lecció fonts i estudis, Sèrie fonts, 1 (Barcelona, 1987), no. 1 (pp. 45–46)]. [53] DACU 341.

[54] LA 2:477* (a. 962), 2:479* (a. 965). See Coral Cuadrada, *El Maresme medieval: Les jurisdiccions baronals de Mataró i Sant Vicenç/Vilassar (hàbitat, economia i societat, segles X–XIV)* (Mataró, 1988), 164; for the dates, see Kosto, "Agreements," 95 n. 44.

clause ends with a promise to act according to "our agreement in this pact and precarial grant" ("nostra . . . *convencia* in hanc pactum et precaria"). The guarantee clause is introduced with the phrase "tale pactum," and *precaria* is found in the opening phrases of the grant, but *convencia* appears here for the first time. The second grant repeats the use of *convencia* in the guarantee clause ("adimpleamus sicut nostra est *convencia*"), but here that term is also included in the dating clause ("Facta precaria vel *conventia*") and the subscription of the scribe ("Azarichus qui hanc precaria vel *conventia* scripsit").[55]

A third document copied into the cartulary of the cathedral (again there is no original for confirmation), if copied accurately, presents the earliest appearance of the orthography *conveniencia*.[56] It is a donation dated 997 by Sendred Donús to the cathedral of a piece of land at La Boadella and a garden in the suburbs (*burgus*) of Barcelona.[57] The grant is called a *donatio* in the dating clause, but contains a lengthy conditional section in which the scribe used other terms to denote the arrangement. Sendred made the donation on condition that ("sub ea videlicet ratione ac tenore") the land be reserved for the use of the present *sacriscrinius*, Bonfill, and after his death for his successors in that position. If the bishop or anyone else violated these terms ("hanc scripturam vel huiusmodi conveniencia disrumpere aut abstrahere"), the lands were to revert to Sendred or his heirs. In the anathema clause, which follows immediately upon this condition, the scribe used the term *convencio*: "whoever acts against this agreement (*convencio*) and violates or disrupts this charter (*carta*) first shall incur the wrath of God . . . and henceforth this grant (*donatio*) with the aforesaid agreement (*convencio*) shall remain firm."[58] As is evident, the scribe separated the idea of condition (*convencio* or *conveniencia*), from the idea of the document as a whole (*donatio, carta*), making these phrases of a kind with the first abstract uses of conditional terms, discussed above.

If the distinction between "condition" and "agreement" in these documents seems ill-defined, that is because it is ill-defined. In theory, the two concepts are easily distinguished: one means "a prerequisite" or "a qualification," the other "a meeting of minds" or "an arrangement." In

---

[55] See also RBorrell 4 (a. 994): "terra culta at complantandum vel ad edificandum . . . in tale nostrum conventum ut non abeas licenciam dare . . . nos abstraxerimus de ista convencione . . . nostrum conventum . . . iste placito . . . quod nostra est convencio . . . de isto convento . . . Facta precaria . . ."

[56] DOliba 7 (a. 982x83), which survives only in an eighteenth-century transcription, reads: "elegit eis bona voluntas que fecerunt convenientia ad Deum et ad Sancta Maria que de alium alaude que adhuc abebant et tenebant non vendidissent et non dedissent . . ."

[57] LA 1:412★. Cit. Gaspar Feliu i Montfort, "El patrimoni de la seu de Barcelona durant el pontificat del bisbe Aeci (995–1010)," *Estudis universitaris catalans* 30 (1994), 61 n. 68.

[58] "qui contra hanc *convencionem* venerit *et istam cartam* extorquerit vel disrumpere temptaverit primitus iram Dei incurrat . . . et in antea *ista donatio cum predicta convencio* firma permaneat" (emphasis added).

practice, however, scribes used the same terms to denote both ideas. Words derived from *convenire* – "to come together" – describe agreements containing conditions, but also the conditions within those agreements. Conditions were, of course, agreed upon by the parties to a transaction, but that is a poor consolation for one attempting to understand the thoughts of those who composed these documents. This ambiguity is a first indication of a transitional period, of scribes cut loose from traditional formulae and forced to improvise.

Dispute settlement

There is plentiful evidence for the use of *convenire* and related terms outside the context of conditional grants. *Convenire* appears in some of the earliest documents from this region in charters of sale, in the common phrase used to denote price: "precio quod inter nos bone pacis placuit atque convenit."[59] Although this phrase could be translated "fitting price" rather than "agreed upon price," the intervening phrase "quod inter nos bone pacis" emphasizes the notion of goodwill and agreement between the parties, rather than acceptability to both. The fact that two of the earliest citations of the term *convenientia* are from agreements associated with the settlement of disputes – a record of judgment and a quitclaim – may be a coincidence. But despite the tradition just documented of the use of the term to denote conditional grants, when *convenientia* first appears in a dating clause as a typological designation, it is not in a conditional grant, but in a dispute settlement.

Scholars have long been aware of the persistence of a strong legal culture in the Catalan counties in the ninth and tenth centuries, a culture centered on the text of the *Liber iudiciorum* and the activity of professional judges. Litigants presented disputes at assemblies (*placita*) presided over by judges and in the presence of secular or ecclesiastical officials (counts, viscounts, bishops, abbots). Plaintiff and defendant presented their claims and provided proof in the form of documents or witnesses. The proceedings we know about usually ended either with a recognition of wrong on the part of one of the litigants, or with a judicial decree.[60] Various types

---

[59] *ACondal* 6 (a. 889). Similarly at *ACondal* 14, 15, 17, 19 . . .; *DVic* 6 (a. 886), 15, 23 . . .; DACU 9 (a. 839), 19, 21 . . .; *CCM* 25 (a. 911), 26, 28, 34 . . .; *DBarcelona* 5 (a. 894), 7 . . .

[60] Josep Maria Pons i Guri, "El dret als segles VIII–XI," in *Symposium internacional*, 1:131–59 provides a useful overview of recent research and problems. See also Bonnassie, *La Catalogne*, 1:183–202, 2:560–66; Iglesia Ferreirós, "La creación del derecho"; Antoni M. Udina i Abelló, "L'administració de justícia en els comtats pirinencs (segles IX–XII)," in *Miscel·lània homenatge a Josep Lladonosa* (Lleida, 1992), 129–45; and Bowman, "Law." For comparative purposes: Roger Collins, "*Sicut lex Gothorum continet*: Law and Charters in Ninth- and Tenth-Century León and Catalonia," *English Historical Review* 100 (1985), 489–512; Collins, "Visigothic Law"; Paul Ourliac,

of records provide evidence for these proceedings. Because form and function frequently overlap, it is not possible to provide a strict typology. Nevertheless, the evidence breaks down roughly into three basic forms: the record of judgment, the quitclaim, and the oath.

Records of judgment, often labeled *notitiae*, record the details of the proceeding or *placitum*. They begin with a statement of the location of the *placitum* and the individuals present, list the pleadings of the plaintiff and defendant and the proof offered by each side, and then note the decision of the tribunal or an order to a judicial officer (*saio*). Beyond these formal elements, the content of the records varies from case to case.[61] These documents are written in an objective style ("ordinaverunt . . .") and record the action of the tribunal rather than of one of the parties.

More common is the acknowledgment, or quitclaim, variously called a *recognitio, professio*, or *exvacuatio*. Although there may originally have been a distinction between a *recognitio* and an *exvacuatio* – the recognition or profession that a statement made is true, as against the dropping of a claim – it does not appear to have survived to the tenth century, and scribes used the terms interchangeably.[62] These documents record an acknowledgment by one party to the dispute either of the facts presented by the other party, or of his or her own inability to present sufficient proofs.[63] Like the *notitiae*, quitclaims begin with a statement of the location and personnel of the tribunal. Where the *notitia* continues with a third-person description of the course of the dispute, however, the quitclaim has a first-person acknowledgment. The exchange of pleadings and detailed description of proofs found in the *notitiae* are absent, although details may be reconstructed indirectly through the content of the acknowledgment.[64] The

---

footnote 60 (*cont.*)

"Juges et justiciables au XIᵉ siècle: Les *boni homines*," *Recueil de mémoires et travaux publié par la Société d'histoire du droit et des institutions des anciens pays de droit écrit* 16 (1994), 17–33; François Bougard, *La justice dans le royaume d'Italie de la fin du VIIIᵉ siècle au début du XIᵉ siècle*, Bibliothèque des Écoles françaises d'Athènes et de Rome 291 (Rome, 1995); *La giustizia nell'alto medioevo (secoli IX–XI)*, 2 vols., Settimane di studio del Centro italiano di studi sull'alto medioevo 44 (Spoleto, 1997).

[61] Joan Bastardas i Parera, ed., "Dos judicis antics (s. IX i XI): La pràctica judicial en el període de la formació nacional de Catalunya," in *Documents jurídics de la història de Catalunya*, 2nd ed. (Barcelona, 1992), 24–25 (a. 862); *CCM* 9 (a. 881); *NH* 11:38 [*VL* 14:25] (a. 879).

[62] *Recognitio*: *ACondal* 16 (a. 904), 35 (a. 913); *DACU* 67 (a. 910); *Pallars i Ribagorça* 113 (a. 910). *Professio*: *ACondal* 38 (a. 913). *Exvacuatio/recognitio*: *ACondal* 53 (a. 917), 181 (a. 977); *DACU* 143 (a. 961x62). *Professio/recognitio*: *CCM* 18 (a. 893). *Professio/exvacuatio*: *CCM* 6 (a. 842), 22 (a. 900). *CCM* 23 (a. 903) works in all three terms: "et sic est ueritas sicut professus sum in uestrorum supradictorum iuditio. Facta recognitione uel euacuatione . . ." See also Eixalada-Cuixà 64 (a. 901). I have not found an example of *exvacuare* used independently.

[63] This party was usually the defendant, but see *ACondal* 181; see also Eixalada-Cuixà 64.

[64] E.g., *ACondal* 35: "recognosco me ego Teudisclus, a peticionibus Sculvane, qui est mandatarius vel advocatus de domna Hemmone, abbatissa, vel ad interrogacione de supra scriptos iudices, veris est in omnibus et veritatem denegare non possum qualiter . . ." Also *NH* 21:11 (a. 875); *CCM* 14 (a. 892x93); Eixalada-Cuixà 64.

dispositive phrase of these documents is the first-person acknowledgment ("recognosco me"), fortified by the subscription of the individual or individuals making the admission or quitclaim.[65]

The third class of document is the sworn judicial oath or *conditiones sacramentorum*. These also begin with details of the location and personnel of the tribunal, but continue by identifying the party or advocate at whose request the oath was being sworn, the matter under dispute, the names of the witnesses, and the text of the oath in the first person ("iuramus . . ."). The oath was customarily subscribed by the witnesses, who testified to long-term possession of land or to having been present at a transfer of property or rights.[66] The sworn publication of testaments and the procedure of *reparatio scripturae*, whereby the content of lost or damaged documents was reconstructed, also involved witnesses and produced *conditiones sacramentorum*.[67]

Other documents do not fit neatly into one of these categories, but combine two or more of the forms and functions. A common combination is that of the *notitia* and the *exvacuatio*. The *notitia-exvacuatio* begins in impersonal narrative form, but switches at some point in the text to a first-person quitclaim.[68] Another variety of document integrates the *notitia* and the oath. Records of *reparationes scripturae* do this to some extent, but this combination is also present in generic records of dispute. The *notitia*, as noted, may record the fact of a sworn oath, identifying the witnesses and the content of their oath. A few documents, however, include at this point in the record partial or full texts of the oaths. Occasionally, separate *conditiones sacramentorum* survive alongside the *notitiae* and show that the text in the *notitia* is an accurate transcription of the relevant parts of the oath.[69] These documents

---

[65] *ACondal* 38, subscribed by 492 inhabitants of the villages making the acknowledgment, is the most striking illustration of this last point. See Gaspar Feliu i Montfort, "Sant Joan de les Abadesses: Algunes precisions sobre l'acta judicial del 913 i el poblament de la vall," in *Homenatge a la memòria del Prof. Dr. Emilio Sáez: Aplec d'estudis dels seus deixebles i col·laboradors* (Barcelona, 1989), 421–34.

[66] E.g., *Pallars i Ribagorça* 188 (a. 962, two witnesses); Eixalada-Cuixà 2 (a. 843, twenty-one witnesses).

[67] Eixalada-Cuixà 57, 58, 59, 60 (a. 879); LA 2:46★ (a. 987), 2:518★ (a. 994); Abadal i de Vinyals, ed., *Els diplomes carolingis*, 1:72–73 (a. 992); *DVic* 27, 28 (a. 898). See José Rius Serra, "*Reparatio scripturae*," *Anuario de historia del derecho español* 5 (1928), 246–53; Bowman, "Law," 191–203; *STCA*, pp. 51–58; Benito-Kosto-Taylor, "Approaches," 48–59.

[68] E.g., Jaume Marquès i Casanovas, "Sobre los antiguos judíos de Gerona," *Sefarad* 23 (1963), 29–31 (a. 983): "Unde sup(r)ascriptus comes et iudices iam dicto uuistrimiro mandatario plures vices interrogaverunt, *et placitos legitimos, mihi dederunt, si possem habere scripturas aut probationem legitimam aut ullum indicium veritatis, unde iam dictum alodem defendere possim a parte de istos sup(r)ascriptos homines cuius assertor vel mandatarius sum*" (emphasis added). Similarly, Joseph Calmette, ed., "Un jugement original de Wifred le Velu pour l'abbaye d'Amer," *Bibliothèque de l'École des chartes* 67 (1906), 66–69 (a. 898). In other cases the quitclaim comes after a judicial decision, e.g., Eixalada-Cuixà 16 (a. 868); similarly, *VL* 13:20 (a. 987); *Pallars i Ribagorça* 297 (a. 995).

[69] Eixalada-Cuixà 3 (a. 843; separate oath is Eixalada-Cuixà 2); *CCM* 5 (a. 842; separate oath is *CCM* 4). *CCM* 6 is a quitclaim, dated the same day, involving the same case. Cf. *CCM* 31 and 32 (a. 921),

maintain the overall form of the *notitia*, interpolating the text of an oath.[70]

A few documents, though issued subsequent to *placita*, do not correspond in any way to these three categories. In some cases, a charter makes an incidental mention of a connection to a tribunal. In 878, Comparat issued a *carta compositionis* in favor of the monastery of Sant Germà de Cuixà. The charter gives the reason for the composition, but also mentions that the composition was ordered by a tribunal.[71] A sale in 969 to Mir III Bonfill, count of Besalú, also turns out, on closer inspection, to be a composition ordered by a tribunal.[72] In other cases the connection to a *placitum* is more obvious. In 923, the monasteries of Sant Genís de Bellera and Santa Maria de Lavaix drew up a *libellus divisionis* recording the boundary between their lands. It includes a *notitia*-like narrative description of the dispute, but is presented as a charter of division issued jointly by the personnel of the two houses.[73] A document from 987 records the *recognitio* and self-*traditio* of one Pere, found guilty of killing his wife. It begins as a quitclaim ("recognosco me"); but since Pere had insufficient funds with which to redeem himself, he had to turn himself over to the judicial officer (*saio*), presumably to become the slave of the plaintiff. Thus the text ends with a *traditio* ordered by the tribunal: "therefore, by order of the judge, I place myself in the hands of the *saio*, and from the hands of the *saio* into the hands of the plaintiff."[74] While these last two documents present anomalous diplomatic forms, the first two are perfectly in accord with ninth- and tenth-century practice. Only the incidental mentions of the *placita* reveal that these were part of a process of dispute settlement. It is highly likely, however, that many other transactions that disguise or remain silent about the motives for the act are in fact the result of judicial orders.

From the late tenth century, a change appears in the documentation of dispute settlement. The tribunal that ordered a division of lands between

---

footnote 69 (*cont.*)

an oath and quitclaim generated by the same proceeding. In other cases, the existence of a separate oath may be assumed, e.g., Bernard Alart, ed., *Cartulaire roussillonnais* (Perpignan, 1880), no. 1 (p. 1, a. 865) [Jean-Gabriel Gigot, ed., "Les plus anciens documents d'archives des Pyrénées-Orientales (865–989)," *Bulletin philologique et historique (jusqu'à 1610) du Comité des travaux historiques et scientifiques: Année 1962* (1965), nos. 1, 2 (pp. 361–69)].

[70] Cf. DACU 252 (a. 997), which begins as an oath.

[71] Eixalada-Cuixà 55: "interpellavit me in judicio Dutila, mandatarius de ipso monasterio . . . et feci me recognitione et, quodiu lege est constitutum, mandaverunt me componere . . ."

[72] *NH* 11:156: "propter ipsum forisfastum quod fecimus et propter ipsum placitum que nos condemnavit et per ipsa legem quod nos debemus componere sic vindimus nos tibi ista omnia."

[73] *Pallars i Ribagorça* 134.

[74] ACV 6/238★: "Propterea sic me trado in manu saioni, de manu saioni in manu petentis, ordinante iudice."

the monasteries of Sant Pere de Camprodon and Sant Llorenç prop Bagà in 987 included in the record of the dispute a penalty clause, leading the scribe to label the document a *notitia cautionis*. In the same year, the brothers Vives and Hugbert settled a dispute concerning a joint inheritance. Unable to decide how to divide their lands, they presented themselves before an assembly presided over by Bishop Vives of Barcelona; the group included at least one professional judge, Orús. With the intervention of the assembly, they reached an accord as to the division (*divisio*) of the lands. The settlement, called a *scriptura divisionis*, was backed up by a fine of 50 *solidi*, to be paid by anyone who violated the agreement. A quit-claim of 996 to the monastery of Sant Cugat del Vallès included a more substantial penalty of 10 pounds of gold, in addition to a threat of excommunication.[75] In 1009, *Uristia* and her mother Bella complained before a tribunal against her uncle Goltred that he was responsible, along with her father, for losing the family patrimony. The judge found no merit in the complaint. Nevertheless, he ordered Goltred to pay the women a compensation of 3 *denarii*, in return for which the women presented a quit-claim, backed up by a penalty of 1 pound of gold. The document is called an *exvacuatio et securitas*.[76] Four years later, Sunifred de Rubí contested before a tribunal the possession of a vineyard held by Maria, widow of the judge Orús just mentioned. Sunifred claimed that the vineyard had been held by his father before the capture of Barcelona, that is, before 985. Neither party was able to present any proofs, so the judges ordered the vineyard to be divided evenly between the two litigants. The *noticie exarationis* ends with a grant by Sunifred to Maria of half of the vineyard, backed up by a penalty of 100 *solidi*.[77]

Two changes should be evident from this survey. These documents show an increased willingness on the part of scribes to break away from the standard forms and combinations of forms discussed above that had long been used to record the outcome of judicial proceedings and to execute judgments. A change in what scribes chose to label the documents does not yet prove that there was a significant change in legal procedure. The documents do not begin with the phrase "In iudicio," but the disputes clearly involve judges imposing decisions upon litigants according to a procedure. Is the tribunal that mediated the dispute between the two brothers in 987 so different from the tribunal that ordered the *libellus divisionis* between the two monasteries in 923? Perhaps not. A second change, however, does hint at the recognition of a need for something beyond standard judicial practices: each of these

---

[75] *VL* 15:34; *ACondal* 207; OR, Sant Cugat del Vallès 83*. Also *DBarcelona* 329 (a.998).
[76] LA 2:568*: "talis petitio inanis et vacua existimamus quia nullam rationem firmitatem habere videmus."   [77] ACB 1–2–1112.

documents turns to the imposition of specific monetary penalties to back up the settlements. While penalty clauses are a common element of tenth-century sales, donations, and exchanges, the use of monetary penalties or pledges is new in judicial records. Furthermore, whereas standard penalty clauses imposed a two- or fourfold penalty (based on the *Liber iudiciorum*), the values in these cases are specific amounts.[78] These are not yet extrajudicial settlements; the security is given in the context of regular procedure. But the inclusion of the penalty clause, even if symbolic, hints at a structural deficiency in the judicial process alongside the diplomatic deficiencies reflected in the new language of the documents. These changes are the context for the introduction of the language of the *convenientia* into documents of dispute settlement.

The first record of a dispute settlement that refers to itself as a *convencio* is an account of proceedings in 988 against Sentemir, accused of hiding the testament of his brother from the beneficiary, the monastery of Sant Cugat del Vallès.[79] It begins in the form of a standard *notitia*, narrating the history of the dispute. The advocate (*assertor*) of the monastery leveled accusations against Sentemir before a *placitum* that included Bishop Gotmar of Girona, Abbot Odó of Sant Cugat, and the famous judge Bonhom. Sentemir denied the accusations, but the advocate produced a trustworthy witness who claimed to have seen the testament and given it to Sentemir to publish. Sentemir refused to make a *professio*, even after he was urged to do so by the judge, and offered to submit to an ordeal. He failed the ordeal[80] and was ordered by the judge to acknowledge that he had told his wife to burn the testament. The judge also ordered that he subscribe a *recognitio*. When the judicial officer (*saio*) wanted to hand him over to the advocate to become the penal slave of the abbey, Sentemir appealed for mercy. The judges suggested ("dederunt consilium") that instead of being reduced to servitude, he could make concessions to the abbey, the bishop, the judge, and the judicial officer. The remainder of the document records, still in impersonal form, the concessions to the abbey, and concludes:

And they established this *convencio* with the agreement (*conventum*) and settlement (*placitum*) that if at any time the said Sentemir should rise up against this agreement (*conventum*) to break it – either he himself or his advocate or his heirs or any man – and thus should wish and act to destroy this pact (*pactum*) and presume to alienate and carry off from the said monastery its grant and everything included above, he shall pay 1 ounce of gold as a penalty to the said monastery to be held forever, and henceforth this pact (*pactum*) and agreement (*conventum*)

---

[78] *ACondal*, pp. 38–40; *CSCV*, 1:liii–liv; Zimmermann, "L'usage," 268–76. Specific values are found in some clauses: *ACondal* 6, 7, 10, 22, 102; *CSCV* 337. [79] *CSCV* 218.
[80] Cf. the interpretation of Bowman, "Law," 149, 151–52, 161–62.

shall remain firm for all time. This *convencio* was completed on the fourteenth day of the kalends of April, in the first year with Hugh the Great reigning. The sign (*signum*) of Sentemir . . .[81]

The language is opaque, the vocabulary is inconsistent (*conventum, placitum, pactum, convencio*), and it is difficult to tell to what precisely the terms refer. Nevertheless, this document participates in the developments just discussed: diplomatic change and use of a monetary penalty. Both reflect problems in the standard judicial process for settlement of disputes. Sentemir did not respect either the initial or the eventual finding of the judge, who was forced first to assent to the extraordinary procedure of the ordeal, and then to propose (rather than impose) what looks very much like an extrajudicial settlement. Sentemir avoided the penal servitude prescribed by the law not because the judge ordered the settlement with the monastery, but because it was "pleasing to both parties" ("Placuit utriusque partibus"). Since the prestige of the *placitum* was insufficient to guarantee the agreement, the monastery arranged for the inclusion of a penal clause.

No similar documents survive before the second decade of the eleventh century, an absence that corresponds to a reduced number of judicial records in the period 990–1010. By the date of the next extant document of this type, alternatives to the traditional *notitia*-based forms were more common. In a document of 1015, Trasoari quitclaimed ("exvacuo me") to Goltred a number of different disputes, which had been heard in an unidentified *placitum*; furthermore, he promised a composition of 2 pounds of gold if he were to raise the issue again. The dating clause refers, in the usual unsure style of the period, to "hec paginola securitatis vel pacificationis et evacuationis"; Trasoari's subscription, however, contains the slightly different phrase "ista securitate vel *pactum conveniencie* et evacuacione."[82] In a *placitum* held before the countess Ermessenda in 1020, Sant Cugat del Vallès prevailed in a claim concerning its rights in an alod near Olèrdola. The defendant offered a quitclaim ("recognosco"), promising to provide the required services and to remain in homage (*ominaticum*) to the abbey. The document ends with a penalty clause in the name of the abbot and the tenant, setting a fine of 100 *solidi*. This scribe also seems to have been at a loss for appropriate terminology,

---

[81] "Et tali convento et placito in huius conventione instituerunt: ut si in aliquo tempore iste iam dictus Sentemirus, adversum huius conventum consurgerit ad disrumpendum, tam ipse quam suum advocatum vel heredum suorum, vel alicuius homo et ita istum pactum confringere voluerit et fecerit, et ista omnia superius comprehensa ad cenobium prefatum vel et ad donationem ipsius auferri vel alienari presumserit, libram auri in vinculo persolvat ad cenobium iam dictum perpetim habitura et in antea istum pactum et conventum firmum permaneat omnique tempore. Facta convencione x.°iiii.° kalendas aprilis anno .i.° regnante Ugo Magno, rege. S+m Sentemiro . . ."

[82] LA 2:537*.

but ended up including the idea of a convention: "hunc pactum scripture largitionis vel definicionis plenam obtineat firmitatem . . . hunc *pactum* definicionis vel largitionis atque *convencionis*."[83] As in the case from 988, the agreement or security clause is still closely connected to the procedure of a *placitum*; this settlement is extrajudicial not in the sense of "outside," but in the sense of "in addition to" the normal process.

A case from 1023 presents an interesting parallel.[84] A clerk of the cathedral chapter of Barcelona named Joan, accused of murder before a comital assembly (*audiencia*), argued that a lay tribunal (*seculare iudicium*) had no jurisdiction in the matter. The case moved before an ecclesiastical court in the cathedral. Since the plaintiffs were unable to produce witnesses, Joan was able to clear himself by oath. This action was not sufficient to settle the matter, however. The parties made a pact (*paccio*), which consisted of a promise on the part of the plaintiffs not to bring up the matter again, under penalty of 300 *solidi*.[85] Like their secular counterparts, ecclesiastical decisions in the early eleventh century had to be supplemented with additional penalties and settlements.

The record of a dispute in 1017 between a widow and her brother-in-law over the lands of her late husband provides evidence for a truly *extrajudicial* convention.[86] The judges ordered an inquiry into the proper disposition of the lands, but were unable to settle a related complaint concerning violence arising from the dispute[87] because the widow refused to accept the expurgatory oath of the brother-in-law. *After* the failure of the formal proceedings, however, the parties reached an accord with the help of the witnesses. This passage follows the dating clause and the subscriptions of the witnesses:

And after this dispute, a *conveniencia* between them was completed on the advice of the aforesaid men, that there should be a pact (*pactum*) or settlement (*paci[ficatio?]*) between them, and [. . .] and they carried it through, each with respect to the other, the said Blanca and the aforementioned Ramon. And whoever tries to break this pact (*pactum*) or agreement (*placitum*), let him not

---

[83] *CSCV* 479. Cf. AAM, Sant Benet de Bages 1240 (a. 1010: "hanc securitatem vel professionem adque evaccuacionem vel pactum stabilitatem"); *CSCV* 102 (a. 973: "Hic est pacto et placito sive et noticia legibus conscriptura . . . Facto pacto et placito," in what is essentially a *carta impignorationis*). [84] ACB 1–2–134*; Bonnassie, *La Catalogne*, 1:185.

[85] "Unde ne ad futurum reiteretur petitcio, ista est ab eis confirmato paccio: In Christi nomine. Ego Teudisclus et Giscafredus et Iohannes, facientes tibi Iohanni levite pactum hoc securitatis ut ab odierno tempore quietus et sine aliqua pulsacione nostrorum supradictorum mortis maneas propinquorum, Stephani scilicet levite et Raimundi, inducimus super nos huius institucionis penam, ut si in postmodum temptaverimus te propter hoc apellare, ccc^{tos} solidos aureos componamus tibi, et insuper hoc firmum permaneat. Acta est huius scripcionis institucio . . ."

[86] OR, Sant Benet de Bages 134.

[87] "repellit eam de dommo sua et maliciose pertraxit pro capillos capitis sui, et dedit ei unum ictum in pectore cum pede . . ."

succeed, [and] let him pay 1 pound of the purest gold into the fisc of the prince, and let this remain forever firm. S(*signum*) Ramon S(*signum*) Blanca, we who together have made this pact (*pactum*) and ordered [it] to be subscribed.[88]

The outcome here is the same as in the cases from 1014 and 1020: a supplemental agreement entered into after a judicial proceeding, backed up by a monetary penalty. The import, however, is different. This settlement occurs after the manifest *failure* of the standard procedure after the widow removed herself from the *placitum* ("abstraxit se de ipsum placitum"). The scribe labeled the main document a "pagina comemoracionis vel subtracionis," focusing attention on the fact that one of the parties withdrew (*subtrahere*) from the agreement. The final settlement was outside normal legal procedures.

Refusal to accept witnesses and withdrawal from a *placitum* is a situation foreseen in the Visigothic law, but the first evidence for this action being taken appears only in 997.[89] After the case in 1017 just discussed, and another from the same year, the next example is a dispute in 1018 between Hug I of Empúries and the countess Ermessenda concerning possession of the alod of Ullastret.[90] In fact, there are several examples in this case of Hug's rejection of the legal order. The case is particularly noteworthy for the extent to which the judges went to devise alternatives to keep Hug at the bargaining table. Hug did not make his initial claim against Ermessenda through judicial procedure. Instead, he approached the countess directly. When Ermessenda proposed a proper *placitum* to resolve the matter, he proposed instead a trial by battle. She refused, claiming that the "Gothic law does not decree that lawsuits should be judged by battle." Hug took the land by force, and Ermessenda initiated a standard legal proceeding with a complaint against him.[91]

---

[88] "Et post quam ista ista [*sic*] altercacio peracta fuit conveniencia inter illos propter consultum predictorum virorum ut fuiset inter illos pactum vel paci[ficatio?] et [siat?] et perpeterunt unus ab alius predicta Blanca et pretaxato Raimundo. Et qui contra istum pactum vel placitum disrumpere temptaverit at nihilum proficiat componat in fisco principi libra auri purissimi et in ante firmum permaneat. S(*signum*) Raimundus S(*signum*) Blanca nos simul qui istum pactum fecimus et firmare rogavimus."

[89] Liber iudiciorum, II.1.25, Additamentum 1 (pp. 71–72, 462); DACU 252. Other early examples: LA 4:279* (a. 1016); DACU 398 (a. 1025), 539 (a. 1041); CSCV 496 (a. 1025), 524 (a. 1032), 527 (a. 1033); cf. CSCV 529 (a. 1033).

[90] DOliba 56 [CCM 77]. This is the first case cited by Iglesia Ferreirós ("La creación del derecho," 202). Many authors have discussed the dispute between Hug and Ermessenda (DOliba, pp. 83–84; Sobrequés, *Els grans comtes*, 23–24; Abadal, *L'abat Oliba*, 216–19; Rovira i Virgili, *Història*, 3:481–83), but none gives a completely accurate account of the course of this very complex dispute.

[91] "Hugo iam dictus requisivit eam ut reddidisset illi alodem . . . Ermessendis . . . voluit se conligare cum illo legaliter ut quemadmodum lex ordinasset, parata fuisset illi respondere, et in iudicio reddere illi omnia quae legaliter iudicata fuissent non debere esse iuris Berengarii praefati, sed Hugonis . . . lex Gothica non iubet ut per pugnam discutiantur negotia."

When the tribunal decided against Hug, Bernat I of Besalú, who was copresident of the *placitum* (along with Bishop Oliba of Vic) *and* Hug's surety (*fideiussor*), refused to accept the ruling. In an attempt to delay the proceedings, he came up with a novel ploy and had the judges confirm their judgment by swearing an oath.[92] Bernat's and Hug's responses are not known, but the oath presumably did not satisfy them. We know this because the judges had to try once again to get Hug to accept their judgment, asking his advocate if he would accept the witnesses offered by the countess. This occurred *after* a judgment had already been given. At this point Hug's advocate refused to accept the witnesses and removed himself from the *placitum*. The remainder of the document records the sworn oath of the witnesses and a second judgment. Hug's response to this second judgment is also unknown.

Despite the concrete circumstances – the dispute over Ullastret – this was a high-level political conflict being played out in the context of a legal procedure; resolution came not through judgments, but through the extrajudicial diplomacy of Oliba. This case is an important reflection, though, of the inadequacy of the traditional legal system to deal with such problems: the conflict could not be resolved through judicial means, because only one of the parties was willing to accept the decisions of the tribunal. The date of this failed *placitum* (1018), coming as it does a few months after the death of Ramon Borrell, corresponds well with the accepted chronology of crisis.[93] But the dispute concerning the widow occurred *before* his death, in 1017, and the first of these failures date from 988 and 997. Other indicators of weakness in the system – the adoption of monetary penalties and the turn to supplemental agreements – are also evident in documentation stretching back into the tenth century.[94] The apparent confusion of scribes and their turn to the language of convention was not simply an empty diplomatic change; judges and litigants were experimenting with a system in which people had lost confidence. As far as judicial procedure is concerned, 1020 may be a crisis point, but it is not a beginning.

---

[92] "Cumque hoc iudicatum fuisset a iudicibus, Bernardus, comes, nolens obedire huic iudicio, tamdiu perseveravit in ipsa contentione quousque excogitavit rem inauditam, faciens confirmari a iudicibus supra dictis iureiurando super altare Sancti Genesii de Orreolis hoc iudicium, quoniam ipse fideiussor erat ex parte Hugonis, ut ipse Hugo talis extitisset in iudicio quemadmodum illi iudices legaliter iudicassent." The phrase "ut . . . iudicassent" is an explanation of Bernat's obligations as *fideiussor*, not a promise made by Bernat.

[93] "Este abandono del proceso, al no querer aceptar los testigos, es el reflejo de una crisis en la sociedad catalana altomedieval, que paulatinamente, a partir del 1020, se ve dominada por la violencia. Esta crisis encuentra reflejos cada vez más evidentes en el proceso" (Iglesia Ferreirós, "La creación del derecho," 202).

[94] Bowman ("Law," 293–97, 309–19) integrates penalty clauses and withdrawal from tribunals into his picture of continuity in disputing practice between 985 and 1060. From the longer perspective presented here, however, these elements may be seen to be less routine.

Oaths

While conditional agreements and records of dispute settlement provide the context for the formulae of the earliest *convenientia*, its institutional foundations appear elsewhere. There are a number of possible precedents for the written oath of fidelity, a document that became closely associated with the *convenientia* in the eleventh century. The evidence for these, however, is more limited than for conditional agreements and judicial records. Oaths associated with judicial practice, including sworn oaths of witnesses involved both in *placita* and testamentary transactions, have survived in significant numbers, as seen above. Decisions to begin keeping written copies of oaths of fidelity, though complex, drew on this tradition. But beyond the simple fact of their written nature, there is little connection between the two types. Judicial oaths share some language and perhaps ritual with oaths of fidelity, but they have no bearing on interpersonal ties.

The language and content of the oath of fidelity draws not on procedural oaths, but on early medieval models of the personal and collective oath. Key phrases from the Catalan oath ("ab ista die in antea fidelis ero"; "adiutor ero"; "sicut homo per drictum debet esse domino suo"; "sine fraude et malo ingenio") first appear in Carolingian capitulary texts from the late eighth and ninth centuries.[95] The oath of fidelity existed in the Visigothic kingdom, as well, and although no example has survived, there is evidence that some were in written form.[96] Written oaths north of the Pyrenees appear almost simultaneously with their peninsular analogues, a coincidence that may point to a common development rather than transmission from one region to the other.[97]

In keeping with his model of a Carolingian-style public order

---

[95] Élisabeth Magnou-Nortier, "Fidélité et féodalité méridionales d'après les serments de fidélité (Xᵉ–début XIIᵉ siècle)," *AM* 80 (1968), 461; Magnou-Nortier, *Foi et fidélité: Recherches sur l'évolution des liens personnels chez les Francs du VIIᵉ au IXᵉ siècle*, Publications de l'Université de Toulouse–Le Mirail, ser. A, 28 (Toulouse, 1976); Matthias Becher, *Eid und Herrschaft: Untersuchungen zum Herrscherethos Karls des Großen*, Vorträge und Forschungen, Sonderband 39 (Sigmaringen, 1993).

[96] Wilhelm Levison, ed., "Iudicium in tyrannorum perfidia promulgatum," in Bruno Krusch and Wilhelm Levison, eds., *Passiones vitaeque sanctorum aevi Merovingici*, MGH Scriptores rerum Merovingicarum 5 (Hanover, 1910; repr. 1979), cap. 6 (p. 534, lines 3–4) [Canellas López, *Diplomática*, no. 147 (pp. 219–20 at 220)]: "Quibus conditionibus reseratis atque perlectis, ad confusionem perfidiae ipsorum subscriptio manus eorum in ipsis conditionibus eis aspicienda ostenditur"; cf. Canellas López, *Diplomática*, nos. 143, 145 (pp. 217–18), and see Michael McCormick, *Eternal Victory: Triumphal Rulership in Late Antiquity, Byzantium, and the Early Medieval West* (Cambridge, 1987), 313. A sworn *securitas* from 642x49 preserved on slate contains the phrase "Iuro ego," departing from analogous formulae (Canellas López, *Diplomática*, no. 119a [pp. 198–99]). Other examples of individual oaths ("iuro . . ."): Canellas López, *Diplomática*, nos. 38, 221 (pp. 141–42, 270).   [97] Magnou-Nortier, "Fidélité et féodalité."

persisting in Catalonia into the eleventh century, Bonnassie has posited the existence of the public oath due to the count. He cites two collective oaths to Ramon IV of Pallars Jussà (1047–98); since one of these refers back to Counts Guillem of Pallars Sobirà (1011–35) and Ramon III of Pallars Jussà (1011–47), he speculates that they have "transmitted the formula" of earlier oaths.[98] But no oath of this type has survived from the tenth century. Oaths may have played a role, too, in relations with the Islamic powers to the south. An Arabic chronicle reports that Borrell II of Barcelona transmitted letters to al-Ḥakam II, caliph of Córdoba, during embassies in 971 and 974 in which he promised "obedience and vassalage" and "love and submission." The vocabulary used in describing these letters differs from that in the text of the oath of the Andalusian lord 'Abd al-Karīm ibn Yaḥyà to al-Ḥakam, transmitted in the same chronicle. Still, from the perspective of the count of Barcelona, the content of the letters may have approximated the personal oaths of fidelity under consideration.[99]

The author of an excellent study of the oaths from the reign of Ramon Berenguer I of Barcelona (1035–76) acknowledges that his analysis begins in the course of an evolution, the previous step of which is poorly known.[100] The survival of a handful oaths from before 1035 opens a window onto this earlier stage (Table 1.1). These first written oaths not only represent the origins of later oaths, but also prove to be a source for understanding the appearance of the earliest *convenientiae*. They are not a homogeneous group. While the oaths from later in the century have a settled formula, beginning with the phrase "Iuro ego," these are more

[98] RBI sd 183*, sd 185*; Bonnassie, *La Catalogne*, 1:139–40.

[99] 'Īsà ibn Aḥmad al-Rāzī, *Anales palatinos del califa de Córdoba al-Ḥakam II, por 'Īsā ibn Aḥmad al-Rāzī (360–364 H. = 971–975 J. C.)*, trans. Emilio García Gómez (Madrid, 1967), §§3, 182, 187 (pp. 44–45, 207, 212–13). The letter from Hugh Capet to Borrell II in 988 suggests that the Capetian king believed that Borrell had sworn fidelity to the caliph: "Qua in parte si fore mavultis nobiscum potius obẹdire delegistis quam Hismahelitis, legatos ad nos usque in pascha dirigite, qui et nos de vestra fidelitate laetificent et vos de nostro adventu certissimos reddant" (Gerbert of Reims, *Die Briefsammlung Gerberts von Reims*, ed. Fritz Weigle, MGH Die Briefe der deutschen Kaiserzeit 2 [Weimar, 1966], no. 112 [p. 141, lines 1–4]). See Ramon d'Abadal i de Vinyals, *Els primers comtes catalans*, Història de Catalunya, Biografies catalanes, 1, [3rd ed.] (Barcelona, [1980]), 332–34; Bonnassie, *La Catalogne*, 1:342 nn. 60–61.

[100] Michel Zimmermann, "Aux origines de la Catalogne féodale: Les serments non-datés du règne de Ramon Berenguer Iᵉʳ," in *La formació i expansió*, 142. The two "earlier" oaths he cites cannot be securely dated to the period before 1035 (RBorrell 119*, *LFM* 531); the same is true of *CSCV* 599. BRI 121*, which concerns a transaction between Ramiro I, king of Aragón, and Sancho (IV) de Peñalén, king of Navarre, dates from 1063x64; see Antonio Ubieto Arteta, "Estudios en torno a la división del reino por Sancho el Mayor de Navarra," *Príncipe de Viana* 21 (1960), 199–200. I have not included *LFM* 158 (below, n. 122), or *HGL*, 3:261 (Bérenger, viscount of Narbonne, to Ramon, son of the count of Cerdanya, and Guifred, archbishop of Narbonne); *HGL* rehearses a résumé given in Guillaume de Catel, *Mémoires de l'histoire du Languedoc . . .* (Toulouse, 1633), 580–81. See above, n. 51.

Table 1.1. *Earliest written oaths from the Catalan counties*

Document	Date	From	To
AME 6/72★	987	Ennec Bonfill	Fruia, bishop of Vic
ACU 163★	992x1002	Ermengol I, count of Urgell	Sal·la, bishop of Urgell
DACU 483	981x1010	Guillem, viscount of Urgell	Sal·la, bishop of Urgell
DACU 485	1017?	Borrell, bishop of Roda	Ermengol, bishop of Urgell
DACU 484	1010x17	Ramon Borrell, count of Barcelona	Ermengol, bishop of Urgell
ACV 9/ii/28★	1017x18#	Pere, bishop of Girona	Borrell, bishop of Vic
ACB 1-2-581	31 May 1019	Deusdé, bishop of Barcelona	(canons of Barcelona)
BRI 120★	1013?x1020?	Ermengol, bishop of Urgell	Guifré II, count of Cerdanya
LFM 583	1010x22?	Ermengol, bishop of Urgell	Guifré II, count of Cerdanya
RBI extra. 2102★	1018x23?	Guifré II, count of Cerdanya	Ermessenda, countess of Barcelona
DACU 487	1010x35	Ermengol II, count of Urgell	Ermengol, bishop of Urgell
DACU 488	1010x35	Guisad de Sallent	Ermengol, bishop of Urgell
DACU 489	1010x35	Bernat de Figuerola	Ermengol, bishop of Urgell

Note:
The exception of Ermessenda and her *son*, Berenguer Ramon, rather than her husband, Ramon Borrell, suggests a date following the latter's death on 8 September 1017; Borrell died on 24 February 1018. See Anscari M. Mundó, "La mort del comte Ramon Borrell de Barcelona i els bisbes de Vic Borrell i Oliba," *Estudis d'història medieval* 1 (1969), 3–15; *CDSG* 173n.

varied. Nevertheless, most refer to themselves with the term *sacramentum*, and those that do not still record, as their primary act, a promise in the first person. Furthermore, despite the fact that these oaths are made to officials – usually ecclesiastical ones – they are of the "private" rather than the "public" variety: none of them is a collective oath of the type proposed by Bonnassie. In the one case in which multiple individuals act as a party to the oath, they receive the oath rather than swear it. For all these reasons, it is appropriate to consider these earliest written oaths as a group.

All but one of the thirteen oaths involve a bishop, either as subject or object of the oath. Members of the lay aristocracy appear (counts of Urgell, Barcelona, Cerdanya; viscount of Urgell), but usually as jurors rather than receivers of an oath. The oaths are concentrated in the northern diocese of Urgell, but all five of the sub-Pyrenean Catalan dioceses (Barcelona, Vic, Urgell, Girona, Roda) are represented. These patterns may simply be a result of documentary survival over time, but the fact that a significant comital documentation survives from this period and that the extent of the ecclesiastical archives of Vic and Barcelona rival that of Urgell suggests that the explanation lies elsewhere. Six of the seven oaths to the bishops of Urgell survive only in the thirteenth-century cartulary of the cathedral, grouped together with later oaths on the last folios of the first volume. Most of the other oaths survive as original or contemporary single-sheet documents. The key factor, then, may not be the effect of a millennium on the state of the archives, but rather decisions by contemporaries about what to preserve as single-sheet documents or in cartulary form.[101] The geographic pattern, for example, persists into the twelfth century: the number of surviving oaths to the bishops of Urgell remains greater than the number from Girona, Vic, and Barcelona.

Some of these documents vary only slightly from the model of the later oath of fidelity. The oath of the viscount of Urgell, for example, is redacted entirely without vernacular terms. The oath of the bishop of Roda includes Saint Mary (as patron of the cathedral) as the object of the oath, lending it a vaguely institutional character. The oaths of Guisad de Sallent (a promise not to make an alliance to the *desonor* of the bishop) and Bernat de Figuerola (a promise to be faithful and to grant the appropriate services concerning the castle of Figuerola), are unusually brief. Others of this group, however, resemble the standard form only loosely. The earliest of the documents included in this sample does not seem to record a ritual, but its content is unquestionably that of an oath, namely a first-person promise of fidelity with respect to a castle: "I, Ennec, who am called Bonfill, am resolved to make this *fides promissionis* to you, Bishop Fruia."[102] The oath of Bishop Deusdé of Barcelona, on the other hand, uses some of the standard formulae, but records a promise that is notably different from most oaths in that it is purely negative and is directed downward in the social hierarchy. The opening line is familiar: "I, Bishop Deusdé, son of the woman Senegundis, swear that from this

---

[101] Below, p. 282.

[102] AME 6/72*: "[Ego Ennegone que vocant Bo]nofilio tibi Fruiane episcopo hanc fidem promissionis constat mihi tibi facere." On Ennec Bonfill, see Bonnassie, *La Catalogne*, 1:176–77.

day forward . . ." The remainder of the text, however, consists only of a list of properties that the bishop promises not to seize from the cathedral chapter. A promise of fidelity and other positive undertakings are absent.[103]

Still others contain significant irregularities. The oath of the count of Urgell to Bishop Sal·la includes the provision that the future bishop would swear fidelity (*fidelitas*) to the count, but this was not the motivating factor for the oath. The count's principal undertaking was a promise that he would invest the nephew of the present bishop with the bishopric within ten days of receiving notice from the bishop and that he would not cause harm to him or the bishopric. All of the aspects of the oath of fidelity (promises not to injure and to aid, for example) are present in the text, but they are secondary to the arrangement for succession. It is this arrangement, not the general promises of fidelity, that was backed up by a pledge.[104] In the second oath of the bishop of Urgell to the count of Cerdanya, the clauses governing the settlement of disputes operate in a counterintuitive fashion. Although the bishop makes the oath to the count, the oath foresees the count as the likely violator of the relationship embodied in the document, giving the oath an oddly reciprocal quality.[105]

Each oath contains at least one negative undertaking, most commonly a promise not to deceive ("non decebre") or not to seize certain properties or rights ("non tolre"). Later oaths to the counts of Barcelona feature long lists of the counties, dioceses, and castles that were not to be violated; this list is already present in the fragmentary oath to the countess Ermessenda. Other negative oaths include promises not to ignore a warning ("non vedare comonir"), not to defy or break faith with the subject of the oath ("no desfidare"), not to deny entry to a castle ("no li vedare entrar"), and not to make a separate agreement without permission ("finem nec treguam . . . no prende"; "societad non avere").

While the content of the oath may be entirely negative, most also contain some form of positive undertaking, commonly a promise of aid ("adiutor ero") to have, hold, or defend (*habere, tenere, defendere*) properties or rights. In those cases where this positive undertaking is coupled with the negative undertaking not to seize or injure, the promise of aid is made in relation to properties already listed. It may, however, stand alone. Some method of requesting the aid is usually added to the promise, normally notification, either in person or by a messenger, of the individual or individuals against whom aid is required. This clause in turn may

---

[103] ACB 1–2–581: "Iuro ego Deusdedit episcopus filius Senegundis femine quia de ista hora in antea ego non tolre nend tolre me sciente neque aliquis homo aut femina per meum consilium."
[104] ACU 163*. Cf. Bonnassie, *La Catalogne*, 1:178–79.   [105] BRI 120*.

support a negative promise, as seen above, not to reject the notification. Promises of aid may include exceptions; the bishop of Urgell, for example, promises to aid the count of Cerdanya, except against the count of Urgell. The other major positive promise is the promise of fidelity ("fidelis ero"). Despite the fact that this promise is present in nearly all later oaths, in this group it is a rarity.[106] Only the oaths of Bishop Borrell of Roda and Bernat de Figuerola contain an explicit promise of fidelity, although related terms appear in other documents ("salva fidelitate"; "no desfidare"; "facere fidantias et fidelitatem"; "fidem promissionis"). The technical terms *senior* and *homo* are likewise frequently missing. This absence of the vocabulary of relationships of fidelity between lords and their men is the most striking difference between these early oaths and those from later in the century. It is also yet another reflection of the transitional state of the documentation.

Several of the oaths contain clauses detailing the procedure in the case of violation of the terms of the oath, often summed up in the term *forisfacere*. These passages offer some of the best early evidence for the existence of the extrajudicial mechanisms for the resolution of disputes seen in the developments in the previous section. Curiously, it is not always the party swearing the oath that is seen as the potential violator. The process usually involves a notification of the violation followed by the payment of a composition (*emenda*). The composition itself may be fixed by a small group of arbitrators (three or four) agreed upon by the two parties. In each case a time limit – 30, 60, or 100 days – is established for payment of the composition. If the emendation is not made or agreed upon, one party may be freed from his obligations under the oath. In one oath, if the arbitrators are unable to reach a decision, the matter progresses to an ordeal by cold water.

Though the evidence is scant, what survives shows that the idea of a written oath, with its own vocabulary and appropriate subject matter, was well developed, though not fully developed, by the start of the reign of Ramon Berenguer I. On the other hand, it is equally clear that the language and formulae of oaths might be put to other uses. The subject matter of some of these documents – castles, treaties, pledges – overlaps with the subject matter of the earliest *convenientiae*. One of the documents discussed is, in fact, paired with a *convenientia* that has survived. This oath/*convenientia* pair raises the question of whether *convenientiae* existed but have not survived for some of these other documents. Later oaths

---

[106] Zimmermann, "Aux origines," 118 ("moins de 10 sur 163 ne débutent pas par cette protestation de fidélité"). Some authors refer to this as "negative fidelity," in contrast to a more positive "aid" (*adiutorium*). Active/passive describes the distinction more accurately. I reserve "negative" for the discrete group of promises stated negatively.

occasionally refer to the *convenientia* with which they are associated; some are even inscribed on the same piece of parchment as the *convenientia*. This is not the case with these early oaths, however; the question must remain unanswered.

Castle tenure

The early oaths of fidelity, especially those dealing with castles, raise the intractable problems of the terms on which castles were held and how the earliest counts of Barcelona and the other Catalan counties organized their military power. The end of the story is extremely well documented in numerous oaths and *convenientiae* from 1050 onward. The state of affairs in the century and a half before this, however, is much less clear. We learn of the names of castles from the ever more frequent use of the castle district (*castrum*) as a geographical designation, but charters of sale or donation and testaments provide more detail only when a castle changed hands. The day-to-day operations of the castles are rarely recorded; no documentary form provides knowledge of anything like the terms set forth at length in a mature *convenientia*.

The current model of historical development in Catalonia posits a rapid change in the early eleventh century, and to demonstrate that change, historians have needed to sketch the earlier situation. A scholarly consensus has developed as to its nature.[107] Castles were of two types: those that were the property of the counts, more common earlier and in the eastern lands of Old Catalonia, and those that were the property of individuals or ecclesiastical institutions, more common in the frontier regions. The latter type arose by comital grant or sale of an existing castle, by an individual's or institution's own initiative in constructing a new castle, or, as is more likely, by the reconstruction of an old site destroyed by Islamic incursions. Both types of castles were held as alods and could be bought and sold freely. The count manned his castles with *vicarii*, local comital officials, perhaps institutional descendants from the Visigothic *tiufath* and the Frankish *centenarius* or *vicarius*. The *vicarius* controlled his assigned territory, the *castrum*, from a comital castle, the *castellum*, and thus combined functions usually delegated to separate officials in Frankish

---

[107] José Maria Font Rius, "Les modes de détention de châteaux dans la 'vielle Catalogne' et ses marches extérieures au début du IXe au début du XIe siècle," *AM* 80 (1968), 405–14; Bonnassie, *La Catalogne*, 1:173–77; Manuel Riu i Riu, "A propósito del feudalismo todavía," in *Estudios en homenaje a Don Claudio Sánchez Albornoz en sus 90 años*, 6 vols. to date (Buenos Aires, 1983–), 2:65–82; Riu i Riu, "Castells i fortificacions menors: Llurs orígens, paper, distribució i formes de possessió," in *Catalunya i França*, 248–60; Michel Zimmermann, "Naissance d'une principauté: Barcelone et les autres comtés catalans aux alentours de l'an Mil," in *Catalunya i França*, 111–35.

territory. His service was rewarded with revenues from a *fevum*, a portion of public lands associated with the castle, as well as with rights to revenues from the alod holders and dependent tenants within the *castrum*.[108]

This consensus is in many respects very unsatisfactory, as even its authors admit. The most serious flaw is the distinction between comital castles entrusted to *vicarii* and castles held independently. It has been argued – with frankly little or no documentary support for Catalonia – that around the year 1000, the institution of the *vicarius* was in transition, with these officials tending to exercise their functions with more and more independence and succeeding in absorbing their "office" into their patrimony. There is scant evidence for the passing of the vicarial charge from one generation to the next in the tenth century; there is no evidence for the terms on which this occurred. Indeed it is more likely that the count maintained a given family as *vicarii* because they were the most prominent landowners in the region, a fact which may explain the acquisitions of some of these families.[109] There is also some evidence that the counts granted vicariates to the sons of important lay and ecclesiastical officials: Sunifred, *vicarius* of Rubí, was the son of Bishop Odó of Girona; Geribert, *vicarius* of Subirats, was the son of Viscount Guitard of Barcelona.[110] Any patrimonialization was de facto, not de jure or de recto. Patrimonial rights even of viscounts in the tenth century to their castles is similarly unlikely.[111] Thus though it is undeniable that there were *vicarii*, their exact relationship to the count and his castles is far from clear.

As for castles held independently, most of the examples of comital alienations do not involve sales or donations to individuals identified as *vicarii* (Table 1.2). In fact, the only beneficiary of such a transaction

---

[108] Cf. Georges Duby, *La société aux XIᵉ et XIIᵉ siècles dans la région mâconnaise*, 2nd ed. (Paris, 1971; repr. 1988), 99–103. Font Rius ("Les modes de détention," 409) refers to confiscation of a *fevum* because of vicarial treason, but does not cite documents or make clear the era in question. The only – ambiguous – example I have found is *DOliba* 7 (a. 982x83).

[109] Bonnassie, *La Catalogne*, 1:240–41, identifies one pair of father and son *vicarii*: Sal·la and Isarn de Solterra. He does not clarify whether Sunifred, son of Morgad de Cabrera, was also a *vicarius*. Nothing is known of the status of the ancestors of the other *vicarii* in his table, Ansulf de Gurb and Guifré d'Orís, although the son of the first, Sendred de Gurb, is cited as a *vicarius* of the castle of Sallent in 1005; see Benet, *Gurb-Queralt*, 33–56 and app. 2 (pp. 240–41). In the dispute in 996 between the monastery of Sant Cugat del Vallès and Sunifred, *vicarius* of Rubí, the latter claimed: "Semper vicharii castri Riorubii consueti fuerunt [devi?]rare predictas aquas" (OR, Sant Cugat del Vallès 83*).

[110] OR, Sant Cugat del Vallès 83*; *DBarcelona* 329. Cf. Matthew Innes, *State and Society in the Early Middle Ages: The Middle Rhine Valley, 400–1000*, CSMLT, 4th ser., 47 (Cambridge, 2000), 237–39.

[111] In 928, Lleopard, viscount of Girona, sold the *castrum* of *Ravinas* to his son, Otger, for 1,000 *solidi* (*ACondal* 91). Riu i Riu, who thought Lleopard was viscount of Barcelona, suggests that this was a simulated sale to enable the viscount to pass on the castle to his heir. Otger, however, was probably preceded in the viscomital position by an elder brother, Unifred. So, while the argument may still be correct, this document may not be the best evidence. See Riu i Riu, "A propósito del feudalismo todavía," 75; Coll i Castanyer, "Els vescomtes," 40–41.

Table 1.2. *Alienations of castles by the counts of Barcelona (950–1000)*[#]

Document	Date	*Castrum*	Sale Price	Beneficiary
DPoblet 1 [CPF 6]	960	La Roqueta		Isarn, *fidelis meus*
MH 101	962x63	Sacama		Digfré, *fidelis noster*
CSCV 65	963	Masquefa	1,000 *solidi*	Ennec Bonfill
DVic 365	964x65	Ceuró	400 *solidi*	Borrell, *fidelis meus*
Benet, *Gurb-Queralt*, app. 1	976	Queralt	200 *pensa de argento*	Guitard, viscount
CSCV 126	977	Sant Esteve	60 *pensa*	Unifred Amat
ACondal 186	980	Cabra		Ervigi
DACU 207	947x86	Figuerola	?	Vidal
ACondal 204 [LFM 268]	987	Miralles		(see of Vic)
ACondal 232	992	Cervelló	100 *pensa de argento*	Ennec Bonfill
DVic 566	992	Meda, Sant Llorenç	300 *solidi*	Bonfill, *levita*
DVic 570	992	Miralles		(see of Vic)

Note:
[#] Cf. Bonnassie, *La Catalogne*, 1:145–48.

identifiable as a *vicarius*, Ennec Bonfill, is not identified as such in the records related to the transaction. It might be expected that if the transfer of the castle was connected in some way to Ennec's vicarial function, his title – if not the precise terms of the grant – would be used.[112] In the grant by Borrell II of Barcelona of the castle of Cabra to Ervigi, son of *Bitarius*, and his wife and son, the beneficiary is not given the title *vicarius*, but the subscription immediately following the count's is that of Erimir *vicarius*. What was the connection of this figure to the castle?[113] If the beneficiaries were not *vicarii*, who were they? Most can be identified as men close to the count, if not set apart by a position (viscount), then

---

[112] *CSCV* 298 (a. 994: "in terra de Bonefilio, vicario"); OR, Sant Cugat del Vallès 86★ (a. 999: "tibi Bonefilio, viccario, filium condam Sinderedi"). Historians have assumed that these references are to the individual appearing in documents from 963 to 997 usually referred to as "Ennego, que vocant Bonofilio" (AAM, Sant Cugat del Vallès 32★; *CSCV* 65, 277, 327, 328; AME 6/72★), a name occasionally found along with "filius (quondam) Sendredi" (*CSCV* 243, 331, 337; *ACondal* 232; cf. OR, Sant Cugat del Vallès 83★, subscribed by "Bonefilio filium Sinderedi condam quę alio vocabulo fungitur Henego").

[113] *ACondal* 186 (a. 980). A *vicarius* named Ervigi is mentioned as alive in *DBarcelona* 96 (a. 970) and dead in LA 2:428★ (a. 997).

by the title of *fidelis* or the use of a cognomen. This class of men is precisely the group, however, upon whom the count drew for his *vicarii*.[114]

Just as the line between the personnel in charge of "comital" and "independent" castles is not clear, so the terms on which these castles were held seem to overlap. The language of comital sales and donations of castles suggests that the grants were made with no conditions. They follow the usual formulae of sale or donation, including phrases such as "we hand over from our right into yours control and power [of these lands], so that whatever you wish to do concerning them, freely in the name of God you shall have full power to do, with all their benefits and profits as your own."[115] These were not, though, totally unencumbered grants. The grant just quoted from contains numerous exceptions of both alodial and comital lands ("quod hodie Borrellus comes ad suum opus tenebat ad suum domenicum"). Nor is it at all clear that the castle (*castellum*) became the freely held possession of the beneficiary. This same grant, of the castle of Cervelló, uses the territorial designation (*castrum*), as well as the terms for smaller fortifications (*turris, rocha*), but never *castellum*.

Many have followed a model proposed by Ramon d'Abadal for how the counts established control in new areas. Once colonists began to install themselves in a region, the count would appoint a *vicarius* to define the limits of a territory and set up a defensive site; the count would also grant a *fevum* to the *vicarius*.[116] This is a good model, but it is purely speculative, for there are no citations of *vicarii* associated with this type of exercise. Documents are entirely silent on the relationships among count, *vicarius*, and castle. A few transactions concerning castles survive that were made without any reference to the counts, but it is likely that the count had ties to these as well.[117] Referring to documents from the first decades of the eleventh century, Michel Zimmermann has written, "The count sells what never belonged to him . . . or what no longer belonged to him; what he sells, on the other hand, continues to belong to him."[118] What difference, then, was there between a *vicarius*, endowed with a fief, in charge of a comital castle, and a castle held by independent grant of the count?

---

[114] Zimmermann, "Naissance d'une principauté," 126; Bonnassie, *La Catalogne*, 1:286.

[115] *ACondal* 232: "de nostro iuro in tuo tradimus dominio et potestatem ut quidquid exinde facere vel iudicare volueris libera in Dei nomine plenam abeas potestatem cum exios vel regresios earum a proprio."

[116] Ramon d'Abadal i de Vinyals, "La reconquesta d'una regió interior de Catalunya: La Plana de Vic," in Abadal i de Vinyals, *Dels Visigots als Catalans*, ed. Jaume Sobrequés i Callicó, 3rd ed., 2 vols., Col·lecció estudis i documents 13–14 (Barcelona, 1986), 1:320–21; Abadal i de Vinyals, *Els primers comtes*, 91–92; Bonnassie, *La Catalogne*, 1:211; etc.   [117] E.g., *ACondal* 91.

[118] Zimmermann, "Naissance d'une principauté," 127; cf. Bonnassie, *La Catalogne*, 1:209–14.

The difficulties in understanding the late-tenth-century situation are best illustrated by a group of documents concerning Miralles, a castle on the western frontier of the county of Osona. In 987, Borrell II of Barcelona donated half of the *castrum* of Miralles to the see of Vic; in 992, his son, Ramon Borrell, granted the other half.[119] The castle thus appears to have moved from the sole possession of the count, to the joint posses- sion of the count and the bishop, to the sole possession of the bishop.[120] At all times, immediate control over the castle was in the hands of Ennec Bonfill. He is not mentioned in the first grant, but at some point there- after, he subscribed the oath to the bishop cited above. He promised "sincere faith (*fides*) concerning your half of the castle," and that he would not knowingly allow injury to come to the bishop from the castle. The count's rights are not mentioned in this document, and no similar written pledge from Ennec to the count has survived. The grant of the second half of the castle is known only from a seventeenth-century notice that reads (in part), "he made a donation to the church of Osona, in the hands of Bishop Fruia, of the other half of the castle of Miralles, which Ennec Bonfill possessed for the count ('por el Conde'), with the condition that during his natural life, the said Bonfill should possess it."[121]

These documents provide many more questions than answers. Was Ennec the *vicarius* for the castle? Was Ennec holding the castle "por el Conde" on the same terms as presented in his oath to the bishop? In other words, do the terms of the first surviving written oath from Catalonia represent the standard terms on which castles were held, whether from a count or a bishop? The terms are similar to what came after, but this says nothing about what came before, and the terms are sufficiently ambigu- ous that they could fit equally well into a regime characterized as public or one where private relationships were most important. Were the terms an innovation, or was it the fact that they were written down that was new? Does the requirement in the second grant that Ennec remain in possession of the castle until his death suggest that he was in danger of losing his position as master of the castle when he was no longer serving the count? Does it suggest that his position under the count was not as precarious as the standard interpretations would suggest?

---

[119] *ACondal* 204 [*LFM* 268] (a. 987); AME 6/72* (a. 987); Juan Luís de Moncada, *Episcopologio de Vich*, ed. Jaime Collell (vols. 1 and 2) and Luís B. Nadal (vol. 3), 3 vols., Biblioteca histórica de la Diócesis de Vich 1, 3 (vols. 1 and 2) (Vic, 1891–1904), 1:196–97 [*DVic* 570] (a. 992).

[120] *ACondal* 204 [*LFM* 268]: "Quantum infra istas affrontaciones includunt, sic dono ego iamdictus comes ad Domino Deo et sancti Apostoli supra scripti de ista omnia superius scripta ipsa med- ietate tota ab integro."

[121] Moncada, *Episcopologio*, 1:197: "hizo donacion á la Iglesia de Ausona en manos del Obispo Froya de la otra mitad del Castillo de Miralles la qual poseia, por el Conde Enego Bonfilio, con tal pacto y condicion que durante su vida natural poseyese aquella dicho Bonfilio."

Two final points: In his tripartite schema of modes of castle holding, Font Rius argues that the "vicarial" regime is entirely separate from the "feudal" regime. The only evidence for the terms of the early "feudal" regime, however, is this oath by an individual known to have acted as a *vicarius*. Was Ennec Bonfill holding the same castle from two individuals under different terms and different regimes, or have historians been overzealous in attempting to establish the novelty of relationships they call "feudal"? It is, after all, supposed to be in part the *vicarial* integration of function into patrimony that lies at the origin of these developments, not the activity of some mysterious protofeudal lords. Font Rius also argues that the origin of the "feudal" regime is to be found in grants for the redevelopment (*ad restaurandum*) of frontier territory, when these initially precarial grants became perpetual. The diplomatic roots of the castle-holding *convenientia* in conditional grants suggest that he may be correct. But while documents from after 1020 show grants of castles *ad restaurandum*, the evidence is too scant for this earlier period. It is impossible in this case to confirm that what seems to have been happening on the level of formula was a true reflection of institutional developments.

EARLY CATALAN *CONVENIENTIAE*, C. 1021–50

These doubts about the development of various regimes of castle holding in the late tenth and early eleventh centuries should not be read as doubts about the fact that this was a society in transition. Litigants found the old mechanisms of settlement and the dispensing of justice inadequate to their needs; they began to make changes within the system and, increasingly, to go outside it. Scribes found the models in their formularies too restrictive and incapable of accurately reflecting the transactions they were asked to record; they experimented with new terms, new phrases, and even new types of documents. Powerful men and women began to require that the promise of fidelity take a written form. It is from this society in transition that the *convenientia* emerged.

The last decades of the tenth century and the first decades of the eleventh witnessed a loosening of documentary formulae in the very areas in which the term *convenientia* first appeared. The "first" *convenientia*, of c. 1021, may now be seen to have drawn transparently on these diplomatic and institutional innovations for clauses concerning conditional grants of castles, oaths of fidelity, dispute-settlement mechanisms, and guarantees. Its most novel aspect is simply its use of the opening formula "Hec est convenientia." Some vernacular technical vocabulary survives in this agreement ("encurgussuda," "comunra," "sine engan lo li faca"),

64

hinting at the language of an oath, but unfortunately no oath has survived. A written oath may have existed. This *convenientia* was included in the *Liber feudorum maior*, the great twelfth-century cartulary of the counts of Barcelona, and an early-fourteenth-century register of that cartulary indicates that the text of an oath followed the text of the *convenientia*.[122] Fortunately, another early oath/*convenientia* pair has survived that further illustrates the close links between these two types of documents in their formative stages.

Scribes used two documents to enshrine an agreement between Count Ermengol II of Urgell and the bishop of Urgell, also named Ermengol.[123] Neither includes a dating clause, and they can be situated in time only by the tenures of the two participants to 1011x35. The *convenientia* is a much shorter and much less complex document than the one between Ermengol II and Berenguer Ramon I, but it contains much of the same language and many of the same institutions. In it the count promises to swear to provide aid when possible to the bishop against all those against whom the bishop requests aid, except the count's own men. There is no indication that this is an oath of fidelity, and no lands are transferred. In fact, unlike the other *convenientia*, this is not an explicitly reciprocal agreement: only the count acts.[124] As in that other document, however, the following elements are present: a promise of aid against all men and women, pledges of castles for maintaining the agreement, and a mechanism for settling disputes arising from the violation of the agreement, with an ordeal as a last resort. Like the other *convenientia*, too, the bulk of this agreement is composed not of undertakings, but of descriptions of guarantees and procedures for dispute settlement. There are other differences: the ordeal here is by cold water, rather than by battle; there is explicit provision for a tribunal to decide an appropriate penalty; and there are considerably more passages in the vernacular. From the point of view of language and formula, however, it is the similarities that stand out.[125] The written oath corresponding to this *convenientia* survives, preserved in the cartulary of the cathedral of Urgell immediately following the agreement. As can be seen from the juxtaposed texts (Figure 1.1), the oath repeats in the first person many clauses that appear in the *convenientia* in the third person. The clauses it omits relate to the content and

---

[122] *LFM* 158 (rubric only): "Sacramentale quod fecit Ermengaudus, comes Urgelli, R. comiti Barcinonensi, post suprascriptam convenientiam." Miquel Rosell surmises that the substitution of "R." for "B.," also found in the rubric to the *convenientia*, is a copyist's error (*LFM*, 1:158 n. 2).

[123] DACU 486, 487.

[124] It is possible that we are only seeing half of the agreement, and that a *convenientia* and oath with different language were drawn up and retained by the count.

[125] The use of the term *parenc(i)a* to refer to the ordeal, for instance, occurs only in these two *convenientiae*.

DACU 486

Hec est convenientia inter Ermengaudo comite et Ermengaudo episcopo, ut *iuret Ermengaudus comes ad Ermengaudo episcopo adiutorium sine engan super omnes homines vel feminas, unde Ermengaudus episcopus lo pregara, exceptus suos homines,* et similiter adiutorium super ipsos iurara *on dret fer no li podra o consel segons sua voluntad* de Ermengaudo episcopo. Et iurara suprascriptus *Ermengaudus comes* ad suprascripto *Ermengaudo episcopo que no.l defidara ne per sacrament no.l comonra, si ipsas pignoras no li toll o no le.n toll* Ermengaudus episcopus suprascriptus *que ui li pegnorara.* Et si Ermengaudus episcopus suprascriptus tollia ipsas pignoras suprascriptas o le.n tollia ad Ermengaudo comite suprascripto que ui li pegnorara, absolutus sia Ermangaudus comes de ipso sacramento que hodie iurara ad Ermengaudo episcopo suprascripto et ipsas pignoras, quod Ermengaudus comes suprascriptus hodie dara ad Ermengaudo episcopo suprascripto, absolutas fiant. Et donat Ermengaudus comes suprascriptus pignoras ad Ermengaudo episcopo suprascripto, cum ipsos castros de Abella cum suos terminos et ipso castro de Boxols et ipsas speluncas de Lavancola et ipso castro que dicunt Odron cum illorum termines. *Quod si fors factura aud fors facturas fa Ermengaudus comes suprascriptus ad Ermengaudo episcopo suprascripto, emen les infra ipsos primos .c. dies quod Ermengaudus episcopus suprascriptus o quererala ad Ermengaudo comite suprascripto e le.n pregara sine engann. Si o emen Ermengaudus comes suprascriptus ad Ermengaudo episcopo suprascripto ad iudicium de duos homines de Ermengaudo comite suprascripto et de duos de Ermengaudo episcopo suprascripto, quod ipsi ambo elegerint; et si de ipso iudicio non concordant inter illos, fatiant parenca ad iuditium Dei in aqua frigida per singulos homines. Et ipsa emenda qui iudgada e per dret faca la Ermengaudus comes suprascriptus ad Ermengaudo episcopo suprascripto aut tale consilium que Ermengaudus episcopus suprascriptus se recipia per sua voluntad;* et si hoc facere noluerit Ermengaudus comes suprascriptus ad Ermengaudo episcopo suprascripto, incurrant ipsas pignoras suprascriptas in potestate de Ermengaudo episcopo suprascripto. Et si emendare noluerit Ermengaudus comes suprascriptus ad Ermengaudo episcopo suprascripto ipsas fores facturas aut fores factura, infra ipsos primos .c. dies que Ermengaudus episcopus suprascriptus o quererala ad Ermengaudo comite suprascripto e le.n pregara sine engann incurrant ipsas pignoras suprascriptas in potestate de Ermengaudo episcopo suprascripto et ipsos homines, qui tenent ipsas pignoras, fient homines de Ermangaudo episcopo suprascripto per ipsa convenientia suprascripta et iurunt ipsi homines suprascripti ipsas pignoras suprascriptas ad Ermengaudo episcopo suprascripto. Quod si incurrunt ipsas pignoras suprascriptas de potestate Ermengaudo episcopo suprascripto, ipsi homines qui tenent ipsas pignoras suprascriptas tennanenn *(sic)* ad Ermengaudo episcopo suprascripto sine male ingenio et sine engann et podstadiut le.n facan sine suo ingann. *Et si Ermengaudus episcopus suprascriptus ipsas emendas aut emenda de Ermengaudo comite suprascripto recipere noluerit o no les li volia perdonar, ipsas pignoras suprascriptas soltas sian. Ista conveninetia suprascripta acsi la tenga Ermengaudus comes suprascriptus ad Ermengaudo episcopo suprascripto per dreta fed sine engann se sciente, exceptus quantum Ermengaudus episcopus suprascriptus solvera Ermegaudo comite suprascripto sine forcia.*

DACU 487

Ego Ermengaudus comes, de ista ora in antea adiutor sere per fide sine engann ad Ermengaudo episcopo filio Guisla supra omnes homines vel homine, feminas vel femina unde Ermengaudus episcopus suprascriptus me pregara, exceptus ipsos meos homines, on dret fer li podre o consel segons sa volentad. Ego Ermengaudus comes de ista ora in antea no desfidare Ermengaudo episcopo suprascripto ne per sagrament no.l comunre si ipsas pignoras no.m tolke ui me pennora o no me.n tol.

Ego Ermengaudus comes de ista ora in antea, si fores factura fac aut fores facturas ad te Ermengaudo episcopo suprascribto, infra ipsos primos .c. dies quod tu Ermengaudus episcopus suprascriptus m.o querellaras o me.n pregaras sine meo engann, si t.o emennare ego Ermengaudus comes ad te Ermengaudo episcopo suprascripto ad iuditium de duos tuos homines et de duos meos si concordant de ipso iudicio, si tu Ermengaudus episcopus rezebre o vols; et si non concordant ipsi homines de ipso iuditio inter illos aut ego noluero recipere illorum iuditio ego Ermengaudus comes ad te Ermengaudo episcopo suprascripto ipsas fores facturas aut fore factura que feites t.aure, emenar les te per iuditium Dei per aqua frigida si tu recebr.o vols o tal consell te.n fare que tu recebras per ta vollentad.

E si tu Ermengaudus episcopus suprascriptus ipsa mea emenna rezebre no la volies o no la.m condonaves per tua bona volentad absolutus sim ego Ermengaudus comes de isto sacramento suprascripto et ipsas meas pignoras ke ui te pennore soltes sian. Ego Ermengaudus comes suprascriptus istum sacramentum acsi.l tenre ad Ermengaudo episcopo suprascripto me sciente com ci es escrit, exceptus quantum Ermengaudus episcopus suprascriptus me solvera sine forcia per Deum et sanctis suis.

Figure 1.1. *Convenientia* and corresponding oath between Ermengol, bishop of Urgell, and Ermengol II, count of Urgell (DACU 486, 487)

details of the pledges. The *convenientia* refers to the oath in the future tense ("iurara"); this suggests that the oath was sworn after the convention was drawn up.[126]

Much of the language in this oath/*convenientia* pair is also found in the earliest written oaths, examined above, which combined the characteristics of both oath and *convenientia*. Here the beginnings of a separation of the oath-convention into two distinct documents are apparent. That scribes were not yet secure with these new written forms may be seen in the text of the pledge granted by Ermessenda to Berenguer Ramon I to bring an end to their conflict of 1020–22.[127] The first half of the document draws on the formulae of a pledge ("Ego Ermessendis comitissa inpignoratrix sum tibi filio meo Berengario comite. Manifestum est enim quia mitto tibi pignoras . . ."). After the list of castles pledged, however, the document slides into the language of *convenientiae* and oaths:

Thus I give to you a pledge that from this day forward I will treat you well and will hold to the settlement and peace that I have sworn to you. And I, the said Ermessenda, will indeed keep and maintain, with respect to you, the said count Berenguer, the oath as it is written, and I will not injure you with respect to it, and if I do injure you with respect to it, within the first forty days after you warn me in the name of the oath, I will redress or pay composition for the wrong, if you wish to accept it . . .[128]

Although this text includes an affirmation common to oaths ("si tenre et adtendre"), it refers to a *separate* written oath ("istum sacramentum quomodo scriptum est"). Despite its beginning, the document serves the same function as documents that begin "Hec est convenientia." It is the written record of some of the details of the agreement (*pax, finis*), identifying pledges, procedures in case of default, and a mechanism for the resolution of conflicts. The scribe is of two minds when he arrives at the dating clause. He begins with "Acta pacta vel convenientia," but continues after Ermessenda's subscription with "qui hanc suppignorationem feci."

The beginnings of a resolution of this scribal experimentation may be seen in the roughly forty *convenientiae* that survive from before 1050 (Table 1.3). Each of these documents includes the term *convenientia*, in the opening formula, in the dating clause, or in the text in a way that

---

[126] A late-twelfth-century oath of fidelity was written and subscribed the day after it was sworn (LA 4:414*). [127] BRI 46* (a. 1022).

[128] "Sic mitto tibi pignus ut ego de isto die in antea bene tibi teneam et adtendam ipsam finem et pacem quam tibi iuravi. Et ego Eremessindis prefata si tenre et adtendre a te Berengarium comitem supradictum ipsum sacramentum quomodo scriptum est ipsum sacramentum et exinde no t.en fors fare, et si ego exinde tibi foras fecero infra ipsos primos xl dies que tu m.en comunras per nomen de sacramentum si t.o drecare o t.o emendare si hoc recipere volueris . . ."

Table 1.3. *The convenientia in the Catalan counties to 1050*

Date	Document	County	Parties	Subject	Castles
1018x26	BRI extra. 2001★	B U	count, count	treaty	x
1010x35	DACU 486	U	count, bishop	mutual oaths	x
1022x35	DOliba 116	R	abbot-bishop, *clericus*	grant *ad edificandum*	
1022 Oct 11	BRI 46★	O G	countess, count	grant *ad edificandum*	x
1023?	DTavèrnoles 49	U	king, abbot	pledge to keep agreement	x
1030	DTavèrnoles 50	U	abbot, son of king	grant, with terms of tenure	x
1032 Apr 2	ACV 9/ii/41★	O	bishop, layman	grant, with terms of tenure	x
1040 Apr 11	AAM, Sant Benet de Bages 1386	O	lay couple, lay couple	dispute settlement	
1040 Jul 30	Òdena 9	O	lay couple, lay couple	conditional sale	
1040 Aug 28	BC 2128★	O	layman, layman	agreement between brothers	x
1040 Nov 5	CPF 21 [CSCV 553]	B	abbot, lay couple	grant *ad plantandum*	x
1040 Nov 30	RBI 48	B	abbot, layman	grant *ad edificandum*	x
1041 Jan 24	BC, MS 729, 4:51r–v	U PJ	count, count	dispute settlement	x
1041 Nov 21	ACB 4–70–413b★	G	layman, viscounts	promise to grant	x
1041 Dec 8	LA 4:58★	B	bishop, lay couple	grant with terms of tenure	
1041 Dec 11?	LA 3:132★	B	viscountess, canons	terms of tenure	
1043 Jan 19	DACU 559	U	*sacer*, laywoman	agreement between siblings	
1043 c.	Extra. 3151	Ber U	count, bishop	treaty	
1043 c.	RBI sd 12★	B U	count, count	treaty	
1043 c.	RBI sd 1	B U	count, count	treaty	
1044 Aug 4	OR, Sant Cugat del Vallès 232★	B	abbot, layman	grant *per fevum* following quitclaim	
1044 Jul 10	RBI 80	B	counts, layman	promise of payment pending grant	
1044 c.	RBI sd 3	B	counts, bishop	promise to keep earlier agreement	
1045 Jul 18	ACU 375★	U	layman, bishop	terms of tenure	x
1045 Jul 31	DPoblet 3	B	layman, layman	terms of tenure	x
1047 May 14	LA 2:23★	B	*sacerdos/iudex*, layman	agreement between relatives	x
1047 Jul 25	DPoblet 5	B	lay couple, layman	grant *per fevum*	
1047 Aug 5	OR, Santa Cecília de Montserrat 54★	O	abbot, lay couple	grant *ad edificandum*	x

Date	Reference	County	Parties	Transaction	
1047 Oct 23	ACU 384★	U	bishop, lay family	terms of tenure	x
1048 Feb 5	RBI 94★	B	lay couple, counts	pledge	x
1048 Oct 4	RBI 99	B	counts, layman	agreement, terms of tenure	
1049 Feb 7	RBI 101★	G	counts, layman	commendation	x
1049 Aug 15	DTavèrnoles 67 [CTavernoles 30]	U	abbot, layman	grant with terms of tenure	
1049 Dec 5	RBI 105	B	layman, layman	grant with terms of tenure	x
1050 Mar 1	RBI 107	B	counts, abbot	commendation	
1050 Jun 9	RBI 110	B	count, count's brother	promise to commend	
1050 Aug 2	ACU 399a★	U	bishop, archdeacon	terms of tenure	x
1050 Aug 2	ACU 399b★	U	bishop, layman	terms of tenure	x
1050 Aug 30	see n. 146	O	lay couple, lay couple	grant *ad edificandum*	x
1050 Nov 5	BC 4143★	U	count, layman	commendation	x

Undatable documents, perhaps before 1050

Date	Reference	County	Parties	Transaction	
1039x50	RBI sd 207★	B	counts, viscount	commendation	x
1032x60	Extra. 3194	C	viscount, viscount's brother	dispute settlement between relatives	x
1035x68	RBI sd 30★	C U	bishop, count	promise to keep agreement	
1037x79	RBI sd 15★	PJ	layman, count	*baiulia*	
1042x62?	VL 10:36	C U	bishop, viscounts	settlement, grant with terms of tenure	x
1043x98	LFM 105	PJ	count, layman	agreement	x
1043x98	RBI sd 16★	PJ	count, layman	commendation	x

Conventiones, c. 1025–50

Date	Reference	County	Parties	Transaction	
1031 Jun 18	CSCV 520	B	monastery, lay family	agreement	
1037 Mar 10	OR, Sant Cugat del Vallès 192★	B	abbot, layman	grant *ad edificandum*	x
1037x38 May 15	ACU 314★	U	bishop, *praepositus*, layman	terms of tenure	
1039 Jul 13	DACU 515	U	bishop, layman	grant with terms of tenure	
1043 Nov 2	ACU 352★	U	canons, lay family	agreement	

Key to Counties: **B**arcelona, **B**erga, **C**erdanya, **G**irona, **O**sana, **P**allars **J**ussà, **R**osselló, **U**rgell

refers to the agreement as a whole.[129] The rapid increase in the numbers of surviving *convenientiae*, especially from *c.* 1040, hints at the importance that the written agreement would come to hold at all levels in this society until the end of the twelfth century.

A small number of *convenientiae* from before 1050 are nearly identical to those conditional agreements in which the terms *conventio* and *convenientia* first appear. Perhaps as early as the 1020s, but definitely by the 1040s, ecclesiastical institutions began to record conditional grants in *convenientiae*. Some of these contracts were directed toward development of resources, either of land, as in standard agrarian contracts referred to as *convenientiae* by scribes of Sant Cugat del Vallès and Santa Cecília de Montserrat, or of a church, as in a grant by Oliba in his capacity as abbot of Sant Miquel de Cuixà.[130] In 1041, the bishop of Barcelona granted by means of a *convenientia* rights to use of water from one of his mills in return for maintenance work on the mill.[131] Other early *convenientiae* are statements of terms under which land was held, such as the document by which Guisla, viscountess of Osona, confirmed her rights to and obligations for four churches held from the cathedral of Barcelona following the assassination of her husband.[132]

The *convenientia* also began in this period to be used for conditional grants and agreements between individuals outside an institutional context.[133] It lent itself particularly well to intrafamily arrangements. Thus in 1040 the brothers Donús Bernat and Guillem Bernat d'Òdena absolved each other of promises made to their father, appointed each other as heirs in the event the first to die had no offspring, promised to follow each other's advice and counsel as well as that of their *boni homines*, and pledged to each other their shares of the *honor* of Òdena as a guar-

---

[129] See also the following documents, which refer to *convenientiae* or *conventiones*: OR, Sant Cugat del Vallès 194★ (a. 1036); *CDSG* 234 (a. 1041); Domènec Sangés, ed., "Recull de documents del segle XI referents a Guissona i la seva plana," *Urgellia* 3 (1980), app. 12 (pp. 234–35) [DACU 601] (a. 1047); Extra. 3157 (a. 1035x69?); RBI sd 32 (a. 1047x71); *LFM* 751 (a. 1014x74), 581 (a. 1035x68); *DOliba* 76 (*post a.* 1043?).

[130] BC 2128★ (a. 1040); OR, Santa Cecília de Montserrat 54★ (a. 1047); *DOliba* 116 (a. 1022x35). The second document is called a *carta donationis* in the dating clause.

[131] LA 4:58★ (a. 1041). Other agreements over water rights referred to as *conventiones*: ACU 352★ (a. 1043), *CSCV* 520 (a. 1031). Sangés, ed., "Recull," app. 12 (pp. 234–35) [DACU 601] (a. 1047) refers back to a written *conventio* in which Bishop Ermengol of Urgell (1010–35) engaged one Mir to construct a castle at Bellveí.

[132] LA 3:132★ (a. 1041?). *DOliba* 76 (a. 1023), a *precaria carta* recording a conditional grant to Sant Miquel de Cuixà, begins with a preface that rehearses the history of the lands involved since a previous grant in 1008 (*DOliba* 39). The preface refers to the underlying agreement as a *convenientia* ("fecerunt convenientiam . . . iam dicta convenientia ad invicem est separata . . . predicta convenientia taliter est reformata . . . iam dicta convenientia ad invicem est disrupta . . . iam dicta convenentia taliter in pristinum statutum est reformata"). The editor suggests that the preface was added after the death of Bishop Oliba in 1046, presumably because it refers to "Oliva abbate tunc temporis." [133] LA 2:23★ (a. 1047); AAM, Sant Benet de Bages 1386 (a. 1040).

antee of the agreement.[134] In 1043, Vives, a priest of the cathedral of Urgell, and his sister Quixol agreed in a *convenientia* to divide land acquired by a testamentary grant. After the death of one of them, the land would pass to the other, then to a third party, and finally to the cathedral.[135]

But the preferred use of these earliest *convenientiae*, especially from *c.* 1045 on, was to record the terms of castle holding, military obligations, and the settlement of disputes concerning these matters. There is, of course, some overlap between this group and ecclesiastical conditional grants. The agreement in which Abbot Guitard of Sant Cugat del Vallès granted land to Bernat Otger as a fief describes, in addition to the usual mention of reservations of demesne lands and services due, the duties of Bernat's subtenant and the obligations of both men if either were to build a fortification (*forteza*).[136] The holder in fief of the church of Sant Esteve de Coll de Nargó owed to the abbot of Sant Sadurní de Tavèrnoles one day's worth of room and board for seven knights and their horses, as well as right of lodging (*alberga*) for the abbot whenever he required it.[137] Two *convenientiae* between the monastery of Tavèrnoles and the Navarrese royal family illustrate the adaption of the ecclesiastical conditional grant for castle tenure. Around 1023, Sancho III Garcés granted the abandoned castle district of Lasquarri to the monastery; the abbot granted the district back to the king for life, along with half of the revenues, on the condition that he "build it up and populate it and maintain peace with the Ishmaelites." The king took the castle district "from the hand of" the abbot, his "lord." Seven years later, the king's son García received tenure of Lasquarri from the same abbot, on the condition that he be the commended man of the abbot for his fief, swear fidelity to him, repopulate and pacify the region, and provide military service to the king if necessary. The agreement ends by stating that García and his sons are to be the commended men of the abbot's successors at Tavèrnoles. The transition in seven years from the language of agrarian contract to the language of military tenure is striking.[138]

After a gap of a decade, *convenientiae* concerning castle holding reemerge abruptly with four documents from 1040–41. In the first two, links to earlier types of documentation are again quite clear. A *convenientia* by which Abbot Guitard of Sant Cugat del Vallès granted the *castrum* of Albinyana to Bernat Otger was modeled on the agrarian contracts

---

[134] *Òdena* 9 (a. 1040).

[135] DACU 559 (a. 1043). See also DACU 370 (a. 1021x23). *HGL* 5:201 (*c.* 1034) is a similar division between Pere, bishop of Girona (1010–51), and his nephew Roger, count of Foix.

[136] OR, Sant Cugat del Vallès 232* (a. 1044).   [137] DTavèrnoles 67 [CTavernoles 30] (a. 1049).

[138] DTavèrnoles 49 (a. 1023?), 50 (a. 1030).

issued by the monastery. The abbot instructed Bernat to "build and construct the *castrum*, so that within seven years you shall have made a strong tower (*turris*) there . . . and around the tower a perimeter wall . . . and you should endeavor to populate the land as best you are able." After the seven-year term, Bernat would receive half of the *castrum* as an alod and the other half as a fief; he would be required to provide military service to the abbey from this new fortification.[139] The grant of the castle of Llimiana by the count of Urgell to the count of Pallars Jussà, recorded in a *convenientia* of the same year, resolved a dispute; it was, in other words, a type of quitclaim.[140]

An agreement between one Umbert and Guerau, viscount of Girona, acting with his son Ponç, concerned a castle that the viscount did not possess at the time, Montpalau. Umbert promised that if the viscount were able to obtain the castle (from the countess Ermessenda) and granted half of it to him, he would hold it from the viscount "in faith, without ill will."[141] Finally, in another *convenientia* of 1041, Guislabert, bishop of Barcelona, granted the episcopal castle of Ribes to his cousin Mir Geribert. This transaction in fact involved four documents: a *carta donationis*; a document without a standard formula (beginning simply "Convenenerunt [*sic*] ut") in which Mir promised to accept the castle on certain terms; an oath; and the *convenientia*, which contained additional terms, including details of the retained demesne (*dominicatura*).[142] The first *convenientiae* for episcopal castles in Urgell appear only a few years later, under Bishop Guillem Guifré (1041–75).[143]

Use of the *convenientia* and written oath for castle holding was not limited to kings, counts, bishops, and abbots. In 1045 Pere Guislabert and Pere Mir agreed to the terms on which the former was to hold the castle of Ponts: the naming of castle guardians (*castlans*), the military service owed, and the extent of demesne to be retained by Pere Mir.[144] Two years later, Arnau Mir de Tost and his wife Arsenda granted by *convenientia* the castle of Artesa to Borrell de Tost, and to Borrell's son after his death.[145] A document from 1050 offers the first example of a private (i.e., nonecclesiastical and noncomital) *convenientia* for the construction (or repair) of

---

[139] CPF 21 [*CSCV* 553] (a. 1040): "castrum construas atque edifices, ita scilicet ut infra septem annorum spatio habeas illic factam unam turrim firmam a petra et calce quinquaginta habentem palmos in altitudine, et in circuitu turris curtale firmum similiter a petra et calce, et terram ad populare studeas, prout melius potueris."

[140] RBI 48 (a. 1040): "definit ad predicto comite Raimundo propter hoc omnes querelas quas habebat de eum in retro de Liminina."

[141] BC, MS 729, 4:51r–v (a. 1041): "per fidem sine enganno."

[142] See below, pp. 191–93.

[143] ACU 375* (a. 1045), 384* (a. 1047), 399a* (a. 1050), 399b* (a. 1050). Cf. ACU 314* (a. 1037x38), a *conventio*.   [144] DPoblet 3 (a. 1045).

[145] DPoblet 5 (a. 1047). See Bonnassie, *La Catalogne*, 2:559.

a castle, a grant of the castle of Vespella.[146] The first private oath/*convenientia* pair, recording terms for the castles of Arraona and Rubí, dates from 1049.[147]

Just over half of the *convenientiae* from before 1050 involve counts and bishops, while a number of others record agreements made by abbots and viscounts. Agreements by nontitled individuals are few, and even in these cases, the individuals are often well-known figures, such as Arnau Mir de Tost (Table 1.3). This distribution is no doubt affected by documentary survival; it is the ecclesiastical documents that have survived in the greatest numbers, followed by those of the counts. But the use of the written word to record agreements, rather than to create legal instruments proving title to land or a debt, might not at first have appealed to those outside this rather limited group. It is perhaps in this sense that the *convenientia* formed at first a "law of the great families."[148]

A number of the earliest *convenientiae* are associated with the county of Osona, but the overwhelming majority are from the counties of Urgell and Barcelona. Again, this geographical pattern may be a question of documentary survival, or, as discussed above, choices by contemporaries about what merited preservation. Nevertheless, the conjunction of the early oaths and *convenientiae* in Urgell is striking. The agreement in *c.* 1021 between the counts of Barcelona and Urgell was heavily influenced by, if not a product of, the scribal culture of Urgell, as is shown by its closeness in language both to the *convenientia* and oath between the count and bishop of Urgell, and to other early oaths from Urgell. The awkwardness of the agreement between Ermessenda and Berenguer Ramon I, on the other hand, may reflect an unfamiliarity with this type of document in Barcelona at this early date. Guislabert, bishop of Barcelona, was involved in three of the earliest agreements concerning Barcelona (1041, 1041, *c.* 1044); this raises the possibility of more regular use of the form at this slightly later date through the efforts of scribes associated with the cathedral. Nevertheless, the initial appearance of the *convenientia* in a northern county is not evidence for southern French influence or transmission, for the counties with the closest

---

[146] ACA, Cancelleria reial, Cartes reials, Papers per incorporar, caixa 1, "57/CII," no. 1 (a. 1050): "Hec est convenientia quam facio ego Deusde et coniux mea Ermessindis ad Arnaldus Bernardi et coniux sua Sancia. Convenientia talis est, quod donamus ad jamdictus Arnaldus et a coniux sua ipso meo castro de Vespela per fevum cum suis terminis et cum suis pertinentiis et donamus ad illos avere unde edificent ipso castro et donamus ad illos cavalleria i de terra vel de mobile unde faciant guardare bene jamdicto castro."

[147] RBI 105 (a. 1049), which includes four documents: (1) *convenientia* between Ramon Sunifred and Bernat Amat de Rubí, his *senior*, concerning the castle of Arraona; (2) *convenientia* between Ramon Sunifred and Bernat Amat concerning the castle of Rubí; (3) oath of fidelity of Ramon to Bernat for castles of Rubí and Arraona; (4) oath of Amat, brother of Ramon, to Ramon concerning the castle of Arraona.   [148] Ourliac, "La *convenientia*," 251.

ties across the Pyrenees were Cerdanya, Girona, and Osona, not Urgell. The castle-holding *convenientiae* that were to become the hallmark of the region appear to be a homegrown variety.

CONVENIENTIAE AND THE "CRISIS" OF CATALAN SOCIETY

These changes in the language and formula of documents correspond to changes in society and its institutions. Some have argued against the reality of such transformations, claiming that they are an illusion created precisely by changes in the nature of the documents: the development of a discursive "new style" that *reveals* information hidden behind the more conventional "old style." Why did this change occur? In the Vendômois, it was a desire to provide more information to the reader, information that was "on the one hand, necessary for the growth of monastic organization itself, the rapid changes of positions among personnel; on the other hand, possible thanks to cultural growth." Changes in vocabulary were simply the result of "new pressure of the vernacular on the Latin of the charters."[149]

However valid this argument may be for the Vendômois, for Catalonia it does not apply. First, the scribes responsible for these earliest *convenientiae* were generally not monks, but clerics associated with cathedral chapters; this is not only true for episcopal documents, but for comital ones as well. Second, administrative reform of the cathedrals generally occurred at the end – not the beginning – of the eleventh century. Third, the relationship between the vernacular and the Latin of the charters was far too complex to allow for "pressure" of a growing vernacular as an explanation for change in the vocabulary of the documents.[150] Finally, the changes in Catalonia are apparent not only in the substance and language of the documents, but in the *process* of documentary change itself. In reading the earliest *convenientiae* and related texts, we may see scribes struggling to understand and to deal with developments in the legal and social order.

On the other hand, the evidence presented in this chapter draws into question the *rapidity* of some of the developments in Catalonia, long seen as the region where change was the most explosive. The historical recon-

---

[149] Dominique Barthélemy, *La société dans le comté de Vendôme de l'an mil au XIVᵉ siècle* (Paris, 1993), 62, 63.

[150] At Barcelona, for example, the dissolution of integral administration of the demesne and the formation of independent episcopal and capitular patrimonies date from 1091; similar reforms took place at Vic in 1098. See Pere Benito i Monclús, "Clergues 'feudataris.' La disgregació del patrimoni de la seu de Barcelona i els orígens del sistema beneficial (1091–1157)," *Anuario de estudios medievales* 29 (1999), 105–19; Freedman, *Vic*, 46–48. On scribes and the language of the charters, see below, pp. 152–56.

struction of the tenth century required to support the idea of a rapid, significant transformation in modes of castle tenure is poorly founded; a new regime certainly took shape in the eleventh century, but without a better understanding of what came before, the speed and degree of change involved cannot be known. Archaeological studies may eventually help to clarify these points.[151] Similarly, the personal and landholding relationships recorded by the scribes in the early *convenientiae* were not entirely new. The parties involved understood them well enough to present their scribes with the challenge of recording complicated systems of oaths and tenures. Here, too, a better understanding of the tenth-century situation is required before the significance of eleventh-century developments may be determined. More positively, deficiencies in the system of comital *placita* that led to the introduction of monetary penalties and withdrawal from tribunals, as well as changes in scribal traditions, are already very apparent as the millennium draws to a close. The changes in these areas seem to take place over three generations, rather than just one, a pace closer to that of economic developments, which also did not occur overnight. But if parts of the chronology in Catalonia are stretched out, as I suggest they should be, that does not diminish the explosive nature and violence of the *political* events of 1020–60. The wheels of the "feudal revolution" need not all turn at the same rate.

One reason for the appearance of rapid change, especially in the judicial order, has been the framing of a simple opposition between public justice and the *convenientia*. Most who have addressed the issue view the proliferation of the *convenientia* as the direct counterpart to the collapse of the public judicial order based on the *Liber iudiciorum*. They argue that as individuals could no longer rely on judges in comital courts to settle their disputes, they turned to private agreements. As the volume of evidence for the *convenientia* rises, the number of *placita* must fall, as if in a zero-sum system.[152] Yet the idea of a crisis of the judicial order is more problematic than the idea of a crisis of comital power,[153] and the material presented here suggests that the relationship between the *convenientia* and dispute settlement was in fact much more complicated. The first full-blown *convenientia* appears decades after the first signs of documentary change in judicial records indicate developments in judicial institutions, and it is a comital treaty rather than an instrument of dispute settlement.

---

[151] Miquel Barceló and Pierre Toubert, eds., *L'incastellamento: Actes des rencontres de Gérone (26–27 novembre 1992) et de Rome (5–7 mai 1994)*, Collection de l'École française de Rome 241 (Rome, 1998).

[152] The view presented by Bonnassie, *La Catalogne*, 2:560–74, has been very influential: Udina i Abelló, "L'administració de justícia," 129; Iglesia Ferreirós, "La creación del derecho," 263–68; Freedman, *Origins*, 66; Bisson, *Medieval Crown*, 24; etc.   [153] Bowman, "Law," 336–70.

In fact, only a small number of these early agreements can be explicitly linked to the settlement of the kind of dispute that might be subject to a comital judicial proceeding. The *convenientia* between the counts of Urgell and Pallars Jussà stated clearly its origin in a dispute. The same can be said of a *convenientia placiti* issued by Bishop Oliba in Rome that records the resolution of a dispute between the see of Vic and the Gurb family.[154] In others, it is likely: the agreement between the brothers at Òdena looks very much like the extrajudicial agreement between the brothers Vives and Hugbert years earlier.[155] But many more of these *convenientiae* do not so much resolve disputes as set up mechanisms for resolving disputes arising from violation of the terms of the agreements. The *convenientia* is not simply a substitute for comital justice. We need to view the *convenientia*, then, not as a functional innovation responding to abrupt institutional change, but as a reflection of more subtle transformations of social relations and power structures. I am not arguing for radical continuity, though elements of continuity did exist; I am proposing a more sophisticated understanding of change, which allows crisis and gradual development to operate as single process.

Whatever its diplomatic antecedents, and however earlier agreements of this sort were committed to memory, what is clearly novel about the *convenientia*, at least by the second decade of the eleventh century, is the fact that it was written down. Why was this step taken? Oliba's explanation in his decree of 1032 is an empty formula: "I have taken care to commit this agreement to writing, so that everyone now and in the future shall know how this was done, and if anyone should hear otherwise, by this he can know the truth."[156] In the case of the agreement between the counts of Barcelona and Urgell, the impulse to write may have been a desire for solemnity, considering the care with which the document was drawn up. But why was it unsubscribed? The complexity of the terms alone would be reason enough for writing it down, but the agreement between the bishop and count of Urgell was much simpler, and some of the early oaths were only one sentence long. The Catalan counties had a long tradition of respect for documentation, but in the late tenth and early eleventh centuries the subject matter of this material expanded greatly; a new flexibility, a response to changes in society, encouraged experimentation and allowed for the development of new forms.

The year 1040 was a watershed: while only seven *convenientiae* survive from before that year, thirty-four date from the following decade. The

---

[154] ACV 9/ii/41* (a. 1032).   [155] Above, p. 47.

[156] "Igitur ego Oliba, Dei ordinante gratia presul, idcirco hanc convenientiam litteris mandare curavi, ut cognoscant omnes tam presentes quam futuri qualiter hoc factum fuerit, et si quis aliter audierit per hoc veritatem cognoscere possit."

global patterns of documentary survival only enhance the significance of this leap: the period 1040–50 is in many collections a trough before a takeoff in the numbers of documents in 1050.[157] Still, the *convenientia* was not yet a regularized form, as can be seen from the variety of uses to which it was put and the frequent recourse to multiple documents to record a single transaction. These agreements were not yet closely linked to the network of castles, but from 1040 on castle-holding *convenientiae* represent an ever increasing percentage of the total. The 1040s also marked the beginning of the use of this form by Ramon Berenguer I – perhaps as early as 1039, certainly by 1043 – who would do the most to regularize and popularize it. It is in the structures he built up using the *convenientia* that a substitute for older institutions may first be seen, and it is during his reign that the written agreement came to function as a new source of order in Catalan society.

[157] Bonnassie, *La Catalogne*, 2:885–91.

Chapter 2

MAKING AGREEMENTS

Close to 1,000 of the written agreements that Catalan scribes identified as *convenientiae* have survived in various forms down to the present day. The earliest such document, as seen in the previous chapter, is a highly complex treaty between two counts, involving issues of castle tenure, inheritance, alliance, commendation, and security. These themes continued to predominate in *convenientiae*. But many written agreements dealt not with the fate of entire counties, but with the disposition of a single castle, or even a tiny plot of land. *Solidi* were numbered not in the hundreds, but in single digits. The actors were not counts, but simple monks, or reasonably well-off peasants. In the minds of scribes, the agreement between Berenguer Ramon I and Ermengol II was of the same species as the following document of 1076:

This is the agreement (*convenientia*) between the woman Adelaida and her son Amat and the woman Ermengarda and her son-in-law Geribert, and Ramon Dalmau. They promise him that they will not sell or pledge to any man or woman the whole alod that they have in Montjuïc or whatever they now ought to have, unless to the aforesaid Ramon Dalmau, if he wishes to receive (it). If, however, he does not wish to receive it, let it be permitted to them to do whatever they wish.[1]

Why did they draw the connection? What was an agreement in eleventh- and twelfth-century Catalonia?

In attempting to address such questions, we must confront an unwieldy mass of evidence. The number and diversity of the eleventh- and twelfth-century agreements enshrined in the new documentary

---

[1] ACB 1-2-1281 (=LA 1:611*): "Hec est convenientia quam faciunt Adalaidis femina et filii sui Amatus et Ermeniardis femina et genero suo Guiribertus et Remundo Dalmacii. Conveniunt ei ut omnem alodium quod habent in Monte Iudaico vel quacumque modo habere debent non vendant neque impignorent aliquo homini vel femine nisi prescripto Remundo Dalmacii, si ipse recipere voluerit. Si autem recipere noluerit, sit eis licitum facere quodcunque voluerint." Cf. LA 1:637*.

form of the *convenientia* encourages attempts at classification, but this proves difficult, especially at the highest levels of generality. One possible index is whether a given agreement is balanced or unbalanced, that is, whether it is presented as mutual undertakings or as an unequal exchange. The distinction may be seen on the level of formula. The opening phrase "Hec est convenientia" is continued in some cases with "que facta est inter" and in others with "quam facit N. ad N.," a differentiation between agreements made *between* parties and those made by one party *to* another.[2] This split is more complicated, however, when applied to the substance of the agreements: many documents with an unbalanced formula record both parties as having acted – that is, both are the subject of a verb in a main dispositive clause – while several ostensibly balanced documents show only one actor. This approach is further weakened by the fact that when only one party acts in a given document, there may be a quid pro quo hinted at in the language of the document itself or evident from another source. Thus the promises in 1060 of Ramon Mir de L'Aguda with respect to the tutelage of the young seneschal, Pere Amat, were in response to the grant of that tutelage, which was recorded in a separate document. Ramon Berenguer I's grant to his brother Sanç of several men and their lands, from a decade earlier, was almost certainly related to Sanç's renunciation of his patrimony in favor of his brother, recorded in a document dated the same day. And a convention that contains a long list of promises of Ramon Guadall to the same count, but none from the count to Ramon, ends with the admonition that the convention be observed without ill will by both parties.[3]

The division of agreements into those recording "horizontal" and those recording "vertical" relationships is also unsatisfying.[4] If notions of horizontal and vertical are based on the seemingly objective index of rank, for example, only the twelve agreements that Ramon Berenguer I entered into with other counts can be considered to be truly between equals.[5] Since, however, in most of these arrangements between counts Ramon Berenguer operated from a position of strength, is it accurate to describe the two parties as equals and the documents as describing

---

[2] Adam J. Kosto, "The *convenientiae* of the Catalan Counts in the Eleventh Century: A Diplomatic and Historical Analysis," *Acta historica et archaeologia mediaevalia* 19 (1998), 197–99.

[3] RBI 253.1*, 253.2* (a. 1060); RBI 110, *LFM* 36 (a. 1050); RBI 331* (a. 1065).

[4] The historiographical influence of this structural metaphor, often applied in the medieval context to distinguish hierarchical from communal or familial relationships, deserves further thought. See, e.g., Susan Reynolds, *Kingdoms and Communities in Western Europe, 900–1300*, 2nd ed. (Oxford, 1997).

[5] Urgell: RBI 120, 230*, 299*, sd 1, sd 12*; Extra. 4726. Besalú: RBI 154*, 210*, sd 11. Cerdanya: RBI 231. Pallars Sobirà: RBIII sd 44*. Sanç: RBI 110.

"horizontal" relationships? Conversely, in the many agreements in which Ramon Berenguer I commended a castle to a nontitled individual, he may have intended to establish greater stability, but the masters of the castles have been seen as presuming to act as his equals in solidifying their formerly precarious hold on castles. Is it correct to characterize these relationships as purely "vertical"? There are elements of vertical and horizontal relationships of power in each of these agreements, and some tend more toward one or the other extreme, but in general this categorization is not particularly useful.

A classification based on a narrower consideration of content is more successful.[6] The varieties of agreement that would remain common throughout the eleventh and twelfth centuries are already apparent in the very earliest surviving *convenientiae*, those from 1045 and earlier: agreements concerning the details of castle tenure, fidelity, and military service; treaties and alliances; conditional agreements for the exploitation of land and rights (other than castles); intrafamily arrangements; documents recording the settlement of disputes; and promises. These categories are in no way absolute; many agreements do not fit well under any of these headings, and there is a good deal of overlap among those that do. Nor are these categories medieval; scribes recognized *convenientiae* as a coherent group, but they did not distinguish subtypes. The groupings proposed here, however, are suggested by the language and content of the documents themselves, and they provide a useful analytical tool. Although the focus here is on *convenientiae*, it is essential to keep in mind the wider documentary context. Older forms from which the *convenientia* developed continued to exist and shared some of its functions, thus *convenientiae* are only a subset of all written agreements; in the case of dispute settlements and agrarian contracts, *convenientiae* are not even the most common form. But this ability of the *convenientia* to serve in various capacities highlights a crucial characteristic of the form: its flexibility. The overlap with other documentary forms also emphasizes the conceptual and institutional links, for example, between agreements concerning castles and those dealing with other aspects of Catalan society. The principal intent of the present chapter is to demonstrate the range of subject matter of the Catalan *convenientia* – the degree to which written agreements spread throughout society. It also provides a closer examination of some of the evidence offered by *convenientiae* for the institutional structures of the Catalan counties in the eleventh and twelfth centuries.

---

[6] On documentary typology, see Robert I. Burns, ed., *Diplomatarium of the Crusader Kingdom of Valencia: The Registered Charters of its Conqueror, Jaume I, 1257–1276*, vol. 1 (Introduction), *Society and Documentation in Crusader Valencia* (Princeton, 1985), 138–44 and works cited there.

Making agreements

In the somewhat murky world of etymologies, Catalonia is the "land of the castellans," while Castile is the "land of castles."[7] Catalonia could make a claim to being a land of castles, as well: close to 400 fortified sites appear in the documentation prior to *c.* 1030, an incredible density. The numbers of castles only increased as the structures of comital authority were transformed over the course of the eleventh and twelfth centuries.[8] Still, the putative etymological distinction highlights a focus in the Catalan documentation not on the castles themselves, but on their personnel and on the relationships between defensive structures, military service, and authority. From the eleventh century, these relationships appear recorded in *convenientiae*; the largest single group of Catalan *convenientiae*, in fact, address the interrelated topics of castle holding, fidelity, and military service. Other varieties of agreements, especially treaties and promises, contain clauses concerning these matters. But as the issues addressed in these other types might go well beyond the topics in question, they will be considered in their broader contexts below. The earliest and most consistent evidence for castle-holding customs is found in comital *convenientiae*, but a substantial group of agreements among the lay aristocracy at lower levels add depth to the overall picture.

Among the documents of Ramon Berenguer I of Barcelona, agreements concerning castle tenure, fidelity, and military service were enshrined in two principal forms: commendations and oath-conventions. The *convenientia* recording or effecting a commendation, sometimes called a *comenda*, includes a notice of a grant – usually, though not necessarily, of a castle – in return for a promise of some form of service.[9] Many *comenda*-conventions include the phrase "commend . . . and grant in fief" ("comendant . . . et donant . . . per fevum"), designating the dual nature of the comital action: commending the castle itself, and granting the fief associated with the castle to its new holder.[10] Others use only one of these two verbs, but achieve the same result.[11] That commendation

---

[7] José Balari Jovany, *Orígenes históricos de Cataluña*, 2nd ed., 3 vols., Biblioteca filológica-histórica 10–11bis (Sant Cugat del Vallès, 1964), 1:59–62; Frederic Udina i Martorell, *El nom de Catalunya* (Barcelona, 1961), 40–42. Castile has its own controversies: Jaime Oliver Asín, "En torno a los orígenes de Castilla: Su toponimia en relación con los árabes y los beréberes," *Al-Andalus* 38 (1973), 319–91.

[8] Michel Parisse and Jacqueline Leuridan, eds., *Atlas de la France de l'an mil: État de nos connaissances* (Paris, 1994), 106–9; *Els castells catalans*, 6 vols. in 7 parts (Barcelona, 1967–79).

[9] Arcadio García, "La 'commenda' de castillos en el siglo XI," *Ausa* 3 (1958–60), 321–28.

[10] RBI 218*, 225, 292*, 296*, 320*, 376*; *LFM* 40; BC 4143*.

[11] *Comendare*: RBI 101*, 419*. *Donare (per fevum)*: RBI 149*, 373*; *LFM* 151. Cf. RBI 445* ("habeat . . . per comendationem"); OM 5:41 ("convenit . . . per fevum").

was seen less as a transfer of property than as an appointment to a position is shown by a number of documents very similar in language to commendations of castles, but in which the thing commended is not a castle but an office: the abbacy of Sant Cugat del Vallès, the seneschalcy of Barcelona, or the position of tutor. In 1089, for example, Berenguer Ramon II commended the tutelage of the castle of Montpalau and its underage master by means of a *convenientia*.[12]

Commendations are balanced in content, in that one party commends, and the other party promises services in return. These services are many and varied, but usually related to the relationship between the two individuals: becoming a "solid man" (*homo solidus*)[13] and swearing fidelity; military activity, such as participation in host and cavalcade or maintenance of castle-guard; and promises to respect the count's military or economic rights. Commendations that require the holder to construct further fortifications on the site highlight the connection between these agreements and ecclesiastical agrarian contracts and grants *ad restaurandum*, documentary forms in which the *convenientia* finds its diplomatic roots. But whereas in the earlier grants the development of the land was the main subject of the agreement, in commendations these matters are secondary.

The oath-convention is the complement of the commendation, but it does not include a notice of a grant. The text is simply a list of the undertakings and services promised, often beginning with a promise of fidelity. In the documentation of Ramon Berenguer I, the services specified in oath-conventions are identical to those found in commendations. Some oath-conventions are for a specific castle or group of castles, in which case the existence of an earlier commendation may be assumed. Often the convention begins in general terms and then continues with clauses concerning the specific castles for which fidelity or service is being promised ("non dezebra eos de ipso castro de . . ."), or of which the holder is to render

---

[12] BRII 62* (a. 1089); RBI 107, 174*, 214*. RBI 253.1*, a *carta donacionis*, contains notice of the commendation; 253.2* is the *convenientia* made "propter baiuliam quam mihi commendatis." In RBI sd 207* the grant is of control over the city of Tarragona. In *CCM* 109, a *comenda* in reverse, the bishop of Girona *submits* La Bisbal to the *baiulia* of the count (see below, n. 64).

[13] While the meaning of *solidus* is clear – "solid" homage is the equivalent of "liege" homage elsewhere in Europe, the principal obligation in a system of multiple homage – the translation of the term presents a problem. The Catalan translation of the *Usatges de Barcelona* gives *sòliu* (Us. 25, 36), meaning "solitary," or "sole," which might make sense in this context. This etymology is not, however, supported by historical linguistics (Joan Coromines, ed., *Diccionari etimològic i complementari de la llengua catalana*, 9 vols. [Barcelona, 1980–91], 8:22). Furthermore, the term *solidus* appears in other contexts in this documentation where this sense is less likely, e.g.: BRI extra. 2001* ("usque Ermengaudus iamdictus habeat solidos Mamacastrum et Alos"); *Gerri* 4 ("post mortem meam libera et solida remaneat predicto cenobio sine ullo retinimento"); AAM, Sant Cugat del Vallès 144 ("abeatis solide et libere prelibatam donacionem"). I have therefore retained the unfortunately awkward "solid." See below, p. 88.

control (*potestas*) on demand.[14] In one oath-convention, twelve separate knights each promised one month's guard duty at the castle of *Palad*.[15]

In other cases the oath-convention is purely general: an individual promises fidelity and services, but not with respect to a specific castle.[16] Four brief conventions of Ramon Berenguer I share an almost identical text, including a partially vernacular affirmation similar to ones found in oaths with the form "Iuro ego": "I, N., will hold and keep to ('o tenre et o atendre') what is written above with respect to you, the said count and countess, in full fidelity and without any ill will ('sine ullo enganno')." Each of these, in which an individual promises to be the "solid man" (*solidus*) of the counts and to respect their holdings generally, would seem to be the oath of a man of relatively low status among Ramon Berenguer's followers.[17] Others contain the more extensive promises of more substantial persons, such as Guerau Alemany de Cervelló or Guillem II of Besalú. Even in these, however, the undertakings remain purely general.[18] What unifies this group of oath-conventions, general and specific, in a formal sense is the fact that they are all unbalanced, at least on the surface. The only major engagements recorded are those of the individual promising service.[19]

A third type of oath-convention, which lies somewhere between the commendation and the general oath-convention, establishes a "money-fief." In these documents, the promise of fidelity is still general, but it is offset by a yearly payment. Like commendations, then, these agreements are explicitly balanced. Ramon Berenguer I did make payments in addition to commendations of castles in other conventions,[20] but in conventions recording a money-fief the money is the *only* compensation granted. Four of the six surviving examples are brief documents, very similar to the brief oath-conventions, but with the addition of a comital promise of 20 ounces of gold per year.[21] A fifth is a temporary money-fief in which the count makes the standard grant of 20 ounces to Guillem Umbert until his father's honor becomes available.[22] A sixth is more complex than the rest, but has

---

[14] RBI 269, 273.1*, 280*, 287*, 321.1*, sd 4.   [15] RBI sd 7.

[16] RBI 154* contains the stock list of counties, dioceses, and castles of the counts of Barcelona more commonly found in oaths with the form "Iuro ego." See Michel Zimmermann, "Aux origines de la Catalogne féodale: Les serments non-datés du règne de Ramon Berenguer Ier," in *La formació i expansió*, 113–14.

[17] RBI 261, 279*, 338 ("Sicut superius scriptum est si o tenre et o atendre ego iamdictus Bernardus vobis predictis comitem et comitissam per directam fidem sine ullo engan"); *LFM* 179.

[18] RBI 154* (middle section), 210*, 328, 337, 407; *LFM* 364.

[19] There are minor exceptions: e.g., in RBI 273.1*, the count undertakes to loan asses for use in the host service he has been promised.   [20] RBI 120, 218*, 373*, 419*, sd 207*; BC 4143*.

[21] RBI 386*, 387, sd 10, sd 14*.

[22] RBI sd 9. Cf. AME 8/87 (a. 1088), involving Bishop Berenguer Sunifred of Vic and Guislabert Mir de Sentfores.

the same effect: in return for promises of fidelity, the counts promise to pay 7 ounces yearly to Bernat Tedmar until they can provide a piece of land (*cavalleria*) for him, at which point the yearly payments were to stop.[23]

Counts were not the only ones to regulate castle tenure and military service by means of *convenientiae*; ecclesiastical institutions did so from an early date, and there is substantial evidence from *c.* 1050 on of similar activity among the lay aristocracy, both within and outside the frameworks of comital authority. The connections between comital and non-comital *convenientiae* in these centuries will be examined in later chapters. For present purposes, it is sufficient to point out that there are disparities between these two groups of records: in the surviving documentation of castle-holding conventions below the comital level, for example, while oath-conventions have survived, they are very rare.[24] The principal difference, however, seems to be that noncomital castle-holding conventions demonstrate more flexibility.

Lords occasionally granted rights and lands – sometimes, though not always, called fiefs – in exchange for guard duty in a castle without actually commending the castle. These agreements could require a certain number of months of service, or they could be purely general.[25] Often this guard duty was in addition to other services promised in return for a grant; the standard services of host and cavalcade were the most common, but the beneficiary of the grant might also be responsible for an annual payment.[26] Other conventions recorded military support from a castle that was not the subject of a commendation. When, for example, Guillem de Terrassa granted a fief to Bertran Guillem *de Ipsis Olleriis* in return for military service in 1142, Bertran promised to defend Terrassa "with the fortress called Castellet that we hold," apparently independently of Guillem. Similarly, in 1155, Pere Bertran de Bell-lloc promised in return for a grant from Guillem Ramon (II) Seneschal, to defend the Montcada domain from his castle of Bell-lloc.[27]

---

[23] RBI 162*. See Bonnassie, *La Catalogne*, 2:755–59. He would have RBI 80 be another money-fief, but this is a payment not for service, but for rights. Cf. Bryce Lyon, *From Fief to Indenture: The Transition from Feudal to Non-feudal Contract in Western Europe*, Harvard Historical Studies 68 (Cambridge, Mass., 1957).

[24] RBI 278, 401; BRII 51; RBIII 312; RBIV 346; OR, Santa Maria de Montalegre 48a*, 79*; ACG 145. General oath-conventions and oath-conventions for holdings that are not castles are also very rare: *LFM* 650, 651; RBIV 286; BC 10106.

[25] BRII 37: "quatuor menses in anno stare in kastro Erapruniano." ACB 1–4–211: "bene guardet ipsum chastrum de Muntbui . . . vi menses in anno id est maio et iunio et iulio et augusti et september et octuber." RBI 462: "guardet ipsam turrem quod est ipsum kastrum."

[26] ACV 6/1821: "faciatis vobis servicium perna i et fogaces iii per unumquemque annum . . . Et propter hoc convenio vobis seniores meos que facio staticam in Cocala."

[27] OR, sense procedència 498 (a. 1142: "cum ipsa forteza quam vocant Chastelet quam habemus"); RBIV 289.

Lords also exchanged lands, rights, or money for promises of general military service without any reference to a specific castle. The conventions sometimes call the land granted a *cavalleria*, but without explicitly linking this unit of land to a fortification.[28] In other agreements, the grant made in return for service consisted of a church and its associated rights. Instead of the rights and exactions that commonly accompanied the grant of a castle, a church was granted along with its "tithes and first fruits and offerings."[29] Churches might rival castles in their potential to generate revenue, and lords required similar military service in return for both types of grants. Grants of privately held churches for military service may have been, however, a fairly localized practice, as six of the nine surviving examples concern only two families.[30]

STRUCTURES OF POWER IN *CONVENIENTIAE*

A closer examination of the details of these agreements dealing with the topics of castle tenure, fidelity, and military service shows how *convenientiae* could articulate structures of power. Much of what parties recorded in these documents amounts to the details of the "feudal contract," a phenomenon that elsewhere in Europe is assumed to have been the subject of predominantly oral transactions. The concept of feudal contract has come in for much criticism, and rightly so, for many commit the error of assuming that the existence of a part of the classical model implies the existence of the whole: if there is a vassal, for example, there must be a fief. The abundant evidence offered by *convenientiae* for the relationships centered around military service and personal ties in Catalonia obviates the need for such extrapolation. The links are explicit in these documents among homage, fidelity, the grant of a fief, military service, and a system of exploitation of the land. It is by no means necessary, however, to discuss these relationships in terms of the classical model; here the critics of feudalism have a point. A focus on specific reciprocal rights and obligations, with an eye toward comparative studies, is the best approach.[31]

---

[28] OR, Santa Maria de Montalegre 84*: "ipsam cavalleriam terre . . . in Terracia." AAM, Sant Benet de Bages 1646: "unam kavalleriam in Ferrerons . . . aliam kavalleriam in Navarcles."

[29] RBIII 169*: "cum suis decimis et primiciis atque oblationibus et ceteris omnibus eidem ęcclesię quolibet modo pertinentibus."

[30] Ricard Guillem de Barcelona made three such grants: RBII 37*; RBIII 164, 169* (see Bensch, *Barcelona*, 155 and n. 75, which conflates RBIII 164 and 169*). Guerau de Rupià and later Guillem de Rupià received oath-conventions for churches in the diocese of Girona (ACG 199, 222; ADG, Mitra 2/206*). Others include: BC 10112; Bernard Alart, ed., *Cartulaire roussillonnais* (Perpignan, 1880), no. 62 (pp. 91–92); RBI 412. Cf. DACU 793, a grant of a parish; AME 13/50, which may contain a commendation of a church.

[31] Susan Reynolds, *Fiefs and Vassals: The Medieval Evidence Reinterpreted* (Oxford, 1994), esp. 15, 480–81. She does not address Catalonia.

The wealth of detail in the Catalan documentation permits research into these questions to ignore the general model and consider specific regional manifestations of relationships of subordination and service. Perhaps because the documentation from Barcelona has been the most intensively studied, it is conventions from Pallars that offer the freshest perspectives.

Hierarchies

As noted, one common function of the *convenientia* was the commendation of a castle. In this context, the verb *comendare* has two syntactical constructions that seem to have the same meaning: the appointment of an individual or individuals to a position of responsibility for control over a castle. A person may commend a castle to a second person, or a person may commend a second person to a third person, with respect to a castle. The convergence of commendations of persons and properties could lead to the creation of complex hierarchies of power, chains of command through which the counts controlled their castles. This type of development is evident in a series of conventions from 1079–80 concerning the castle of Talarn, a strategic outpost of the counts of Pallars Jussà, in the shifting border region between that county and Pallars Sobirà.[32]

In September 1079, Ramon IV and the countess Valença commended the castle of Talarn to Guilamany Hug, with a standard set of conditions. Guilamany received a fief (*fevum*) and in return promised to perform various services and fulfill various obligations. These included a provision that he should accept as a lord (*senior*) whomever Ramon requested. This last clause indicates that Guilamany did not occupy the highest possible position in the hierarchy, a condition also hinted at by the fact that his fief was restricted to demesne not held by two other individuals, Ramon Mir and Berenguer Mir.[33] Guilamany's position was similar to that of Oliver Bernat, who entered a convention for the same castle six months later. The text of this agreement follows very closely the text of the convention with Guilamany, including identical rights to exploitation of the demesne. But while Guilamany promised to accept an unnamed lord, Oliver was required to accept either the viscount (Arnau Bernat) or Guillem Folc de Galliner.[34]

This next layer in the hierarchy can be reconstructed by reference to an agreement of December 1079, by means of which the count and countess not only commended the castle of Talarn to Guillem Folc, but

---

[32] RBII 42.1*, 42.2*, 42.3*, and 42.4* are copies on a single parchment; RBII 55* is a separate original. For clarity, they are cited below by numbers from the printed edition of the *LFM* (72, 74, 75, 73, 76), although transcriptions are from the originals.
[33] *LFM* 72. I have been unable to identify these last two individuals.   [34] *LFM* 74.

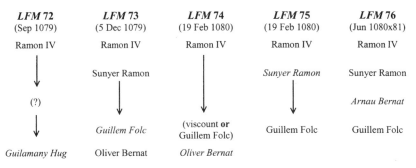

LFM 72	**LFM 73**	**LFM 74**	**LFM 75**	**LFM 76**
(Sep 1079)	(5 Dec 1079)	(19 Feb 1080)	(19 Feb 1080)	(Jun 1080x81)
Ramon IV	Ramon IV	Ramon IV	Ramon IV	Ramon IV
	Sunyer Ramon		*Sunyer Ramon*	Sunyer Ramon
(?)				*Arnau Bernat*
	Guillem Folc	(viscount **or** Guillem Folc)	Guillem Folc	Guillem Folc
Guilamany Hug	Oliver Bernat	*Oliver Bernat*		

Figure 2.1. Chain of command for the castle of Talarn (1079–80x81) I
(names in *italic type* are the individuals directly involved in the agreements with the count)

situated him securely in the chain of command by commending *to him* Oliver Bernat as a commended man (*homo comendatus*). This document reveals yet another layer: Guillem Folc was to be the commended man of Sunyer Ramon, the count's brother.[35] The grant to Sunyer came two months later, in a document issued on the same day as the convention with Oliver Bernat.[36] This convention reconfirmed the commendation of Guillem Folc to Sunyer. As for the viscount, Arnau Bernat, the count seems to have decided to place him on still another level in the chain of command: he was granted the castle of Talarn in June 1080, with the provision that Guillem Folc should be his commended man, but that *he* (the viscount) should be the commended man of Sunyer Ramon.[37] The structure of the hierarchy can be recreated and checked by aligning the various elements revealed in the documents (Figure 2.1).

The count was clearly not following a blueprint from the start, as he was unable to tell Guilamany Hug in September whom he would have to accept as his lord, or Oliver Bernat in February whether it would be the viscount or Guillem Folc. The final disposition of the castle must have been cobbled together over the course of ten months, certainly in response to political pressures that do not emerge from the sources. Furthermore, the situation at the lowest level is not entirely clear. Did Guilamany Hug fall out of the system? Were Ramon Mir and Berenguer Mir in the same position as Guilamany Hug and Oliver Bernat? Why were Guilamany Hug and Oliver Bernat not mentioned in the agreements with Sunyer Ramon or Arnau Bernat? If Guilamany Hug did not fall out of the system, and if Ramon Mir and Berenguer Mir *also* held the castle on similar terms, we might imagine four individuals on the

---

[35] *LFM* 73.   [36] *LFM* 75.
[37] *LFM* 76. The date should be 1081 only if the agreement was completed before 24 June.

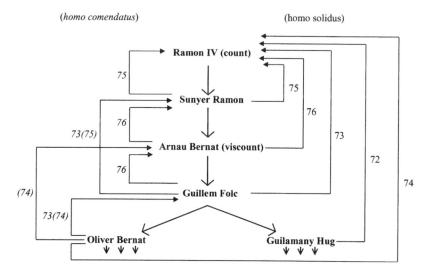

Figure 2.2. Chain of command for the castle of Talarn (1079–80x81) II

bottom level of the hierarchy. These questions must remain unanswered. Still, the lack of internal contradiction in a set of five separate agreements, closely spaced in time, suggests that the count's arrangements for the castle of Talarn were not haphazard.

What terms apply to the individuals appearing in these five documents? Three are easily comprehended: *senior*, *solidus* and *homo comendatus*. The *senior*, or "lord," is any individual higher up in the hierarchy, whether or not the immediate superior. *Senior* may be used in reference to two individuals at different levels of the hierarchy in the same document. Thus Arnau Bernat is the lord of Guillem Folc, while Sunyer Ramon is the lord of Arnau Bernat *and* Guillem Folc. Likewise, *homo comendatus* is the status of an individual with respect to his *seniores*. Here, too, the relationship is not limited to the next person up in the hierarchy: Guillem Folc is the *homo comendatus* of Arnau Bernat as well as of Sunyer Ramon and of the count and countess. The term *solidus*, however, is strictly limited to an individual's relationship with the top of the hierarchy: the count and countess. One may be, therefore, simultaneously a *homo comendatus* and a *homo solidus*.[38] The lord of a *homo solidus*, here the count, may be referred to as the *solidus senior*.[39] These relationships for the castle of Talarn are shown in Figure 2.2.

[38] E.g., *LFM* 73: "sit eorum homine comendatus et illorum solidus."

[39] The use of the term *solidus*, though *not* of *comendatus*, is especially common in conventions from Barcelona, e.g.: RBI 149*, 174*, 214*, 253.2*, 373*; "melior senior" also appears. See Bonnassie, *La Catalogne*, 2:743–46.

While *senior, solidus,* and *homo comendatus* appear to be relative distinctions, two other terms found in the documents concerning Talarn are supposed to be more absolute: *castellanus* (Cat. *castlà,* pl. *castlans*) and *caballarius* (>Cat. *cavaller,* "horseman"; cf. Fr. *chevalier,* Cast. *caballero*). This *castlà* is usually conceived of as the individual with direct operational control over the castle, charged with providing for its defense by commanding a group of *caballarii.* The *castlà* was appointed by the master of the castle (Eng. castellan, Fr. *châtelain*), who either constructed the castle or received it by commendation from the count.[40] In these documents concerning the castle of Talarn, however, the term *castellanus* is applied to both of the bottom two levels of the hierarchy: the texts imply that both Oliver Bernat and Guillem Folc are *castellani.* An additional reference in the convention with Guillem Folc shows only that *castellani* are below Sunyer Ramon in the chain of command. Matters are further complicated by the fact that the convention with Guilamany Hug indicates that he may be a *caballarius.* We should not picture, then, a well-ordered system of recognized ranks, after the fashion of a modern military organization. It is more likely that the terms were taken at face value and were situation specific. The *castlà* was someone associated principally with the castle, thus there might be more than one *castlà* for any given site. The *caballarius,* on the other hand, was associated principally with his horse, rather than a particular castle; he was defined by his ability to fight rather than by his ability to organize and command.[41] The functions of "castellan," *castlà,* and *cavaller* were without a doubt present in the medieval conception of military hierarchy, but they were not applied as consistently as historians sometimes assume.

Obligations

Whatever terms were ultimately recorded in a castle-holding *convenientia,* the transaction behind the document was at some level always a

---

[40] This distinction is repeated in the literature, even though there is no separate term in the documents for the master of the castle: castellan/châtelain. See, e.g., Bonnassie, *La Catalogne,* 571 n. 151. This is a good example of the model shaping the evidence.

[41] *Caballarius* appears in only four documents from this period in Pallars (RBII 42.1*; BRII 25*, 54*; LFM 81). In conventions from Barcelona: BC 4143*; RBI 218*, 419*; OM 5:41. Each of these documents deals with frontier castles. *Castellanus* is common in Pallars (RBII 44*; BRII 64; RBI sd 21* [*castla*] . . .) and Barcelona (RBI 101*, 218*, 225, 296*, 320* . . .). See Bonnassie, *La Catalogne,* 2:571–73. In some documents from Cerdanya the scribal formula "contra omnes homines vel feminas" is extended to "castellanum vel castellanos, *castellanam vel castellanas*" (LFM 534; emphasis added); I have not found evidence, however, of a female *castlà,* though see Thomas N. Bisson, *Tormented Voices: Power, Crisis, and Humanity in Rural Catalonia, 1140–1200* (Cambridge, Mass., 1998), 34 (the lady lord of Mediona), and CSCV 612; cf. Fredric L. Cheyette, "Women, Poets, and Politics in Occitania," in Theodore Evergates, ed., *Aristocratic Women in Medieval France* (Philadelphia, 1999), 162.

balanced one. The count granted control of the fortification, and usually various lands and rights of exploitation along with it; in return, he was owed various services. More detailed study of these various obligations is needed. Historians have distinguished between, for example, host and cavalcade, defining the former as a larger-scale foray led by a lord, the latter as a smaller raid led by a *castlà*.[42] But since these terms often appear together in the stock phrase "hostes et cavalgadas et curtes et placitos et servicia," probably a mnemonic phrase along the lines of the Anglo-Saxon "sake and soke and toll and team," is this distinction universally valid?[43] What does it mean to say that cavalcade service was due to the count, if any outing led by the count was by definition the host? Furthermore, these obligations were subject to temporal and regional variation. In Barcelona until around 1058, for example, the obligations listed in conventions were limited to host, cavalcade, and war (*guerra*); only after that date do the obligations to perform *placita, curtes, (ob)sequia*, and *directum* emerge. While the first three in this list are also found in other counties, the last, *directum*, is limited to Barcelona. Are these differences purely a result of variations in scribal formulae, or do they have a deeper significance?

One set of obligations that have received particularly little attention are those undertaken by the recipient of a commendation with respect to subordinates. The master of a castle would promise the count to make any *castlans* repeat the undertakings that he himself was making in the *convenientia*: to swear fidelity, to render control of the castle (*potestas*), and to become the man (*homo*) of the count. The count's control over the chain of command was thereby strengthened. The count also strictly controlled the replacement of the personnel manning his castle, a procedure closely linked to the concept of *adopertura*.[44]

When the relationship between a position or a fief and its holder was broken, the position was said to be "open," or in *adopertura* (*apertura, obertura, opertura*). A castle, for example, was said to become open (*venire in*

---

[42] Bonnassie, *La Catalogne*, 2:572–73. Cf. James F. Powers, *A Society Organized for War: The Iberian Municipal Militias in the Central Middle Ages, 1000–1284* (Berkeley, 1988), 158.

[43] RBI 269. See Regula Matzinger-Pfister, *Paarformel, Synonymik und zweisprachiges Wortpaar: Zur mehrgliedrigen Ausdrucksweise der mittelalterlichen Urkundensprache*, Rechtshistorische Arbeiten 9 (Zurich, 1972); Michel Zimmermann, "Glose, tautologie ou inventaire? L'énumération descriptive dans la documentation catalane du Xème au XIIème siècle," *Cahiers de linguistique hispanique médiévale* 14–15 (1989–90), 309–38.

[44] *GMLC*, s.vv. *adobertura, apertura*; Eulalia Rodón Binué, *El lenguaje técnico del feudalismo en el siglo XI en Cataluña (contribución al estudio del latín medieval)*, Publicaciones de la Escuela de filología de Barcelona, Filología clásica, 16 (Barcelona, 1957), s. vv. *adaperire, apertura*. While present elsewhere, the term is most common in documents of Pallars Jussà. The obligation to place a castellan with the permission or advice of the count (or, phrased negatively, not to place a castellan without his permission) is very common in the conventions of Ramon Berenguer I, although the term *adopertura* is not commonly used: RBI 101★, 225, 296★, 320★, etc.

adopertura) with respect to (*de*) the former holder. In castle-holding conventions, the position in question was always the command of a castle, although *adopertura* was also used in reference to other positions.[45] The most common reason for a rupture of this kind was the death of the holder, as is reflected in the ubiquitous phrase "if he should die . . . or if [the castle] should in any way become open."[46] Another scenario, highly likely but impossible to demonstrate, was that the holder of the position had violated the convention with his lord and/or switched his allegiance to another lord.[47]

The conventions from Pallars Jussà reveal two facts about *adopertura*. First, a castle could become open at any level of the chain of command below the count. In a grant by Ramon IV to Ramon Pere of the castle of Mur and the grant (discussed above) by Ramon IV to Sunyer Ramon of the castle of Talarn, *castlans* are explicitly the subject of the *adopertura* clause.[48] In a related convention, between Ramon IV and Guillem Folc, the possibility is presented of Talarn coming into *adopertura* with respect to Sunyer Ramon, the count's brother and most direct subordinate. A fourth convention indicates that *adopertura* might apply even at the level of the *caballarius*.[49] Second, the count had ultimate control over the vacancy, at any level. Even though the responsibility for the replacement might fall to a subordinate, the count had the last word. In a grant by Count Bernat Ramon of Pallars Jussà (1112–24) to Guillem Ramon de Galliner, it was Guillem Ramon and not the count who had to replace a missing *castlà*, but with the count's advice.[50] Even when this counsel was not explicitly required, however, the count's control was evident. A convention between Ramon IV and Guitard Guillem de Meià records the hierarchy over the castle of Llimiana (Figure 2.3). If the castle fell open with respect to Ramon Brocard, Guitard had to replace him with another *castlà* who was to be subject to the orders and will ("mandamentum et voluntatem") of the counts. The situation is less clear if the castle fell open with respect to Guillem Folc; Guitard may have had the responsibility for filling this vacancy as well, but again it was "on the advice and

---

[45] RBI 231 foresees the episcopacy of Vic falling *in adopertura*.

[46] E.g., RBII 42.4*: "si obierit . . . aut ullo modo venerit de eo inobertura."

[47] E.g., RBI 204: "Et illi faciant ei hostes et cavalcades et servicium que facere debent [ad] Bernardum iam dictum et ad Raimundum seniorem suum. *Et si ipsi facere noluerint* aut per aliquo modo adoperti fuerint ipsi fevi sive per istis sive per aliis . . ." (emphasis added).

[48] RBII 6*: "Et si per quecumque modum venit in obertura de ipsos castellanos." RBII 42.3*: "Et si morierint ipsos castellanos qui modo sunt in Talarn, aut ullo modo venit inobertura de eos." Cf. RBIII 26* (=Extra. 3293): "si de ipsos seniores veniunt in adobertura ipsos kastros," where *seniores* most likely refers to *castlans*.

[49] RBII 42.4*. Cf. RBI sd 29: "et convenit Raimundo comite que de ipsa prima honore que Deus illi dederit aud venerit in adobertura que donet ad Bertran Enech duas chavallerias de terra."

[50] RBIII extra. 3601.1*: "cum consilium de suo comite."

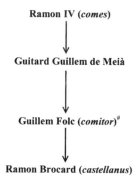

Ramon IV (*comes*)

↓

Guitard Guillem de Meià

↓

Guillem Folc (*comitor*)[#]

↓

Ramon Brocard (*castellanus*)

Figure 2.3. Chain of command for the castle of Llimiana (1079)

Note:
[#] This does not seem to be the use of *comitor* described by Bonnassie, that is, a member of the comital inner circle (*La Catalogne*, 2:785–88); Guillem Folc is fairly low down in the hierarchy. *Comitor* is used in Bonnassie's sense in its only other appearance in these documents (RBII 19).

by the order of the said count and countess."[51] In other cases, however, the count had *direct* control. A convention between the counts Ramon IV of Pallars Jussà (1047–98) and Artau II of Pallars Sobirà (1081–*c.* 1115), in which Ramon commended Llimiana and Mur to Artau, states that the lords (*seniores*) who hold the castles shall be the commended men of Artau, but that in the case of a vacancy Ramon shall replace them.[52]

The holder of a castle was also required to respect certain rights of the count or other superior. These often included lodging rights (*statica*) and rights to exploitation of his reserved lands (*dominicum*). The most important right, indeed the central element in the entire scheme of castle control, was the rendering of *potestas*, or control over the castle, on direct or indirect request of a superior in the hierarchy.[53] In conventions with the count, his men promised to render *potestas* directly to him, but also to intermediate lords. The count could also explicitly retain *potestas* in a grant of a castle.[54] Castles were the key to power in this region, and prom-

---

[51] RBII 44★: "ad consilium et mandamentum de supradicto comite et comitissa." Also RBII 6★: "alteros castellanos que ibi erunt sint ibi ad volumptate et mandamentum omni tempore de predicto comite et comitissa."

[52] RBIII 26★ (=Extra. 3293): "mittat ibi Raimundo comite alios seniores ad sua volumptate et ad suo mandamento." Also RBII 42.3★: "alios castellanos, que mitant comes et comitissa predicti in Talarno et in Sot terras." RBII 42.4★: "aliud castellanum que mitant comes et comitissa in Talarn et in Sots terras."

[53] Michel Zimmermann, "'Et je t'empouvoirrai' (Potestativum te farei): A propos des relations entre fidélité et pouvoir en Catalogne au XIᵉ siècle," *Médiévales* 10 (1986), 17–36.   [54] RBII 19.

ises of *potestas* were the key to control of castles. Counts were careful to make clear their rights: the obligation to render *potestas* is present in nearly all of the conventions involving a grant of rights over a castle, in whatever county.

An interesting group of conventions, however, contain clauses that seem to undermine the entire structure of the hierarchy by removing this crucial element.[55] Three of these documents concern the castle of Orcau, in Pallars Jussà. In 1056x57, Ramon IV and Valença promised Ramon Mir d'Orcau and his wife Maria that they would *not* ask them or their heirs for the *potestas* of the castle of Orcau. If they did, Ramon Mir and Maria were not to give it to them, unless the castle had been judged forfeit by a tribunal conducted by other barons (*barones*). In this case, the promise was the entire content of the *convenientia*. This agreement was repeated in a different, more complex convention, perhaps drawn up just before Ramon Mir's death. This second document contains engagements not present in the first, but it also includes nearly identical language in which the counts promise not to demand *potestas*. This undertaking is reinforced by a clause in which Ramon Mir promises that the counts are to have the same demesne rights in the castle that they held when his father was in charge, except for the *potestas* of the castle. The agreement was renewed once again in 1088, this time between Ramon IV and Ramon Mir's fourth son, Tedball Ramon. This convention adds the interesting detail that the no-*potestas* clause was to end with Tedball Ramon: after his death, his heirs and subordinates would be required to give *potestas* to the counts.[56] In other cases, however, the no-*potestas* clause was extended to the next generation.[57] This provision could be applied to more than one castle simultaneously. In one instance a *castlà* purchased this concession from his lord.[58] Two other unorthodox clauses concerning *potestas* appear in documents involving Ficapal de Vallferrera. In 1076, Ficapal got Ramon IV and Valença to assent not to grant *potestas* of the castle of Gilareny to someone whom Ficapal had not appointed (*aclamare*). In an undated agreement of roughly the same time between the same counts and a Ramon Geribert, the latter stated that he would, if it became necessary, render *potestas* of the castle of Orrit to Ficapal, but only in the presence of the counts.[59]

---

[55] Zimmermann, "Et je t'empouvoirrai," 27–28; Bonnassie, *La Catalogne*, 2:766.

[56] RBI 208* (a. 1056x57); *LFM* 65 (a. 1071x72); BRII 54* (a. 1088). For the dates, see Kosto, "Agreements," 199 n. 166.

[57] RBIII sd 8*: "Et mandavit Raimundus comes que non donasset potestatem Arnallus iamdictus de ipso castro de Talarn a Petro comite, si non erat per bauzia conprobata." Also, RBI 163: "non demandet Remundus iamdictus de ipso castro de Reverte potestatem."

[58] RBI 141. Also Extra. 3271, in which a debtor renounces his right to *potestas* over a castle for the duration of the loan.   [59] RBII 1 (a. 1076); RBI sd 24 (a. 1053x98).

Such diminutions of the right of *potestas* seem to be limited to this region; the only examples from outside Pallars are from the neighboring county of Urgell, both involving Arnau Mir de Tost, who was closely connected to the comital family of Pallars.[60] Bonnassie cites these documents as a reflection of the singular weakness of Ramon IV, but this is somewhat of an overstatement. The dates of these documents span the entire reign of Ramon IV, both before and after his reestablishment of control in the county in the early 1070s.[61] Still, it seems clear that the difference in power between Ramon IV and his subordinates was not as great as that enjoyed by some other counts. In 1050, Arnau Mir de Tost was able to extract an analogous concession from Ramon Berenguer I; this was not a promise not to demand *potestas*, but a much lesser concession not to demand rights of lodging (*statica*).[62]

Conventions from Pallars Jussà also show a regional variation on the institution of the *baiulia*. Recent work has demonstrated the importance of the bailiff (*baiulus*) for the development and functioning of *seigneurie banale* and, later, the administration of the count-kings in Catalonia. The area under control of the bailiff is called, often, the *baiulia*, but this term also has a more general meaning of "protection" or "tutelage." The most common use in this sense is for control over the person and goods of a widow or a minor. *Baiulia* may also indicate protection in a still more general sense, such as that suggested by the submission of Catalonia in 1116 to the *baiulia* of the papacy.[63] The *convenientia* could be used to establish a *baiulia*, either by grant, such as in the commendation of the *baiulia* of the seneschalcy of Barcelona and its associated castles to Ramon Mir de L'Aguda in 1060, or by submission, such as in the convention between Bishop Pere of Girona and Ramon Berenguer I concerning La Bisbal or documents drawn up during the minority of Ramon Berenguer III (1096–1131).[64] It was more common, however, for a count to commend a *baiulia* than for him to receive one by submission, and payments to the counts connected with such grants were rare in the eleventh century.[65] But in a group of acts from Pallars Jussà, the holder of a prop-

---

[60] DACU 797 (cit. Bonnassie, *La Catalogne*, 2:766 n. 131); BC 4133.

[61] Bonnassie, *La Catalogne*, 2:618.   [62] BC 4143*.

[63] *GMLC*, s.v. *baiulia*; Rodón Binué, *El lenguaje*, s.v. *baiulia*; Bonnassie, *La Catalogne*, 2:597–98, 606–8, 707, 761; *FA*, esp. 1:66–69; Paul Kehr, *Das Papsttum und der katalanische Prinzipat bis zur Vereinigung mit Aragon*, Abhandlungen der preussischen Akademie der Wissenschaften, Jahrgang 1926, Philosophisch-historische Klasse, no. 1 (Berlin, 1926), 56–57.

[64] RBI 253.2* (a. 1060); *CCM* 109; below, pp. 164–65.

[65] AME 9/20; AAM, Sant Cugat del Vallès 123; BRII 58. Cf. ADG, Pia Almoina, Fonolleres 13, grant of a bailiwick in return for an annual render; RBIV 15*, submission to protection without mention of payment; RBI 434*, intermediary named for only part of the render. Us. 120 refers to the payment of a *censum* with respect to a *baiulia*. See also RBI 280*, 296*. For the twelfth century, see below, pp. 264–66.

erty, frequently a castle, submitted directly to the *baiulia* of the counts by means of a *convenientia*, without mention of an intervening comital official. In return for this protection the count received a payment, usually termed a *receptum*.[66]

These documents adhere loosely to a common formula. After the usual introduction ("Hec est conveniencia qui est facta inter . . ."), there follow three standard elements, appearing in no particular order: (1) The immovable in question is defined. While this is most often a castle, churches, *villae*, and unspecified alods also figure in these documents. Often more than one type appears in a single convention. (2) The *baiulia* (*bagulia*, *baglia*, *baiolia*) is recognized. Either the counts acknowledge or promise (*convenire*) that they hold the property under their protection, or the other party grants the property to the count and countess as a *baiulia*. The protection is promised against all men and women. (3) A *receptum* is defined.[67] This is always a yearly payment, usually consisting of round-cakes (*fogazas*), wine, and grain (wheat, oats, or barley), with the occasional pig, sheep, or unspecified meat. When the *baiulia* is for a castle, the amounts may be stated in a more utilitarian fashion: bread and wine and meat for twenty horsemen, or oats for sixty horses. When multiple properties are in question, the *receptum* may appear grouped together as all coming from one of the properties, or as divided among the properties. The direct connection between the *baiulia* and the *receptum* is usually made explicit with a phrase such as "per hoc."

While these three elements appear in all or nearly all of the documents, other elements appear more sporadically. The convention usually provides for the continuation of the *baiulia* into the future, by implicating the heirs of the count, the heirs of the other party, or both. This is accomplished either by a statement to that effect, or by the inclusion of the heirs in question as actors in the document. A variety of services and duties also appear in the texts. The grantor may promise the count access (*intrare et exire*) and military service (*guerregare*), aid in holding the property, or that no harm shall come to him from the property.[68] The grantor may declare himself to be the man of the count with respect to the convention or, conversely, the count may declare himself to be the lord of

---

[66] The following documents are included in this analysis: RBI 428★, sd 22★, sd 25★, sd 27★, sd 28★; RBII 20; BRII 17★, 67★; RBIII 49★; *LFM* 81. RBII 20 and RBIII 49★ appear to be two variant versions of the same agreement. See also Jesús Lalinde Abadía, *La jurisdicción real inferior en Cataluña ("Corts, veguers, batlles")*, Publicaciones del Seminario de arqueología e historia de la ciudad 14, Estudios, 1 (Barcelona, 1966), 61–62.

[67] Bonnassie, *La Catalogne*, 2:585–86. BRII 43★, which does not involve a *baiulia*, contains a promise of a *receto*.

[68] *LFM* 81 employs the more general term for the body of comital rights, *comtivum*: GMLC, s.v. *comitiuum*; Rodón Binué, *El lenguaje*, s.v. *comitivum*.

the grantor. The grantor may also commend to the count a member of the next generation. One or the other of the parties may promise to act without ill will. Finally, the texts are usually dated, although not always very exactly, and subscribed by the count(s), the other party, and on occasion two to four witnesses.

The historical context clarifies the function of these unique *convenientiae*. In September 1097, Ramon Mir and Ramon Arnau granted Count Ramon IV *baiulia* over the castle of Castellet along with a *receptum*. The *receptum* was to be equal to the one that they had given to Artau I of Pallars Sobirà (1049–81), revealing this as a castle that Ramon IV had reclaimed, either by treaty or by force, from his cousin and rival.[69] Many, if not all, of the documents considered here may be interpreted in this light. The convention establishing a *baiulia* was one of the means by which Ramon IV maintained, established, or reestablished control over his territories and castles during his wars with Artau I. When compared to other conventions with men who had recently submitted, such as the conventions with no-*potestas* clauses discussed above, the *baiulia* is quite onerous. It is perhaps for this reason that the only examples that have survived are conventions with individuals not known to have been particularly powerful. Submission to *baiulia* by convention continued under the next count, Pere Ramon (1098–1112); he took under his protection the castle of Alós by this means.[70] By the second half of the twelfth century, however, while the *baiulia* is still found in the charters of Pallars Jussà, it is no longer associated with the form of the *convenientia*.[71]

A smaller set of conventions, all contemporaneous with the group just examined, establish relationships that appear identical to the *baiulia*, but without using the term; instead, they refer to the count as a *patronus*.[72] All the documents deal with castle holding; all create a relationship with the count under which the count is granted rights of entry and military activity (*intrare et exire et guerregare*) and receives an annual *receptum*, along with other services. In addition, the grantor promises not to choose another patron (*patronus*). The distinction between count as *patronus* and count as holder of a *baiulia* is not particularly clear; indeed, it may not exist. The salient fact is that the count receives payment in kind for his "protection." Granted, this protection was not necessarily very effective; memorials of complaint (*querimoniae*) reveal that the count's *baiulia* was violated.[73] *Convenientiae* describe ideal situations; when we are privileged

---

[69] RBIII 49*. [70] RBIII sd 11*.

[71] *LFM* 94; Pilar Ostos Salcedo, ed., "Documentación del Vizcondado de Vilamur en el Archivo Ducal de Medinaceli (1126–1301). Estudio diplomático y edición," *Historia. Instituciones. Documentos* 8 (1981), doc. 4 (pp. 327–28). [72] RBI 354*; BRII 43*; Extra. 3252*. Cf. RBI sd 23*.

[73] RBI sd 34; *LFM* 130. Cf. RBI sd 32.

to have evidence for the actual conditions, they may be far from this ideal. Nevertheless, the *baiulia*, like the no-*potestas* clause, represents a regional variation in the use of the written word to maintain and establish control.

TREATIES

Many *convenientiae* concerning castle holding, military service, and fidelity, went beyond the simple grants and lists of obligations seen in commendations, oath-conventions, and related documents. The agreement of *c.* 1021 between Berenguer Ramon I and Ermengol II is a perfect example: in addition to commendation, castles, fidelity, and associated pledges, the two counts negotiated the details of the succession of their respective counties. We may define these broader agreements as treaty-conventions. Some treaty-conventions contain elements that stand alone in other agreements. A treaty of 1062 between the counts of Barcelona and Urgell, for example, begins (and continues at length) as an oath-convention, and in a treaty of 1051 between the same two counts, Ramon Berenguer I begins by granting to Ermengol III a castle in fief and promising a yearly payment.[74] Nevertheless, all of these documents deal with matters beyond simple statements of fidelity and grants of castles.

In a formal sense, these agreements are, like *comenda*-conventions, explicitly balanced, in that both parties have obligations; but while in commendations the undertakings are limited to a grant of a position and lands on the one hand, and standard obligations of service and payment on the other, treaties describe duties that are much more complex. Perhaps for this reason, this category contains mostly agreements among the highest members of the aristocracy. The treaty-conventions of Ramon Berenguer I, for example, include five agreements with the count of Urgell, one with the count of Cerdanya, one with the count of Besalú, and one with the viscounts of Béziers. The remaining agreement is with Alemany Hug de Cervelló, one of the more powerful of Ramon Berenguer's men on the frontier.

The five *convenientiae* between the counts of Barcelona and Urgell address the subject of military alliances, first against Count Ramon Guifré of Cerdanya, then against Islamic frontier lords.[75] They include clauses regulating the division of spoils, promising mutual aid, and forbidding one party to make peace with the common enemy without the consent of the other. The agreement with Ramon Guifré is also a military alliance directed toward recovery of frontier lands and contains

---

[74] RBI 299* (a. 1062), 120 (a. 1051).   [75] RBI 120, 230*, 299*, sd 1, sd 12*.

many of the same clauses. The convention with Alemany Hug, although on a smaller scale, is similar: Alemany Hug and the count agree on the terms for holding the castle of Santa Perpètua, and the count promises to aid Alemany Hug against – and not to make any agreements with – his enemies.[76] Similar treaty-conventions survive from the eleventh century between Ramon Berenguer I's sons and Ermengol IV of Urgell (1066–92), between the counts of Pallars Jussà and Pallars Sobirà, between Ermengol III of Urgell (1038–66) and Arnau Mir de Tost, and between the counts of Empúries and Rosselló, among others.[77] The ties created were not necessarily military. Some treaty-conventions record proposed marriage alliances, such as those between Ramon Berenguer I's sister-in-law, Llúcia, and Guillem II of Besalú, or between Ramon Berenguer IV and Blanca of Navarre.[78] Others record terms of succession or submission. In a *convenientia* of 1068, Ramon Berenguer I and Raimond Bernard, viscount of Béziers, and their families promised each other rights to lands in Carcassonne, Razès, Toulouse, Narbonne, and Minerve, if either should die without heirs.[79] A century later, after the death of Raimond des Baux, his wife and son submitted to Ramon Berenguer IV by means of a treaty-convention and a number of oaths.[80]

Bonnassie, limiting his evidence to the earliest documents, distinguished three types of these *convenientiae* between magnates: alliances, sometimes defensive, but often directed against a third party; nonagression pacts; and peace treaties. From a broader chronological and geographical perspective, another aspect of treaty-conventions stands out: their use to effect prospective grants and divisions of territory.[81] The agreement in 1053 between Alemany Hug and Ramon Berenguer I on terms for holding the castle of Santa Perpètua was only to take effect *after its recovery*. Ramon IV of Pallars Jussà made a similar promise in a *convenientia* of 1088: "If God grants to Count Ramon the land of Vallferrera, vills and castles, the count should grant it to *Orseth* and *Drocho* . . ."[82] This type of arrangement became much more common as the *Reconquista* gathered steam. Ramon Berenguer III and Artau II of Pallars Sobirà may have subscribed a convention detailing their arrangements for the seizure

---

[76] RBI 231, 143★.
[77] RBII 69, 69dup; RBIII 26★=Extra. 3293; BC 4118★; ADPO B4, 74★. Cf. RBI sd 191★.
[78] RBI sd 11; RBIV 214★; Aurell, *Les noces du comte*, 281–87, 372–73, 468; and below, pp. 171–72.
[79] *LFM* 816. See below, p. 259.   [80] *LFM* 887, 888.1, 888.2.
[81] Bonnassie, *La Catalogne*, 2:567–68. On prospective grants: Cheyette, "Sale," 863–64; Robert Bartlett, *The Making of Europe: Conquest, Colonization and Cultural Change, 950–1350* (Princeton, 1993), 90–92.
[82] *LFM* 102: "si Deus dederit ad Raimundo comite ipsa terra de Val Ferrera, villas atque castros que donet illa ad Orseth et Drocho . . ."

of Tortosa.[83] As early as 1136, the young Ramon Berenguer IV offered to Guilhem VI of Montpellier rights to the city of Tortosa, should he capture it, in return for a promise of fidelity.[84] In the previous year, he granted to Deusdé, one of the men of the viscount of Cardona (Osona), rights in the *parias* and promised him an *honor* of fifty *cavalleriae* bordering València when sufficient land had been reconquered. In return he received promises of fidelity and a payment of 200 *morabetins*. In the Treaty of Carrión of 1140, Ramon Berenguer IV planned with Alfonso VII of León-Castile the division of the yet-to-be-conquered lands of García IV Ramírez of Navarre.[85] In 1147, he negotiated an agreement with the Genoans, who had just assisted in the conquest of Almería, by which they would receive a one-third interest in the city of Tortosa in return for their aid in taking the city.[86] In 1148, he granted to Ermengol VI of Urgell rights to a third of the city of Lleida, in advance of its conquest, again in return for promises of fidelity and service. After conquering the city, he subscribed an agreement there (1156) with the king of León-Castile reaffirming the division of Navarre.[87] The most striking of these agreements are the treaties of Tudillén (1151) and Cazola (1179) between the count-kings of Catalonia-Aragón and the kings of León-Castile, by which the rulers established spheres of influence in the yet-to-be-conquered portions of the Iberian Peninsula.[88]

A few written treaty-conventions not involving counts have survived, almost all of which date from the twelfth century; no two are exactly alike. Some recorded positive undertakings, usually a promise of unspecified aid to the other party. In others the promise was negative, not to harm or allow harm to come to the other party. They also varied widely in length and complexity. An undated, unsubscribed *convenientia* between Ramon Sunifred and Pere Geribert consists in its entirety of simple mutual promises: "I N. promise you N. that I will be your *fidelis*,

---

[83] Francisco Diago, *Historia de los victoriosíssimos antiguos condes de Barcelona* (Barcelona, 1603; repr. Valencia, 1974), fols. 143r–144r (lib. 2, cap. 80). Diago's summary (in Castilian) suggests language typical of a *convenientia*.

[84] RBIV 73*; see Antoni Virgili, "Conquesta, colonització i feudalització de Tortosa (segle XII), segons el cartulari de la catedral," in *La formació i expansió*, 276.

[85] RBIV 66* (a. 1135), 96* (a. 1140).

[86] RBIV sd 6*, sd 10*; see Shideler, *Montcadas*, 97 n. 35. A similar promise to Guillem Ramon (II) Seneschal, made around the same time, was couched as a charter of donation rather than a *convenientia* (RBIV 189.1*). The interest of the Templars in the city depended on a grant of 1143 of a one-fifth interest in all lands reconquered (RBIV 159*); a separate grant for Tortosa has not survived.   [87] RBIV 202* (cf. *LFM* 163); *LFM* 30 [*DI* 4:91].

[88] *LFM* 29 [*DI* 4:62]; ALI 267*, 268*. For a political analysis of these treaties, see Andrea Büschgens, *Die politischen Verträge Alfons' VIII. von Kastilien (1158–1214) mit Aragón-Katalonien und Navarra: Diplomatische Strategien und Konfliktlösung im mittelalterlichen Spanien*, Europäische Hochschulschriften, Reihe III, Geschichte und ihre Hilfswissenschaften 678 (Frankfurt am Main, 1995), esp. 116–26, 243–48.

to the best of my ability, in retaining your *honor* and everything that you possess today or will possess in the future."[89] A *convenientia* between Galceran de Sales and Bernat de Romanyà in 1183 was much more involved. Bernat promised not to make war against Galceran or in any way harm him or allow harm to come to him from his castle of Romanyà. Galceran, in return, promised that if there were to be a conflict between them, he would not attack Romanyà. Bernat also promised not to establish any new customs (*novitates*) in the lands subject to the castle and paid to Galceran the sum of 200 *solidi*.[90]

In the example just cited, it is possible that Bernat held Romanyà from Galceran, but this is not revealed in the agreement. The absence of this type of information is common. A promise of aid might be with reference to a certain property, but agreements often fail to describe the relevant tenurial arrangements. For example, in a *convenientia* of 1191, Berenguer de Barberà promised Guillem Ramon de Montcada that no harm would come to him from his "house called *Turris*"; in return, Guillem Ramon promised to guarantee the safety of the property. The document does not refer to Guillem Ramon as Berenguer's lord, nor does it describe *Turris* as held from Guillem Ramon. Berenguer may in fact have been Guillem Ramon's man and may have held the site from him, but the convention was solely concerned with their mutual promises, independent of land, status, or any specific personal relationship.[91] The property in question might also be held in common, as by multiple guardians of a castle. This was the case in 1123 when the brothers Bernat and Guillem de Voltrera and Umbert and Guillem de La Tallada promised each other aid and fidelity concerning the castle of Fonolleres.[92]

Like treaties at the comital level, agreements at lower levels included exceptions for certain persons. Thus when in 1121 Ponç Guerau II, viscount of Girona, and Arnau de Castellbò swore aid and fidelity to each other, each explicitly excepted from the agreement his immediate superior, his relatives, and his men. Alternatively, aid promised in a treaty could be directed against a particular individual, as when sometime after 1150 Pere de Puigverd promised to help Pere de Bellvís in his conflict (*guerra*) with the count of Urgell.[93]

[89] LA 1:105*: "Hec est convenientia que facta est inter Raimundum Seniofredi et Petrum Gerberti. Convenio ego Petrus Gerberti tibi Raimundo Seniofredi quod fidelis tibi ero ad retinendum tuum honorem et ad omnia que hodie habes vel in antea habebis secundum meum posse. Item ego Raimundus Seniofredi convenio tibi jamdicto Petro quod fidelis ero tibi ad retinendum tuum honorem et ad omnia que hodie habes vel in antea habebis secundum meum posse."

[90] ALI 343.

[91] ALI 589: "illa domo mea que vocatur Turris." Similarly AAM, Sant Cugat del Vallès 159; *Remences* 6.

[92] ADG, Pia Almoina, Fonolleres 15. Similarly ACA, Diversos, Varia 10 (Vilanova Roselló), leg. 1, doc. 5, no. 2 (p. 2).   [93] BC 4226; *DPoblet* 127.

DISPUTE SETTLEMENT

Negotiation always played a role in the settlement of disputes in the medieval West; the evidence for these settlements, however, is often overshadowed by formal records of formal judgments.[94] In Catalonia, these were the products of a Visigothic-Carolingian judicial order grounded in a written code, the *Liber iudiciorum*. The decline in the numbers of these records in the eleventh century has been used to support the argument that the institutions that had generated them were in a state of crisis. Critics of this line of thought have rightly pointed to the evidence for negotiated settlement in earlier periods, but they fail to explain the decline of the traditional types of records. Neither approach, however, adequately addresses the question of the rise of new documents of dispute settlement. It was argued in the previous chapter that the change in the nature of the documents in late-tenth- and early-eleventh-century Catalonia reflects real changes in the way disputes were conducted. But it is possible to press the issue further. Why did procedures, which had existed earlier without generating records, begin to produce records? The creation of a record in itself imparts a degree of formality to a process, but the documents refuse to yield evidence for a consistent, organized, and regular system. Furthermore, why did this change coincide with changes in the old procedures? This was hardly a necessity.

The relationship between the *convenientia* and procedures for the settlement of disputes in Catalonia was highly complex. The written convention was used early on and throughout the eleventh and twelfth centuries as a means for recording agreements supplementary to, or outside, the old comital *placitum*. Thus it is possible to see in *convenientiae* concerning military alliances or the tenure of castles evidence for underlying disputes. The marriage agreements between the houses of Barcelona and Besalú, for example, were arranged in the course of an ongoing conflict which had a judicial aspect.[95] The commendation of the castle of Fornells to Hug Guillem in 1049 occurred the day after Hug Guillem's quitclaim of that same castle, an act that was likely the outcome of a dispute.[96] Because such connections to conflicts are often obscured or hidden, what the *convenientia* reveals about the nature and mechanics of dispute settlement can only be a partial picture. This is all the more

---

[94] For discussion of and citations to the most important studies, see: Patrick J. Geary, "Extra-judicial Means of Conflict Resolution," in *La giustizia nell'alto medioevo (secoli V–VIII)*, 2 vols., Settimane di studio del Centro italiano di studi sull'alto medioevo 42 (Spoleto, 1995), 1:569–70 and nn. 1–3; Geary, "Vivre en conflit dans une France sans état: Typologie des mécanismes de règlement des conflits (1050–1200)," *Annales: Économies, sociétés, civilisations* 41 (1986), 1108 and nn. 4–13; and works cited above, p. 43.   [95] Below, pp. 170–75.

[96] RBI 101*, 100*. In the eschatocol of the latter document, the term *conveniencia* has been deleted and replaced by "difinicione et exvacuacione."

true because *convenientiae* represent only a portion of the available evidence. A comprehensive understanding of how people resolved their conflicts in the eleventh and twelfth centuries requires that the study of conventions be supplemented by a complete investigation of all documents associated with judgment and settlement.[97] Therefore, although supplementary documentation is sampled in what follows, the picture presented can only be tentative. Finally, *convenientiae* on a wide range of subjects established ad hoc procedures for the settlement of disputes arising from the agreements themselves. Such procedures may be seen in the *convenientia* of *c.* 1021. They are even more evident in a series of agreements between the counts of Pallars Jussà and Pallars Sobirà. One of the many documents from this dossier is a *convenientia* in which the counts Ramon IV and Artau I spell out how they would go about resolving a conflict: they set a date and place for a *placitum*, appoint arbiters, and specify details such as ordeals, essoins, and pledges.[98] This agreement and similar documents are not so much products of disputing processes as they are formative of those processes. These additional sources only add to the complexity of the problem.

In studying the disputes of the cathedral of Vic in the twelfth century, Paul Freedman hesitantly adopted a threefold typology of the new documentation of settlement: "the *diffinitio*, in which one party unilaterally renounces its claim, the *concordia*, a reconciliation and compromise, and the *placitum*, a hearing before an ad hoc tribunal."[99] He demonstrated, however, the inconsistency of this model, showing how elements of compensation and third-party intervention entered into each type of agreement. He concluded that the similarities among the three "procedures" were more important than their differences. Scribes, from Vic and elsewhere, added the term *convenientia* to these records of dispute settlement, but this does little to clarify matters. It is often impossible to distinguish, on the basis of content, between *convenientia*, *concordia*, *diffinitio*, and *placitum*. Scribes in the eleventh and twelfth centuries were released from the framework of their early medieval formularies, which had presented them with the three principal options described in chapter 1: *notitia*, *exvacuatio*, and *conditiones sacramentorum*.[100] Faced with a more flexible procedure to record, they failed to create standardized types of records. But they nevertheless created records, and that in itself is significant. The diffusion of the written agreement as a means of ordering relationships touched dispute settlement, as well.

The scribal confusion evident in the earliest documents to depart from

---

[97] Bowman, "Law," accomplishes this for the late tenth and early eleventh centuries. For what follows, see esp. chapters 3, 6.   [98] RBI sd 18. See below, pp. 139–40.
[99] Freedman, *Vic*, 124–25.   [100] Above, pp. 44–46.

the old formulae for records of judgment was hardly dispelled in the course of the eleventh and twelfth centuries. A few of these conventions adopt the form and opening of the *convenientia* familiar from castle-holding agreements, but others reflect the ad hoc creativity of their composers. This inventiveness may be seen in opening phrases ("Hec est conveniencia et memoria"; "Hec est conveniencia de placito"; "Hoc est placitum et conuenientia"; "Hec est scriptura pacis et concordie et conuenientie"; "Hec est conveniencia evacuacionis"); in penalty, dating, and signature clauses ("hanc definicionem vel convenienciam"; "fuit facta ista difinicio et conveniencia"; "hanc evacuationem vel diffinitionem seu convenientiam"); and in the internal inconsistencies of documents ("Hęc est carta recognicionis . . . Facta carta ista et conveniencia"; "Hoc est placitum finis et concordie . . . hoc placitum et convenientia firma permaneat"; "Hec est conveniencia . . . hanc exvacuacione rogavi scribere"). Variations on a neutral notification formula ("Notum est omnibus") are also quite common.[101]

Sometimes, however, the reason the scribe labeled the document a convention is reasonably clear, as when the outcome of a dispute was itself a transaction commonly couched in a *convenientia*. This was the case in a settlement, titled a *placitum finis et concordie*, between Pere de Berga and Guillem de L'Espunyola in 1148 concerning a dispute over the castle of L'Espunyola. Guillem promised not to injure Pere and granted him entry and use of the castle; Pere, in return, promised not to injure Guillem and to help him defend the castle. The agreement was essentially a treaty-convention, a fact recognized by the scribe, who in the penalty clause referred to it as "hoc placitum et convenientia." The settlement ("hec est carta convenientie") in 1156 that brought to an end a dispute over the castle of Avinoçar between Assalid de Güel and Berenguer Roig involved a grant in fief of the castle by the former to the latter in return for promises of homage, *potestas*, aid, and castle-guard. It was, in other words, very similar to a classic *comenda*-convention.[102] A long-running dispute between the monastery of Sant Benet de Bages and Mir Guillem de Castellcir was settled in 1145 when Mir Guillem quitclaimed the disputed lands, and the monastery returned them as a grant for life against the payment of a census.[103] The scribe labeled this arrangement a *donum vel convenientia*; it is similar to many other *convenientiae* involving the monastery's tenurial arrangements that are not clearly connected to the

---

[101] Familiar form: ALI 26; ACG 400.1; Extra. 3462. Headings: BC 3957*; *LFM* 649; *CCM* 179, 281; DACU 1260. Penalty, dating, and signature clauses: *CSCV* 882; ALI ap. 2*; LA 3:112*. Internal inconsistencies: *Gerri* 95; RBIV 207; DACU 1043. Notification formula: MEV, MS 283, no. 81.2 (fols. 40v–41r).   [102] RBIV 207 (a. 1148), 303 (a. 1156).

[103] AAM, Sant Benet de Bages 1686.

settlement of disputes. In other cases, the use of the term *convenientia* indicates a conditional or compensatory element to the agreement bringing a dispute to a close; this was often the case with quitclaims.[104]

Although *convenientiae* lack the formalism of earlier judicial records, they share some of the characteristics of that documentation. Like judicial documents of an earlier era, they often begin with a narrative of the history or at least the topic of the dispute. The notification formula ("Notum sit omnibus") frequently introduces such a passage.[105] While earlier records of judgment were quite informative about the various steps of procedure, however, these texts are much less forthcoming. They occasionally mention which party initiated the complaint (*querelare*), or apply the term *placitum* to the assembly (although just as often *placitum* seems to refer to the settlement itself); one even states that documents were examined as proof. But no standard process is evident.

As in earlier records of judgment, opening narratives often identify or characterize the individuals before whom the parties settled their dispute. In earlier records these were invariably identified as professional judges; the terms used to designate them in these conventions vary considerably. *Boni homines* are common, but also *boni viri, nobili viri homini* [*sic*], *prudentes et nobiles viri*, and *probi homini*.[106] Although the *boni homines* had in the past been a recognized category, the additional use of these other, similar terms raises the question of whether they still represented an identifiable group. The terms – *nobilis, prudens, probus* – seem to refer to quality rather than to function. In other words, there does not appear to have been a set group before whom disputes were settled; the presence of a group was important, as was the social standing of the members of that group, but it was not necessarily composed of particular individuals.

Who were these good, noble, and upright men? The complaints (*querimoniae*) of Arnau Ramon against his lord Guitard de Caboet were resolved with the counsel of Guitard's own *boni homines* and his wife. Similarly, a dispute between the sacristan of Sant Vicenç de Cardona and a priest of Sant Miquel de Cardona was settled before the abbot and all the canons of Sant Vicenç.[107] In only one of these *convenientiae* was the panel described as elected by both parties, at Sant Benet de Bages in

---

[104] LA 3:149*, 4:271*; Josep Maria Marquès i Planagumà, ed., *El cartoral de Santa Maria de Roses (segles X–XIII)*, Memòries de la Secció històrico-arqueològica 37 (Barcelona, 1986), no. 23 (pp. 48–49); RBIII 226; DPoblet 48.

[105] E.g., LA 4:271*: "Manifestum sit omnibus diu fuisse controversiam inter Guilelmum de Turredella et canonicos sedis Barchinonensis super quodam manso qui est in Penitensi in loco qui dicitur Pug Rog, dicentibus utrisque et afirmantibus predictum mansum iure hereditario sibi debere contigere."

[106] *Boni homines*: BRII 21; ACV 6/2455. *Boni viri*: LA 1:393*. *Nobili viri homini*: RBIV 303. *Prudentes et nobiles viri*: CCM 281. *Probi homini*: ALI 26.   [107] BC 3957*; BC, MS 729, 4:75v–76r.

1145.[108] *Iudices* are surprisingly rare, and at the cathedral of Barcelona in 1079, the assembly appears to have been composed of simply whoever happened to be there that day: "*boni viri*, clerical and lay, of the city of Barcelona."[109] This last example seems to represent the most common situation.

The extent of the involvement of these individuals in the proceedings is also difficult to determine. In a number of cases, the document listed their names; this alone may have been sufficient to lend their influence to the settlement. Unlike the judges in earlier conflicts, however, they were included only occasionally among the subscribers, and with no apparent pattern. A dispute between Guillem Ramon I de Castellvell and Bernat Guifard was settled in the presence of eight named individuals and "many other knights who were there," but only two of those named subscribed. The abbot of Sant Joan de les Abadesses along with the archdeacon of Besalú and the schoolmaster of Girona participated in the settlement of a dispute between the bishop of Girona and Galceran de Sales, but only two of the three subscribed.[110] Often the conventions simply state that the dispute was settled in the presence of certain men. In others, it was "with their counsel" or their "intervention." The highest degree of involvement is suggested of those who approved (*laudare*) or actually judged (*iudicare*) the settlement.[111] At Sant Benet de Bages in 1145, the parties appointed the arbiters in order that "whatever the said chosen 'approvers' (*laudatores*) approve, they shall carry it out without delay."[112] These distinctions between counsel, approval, and judgment may reflect important procedural differences, but here the evidence is silent.

High secular and ecclesiastical officials certainly continued to play a role in these procedures. We catch occasional glimpses of the count intervening in this system, although on terms alien to the old comital *placitum*. In 1122, Ramon II, viscount of Cerdanya, and Arnau Bertran de Torrelles brought a dispute before Ramon Berenguer III and gave guarantees to the count that they would settle their dispute. The count did

---

[108] AAM, Sant Benet de Bages 1686: "elegerunt viros probos, viros consiliarios, viros equo animo, cuncta agentes quibus prescripti altercatores spondentes, quia quicquid predicti viri electi laudatores, id est Guilelmus prior Stagnensis et Raimundus Reinardi, eius socius, vir nobilis et omni scientia seculari eruditus, laudassent, et ipsi sine mora facerent."

[109] LA 1:393* ("presentibus bonis viris Barchinone urbis clericis ac laicis"). See also *CCM* 249 ("Berengarius caput scole atque iudex").

[110] ALI ap. 2* ("alios milites qui ibi multi fuerunt"); *CCM* 249.

[111] *Presentia*: LA 1:393*; ACV 6/2455; ALI ap. 2*. *Consilium*: BC 3957*; DACU 1469. *Interveniens*: *CCM* 249. *Laudare/iudicare*: RBIV 207, 303; BRII 21 (cf. *CCM* 281: "per laudamentum atque consilium").

[112] AAM, Sant Benet de Bages 1686: "quicquid predicti viri electi laudatores . . . laudassent et ipsi sine more facerent."

not render judgment, but "gave permission" that they should hold a *placitum*; they reached an agreement not with the advice of the count, but with the counsel and assent of their own men.[113] In 1166, Guillem, *precentor* of the cathedral of Girona, and Arnau Guifré appeared before the court (*curia*) of Alfons I of Barcelona. The settlement of their conflict looks more traditional, in that a solution was dictated by the order of Alfons and with the advice of his court, including the bishop of Barcelona and the seneschal, Guillem Ramon (II). But the language is very different. The *curia* did not judge (*iudicare*); a decision was "established between them" (i.e., the litigants); this suggests a negotiated settlement. A grant by the count-king to the "loser" of additional lands on the same day may have been part of a compromise.[114]

The negotiated settlement recorded in a written convention also penetrated the highest levels of the church hierarchy. Two conventions from Urgell describe conflicts resolved with papal intervention. In 1140, Guillaume, archbishop of Arles and papal legate, fixed the disputed boundary between the dioceses of Urgell and Roda. He did this with the counsel ("cum consilio") of the counts of the two Pallars, Ramon Pere II d'Erill, and the abbots of Sant Sadurní de Tavèrnoles and Santa Maria de Lavaix; in the presence of ("in presencia") various ecclesiastical officials of the two dioceses; and "in the sight of ('in conspectu') many others, laymen and clerics." The various descriptions may indicate different levels of involvement or influence, though again this is far from certain; the scribe may simply have been searching for synonyms. The list of subscribers included the counts of Pallars, Ramon Pere d'Erill, and the archdeacons of Urgell and Roda, all of whom were among those present or those giving counsel.[115] In 1170, a dispute between the monasteries of Santa Maria d'Alaó and Santa Maria de Ripoll was settled at a council held at Tarragona. The abbot of Ripoll had complained to the pope about a usurped church. The pope ordered the abbot of Alaó to settle the matter by the judgment (*judicium*) of the bishop of Tortosa. The settlement was not described as a judgment, however, but as having been reached "with the counsel and approval" ("laudamento et consilio") of the bishops of Tortosa and Lleida. A dispute in 1131 between the abbot of Sant Cugat del Vallès and Jordà de Sant Martí was settled "with the

---

[113] *LFM* 649: "venerunt ad querimoniam ante comitem Raimundum Berengarii de hoc suprascripto honore et per hanc querimoniam firmaverunt directum in potestate comitis ut facerent sibi ad invicem. Et dedit licenciam prephatus comes ut de hac querimonia facerent placitum inter se, et ipsi cum consilio et laudamento suorum hominum fecerunt placitum sicut in pagina fuerit insertum."   [114] ACG 400.1 ("positum fuit inter eos"), 400.2.

[115] DACU 1469 [*VL* 11:9]. On Guillaume, see Stefan Weiß, *Die Urkunden der päpstlichen Legaten von Leo IX. bis Coelestin III. (1049–1198)*, Forschungen zur Kaiser- und Papstgeschichte des Mittelalters 13 (Cologne, 1995), 142–44.

counsel and approval" ("consilio et laude") of Oleguer, archbishop of Tarragona.[116]

The evidence of the *convenientiae* that explicitly concern the settlement of disputes corresponds to Freedman's findings for the documentation for Vic in the twelfth century. It also corresponds to the findings of a preliminary survey of additional records related to settlement in Catalonia that are not labeled *convenientiae*.[117] Records of the resolution of conflicts in this period lacked consistent patterns and formalism. Nevertheless, their shared institutional vocabulary suggests that litigants did follow certain procedures. Part of the problem in identifying these procedures is local and chronological variation, topics that have received little attention. The partial evidence offered by dispute-settlement *convenientiae* provides only incomplete answers to the important questions of change in judicial procedure in medieval Catalonia.

EXPLOITING THE LAND

Peasants of the Catalan counties at the turn of the millennium were free in terms of personal status, but that did not mean that they held their lands in complete independence. True freeholds were rare, as lords inevitably established superior rights and jurisdictions over peasant lands. The terms of tenure were light and almost never included personal service, but they remained terms of tenure. Seigneurial pressure on the peasantry increased, especially in the mid-eleventh and mid-twelfth centuries, but, as recent research has shown, favorable conditions persisted.[118] Because no uniform custom of tenure had developed, each landholding agreement represented an individual negotiation. The results of these negotiations were occasionally drawn up as *convenientiae*, the flexibility of which again came into service. Most of the available evidence concerns peasant tenure from ecclesiastical institutions, but conventions for the exploitation of land proved useful across a broad spectrum of Catalan society.

Convenientiae establishing agrarian contracts share formal characteristics with *convenientiae* concerning castle holding and relationships of fidelity.[119]

---

[116] Antoni Bach, ed., "Els documents del priorat de Santa Maria de Gualter de l'Arxiu Episcopal de Solsona (segles XI–XIII)," *Urgellia* 8 (1986–87), app. 21 (pp. 238–39, a. 1170); *CSCV* 909 (a. 1131). [117] Kosto, "Agreements," Table 6.2 (pp. 464–67). [118] Freedman, *Origins*, 73–79.

[119] Freedman, *Origins*, 95. On agrarian contracts generally: Lluís To Figueras, "Le mas catalan du XIIᵉ s.: Genèse et évolution d'une structure d'encadrement et d'asservissement de la paysannerie," *Cahiers de civilisation médiévale* 36 (1993), 151–77; Roland Viader, "Remarques sur la tenure et le statut des tenanciers dans la Catalogne du XIᵉ au XIIIᵉ siècle," *AM* 107 (1995), 149–65; Pere Benito i Monclús, "Senyoria de la terra i tinença pagesa: Estudi sobre les relacions contractuals agràries al comtat de Barcelona des de la fi dels sistemes d'explotació dominical als orígens de l'emfiteusi (segles XI–XIII)" (Tesi de doctorat, Universitat de Barcelona, 2000).

Agrarian contracts recorded grants of land by an institution or individual to another individual or group, made with the condition that the recipient(s) cultivate the land or develop it in some way.[120] In addition, the tenant(s) had to pay a yearly sum consisting of a portion of the profits earned from the land or, rarely, a fixed quantity of produce. From the mid-eleventh century, there begin to appear in these contracts new elements that recall the terms of castle-holding agreements, including promises of fidelity, prohibitions against choosing another lord (*senior*) for the property, and statements that the land was to be held in service and fidelity.[121] Provisions that limited the contracts to grants for life or for the life of the beneficiary and one of his or her heirs gave way to language that implied perpetuity. A better understanding of the parallel development of castle-holding and agrarian regimes must await the findings of studies in progress on agrarian contracts. What follows is limited to those agrarian contracts that scribes labeled *convenientiae*.

Most of the surviving agrarian contracts come from ecclesiastical archives. This characteristic of the evidence is partly a result of the fact that these archives are the best preserved, but cathedrals, churches, and monasteries were also most likely to possess sufficient lands to require the development of regular systems to exploit them. A second pattern of documentary survival is more problematic: the vast majority of these contracts come from the county of Barcelona, specifically from the archives of the monasteries of Sant Benet de Bages and Sant Cugat del Vallès, and the cathedral archive of Barcelona. While the size of the archives involved no doubt contributes to this bias, there may be more to this geographical pattern. The earliest agrarian contracts identified, dating to the mid-tenth century, concern Sant Cugat and the cathedral of Barcelona, and they are fairly common in the documentation from Sant Cugat in the first half of the eleventh century. The chronology for the county of Urgell is very different. While donations to the cathedral with usufruct reserved to the donor are common in the eleventh century, specialized grants (Cat. *arrendaments*) do not appear until the twelfth. The earliest agrarian contract from the archive of the cathedral of Urgell written in the form of a grant from the church is dated 1106. The situation is similar for institutions in the county of Girona. Studies to date have been primarily local and have focused on the abundant evidence from Barcelona; more broadly based examinations promise to reveal interesting patterns and lines of influence.[122]

---

[120] This activity was expressed in a variety of ways: *construere, (re)edificere, condringere/condirigere, ad culturam perducere, excolere, meliorare, laborare, restaurare, exercere, complantare, expletere, erigendere* . . .

[121] OR, Sant Cugat del Vallès 626; AAM, Sant Benet de Bages 134, 1591; etc.

[122] Urgell: DACU 1235; see Bonnassie, *La Catalogne*, 1:245 n. 123. Girona: Lluís To Figueras, *El monestir de Santa Maria de Cervià i la pagesia: Una anàlisi local del canvi feudal: Diplomatari segles*

The agrarian contracts recorded using the language of the *convenientia*, which represent a small percentage of the whole, are not recognizably different in substance from those that survive in other forms. Nevertheless, these few examples indicate an awareness at some level on the part of the scribes of the functional and formal relationships between the agrarian contract and other types of conventions. In some contracts, the connection remains implicit, as the term *convenientia* appears only in the phrase introducing the conditional clause ("tali convenientia ut"); as noted earlier, this was only one of a number of options available to a scribe who needed to express a condition.[123] In other cases, however, scribes made the connection plain by referring to the agreement itself as a convention. In most cases, they did so not by employing the formula "Hec est convenientia," but rather by inserting the term into the penalty clause: "if you . . . remove yourself from the abovewritten *convenientia*, you shall likewise pay a composition to us of another ounce of the best gold."[124] In twelfth-century documents from the cathedral of Barcelona, terms for convention and grant (*donum et convenientia*) were paired in the penalty clause.[125] Dating clauses included similar language.[126]

These formal patterns are important in that they offer strong support for the diplomatic continuity of these agrarian contracts with early medieval conditional agreements. In Italian documents, for example, the term *convenientia* appears in the same three parts of the act as it does in these contracts: the phrase introducing the conditional clause, the penalty clause, and the dating clause.[127] This similarity cannot have been a case of strict adherence to an early medieval formula by Catalan scribes of the eleventh and twelfth centuries. The earliest surviving agrarian contracts, from the 950s and 960s, antedate by a century the earliest agrarian contracts to include the term *convenientia*. Furthermore, this language appeared only at the time when other types of written conventions were becoming common. It could be argued that this is an example of scribes expressing similar ideas in a similar fashion, but the degree of formal resemblance seen in these documents points rather to a common and enduring notarial tradition.

X–XII, Publicacions de la Fundació Salvador Vives Casajuana 110 (Barcelona, 1991), 144–46; but see *CDSG* 263 (a. 1052). Barcelona: Francesch Carreras y Candi, *Notes sobre los origens de la enfiteusis en lo territori de Barcelona* (Barcelona, 1910); Raimundo Noguera de Guzmán, "El precario y la 'precaria' (Notas para la historia de la enfiteusis)," *Estudios históricos y documentos de los archivos de protocolos* 2 (1950), 250–54.   [123] E.g., LA 1:289*, 1:328*, 1:535*, 2:78*.

[124] OR, Santa Cecília de Montserrat 59*: "si tu . . . de hac de suprascripta conveniencia te abstraxeris, similiter componas nobis suprascriptis aliam unicam auri obtimi."

[125] LA 2:157*; similarly, LA 3:109*, 4:451*, 4:452*.

[126] LA 3:139*, 4:376*; AAM, Sant Benet de Bages 152; etc.

[127] Adam J. Kosto, "The *convenientia* in the Early Middle Ages," *Mediaeval Studies* 60 (1998), 40–49.

A number of agrarian contracts do employ the form "Hec est convenientia," but again it is difficult to determine why this is so. Part of the answer may lie in local variation: several of these agrarian *convenientiae* concern the monastery of Sant Benet de Bages.[128] But the background of a contract may have been equally important. Some of the elements in these agreements are reminiscent of the details of other types of *convenientiae*. A convention in 1088 between the prior of Bages and one of his tenants was described as having been reached in the presence of two monks and two laymen. The contract also suggested that these four men advised on the terms, namely that no *census* would be required, but that the tenant would become the man (*homo*) of the prior. The role of these advisors recalls the clauses that regulate the settlement of disputes in castle-holding conventions, in which conflicts were to be adjudicated by two men representing each party. This contract, therefore, may represent the resolution of a conflict between the prior and the tenant; in labeling the document a *convenientia*, the scribe was highlighting this aspect of the agreement.[129]

In other cases, contracts with the formula *Hec est convenientia* describe particularly complex transactions. For example, in 1068, Guitard received a grant from Sant Cugat del Vallès of the manse of El Vendrell on the condition that he work the land and return half of the profits to the monastery. The agreement required Guitard's fidelity to the monastery; as noted above, this was an increasingly common condition for agrarian contracts. On the other hand, the agreement also included the unusual provisions that the monastery would provide half of the oxen required for working the demesne, as well as 2 *sesters* of barley every year to defray Guitard's expenses for transportation. A contract in 1094 between the bishop and canons of Barcelona and Guillem Donús also contained unconventional terms, such as promises by the bishop to process all of the grain destined to the canons at Guillem Donús's mill, and terms for the construction of an additional mill.[130] These two agreements highlight the continued flexibility of the labor market in the second half of the eleventh century; tenants were still able to obtain beneficial terms. The fact that these agreements were labeled conventions emphasizes the bargaining process involved in their creation.

Of the other major types of landholding agreements, the lease was the most similar to the agrarian contract. It also took the form of a grant by an individual or institution to another against a yearly payment. But whereas the agrarian contract specified that the land was to be held for

---

128 AAM, Sant Benet de Bages 163=1579, 175, 1554, 1628. Cf. *VL* 9:19; ACB 1–1–480.
129 AAM, Sant Benet de Bages 1591.
130 OR, Sant Cugat del Vallès 314* (a. 1068); LA 1:621* (a. 1094).

the purposes of agricultural labor (*ad laborandum, ad edificandum*), the lease was silent on this point. Furthermore, where the rent due for an agrarian contract was most often a portion of the harvest, the holders of leases usually enjoyed – or labored under – fixed rents. Of course, much of the land granted in this fashion was agricultural land, and such land was going to be worked. The fixed rent was often agricultural produce, and the land was often improved in the manner of an agrarian contract. In a lease from Sant Benet de Bages in 1104, for example, the prior specified that when the land reverted to the monastery at the death of the beneficiary, it was to be "with every improvement."[131]

Leases were easily adaptable, however, to other types of revenue-generating property, such as churches, ovens, or the lands associated with clerical offices.[132] Leases also offered the opportunity for an institution to meet its needs in a very specific fashion. The canons of the cathedral of Barcelona, for example, granted lands in return for a yearly provision of spiced wine and pastries.[133] While agrarian contracts usually provided for the extension of the agreement into the future, by allowing for the heirs of the original beneficiary to remain on the land, leases were more commonly presented as simple grants for life. As with many of these agreements, however, the form conceals a more complicated reality. A lease might concern lands that had been held by a beneficiary's parent, or lands that the beneficiary himself had donated to the grantor of the lease.[134] In the twelfth century, these agreements began to be presented as perpetual.[135]

Scribes also couched transactions between institutional landholders and their tenants as grants "in fief." In the context of most castle-holding conventions, the fief comprised the lands and rights associated with the castle, held unconditionally. That is not the case in these conventions, in which the fief was susceptible to a wide variety of terms of tenure.[136] The abbot of Sant Sadurní de Tavèrnoles granted a church in fief, along with two-thirds of the revenues. The abbot of Sant Cugat del Vallès granted a manse as a protectorate, cultivated land, and fief ("per baiulia et laboracionem et fevum"), along with a vineyard in fief ("ad fevum"), with no division of revenues, but against a onetime countergift of 70 *mancusos*.[137]

---

[131] AAM, Sant Benet de Bages 1625: "cum omni melioratione que melioraveris."
[132] *CDSG* 469; *CCM* 124; Cebrià Baraut, ed., "Set actes més de consagracions d'esglésies del bisbat d'Urgell (segles XI–XII)," *Urgellia* 2 (1979), app. 3 (pp. 485–86).
[133] ACB 1–1–2179=LA 4:197*; LA 3:159*.   [134] AAM, Sant Benet de Bages 166; *CDSG* 263.
[135] AAM, Sant Benet de Bages 1791; *CSCV* 1019; *CCM* 357.
[136] Bonnassie, *La Catalogne*, 2:746–48. The lack of consistency in the documents of ecclesiastical institutions is even greater than he suggests.
[137] DTavèrnoles 88 [CTavernoles 41]; AAM, Sant Cugat del Vallès 123. Other countergifts: *DPoblet* 51; AAM, Sant Benet de Bages 128.

The canons of Urgell granted an alod in fief (!) for life (!!) against the payment of a *tasca*. The abbot of Sant Cugat, on the other hand, granted a manse and vineyard as a fief to a tenant and his descendants, while renouncing the tithe and *tasca* that was once due from the property.[138] What unites these disparate grants is the requirement of service and fidelity, analogous to the service and fidelity required of the recipients of grants of castles. In the last grant mentioned, for example, service and fidelity seem to be the *only* requirements of tenure. But as noted above, service and fidelity were increasingly part of agrarian contracts and leases. Meanwhile, there exist conventions for which the only requirement was service and fidelity, with no mention of a fief.[139] The inconsistency is too widespread to be an illusion caused by the occasional misuse of the term by a scribe. Outside the context of the grant for military service, it is impossible to define the fief with precision.

Agrarian contracts, leases, and grants in fief all present the tenurial relationship as created by a grant *to* the tenant. Agreements with institutions were also expressed as conditional grants *from* the tenant, in which the condition or the entire document was labeled a *convenientia*. The simplest, though few in number, were grants with the use reserved, whereby the donor retained use of the property for life with no obligations, after which full rights would revert to the institution.[140] Conditions that scribes labeled *convenientiae* were normally more complicated or unusual. Santa Eulàlia del Camp received a grant of rights to pledges worth 100 *morabetins* in return for a promise of weekly prayers for the soul of the donor and his family. Pere, sacristan of the cathedral of Barcelona, made an extensive grant of lands, rights, and money to the cathedral community, with the intent of increasing the almsgiving activity of the church; he included detailed instructions as to his desires in the agreement.[141] Other similar conventions concerned livestock and grazing rights.[142] The condition to such a grant could also be the acceptance of the donor into the community receiving the grant. It might take the form of a simple promise of support, as when the community of Sant Salvador de Bellver undertook to maintain the donors in retirement ("victu et vestitu") in exchange for their grant of four *peciae* of land.[143] But these agreements also served as contracts of oblation, or self-oblation. In 1173, a brother and sister granted extensive lands to Sant Cugat del Vallès on the condi-

---

[138] DACU 1159; *CSCV* 1041. Other life grants: AAM, Sant Benet de Bages 128. Other yearly payments: ACV 6/1693; AAM, Sant Benet de Bages 128; *CSCV* 1129.

[139] OR, Sant Llorenç del Munt 229*; BC, MS 729, 4:76r–v, renewed by 4:76v, 4:89r.

[140] DACU 1223; *DPoblet* 45; cf. DACU 1226, where the condition is expressed by the phrase "tali convenientia ut."   [141] *Santa Anna* 350; LA 4:1*, 4:6*.   [142] *DPoblet* 471; *LBSC* 316.

[143] ACV 6/1192. Similarly ADG, Mitra 17/112*; *CSCV* 762.

tion that the sister be maintained in the priory of Santa Maria de Santa Oliva, and that the brother be buried in the cemetery of Sant Cugat. In the second half of the twelfth century, this type of agreement was adopted by the military orders.[144]

Other conventions recorded not grants by one party to the other, but acknowledgments by one or both parties of the terms of tenure. Thus around the year 1100 the men (*homines*) of Sas subscribed conventions with the prior of Santa Maria de Lavaix by which they recognized that they held a certain alod from him; the document specified the renders due from each of the eight inhabitants.[145] An agreement of 1126 recorded the same type of transaction, but in slightly different language: the provost Bernat Ponç accepted an alod from the hands of the canons of the cathedral of Urgell, promising in return various fixed rents.[146] These conventions were unbalanced, in that only one party was doing the accepting or acknowledging. Others avoided this appearance by simply recording, in an objective manner, the terms of holding.[147]

The variety of tenurial arrangements found in *convenientiae* demonstrates the flexibility of the form. It served as well in the context of land-management practices as it did in the context of castle holding and dispute settlement. The numbers of these documents demonstrate the important role written agreements came to play – for institutions, but also for individuals, including peasants – in establishing social and economic structures within Catalan society.

FAMILY SETTLEMENTS

Intrafamily arrangements were among the first Catalan *convenientiae*. These earliest conventions included agreements concerning inheritances and the disposition and succession of family lands at various levels of society.[148] The *convenientia* by which Ramon Berenguer I promised to commend certain lords to his brother, Sanç, was part of an agreement whereby the latter abandoned his claims to the family patrimony. But most such arrangements within comital families, because of the lands, rights, and issues involved, are essentially treaties. Agreements between Ramon Berenguer II and Berenguer Ramon II, for example, were

---

[144] *CSCV* 1085. Similarly *CSCV* 1022; Manuel Serrano y Sanz, *Noticias y documentos históricos del condado de Ribagorza hasta la muerte de Sancho Garcés III (año 1035)* (Madrid, 1912), 277 n. 2; OM 17:53 (a. 1187), 23:213 (a. 1191).

[145] Ignasi M. Puig i Ferreté, ed., *El cartoral de Santa Maria de Lavaix: El monestir durant els segles XI–XIII* (La Seu d'Urgell, 1984), no. 39 (p. 89). Similarly, AAM, Sant Benet de Bages 1659; DTavèrnoles 130 [CTavernoles 60].   [146] DACU 1377.

[147] Puig i Ferreté, ed., *Lavaix*, no. 46 (p. 95); AAM, Sant Benet de Bages 1593; ACG 208.

[148] Òdena 9; DACU 559; LA 2:23*; HGL 5:201.

designed to halt a civil war, not a family squabble.[149] At lower levels, *convenientiae* of this sort remain rare until the 1080s, though they appear more consistently thereafter.[150] The subjects they address are the same as those found in the earliest exemplars.

Matters of inheritance were the most common. The *convenientia* served in some situations as a substitute for the testamentary document itself. In one case, the substitution was very simple: a husband granted to his wife 100 *mancusos* after his death if they had no children, as well as the right to recover her personal property. In another, a father granted to his son various properties for life, but with the condition that they should pass to other individuals outside the family after the son's death. Usually, however, these conventions involved promises by both parties, such as in agreements between brothers in which each assigned his property to the other in case of his death.[151] Variations on this type involved grants between the parties during their lifetimes, or reserved rights for third parties.[152]

In other cases where intrafamily *convenientiae* concerned inherited rights and lands, they served a function analogous to executory documents, such as donations made by the *marmessors* or *elemosinarii* of the deceased to churches to fulfill the terms of a testament.[153] For example, in 1179 the brothers Guillem, Pere, and Arnau de Balenyà entered a *convenientia* "according to the terms of the testament of Guillem de Balenyà, their father, concerning the *honor* that he left to them and divided among them in that testament." The agreement addressed the terms by which several castles and other lands were to be held. In addition, the brothers confirmed the order of succession to the lands that their father had specified. A notable example of this type of agreement was the *convenientia* of 1087 that carried out the testamentary instructions of Ramon Folc I, viscount of Cardona (Osona). The dowager viscountess and the viscount regent (Folc II, Ramon Folc's brother) commended the family *honores* to the late viscount's son-in-law, who was to hold them from the viscounts as their man (*homo*) until he could pass them on to the intended beneficiary in the next generation.[154] This type of intrafamily conven-

---

[149] RBI 110; *LFM* 36. RBII 48* refers to a *scriptura convenientie*; the surviving documents are not themselves *convenientiae* (below, p. 163).

[150] I have located only five examples from the period 1050–80: DACU 659; ACV 6/1618; *CDSG* 265; RBI 281; AAM, Sant Benet de Bages 1509.

[151] OR, sense procedència 412; AAM, Sant Benet de Bages 1509; ACV 6/1618. See also DACU 659; BC 2653.

[152] ACB 1–5–463=LA 4:274*; ACV 6/1085; DACU 1017.

[153] On this part of the testamentary process, see *STCA*, pp. 135–44; Nathaniel L. Taylor, "The Will and Society in Medieval Catalonia and Languedoc, 800–1200" (Ph.D. diss., Harvard University, 1995), pp. 96–103. In addition to examples cited below, see: DACU 659; BC 2653; *CDSG* 459.

[154] ADG, Pia Almoina, Girona "subratllat" 1 (Testaments) (a. 1179: "iuxta tenorem testamenti Guilelmi de Balanano patris eorum de honore quem eis in ipso testamento divisit ac dimisit); BC, MS 729, 4:196v–97r (a. 1087).

tion might also substitute for an execution of an oral testament, as in an agreement between two brothers in 1181 reached "because our father declared his [wishes as to the disposition of his] affairs, but they were not written."[155]

Testators also employed *convenientiae* to guarantee the execution of their testaments. This was the case in the agreement between an uncle and nephew in 1062x63 by which the uncle granted a tower to his nephew, with the condition that the nephew see to the disbursement of 40 ounces of gold as specified in his testament. Parties to these conventions did not, however, always adhere to the apparent desires of deceased relatives. In 1173, Bertran de Butsènit and his wife granted extensive lands and rights to their daughter and her fiancé, with the condition that they should provide honorably for a second daughter, Ermessenda, or at least grant to her 2,000 *solidi* as a dowry. Three years later, and following the death of the father, Ermessenda was married, but the 2,000 *solidi* had apparently not been transferred. The sisters and their husbands came to an agreement "concerning the 2,000 *solidi* that the aforesaid Ramon de Montseré and his wife Sança were to have given to Ermessenda according to the instructions of Bertran, Ermessenda's father, now dead." Ermessenda and her husband quitclaimed half of the sum, while Sança and her husband promised to grant the remaining 1,000 *solidi*, half in coin, half in kind. If Ermessenda died childless, her husband was to return the sum to his brother-in-law; if he refused, the brother-in-law would have rights to 1,000 *solidi* in the land assigned to Ermessenda as her dower.[156]

Some of these conventions, while addressing matters of inheritance, also recorded the attempts of relatives to establish tenurial relationships during their lives. The parties involved did not necessarily view these arrangements with confidence. In 1120, Pere Guillem and Bernat Guillem along with the latter's wife, Rossa, agreed to live together during their lifetimes, with the couple agreeing to maintain Pere Guillem to the best of their ability. If Pere Guillem died first, all of his lands were to pass to the couple, but if Bernat died first, Pere Guillem and Rossa were to continue to live together. The brothers must have recognized that this might not work, for they added the clause, "if they are not able to live together, let each have his own."[157] Similarly, the intent of the parties to a contract of dowry (*exovar*) in 1133 was that the new couple would share the family *honor* with the grantors, the mother and the brother of the

---

[155] OM 2:305: "facimus carta convenientia propter hoc quod nostro pater mandavit suas kausas ad obitum suum et non fuerunt scriptas."

[156] RBI 281 (a. 1062x63); DPoblet 451 (a. 1173), 558 (a. 1176: "de dua milia solidos qos daturus erant predictum Raimundus de Mont Sere et uxoris sue Sanice ad Ermessen per iusionem Bertran, patris Ermessendis qui iam hobit"). Cf. BRII 66.

[157] RBIII 227: "et si non possunt stare in simul unusquisque abeat suum." Cf. *Santa Anna* 293.

bride; if this arrangement was untenable, the *honor* was to be split among them evenly.[158] In a contract from 1132, the couple would receive, in addition to the initial grant of half of the family *honor*, one-third of the movables if the family had to break up.[159]

Children were another common subject of these agreements, and a number of conventions were directed toward establishing tutorships (*baiuliae*). One of the more conspicuous examples involved Berenguer Ramon de Montcada and his cousins. The agreement formed part of the extensive intrafamilial negotiations of the various branches of that family around the year 1100. Berenguer Ramon and his cousins made each other heirs, if Berenguer Ramon were to die childless, or if the cousins died first "without any lay brothers" or children; if Berenguer Ramon had a child, however, the cousins were to have tutorship of that child and the lands. Such arrangements were not restricted to the highest levels of the aristocracy, as shown by the detailed clauses of the *convenientia* entered into in 1138 by Pere and Berenguer de Sentmenat. First, they agreed to share whatever they possessed jointly, with full rights after the death of one of the brothers to pass to the survivor, if there were no children. If the deceased brother left sons, the uncle would have tutorship over them; when they came of age, the children would hold their lands from the uncle during their lifetimes. If there were only a daughter, the uncle was to arrange a good marriage for her, while maintaining the lands during his lifetime; after his death, the lands would pass to the daughter.[160]

Between bequests, tutorships, and tenurial arrangements among the living, these *convenientiae* could become quite complex. A convention of 1119 provides a particularly intricate example of the intrafamily arrangement. It involved a set of parents with their four children and the wives of two of those children. Rules were established for distribution of the lands after the death of both parents, but the agreement also stated how the lands were to be held until that time, addressed the status of a debt of the parents to one of the daughters, and established a procedure for the settlement of disputes and a fine.[161]

---

[158] ACV 6/1181. Cf. BC 3993.

[159] AAM, Sant Cugat del Vallès 144: "Dum autem mecum simul habitaveritis, sitis uni domini et heredes domus mee, ita ut ametis meum sicut et vestrum et ego vestrum sicut meum, et omne meum et vestrum negocium sit unum. Si vero, quod absit, aliquo modo nobis invicem separaverimus, tunc abeatis solide et libere prelibatam donacionem, et de mobilibus que tunc habuerimus habeatis terciam partem." Although the *convenientia* was ideally suited to the flexible nature of the marriage contract (as in BC 1810), marriage agreements usually took other forms. See Jesús Lalinde Abadía, "Los pactos matrimoniales catalanes (Esquema histórico)," *Anuario de historia del derecho español* 33 (1963), 133–266.

[160] RBIII 66 ("sine fratris laicis"; see Shideler, *Montcadas*, 40); RBIV 82 (a. 1138).

[161] BC 2801 (a. 1119). Additional examples: BC 2794, 3999; ADG, Pia Almoina, Cassa de la Selva 528.

In other intrafamily agreements, matters of inheritance were not at issue. Conventions recorded a simple pledge between brothers, or an agreement addressing the details of how family land was to be held.[162] They also detailed the terms of relationships between nephew and uncle. One such transaction involving testamentary dispositions has been mentioned. Another recorded an oath-convention of a nephew to his uncle.[163] The negotiations between Mir Ballouí, canon of the cathedral of Barcelona, and his nephew Ramon Mir over family lands at Argentona resulted in at least three *convenientiae*.[164]

A number of the intrafamily agreements that have survived deal with that most common subject of conventions, castles. The specific transactions varied considerably from agreement to agreement. In 1053, the brothers Pere and Guillem promised each other mutual aid in a *convenientia* concerning a pledge of a one-eighth interest in the castle of Fonolleres. In 1085, Berenguer Ramon de Montcada pledged the castle of Vacarisses to his uncles as a guarantee of his fidelity. In 1124 Ponç de Cervera and his brother Ramon agreed to share the castle of Passanant. They would alternate direct control on a yearly basis, but each would always have right of entry. In 1132, Gombau and Guillem granted to their brother Pere Ponç one-third of their rights in the castle of Miralles in return for his protection. And in 1149, in another example of potential familial discord, Agnès de *Murezeno* promised to grant the castle of *Murezeno* to her son, Bernat de Montesquiu, and his wife if they all could not agree to live together.[165]

John Shideler has described the pledge of Berenguer Ramon de Montcada to his uncles as "more typical of settlements reached between lineages than of those between close relatives." He points to this, and to the convention between Berenguer Ramon and his cousins years later, as evidence of the "feudalization of family relations."[166] The documentation just surveyed does not support this claim. While fiefs, castles, oaths,

---

[162] ACV 6/1140; DACU 1590; LA 3:23*. Cf. *CSCV* 850 ("Advenit nobis per donacionem eiusdem fratris meis Mironis et per convenienciam quam fecit mecum in vita sua"); OR, Sant Cugat del Vallès 477* ("Omnia quidem sicut suprascripta sunt et ut in convenientia resonat que facta est inter me et Berengarium Arnalli, fratrem meum, dono"). Numerous other references to conventions may be found in testamentary documents, e.g., DACU 1262 ("Et ipsum suprascriptum honorem sic teneat Miro frater meus pro filia mea Ermengardis et per virum suum sicut et per me tenet et quomodo resonat in ipsa convenientia").   [163] LA 2:235*.

[164] LA 2:502*, 2:506*, 2:511*; cf. LA 2:503*. The relationship between nephew and maternal uncle in medieval society is an important theme, but in these cases the uncle in question is not always the maternal uncle. For Catalonia, see most recently Ruiz-Domènec, *L'estructura feudal*, 101–5.

[165] *CDSG* 265 (a. 1053); BRII 19 (a. 1085; see also BRII 18, 20); OM 1:136 (a. 1124); *Santa Anna* 212 (a. 1132); RBIV 213 (a. 1149). In ACA, Diversos, Varia 10 (Vilanova Roselló), leg. 1, doc. 5, no. 2 (p. 2), it is not clear whether the parties are relatives or unrelated castellans.

[166] Shideler, *Montcadas*, 57–58.

and homage occasionally entered into intrafamily settlements, they were not the normal subject. These written agreements differed considerably in substance from the castle-holding conventions with which the counts organized their power. They do demonstrate, however, the flexibility and utility of the written agreement, in the form of the *convenientia*, within the family. The *convenientia* helped to articulate structures not only among various elements of society, but within its most basic units.

PROMISES

We have already noted within *convenientiae* that dealt with castle tenure and related subjects a split between balanced and unbalanced agreements: commendations, in which both parties acted or were to act, and oath-conventions, in which the undertakings of only one of the parties was recorded. These unbalanced, one-sided agreements form a subset of *convenientiae* even outside the realm of castle-holding arrangements. Whereas the undertakings in oath-conventions might be quite vague, those in promise-conventions could be very wide-ranging and specific. Consider, for example, the list of promises in the agreement between Mir Geribert and his family and the count of Barcelona at the time of Mir Geribert's ultimate submission in 1059. Mir Geribert, his wife, and two of his sons promised the counts: to make their other sons quitclaim various disputed castles and *honores* when they reached the age of majority; to make their other sons sign the charter, which they themselves had signed on the same day, by which they granted the Castell de Port to the count; to make those sons swear fidelity to the count; to return various disputed rights in the Penedès; not to require payment of a relief (*acapte*) from Bishop Guillem of Vic without comital permission; to provide aid as promised in their written oaths; to secure their castle of Olèrdola with comital supervision; to make the present and future masters of Eramprunyà and Olèrdola promise fidelity and control (*potestas*) of the castles to the counts; and, finally, to do right concerning the tower of Caldes. From this long list of promises, the only clauses that might be found in oath-conventions are the promise of aid and the obligations concerning control of the castles. The submission of Bishop Guislabert at the end of the first phase of the rebellion against Ramon Berenguer I (*c.* 1044) is presented in the form of a promise to keep oaths not recorded in the document itself.[167] Other promise-conventions reached farther afield, such as the promise of Guillem Bernat de Queralt to present char-

---

[167] RBI 239*, 240* (a. 1058); sd 3 (*c.* 1044); below, pp. 194–95. See also RBI 268*, 331*; Extra. 4726.

ters in the course of a judicial proceeding, or the promise of the viscounts of Béziers in 1070 not to alienate various abbeys.[168] Just as it is reasonable to assume in the case of many of the oath-conventions a preceding commendation, many of these unbalanced promise-conventions conceal the action of the other party. The label *convenientia* may in fact be a marker that a one-sided action is in fact the outcome of a process of negotiation. In any case, promises are more often found as elements of the varieties of agreements described above than as independent documents.

Other categories are possible. A group of the *convenientiae* of Ramon Berenguer I all concern financial arrangements: three grants of rights of minting and the associated profits against a yearly payment of grain; a convention granting milling rights in Barcelona, again against payments in grain; a settlement of the value of the bailiwick of Cervera; the acquisition of a quitclaim of lodging rights (*albergas*) in return for a yearly payment of fifty pigs (to be made by the count's bailiff); and the promise of a payment of 6 ounces a year for the profits of the parish of Sant Pere de Vilamajor. The flexibility of the *convenientia* contributed in these examples to early experiments in comital fiscality.[169] A separate group of *convenientiae* from the second half of the twelfth century concern the construction, maintenance, and exploitation of mills. Another fairly homogeneous group concerns pledge agreements.[170] Close analysis of these and other different groupings would aid in our understanding of various institutions. But from the variety of agreements presented so far, the flexibility of the *convenientia* should be clear; this flexibility is precisely what allowed for the diffusion of the written agreement. The principal use of the form was in the regulation of the military and political affairs of the aristocracy, through commendations, oath-conventions, and treaties. Still, the *convenientia* could be adopted by other segments of society for other purposes: negotiated settlements, either in association with or separate from other processes of judgment; arrangements within families; and agreements for the tenure and exploitation of land and rights much less exalted than castles.

The *convenientia* competed in many of these arenas, as noted, with other documentary forms. The foregoing analysis suggests the possible

---

[168] RBI sd 6; ALI 275.2* (a. 1070).

[169] RBI 182*, 228*, 361*; 99; 434*; 358; 80. No further early commissions like the one for Cervera have emerged from the comital archives to support the hypothesis that the administrative structures visible in mid-twelfth-century documents were "basically traditional," as suggested by Bisson (*FA*, 1:23–24 and n. 2).

[170] Mills: AAM, Sant Benet de Bages 1705; RBIV 322; OM 11:2142; OM, vol. 179, no. 143 (fol. 59r–v); *LBSC* 215; ALI 502*; DACU 1880. Pledges: ACG 57; *Santa Anna* 82, 95; RBI 425; BC 3076; ACV 6/1572.

significance of scribal choice in certain cases. In intrafamily arrangements, the *convenientia* appears to record particularly complex sets of
undertakings. Similarly, the agrarian contracts and tenurial arrangements
embodied in *convenientiae* are often quite irregular in some fashion. In the
case of dispute-settlement conventions, *convenientiae* may highlight the
negotiated nature of the final agreement, whatever the actual mechanism.
Indeed, this focus on negotiation may be understood beyond those agreements explicitly connected to a confrontational context, such as promise-
conventions. Negotiation of these agreements implies some degree of
mutual expectation of adherence to the terms. Although we have examined in detail how, and about what, these agreements were made, we may
come closer to understanding the exact nature of the *convenientia* in
examining how they were kept.

Chapter 3

KEEPING AGREEMENTS

Making agreements is one thing; keeping them is another. We are much less well informed about this second aspect of the process. Individual cases did end up in courts or other dispute-settlement fora that have left records, and here we can see an enforcement mechanism at work. Such cases are, however, few and far between, and furthermore only show that certain agreements failed. What about those agreements that worked, or at least did not break down to the point where they generated a record of a dispute? How were agreements kept? The agreements themselves give indications. Some *convenientiae* contain simple penalty clauses, though others address the issue of guarantees at great length, as was the case in the *convenientia* between Berenguer Ramon I and Ermengol II of *c.* 1021. Parties proposed various types of real and personal sureties, and they detailed procedures to be followed in case of violations. The threat of these sanctions certainly played a role in encouraging adherence to agreements, but sanctions are, like dispute-settlement procedures, negative factors, potential consequences of a change in the status of the agreement. Other factors contributed to the maintenance of agreements in a less mechanical fashion. The oath is one such element; we must revisit its relationship to the *convenientia* in order to understand more fully the nature of agreements. The written word is another, for the very inscription of the *convenientia* on parchment was a part of the process of making sure that it would be kept.

PENALTY CLAUSES

Penalty clauses, inherited from ancient and late antique formulae, are a standard part of many documentary types across Europe before *c.* 1200, when they begin to disappear. They threaten the potential violator of an agreement with spiritual, financial, or other consequences: damnation, excommunication, anathematization, fines based on the value of the object of the agreement, or a fixed sum. A grant by Berenguer Ramon I to the abbey of Sant Cugat del Vallès closes with the warning: "And whoever attempts to violate this grant, first let him incur the wrath of God, and let him pay a fourfold composition for everything above to the said institution just as the holy fathers have sanctioned."[1] Such clauses are not static formulae: the earliest surviving documents contain only financial penalties; from the tenth century, temporal and spiritual penalties appear side by side, with the spiritual receiving priority; from the mid-eleventh century, the trend reverses; and from *c.* 1130–35, spiritual penalties have all but disappeared. These changes track the long-term fortunes of comital power, though in this case, too, documentary formulae do not reflect as precisely as some suggest the political crisis of 1020–60.[2] But were such penalties in fact effective, and were they even meant to be so?[3] The pattern in the Catalan evidence suggests that the temporal penalties, at least, were: they only made sense in an environment where they could be enforced. In periods of particularly weak comital power – such as the first half of the eleventh century – they had no place. While an excommunication might be ignored, however, the efficacy of spiritual penalties pertaining to the afterlife was unverifiable. On the other hand, there is no independent evidence for penalties paid in cases of violation, and for agreements that were kept, it is impossible to know the precise role played by the threat of sanction.

In this as in other areas, the *convenientia* departs from previous documentary forms. Most *convenientiae* do not indicate the consequences of violation, but those that do often address those consequences outside a formulaic penalty clause; discussions of consequences can expand to become part of the substance of the agreements themselves. They offer a wider range of guarantees and offer more detail about the procedures involved. The question of how agreements were kept can thus be pushed a little further beyond the heuristic roadblock presented by formulaic

---

[1] *CSCV* 436: "Et qui contra hac largicione venerit ad inrumpendum, primum iram Dei incurrat componatque prenotata omnia ad domum prelibatum in quadruplum prout sancti Patres sanxerunt."

[2] Michel Zimmermann, "Protocoles et préambules dans les documents catalans du Xe au XIIe siècle: évolution diplomatique et signification spirituelle," *Mélanges de la Casa de Velázquez* 10 (1974), 50–74; Zimmermann, "Le vocabulaire latin de malédiction du IXe au XIIe siècle: Construction d'un discours eschatologique," *Atalaya: Revue française d'études médiévales hispaniques* 5 (1994), 39–44, 49–54; Jeffrey A. Bowman, "Do Neo-Romans Curse? Law, Land, and Ritual in the Midi (900–1100)," *Viator* 28 (1997), 7 n. 22. Cf. Lester K. Little, *Benedictine Maledictions: Liturgical Cursing in Romanesque France* (Ithaca, 1993), 52–59; Frank M. Stenton, ed., *Transcripts of Charters Relating to the Gilbertine Houses of Sixle, Ormsby, Catley, Bullington, and Alvingham*, Publications of the Lincoln Record Society 18 (Horncastle, 1922), xxxii–xxxiii.

[3] Joachim Studtmann, "Die Pönformel der mittelalterlichen Urkunden," *Archiv für Urkundenforschung* 12 (1932), 330–54.

penalty clauses. The most basic guarantee clauses in *convenientiae* do not even define a penalty; they simply state that the agreement should be kept: "If anyone should infringe upon this, let him not prevail."[4] Penalty clauses that specify monetary damages are more common. Generally, no precise value is specified; rather the violator is charged a penalty equal to a multiple of the property at issue – usually double, occasionally triple or quadruple.[5] Such multiple penalties are common in sales, donations, exchanges, and pledges, and find roots in Visigothic law.[6] In a simple *convenientia*, the value at issue might be clear, but this was often not the case. Consider the following example. In 1157, Bernat de Manlleu and his wife Ermessenda commended to Bernat de Rocafort and his son Bernat the castle of Castelladral; the grant included one-half of the tithe (*decima*), one-half of the revenues of justice (*placita*), three manses, two months of lodging in the castle (*statica*), and *cavalleria* worth 10 *sesters* of wheat. In return the Rocaforts were to become the commended men of Bernat de Manlleu, granting *potestas*, promising fidelity, serving in hosts and cavalcades, and performing other standard duties. The agreement ends with the clause threatening a twofold composition payment in case of violation.[7] How was this to be calculated? The three manses and even the two months of *statica* might have some known value, but variable future interests (*decima*, *placita*) could not. It is possible that standard values for military and other services owed to lords had been developed, but there is no evidence for commutation in this period.[8] The only item in this agreement with a stated value is the *cavalleria* worth 10 *sesters* of wheat, and even this was an annual income. The value of such damages would have to be the subject of a future dispute. Claims for specific monetary damages do appear in judgments, but for losses, not penalties.[9] Nonspecific damages may have been empty threats.

---

[4] OM 23:245: "Si quis hoc infrigerint non valeant."

[5] E.g., RBIV 289 (double); AAM, Sant Benet de Bages 1686 (triple); LA 4:271* (quadruple).

[6] *CSCV*, 1:liv; *ACondal*, pp. 38–40; Michel Zimmermann, "L'usage du droit wisigothique en Catalogne du IXe au XIIe siècle: Approches d'une signification culturelle," *Mélanges de la Casa de Velázquez* 9 (1973), 268–76; also above, pp. 47–48; P. D. King, *Law and Society in the Visigothic Kingdom*, CSMLT, 3rd ser., 5 (Cambridge, 1972), 208–20, etc.; Liber iudiciorum, VIII.1.7 (p. 316), etc. Cf. Michel Zimmermann, ed., "Un formulaire du Xème siècle conservé à Ripoll," *Faventia* 4:2 (1982), 80–81 (fixed values).   [7] AAM, Sant Benet de Bages 1716.

[8] Cf. Frank M. Stenton, *The First Century of English Feudalism, 1066–1166*, 2nd ed. (Oxford, 1961), 178–91; John W. Baldwin, *The Government of Philip Augustus: Foundations of French Royal Power in the Middle Ages* (Berkeley, 1986), 171–73; Heinrich Mitteis, *Lehnrecht und Staatsgewalt: Untersuchungen zur mittelalterlichen Verfassungsgeschichte* (Weimar, 1933), 613–15.

[9] E.g., RBIV 305*: "Deinde conquestus est Petrus de domino suo comite quod ivit cum eo in Narbonenses partes et in Aragonem, et fecerat ibi multas perdedas, et non erat paccatus, neque de servicio neque de ipsis perdedes . . . Super hoc iudicaverunt Petrum debere probare per testes uel per averamentum secundum morem Barchinonensis curie quod sibi deficit de istis perdidis, et quod probaverit uel averaverit, reddat ei dominus comes." Cf. Us. 34.

Perhaps because of this, some agreements specify fixed monetary penalties. The monastery of Sant Benet de Bages and Adalbert Bon agreed to a penalty of 1 ounce of gold, weighed according to the standard of Barcelona, to guarantee an agrarian contract.[10] In a similar agreement involving the see of Barcelona, the penalty was 200 *morabetins*; the same penalty applied in an agreement between Pere and Berenguer de Sentmenat to possess all of their property jointly.[11] Nevertheless, such specificity was exceptional. The spiritual penalties that flourished in other documentary forms in these years only rarely appear in this documentation,[12] although a treaty of 1168 between Alfons I and Sancho VI of Navarre includes a secular analogue of anathema, stating that the violator will be considered a "knave and traitor."[13]

Guarantees of *convenientiae* more often concerned not external penalties, but the subject of the agreements themselves. At a minimum, this was a statement invalidating the agreement. In the case of the commendation of the abbacy of Sant Cugat del Vallès to Andreu Sendred, for example, if the abbot failed to adhere to the agreement, the abbacy was to revert to the counts, Ramon Berenguer I and Elisabet. The *convenientia* for the castle of Talladell dictates similar consequences if Ramon Guifré de Vilamur were to fail to keep his commitments.[14] A more complex type of guarantee linked the penalty to an element of the agreement. As part of an agrarian contract, a later abbot of Sant Cugat received 70 *mancusos*, the same amount defined as the penalty for violation of the agreement by either party.[15] In the commendation of the viscounty of Cerdanya in *c.* 1068, the viscount pledged back to the count the very lands and castles that had been granted; if he violated the agreement, he would lose his pledge (*pignus*).[16] The result here is the same as a simple reversion or invalidation of the agreement, but it is structured in terms of a pledge of real property, another common mechanism of guarantee.

SURETIES

The simplest type of real surety was the offer of a pledge of property that was not a direct subject of the agreement.[17] In return for the commendation of the castle of Fornells in 1049, for example, Hug Guillem and his wife pledged all of their alodial lands in the county of Girona; in case of default, these lands would be at the disposition of the count.[18] Similarly, the

---

[10] AAM, Sant Benet de Bages 148. [11] LA 2:157*; RBIV 82.
[12] RBI 446; AAM, Sant Benet de Bages 1625. [13] ALI 64* ("proditor et alevosus"). Cf. PEI 71.
[14] RBI 107, 373*. Cf. RBI 253.2*. [15] AAM, Sant Cugat del Vallès 123.
[16] *LFM* 598. Similarly, *LFM* 636.
[17] Cf. Jehan de Malafosse, "Contribution à l'étude du crédit dans le Midi aux Xe et XIe siècles: Les sûretés réelles," *AM* 63 (1951), 105–48.
[18] RBI 101*. Cf. RBI 182*.

castellan of Cartellà offered in pledge to his lords the castle of Tudela, which he also held from them, and which he would forfeit if any harm should come to them from Cartellà. He then pledged his entire *honor* that he held from them as a guarantee of the agreement as a whole.[19] Reversing the direction of the pledge in these situations, Arnau Mir de Sant Martí promised one of his *castlans* for Eramprunyà that if he did not acquire for him certain revenues (presumably as payment for his service), the *castlà* should have "that land that the said Arnau pledged to him."[20] This type of guarantee was not limited to simple agreements for castle tenure. Arnau Mir de Tost was able to extract from Ramon IV of Pallars Jussà a pledge of four castles that he would keep the agreements entered into at the time of his marriage to Arnau's daughter, Valença.[21] Lower down the social hierarchy, three brothers promised that if they should fail to warrant the lands that they were granting, they would give up their rights to certain other alods.[22]

In all of these cases, the property pledged was not immediately handed over to the individual in need of a guarantee; transfer of control would only occur in case of forfeit. When the forfeited property was fortified and under guard, the transfer might not be very smooth. Parties to agreements addressed this by turning to personal sureties. Personal sureties – individuals, as opposed to property, serving to guarantee transactions – operate in a number of different ways: by using influence to encourage the debtor to perform (Fr. *garant influent*; Ger. *Verwendungs-* or *Repressalienbürge*); by forcing the debtor to perform (*garant exécuteur*; *Executionsbürge*); by compensating the creditor in case of a debtor's failure to perform (*garant dédommageant*; *Schadlosbürge*); or by performing the debtor's obligation itself, whether payment or action (*garant payant* or *exécutant*; *Zahlungsbürge*).[23] All of these various functions appear in Catalan agreements, though with some overlap. Personal sureties receive a variety of designations, some shared with real sureties (*pignus, fidancia,*[24] *firmantia, guadium*), others referring specifically to people and their actions (*debitor, federator, fideiussor, guarantus, guarantor, manulevator, obses, ostaticum, pagator, plevius, tenedor*). The terms are not applied with absolute consistency.

---

[19] RBIII 312, with Extra. 3209; cf. RBI 306*.

[20] BRII 37: "ipsam terram quam Arnaldus predictus misit ei in pignus."

[21] RBI 171*. Cf. BC 1810.   [22] RBI 255.

[23] John Gilissen, "Esquisse d'une histoire comparée des sûretés personnelles: Essai de synthèse général," in *Les sûretés personnelles*, 3 vols., Recueils de la Société Jean Bodin pour l'histoire comparative des institutions 28–30 (Brussels, 1969–74), 1:50–69.

[24] Although the term *fidancia* may refer to personal sureties (e.g., RBIV 333*), it usually seems to refer to a type of oath: RBI sd 207* ("faci[at] eis fidancias et sacramentos quales alii illorum homines eis iurant"); *LFM* 40 ("faciat eis fidancas et fidelitatem"), 534 ("tales fidancias ei de predictis castellis et omnibus eorum fortedis ei faciant et fidem teneant et attendant per[h]enniter sine ullo engan"), 627 ("quales fidancias et conveniencias facit ad prephatum comitem, tales illi faciat facere ad patrem suum, et ambo donent predicto comiti obsides et federatores"). In this last example, *fidancia* is distinguished from the forms of personal surety.

Personal sureties often complemented real sureties. Parties might appoint an executing surety, a particular individual to assure that defaulted property, whether or not it was a subject of the agreement, was handed over. In the most common situation, the real surety would be a castle and the personal surety, its guardian.[25] An offensive alliance between Pere Ramon, count of Pallars Jussà (1098–1112), and the brothers *Orseth* and Berenguer *Madex* stands out because each side pledged a different castle along with its castellan. Pere Ramon and the brothers promised each other not to reach a separate peace with Ficapal de Vallferrera. The brothers pledged the *torre* of Ribera "in the power (*potestas*) of Company, so that if they did not keep this *conveniencia* with Count Pere, Company should grant *potestas* to Count Pere of that *torre* of Ribera in upright faith, without ill will concerning Count Pere." Likewise, the count pledged his castle of Arboló in the *potestas* of Ramon Ramon, who was to turn over control to the brothers if the count violated the terms of the agreement.[26]

Usually only one party provided such a pledge. In his submission to the count of Barcelona in 1054, Guillem II of Besalú offered two pledges: Ramon Ademar, along with his castle of Finestres, which was a subject of the agreement, and Ramon Bernat, along with his castle of La Guàrdia, which was not.[27] Three years later, in an agreement between the same two men, the terms governing the pledges were more strict. Guillem II pledged the castle of Colltort, but the counts added that whoever held the castle was not to grant *potestas* to either count while the castle was in pledge.[28] Bishop Guislabert of Barcelona, as part of his submission to Ramon Berenguer I, offered as a pledge the episcopal castle of Castellbisbal. Much of this agreement details the responsibilities of the castellan of that castle, Ramon Guillem, if the bishop were to violate his promises.[29] By the terms of an agreement between Bernat Guillem de Queralt and Berenguer Ramon II in 1089, Bernat commended to the count three *castlans* of Queralt, who were to deliver themselves into the *potestas* of the count along with the castle of Queralt should Bernat Guillem violate the agreement.[30]

---

[25] Cf. Andrea Büschgens, *Die politischen Verträge Alfons' VIII. von Kastilien (1158–1214) mit Aragón-Katalonien und Navarra: Diplomatische Strategien und Konfliktlösung im mittelalterlichen Spanien*, Europäische Hochschulschriften, Reihe III, Geschichte und ihre Hilfswissenschaften, 678 (Frankfurt am Main, 1995), 284–326.

[26] Extra. 3197: "mitunt in pignora Orset et Berenger ipsa torra de Ribera ad ipso chomite in potestate de Compang, quod si non tenebant ista conveniencia ad Petrus chomes, donasset Chompang potestate ad Petro chomite de ipsa torra de Ribera per directa fide sine suo engan de Petro chomite."　　[27] RBI 154*; see below, pp. 170–71. Cf. RBI 378, sd 11.

[28] RBI 210*. Similarly, RBI sd 18, sd 20 (below, pp. 139–40).　　[29] RBI sd 3; below, pp. 194–95.

[30] BRII 59*.

126

Although these personal sureties undertook to perform the debtors' obligations on their own, they were not risking much. They pledged *potestas*, but *potestas* was, in the first place, not something that was theirs to keep and, second, something that they were capable of giving up at any moment (though they might not be willing to do so).[31] Castle guardians in control of pledged castles were not, however, the only form of personal surety available. Some individuals are named as guarantors of agreements without being given specific tasks; these are presumably influencing sureties. By the terms of a *convenientia* with Count Guillem I Ramon of Cerdanya (1068–95) for the castle of Lordat, Raimond de Niort was to offer as sureties (*obsides et federatores*) "those men whom the said count should request, through whom he might be faithful, so that he might maintain and adhere fully to everything as it is written."[32] Bernat Isarn, as part of his promise of service to Ramon Berenguer I, named two individuals as *fideiussores* "that he would hold and adhere to all this with respect to the said count without ill will"; the agreement does not detail particular responsibilities.[33] In one case, a surety was bound to aid the injured party against the violator, presumably as an enforcing surety, to compel adherence to the agreement.[34]

Many agreements assigned personal sureties a monetary value, thereby indicating that they fulfilled a paying or compensating role. Such sureties might serve to guarantee a simple debt. For example, Ramon Berenguer I offered two sureties (*plivii*) for a promised yearly payment of 6 ounces of gold from the *parias* to Ramon Mir d'Hostoles, and Guillem Ramon (II) Seneschal and Pelegrín de Castillazuelo promised to serve as *debitores* and *pagatores* for a debt of 1,500 *morabetins* owed by Alfons I.[35] The surety could also guarantee not a debt already incurred, but payment of a possible future penalty. Thus Bishop Berenguer Sunifred of Vic, in a *convenientia* for the castle of Sentfores, offered Guislabert Mir two *fideiussores* for payment of a money-fief for three years, but a separate *fideiussor* who was to compensate Guislabert Mir if the bishop failed to grant him his *cavalleria* at the end of that period.[36] A document from 1061 records a grant of sureties made three years after an initial agreement, suggesting that such measures were seen as extraordinary. Ricard Altemir had failed to perform the construction at Tàrrega required in his convention and oath to Ramon Berenguer I of 1058. No guarantees had been specified

---

[31] In the agreement of 1054 (above, n. 27), Ramon Ademar agreed to act as a pledge on the condition that Ramon Berenguer not make him give up possession of the castle if Guillem violated the agreement! (RBIV ap. 10*).

[32] *LFM* 627: "ambo donent predicto comiti obsides et federatores illos homines quos ei requisierit prephatus comes, per quos bene sit fidus."

[33] OM 5:41: "donet ei fideiussores . . . ut hoc totum teneat et atendat ad predictum comitem sine engan." Similarly, CCM 145.　　[34] Extra. 3233.　　[35] RBI 80; ALI 55*.　　[36] AME 8/87.

in the original agreement, so the count obtained from Ricard a grant of three sureties (*fideiussores*) for 1,000 *solidi* each that he would complete the works within a given term; if he failed, they were to pay the fine to the count within fifteen days.[37] Similarly, in a peasant recognition oath to the see of Vic in 1194, Pere Poc offered Ranulf as a *fideiussor* who was to pay 20 *solidi* to the see if Pere broke the agreement.[38]

Twenty *solidi* may have been enough to constitute an effective threat in the eyes of a peasant, but this was a paltry sum compared to the values assigned in contemporary *convenientiae* to sureties generally called hostages (*ostatici, obsides*). A hostage is a person held or potentially deprived of liberty by a second person in order to guarantee an undertaking by a third person. On the one hand, hostages are distinguished from other forms of personal surety in that they are subject to a physical, rather than a moral or financial obligation; they thus share the characteristics of real sureties, in that it is their bodies as physical objects that fulfill the function of guarantee. On the other hand, hostages are distinguished from captives. For an individual to act effectively as a hostage, both parties to an agreement must recognize the individual as such; although there are situations in which previously seized individuals become hostages, generally hostages are requested and granted, not taken.

The Catalan sources generally adhere to the core elements of this definition.[39] First, hostages are not captives. The family of Arnau Isarn made a donation to the see of Urgell in 1103 in order to gain a proper burial for him because he had failed to redeem his brother, who was serving as a hostage (*ostaticum*) in place of Arnau, who had fallen into captivity (*captivitas*).[40] Second, hostages are third parties. Ermengol III of Urgell granted to the counts of Barcelona two hostages (*obsides*) as a guarantee that he would make Guillem Guifré, bishop of Urgell, renounce his fidelity to the count of Cerdanya. In the same agreement he promised to make five of his men along with other *comitors* of Urgell who were also men of Ramon Guifré of Cerdanya renounce their fidelity to that count and support the alliance of the houses of Urgell and Barcelona. As these individuals stood surety for themselves, they were not hostages; the document refers to them as "pledged" ("faciat impignorare").[41] I have seen only one case in which the term hostage refers to principals in the agreement. In a *convenientia* of submission to Alfons I in 1170, Berenguer

---

[37] RBI 218*, sd 94* (a. 1058); 266* (a. 1061).
[38] ACV 6/2570. This document is analogous to peasant recognitions and commendations; see Freedman, *Origins*, 91–99. See also Extra. 3462, which deals with pledges for composition payments incurred for imprisonment (cf. Us. 15).
[39] Though not always: e.g., *DBarcelona* 217.
[40] DACU 1203: "Arnallus Isarni cecidit in captivitatem et misit fratrem suum ostaticum propter se ut adquireret et redimeret eum."   [41] RBI sd 2*.

de Correà and his son swore to the count that they would uphold the agreement, and to this end made their lords Ponç III, viscount of Cabrera (Girona), and Ponç de Santa Fe, along with his son Ponç, and their own vassal Arnau d'*Angela* also swear an oath to the count. If Berenguer and his son violated the agreement, all of them – "we and our said lords and Arnau d'*Angela*" – were to hand themselves over as hostages to the count.[42] This example is also distinct in that the hostages here are not assigned financial values. Most, though not all, Catalan hostages served to guarantee monetary obligations,[43] whether debts or penalties; some were to be redeemed by the debtor, while others were personally liable for payment.

Seven of Ramon Berenguer I's conventions involved the granting of hostages; three of these were with the count of Urgell. The counts concluded the first two agreements in preparation for their joint assault on the count of Cerdanya. In one, the count of Barcelona granted hostages to his northern cousin for 20,000 *solidi*, or 200 ounces of gold. The document lists five individuals (Amat Elderic, Ramon Guillem de Montcada, Mir Guifré, Geribert Mir, and Berenguer Ramon), responsible for 4,000 *solidi* (80 ounces) each in gold, silver, horses, mules, and coats of mail (*alsbergs*).[44] In return, the count of Urgell guaranteed his undertaking with hostages for an equal sum, although broken down differently: four sureties for 4,000 *solidi* each (Ricard Altemir, Arnau Mir de Tost, Isarn Ramon de Caboet, and Hug Guillem) and two for 2,000 each (Dalmau Isarn and his brother Bernat).[45] In each case the only detail given as to how the arrangement worked is that each set of hostages was given into the control (*potestas*) of the opposite count.

These agreements can be dated to 1043x44. The third agreement between the two counts, from two decades later, contained better arithmetic and slightly more detail on the procedures involved. Count Ermengol named five hostages for 10,000 *solidi*, one of whom had acted as a hostage in the earlier agreement (Dalmau Isarn; the others were Guitard Guillem de Meià, Brocard Guillem, Pere Mir, and Ramon Mir). In case of default, the five fell under the control ("incurrant in potestatem") of the count of Barcelona. If one of them died, the count of Urgell had to replace him. If a dispute arose concerning the hostages, it was to be submitted to judgment. Unlike the first two documents, this one is subscribed, and the subscriptions

---

[42] ALI 86: "nos et predicti seniores nostri et Ar(naldus) de Angela veniamus obsides in manum vestram a potestate vestra."   [43] Below, n. 54.

[44] RBI sd 1. A sixth hostage, Bernat Otger, was listed and then deleted. Cf. RBI sd 1bis.

[45] RBI sd 12*. In each case the arithmetic does not come out correctly: the gold equivalents add up to 400 ounces, rather than the 200 given as the equivalent in the texts. That is, in the total, the ratio is given as 100 *solidi* to the ounce, while in the individual figures it is 50 *solidi* to the ounce, the correct equivalence in this period (Bonnassie, *La Catalogne*, 1:388).

of the five hostages follow immediately that of the count himself.[46] Hostages for similar sums appear in other dealings between these two counts,[47] and they continued to be employed as a method of guarantee in the relations between their sons. To secure an agreement, Ermengol IV and Ramon Berenguer II granted each other, in addition to one castle apiece in pledge, ten hostages for 200 ounces of gold.[48]

Recourse to hostages was not limited to agreements between counts.[49] In 1061, Ponç Guerau I, viscount of Girona, secured an agreement with Ramon Berenguer I with a grant of ten hostages from among his men for a total of 20,000 *solidi*. In case of default, they fell under the control ("incurrant et veniant in potestatem") of Ramon and had ten days in which to redeem themselves, that is, pay their value to the count. Here too, if one of the hostages died, the viscount had to replace him, but he also had to replace any hostage who left his service. Eight of the ten hostages subscribed the document along with Ponç.[50] Four years later, Guerau Alemany (I) de Cervelló backed up an agreement with the count with a grant of five hostages for 2,000 *solidi* apiece. Two of these hostages, though, were only temporary; they were to serve in that capacity until the following Easter (four months later), at which point they were to be replaced with two others.[51] Finally, in an agreement announcing plans for the recapture of Tarragona, Guerau Alemany (II) de Cervelló, Arnau Mir, and Deusdé Bernat offered into the *potestas* of Berenguer Ramon II and Berenguer Sunifred, bishop of Vic, hostages for 2,000 *nummi* apiece as guarantees that they would hand over certain castles; if they failed to do so, the hostages had to redeem themselves.[52]

The key to how these hostages functioned lies in the phrase "in potestate." The hostages were not simply personal sureties for payment; their bodies served as real surety when kept under the control of another person. A *convenientia* in the 1050s between Guillem Guifré, bishop of Urgell, and Ramon Guifré of Cerdanya specifies that if Guillem failed to keep the agreement, his five hostages for 1,000 *solidi* each had to enter into the power of the count, "in the castle of Sant Martí, within the *solarium*, and from there they should not depart until the said funds have been given for them."[53] The hostages in an agreement between the viscounts

---

[46] RBI 299*.   [47] RBI sd 2*, sd 37; Extra. 3154=3204.   [48] RBII 69. See also RBI sd 11.
[49] In addition to the documents cited below, see RBI sd 32; RBIV 333*.   [50] RBI 268*.
[51] RBI 337.
[52] ACV 9/ii/75*. Lawrence J. McCrank, "Restauración canónica e intento de reconquista de la sede Tarraconense, 1076–1108," *Cuadernos de historia de España* 61–62 (1977), 212–21, misinterprets the role of the hostages in these documents.
[53] RBI sd 30* (=Extra. 4744.3): "in kastrum Sancti Martini intus in ipso solario, et inde non deses- chant usque eis prescriptum avere abeant donatum." For *solarium*, see Bonnassie, *La Catalogne*, 1:497 n. 70.

of Béziers and Ramon Berenguer I in 1070 had ten days after a default and failure to amend to report to "either the city of Carcassonne, or the castle of Saissac, or the castle of Laurac, or the castle of Rennes . . . and they shall not depart from there without the permission and will of the said count . . ." As no monetary value had been assigned to these hostages, they were required simply to "emend" any violation of the agreement.[54]

Documents from the next century confirm this procedure: hostages were to go to a particular place and remain there at the will of their holder. An agreement between Alfons I and the merchant *Trepelizinus* for a voyage to Constantinople – apparently in connection with a proposed marriage alliance between the house of Barcelona and the imperial family – includes a provision that if the count did not pay the merchant by the deadline, six barons were to serve as hostages at Marseille, where they were to remain within the walls until the debt was paid.[55] In the Treaty of Sahagún in 1170, Alfonso VIII of Castile offered Alfons I three hostages for tribute payments owed by Ibn Mardanīš (Lobo) of València and Murcia; they were to enter into the hand and *potestas* of Alfons I until the terms of the agreement were met, and they were not to depart without permission.[56] The twelfth-century evidence also reveals two further procedural developments. First, hostages acted for themselves in agreements; second, the holder of the hostages was not responsible for the cost of their maintenance. In 1157, Bishop Lope of Pamplona subscribed an agreement whereby he served as a hostage for Sancho VI of Navarre at the behest of the pope, promising not to depart without the count's permission; in a later agreement he promised to reimburse Ramon Berenguer IV for the costs of his hostageship.[57]

Some of the procedures for these agreements may have been adapted from the world of comital finance. Ramon Berenguer IV and Alfons I offered hostages for a series of heavy debts: 7 to Guillem Mainard for 2,500 *morabetins* in 1159;[58] 7 to Guilhem Leteric for 4,700 *morabetins* in 1157, followed by 10 for 6,700 *morabetins* in 1160, along with 6 more for the 6,000 *morabetins* remaining in 1162, and then 16 for 22,600 *solidi* in

---

[54] ALI 275.2*: "omnes ostatici iam dicti revertantur in potestatem de iam dictis Barcheonensi comite et comitissa et filio eorum Remundo aut in civitate Carcassona aut in castro de Sexag aut in castro Laurag aut in castro Redes aut in uno de istis castris quo commoniti fuerint ut ibi revertantur."

[55] ALI extra. 2621*; Shideler, *Montcadas*, 120–21; Ernest Marcos Hierro, *Die byzantinisch-katalanischen Beziehungen im 12. und 13. Jahrhundert unter besonderer Berücksichtigung der Chronik Jakobs I. von Katalonien-Aragon*, Miscellanea Byzantina Monacensia 37 (Munich, 1996), 142–43; Paul Magdalino, *The Empire of Manuel I Komnenos, 1143–1180* (Cambridge, 1993), 102.

[56] ALI 85*; Büschgens, *Die politischen Verträge*, 64–69. See also OM 11:2207.

[57] RBIV 297*, 316*. On this episode, see José Goñi Gaztambide, *Historia de los obispos de Pamplona*, vol. 1, *Siglos IV–XIII* (Pamplona, 1979), 404–8.

[58] RBIV ap. 6*. This transaction was a renegotiation of an earlier debt.

the reign of Alfons I;[59] 20 to Guilhem VII of Montpellier for 24,000 *morabetins* in 1171.[60] The agreements with Guilhem Leteric include the oaths of each of the hostages; the agreement with Guillem Mainard also refers to a separate document containing oaths.[61] Hostages granted to Guilhem Leteric had to declare themselves individually responsible for the entire sum; these agreements also included lists of secondary guarantors with the evocative designation of *manulevatores*. Comital accounts show that the count was paying the expenses of his hostages.[62]

In all of these conventions, hostages were chosen from among the most powerful men of the person offering the guarantee. Sancho VI of Navarre offered Bishop Lope of Pamplona; Alfonso VIII of Castile employed Counts Nuño Pérez and Pedro Manrique de Lara;[63] Ramon Berenguer I and Ramon Berenguer IV both turned to the Montcada family, the Ermengols of Urgell to Arnau Mir de Tost and other *comtors*. Lesser figures turned to their own vassals and even their lords.[64] The service of particular individuals may not have been as important as the service of members of a particular group or family. The Genoese consul Enrico specified hostages for the treaty of 1153 with Ramon Berenguer IV for the seizure of Tortosa as follows:

One will be [one] of the sons of Guillem Ramon Seneschal, and a second will be Berenguer de Torroja or his brother Arnau or his nephew Ramon; the third will be Guillem de Castellvell or his brother Arbert or his son Guillem. The fourth will be one of the sons of Pere Bertran de Bell-lloc, or Guillem de Cervera or his brother, or Guillem Pere de Castellet or his son, or Dalmau de Peratallada or his brother or son. From these aforesaid eight [*recte* seven] lineages (*genera*) the count will give five hostages . . . with the noble Arnau de Llers, who is the eighth.[65]

Among the hostages for a debt of Alfons I to Guilhem Leteric were Sanç, the king's brother, and the unnamed sons of Ramon Folc III, viscount

---

[59] RBIV 296* (a. 1157); sd 15*, ap. 8* (a. 1160); ap. 9*, ap. 9dup* (a. 1162); ALI extra. 3627*. See also above, n. 35.   [60] ALI 105*.

[61] "sub illo sacramento quod tibi fecimus in alia carta."

[62] ALI 140* ("remansit in debito super dominum regem ad persolvendum, computatis similiter pignoribus supradictorum burgensium, xxi milia et dcc solidos melgorienses, preter expensam et conductum hostaticorum").

[63] Büschgens, *Die politischen Verträge*, 65; Simon Barton, *The Aristocracy in Twelfth-Century León and Castile*, CSMLT, 4th ser., 34 (Cambridge, 1997), 269–70, 282–83.   [64] ALI 86.

[65] RBIV 266quad*(=266quin*): "Quorum obsidum erit unus ex filiis Guilelmi Raimundi Dapiferi, et alius erit Berengarius de Torroia aut frater eius Arnaldus aut nepos eius Raimundus. Tercius erit Guilelmus de Castelvel aut frater eius Arbertus aut filius eius Guilelmus. Quartus erit unus ex filiis Petri Bertrandi de Bello Loco, aut Guilelmus de Cervaria uel frater eius, aut Guilelmus Petri de Castelet, vel filius eius, aut Dalmacius de Perataiada aut frater eius vel filius eius. Ex supradictis viii generibus dabit comes v obsides quales habere potuerit cum ipsa companna Arnalli de Lercio, que est in octavo numero."

of Cardona (Osona), Guillem de Castellvell, Jofre I, viscount of Rocabertí (Peralada), Bertrand des Baux, Porcell, and Guillem Ramon Gantelm.[66]

Why were such individuals chosen? In some cases, though certainly not all, the captivity of a son would increase pressure on the father to pay, and whether it was the father or the son who was held, the families of great barons and royal financiers would be better able to pay redemptions at the high values set. The existence of hostages for different amounts within individual agreements suggests that the figures might have been established on the basis of ability to pay. If it were just a question of money, however, it is unlikely that hostages would have been an effective mechanism of guarantee. A party could decide to violate the agreement and foot the bill for his hostages. Furthermore, the repetition of certain very high figures for hostages in the agreements (10,000 or 20,000 *solidi*) suggests that these were simply formulae. The primary concern of a party to a *convenientia* was the performance of the agreement, not compensation for a default. Ramon Berenguer I, especially after his treasury had been enriched by the *parias*, was certainly not in need of additional sources of income.

In the case of hostages for debts, such as those granted to Guilhem Leteric, the ability to pay is clearly paramount. In the *convenientiae*, however, other factors predominate. Alfonso VIII of Castile proposed a replacement for Count Pedro Manrique de Lara if he should cease to be a vassal of the king. Similarly, Ponç Guerau I had to replace not only hostages who died, but any who "may separate themselves from the lordship or benefice of the said viscount."[67] Combined with the usual requirement of confinement, these cases suggest that a good hostage was someone whose service, rather than his resources, was valuable. The best hostage might have been someone whom the other party would not want as an adversary, or someone whose absence would significantly diminish an opponent's power. Elements of honor or of duty to one's subordinates when they were serving as hostages may be involved here, perhaps revealing a nascent set of noble mores: the hostages received by Ramon Berenguer I from the viscounts of Béziers were forbidden to *desexire*, a term more generally used in the context of rejection of lordship.[68]

---

[66] ALI extra. 3627*. Porcell is probably Porcell (II) de Caldes; see Thomas N. Bisson, "Ramon de Caldes (*c.* 1135–1199): Dean of Barcelona and King's Minister," in *Medieval France*, 190 n. 21.

[67] RBI 268*: "Et si predicti ostatici mortui fuerint, aut aliquis ex illis, aut se separaverint a senioratico vel beneficio predicti vicecomitis, iamdictus vicecomes restituat alios hostaticos vel hostaticum in loco illorum vel illius in potestatem de iamdictis comite et comitissa sine illorum engan."

[68] *GMLC*, s.v.

PROCEDURE

Whatever the nature of the guarantee, and whether or not there was a guarantee, some conventions indicated simply that default would lead to loss of the pledge or annulment of the agreement. In others, however, the penalty clauses and guarantees only came into effect after a process. This is described completely in only a few documents, but elements in others correspond to these fuller accounts. The process as it appears in the *convenientiae* of Ramon Berenguer I and his immediate successors includes four steps: default, warning, opportunity to amend, and application of sanctions.

The language used to describe the violation of the agreement is in most cases very general, not referring specifically to the terms of the convention, but simply foreseeing that the convention would not be adhered to. Phrases such as "If N. does not keep and adhere to" ("Si . . . non tenuerit et non attenderit"),[69] echoing the positive vernacular oath "si o tenre et o atenre," are common. Alternatively, the default could be described in an active fashion as violating the agreement, in which case scribes had a more colorful vocabulary on which to draw: *infringere, passare, se abstrahere, transgredere, facere malum, facere forsfacturam, disrumpere, minuare.* Two or more of these terms often appear in conjunction.

The violation led to a summons or notification by the counts that they considered the agreement violated. The most common term used for this action was "to warn" (*commonere*), as in the phrase "after they warn him . . . in the name of this *convenientia*." [70] "Complain," "order," and "demand" (*querelare, mandare, requirere*) appear less frequently.[71] The summons could be delivered by the counts themselves, or by their messengers (*missi, nuncii*). Some of the documents specify that these messengers are not to be detained or abused (*reguardum habere*), and that the summoned individual should not ignore the warning ("non vedet se inde cumunir"). This language recalls that used to describe the treatment of messengers who demand *potestas* of castles.[72]

The violator was granted a certain period within which to respond to this summons. The length of this period in conventions is anywhere from fifteen days to six months and was subject to change over time

---

[69] RBI 287*.

[70] RBI 154*, 268* ("postquam predicti comes et comitissa comonuerint inde iamdictum vicecomitem per nomen aut in nomine de ista convenientia"), 287*, 292*, 299*, sd 11, sd 207*; ALI 275.2*.

[71] *Querelare*: RBI 320*, 328. *Mandare*: RBI 296*, 321.1*, 376*; Extra. 4726; OM 5:41; *LFM* 40. *Requirere*: RBI 162*, 273.1*.

[72] RBI 268*, 299*, sd 4; cf., e.g., RBI 331*. *Vetare* also carries judicial connotations (Jan Frederik Niermeyer, *Mediae Latinitatis lexicon minus*, ed. C. van de Kieft [Leiden, 1976; repr. 1993], s.v.).

Table 3.1. *Grace period before default in
convenientiae of the eleventh-century counts of
Barcelona*#

Document	Date	Period (Days)
RBI sd 3	1039x50	[1]20
RBI sd 207★	1039x50	60/30
RBI 120	1051	100
RBI 154★	1054	180/90
RBI sd 11	1054	30/15
RBI 162★	1055	20
RBI 225	1058	60
RBI 268★	1061	60
RBI 273.1★	1062	40
RBI 287★	1062	60
RBI 296★	1062	60
RBI 299★	1062	50
RBI 292★	1063	60
LFM 40	1064	40
RBI 328	1064	15
RBI 320★	1065	30
RBI 321.1★	1065	30
RBI 358	1065	30
RBI 376★	1067	30
ALI 275.2★	1070	20
OM 5:41	1071	30
RBII 69	1076x82	30/10
RBII 67★	1078x82	30
BRII 59★	1089	30
BRII 62★	1089	30

Note:
Undated: RBI sd 4 (1052x71); Extra. 4726 (1066x76);
both 60 days. In conventions of other counts: RBI 306★
(Pallars, a. 1064), 100 days; BRII 70★ (Besalú, a. 1089), 30
days; *LFM* 598 (Cerdanya, a. 1068x95), 30 days; *LFM* 698
(Empúries/Rosselló, a. 1085), 40 days.

(Table 3.1).[73] During this period, one of four things could happen. First,
the individual could pay or perform a penalty (*emendare*), which seems to
have been set by an ad hoc judicial assembly. This, at any rate, is the most

[73] Other examples: ACV 9/ii/76, 30 days; ACB 1–2–1253, 40 days; LA 4:308★, 30 days; RBIV 266★,
15/40 days; RBI sd 30★=Extra. 4744.3, 30 days; ACA, Diversos, Varia 10 (Vilanova Rosselló), leg.
1, doc. 5, no. 2 (p. 2), 10 days; AAM, Sant Cugat del Vallès 159, 10 days; ALI 589, 30 days; *Remences*
6, 30 days. See also two related documents of Ramon Berenguer I: RBI sd 2★, 15 days; RBI 266★,
15 days. The preference for a sixty-day grace period was particularly strong during the period
1058–64.

likely interpretation of the common phrase "according to the judgment of those men whom the said count and countess, or one of them, shall order to judge this matter."[74] A few of the documents specified the quality of the judges (*boni homines, iudices, barones homines*) or named them. In one convention between the counts of Barcelona and Urgell, the judges were to be appointed by both sides: "according to the judgment of four men whom the said count of Barcelona shall choose, and four others whom the said count of Urgell shall choose."[75] The counts could accept this penalty, or they could decline it. Second, the violator could reach an accord with the count, variously described as a *placitum* or *condonamentum*. Several documents add that this would be done on the counts' mercy, suggesting that the accord would result in a lesser penalty than that dictated by the judges.[76] Third, before or after a penalty was offered, the counts could pardon (*perdonare, absolvere*) the violation. This, too, was done on the counts' mercy, although a few of the documents suggest potential problems with this solution when they add that the pardon should be "with free will" or "freely, without force" ("libenti animo," "per gratum sine forcia").[77] Fourth and finally, if the summoned party failed to make amends, or if the counts rejected the proffered penalty, as was their right, the convention was violated and the sanctions (pledges, hostages, etc.) came into effect. Many of the documents add that the sanctions had to be observed peacefully ("sine ira et marrimento," or "sine rancura") by the violator and his family and associates (*amici*). This even applied to the count of Barcelona. In an agreement to provide a certain Bernat Amat with pigs in return for the lodging rights (*alberga*) of Terrassa, failure on the part of the count was to result in the reversion of the rights to Bernat "without the anger or hindrance or ill will of the said count and the lady countess Almodis, and their children."[78] The count's default is foreseen, it should be noted, in only two other cases.[79] *Convenientiae* were Ramon Berenguer I's instrument of power, and scribes inserted these clauses in his documents primarily for his benefit.

In three exceptional cases, two involving counts of Urgell and one

---

[74] RBI 328: "ad iuditium de illis hominibus quas predicti comes et comitissa aut unus illorum mandaverint hoc iudicare." Also RBI 162*, 320*, 321.1*, sd 3; OM 5:41; Extra. 4726. RBI 321.1*, a twelfth-century copy, reads in error *vindicare* for *iudicare*. On one case (RBI 296*) the phrase ends "miserint ad iudicandum ipsum placitum," suggesting a confusion between this dictated penalty and a negotiated settlement.

[75] RBI 162*, 174*, sd 3; OM 5:41; Extra. 4726 ("ad iudicium de quatuor homines quos iamdictus comes Barchinonensis eligat et de alios quatuor quos iam dictus Urgellensis comes eligat").

[76] RBI 268*, 296*, 321.1*, 376*; OM 5:41. Cf. RBI 419*.

[77] RBI 154*, 225, 287*, 292*, sd 4; *LFM* 40.

[78] RBI 358: "sine ira et marrimento et mala voluntate de iam dicto comite et de domna Almodis comitissa et de filiis illorum."   [79] RBI 80, 143*.

involving the viscounts of Béziers, a further procedural mechanism was put in place to insure the stability of the agreements. The agreement of 1062 between Ramon Berenguer I and Ermengol III provides for the possibility of a dispute concerning hostages. The two counts would choose judges to arbitrate the dispute. If the judges could not reach an agreement, the dispute would move to trial by battle. In an agreement with Ermengol IV, a judicial duel is specified if the eight judges elected by the counts to decide the penalty for Ermengol's default could not agree.[80] In the agreement with the viscounts of Béziers, a judicial duel is called for if they were to refuse to amend a default.[81]

In the end, these procedures for the settlement of disputes, like the specific guarantees provided by pledges and hostages, were heavily dependent on the willingness of parties to observe the various terms. In some cases, the many layers of judgments, pledges, and waiting periods seem to suggest that the parties expected the rules to be broken. Guarantees could be added to guarantees without end. In 1090, Guillem Hug offered Arnau Arnau de Llers and his son as pledges to Bernat II of Besalú. If Guillem Hug violated the agreement and ignored the summons, the pledges were to be summoned to amend the wrong. If they failed to do so, they were to pay 200 ounces of Valencian gold in kind. If they failed to pay, then some of Guillem Hug's lands would become forfeit to the count, and the pledges were to assist the count in recovering them.[82] But what was the next step? What would happen if the pledges did not support the count? The count's only remedy would be to resort to force.

While spiritual sanctions predominate in other documents of the eleventh century, in the comital *convenientia* they – like verbal invocations and devotion formulae – are nowhere to be found.[83] It is as if the *convenientia* were a document from another period, from the tenth or the later twelfth century, when comital power was more consistently strong. If the convention is seen as an instrument of comital control, however, the ultimate reliance on force makes sense. Force was the ultimate guarantee behind the *convenientia*, just as it had been the ultimate guarantee of the decisions of comital *placita*. Even if the count was not always in a position to use his power, the *convenientia*, like the *placitum*, offered him a means of claiming it.

---

[80] RBI 299*; Extra. 4726.   [81] ALI 275.2*. Also RBI sd 18 (below, pp. 139–40).
[82] BRII 70*; see Gaspar Feliu i Montfort, "Existí el comte Bernat III de Besalú?" *Acta historica et archaeologica mediaevalia* 19 (1998), 391–402, which demonstrates that Bernat II and "Bernat III" are the same person.
[83] Adam J. Kosto, "The *convenientiae* of the Catalan Counts in the Eleventh Century: A Diplomatic and Historical Analysis," *Acta historica et archaeologica mediaevalia* 19 (1998), 196–97, 200; cf. 222.

CASE STUDIES: PALLARS AND EMPÚRIES/ROSSELLÓ

A series of settlements between the counts of the two halves of Pallars illustrate in a fuller context the complexity of procedures involved in the keeping of agreements. Ramon IV of Pallars Jussà (1047–98) and Artau I (1049–81) and II (1081–c. 1115) of Pallars Sobirà were not only frequent opponents on the battlefield; they often found themselves opposing each other in litigation.[84] Their disputes may be traced over half a century through a rich series of conventions and other documents. The conventions, which are often very difficult to interpret, stand out because of their concern not only with settlement itself, but with the procedures of settlement. These enter into the documents in three ways. First, conventions record agreements that arrange and explicitly guarantee the process of settlement. Second, conventions record grants or exchanges of property made in order to bring a dispute to a close. Third, conventions record arrangements guaranteeing the stability of the outcome of these settlements.

The first of these conventions between the two counts is dated 1064. It is called a *convenientia* only in the closing formulae. The title makes clear its subject: "This is the written commemoration of the settlement and quitclaim (*fine et perdonamentum*)."[85] The specifics of the dispute are not recorded in the text. Artau I promised to keep the agreement and offered specific assurances. He named a castle to serve as a pledge (*pignus*) for the agreement and explained how the pledge would function. If Artau did not keep the agreement and did not make amends within 100 days of being notified of the breach of the agreement, the castle pledged would pass freely to Ramon. Three years later, on a day appointed in a previous agreement (now lost), Artau quitclaimed a long list of castles and lands to Ramon, including many of the lands he had granted to Ramon in the agreement from three years before, on the condition that they hold another *placitum* to settle their differences.[86] The document provides no details concerning this future meeting. Although the quitclaim included all of the *villae* exchanged in the earlier agreement, as well as the monas-

---

[84] See Bonnassie, *La Catalogne*, 2:612–18; Ferran Valls i Taberner, "Els orígens dels comtats de Pallars i Ribagorça," *Estudis universitaris catalans* 9 (1915–16), 1–101; Lydia Martínez i Teixidó, *Les famílies nobles del Pallars en els segles XI i XII*, Estudis 3 (Lleida, 1991).

[85] RBI 306★: "Hec est scriptura rememoracionis de fine et perdonamentum."

[86] RBI 378: "Hec est conveniencia que facta est inter Raimundo comite, [filio Ermessen] comitessa, et Artallo comite, filio Estefania. Facit predictus Artall finem ad predictum Reimundo comite de ipsa onore sua quem tenet predictus Reimundo comitem ad diem primum de ipsa quatuor tempora de iunio que inter ipsos est nominata." This passage refers to the ember day following Pentecost, which fell on 30 May in 1067, the date of the document. Meetings (*placita*) were often set up in advance, although often not for a specific day, but for a range of days (e.g., within thirty days, within one hundred days). In one case a meeting was put off indefinitely, pending the outcome of a war (*LFM* 128).

tery of Santa Maria de Lavaix, only one castle (Enrens) was affected. This suggests that the other castles were the intended subject of the *placitum*. Artau gave several castles in pledge that he would keep the present agreement, and he swore an oath to that effect. No record of Ramon's pledge has survived.

The next documents are a series of four undated conventions, probably from *c.* 1080. They may be closely related, referring to a single dispute and accompanying process of settlement. It is impossible to prove this conclusively, despite the fact that the four have considerable overlap in the persons and places involved. Even if they do not represent a single incident, however, they are all a part of the long-term dispute between the two counts.[87] Although the language of these texts is sometimes confusing, they offer more information than the first two conventions about the details of the process. The richest of these documents is an agreement between Ramon IV and a Count Artau in which they essentially agreed to agree: "This is the *convenientia* that Count Ramon and Count Artau made, that they would do right to each other with respect to the conflicts that they have."[88] After this statement of intention, they went on to agree on how they would go about agreeing. First, a day had to be set for a *placitum*; the text is not particularly lucid here, but it seems to suggest that it was to fall within the thirty days following a given date, upon demand of one of the parties.[89] A place was appointed for the meeting, as were the judges. If the barons (*barones*) from each side could arrive at a decision, that decision would be binding on the two counts. If they could not agree, however, the decision would be made by ordeal. If either did not appear and had a legitimate excuse, the *placitum* was to be held within the next thirty days, on a day set by the party who did appear. Finally, each count assigned a pledge to assure his performance of the judgment. The pledges were, as was usual, castles. The *potestas* of each castle was granted to a third party, who swore to render the castle to the aggrieved count in case of a failure to comply with the judgment. Specifically, Ramon handed over the castle of Talarn to two of his barons, Pere Ramon (I) d'Erill and Mir Guirreta (II) de Bellera, while Artau handed over Salàs to two of his men, Guillem Guitard de Vallferrera and Ramon Bernat. Talarn and Salàs sit less than 5 km apart on the banks of the Noguera

[87] RBI sd 17*, sd 18, sd 19*, sd 20. For texts and dating, see Kosto, "Agreements," 230–33.
[88] RBI sd 18: "In Dei nomine hec est convenieniencia [*sic*] quem faciunt Raimundo comite et Artallo comite que se faciunt directos de ipsas querelas que abet unus quisque de alio usque ad istum diem." Artau II succeeded his father in 1081.
[89] "Et convenit Raimundo comite ad Artallo comite que de ipso die in antea, de mediante die augusti usque infra xxxª dies, quod si Artallo comite primus mandaverit ipsum placitum a Raimundo comite, faciat ad illum directum. Et si Raimundo comite primus mandaverit ipsum placitum ad Artallo comite, infra ipsos xxx dies iamdictos, faciat ad illum directum Artallo."

Pallaresa, at the frontier of Pallars Jussà and Pallars Sobirà; Pere Ramon and Mir Guirreta were two of Ramon IV's most powerful men. These pledges were of a very high value.

A second *convenientia* also discusses the mechanics of settlement, rather than substantive issues; it is complicated, however, by the involvement of the king of Aragón, Sancho Ramírez (1063–94). The scribe labeled it an agreement concerning pledges – "This is the *conveniencia* concerning the pledges that Count Ramon and Count Artau grant to each other" – but it is more complicated than a simple exchange of guarantees.[90] A secondary dispute between Artau and the king was to be resolved before, or at the same time as, the dispute between Artau and Ramon. This is confirmed by a passage deleted from the convention just discussed: Artau and the king were to "do right" with respect to one another on the same day as the *placitum* between Artau and Ramon.[91] It also seems that the king was being engaged to arbitrate the dispute, for Ramon and Artau agreed that if the king did not appear at the *placitum*, they would hold it before the king's men, just as if it were before the king. As in the previous convention, a time and a place were set for the *placitum*, judges were named, and pledges were granted for the counts' appearance.

The two other documents refer not to the mechanics of the disputes, but to the content of the settlement. It is for this reason, no doubt, that only these two documents were included in the *Liber feudorum maior* (*LFM*); portions of the first two documents that were not repeated in the second two, referring only to process, not results, became irrelevant once the dispute was settled. The scribe labeled the first document a "conveniencia et fine et perdonamento"; the use of the same terms seen in the convention of 1064 to refer to an agreement ending a dispute is noteworthy.[92] In the first section of the agreement, Ramon granted and quitclaimed to Artau various castles and other lands; in the second, Artau granted and quitclaimed to Ramon a different set. In addition, each forgave the other all past injuries, promised not to build castles in the other's territory, and promised to keep the agreement. That this was a settlement of a dispute is clear from the language ("fine et perdonamento," "forasfacturas") and from the fact that the convention was executed "in the presence and by the order of King Sancho"; this was not so much a mutually agreed compromise as it was a settlement imposed, with an unknown degree of persuasion, by a third party.[93] It thus corresponds to the procedural agreement above that designated the king as arbiter.

---

[90] RBI sd 20: "Hec est conveniencias de pignoras que se mittant Raimundo comite et Artallo comite."

[91] RBI sd 18: "[Similiter convenit Artallo comite que faciat directum ad ipso rege ad ipsum diem. Et rege ad illum.]"   [92] RBI sd 17★.   [93] "in presencia et mandamento de Sancio rege."

The last document of the four is nearly identical to the second half of the balanced agreement just mentioned: this convention, subscribed only by Ramon and Artau, records solely the donations and quitclaims of Artau to Ramon, with some minor alterations.[94] This is, perhaps, a working document from the negotiations leading to the final compromise. The date given of the third week of July would be a week before the final agreement, formally composed before the king on 26 July. It should not be surprising that a dispute of this sort could be ended by an exchange of castles, especially considering that the castles themselves were the most likely subject of the dispute.

A *convenientia* dated 20 July 1094 describes a last eleventh-century compromise between the two houses. The document, the bulk of which concerns the commendation of Llimiana and Mur by Ramon IV to Artau II, begins with a grant, as alods, of the castles of Castellet and Claverol and the Vall d'Escós. These were given in return for – or, more accurately, as part of – the agreement ("fine et perdonamento") assented to by Ramon with respect to lands disputed from the time of Artau's father.[95] A *carta commutacionis* dated three weeks later (9 August 1094), in which Claverol and Castellet are included in a much more extensive exchange of castles, provides further evidence that the context of the act was the settlement of a dispute.[96] The complex series of agreements of *c.* 1080 had not put an end to the conflict between these two counties.

Eight documents survive to chronicle the course of this thirty-year period of a much longer dispute between the counties of Pallars Jussà and Pallars Sobirà. The parties employed a wide range of sanctions, guarantees, and disputing procedures: real sureties of castles and other lands; executing sureties to ensure their delivery; promises; oaths; quitclaims; and *placita* involving judges, ordeals, and the participation of the king of Aragón. The constant need for new negotiations indicates that despite all of this, the individual agreements were not in fact kept. Does this mean that the various mechanisms for keeping agreements failed? In one sense, yes. In a broader sense, however, the agreement between the two counts is not to be found in the individual arrangements, but rather in the ongoing process: the agreement to remain in a constant state of negotiation, mediated and propelled along by these various mechanisms of guarantee. Because of the structures established, violation of one agreement led directly into the formation of a new one. From this perspective,

---

[94] RBI sd 19★.

[95] RBIII 26★ (=Extra. 3293): "hoc facit per fine et perdonamento que Artallo comite facit a Raimundo comite de tota ipsa honore que abebat ad illo querelata qui fuit de Artallo, suo patre." Claverol and Castellet were among the castles quitclaimed by Artau I to Ramon IV in the dispute from *c.* 1080.

[96] RBIII 27★: "Et desino [vobis] ipsas querellas . . . Et definimus vobis ipsa querella . . ."

the guarantees succeeded. These particular *convenientiae* were not end-points, but intermediate stages in a developing relationship; pledges, guarantors, and settlement procedures kept the process alive. In the same way that donation of a certain piece of land established a framework for a relationship between a family and a monastery, a relationship that could be reaffirmed by repeated donation of the same piece of land,[97] *convenientiae*, disputes about *convenientiae*, and their guarantees established a framework for the relationship between these two counts. Not all written agreements functioned in this way, but the example of the counts of Pallars encourages a broader conception of what it meant to keep an agreement in medieval Catalonia.

A series of agreements between the counts of Rosselló and Empúries-Peralada reveals a different set of guarantee mechanisms, highlighting the importance of regional differences and individual political circumstances in the maintenance of agreements. Although the two regions had been governed separately since 991, they remained closely related, with each count maintaining lands, rights, and interests in the other's territory.[98] Thus in a *convenientia* of 1085, Hug II of Empúries promised Guislabert II of Rosselló not to seize the *honor* held by the latter in the counties of Empúries and Peralada; the bishopric of Elna; the viscounties of Tatzó (Rosselló), Empúries, and Peralada; and a number of monasteries and castles both north and south of the Alberes mountains, the geographical boundary between the regions. The terms for distribution of judicial revenues reveal the extent of the connections. If both counts were present at a *placitum*, they would split the proceeds; each count had to inform the other of any *placita* taking place in his territory to give him the opportunity to attend. Hug's *convenientia* even promises the count of Rosselló rights of *statica* in the town of Empúries, with permission to collect all comital revenues during his stay.[99]

If Hug violated the agreement, he was to do right to Guislabert within forty days of a formal warning at the Coll de l'Espill,[100] where the dispute would be judged by the *boni homines* of the two counts. If Hug failed to appear at the appointed place within the appointed time, pledges would incur, "as it states in the *scriptura pignoracionis* that I granted to you."[101]

---

[97] Barbara H. Rosenwein, *To Be the Neighbor of Saint Peter: The Social Meaning of Cluny's Property, 909–1049* (Ithaca, 1989), 49–77.

[98] Santiago Sobrequés, *Els barons de Catalunya*, 4th ed., Història de Catalunya, Biografies catalanes, 3 (Barcelona, 1989), 7–17, 38–41.

[99] *LFM* 698. This agreement was an advance upon an earlier arrangement: ADPO B4, 74*. See also RBI sd 191*.

[100] A pass in the Alberes on the border between the two counties (*LFM* 709; Ramon d'Abadal i de Vinyals, ed., *Els diplomes carolingis a Catalunya*, vol. 2 of *Catalunya carolíngia*, 2 parts, Memòries de la Secció històrico-arqueològica 2 [Barcelona, 1926–52], 2:393–94).

[101] "sicut resonat in ipsam [[scripturam pignoracionis quod ego tibi feci."

This document also survives, dated on the same day as the agreement.[102] In it, Hug pledged his half of the abbey of Sant Pere de Rodes along with his half of the bishopric of Elna. The document repeats the provisions for warning, waiting period, and judgment contained in the *convenientia*, but foresees additional problems. If the pledges of either party were encumbered – Hug's *scriptura pignoracionis* refers explicitly to the counter-pledges that Guislabert offered to him – the *boni homines* were to decide about their disposition. If Hug's men refused to take part in the judgment, and Hug refused to recognize the judgment of Guislabert's men, immediately Guislabert's pledges were to be released and Hug's would incur.

While the pledges offered by Hug demonstrate again the close territorial ties between the two counties, they also show how political and geographical circumstances inevitably affected security arrangements for agreements. Sant Pere de Rodes lay clearly within the county of Empúries, yet Guislabert had a half interest in it; similarly, Elna was in the county of Rosselló, yet Hug claimed rights there. While Guislabert could easily have seized the revenues of the bishopric, he would have had a harder time claiming Sant Pere de Rodes. The role of the *boni homines* would thus have been particularly important here, not only as judges, but also as enforcing sureties. Jofre III of Rosselló (1113–64) renewed these agreements on identical terms with Ponç Hug I (1116–53x54) in 1121 and Hug III (1153x54–73) in 1154.[103] While the agreements between the counts of Pallars Jussà and Pallars Sobirà referred freely to the tensions between the two, these agreements suggest a steady condition of peace. This was not the case. Jofre III sided with Ramon Berenguer III in his war with Ponç Hug I in 1128, and in 1147 the two came into direct conflict over the castle of Requesens.[104] As in the case of Pallars, however, the framework provided by *convenientiae* and guarantee mechanisms that were perhaps wishful thinking nevertheless allowed for the easy resumption of a state of peace; in the short term, the agreements were broken, but in the long term, they were kept.

OATHS

The agreements of 1121 and 1154 between the counts of Empúries and Rosselló produced not only *convenientiae* and *scripturae pignorationis*, but oaths. These included, unusually, dating clauses that show that they were

---

[102] *LFM* 699.
[103] *LFM* 700, 701, 704, 705. The agreement may have been renewed again in 1165 (Sobrequés, *Els barons*, 57 [n. 37], citing *NH* 25, p. 95).
[104] *LFM* 711, 712; Sobrequés, *Els barons*, 11–12, 15–16, 40.

subscribed on the same days as the other documents. In each, the count of Empúries swore fidelity to the count of Rosselló, promising aid "just as stated in the *scriptura conveniencie* that I granted to you and subscribed."[105] Were these oaths also guarantees? The possibility that the oath of fidelity served as another layer of guarantee for *convenientiae* is particularly important in the case of those *convenientiae* concerning grants of castles and promises of military service.[106] The oath, along with the act of homage and the grant of a fief, is one of the classic constituents of the vassalic contract. This model does not apply universally in southern lands, where fidelity may exist independently of homage or a corresponding grant of a fief.[107] Nevertheless, a parallel trio does appear in the Catalan evidence: a *convenientia* in which one party grants land and the other party promises services; an oath of fidelity, in which one party swears that he or she will behave in certain ways, many of which echo undertakings recorded in the *convenientia*; and allusions or explicit references in one or both of these documents to the ritual of homage. Such oath/convention/homage groupings may be pieced together for several of Ramon Berenguer I's *convenientiae*.[108] A few oaths even refer specifically to their attendant *convenientiae*.[109] The oath and *convenientia* thus form a natural pair, and while the oaths do not themselves contain penalty clauses, they implicitly add the threat of additional sanctions – spiritual punishment for perjury and temporal loss of honor – for violation of the contract represented by the *convenientia*.[110]

Yet the relationship between oath and *convenientia* is not that simple. The oath was not merely an extended penalty clause, an added guarantee of the agreement represented in the *convenientia*. First, oaths and

---

[105] *LFM* 702 ("sicut resonat in scripture conveniencia quam ego tibi feci atque firmavi"), 706 ("sicut scriptura conveniencie dicit, quam ego feci tibi atque firmavi").

[106] Ourliac, "La *convenientia*," 245: "Certains actes indiquent nettement que le serment et la *fides* ont été ajoutés à la *convenientia*, apparemment comme un supplément de garantie."

[107] Élisabeth Magnou-Nortier, "Fidélité et féodalité méridionales d'après les serments de fidélité (Xᵉ–début XIIᵉ siècle)," *AM* 80 (1968), 457–77. This assumption could be usefully extended to northern lands, as well; see Susan Reynolds, *Fiefs and Vassals: The Medieval Evidence Reinterpreted* (Oxford, 1994), 11.

[108] E.g., RBI 218* ("stet in illorum hominatico"), sd 94*; 296* ("sint illorum homines"), sd 137*; 287*, sd 117* ("sicut homo debet esse fidelis ad seniorem suum cui manibus se comendat"); 292*, sd 61* ("sicut homo debet esse fidelis ad seniorem suum cui manibus se comendat"); 443* ("quod homo debet facere per suum meliorum seniorum"), sd 201*; 320* ("sicut homo debet esse suis senioribus quibus manibus se comendat"), sd 92*. Cf. RBIII extra. 3601.1*, sd 40*; RBII 2*, with *LFM* 96; ACV 9/ii/71=9/ii/72=9/ii/73, 9/ii/74=RBII 43.1*.

[109] RBIII 236*, 241.2*, with *LFM* 700, 520 (cit. Michel Zimmermann, "Aux origines de la Catalogne féodale: Les serments non datés du règne de Ramon Berenguer Iᵉʳ," in *La formació i expansió*, 143 n. 181); RBI sd 137*, 296*. See also Magnou-Nortier, "Fidélité et féodalité," 461–62, 468–69.

[110] Lothar Kolmer, *Promissorische Eide im Mittelalter*, Regensburger historische Forschungen 12 (Kallmünz, 1989), 314–35.

conventions do not always survive in pairs; the existence of one does not necessarily imply the existence of the other. In some cases this could be a question of archival practice, but it is unlikely, for example, that when the count commended a castle to a lord, separate *convenientiae* were in all cases drawn up between the count and each of that lord's *castlans*; separate oaths, however, do survive.[111] Two oaths to Ramon Berenguer I include lists of those who swore fidelity, eight in one case, ten in the other.[112] Second, oaths may accompany documents that are not standard *convenientiae*. The countess Ermessenda swore a long oath at the time of her quitclaim (*vendicio et evacuacio atque definicio*) of lands to her grandson in 1057, while Bernard Odo swore an oath to Ramon Berenguer I after selling him his castle of Dorna in 1069.[113] Scribal creativity, flexibility, and in some cases inconsistency allowed for such pairings.

Even when standard oath/convention pairs do exist, the functional distinction between them is not always clear. In some cases the oath is simply a short adjunct to a more detailed convention, but in others the oath recapitulates at length the content of the *convenientia*, making specific references to its terms. This close verbal connection between oath and convention was present in the earliest surviving pairs, such as the documents describing the agreement between the count and bishop of Urgell discussed in chapter 1. This apparent redundancy continued well after this period of crystallization of the form of the *convenientia*. Both the oath and *convenientia* of Bernat and Mir Riculf for the castles of Balsareny and Gaià in 1062, for example, specify that the brothers are to aid the counts in defending: the city and county of Barcelona, along with their fortified sites; the city, county, and bishopric of Girona, along with their fortified sites; the city of Manresa, county of Osona, and see of Vic, along with their fortified sites; the county of Penedès; the castles of Cardona, Tàrrega, Camarasa, Cubells, Estopanyà, Canelles, and Purroi; and the *parias*. Each document also records the promise of the brothers to grant *potestas* of the castles of Balsareny and Gaià on demand, as well as instructions for how the agreement should be kept after the death of various parties.[114] Significant differences remain between the two documents, even on the level of content: only the *convenientia* includes the undertakings of the counts, the detailed listings of services due, and the procedures for dispute settlement, while only the oath contains the brothers' promise not to harm the counts and mention of the possibility of release from the agreement. Nevertheless, the repetition of so much of the detail

---

[111] E.g., *LFM* 41, 42, 43, 140 (rubric only); RBorrell 119*; RBI sd 109*, sd 136*.
[112] RBI sd 112, sd 144. RBI sd 53 appears to be from eleven members of the *curia* (cit. Zimmermann, "Aux origines," 125 n. 77). See also RBI sd 186, a multiple oath to the count of Pallars Jussà.
[113] RBI 206*, sd 173*; *LFM* 825, with ALI 275.8*.   [114] RBI 296*, sd 137*.

of the *convenientia* in the text of the oath blurs the lines between the two forms.

Conversely, the fact of an oath may be recorded in the *convenientia*. A *convenientia* of 1183 between Bernat de Romanyà and Galceran de Sales reports that Bernat "swears with his own hands on the four gospels" not to attack Galceran or his heirs from the fortification of Romanyà. A similar agreement between Berenguer de Barberà and Guillem Ramon de Montcada in 1191 includes the passage "And I swear by God and the four holy gospels to you and your successors that I will adhere to and fulfill all this, just as it is said above." Ponç Guerau II, viscount of Girona, and Arnau de Castellbò swore mutual oaths in a *convenientia* of 1120, Arnau on the gospels, Ponç on the gospels and relics.[115] While the agreement between Galceran de Sales and Bernat de Romanyà maintains the third-person discourse common in eleventh-century *convenientiae*, the other two employ the first person ("convenio . . . promitto . . . iuro"), adopting the style of the oath.[116] In these examples, the *convenientia* essentially includes the oath, obviating the need for a separate record. This absence of a clear distinction between oath and convention allowed for the development of regional practices in the production and retention of written agreements.

Although Ramon Guifré of Cerdanya undertook a program of castle management similar to the program of his contemporary, Ramon Berenguer I, the evidence for his activity consists not of *convenientiae*, but of oaths. These fall into two categories: four shorter oaths, beginning with the standard formula "Iuro ego," and thirteen generally longer oaths beginning "De ista ora in antea."[117] The long-form oaths are considerably more detailed than the shorter oaths, and while they do not contain promises of services, they do contain clauses prohibiting other alliances or mandating renewal of the oath to the count's heir within a certain number of days following the count's death. Some of these documents – unlike almost all of the oaths to Ramon Berenguer I – include a witness list (*visores, auditores*) or dating clause.[118] It is possible that separate *convenientiae* existed and have been lost, but with this level of detail and especially formality, the long written oath may simply have acted as a substitute in the Cerdanya of Ramon Guifré for the *convenientia*. This

---

[115] ALI 343 ("propiis manibus iurat super sancta iiii^{or} evangelia"), 589 ("iuro tibi et successoribus tuis attendere et complere per Deum et sancta iiii evangelia"); BC 4226. See above, p. 100.

[116] Cf. Zimmermann, "Aux origines," 144–45.

[117] Additional oaths not considered: *LFM* 573, 574 (rubrics only).

[118] Long form: RBI sd 188, sd 193*, sd 194, sd 195; *LFM* 532, 554, 556, 581, 594, 596, 597, 653, 683. Short form: RBI sd 189, sd 190*; *LFM* 537, 592. In the printed edition of the *LFM*, the oaths with the form "Iuro ego" range from 11–23 lines (mean 17.6), while the "De ista ora" variety range from 21 to 89 lines (mean 53.3).

tradition may date back to the time of Ramon Guifré's father. The first document in the *Liber feudorum Cerritaniae* – an early-thirteenth-century cartulary extracted from the *LFM* – is a long oath with the form "de ista ora" for the castles of Sant Esteve and Castellfollit.[119] The use of the long-form oath continued under Guillem I Ramon of Cerdanya (1068–95), but the documentary situation in this reign is much more complex. Formulae become increasingly irregular, and oath, convention, and also *placitum* overlap. The percentage of short-form oaths increases, and the "Iuro ego"/"De ista ora" distinction breaks down.[120] Each of the five conventions from Guillem's reign has an associated oath, but three of these are short form and two are long form, thus it is impossible to suggest that the short-form oath was an adjunct of a separate *convenientia* and the long-form oath was a replacement for it. One of the *convenientiae* ends with a sanctification formula, "Per Deum et hec sancta," more commonly found in oaths.[121]

The records of Ramon Berenguer III show a shift toward the use of the oath rather than the oath/*convenientia* pair of his grandfather. In the home counties of Barcelona, Osona, and Girona, this may be explained by the fact that relationships that Ramon Berenguer III renewed in the twelfth century were often based on *convenientiae* and oaths drawn up during the reign of Ramon Berenguer I; the one surviving antecedent *convenientia* makes the transgenerational relationship explicit.[122] The drafting of a new *convenientia* under Ramon Berenguer III may have been considered superfluous. Similarly, in his acquisitions of Cerdanya and Besalú the count also renewed earlier agreements establishing fidelity and comital control over castles;[123] the choice of formula in these cases would have been governed by local traditions that blurred the distinction between oath and *convenientia*. But this preference for oath over convention is apparent in cases that cannot be explained by adherence to traditions. The count was the corecipient of the oath sworn by Ramon Renard, the *castlà* of Font-rubí, to Bernat Berenguer, an intermediate

---

[119] *LFM* 531.

[120] RBII 72*, 75, 77*, 78*, 79*, 80, 81, 82, 83*; *LFM* 220=551, 221=553, 411=536, 533, 546, 588, 599, 600, 601, 602, 603, 604, 605, 606, 625, 626, 628, 629, 636, 637, 638, 639, 640, 641, 654, 659, 662, 664, 668, 675, 686, 687. Oaths not considered: *LFM* 563, 575 (rubrics only). There are 37 oaths in the printed edition of the *LFM*, ranging from 8 to 82 lines in length (mean 33; cf. 34 for the 62 printed oaths to Ramon Berenguer I and/or his wives). Fourteen of the oaths are longer than 40 lines.   [121] *LFM* 534.

[122] RBI 292*: "Et predictus Udalardus similiter facit predictam convenientiam ipsi filio de iamdicto comite qui tenuerit Barchinonam post mortem iam dictis comite et comitissam . . . et predicti comes et comitissa supra predictas convenientias comendant predictum Castrum Vetulum Vicecomitale iam dicto Udalardo, et donant ei per fevum ipsum vicecomitatum de Barchinona et ipsum fevum de iam dicto castro sicut avus et proavus iamdicti Udalardi tenuit ipsum fevum per comitem." In addition to documents discussed below, pp. 220–23, see RBIII 284*, 310* (cf. 142*, 213 dup*).   [123] Below, pp. 223–25.

castellan, in 1123. The corresponding *convenientia* is not between Ramon Renard and the count, but between the castellan and the *castlà*; it mentions the count only as the ultimate lord.[124] A decade earlier, following his altercation with a townsman of Barcelona named Ricard Guillem over the castle of Arraona, the count discovered that he was unable to locate the oaths (*sacramentorum scripture*) of the *castlans*, Jofre de Santa Coloma and Ramon Gausbert.[125] He was forced, therefore, to absolve them from their oath (*sacramentum*) and homage (*ominaticum*).[126] It was the written oaths of *castlans*, rather than a *convenientia* with their lord, that were the proof of the count's power.

North of the Pyrenees in Carcassonne and in Provence, the count's activity was of a different nature: the documentation records the settlements, alliances, and submissions involved in the count's military conquest of these regions rather than renewals of earlier arrangements. Here, too, the shift toward the oath is seen: few standard *convenientiae* have survived.[127] In Carcassonne, oaths to the count concerned his attempts to rein in Bernard Ato, viscount of Béziers.[128] A number were explicitly directed against the viscount of Béziers: the oath of approximately 500 of the *homines* of Carcassonne to the count; a series of 5 oaths from local castellans; and an oath of Ramon Berenguer's half brother, Aimery, viscount of Narbonne.[129] Oaths of the viscount Bernard Ato and his sons, Roger and Raimond Trencavel, were promises to keep a settlement with the count.[130] An oath of Viscount Pierre of Minerve dealt with his proposed marriage to a sister of Ramon Berenguer III, apparently another attempt to secure an alliance.[131] These were not simple oaths of fidelity

---

[124] RBIII 261.1*, 261.2*. The count had received an oath from the senior castellan, Berenguer (I) de Queralt, in 1121 (RBIII 230*).

[125] RBIII 174*; see also 173. On Ricard Guillem, see Bensch, *Barcelona*, 154–57, and works cited there.

[126] It is unclear whether RBIII sd 24* and sd 25* are the missing oaths or new ones sworn after the fact. These were sworn to Countess Douce, as well, and thus must date from after 1112.

[127] See RBIV 73*.

[128] The chronology of events is almost impossible to divine, as many of the documents are undated or survive only as rubrics from the *LFM*, and the late-twelfth-century memorial on which most historians have based their accounts is very unreliable. See Cheyette, "Sale," 857–60, for a novel attempt at reconstruction.

[129] *LFM* 832, 849 (rubric only), 809. Cheyette ("Sale," 860) suggests that the first document dates from 1120, while the second is from 1113. Sobrequés puts the first in 1105 and the third in 1112 (*Els grans comtes*, 144–45). Whatever the date of *LFM* 849, *LFM* 850 and 851 (below, n. 131) are probably not contemporary, *pace* Cheyette.

[130] *LFM* 845, 846, 847. *LFM* 848 is another oath of Bernard Ato. Cf. RBIII sd 2.1*=RBI 392.2a*, RBIII sd 2.2*=RBI 392.2b*; *LFM* 844; *HGL* 5:443; from which the context and terms of the settlement may be reconstructed.

[131] *LFM* 849, 851. Cheyette ("Sale," 859 n. 136) suggests this identification of "viscount Pierre." The sister, Amabilia, is known only from the rubric to *LFM* 851 (the document itself has not survived): "Sacramentale Petri, vicecomitis, super honore Carcassonae [et Redes et de matrimonio

for castles, but complex engagements that took the place of *convenientiae*. The records from Provence confirm the trend: only four oaths, and no conventions, survive from the count's campaigns of 1113–16 and 1123–26.[132]

Again, archival practice may explain these patterns, but it is striking that records preserved by the counts of Barcelona for their trans-Pyrenean holdings, while generally different from those for their older territories, are the same types of records preserved by local powers in those northern regions. The Trencavel cartulary (*Liber instrumentorum vicecomitalium*), compiled in two stages beginning around 1186x88, preserves acts relating to the lineage that held Albi, Carcassonne, Razès, Béziers, Agde, and Nîmes: precisely the areas in which Ramon Berenguer III was active. Of the 585 acts, which date between 1028 and 1214, 321 are oaths of fidelity, while only 57 are *convenientiae* and 79 are documents concerning fiefs. A few of the oaths refer to separate *convenientiae*, but most stand alone; the power of the Trencavels rested on the oath.[133] The cartulary of the Guilhems of Montpellier, compiled at the beginning of the thirteenth century, shows a similar imbalance: of 570 documents, close to 150 are oaths, while conventions and similar documents number close to 30.[134] In the regions north of the Pyrenees, despite the presence of the *convenientia*, the oath was seen as the essence of the agreement.

If generally in the Midi and occasionally in Catalonia the oath appears as the most important element of the agreement, then its role cannot be limited to a guaranteeing function. It did add a form of security in some cases, but the relationship between oath and *convenientia* was much more complex. The classical tripartite model of the feudal contract tends to encourage an analytic approach to such institutions: because the investiture of the fief, the homage of the vassal, and the oath of fidelity have

<hr/>

ineundo cum Amabilia, sorore eiusdem comitis]." See now Martin Aurell, "Du nouveau sur les comtesses catalanes (IXe–XIIe siècles)," *AM* 109 (1997), 372.

[132] Below, pp. 258–59.

[133] Montpellier, Société archéologique de Montpellier, MS 10 (consulted on microfilm at the Archives départementales de l'Hérault); Hélène Débax, "Le cartulaire des Trencavel (*Liber instrumentorum vicecomitalium*)," in Olivier Guyotjeannin, Laurent Morelle, and Michel Parisse, eds., *Les cartulaires: Actes de la table ronde organisée par l'École nationale des chartes et le G.D.R. 121 du C.N.R.S. (Paris, 5–7 décembre 1991)*, Mémoires et documents de l'École des chartes 39 (Paris, 1993), 291–99. Oaths containing possible references to a separate *convenientia*: nos. 19, 20, 21, 22, 23, 58, 59, 101 [*HGL* 5:139], 147, 223, 227, 271, 340, 345, 380 (fols. 5v–7r, 14v–15r, 30v–31r, 49v, 68v, 71r, 88r–v, 113r, 115v–16r, 138r–39r).

[134] [A. Germain, ed.,] *Liber instrumentorum memorialium: Cartulaire des Guillems de Montpellier* (Montpellier, 1884–86). Documents of the form "Hec est convenientia" are few: nos. 152 (=RBIV 73*), 213, 380 (pp. 284–85, 368–70, 563); cf. nos. 40, 59, 64, 501, 503, 523 (pp. 69–72, 100–101, 112–13, 684–85, 686–87, 702–3); 43, 44, 45, 58, 61, 65, 67 . . . (pp. 75–83, 99–100, 103–8, 113–16, 119–21 . . .). See also Hideyuki Katsura, "Serments, hommages et fiefs dans la seigneurie des Guilhem de Montpellier (fin XIe–début XIIIe siècle)," *AM* 104 (1992), 155–56.

separate histories, they remain separable. This eases efforts to deconstruct feudalism – thus southern France possesses "fidelity without a basis in land, feudalism without a basis in the oath, and an aristocracy without vassals"[135] – but remains dominant even when the institutions are combined into a single process.[136] The Catalan documentation challenges the orderliness of this scheme, in that the written oath and *convenientia* not only make explicit the reciprocal obligations of the two parties that remain implicit elsewhere, but also overlap in content. The Catalan oath is not simply an oath of fidelity; the *convenientia* is not simply a written record of investiture. What precisely is the connection between the two? The analytical approach has held in attempts to answer this question, as well. Thus the oath "finds its natural place following an agreement," or it "corresponds to an agreement, to a *convenientia*; in expressing it in a Christianized ritual, it renders it valid and effective."[137] The shared form and content of the *convenientia* and oath, however, suggest that both reflect aspects of a single process of agreement that is best considered as a whole.[138]

That is not to say that oath and *convenientia* are identical. In general, there are important formal and conceptual differences. The *convenientia* may involve lineages, while the oath is a personal undertaking, thus the *convenientia* can include a prospective element not brought out in the oath.[139] The oath, meanwhile, is firmly grounded not only in first-person discourse, but also in the present tense; many *convenientiae* take on the style of a notice, in the third-person past tense. Matrilineal identification of the parties in the oath, normally not found in the *convenientia*, highlights both the individual nature and the immediacy of the action.[140] The *convenientia* carries with it the notion of bilateral agreement (even if this is not always the case), while the oath is purely unilateral. Similarly, the

---

[135] Magnou-Nortier, "Fidélité et féodalité," 476: "une fidélité sans support foncier, une féodalité sans support juré, une aristocratie sans vassaux."

[136] E.g., Katsura, "Serments, hommages et fiefs," 143: "il reste à examiner pour chaque région si l'on peut trouver dans les sources les éléments qui fondent la féodalité classique – serment de fidélité, hommage et fief –, et à quelle époque ils remontent."

[137] Magnou-Nortier, "Fidélité et féodalité," 462 ("Ce serment semble trouver place naturelle à la suite d'un accord"); Zimmermann, "Aux origines," 143 ("Chaque serment répond à un accord, à une convenientia; en l'exprimant dans un rituel christianisé, il le rend applicable et efficace"). Zimmermann's remarkable study should be consulted for all that follows here.

[138] Bonnassie, *La Catalogne*, 2:737: "Dans l'esprit des hommes de ce temps, convention, hommage et serment forment en effet un tout indissociable et il est impossible de dire, par exemple, lequel de ces trois actes engendre les obligations vassaliques."

[139] Bonnassie, *La Catalogne*, 2:738; cf. Ourliac's notion of the *facteur temps* ("La convenientia," 248).

[140] Zimmerman, "Aux origines," 112, 144–45. For various explanations of matrilineal identification, see: Ruiz-Domènec, *L'estructura feudal*, 90–92, esp. 91 n. 86; Martin Aurell, "La détérioration du statut de la femme aristocratique en Provence (Xᵉ–XIIIᵉ siècles)," *Le Moyen Âge* 91 (1985), 15–17; Aurell, *Les noces du comte*, 72–73.

convenientia deemphasizes the subordination of one party to the other, while this is what defines many oaths. Oaths are more likely than *convenientiae* to contain vernacular terms, and they are much more likely to be undated. Still, the frequent exceptions to these rules – oaths mentioning future generations; *convenientiae* redacted in the first person or the present tense, undated, or with matrilineal identifications; unbalanced opening formulae – undermine the notion that they are defining characteristics. These exceptions, along with the potential for substantive overlap noted above, are made possible by the fact that both the *convenientia* and the oath form part of a single process.

This process was a ritual, a performance, a complex mixture not only of words, but also of sights, sounds, gestures, and touches with complementary functions.[141] The ritual aspects have been considered most intensively in the case of *convenientiae* including homage, where the powerful image of a kneeling man placing his hands between the hands of his lord provides a focus. Homage has left traces in the illuminations of the comital cartularies, as well as in the documents themselves, where oaths and *convenientiae* alike refer to commendation with the hands.[142] But homage was not essential to the formation of an agreement; even in castle-holding *convenientiae* and oaths of fidelity, references to homage are rare before the mid-twelfth century.[143] In the absence of homage, other ritual aspects of the formation of the agreement emerge. Parties inevitably swore their oaths, whether or not they were oaths of fidelity, on an altar or relics.[144] Because the essence of the *convenientia* was a promise, an oath or other solemnification would have been part of all such agreements, from high-level treaties to agrarian contracts, even if no separate document was produced. The fact that documents were produced adds

---

[141] Zimmermann, "Aux origines," 143; Jean-Claude Schmitt, *La raison des gestes dans l'Occident médiéval* (Paris, 1990), esp. 16, 62, 98–100, 296–98, on gestures associated with oaths and homage; Bernard J. Hibbitts, "'Coming to Our Senses': Communication and Legal Expression in Performance Cultures," *Emory Law Journal* 41 (1992), 873–960. I have not explored here the implications and problems of considering the oath/*convenientia* complex as political ritual. See, e.g., Janet L. Nelson, *Politics and Ritual in Early Medieval Europe* (London, 1986); Gerd Althoff, *Spielregeln der Politik im Mittelalter: Kommunikation in Frieden und Fehde* (Darmstadt, 1997); Philippe Buc, "Ritual and Interpretation: The Early Medieval Case," *Early Medieval Europe* (forthcoming). Although such approaches are more readily available to scholars working with narrative sources, diplomatic records, especially records of dispute settlement, are susceptible to this type of analysis: Geoffrey Koziol, *Begging Pardon and Favor: Ritual and Political Order in Early Medieval France* (Ithaca, 1992); Stephen D. White, "Proposing the Ordeal and Avoiding It: Strategy and Power in Western French Litigation," in Thomas N. Bisson, ed., *Cultures of Power: Lordship, Status, and Process in Twelfth-Century Europe* (Philadelphia, 1995), 89–123; Bowman, "Do Neo-Romans Curse?"

[142] Bonnassie, *La Catalogne*, 2:741; Zimmermann, "Aux origines," 122. Below, p. 284.

[143] Zimmermann, "Aux origines," 122–23; below, p. 261–62.

[144] Zimmermann, "Aux origines," 115.

another ritual element: though the process is poorly understood, the redaction of charters was in itself ceremonial.[145]

Important specifics of the ceremony such as the staging and the order of events have not yet been recovered; Catalonia has no Galbert of Bruges to narrate the scene.[146] Some of its sounds, however, have survived, for *convenientiae* and especially oaths preserve words and phrases in the vernacular, words and phrases that may offer direct testimony for the speech of the juror. The presence of such words and phrases raises many difficult questions. An older tradition of philological scholarship maintained that from the fifth, sixth, or seventh century, Latin and Romance existed as independent languages; the former was the spoken and written language of the educated elite, while the latter was the language – spoken only – in general use among the population. Roger Wright suggested in 1982 that this was not the case. Before the late eighth century, he argued, "Latin" and "Romance" were one; "Latin" was simply the written mode of the common tongue, an attempt to record in an archaic system a language that had evolved away from the roots on which the written system was originally based. A "Latin" language distinct from "Romance" vernaculars was created by Carolingian pronunciation reforms, associated principally with changes in the liturgy; these reforms mandated an archaic pronunciation to correspond to the archaic writing system still in use. A separate written system was required to represent the nonarchaic pronunciation systems. Thus the ground was prepared for the development of "Latin" and "Romance" as separate languages. The Iberian Peninsula is an exception in that the Roman liturgy, and thus the Carolingian pronunciation reforms attached to it, were not introduced until 1080.[147] Wright's thesis has not been universally accepted, but it has reinvigorated the field. An important development has been the expansion of the Latin-Romance debate beyond questions of definition to issues of communication and literacy. Whether a language, written or spoken, is "Latin" or "Romance" is in the end less important than who understood the language, to what degree, and in what context.[148]

---

[145] Zimmermann, "Aux origines," 143–44, 148, offers suggestions; cf. Rosamond McKitterick, *The Carolingians and the Written Word* (Cambridge, 1989), 94–98.

[146] Galbert of Bruges, *De multro, traditione, et occisione gloriosi Karoli comitis Flandriarum*, ed. Jeff Rider, Corpus christianorum, Continuatio mediaevalis, 131 (Turnhout, 1994), cap. 56 (pp. 105–6).

[147] Roger Wright, *Late Latin and Early Romance in Spain and Carolingian France*, ARCA Classical and Medieval Texts, Papers and Monographs 8 (Liverpool, 1982); Wright, *Early Ibero-Romance: Twenty-one Studies on Language and Texts from the Iberian Peninsula between the Roman Empire and the Thirteenth Century*, Estudios lingüísticos 5 (Newark, Del., 1994).

[148] See Michel Banniard, *Viva voce: Communication écrite et communication orale du IVᵉ au IXᵉ siècle en Occident latin*, Collection des études augustiniennes, Série Moyen-Âge et temps modernes, 25 (Paris, 1992); Banniard, "Language and Communication in Carolingian Europe," in Rosamond McKitterick, ed., *The New Cambridge Medieval History*, vol. 2., *c. 700–c. 900* (Cambridge, 1995),

The evidence under consideration here – written oaths from Catalonia – represents a special case for two reasons. First, even if Wright's hypothesis is correct, Catalonia, unlike the rest of the Iberian Peninsula, was exposed to Carolingian liturgical reforms from an early date; as in many other aspects of its history, the region is closer to the Carolingian heartland than to its immediate Iberian neighbors. The questions of the impact of the Carolingian reforms, whether in pronunciation or orthography, and the speed of their spread, are thus relevant here in a way that they are not elsewhere on the peninsula.[149] Second, the Latin of charters has been considered as a distinct problem. The Latin of diplomatic texts is often viewed as deficient, the product of poorly trained scribes combining scraps of "Latin" formulae with "Romance" words and syntax to produce what may be considered either "a vernacularized variety of medieval Latin" or Romance with a "camouflage" or "veneer" of Latin. Even in the case of a text following Latin rules of orthography, Romance syntax and vocabulary similar to the vernacular could make a "Latin" charter read aloud with vernacular pronunciation intelligible to a "Romance" speaker.[150] It is possible to argue that the Latin of charters represented a different linguistic register, corresponding to a particular social function and professional class.

695–708; McKitterick, *The Carolingians*, 7–22. Wright was not a lone pioneer: Marc van Uytfanghe, "Histoire du Latin, protohistoire des langues romanes et histoire de la communication: A propos d'un recueil d'études, et avec quelques observations préliminaires sur le débat intellectuel entre pensée structurale et pensée historique," *Francia* 11 (1983), 579–613; Michael Richter, *Studies in Medieval Language and Culture* (Dublin, 1995). See most recently József Herman, ed., *La transizione dal latino alle lingue romanze: Atti della Tavola rotonda di linguistica storica, Università Ca' Foscari di Venezia, 14–15 giugno 1996* (Tübingen, 1998).

[149] Cf. on reform in chant, John J. Contreni, "The Carolingian Renaissance: Education and Literary Culture," in McKitterick, ed., *The New Cambridge Medieval History*, 743–44. On the historical development of Catalan generally, see Antoni M. Badia i Margarit, *La formació de la llengua catalana: Assaig d'interpretació històrica*, 2nd ed. (Barcelona, 1981).

[150] António Emiliano, "Latin or Romance? Graphemic Variation and Scripto-linguistic Change in Medieval Spain," in Roger Wright, ed., *Latin and the Romance Languages in the Early Middle Ages* (London, 1991), 233; Wright, *Late Latin*, 148, 240–44. See also Thomas J. Walsh, "Spelling Lapses in Early Medieval Latin Documents and the Reconstruction of Primitive Romance Phonology," in Wright, ed., *Latin and the Romance Languages*, 205–18; Wolf-Dieter Lange, *Philologische Studien zur Latinität westhispanischer Privaturkunden des 9.–12. Jahrhunderts*, Mittellateinische Studien und Texte 3 (Leiden, 1966); Maurilio Pérez González, *El latín de la cancillería castellana (1158–1214)*, Acta Salmanticensia, Filosofía y letras, 163 (Salamanca, 1985). Philologists are drawn to the diplomatic evidence, as it often provides some of the earliest exemplars of written vernacular. For Old Provençal: Clovis Brunel, ed., *Les plus anciennes chartes en langue provençale: Recueil des pièces originales antérieures au XIIIᵉ siècle, publiées avec une étude morphologique*, 2 vols. (Paris, 1926–52); Max Pfister, "Die Anfänge der altprovenzalischen Schriftsprache," *Zeitschrift für romanische Philologie* 86 (1970), 306–13. Generally: Georges Straka, ed., *Les anciens textes romans non littéraires: Leur apport à la connaissance de la langue au Moyen Âge: Colloque international organisé par le Centre de philologie et de littératures romanes de l'Université de Strasbourg du 30 janvier au 4 février 1961*, Actes et colloques 1 (Paris, 1963); Françoise Vielliard, "Les langues vulgaires dans les cartulaires français du Moyen Âge," in Guyotjeannin, Morelle, and Parisse, eds., *Les cartulaires*, 137–50.

Two languages certainly existed by the eleventh century in Catalonia: Latin and Catalan, a Romance language already distinct from Occitan and Aragonese. A late-eleventh-century sermon collection that includes sections of Latin texts followed by translation and commentary in Catalan is sufficient proof. The independent existence of Catalan is even more evident in the twelfth century, when we can point to a Catalan translation of the *Liber iudiciorum* and perhaps also of the *Usatges de Barcelona*.[151] As for the Latinity of the charters, while they have their own rhythm, the argument that they were the product of semiliterate scribes is not entirely convincing. First, the use of formulae and the generally conservative nature of the language of the charters makes it difficult to judge the overall Latinity of the scribes of these texts. Second, charter scribes might in fact be very well trained: Guibert, *grammaticus* and head of the cathedral school of Vic, redacted at least three documents, a testamentary grant and two judicial records.[152] Finally, while their language is not that of Cicero, it is difficult to lump these documents together with charters written in "Leonese Vulgar Latin." Generally, their language is Latin – "post-classical, simple, and tolerably correct," but Latin nonetheless.[153]

These facts make the appearance of vernacular terms in the written oaths all the more puzzling. It is possible to view the vernacular terms as a direct transcription of the words of the juror.[154] While there are occasional examples of entirely vernacular oaths, however, normally only certain words and phrases appear in Catalan. One could imagine scribes transcribing a vernacular oath into Latin, turning to the vernacular for technical terms for which no Latin equivalent was readily available.[155] Yet

[151] Jordi Bruguera and Joan Coromines, eds., *Homilies d'Organyà: Edició facsímil del manuscrit núm. 289 de la Biblioteca de Catalunya*, Llibres del mil·lenari 1 (Barcelona, 1989); Anscari M. Mundó, ed., "Fragment del *Libre jutge*, versió catalana antiga del *Liber iudiciorum*," *Estudis universitaris catalans* 26 (1984), 155–93. The earliest manuscript of the Catalan text of the *Usatges* dates from the second half of the thirteenth century, but the text itself may date from the twelfth. See Joan Bastardas i Parera, *Sobre la problemàtica dels Usatges de Barcelona* (Barcelona, 1977), 22; Mundó, ed., "Fragment," 182.

[152] ACV 9/ii/29*, 9/ii/41*, 6/1016; see Josep M. Masnou, "L'escola de la catedral de Vic al segle XI," in Imma Ollich i Castanyer, ed., *Actes del Congrés internacional Gerbert d'Orlhac i el seu temps: Catalunya i Europa a la fi del 1r mil·lenni: Vic-Ripoll, 10–13 de novembre de 1999*, Documents 31 (Vic, 1999), 621–34. Cf. RBIII 132*: "(s.m.) Renaldi gramatici Barchinonensis, qui hoc scripsit."

[153] To borrow the phrase of Thomas Bisson (*FA*, 1:11). See Carmen Pensado, "How Was Leonese Vulgar Latin Read?" in Wright, ed., *Latin and the Romance Languages*, 190–204; Wright, *Late Latin*, 165–75.

[154] E.g., Clovis Brunel, "Les premiers exemples de l'emploi du Provençal dans les chartes," *Romania* 48 (1922), 362: "les plus anciennes chartes provençales sont des serments de fidélité . . . Leur conservation en langue vulgaire est due en partie à la même cause qui nous a valu la transmission des serments de Strasbourg. Comme on l'a déjà remarqué, il faut l'attribuer au désir de reproduire sans traduction, qui pourrait fausser le sens, des formules consacrées d'engagement grave."

[155] E.g., Brunel, "Les premiers exemples," 335–36: "Dans l'Europe méridionale, les rédacteurs des actes ont d'abord employé la langue vulgaire au milieu de phrases latines, quand leur ignorance ne leur permettait pas d'exprimer autrement leur pensée."

it is verbs, not nouns, that comprise the bulk of the vernacular lexicon of oaths, verbs for which a scribe would have had no trouble finding a Latin substitute: *esse, habere, jurare, tenere, tollere, ferre, vetare, decipere, commonere* . . .[156] The similar presence of vernacular words in early medieval Italian documents has been explained by the observation that the formulaic passages are more "correct," while the passages that pertain to the substance of the particular transactions are composed in a free style in order to represent more accurately the intentions of the parties.[157] In these oaths, however, it is just the opposite. The vernacular terms often provide a formulaic framework for the oath, introducing each new significant engagement ("non dezebre . . . no la tolrei . . . adiutor te sere . . . comonir no men devedare . . ."); it has been suggested that these were the *only* words actually spoken by the juror, intoned responsively with a reading, in Latin, of the details of the engagements either from an oath composed in advance or from the *convenientia* itself.[158] Finally, Wright has postulated that the appearance of distinct vernacular sentences in four Italian charters of the 960s – sentences that appear elsewhere in "normal Latin" – represents an attempt on the part of lawyers "to see if the reformed orthography aided vernacular reading back to, or by, the depositor." Here, he writes, "the invention of Latin speech had led to experimentation in Romance writing."[159] This theory is possible for the Catalan case, but the timing is wrong, and in any case the use of the vernacular in the eleventh century seems too widespread for an experiment.[160]

Part of the difficulty in analyzing the problem of the presence of vernacular terms in the written oath is the starting point of this line of inquiry: that the oath is in some way a transcript of a fundamentally oral act, a complement to a *convenientia* more firmly grounded in the written word. The presence of vernacular terms in *convenientiae*, as well, raises the possibility that they, too, were read aloud and understood – either by translation from the written Latin into a spoken Catalan, or – and I believe this to be more likely – in Latin intelligible to the parties. Vernacular passages in *convenientiae* also confirm the influence of the ceremonies surrounding oath and *convenientia* on the composition of those

---

[156] Zimmermann, "Aux origines," 145–47.

[157] Wright, *Late Latin*, 62, citing Francesco Sabatini, "Dalla 'scripta latina rustica' alle 'scriptae' romanze," *Studi medievali*, 3rd ser., 9 (1968), 328–35.

[158] Zimmermann, "Aux origines," 145–48.

[159] Wright, *Late Latin*, 144; for the texts, see Ruggero M. Ruggieri, ed., *Testi antichi romanzi*, 2 vols., Testi e manuali 29–30 (Modena, 1949), nos. 5, 6, 7, 8 (2:21–28 and plates).

[160] Wright (*Late Latin*, 148) cites an oath composed completely in Catalan (first published as Joaquim Miret i Sans, ed., "Pro sermone plebeico," *Boletín de la Real academia de buenas letras de Barcelona* 7 [1913–14], 105–6), suggesting that it was "designed to aid performance." In contrast to Languedoc and Provence (above, n. 154), such entirely vernacular oaths were rare in Catalonia.

documents. Conversely, the formulae of the oaths employed are firmly grounded in a *written* tradition dating back to the Carolingian period: the words spoken echoed traditions of the documentary scribes, rather than vice versa.[161] Furthermore, the oaths refer not only to written *convenientiae*, but also to their own written nature: "Sicut superius scriptum est . . ." Written and oral are inextricably linked in the ritual of agreement.[162]

The spoken words of parties to an agreement were essential; without them, there would be no reason for the production of a document and nothing to write down. Nevertheless, the integration of oral and written in the course of the ritual surrounding the agreement shows that *convenientiae* and written oaths were very much a part of the process. This was perfectly natural in a region so imbued with the written word. Documents did not simply serve as repositories of the memory of an event; they were a constitutive part of the event itself. Parties literally made an agreement by having it written down.[163] Because of this, the function of *convenientiae* and written oaths goes beyond their potential use as proofs in future disputes, where their utility in many cases would have been limited by the absence – regular in oaths, occasional in *convenientiae* – of standard formulae of authentication such as dating clauses, witness lists, and subscriptions.[164] As integral elements of the ritual that created an agreement, *convenientiae* and written oaths added an additional layer of guarantee: the agreement was more secure because the written word was involved. The precise role of writing in the creation of the agreement varied from place to place and over time, reflecting different aspects of

[161] Magnou-Nortier, "Fidélité et féodalité," 458–61. A similar argument may apply to the Strasbourg Oaths of 842. See Ruth Schmidt-Wiegand, "Eid und Gelöbnis, Formel und Formular im mittelalterlichen Recht," in Peter Classen, ed., *Recht und Schrift im Mittelalter*, Vorträge und Forschungen 23 (Sigmaringen, 1977), 62–72; Wright, *Late Latin*, 122–26. As I am arguing for the Catalan oaths, the Strasbourg texts themselves are unlikely to represent a simple verbatim transcription of oaths sworn. They are preserved in a literary, not a legal, text – Nithard's *Histories* – where they fulfill a rhetorical function; furthermore, the sole manuscript of the oaths dates from perhaps fifty years after the event. See Janet L. Nelson, "Public *Histories* and Private History in the Work of Nithard," *Speculum* 60 (1985), 266–67; Rosamond McKitterick, "Latin and Romance: An Historian's Perspective," in Wright, ed., *Latin and the Romance Languages*, 138–39 and n. 1; McKitterick, "Introduction: Sources and Interpretation," in McKitterick, ed., *The New Cambridge Medieval History*, 11–12.
[162] Cf. Julia M. H. Smith, "Oral and Written: Saints, Miracles, and Relics in Brittany, c. 850–1250," *Speculum* 65 (1990), 309–43.
[163] Cf. Zimmermann, "Aux origines," 143: "Le serment (sacramentale) apparaît par conséquent comme la conjonction indissociable de deux gestes: le serment oral prêté sur les reliques et l'écriture; deux gestes, mais un seul agent: la propria manus du fidèle . . . Le vassal jure fidélité en écrivant le texte."
[164] Cf. the comments of Brigitte Bedos-Rezak, "Diplomatic Sources and Medieval Documentary Practices: An Essay in Interpretive Methodology," in John Van Engen, ed., *The Past and Future of Medieval Studies*, Notre Dame Conferences in Medieval Studies 4 (Notre Dame, 1994), 323.

the complex processes that generated and confirmed a meeting of minds between individuals. But whether in the form of *convenientiae* in Barcelona, long oaths in Cerdanya, or entirely vernacular oaths in Languedoc, the written word served alongside the spoken word and ritual gestures to make agreements – and to insure that they would be kept.

Chapter 4

FOUNDATIONS (THE ELEVENTH CENTURY)

The trickle of *convenientiae* that began in the 1020s and continued through the 1040s became a flood from 1050 on. Fewer than 50 survive from the first half of the eleventh century; over 600 are preserved from the second half. Counts, viscounts, bishops, abbots, clerks, castellans, and peasants from every county all took advantage of the new form to record their agreements. These multiplying agreements are not isolated from one another; rather, they overlap, forming networks and structures. A single agreement between two individuals is of only limited import. Hundreds of agreements within a community begin to shape the social order.

Since the richest concentration of agreements for this period concerns castle holding, the development of structures based on written agreements is most easily seen in a consideration of that subject. What was a castle in eleventh- and twelfth-century Catalonia? As research into the phenomenon of concentration of habitats in fortified sites on the Italian peninsula (*incastellamento*) has made clear, the castle of the tenth to twelfth centuries was much more than a fortified site or building. It served administrative, political, economic, military, and even symbolic functions that varied from region to region.[1] For Catalonia, a distinction has been drawn between the *castellum*, or fortified site, and the *castrum*, or administrative territorial unit, usually centered on a *castellum*, but this distinction is – like the related distinction between castellan/*châtelain* and *castlà* – as much an historiographical construct as it is an accurate representation of contemporary terminology: sources are not as consistent in their use of these terms as they might be. While the idea of territorial circumscriptions controlled from fortified buildings describes well the prevailing structures of power, the term *castrum* designates in contemporary

---

[1] Miquel Barceló and Pierre Toubert, eds., *L'incastellamento: Actes des rencontres de Gérone (26–27 novembre 1992) et de Rome (5–7 mai 1994)*, Collection de l'École française de Rome 241 (Rome, 1998).

documentation both castle and castle district, while fortified sites of various sizes received a wide variety of labels.[2] For the purposes of castle-holding *convenientiae*, the realities of power in the eleventh and twelfth centuries meant that possession of a fortification entailed economic and political control of the surrounding countryside. A grant of a *castrum*, in the sense of a territorial division, included a grant of the fortified site that was at its center. Fortifications of whatever size provided a base for the extension of military force into the neighboring area, whether or not this power was restricted within a territorial boundary conforming to an older administrative district. Control over castles as administrative districts and control over castles as sources of power are thus two aspects of the same general phenomenon, and an examination of structures of castle tenure has implications beyond the construction of hierarchies of military command. The particular details of the rights and obligations of those with interests in the castles, particularly with regard to *potestas*, were worked out in *convenientiae*.

We must begin with comital *convenientiae*, for these account for approximately half of the *convenientiae* from the second half of the eleventh century. This does not correspond to overall patterns of documentary survival, since the extant comital archives are dwarfed by the combined ecclesiastical holdings for the same period. At first, the *convenientia* was above all an instrument of the counts. It has been argued that in adopting the *convenientia*, the counts were accommodating themselves to a system that had developed among the lesser aristocracy. But, as will be detailed below, the *convenientia* did not begin to flourish among the lay aristocracy until *c.* 1070. The Catalan dioceses, under the leadership of powerful lord-bishops, played a role, too, in the spread of the network of castle holding, as did some monasteries. The mechanics of castle tenure and the written forms involved in the process are more likely to have been inspired by the practice of these ecclesiastical institutions than by the habits of unruly castellans. But it was the counts – especially Ramon Berenguer I of Barcelona – who were the innovators. It is they who did the most to introduce the idea of a system of relations based on written agreements.

---

[2] *GMLC*, s.vv. *castrum, castellum*; André Constant, "Châteaux et peuplement dans le massif des Albères et ses marges du IXe siècle au début du XIe siècle," *AM* 109 (1997), 443–66; Manuel Riu i Riu, "Castells i fortificacions menors: Llurs orígens, paper, distribució i formes de possessió," in *Catalunya i França*, 248–60. In neighboring Béziers, the semantic distinction between *castrum* and *castellum* was in place only by the twelfth century; see Monique Gramain, "*Castrum*, structures féodales et peuplement en Biterrois au XIe siècle," in *Structures féodales et féodalisme dans l'Occident méditerranéen (X^e–XIIIe siècles): Bilan et perspectives de recherches: École française de Rome, 10–13 octobre 1978*, Colloques internationaux du Centre national de la recherche scientifique 588 (Paris, 1980), 122–29.

COUNTS

Barcelona

The earliest *convenientiae* are too few and diverse in form to support generalizations about documentary form; the only element that unites the agreements is the appellation *convenientia*. With the seventy-one *convenientiae* to which Ramon Berenguer I (1035–76) was party, patterns begin to emerge.[3] But an analysis of the language of these documents shows that while there are recurring elements, on the whole *convenientiae* are considerably less formal than most contemporary documents. Perhaps consistency is not to be expected. While there is evidence that a dedicated comital chancery was developing in the eleventh century,[4] the preparation of documents involving the count was not yet sufficiently regularized that we may conceive of an institution scrupulously following particular rules and forms. Furthermore, although scribes often revealed their own names in documents that they prepared for the count, few names are repeated, and a distinction between scribes working for the count and those associated with the writing offices of ecclesiastical institutions is difficult to establish. Nevertheless, formulae recorded in the tenth-century formulary from Santa Maria de Ripoll found widespread use, as the monotonous consistency of the sales, exchanges, and pledges that make up the bulk of the surviving records attests. Among *convenientiae* consistency and formality are notably lacking.

Medieval documents, like modern ones, contain discrete elements designed to serve a functional purpose (such as listing the names of those who witnessed a transaction) or simply to lend a degree of formality to the written record. Most of these elements appear at the beginning (protocol) and end (eschatocol) of a document. In *convenientiae*, they are often missing. The standard formulae for gift, sale, and pledge, for example, begin with a verbal invocation, a brief phrase invoking the support of the deity for the act (e.g., "In nomine Domini"); this is present in only five of Ramon Berenguer I's conventions (7 percent). In approximately one-third of all the documents concerning Ramon Berenguer I and his third wife, Almodis, the devotional formula "gratia Dei" is included in the counts' titles (e.g., "Remundus gratia Dei Barchinonensis comes hac marchio"); in *convenientiae*, it is present only four times (6 percent). Documents almost always end with a dating clause; it is lacking

---

[3] For what follows, see Adam J. Kosto, "The *convenientiae* of the Catalan Counts in the Eleventh Century: A Diplomatic and Historical Analysis," *Acta historica et archaeologica mediaevalia* 19 (1998), 192–214.

[4] Bonnassie, *La Catalogne*, 1:169; Josep Trenchs Òdena, "La escribanía de Ramón Berenguer III (1097–1131): Datos para su estudio," *Saitabi* 30 (1981), 12–16.

in fifteen of the *convenientiae* (20 percent). Similarly, documents usually include the subscriptions of at least one of the parties to the transaction and one or more other individuals (witnesses, subscribers, other interested parties, etc.); the subscription of at least one of the parties is absent in twenty-three of the *convenientiae* (32 percent), while thirty-two (45 percent) lack additional subscriptions.

The absence of subscriptions and a dating clause has juridical significance, as noted in the last chapter. But setting aside any strictly juridical content of these particular elements, their absence corresponds to the general lack of formality indicated by the patterns of use of invocation and devotion formulae. This lack of formality is above all a reflection of the novelty of the *convenientia*; scribes had no models from which to work. A similar freedom is apparent in Catalan memorials of complaint from the mid-twelfth century.[5] A standard *convenientia* did develop, and we can see here its genesis, with the concentrated activity of scribes producing documents for the comital court and having recourse to recurring elements. Yet the *convenientia* remained flexible and informal, especially when compared to an earlier documentation.

There remains enough formal consistency in these agreements, however, to reveal a significant shift around 1058, evident in a change in the formula of the opening clause. The most consistent, if not defining, element of the *convenientiae* of Ramon Berenguer I, and indeed most eleventh-century *convenientiae*, is the initial phrase: "Hec est convenientia." The names of the parties to the agreement generally follow these words. Before 1058, this identification is usually in the form "que est facta inter N. et N.": this is the agreement *between* the count and so-and-so. After 1058, this changes to "que facit N. ad comitem": this is the agreement that so-and-so makes *to* the count. "Agreement" is almost the wrong word here; "undertaking" or "promise" might fit better. But the phrase appears in this form even when the count is also making promises, that is, when the content of the agreement is explicitly balanced – *between* individuals. So this formal shift must indicate more than just a change in substance. Might it be a piece of political symbolism? Many studies have demonstrated the importance of documentary formulae for making such statements.[6] What statement is being made here?

Just as a change in formula is evident in the *convenientiae* of Ramon Berenguer I beginning around 1058, there is a change in the number of agreements in which he was involved. Although the numbers of

---

[5] Thomas N. Bisson, *Tormented Voices: Power, Crisis, and Humanity in Rural Catalonia, 1140–1200* (Cambridge, Mass., 1998), 74. [6] Above, p. 5.

convenientiae had been gradually increasing from the beginning of the reign, the rate of increase seems to take off in this period: eighteen datable conventions survive from the ten years before January 1058; thirty-two survive from the ten years following that date. The increase parallels a rise in the overall amount of surviving comital documentation in this period and thus on its own is meaningless. There is other evidence, however, that suggests that these numbers are not simply a result of better rates of documentary survival: the nature of the agreements changes. Agreements with explicitly balanced content give way to agreements with explicitly unbalanced content. Of Ramon Berenguer I's nine treaty-conventions, for example, five date from before 1058, two from 1058, and only two from the remaining eighteen years of his reign. After 1058, the most common varieties of *convenientiae* are the various oath-conventions. This pattern in the evidence suggests that Ramon Berenguer I began around 1058 to use the *convenientia* in a new way. Whereas before it had been principally a tool for making agreements, either with neighboring counts or with overmighty castellans, now it was an instrument of power. This new function was reflected in the change of formula: the count no longer made conventions *with* people; people made conventions *to* him. In the context of these formal and substantive changes, the increase in numbers appears not as question of documentary survival but as evidence of a more active comital chancery. More agreements survive because Ramon Berenguer I's scribes were creating more of them.

These changes in the number and nature of conventions coincide almost exactly with the major turning point of Ramon Berenguer I's reign. In June 1057, the countess Ermessenda sold to her grandson her rights to the counties of Barcelona, Girona, and Osona, as well as a large number of castles, and swore fidelity to him; she retired to the castle of Besora where she died nine months later. In 1058, he made alliances with the counts Ermengol III of Urgell and Ramon Guifré of Cerdanya and took up, once again, the campaigns against the *taifa* kingdoms. Finally, in 1059, the count achieved the final submission of the rebel Mir Geribert and his supporters. With his major conflicts in order, and with an impressive increase in income from the *parias*, Ramon Berenguer I could turn to solidifying and ordering his control over the region. He started to purchase castles and bind their guardians to him by oath and *convenientia*.[7] A system of castle tenure based on written agreements began to emerge: Castell Vell and Castell Nou of Barcelona, Tàrrega, Orís, Solterra, Cervià, Begur, Montagut, Querol, Pinyana, Pontils, Balsareny, Gaià,

---

[7] RBI 206*, 230*, 231, 239*, sd 38*, sd 173*. See Sobrequés, *Els grans comtes*, 48–49, 52, 54–55; Bonnassie, *La Catalogne*, 2:640–41, 644, 664, 687–98.

Foundations (the eleventh century)

Estopanyà, Clarà, Púbol, Talladell, Pontons, Casserres . . . all within a decade.[8]

A decrease in the number of surviving conventions begins in the final years of the reign of Ramon Berenguer I, but the near disappearance of such agreements during the reigns of his sons is still striking. Only two agreements with the form "Hec est convenientia" survive from the period of the joint reign of Ramon Berenguer II (1076–82) and Berenguer Ramon II (1076–96): a treaty between the two brothers and Ermengol IV of Urgell concerning the war against Zaragoza and the distribution of income from the *parias*,[9] and the settlement of a dispute between the see of Vic and the Queralt family concluded before, or perhaps at the order of, Ramon Berenguer II.[10] Despite the fact that the brothers were at odds throughout the period of their joint reign, no *convenientiae* survive among the few artifacts of their attempts to reach a negotiated settlement. A *definitio atque pacificatio* mentions conventions between the two, but is not itself constructed as one.[11]

Even these would be treaty-conventions, however; commendations and oath-conventions dealing with the terms of castle holding are entirely absent from the comital documentation in these years. Ramon Berenguer I's testamentary instruction to his castellans not to grant control (*potestas*) of their castles to the brothers until a full year after his death may have dealt a blow to their chances of renewing the many castle-holding agreements established by their father. The same may be true of oaths of fidelity. Only two oath texts have survived, one of Arnau Mir de Sant Martí for the castles of Olèrdola and Eramprunyà, and a generic oath from which the list of the jurors' names has been removed.[12] The brothers did continue to grant lands and castles. Some of these grants appear to be outright donations, but those that include terms that would have been found in a *convenientia* of the reign of Ramon Berenguer I, such as requirements for the construction of fortifications, are written as

---

[8] RBI 218*, 225, 253.2*, 269, 273.1*, 280*, 287*, 292*, 296*, 320*, 321.1*, 373*, 376*; *LFM* 40, 151.

[9] RBII 69, 69dup. See Sobrequés, *Els grans comtes*, 99–100. RBII 69 contains a supplementary agreement not found in RBII 69dup.   [10] AME 9/36=9/59.

[11] RBII 39*, 71; 48*: "absolvo te Berengarium prenominatum de ipsa scriptura convenientie quam mihi fecisti per filiam Roberti Giscardi . . . quod resonat in ipsis scripturis quas fecimus fieri in Cervera de nostris convenientiis." Each of the first two signatures represents two single-sheet documents that have been sewn together. Francisco Diago recorded the existence of at least two documents that may have been these *convenientiae* (*Historia de los victoriosíssimos antiguos condes de Barcelona* . . . [Barcelona, 1603; repr. Valencia, 1974], fols. 132v–33v [lib. 2, cap. 68]). See also Gerónimo Pujades, *Crónica universal del principado de Cataluña*, 8 vols. (Barcelona, 1829–32), 8:2–4 (lib. 16, cap. 1); Bofarull, *Los condes*, 2:111; Sobrequés, *Els grans comtes*, 97–100.

[12] RBII 73*, 74. The latter text ends "Isti homines habent iuratum istum sacramentum," without listing any names; the parchment is cut just below this last line.

163

simple grants (*cartae donationis*).[13] Even the commendation by Ramon Berenguer II and his wife, Mahalda, of the castle of Font-rubí – in most respects a typical commendation, undated, and with the phrase "qui hanc convenientiam fecit" in one of the subscriptions – begins with the formula of a donation: "hec est donatio."[14] Ramon Berenguer II did not adopt his father's methods.

The reduced number and irregularity of conventions continued under the independent reign of Berenguer Ramon II, even after his nephew, Ramon Berenguer III, began to appear in documents with the comital title.[15] Two of the three documents with the form "Hec est convenientia" are associated with the settlement that defused the tensions following the assassination of Ramon Berenguer II by Berenguer Ramon II and established the tutelage of the young Ramon Berenguer III and his lands.[16] The first two are a pair of unbalanced agreements. In one, which was given the unorthodox designation "convenientia et baiulia et donatio," Ponç Guerau I, viscount of Girona, and his son Guerau Ponç granted ("donant") the *honor* of Ramon Berenguer III to his uncle for a period of eleven years. They also promised to receive the castles of the *honor* back from the count and to provide standard services. This transaction was a new one for a comital *convenientia*, although it is perfectly in line with the diplomatic roots of the document in the precarial grant and agrarian contract. In the other agreement, the count promised the viscount "and the other men holding the *honor* of the son of count Ramon Berenguer (II) who shall place themselves temporarily with the said *honor* under the tutelage and command of the said count Berenguer (Ramon II)" that he would not alienate the lands under his charge and that he would return them upon completion of the term. While this convention is partly a simple promise to Ponç Guerau recording the count's half of the bargain, the language suggests that this represents another novel use for the *convenientia*: a public pronouncement.[17] A third document associated with the settlement, the submission by Bernat Guillem de Queralt of lands to the tutelage of the count, also breaks with the regular forms: "Let all men be informed how Count Berenguer and Bernat Guillem, with the intercession of qualified men

---

[13] RBII 3*, 4*, 31, 41*, 65; *HGL* 5:335.2; *DPoblet* 24, 28 [*LBSC* 19], 29. [14] RBII 67*.

[15] The earliest such document is a grant of 23 August 1090 (cit. Bofarull, *Los condes*, 2:140; Sobrequés, *Els grans comtes*, 124–25).

[16] Sobrequés, *Els grans comtes*, 109–12; Shideler, *Montcadas*, 25–28; Benet, *Gurb-Queralt*, 139–44.

[17] BRII 34*, 35*. Benet writes, "El segon és la resposta del primer, i una crida, per part del comte Berenguer, als que vulguin fer el mateix conveni en les condicions esmentades" (*Gurb-Queralt*, 141). Changes are evident in BRII 34 to add Guerau Ponç to the agreement, whereas he is absent from BRII 35; this suggests that the order of composition of the documents is the reverse of what Benet proposes.

(*boni homines*), came to an agreement, making this pact and *convenientia* between themselves."[18]

All three of these documents are irregular in form, in content, or in both, when compared with the types dominant during the reign of Ramon Berenguer I. The only standard *convenientia* involving Berenguer Ramon II is the commendation of the tutelage of the castle of Montpalau and its underage castellan to Arnau Jofre.[19] In this case, however, the scribe may have been using an agreement from the reign of Ramon Berenguer I as a model.[20] Six days earlier the same scribe composed an oath-convention of Arnau Mir de Sant Martí, who was promising control (*potestas*) of the castles of Eramprunyà and Olèrdola (part of the *honor* of Ramon Berenguer II) for the term of the comital tutelage discussed above. The document refers to itself as a convention in the text ("hec supra scripta convenientia") and in a subscription, but begins "Sit omnibus presentibus et futuris manifestum."[21] With the exception of the straightforward grant of Montpalau, the temporary castle-holding arrangements enshrined in these unorthodox conventions are the only examples of documents recording the terms of castle holding from this period. In this, as in the very low number of oaths, Berenguer Ramon II's tenure was a continuation of his brother's reign.[22]

The small number of conventions involving these two counts – only six in over twenty years – must be considered in the context of the overall drop in numbers of comital documents surviving from this period. Documents from the reigns of Ramon Berenguer III (1096–1131) and Ramon Berenguer IV (1131–62) suggest that the acts of Berenguer Ramon II issued after the assassination were declared void at some point. One historian has suggested that the intentional destruction of these documents may explain the falloff.[23] This is possible, but that would only account for the absence of documents from *after* 1082. Furthermore, this hypothesis does not explain the changes in the *formulae* of these documents. It seems unquestionable that internecine struggle derailed the

---

[18] BRII 59*: "Certum sit omnibus hominibus qualiter B(erengarius) comes et B(ernardus) Guilelmi intervenientibus bonis hominibus ad concordiam veniunt, hoc pactum et convenientiam inter se facientes." Extra. 3233 may be a codicil to this agreement: "Hanc conventionem et placitum quod est presentialiter factum inter Berengarium comitem et Bernardum Guilelmi, si comes fregerit eum et non atenderit, mandat prescriptus comes vicecomiti Deusde (viscount of Tarragona, 1083–98) ut adiuvet de hoc filio Remundi Berengarii atque Bernardo Guilelmi per fidem sine ingenio usquequo fiat emendatum quod de prescripto placito fuerit hactum. S(*signum crucis*) Berengarii comitis qui hoc iussit facere [S(*signum crucis*) Deusde vicecomitis (*deleted, cross not pointed*)] S(*signum crucis*) Guilelmi Umberti S(*signum crucis*)m Deusdedit."

[19] BRII 62*. BRII 88 is an oath of Arnau Jofre to the count, in the same hand as the convention.

[20] RBI sd 52*, an extended oath to Ramon Berenguer I for Montpalau.   [21] BRII 61*.

[22] As during the joint reign, the count granted castles by *carta donationis*: LBSC 22; BRII 84.

[23] Sobrequés, *Els grans comtes*, 108, 139–40.

program of acquisition and organization of castles initiated by Ramon Berenguer I. The sons failed to build upon, or even maintain, the work of the father; in the process the *convenientia*, the tool used by the count to perform this work, fell into disuse at the highest political levels in the county of Barcelona. But beyond its borders, and even within the county in other milieux, it continued to spread.

Pallars Jussà

After a single convention datable to the reign of his father, Ramon III (1011–47), there are fifty-four conventions in which Ramon IV of Pallars Jussà (1047–98) is a participant. Twenty of these are undated, so it is difficult to draw chronologically precise conclusions.[24] Still, the beginnings of the use of *convenientiae* in Pallars Jussà are reasonably clear. Very few of the datable documents fall before 1060, and many of the undated documents can be dated to after 1055, the year of the marriage of Ramon IV to Valença de Tost. In the single convention from the reign of Ramon III, that count accepted the overlordship of Ermengol III of Urgell in return for a yearly payment.[25] The scribe of this document, dated 1040, was the priest Vidal. Vidal enjoyed a long career in the service of Arnau Mir de Tost, and it is in that capacity that he penned the first three datable conventions of Ramon IV.[26] He may thus be said to have introduced the form into this region. Still, the delay in increased numbers of datable *convenientiae* until the 1060s allows for possible influence from Barcelona.

The individuals appearing most often as parties to these conventions are Ramon IV's neighbors and frequent adversaries, the counts of Urgell and Pallars Sobirà.[27] The majority of the conventions, however, were contracted with the many castle-holding families of the region, including the viscomital family of Vilamur, the Bellera, and the Orcau.[28] Indeed, only six of the fifty-four documents do not deal explicitly with castles, either

---

[24] See Kosto, "The *convenientiae* of the Catalan Counts," Table 3 (pp. 220–21). On Pallars in the eleventh century, see Ferran Valls i Taberner, "Els orígens dels comtats de Pallars i Ribagorça," *Estudis universitaris catalans* 9 (1915–16), 40–101; Lydia Martínez i Teixidó, *Les famílies nobles del Pallars en els segles XI i XII*, Estudis 3 (Lleida, 1991).

[25] RBI 48. See also RBorrell 119★ (an oath).

[26] RBI 141, 163, 168★. Other documents involving Arnau Mir de Tost written by Vidal: DACU 564 (a. 1042), 596 (a. 1046); DPoblet 5 (a. 1047); RBI 171★, 172, 173★ (a. 1055), 191★ (a. 1056); BC 4118★ (a. 1058). His hand can also be found on RBI 230★ (a. 1058), a convention between the counts of Barcelona and Urgell, and perhaps RBI 163 (a. 1055).

[27] Urgell: RBII 19; BRII 28, 64; cf. Extra. 3271. Pallars Sobirà: RBI 306★, 378, 449★, sd 17★, sd 18, sd 19★, sd 20; RBIII 26★=Extra. 3293.

[28] Vilamur: RBI 354★, sd 21★; *LFM* 128; RBII 55★; BRII 85. Bellera: Extra. 3252★; RBI sd 26. Orcau: RBI 208★; BRII 54★; *LFM* 65.

as the object of the convention, or as a guarantee.[29] So as for Ramon Berenguer I, for Ramon IV the *convenientia* was an instrument with which to manage his castles. But as noted in chapter 2, while in the commendations of Ramon Berenguer I the count's undertakings are limited to a grant of a castle, office, or lands, Ramon IV's commendations tend to include additional comital promises, such as one not to demand control (*potestas*) of the castle. The fact that Ramon IV's subordinates were in a position to ask for such concessions suggests that the differences in power between the count and his men were not as great as in Barcelona, and that these agreements were therefore more truly reciprocal.

Comparison of this series of *convenientiae* with the one from Barcelona is in this respect instructive. In general the conventions from Pallars Jussà exhibit a greater degree of formal balance, seen in the persistence of the balanced opening formula, as well as the frequent presence of the subscriptions of both parties to an agreement. This formal aspect is mirrored in the content of the documents: there are fewer documents in which only one party acts, and many of the documents, including treaties, are explicitly linked to the settlement of conflicts. Ramon IV used the *convenientia* and oath in a fashion similar to his neighbors to the southeast to order his relationships with his subordinates, allies, and adversaries, especially in dealing with castles. The power that he was in a position to exercise, however, was of a different degree, so he and his scribes developed a type of agreement that was appropriate to his circumstances.

Other counties

Outside Barcelona and Pallars Jussà, comital *convenientiae* are more rare. In Cerdanya, the form took hold only in the 1070s: after one between Ramon Guifré (1035–68) and the bishop of Urgell,[30] five survive from the reign of his son, Guillem I Ramon (1068–95): two more with the bishop of Urgell, and three castle-holding conventions, one each with a viscount, a castellan, and a *caballarius*.[31] The two agreements with the bishop, both of which go beyond simple descriptions of the terms of castle holding, begin with the phrase "Hec est convenientia *et placitum*." The same phrase may be found in the opening of the text of an agreement between Guillem I Ramon and the party opposed to Berenguer Ramon II in 1084.[32] Earlier echoes of this phrase are present in an agreement ("brevis de placitum") of 1064 between Ramon Guifré and the

---

[29] The exceptions are: RBI sd 15*, sd 22*, sd 29; BRII 17*, 25*, 85.
[30] RBI sd 30*=Extra. 4744.3.   [31] BRII 73*; *LFM* 218, 534, 598, 627.
[32] Partially transcribed in Pujades, *Crónica*, 8:53–54, and Bofarull, *Los condes*, 2:132–33. The original may be in the Cardona archive at Seville (Archivo Ducal de Medinaceli).

villagers of Meranges: "all the men of the said vill made a *placitum* or *convenientia* . . . the count and countess made a *placitum* and *conventum* with all the men of the said vill."[33] In Cerdanya, then, agreements other than those concerning simply the tenure of castles employ the term *placitum*, alongside or independently of *convenientia*.[34] Despite the fact that no castle-holding conventions survive from the reign of Ramon Guifré, it would be incorrect to argue that he did not set down the terms of relationships with his subordinates in written documents. As seen in chapter 3, this was accomplished by means of oaths. Similarly, under Guillem I Ramon, the *convenientia* and *placitum* overlapped with a variety of oaths. The use of the written word in organizing power was strong in Cerdanya, but the forms the writing took were different, perhaps because of an earlier local tradition.

Of the remaining counties, Urgell supplies the most comital *convenientiae* from this early period: fourteen, half of which are with the counts of Barcelona. Fourteen is nevertheless a very small number given the proportion of conventions from before 1050 associated with this county. Of the six conventions between the counts of Urgell and Ramon Berenguer I, five were composed during the reign of Ermengol III (1038–66). Five additional conventions survive from the records of this count: a group of three transactions with Arnau Mir de Tost in 1057–58 and two conventions between the count and Bishop Guillem Guifré of Urgell.[35] The first of the agreements with Arnau describes the conditions under which Arnau held the castle of Casserres from the count; the second two created an alliance between the two, for which they exchanged castles as pledges. The agreements with the bishop record a pledge to keep a promise to hand over the castle of Solsona and a general promise of the count to protect the episcopal patrimony. The *convenientia* with Ramon Berenguer I and a second with his sons are the only ones remaining from the reign of the next count, Ermengol IV (1066–92).[36] From the brief reign of his son, Ermengol V (1092–1102), there are two more, both castle-holding agreements.[37] As in Pallars Jussà, scribes treated the *convenientia* as a more formal type than did their counterparts in Barcelona.

After a group of conventions from the 1050s concluded between Ramon Berenguer I and Guillem II of Besalú (1052–66), which appear to have been established through the initiative of the count of Barcelona (see below), no conventions of the counts of this region survive until four

---

[33] *LFM* 591: "faciunt placitum vel convenienciam omnes homines de predicta villa . . . comes et comitissa faciunt placitum et conventum cum omnes homines de iam dicta villa."
[34] Cf. BRII 52*; *LFM* 595.
[35] BC 4118* (two documents with the same date), 4133; DACU 672, 733.
[36] Extra. 4726; RBII 69.   [37] BC 4561*; BC, MS 941, fol. 482*.

from late in the reign of Bernat II (1066–1111). The two commendations and two general oath-conventions do not follow a single formula.[38] It is difficult to judge how representative this group is, since the surviving documentation from this period for Besalú is limited and primarily ecclesiastical. A long collective oath to Bernat II includes the names of some twenty individuals and castles, but only one additional oath or convention has survived.[39]

Aside from the agreements with the counts of Barcelona and Pallars Jussà noted above, only one document has survived recording a possible eleventh-century *convenientia* of a count of Pallars Sobirà.[40] In Empúries and Rosselló, meanwhile, comital *convenientiae* are limited to the agreements pertaining to the perennial dispute between the counts. The initial agreement (1069x78) is described as the "notitia de ipsa convenientia"; an accompanying oath refers to "the *convenientiae* that I promise."[41] The renewal of 1085 corresponds more closely to the norm: "Hec est conveniencia quod ego, Ugo, comes, facio tibi."[42] The *Liber feudorum Cerritaniae* preserves many detailed oaths to Guislabert II of Rosselló (1074–1102). These are not as extensive as the oaths to the counts of Cerdanya, but it is possible that as in Cerdanya oath and convention were merged into a single type of written record. A document from the long reign of the previous count, Jofre II (1013–74), lists the pledges granted by one of his men "that he should hold well those *convenientiae* or those oaths that he has sworn to him."[43]

Simply from the chronology of the foregoing survey, it appears that it was Ramon Berenguer I who took the lead in the use of the *convenientia*, for relationships with other counts, but especially for the creation of structures of castle holding. Changes in the surviving conventions of that count reveal an intensification of this effort from 1058. Ramon IV of Pallars Jussà engaged in a similar effort from the late 1060s. Castle-holding conventions of the counts of Urgell, while few in number, also appear only in the late 1060s and 1070s; in Besalú, it is not until the 1080s and 1090s. Elsewhere – Empúries, Rosselló, Pallars Sobirà – the evidence becomes quite thin, but enough survives to document the spread of the form throughout the Catalan counties. The use to which the *convenientia* could be put was

---

[38] BRII 33* (a. 1086), 42* (a. 1087), 70* (a. 1089); RBIII 62* (a. 1099). See Gaspar Feliu i Montfort, "Existí el comte Bernat III de Besalú?" *Acta historica et archaeologica mediaevalia* 19 (1998), 391–402.

[39] *LFM* 500. Extra. 4738 may be an additional contemporary collective oath, or another version of *LFM* 500. RBIII 60.1* and 60.2* record the donation of the castle of Navata *to* the count and the oath of the castellan. [40] Extra. 3300*.

[41] ADPO B4, 74*: "Haec est notitia de ipsa convenientia." RBI sd 191*: "ipsas convenientias que convenio." [42] *LFM* 698.

[43] *LFM* 751: "ut bene teneat ipsas conveniencias vel ipsos sacramentos quos ei iuratos habet." Additional oaths to Guislabert II of Rosselló: *LFM* 710, 720, 721, 722, 723, 724, 725, 741, 742, 759.

certainly influenced by the relative power of various counts: Pallars Jussà offers the clearest example. Similarly, the impact of the particular written form represented by the *convenientia* depended on precedent local traditions; this may explain the relationship between the convention and the written oath in Cerdanya. The picture presented here is certainly strongly affected by vagaries of documentary survival, but overall chronology, changes in form, and patterns of survival of other documentary types help to bypass that potential obstacle. Still, if Ramon Berenguer I was responsible for the spread of the *convenientia* as a means of structuring relationships, we should try to trace the process more closely. We can begin to accomplish this by moving from a consideration of the *convenientia* per se to an examination of how these agreements worked in a broader context.

Convenientiae *in context: Barcelona and Besalú*

How did mechanisms for making and keeping agreements function in this society? How exactly were they used? Were they effective? The attempt of Ramon Berenguer I to form an alliance with Guillem II of Besalú during the years 1054–57 produced unusually numerous and detailed records, including several *convenientiae*. It reveals in greater detail how conventions played a role in the process, and the early progress of the efforts of Ramon Berenguer I to impose on the region a system based on written agreements.[44] The action unfolds in three phases, each of which centers on a *convenientia*. In 1054, desperately searching for allies in his conflict with his grandmother, the countess Ermessenda, Ramon Berenguer turned to the notoriously irascible count of Besalú. A convention dated 11 September 1054 ("[Hec sunt] placita sive convenien-cie") relates that the count of Besalú came to the city of Barcelona, where at a *placitum* he became the man of the count of Barcelona, commending himself and swearing fidelity. Much of the document, such as the promises of aid for the standard list of counties, reads like an oath-convention. Other clauses reveal the specific goals of this agreement. Ramon Berenguer's first concern was to recover control of the double castle at Finestres and the castle at Colltort, which had been the subjects of a transaction between their fathers, Berenguer Ramon I and Guillem I. He requested the return of the original charter, or, failing that, an oath that Guillem would turn it over when he could find it. He then had Guillem recognize his rights in the castles, hand over *potestas* of the castles, and compose another charter, returning the castles to Ramon Berenguer on the same terms by which they had been granted to Guillem I. Ramon

---

[44] Benito-Kosto-Taylor, "Approaches," 62–68.

Berenguer's second concern was territorial jurisdiction. Guillem promised that if he was wronged by anyone from the counties of Barcelona, Osona, or Girona, he would not take matters into his own hands until first complaining to the count and giving the count three months to pursue the matter by judicial means. In order to address further his first concern, Ramon Berenguer arranged that the guarantees for the agreement be the castles of Finestres, with their castellan Ramon Ademar, and the castle of La Guàrdia, with its castellan Ramon Bernat.[45]

The guarantees of this convention were spelled out in three additional documents, each of which refers back to the primary agreement.[46] Two of these are nearly identical in language and record the pledges of castles mentioned in the convention. One has as its primary subject the castles of Finestres and Ramon Ademar, mentioning Colltort and La Guàrdia only at the conclusion. The other addresses Colltort and its castellan, mentioning Finestres only in the final clauses. Each document refers several times to "our *convenientia* that is written between me and my lord, the said Ramon." In the third document ("Notum sit omnibus quia sub ista convenientia"), Ramon Ademar submitted himself to the count of Barcelona as a pledge for the count of Besalú for "those *convenientiae* that he promised to the said count Ramon," on condition that the count of Barcelona allow him to remain in possession of the castles.[47]

As part of the negotiations surrounding this alliance, Ramon Berenguer arranged for the count of Besalú to marry his new sister-in-law, Llúcia.[48] The second set of documents deals with this marriage agreement. Two of the documents, a *scriptura dotis* and a donation *causa sponsalitii*, bear the date 11 December 1054, exactly three months after the first convention. In the first, the count offered as a dower one-tenth of all his possessions, as was required by the *Liber iudiciorum*; in the second he added donations of the counties of Berga and Ripoll, with all their possessions.[49] In detailing the extent of the second donation, the

---

[45] RBI 154*.

[46] RBI sd 31*, sd 209* ("sicut scriptum est in nostra convenientia que est scripta inter me et iamdictum seniorem meum Remundum"); RBIV ap. 10*. Lluís G. Constans i Serrats, ed., *Diplomatari de Banyoles*, 6 vols. (Banyoles, 1985–93), nos. 76, 77, 79 (2:31–34, 37–38), dates all three of these to 1057, associating them with the convention between the two counts of that date. As Ramon Bernat and the castle of La Guàrdia are not mentioned as pledges in the 1057 convention, however, it seems clear that these three documents are ancillary to RBI 154*. Furthermore, RBI sd 31* appears to be cut from the same piece of parchment as RBI 154*. Constans i Serrats, ed., *Banyoles*, no. 76 (2:21–25), misidentifies RBIV ap. 10* as RBI sd 10.

[47] Both halves of this chirograph survive (RBIV ap. 10*, ap. 10dup); each is in a different hand, but each leaves out the count's counterpromise, which is added in as a correction.

[48] See now Aurell, *Les noces du comte*, 281–87.

[49] RBI 156, 157. On these types of marriage agreements, see Bonnassie, *La Catalogne*, 1:258–62, and Jesús Lalinde Abadía, "Los pactos matrimoniales catalanes (Esquema histórico)," *Anuario de historia del derecho español* 33 (1963), 149–71.

document refers back to a "*conveniencia* that is written between me (i.e., Guillem II) and Ramon, count of Barcelona, and the countess Almodis."[50] The reference is not to the initial convention, but to another one, undated, but presumably very close in time to the first.[51] This second convention records Ramon Berenguer's promise to donate the counties, as well as further undertakings with regard to the proposed marriage. The donation was to be carried out by the feast of Saint Martin, that is, Friday, 11 November 1054, exactly two months following the first convention; the wedding was to take place on the following Sunday. As it turned out, the proceedings suffered a delay of one month, as the marriage documents were not composed until 11 December (also a Sunday). The guarantees given for this agreement were of a different nature than those for the first convention. In addition to two castles with their castellans (Milany and La Portella), Guillem offered ten hostages, including the bishop of Elna, for 20 ounces of gold each.

It is impossible to know if the parties adhered to most early comital *convenientiae*. In this case, the outcome is known: the agreements collapsed. A formal complaint (*querela*) of the count of Barcelona against the count of Besalú survives that lists violations of clauses contained in each of the two sets of agreements just discussed:[52] (1) After becoming the man of Ramon, swearing fidelity, and promising in writing not to abuse him or defy him (in the first convention), Guillem did precisely that, declaring himself to be an enemy and raiding in his territory and "doing bad things." (2) He had promised that he would send him pledges (either convention) and failed to do so. (3) He had promised to return the charter for Finestres and Colltort (first convention) and failed to do so. (4) He had granted to him hostages for 10,000 *solidi* (200 ounces of gold), but then unilaterally relieved them of their obligations (second convention). (5) He had promised to provide a replacement if one of these hostages died, and failed to do so. (This clause is not included in the second convention; it might refer to Berenguer, bishop of Elna, who died in 1054.) (6) Before declaring himself an enemy, he claimed that Ramon ought to lose his *honor* and his men, and that he would take him captive and make him redeem himself. (This is an extraordinary complaint about what is essentially an insult; it was not foreseen in the conventions.) (7) He and his men built fortresses on the count's frontier. (Again, this was not specifically mentioned in the conventions, but might be considered under a general heading.) (8) He repudiated the count's sister-in-law, given to him in marriage (second convention; despite the fact that it is

---

[50] RBI 157: "sicut est scriptum in conveniencia que est scripta inter Remundum comitem Barchinonensem et Adalmus comitassam et me."   [51] RBI sd 11.   [52] RBI sd 35.

buried deep in the list, this is the principal complaint.) (9) He named the countess Almodis as a pledge for 50 *solidi* a year to Ponç I Hug, count of Empúries, but subsequently relieved her of the obligation.[53]

About half of the specific complaints, then, were drawn directly from the conventions. The provisions for pledges and hostages were entirely ineffective, and the agreement collapsed. It is not at all clear precisely when this occurred. It has been observed that this rejection of comital authority is a perfect reflection of Ramon Berenguer I's weakness during these years. Bonnassie has plausibly suggested that Guillem II's defiance of the agreements was engineered by the countess Ermessenda. Soon afterward, though, the count of Barcelona regrouped and was in a position to try one more time to come to an understanding with his neighbor.

The third set of documents is dated 4 October 1057.[54] The centerpiece of this group is, once again, a *convenientia*. In it, Guillem II repeats many of the promises, including those of homage and fidelity, made in the first agreement; the only additional specific clause is a limitation of Guillem's required service in the comital host to the Islamic frontier. As a pledge for this agreement, Guillem offered once again the castle of Colltort, now under the control of Guillem, bishop of Vic. The document appears to be a simple chirograph, but the other half of the chirograph pair is not a duplicate but rather a continuation of the text of the convention, beginning "And on account of the above-written *convenienciae*" ("Et propter has conveniencias superius scriptas"). This section records the settlement of all the disputes between the counts, but reiterates the superior right of the count of Barcelona to the castles of Finestres and Colltort and the continuing validity of Guillem II's oath of fidelity. This portion of the document also includes a series of clauses that illustrate Ramon Berenguer I's attempt at finding a different means for assuring compliance, namely, mutual deterrence. Guillem promised to destroy the fortifications in progress at Vilademuls and not to rebuild them. If he failed to destroy them, Ramon Berenguer would build fortifications nearby. Ramon Berenguer promised, however, not to grant this fortress to anyone from Guillem's territory and to destroy it as soon as Guillem destroyed his castle at Vilademuls. The third document in the set is the grant in pledge of the castle of Colltort, along with its guardians, the bishop of Vic and Eneas Mir, for the maintenance of "the said *convenientia* that was written between me and him on 4 October."

---

[53] "Item iamdictus Guilelmus comes misit in plivio comitissam uxorem iam dicti Remundi comitis, per quingentos solidos per unumquenque annum, ad Pontium comitem Impuritanensem; et dimisit eam incurrere." This is not very clear; the last sentence may be incomplete.

[54] RBI 210*, 211* ("prescriptum illam convenientiam que fuit scripta inter me et illum iiii nonas octobris"), sd 5.

The outcome of this final set of agreements is not specifically known, although Ramon Berenguer I did not appear to have any further trouble with Guillem II in the remaining nine years of the latter's life. Llúcia was married off to Artau I of Pallars Sobirà the following February. This arrangement, too, is known through a cluster of documents centered on a convention. In the convention, Artau promised to give six castles in Pallars to Llúcia. Control over two of these was to be granted to the counts of Barcelona, while the other four were to be under the control of Llúcia herself. This grant was made in addition to the grant of dower (*titulus dotis*) assigning the portion of the husband's property (*decima*) specified by the *Liber iudiciorum*. The convention also stated that the castellans of the castles granted were to swear fidelity to Llúcia and to the counts.[55] Two of these oaths survive in written form, identical in language except for the names of the castellans and the castles; each refers specifically to "those *convenientiae* that he promised to you."[56]

With the third agreement with Guillem II of Besalú in 1057 and the marriage pact with Artau I of Pallars Sobirà in 1058, Ramon Berenguer I was coming to the end of his use of the *convenientia* as a instrument for high-level treaties. He contracted two more in 1058 with the counts of Urgell and Cerdanya in preparation for the resumption of attacks on the *taifa* states, and then only two more in the remaining two decades of his rule. His experience with Guillem II had perhaps convinced him and his scribes to rethink the role of *convenientiae*. What is important, however, is that he continued to use them. Ramon Berenguer saw the potential of the written word as an instrument of power. He remained faithful to the concept even though it was not always effective.

This obsession with writing can be seen in the numbers of documents involved in each step of the dispute, often three or four at a time.[57] It can be seen in Ramon Berenguer I's concern to get an original charter back from Guillem II, even though he required a new one to be drawn up, and even though the system of comital courts that relied on such documents was moribund. It can be seen in Ramon Berenguer's first complaint that Guillem had violated promises made *in writing*. And it can be seen, above all, in the creativity of the scribes, who continued the process of experimentation. Many of the documents were new forms, such as complaints (*querimoniae*), oaths, lists of hostages, and *convenientiae*. Freed from

---

[55] RBI 217*; RBIII sd 44*. RBI 217* should be dated 1058, not 1057, placing the marriage *after* the settlement with the count of Besalú. Cf. Sobrequés, *Els grans comtes*, 49; Bofarull, *Los condes*, 2:74; Aurell, *Les noces du comte*, 287–88.

[56] RBI sd 129*; sd 139: "illas convenientias quas habet convengudas ad vos."

[57] This is also true of the acquisition of the counties of Carcassonne and Razès, although the documentation involved in that agreement was more orthodox: RBI 393*; *LFM* 816 (a *convenientia*), 817, 819, 839; *HGL* 5:284, etc. See Cheyette, "Sale," 830–39.

formulae, or perhaps forced to break with formulae, they created ever increasing varieties of new instruments. The obsession was not universal. The count of Besalú paid no attention to his written agreements, and of the many documents to survive from that region, very few involve the count. But elsewhere, especially in Barcelona in the second half of the reign of Ramon Berenguer I, it was in full force.

LAY ARISTOCRACY

Proponents of the "feudal revolution" in Mediterranean Europe argue that after an initial period of crisis, regional princes – in Catalonia, Ramon Berenguer I – rebuilt their power in part by adopting the habits of the rebellious nobles and castellans who had threatened them in the first place. The implication here is that the *convenientia*, and by extension the systems of castle tenure that it enshrined, was in the first instance a tool of the lay aristocracy.[58] If this is the case, Ramon Berenguer I would not be a great innovator, but a desperate mimic. While the castle-holding practices of the counts and lay aristocracy before the second third of the eleventh century remain in the shadows, the increased evidence from that point on allows for a testing of this hypothesis. In contrast to some other regions of Europe, literate habits in Catalonia were common beyond ecclesiastical and comital milieux. If, in the context of an overall growth of surviving documentation, the count were adopting the methods of his inferiors, evidence for those methods among the lay aristocracy should at least be concurrent with, if not antedate, similar evidence in the comital documentation. In fact, this is not the case.

The conventions that have survived from before 1050 primarily record agreements involving counts and ecclesiastical institutions. Of the few private conventions, the three that record grants of castles date from the very end of that period (1045–50);[59] another four survive from the period before 1058, when Ramon Berenguer I's intensified use of the convention began.[60] Only after that point, and in fact with a lag of about a decade, do private conventions begin to appear in any number. Ramon Berenguer I

---

[58] E.g., Pierre Bonnassie, "Du Rhône à la Galice: Genèse et modalités du régime féodal," in *Structures féodales*, 22, 37: "Les nouvelles structures, nées spontanément dans la fièvre des violences, s'affermissent et s'institutionnalisent. Les agents de cette normalisation sont essentiellement les comtes de Barcelone . . . Il est clair que [la troisième phase, celle de la reconstruction des pouvoirs] n'a pu se développer qu'à partir des éléments qui s'étaient dégagés au temps des troubles."

[59] *DPoblet* 5 (a. 1047); RBI 105 (a. 1049); ACA, Cancelleria reial, Cartes reials, Papers per incorporar, caixa 1, "57/c11" (a. 1050). *DPoblet* 3 (a. 1045) records the terms of a castle-holding agreement, but not the grant of the castle. BC, MS 729, 4:51r–v (a. 1041) and *Òdena* 9 (a. 1040) concern castles, but not grants of castles of this type.

[60] ACV 9/ii/50 (a. 1052); RBI 153 (a. 1054), 204 (a. 1057); *Òdena* 10 (a. 1054).

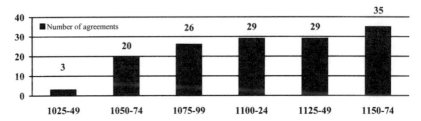

Figure 4.1. Castle-holding agreements among the lay aristocracy (1025–1174)

may indeed have reconstructed his formerly "public" power on the basis of aristocratic practices. In the particular case of the *convenientia*, however, the count was not appropriating the methods of castellans. Extensive application of the written *convenientia* spread not upward, but downward.

Once the lay aristocracy adopted written methods, however, their use increased rapidly. The chronological distribution of a sample of 150 documents from the period 1050–1200 recording the terms of castle tenure among the lay aristocracy suggests that the regime of written castle-holding agreements was instituted very quickly in the period 1050–74 (Fig. 4.1).[61] Furthermore, once the aristocracy had adopted this form, they were more persistent in its use than were the counts. The numbers of comital *convenientiae* from the reigns of Ramon Berenguer II and Berenguer Ramon II, and even the early reign of Ramon Berenguer III, are quite small. The numbers of agreements among the lay aristocracy, in contrast, continue to grow. It is also significant that the majority of these documents before 1100 (37 of 46, or 80 percent) maintain the strict conceptual division between the commendation of a castle and the grant of lands and rights associated with that castle. In many of those that do not, the language is so ambiguous that it does not provide a satisfying counter-example.[62] In fact, this pattern provides another indication of Ramon Berenguer I's importance for the establishment of the regime of conventions among the lay aristocracy and for the survival of a "public" conception of control over castles. None of the three grants before 1050

---

[61] Kosto, "Agreements," Table 6.1 (pp. 402–6). The sample is of private grants of castles, that is, transactions not involving either the count or an ecclesiastical institution. The list includes both commendations and grants in fief of castles, some of which do not strictly follow the standard *convenientia* form. Outright transfers of castles (i.e., sales, or clear cases of grants as alods) have been omitted, as have documents recording grants of lands on which castles were to be constructed. Neither of these types of transactions provides evidence for an ongoing relationship between two parties with respect to an existing castle. The sample comprises, therefore, documents of any type that recorded the establishment of links in chains of command over castles.

[62] E.g., RBI 471: "Donant namque . . . ipsum castrum de Tagamanent . . . Insuper donant unam cavaleriam" (here the concept of commendation is absent, but the grant of the castle is recognized as something separate from the grant of associated lands).

makes clear the grant/commendation distinction: two are grants in fief of castles; one is a *donatio* of a castle that does not use the term *commendare*. In agreements from after *c.* 1050, the concept of commendation is almost always present, and the castle itself is only rarely a fief. The lay aristocracy adopted not only comital documentation, but the comital conception of the system of castle tenure.

EPISCOPAL CASTLES

Bishops were as much a part of the eleventh-century changes in Catalan society as were secular lords; indeed, bishops frequently came from the powerful families that directed the course and pace of these changes. Like the counts, they were powerful men in a society where access to and use of power was very fluid. Did the fact that they were charged with the conservation and exploitation of an undying institutional patrimony affect their actions? What role did they play in the establishment of new structures for Catalan society and in the diffusion of *convenientiae* as a means for developing and maintaining these structures?

One approach to these questions is to examine the networks of castles acquired and developed by various dioceses, for like the counts, they controlled castles and military resources. And like the counts, they used written agreements to structure these relationships: bishops and cathedral chapters entered into *convenientiae* that defined their rights in castles and their relationships with guardians of castles and their retainers. While the outlines of comital castle holding are fairly well known, and many of its details have been examined above, the subject of episcopal castle holding has only rarely been addressed.[63] Castles were the focus of the military power of the Catalan bishops, not only as defensive sites, but as a source of armed service. Thus the study of the development of episcopal castle holding can improve our understanding of the formation of new structures of power. Compared to the volume of evidence found in the central comital archive, the number of conventions from most of the dioceses is limited. Here too, then, *convenientiae* need to be

---

[63] Freedman, *Vic*, 90–114, stands virtually alone. Cf. Heinz Dopsch, "Burgenbau und Burgenpolitik des Erzstiftes Salzburg im Mittelalter," in Hans Patze, ed., *Die Burgen im deutschen Sprachraum: Ihre rechts- und verfassungsgeschichtliche Bedeutung*, 2 vols., Vorträge und Forschungen 19 (Sigmaringen, 1976), 2:387–417; Olivier Guyotjeannin, *Episcopus et comes: Affirmation et déclin de la seigneurie épiscopale au nord du royaume de France (Beauvais-Noyon, X^e–début XIIIe siècle)*, Mémoires et documents publiés par la Société de l'École des chartes 30 (Geneva, 1987); Giancarlo Andenna, "La signoria ecclesiastica nell'Italia settentrionale," in *Chiesa e mondo feudale nei secoli X–XII: Atti della dodicesima Settimana internazionale di studio Mendola, 24–28 agosto 1992*, Miscellanea del Centro di studi medioevali 14, Scienze storiche 59 (Milan, 1995), 111–47; George W. Dameron, *Episcopal Power and Florentine Society, 1000–1320*, Harvard Historical Studies 107 (Cambridge, Mass., 1991), 43–49, and works cited there.

examined in the more general context of documentation concerning episcopal castles.

The extent of episcopal control over castles varied across time and from diocese to diocese. Papal confirmations, though incomplete, illustrate these differences. Privileges of Alexander III granted to the see of Barcelona in 1169 and again in 1176 listed nine *castella*, in addition to the episcopal palace, Regomir gate, and "archdeacon's towers" of Barcelona.[64] Alexander III's privilege to the see of Urgell in 1165, in contrast, listed twenty-four castles, nearly three times as many as at Barcelona at roughly the same date. Urgell had not always been so well established: a privilege of Agapetus II (951) listed only the castle of Sanaüja.[65] Yet these papal bulls, while useful for comparison, prove incomplete guides. Further study of the available documentation reveals that the see of Urgell had an interest in no fewer than 100 castles in the eleventh and twelfth centuries, including both major and minor fortifications. The "second consecration" of the cathedral in 1040, for example, listed along with the *castrum* of Guissona seventeen *castella* within its borders.[66] Benedict VII's confirmation to the see of Vic in 978 listed only the castles of Montbui and Tous, though in the eleventh and twelfth centuries the see had interests in as many as thirty-eight castles.[67] The see of Girona, no doubt because of its location away from the frontier, was the least implicated in the network of castle holding, and papal confirmations do not mention any castles among the possessions of the diocese.[68] Still, Girona had ties to eighteen castles in the eleventh and twelfth centuries. While the experiences of the various dioceses were different, all were involved in the system. All, too, followed roughly similar patterns of development.

Beginnings

Bishops Arnulf of Vic, Odó of Girona, and Aeci of Barcelona participated in the Catalan expedition against Córdoba in 1010. Aeci died on the battlefield, Arnulf and Odó soon thereafter. Their role in the campaign is just one proof that before and after reform currents and the Peace of God swept through the region, bishops were leading forces into conflicts with foes both Islamic and Christian.[69] It was in the late tenth

[64] Barberà, Castellbisbal, El Llor, Ribes, Sitges, La Granada, Banyeres, Montmell, and L'Albà, the last mentioned only in the document of 1176: LA 1:32*, 1:33* [J-L 11624, 12720].

[65] Cebrià Baraut, "La data de l'acta de consagració de la catedral carolíngia de La Seu d'Urgell," *Urgellia* 7 (1984–85), app. 3 (pp. 528–29) [DACU 123; J-L 3654] (a. 951); DACU 1599 [J-L 11231] (a. 1165); cf. DACU 271, 324, 1170, 1523 [J-L 3918, 3993, 5699, –].

[66] Cebrià Baraut, ed., "Les actes de consagracions d'esglésies del bisbat d'Urgell (segles IX–XII)," *Urgellia* 1 (1978), app. 51 (pp. 126–28) [DACU 528].   [67] *DVic* 445 [J-L 3794]; Table 4.1.

[68] E.g., CCM 20, 70, 216.

[69] Sobrequés, *Els grans comtes*, 8. For two later examples, see Freedman, *Vic*, 103.

Table 4.1. Transactions involving castles of the diocese of Vic, by episcopacy, tenth to twelfth centuries

	Tous	Artés	Montbui	Font-rubí	Esparreguera	Les Espases	Miralles	Meda	Llancra	Vilagelans	L'Espelt	Calaf	Ocelló	L'Aguilar	Viladémager	Eures	Malla	Voltregà	Aguilar	Llavinera	S'Avellana	Copons	Montfalcó	Veciana	Quer	Oris	Solterra	Revell	Sentfores	Torroella	Monlleó	Briançó	Pomar	Palau Episcopal	Palomera	Taradell
(to 972)	+																																			
Fruia (972–93)	O		O	+	+	+	+																													
Arnulf (993–1010)			O	+	−	−	+	+	+																											
Borrell (1010–17)	O		O	+																																
Oliba (1017–46)	O		O							+	+	+	O	+	+	+																				
Guillem de Balsareny (1046–76)	O							O		O	O	O	O				±	+	O	O	O	O	−	−	−	+	+	+	+	+						
Berenguer Sunifred (1076–99)	O							O		O	O	O	O					O	O	O	O	O	O	−	−	O	O	O	+	+	+	+	+			
Guillem Berenguer (1099–1101)	O																	O												+	+	+	+			
Arnau de Malla (1102–9)												O		O				O							−						O	O	O	O		
Ramon Jofre (1109–46)	O	O	O					O		O	O	O	O	O		O										O									O	
Pere de Redorta (1147–85)	O	O														O																O	O	O	O	O
Ramon Xetmar (1185–94)	O	O										O														O									±	O

Key: O subject of transaction(s) + acquired − alienated ± acquired and alienated

and early eleventh centuries, however, that bishoprics first acquired or established ties to particular castles. Many were on the frontier and had been acquired with the assent or encouragement of the counts of Barcelona and Urgell. After the sack of Barcelona in 985, the counts were looking for allies in developing the frontier, and the well-endowed ecclesiastical institutions, headed by their relatives and relatives of their viscounts, proved ready to assist. Even at this early stage bishops appointed guardians for the castles, but they were usually held on ambiguous terms with no mention of specific military services due to the bishop. Still, this early evidence points to the forms of documentation and types of relationship that would later be developed by the counts, and in some cases by the bishops themselves.

The early presence of the bishops of Barcelona was strongest in the Penedès, the coastal plain south and west of Barcelona. Throughout the tenth century, the frontier was located in this region. The counts of Barcelona focused their efforts at reconquest there, and the bishops of Barcelona worked alongside them in their efforts to regain the territory. It was as a result of this activity that during the course of the tenth century the bishops acquired rights in various castles. Despite the participation of Aeci in the raid of 1010, at this early stage the concern of the diocese was not as much with military affairs as it was with repopulation. The process may have begun as early as the pontificate of Teuderic (900–931),[70] but the first evidence for possible episcopal control over fortifications in the region refers to his successor, Guilara. In 950×51, Guilara granted lands at La Granada to *Sisovallus*, to be held by him and his descendants from the church.[71] Although no mention was made of a fortification, one must have been in place by at least 1000×1002 and 1003, when La Granada was destroyed during Islamic incursions. The see maintained its rights, and later bishops sold and exchanged lands to raise funds to restore the tower (*turris*).[72]

La Granada failed to develop into an independent center of military strength for the see in the eleventh and twelfth centuries; this was not the case with the complex of coastal fortifications centered on Ribes.[73] In the franchise charter granted to the inhabitants of Ribes in 990, Bishop

---

[70] Gaspar Feliu i Montfort, "Els inicis del domini territorial de la seu de Barcelona," *Cuadernos de historia económica de Cataluña* 14 (1976), 52.

[71] LA 4:356★. See Feliu i Montfort, "Els inicis," 53; Sebastián Puig y Puig, *Episcopologio de la sede Barcinonense: Apuntes para la historia de la iglesia de Barcelona y de sus prelados*, Biblioteca histórica de la Biblioteca Balmes, ser. 1, 1 (Barcelona, 1929), 91.

[72] LA 4:355★ (a. 1005), 2:343★ (a. 1009), 2:324★ (a. 1012). Gaspar Feliu i Montfort, "El patrimoni de la seu de Barcelona durant el pontificat del Bisbe Aeci (995–1010)," *Estudis universitaris catalans* 30 (1994), 58–59 and n. 55, cites another document referring to the reconstruction of La Granada (ACB 1–2–1416=LA 1:277★). For the dating of the incursions, see Sobrequés, *Els grans comtes*, 4–6.

[73] José Maria Coll, "Los castillos de San Pedro de Ribas, La Geltrú, Sitges y Miralpeix," *Analecta sacra Tarraconensia* 32 (1959), 237–53; CPF, 1:672–74; though both should be used with caution.

Vives claimed that the see had acquired the *castrum* by *aprisio* under the reigns of his predecessors Guilara (937–59) and Pere (959–72).[74] Any fortifications at Ribes would have been destroyed during al-Manṣūr's campaign of 985, and this grant of 990 did not describe military arrangements for the site. By 1002, the bishops had lost control of the castle and had complained to the papal court, which directed letters to the violator of episcopal lands, Geribert.[75] Geribert died around 1014, but Ribes was still in the hands of his wife, Ermengarda, when she composed her testament in 1029.[76] Episcopal castle holding to the west of the river Foix started at a similar time. The earliest reference to a castle at Montmell is also found in a franchise charter granted to the inhabitants in 974, again by Bishop Vives.[77] Like the charter for Ribes, the grant does not describe any military arrangements. This castle, too, was probably overrun during al-Manṣūr's campaign in 985, and the addition of the subscription of Bishop Aeci to the very end of the witness list indicates that the grant was renewed during his tenure.

The see of Barcelona had an early interest in at least two other sites in the Penedès. In 959 the see received a grant to establish a castle at Freixe, on the banks of the Gaià. This project was perhaps overly ambitious, as the development of the area did not in fact get underway for another two centuries.[78] In 1032, Bishop Guadall granted the site of Banyeres, 15 km to the west, to Mir Llop Sanç, who along with his father had built the castle and had overseen the population of its lands. Banyeres was held for agricultural services at that point; the grant did not refer to military arrangements.[79]

---

[74] LA 4:368★.

[75] LA 4:387★. Fidel Fita's suggestion ("Bula inédita de Silvestre II," *Boletín de la Real academia de la historia* 18 [1891], 248), adopted by Font Rius (*CPF*, 1:672), that Geribert was refusing to recognize his vassalage to the bishop for Ribes because he had restored or reconquered the castle does not persuade. First, no mention is made of vassalage in the text of the letter, nor is there evidence for recognitions of "vassalage" or "homage" to the bishops at this early date. Second, the site was in the hands of the bishop in 990, and there is no evidence for another Islamic incursion until 1000x1002, which is contemporaneous with the date of this papal letter. Geribert's seizure of the castle may be related to the return of his brother, the viscount Udalard I, from captivity in 991 and his subsequent loss of power (Francesch Carreras y Candi, "Lo Montjuích de Barcelona," *Memorias de la Real academia de buenas letras de Barcelona* 8 [1906], 316–17).   [76] LA 4:375★.

[77] LA 4:394★; *CPF*, 1:677–78.

[78] LA 4:435★. See *CPF*, 1:678–79; Feliu i Montfort, "Els inicis," 53.

[79] LA 4:329★. See Bonnassie, *La Catalogne*, 2:748 and n. 55, citing LA 4:328★; I have not found additional evidence for episcopal control of the castle of Tomoví, cited there. LA 4:437★, the first evidence for a third site, the castle of L'Albà (10 km north of Freixe), is almost certainly a forgery. The document is a *convenientia* between Bishop Vives and Guitard de Mura in which Vives makes a grant *ad edificandum* in return for promises of *potestas* and other services. Although this cannot be demonstrated by more conclusive prosopographical evidence, the document, if authentic, would push back to 978 the earliest appearance of many terms for relationships and institutions that developed fully only in the mid-eleventh century: *castlans, potestas, fidelitas*, hosts and cavalcades, not to mention the use of a toponymic and the term *convenientia* itself. Furthermore, the penalty of 2 pounds of gold would be one of the earliest mentions of this metal in Catalonia (see Bonnassie, *La Catalogne*, 1:372–76). Of course this is precisely the geographical area where early mentions of gold would be expected. See, *contra*, DBarcelona, p. 155.

To judge by the toponym, the most important episcopal castle held by the bishops of Barcelona was not in the Penedès, but north of Barcelona at a site in the Vallès overlooking the Llobregat now known as Castellbisbal. Although an earlier origin has been proposed,[80] the first concrete evidence for the existence of the castle – and by extension from the toponym, of episcopal control over the castle – is in charters from 1012 and 1014.[81] As for two other sites in the Vallès mentioned in the papal bulls of 1169 and 1176, El Llor appears in the testaments of Bishop Vives (989 and 995), but not as a castle,[82] while traces of Barberà are only fleeting. Barberà came under episcopal control through a testamentary grant in 1005.[83] In 1068, Adalbert Guitard and his wife Nèvia commended the castle to Berenguer Ramon and his wife and children in return for military service. Whatever control the bishop had at Barberà seems to have vanished by this date.[84]

Thus the bishops of Barcelona were from the late tenth century closely tied to the work of repopulation of the frontier, and that work gained them the tenure of several castles, especially in the Penedès. But while they certainly encouraged the construction and maintenance of fortifications – the pledges destined for the reconstruction of the *turris* at La Granada are the best evidence of this – the surviving documentation offers little evidence for the terms on which these fortifications were held from the see.

The bishops of Vic began to acquire and build castles during the reign of Count Borrell II of Barcelona (947–92). Seventeen different sites appear as *castra* in documentation from Vic from the first half of the tenth century, always as territorial designations (Cat. *castells termenats*) rather than as fortifications per se. Later, some of these were unquestionably episcopal castles.[85] Tous had entered the episcopal patrimony in 960 by means of a pious donation of Borrell II, which described Tous as "within the territory of the castle of Montbui," providing the first evidence for that castle, as well.[86] Both of these sites were located on the western frontier of the diocese, to the north of the frontier castles of the see of

---

[80] *Els castells catalans*, 6 vols. in 7 parts (Barcelona, 1967–79), 2:32–33.   [81] LA 2:162★, 4:374★.

[82] LA 1:46★, 4:150★.

[83] LA 3:218★; also 3:217★, 3:219★, 3:220★, 3:221★, 3:222★. See also Feliu i Montfort, "El patrimoni," 62; *Els castells*, 2:8.   [84] *Els castells*, 2:10–11.

[85] *Castra*, with dates of first appearance in documentation: Torelló, 881 (*DVic* 2); Sant Llorenç, 881 (*DVic* 4); Gurb, 886 (*DVic* 6); Besora, 885x87 (*DVic* 8); Tona, 888 (Enrique Flórez et al., *España sagrada* . . ., 51 vols. [Madrid, 1747–1879], vol. 28, app. 3 [pp. 246–48]); Casserres, 898 (*DVic* 26); Centelles, 898 (*ACondal* 10); Voltregà, 902 (*DVic* 32); Lluçà, 905 (*Catalunya romànica*, 27 vols. [Barcelona, 1984–98], 2:253–54); Oristà, 908 (*DVic* 43); Taradell, 910 (*DVic* 51; cf. 22); Sentfores, 911 (*DVic* 54); Orís, 914 (*DVic* 58); Cornil, 917 (*DVic* 72); Malla, 924 (*DVic* 111); Oló, 930 (*DVic* 153; cf. 126); Gaià, 936 (*DVic* 174). Cf. Bonnassie, *La Catalogne*, 1:124–25, for a similar list focusing on the southern frontier after 985.   [86] *DVic* 328: "in terminio de castro Montebui."

Barcelona. Before his death, Fruia (972–93) acquired four additional castles in that region for his church, three of which were deep within the territory of the county and diocese of Barcelona: Font-rubí, Esparreguera, and Les Espases.[87]

The fourth of these frontier castles was Miralles. The count of Barcelona granted the site to the see of Vic in two separate donations, in 987 and 992, that left the bishopric with ultimate control of the castle, but immediate possession in the hands of Ennec Bonfill, the *vicarius* of Cervelló.[88] Borrell II granted half of the castle to Vic in January 987. Before 1 March of that same year, Ennec Bonfill, already the guardian of Miralles for the count, offered a *fides promissionis* to the bishop for that half of the castle by means of the earliest surviving written oath for a castle in Catalonia. In November 992, the new count, Ramon Borrell, granted to the new bishop, Arnulf, the other half of the castle, with the condition that Ennec Bonfill hold it during his lifetime.

It is impossible to determine whether it was the counts or the bishops who were the force behind the concentration of episcopal fortresses on the frontier. The counts of Barcelona took a renewed interest in involving other powers in the defense and repopulation of the area after al-Manṣūr's incursion of 985, and the grant of Miralles certainly fits into this pattern. But Fruia's aspirations for Vic began before this date, and some of the frontier castles of the diocese were not acquired directly from the count. His attempts to establish a fortification at Montbui suggest that he was pursuing an independent program.[89] The bishops also possessed at this time at least one castle closer to the see, at Artés. Early documentary references to Artés do not describe it as a *castrum*, but the core structure of the castle, most of which dates from the twelfth and fourteenth centuries, is a tower measuring 6x10m, dating from the tenth century.[90]

Arnulf (993–1010) continued Fruia's policies, although with less zeal. His membership in the viscomital family gave them a monopoly of power in the city of Vic, and soon after taking office he exchanged the outlying castles of Esparreguera and Les Espases for an alod closer to the city.[91] Toward the end of his term, however, he acquired for the diocese the castle of Meda as a testamentary bequest, and in his own testament

---

[87] *DVic* 513, 517.

[88] *DVic* 528 [*LFM* 268; *ACondal* 204], 570; *AME* 6/72★. See Juan Luís de Moncada, *Episcopologio de Vich*, ed. Jaime Collell (vols. 1 and 2) and Luís B. Nadal (vol. 3), 3 vols., Biblioteca histórica de la Diócesis de Vich 1, 3 (vols. 1 and 2) (Vic, 1891–1904), 1:193–94, 196–97; Abadal, *L'abat Oliba*, 167–68, 179–80. A *castrum* at Miralles is first cited in 960 (*DPoblet* 1; *CPF* 6). On Ennec Bonfill, see Bonnassie, *La Catalogne*, 1:173–77.

[89] *ACV* 9/ii/30★: "chastra funditus everterentur preter quod Fruia episcopus incoavit facere in turrim Monteboi."

[90] *DVic* 12, 182; X. Sitjes i Molins and Antoni Pladevall i Font, "El castell bisbal d'Artés," *Ausa* 8 (1975–79), 334, 341–42.   [91] *DVic* 571, 572.

he left to the canons of Vic the castle of Llanera.[92] The seven-year tenure of Arnulf's successor, Borrell (1010–17), saw the addition of five more fortifications to the diocesan lists: the towers of Vilagelans and L'Espelt, by testament and donation, respectively; Santa Perpètua and Barberà, by purchase; and the frontier site of Calaf.[93] Ramon Borrell had granted Calaf to the viscounts of Osona, but sometime after the accession of Bishop Borrell the family's rights were transferred to the see.[94] It is probable that at this point there was not yet a functional fortification at Calaf, for in 1015 the bishop granted the region to Guillem de Mediona with the condition that he construct defenses there. Borrell made a similar grant four months later at a nearby site called Riquer.[95]

Thus when Oliba began his long pontificate (1017–46), the diocese of Vic controlled a string of important castles on the frontier – Font-rubí, Miralles, Montbui, Tous, L'Espelt, Calaf, Llanera – as well as a few on the near side of the Llobregat (Artés and Meda). Miralles may still have been held by Ennec Bonfill, and Calaf was in the hands of Guillem de Mediona, but the rest remained under direct control of the bishop. The sites he controlled, however, may not have been particularly effective defenses, given the devastating and lasting effects of the Islamic incursions. Oliba moved to change that situation. In 1023 he entered into an agreement with Guillem de Mediona in which he transferred to him immediate control over three episcopal frontier castles: Montbui, Tous, and Ocelló. In return, Oliba acquired lordship over an additional castle in the Plain of Vic, L'Aguilar. The stated goal of this grant was to rebuild and establish fortifications at the frontier sites, as Guillem had earlier undertaken to do at Calaf. This agreement left most of the major episcopal possessions in the hands of Guillem, who also controlled in his own right the frontier fortresses of Clariana (between Calaf and Tous) and Mediona (near Font-rubí). Oliba had made Guillem, already a powerful presence on the frontier, the superintendent of episcopal castles in that region.[96] In his testament, composed in 1032, Guillem adhered to the conditions set out in the agreements with the diocese, leaving L'Aguilar,

---

[92] ACV 9/ii/15*, 9/i/96*, 9/ii/18*.   [93] ACV 6/816*, 6/343; RBorrell 106*.

[94] *DOliba* 130 (a.1038): "Querelavit autem se de Borrello, episcopo, ipsius antecessore, quod iniuste tulisset de eorum iure castrum Calaf cum auloaudibus et terminis sibi competentibus. Protulitque chartam quam Reimundus condam comes et uxor eius Ermesindis fecerant patri suo Reimundo condam vice comiti. Ad hec iam dictus pontifex, quamvis multi multa obicerent prefate carte, ostendit scripturam quam prefatus comes et uxor eius fecerant katedrali ecclesie Sancti Petri Sedis Vicho de iam dicto castro cum alaudibus et terminis sibi pertinentibus." Abadal (*L'abat Oliba*, 180) thought that the initial grant to the viscounts must have been made in the early 990s, but the document produced by the viscount Folc I of Osona (1036–40) was a grant to his father, the viscount Ramon (1007x9–14).

[95] Abadal, *L'abat Oliba*, 181–83; ACV 9/ii/16*, 9/ii/19*. There is no mention in later documentation of a castle at Riquer.   [96] AME 8/114*; ACV 9/ii/30*; Abadal, *L'abat Oliba*, 181–89.

Montbui, and Calaf to various successors to be held in the service of Saint Peter, the patron of the cathedral of Vic.[97]

Following the settlements with Guillem de Mediona in the 1020s, for the remainder of Oliba's tenure, and indeed until after 1050, episcopal involvement with castles was limited to a series of disputes: a debate with the Gurb family over the boundaries between the castle districts of Tous and La Roqueta (1030); an internal conflict between the archdeacon and the canons over L'Espelt (1031); and a dispute with the viscomital family over the castle of Calaf (1038).[98] Only the last posed a direct challenge to episcopal authority, and in its resolution, the apparent episcopal policy in dealing with castles is confirmed. The bishops accepted the claims of the Cardona family to Calaf, but got them to grant the castle to the diocese with the condition that they were to retain possession under the patronage (*patrocinium*) of the see. Oliba was perfectly willing to give up immediate control over castles, especially those on the frontier, as long as he could maintain the ultimate rights.[99]

The extent of those rights, at this point, was not fully articulated. In the first agreement with Guillem de Mediona for Calaf, the bishop retained enough land to work five pairs of oxen and the right of free entry at the castle. At Tous, Ocelló, L'Aguilar, and Montbui, the bishop claimed a yearly payment in recognition of his lordship and the right to the cultivated demesne. Similarly, when Calaf fell into the hands of the Cardona family, Oliba obtained a yearly payment from them as well. On the surface, then, the episcopal interest in castles at this stage was purely economic. With the important exception of the documents concerning Ennec Bonfill, there was no mention in these early castle-holding agreements of military service due to the bishop, protection against injury, or fidelity. Like precarial grants and franchise charters, these agreements transferred immediate control of land to a person, who was to improve or settle it to the ultimate benefit of the grantor. What was different in these grants is that the land included a fortification.

---

[97] ACV 9/ii/35*; AME 13/52*, 8/108*. Tous was not left explicitly to Vic, but to Ramon, son of Bernat. Bernat was presumably the Bernat de Tous listed as a *marmessor* and was Guillem's *vicarius* for Tous (cf. ACV 9/ii/32*). Tous disappears from the episcopal records for nearly fifty years after this.

[98] ACV 9/ii/32*, 9/ii/34*=6/1390; AME 13/53*, 13/56*. Odilo Engels, "Die weltliche Herrschaft des Bischofs von Ausona-Vich (889–1315)," *Gesammelte Aufsätze zur Kulturgeschichte Spaniens* 24 (1968), 13 n. 72, citing BC, MS 729, 1:318 (no. 82), notes a donation to Vic by the countess Ermessenda of the castle of Vilademàger in 1023, but there is no further evidence of this connection.

[99] Although he did the same with Eures, close to Vic. Berenguer Ramon I of Barcelona left Eures to the see of Vic in his testament (ACV 9/ii/44*); the bishop granted it to Bernat Sunifred in the following year (ACV 9/ii/38*=9/ii/39*). Although neither of these documents mentions a castle on the site, it was later the location of an episcopal castle (Freedman, *Vic*, 103).

Ramon d'Abadal saw Guifré, a judge active in the region of Vic, as the mastermind of this episcopal scheme for developing castles: he subscribed each of the agreements with Guillem de Mediona, as well as the agreement intended to establish a castle at Riquer. As a judge, he oversaw the see's compromise with the viscounts over Calaf and presided over the disputes involving Tous and L'Espelt. The labeling of the agreement in 1023 with Guillem as a *pactum precariae* was, states Abadal, "Guifré's brilliant – and intentional – exhibition of his own knowledge."[100] But these arrangements were not entirely original; the bishops of Barcelona were managing their frontier castles in a comparable fashion, with documents similar in form to the agreements from Vic. And these documents did not yet address the issues of power inherent in subordinate castle holding. How was a hierarchy established? How was control partitioned among the members of the hierarchy? How were relationships between members of the hierarchy envisaged, written down, and governed? If Guifré was behind this activity, at this early stage he had managed only to deal with the most basic questions of immediate and ultimate rights, while the system itself, in practical terms, was rapidly becoming more complex.

Just as Oliba delegated responsibility to Guillem, Guillem distributed his own power over the episcopal castles. Guillem listed among the executors of his will Guillem "de Montbui," Ermemir "de L'Aguilar," and Bernat "de Tous." Bernat had appeared in the dispute over the boundaries of Tous as the vicar (*vicarius*) of the castle. The others presumably held similar positions at the castles of Montbui and L'Aguilar. These were not, however, the *vicarii* of an earlier era: official representatives of the count at a castle, such as Ennec Bonfill was before he took on a new lord. They were, rather, the subordinates of Guillem the frontier boss, answerable – as far as we can tell from the evidence – only to him. They were already *castlans*. The documentation was beginning to change to fit the altered circumstances. In the original agreement with Guillem for Calaf, the bishop reserved the right of entry, a right that would become standard in the following decades. Even the language of the oath of Ennec Bonfill to the bishop in 978 was very similar to the language of analogous later documents.

The fact that the system was still in its early stages and that the documentation did not yet clearly specify rights and obligations may have

---

[100] Abadal, *L'abat Oliba*, 186. It is tempting to speculate about the possible influence of the *grammaticus* Guibert, who arrived from Lodi in 1015 to reorganize the cathedral school, and who subscribed ACV 9/ii/30* and 9/ii/34*. See Josep M. Masnou, "L'escola de la catedral de Vic al segle XI," in Imma Ollich i Castanyer, ed., *Actes del Congrés internacional Gerbert d'Orlhac i el seu temps: Catalunya i Europa a la fi del 1r mil·lenni: Vic-Ripoll, 10–13 de novembre de 1999*, Documents 31 (Vic, 1999), 621–34.

caused confusion or tempted individuals to see what they could get away with. In his testament, Guillem left Tous not to a member of the cathedral community, as he had promised, but to the son of the *castlà*, with no mention of episcopal rights. Similarly, Gombau de Besora, in his testament, disposed of rights in Montbui without mention of episcopal overlordship.[101] It was left to later bishops to address these problems.

From 942 to 1040, the see of Urgell was occupied by members of the viscomital families of Osona and Conflent.[102] The bishops were slow to acquire castles during most of this period. The earliest mention of an episcopal fortification is the only such reference from the episcopacy of Guisad II (942–979/80): the papal confirmation of Agapetus II (951) refers to the *castrum* of Sanaüja, in the Segarra. The origin of the see's rights in this distant site is unknown, but most of the castles acquired during the reign of Guisad's successor, Sal·la (981–1010), can be traced to Borrell II of Barcelona. In 986, a certain Vidal granted the castle of Figuerola to the see, to be held by him and his son against a payment of a *census*; he had acquired it by purchase from the count of Barcelona.[103] Bishop Sal·la obtained the castle of Carcolze as a forfeited pledge from Borrell in 995. He then sold it to the sacristan of the cathedral, who sold it in turn to Guillem de Castellbò, viscount of Urgell, who finally sold it back to the bishop at cost in the following year. The bishop immediately granted the castle to the see, to be held by his nephew for life.[104] In 1002, the bishop successfully claimed rights for the see in the castle of Queralt, which in 976 had been sold by Borrell to the viscount of Barcelona.[105] Finally, Borrell's son, Ermengol I of Urgell, left the castle of Conques to the see in his testament of 1007.[106]

Most of these castles were granted directly to the see, rather than to the bishop. This pattern changed under Sal·la's successor, Sant Ermengol (1010–35). At his death, Ermengol donated four castles to the see, each of which he had acquired personally between 1022 and 1031: La Rua, Cornellana, Bordell, and Fontanet. The first three he had purchased outright; he received Fontanet as compensation for an injury committed by the son of the holder.[107] Ermengol's most significant acquisition,

---

[101] *DOliba* 146.
[102] Guisad II, brother of Guadall II, viscount of Osona; Sal·la, son of Isarn, viscount of Conflent; Sant Ermengol, son of Bernat, viscount of Conflent; Eribau, son of Ramon, viscount of Osona, and himself titular viscount from *c.* 1033. See Ferran Valls i Taberner, "La primera dinastia vescomtal de Cardona," *Estudis universitaris catalans* 16 (1931), 112, 124–32; Joaquim Miret i Sans, "Los vescomtes de Cerdanya, Conflent y Bergadà," *Memorias de la Real academia de buenas letras de Barcelona* 7 (1901), 138–40.   [103] DACU 207.   [104] DACU 239, 243, 244.
[105] DACU 278. The origin of the bishop's rights is not clear. See Benet, *Gurb-Queralt*, 45–49 and app. 1 (pp. 239–40).   [106] DACU 300.   [107] DACU 378, 383, 420, 445, 461, 463, 478.

however, was of the *civitas* of Guissona. He personally led the reconquest of the site between 1019 and 1024. After successfully defending his rights there against the usurpations of Guillem de La Vansa in a dispute settled in 1024, he granted the city to the see in his testament.[108] Direct grants of castles to the see, in contrast, were rare. The canons received once again a grant of the castle of Figuerola, this time from Bernat, the son of Vidal, the original grantor; this renewed the arrangement there for another generation.[109] The see also acquired directly a reversionary interest in the castle of Coscó, which was not claimed until 1066.[110]

Bishop Eribau (1036–40) was very effective during his brief tenure in defending and extending the rights of the diocese. While he directed most of his energies toward defining ecclesiastical territory,[111] he consolidated the see's hold on its fortifications, as well. In 1036 he arranged for Ermengol II of Urgell to donate to the see half of the rights that he claimed "by comital right" in the city of Guissona. In the same year, the canons acquired a recognition by a lord that he retained no rights in the castle of Cornellana by virtue of his earlier donation.[112] Eribau's testamentary donation to the see, prepared in advance of the pilgrimage on which he died in 1040, of reversionary rights in the castle of Llanera, and the "second consecration" of the cathedral on the following day brought his work to a close (1040).[113]

At the end of this first period in the development of episcopal castle holding in Urgell, the see controlled a number of castles on the frontier, particularly in the Solsonès and Segarra, but only a few scattered sites further north. Most of the castles were acquired by grants from the bishops to the cathedral, usually in their testaments. We know very little about the tenurial relationships in effect at these castles. At Figuerola, the castle lords' responsibilities were limited to payment of a *census* of bread and wine. A later inventory, dated 1046, of lands held by Arnau Mir de Tost from the see shows that he held a castle from the bishops of Urgell for which he owed homage, but only homage.[114] Similarly, a quitclaim by the bishop and canons in 1046x47 referred back to a written agree-

---

[108] Domènec Sangés, ed., "Recull de documents del segle XI referents a Guissona i la seva plana," *Urgellia* 3 (1980), app. 2 (pp. 227–30) [DACU 391]: "ipse de manibus paganorum multo labore abstraxerat et prout melius potuit edificaverat, et adhuc Deo auxiliante edificat"; DACU 463, 478. On the dispute see Abadal, *L'abat Oliba*, 177–78.   [109] DACU 441.

[110] DACU 396, 794.

[111] E.g., ACU 314*; DACU 525, 530; Baraut, ed., "Les actes," app. 52 (pp. 128–31).

[112] DACU 491 ("per vocem comitalem"), 491bis; Sangés, ed., "Recull," app. 7 (p. 232) [DACU 512].

[113] DACU 527; Baraut, ed., "Les actes," app. 51 (pp. 126–28) [DACU 528]; *VL* 10:34.

[114] DACU 596: "Hoc totum predictum dedit iam dictus Eriballus supra dicto Arnallo, sine quod non accepit de eo nullam rem nisi solo ominatico."

ment (*conventio scripta, convenientia*) in which Sant Ermengol commissioned the construction of castles at Bellveí, near Guissona; it did not offer any further details as to the earlier conditions of tenure.[115] The earliest oaths of fidelity to the bishop and the canons of Urgell for specific castles date from the 1030s, for Figuerola and La Rua, but these, too, said little about how the castles were held. Bernat simply promised to be faithful with respect to the castle of Figuerola and not to deny the bishop's right of entry. The oath for La Rua was slightly more detailed; Guillem promised to help defend the castle, not to aid anyone attempting to seize the castle, and not to place anyone in the castle without permission.[116] These undertakings were, however, still far from a promise of specific military service. In 1040, the see of Urgell was only marginally involved in the business of developing and organizing the sources of its military strength.

Early evidence for episcopal castle holding at Girona is the thinnest. Ninth-century imperial confirmations to the see mention two castles, but these were abandoned late antique fortifications.[117] Similarly, *Tolon(e)* (Peralada) appears in the early episcopal documentation, but only as a place name; no episcopal control is evident.[118] The episcopal castle in Girona about which the most information has survived is the fortification at La Bisbal. Count Guifré II Borrell of Barcelona (897–911) may have granted La Bisbal to the see in the late ninth century; the see began to buy lands around the church of Santa Maria de Fontanet in the early tenth century, and from 1002 the place became known as "Santa Maria Episcopale." La Bisbal (<*Episcopale*) was the subject of the earliest surviving episcopal *convenientia* from Girona, namely the submission of La Bisbal to the protection (*baiulia*) of the count of Barcelona by Bishop Pere in 1051. This document did not mention any type of fortification, but this may have been part of Ramon Berenguer I's program of acquisition of castles during the 1050s and 1060s.[119] Sant Sadurní de l'Heura, first mentioned in a ninth-century diploma, was from the tenth century associated with the *precentores* of the cathedral; it was thus technically part of the patrimony of

---

[115] Sangés, ed., "Recull," app. 12 (pp. 234–35) [DACU 601].

[116] DACU 489, 531. DACU 488 is an oath from Guisad de Sallent to Bishop Ermengol, but it does not refer to the castle of Sallent, which appears in the documentation as under the control of the see only later in the century (DACU 983).

[117] "Castellum Fractum"; "uillam Uellosam cum suo castello": *CCM* 2, 7, 10, 11, 21; Ramon Martí Castelló, "Els inicis de l'organització feudal de la producció al bisbat de Girona (Col·lecció diplomàtica de la seu, anys 817–1100)," 3 vols. (Tesi de doctorat, Universitat Autònoma de Barcelona, 1988), 1:167–68.

[118] *CDSG* 162; *CCM* 94, 121. *CDSG* 79, which mentions Finestres, is a forgery.

[119] Martí Castelló, "Els inicis," 1:112, 169; *CCM* 109 [*CDSG* 258].

the chapter, not that of the bishop. There is no evidence of a castle there, however, before 1052.[120]

The see of Girona had limited interests in several other castles in the region, but it is impossible to reconstruct the nature of these relationships from the meager surviving evidence. The document in which the countess Ermessenda returned various properties that she held from the see, for instance, named five castles: Palau-sator, Púbol, Vilafreser, Montpalau, and Blanes. Yet there is no evidence of episcopal connections to these castles before her grant.[121] Other castles were donated or pledged to the see, but similarly no evidence has survived of connections between the bishops and the guardians of these sites. In 1020, Ermessenda and Berenguer Ramon I granted a "turre rodona" near the cathedral to the see.[122] In the case of Aro, Bishop Pere was a codonor with his sister, the countess Ermessenda, of the castle to the monastery of Sant Feliu de Guíxols in 1041. The castle remained under monastic control for the remainder of the eleventh and twelfth centuries, and there is no further evidence of episcopal interest in this site.[123]

Four bishops

In the course of the eleventh century, bishops increased the numbers of castles associated with their dioceses, and they articulated and systematized these relationships by means of oaths and conventions. While the earliest oaths and conventions appeared at various times in the different bishoprics, the new structures were consolidated in each diocese during the long mid-century pontificates of a group of particularly powerful bishops: Guislabert of Barcelona, Berenguer Guifré of Girona, Guillem de Balsareny of Vic, and Guillem Guifré of Urgell. Whether from old comital and viscomital families or the new castellan lineages, all were embroiled in the conflicts surrounding Ramon Berenguer I and thus very familiar with the new politics of castle holding. The conventions of this early period provide details of the military service due to the bishops and often focus on the issue of *potestas*.

[120] Gabriel Roura, ed., "Un diploma desconegut del rei Odó a favor del seu fidel Wicfrid (888–898)," in *La formació i expansió*, 66; Josep Maria Marquès i Planagumà, ed., "La senyoria eclesiàstica de Sant Sadurní de l'Heurà, fins al 1319," *Estudis sobre temes del Baix Empordà* 3 (1984), app. 1 (pp. 82–83); CCM 87 [CDSG 208]; CDSG 241 [Marquès i Planagumà, ed., "La senyoria," app. 2 (pp. 83–84)]. The castle is also mentioned as a boundary in a grant of 1075 (Marquès i Planagumà, ed., "La senyoria," app. 8 [pp. 91–92]).

[121] CCM 120 [CDSG 282]. It is not clear whether the site ("turrem de Palacio") in question is Palau-Sator or Pals. Cf. CCM 67; CDSG 137; Martí Castelló, "Els inicis," no. 126 (2:51); RBI 316*.

[122] CCM 80. Cf. RBI 193*, sd 52*, sd 63.1*. The tower was "sold" by Ermessenda to Ramon Berenguer I in 1057 (RBI 206*), after which date it appeared regularly in the stock lists of comital properties in oaths of fidelity (e.g., RBI 299*, sd 122*, sd 173*; RBIII 142*, 284*; LFM 239 . . .).

[123] Flórez et al., *España sagrada* . . ., vol. 43, app. 30 (pp. 437–39); *Els castells*, 2:638 (n. 10).

In 1039, Folc Geribert returned the castle of Ribes to the see of Barcelona, recognizing that it had been held unjustly; this grant was perhaps the price of admission into the cathedral community for Folc, who later appears as a *levita*.[124] The bishop to whom Folc made the grant was his cousin Guislabert (1035–62), who was also head of the viscomital lineage.[125] Two years later, Guislabert granted the castle back to Folc's brother, Mir Geribert. It is tempting to see some connection between this grant and the opposition during these years to the count of Barcelona, an opposition in which both the bishop and Mir Geribert played leading roles. At the same time, however, it must be stressed that in the complex series of documents effecting this grant, the see was very careful to maintain its seigneurial rights over the castle, rights that it would exercise for the next four centuries.

Four documents, only one of which is dated, recorded the various parts of this transaction.[126] In the first, a *carta donationis*, Bishop Guislabert granted the castle of Ribes to Mir Geribert, his wife Guisla, his son Bernat, and another unnamed son after Bernat's death. As a condition of tenure, both of the sons had to become members of the cathedral community. The castle was to be held for life in service and fidelity to the cathedral and its bishops. After the death of the last son, the castle was to revert to the cathedral. The bishop retained for the term of his life, however, the castle of Sitges, located within the territory associated with Ribes, as well as one-half of the vineyards of Ribes. Sitges would revert first to Mir and his sons after the death of the bishop, but eventually back to the cathedral with the rest of the grant. A second document recorded the undertakings ("Convenenerunt [*sic*] . . .") of Mir Geribert and Guisla with respect to the grant of Ribes. They received the castle from the hand of the bishop (*aprehendere per manum*); they promised to remain in the homage (*hominaticum*) of the bishop and to swear fidelity to the cathedral and the bishop (*iurare fidelitatem*); they promised not to take the castle from the *castlans* (*castellani*) who held it or give it to other *castlans* without permission of the bishop; they promised to make those *castlans* swear not to grant *potestas* of the castle to Mir's sons when they reached age fifteen until the sons entered into the homage of and swore fidelity to the

---

[124] LA 4:367*; 4:377*: "que fuerunt de dominicatura Fulchonis levite."

[125] Guislabert also controlled Piera and La Guàrdia as head of the viscomital lineage, as can be seen from three transactions with his nephew, the viscount Udalard (II) Bernat, all dated 17 February 1058 (RBI 219*, 220, 221). Although the documents describe Guislabert as bishop, none refers to the canons or the cathedral.

[126] LA 4:371*, 4:372*, 4:373*, 4:377*. Single-sheet exemplars: ACB 4–70–411*=LA 4:377*; ACB 4–70–413*=LA 4:371*, 4:372*; ACB 4–70–61 (transcription of a. 1345)=LA 4:371*, 4:372*, 4:377*.

bishop; finally, they agreed that after the death of the sons the castle would revert to the cathedral. A third document, an undated oath ("Iuro ego . . ."), appears to correspond to the agreement just described. This oath has two interesting features. First, it was sworn only by Mir; Guisla may have sworn a separate oath that has not survived, or the oath of the husband may have been considered sufficient. Second, the oath repeated the condition (*stabilimentum*) described in the agreement that the sons would not receive the castle without first swearing fidelity. In the last document, a *convenientia* between the bishop and Mir and Guisla, the bishop promised to give them the castle of Ribes on the condition that he keep the castle of Sitges and one-half of the vineyards in the territory of Ribes as his demesne. On the other hand, the *castlà* in Sitges was to be the man (*homo*) both of Mir, Guisla, and their sons, *and* of the *castlans* of Ribes. The terms of reversion found in the other documents appear here, too, as does the condition of fidelity to the bishop's successor. The bishop and cathedral also agreed not to require anything else of Mir and his family with respect to Ribes.

Why did the bishop's scribes compose at least four documents to record what was essentially one transaction? These documents demonstrate again the important distinction between donations (grants of land associated with a fortification) and commendations (appointments to positions of control over a fortification). The *carta donationis* refers to the "*castrum* called Ribes, with its borders, appurtenances, and associated lands," that is, *castrum* in the sense of a territorial division centered on a castle.[127] It established the borders of the land, the various conditions under which it was held, and the terms of reversion. The document beginning "Convenenerunt . . ." refers, however, to the "*castrum* called Ribes with all of its towers and the fortifications located within it, together with all of their associated lands," that is, *castrum* in the sense of a collection of fortifications.[128] This document and the associated oath dealt entirely with the military aspects of Ribes and its control.

The *convenientia*, which refers both to military and territorial aspects of the transaction, embodied the entire agreement, and may in fact have been the first document composed; it described the complicated compromise that lay behind all of the other documents. Because of his brother's donation, Mir had lost control of this important castle, so close to his seat of power in Olèrdola. His main concern was to regain immediate command over the fortifications. Bishop Guislabert's main concern

---

[127] LA 4:377*: "castrum vocitatum Ribas cum eius terminis et pertinenciis et adiacenciis eius." See Bonnassie, *La Catalogne*, 1:174–75.

[128] LA 4:371*: "castrum vocitatum Ripas cum omnibus turris et forticiis que in eius terminos sunt aut in antea erunt simul cum omnibus eorum aiacenciis."

was not immediate military control, but the revenues and ultimate control. Thus the settlement: Guislabert kept Sitges, the secondary fortification, as well as half of the vineyards associated with the castle of Ribes;[129] Mir received Ribes, as well as immediate influence over Sitges, whose *castlans* had to be subordinate to him as well as to the *castlans* under his control at Ribes. Guislabert, however, also had an institutional responsibility to maintain the see's ultimate rights and to insure that whatever Mir's bellicose plans, they would not be directed against him and his church. This explains the requirements that Mir swear fidelity to him, and, more importantly, that the heir of Ribes be a member of the cathedral community. For added security, the bishop included in the later documents that this heir had to swear an oath of fidelity as well. These documents are surprisingly complex for the first evidence of episcopal castle-holding arrangements. Homage, fidelity, oaths, distinctions between commendation and grant and between castle and castle district: all find a place in these agreements. In the case of the *convenientia* of *c.* 1021 between Berenguer Ramon I and Ermengol II, it was necessary to posit earlier institutional developments to explain the maturity of the vocabulary. The individuals who conceived of the terms of compromise in these episcopal documents and the scribes who composed them were able to draw on an additional twenty years of evolution in these forms.

This set of documents also contains the first evidence for the secondary fortification of Sitges, although its early history is difficult to separate from that of Ribes. The same is true of another minor site, the tower (*turris*) of Miralpeix. In 1057, Guislabert and Mir granted Miralpeix, then an "uninhabitable" location, to Arnau Arluí, half in alod, half in fief, on the condition that he repopulate the area and not proclaim a lord (*senior*) other than Mir and his heirs. The grant indicates that Mir's interest in the tower was based on an earlier grant by the bishop.[130] Thus both the immediate lord and the ultimate lord participated in this grant.

Having established these rights in Ribes and Sitges for the see, Bishop Guislabert was more successful in maintaining them than his predecessors had been. In his testament, Mir left the castle of Ribes to his wife, Guisla, if she remained a widow; if she remarried, the castle would pass to his sons Bernat and Arnau, on condition that they hold it from the bishop. They could not sell or otherwise alienate the castle, even at the

---

[129] In a document of 1059 (LA 4:370★), Guislabert refers to a piece of land at Ribes that he retained for his own use "when I acquired the castle" ("cum adquisivi ipsum castrum"). The subordination of the *castlans* at Sitges to those at Ribes and the more recent establishment of Sitges support the notion that Sitges was a secondary fortification in the region.

[130] LA 4:378★. LA 4:391★ is an undated collective oath for the "castle" of Miralpeix. Joan Llopis Bofill, *Ensaig histórich sobre la vila de Sitges* (Barcelona, 1891), 23 n. 4, cites a document of 1037 supposedly from the *LFM* referring to control of Sitges by the canons of Barcelona.

request of the see.[131] After Mir's death, the particular services due to the bishop for the castle were specified for the first time. A convention transferring the episcopal lands, including the castle of Ribes, held by Mir and Gombau de Besora to Guisla and her sons by Mir (Gombau, Arnau, and Ramon) stated that the new lords had to remain in homage to the bishop and participate in the military adventures of the bishop or his successors.[132]

A few months after arranging affairs at Ribes, Guislabert turned his attention to a location close to the *castella* of La Granada called Mal Consell, which had been acquired by the see in 1012. After reasserting the see's rights in a dispute, the bishop granted the site to the erstwhile usurper by means of castle-holding *convenientia* ("Sub ista convenientia ...").[133] Under the terms of the agreement, Bernat Sendred and his wife were to hold Mal Consell "in service and fidelity of God and Santa Creu and Santa Eulàlia (i.e., the cathedral) and the church of Sant Miquel de Barcelona and the lord-bishop Guislabert and the monastery of Sant Cugat."[134] Of these many masters, they had to swear fidelity only to God, the bishop, and the cathedral. They promised the bishop *potestas* of the fortification (*forticia*), that they would not allow any harm to come to the bishop from their lands, and that they would not deny him entry; this last clause was written in the vernacular ("devedad noli sia"). Bernat and his wife also promised not to build another fortification or allow one to be built without episcopal permission. The agreement contained clauses establishing time limits for emendations of violations, and for renewal of the agreement after the bishop's death.

The first descriptions of seigneurial arrangements at Castellbisbal appear two years later, in the *convenientia* between Ramon Berenguer I and Bishop Guislabert that marked the close of the first stage of the crisis of that count's reign. The bulk of the document contains a description of the pledge provided by the bishop that he would keep his promises, namely Castellbisbal.[135] The convention specified that if the bishop violated the agreement, the *castlà* of Castellbisbal, Ramon Guillem, was to render *potestas* of the castle to the counts. Furthermore, if the bishop changed *castlans*, the new *castlà* would have the same responsibility as a pledge. This latter point shows that the bishop retained immediate

---

[131] LA 4:379*.
[132] LA 4:369*: "albergen cum predicto episcopo in hostes et in cavalcatas dum vivus fuerit. Post obitum quoque eius similiter faciant cum successoribus suis."
[133] LA 4:364*=1:359*; see also 4:365*, 4:362*, 4:363* (a. 1042).
[134] LA 4:364* (=1:359*): "in servitio et fidelitate Dei et Sancte Crucis Sancteque Eulalie et Sancti Michaelis ecclesie Barchinonensis et domini Guilaberti episcopi et Sancti Cucuphtais cenobii."
[135] RBI sd 3. Cf. RBI sd 39*; Puig y Puig, *Episcopologio*, 109–10; Sobrequés, *Els grans comtes*, 42; *Els castells*, 2:33; Bonnassie, *La Catalogne*, 2:697; and above, pp. 118, 126.

control of the castle; he had the power to name its guardian. He would only lose control of the castle to the counts if he violated the agreement. This is, of course, the first mention of a guardian for this castle. That guardian, Ramon Guillem, was the first of a line of *castlans* of Castellbisbal from the important Barcelonese lineage of the Castellvell. On preparing for pilgrimage in 1058, Ramon granted the castle to his son, Gombau, to be held from the bishop of Barcelona.[136]

Guislabert also acquired control, if only for a short time, of another major castle of Barcelona, though not in the city itself: the Castell de Port on Montjuïc. In 1058, Bernat, the eldest son of Mir Geribert, granted the castle to the see of which he was a member. Shortly thereafter, the count acquired the castle as part of the settlement that brought to a close Mir's revolt.[137] Because of the identity of its leader, the see of Barcelona became enmeshed in the castle-holding politics of its region. But Guislabert did act with institutional, rather than familial, interest in mind, and he established the foundations for future episcopal involvement in the new structures of power.

It is tempting to see Guillem de Balsareny of Vic (1046–76) as a transitional figure, overshadowed as he is in modern historiography by his more famous predecessor, Oliba, and his more ambitious successor, Berenguer Sunifred. In the context of episcopal castle holding and its documentation, this would be an error. Where Oliba had shown an early interest in only a few castles, Guillem's activity lasted throughout his reign and involved three times as many sites. Furthermore, the documentation for these transactions developed very quickly toward what would become canonical forms: the oath, and the *convenientia* in which a lord commended a castle to a subordinate and granted him a fief associated with the castle, in return for promises of fidelity, aid and defense, *potestas* of the castle on demand, and military service.

Guillem's first act involving castles reveals this new sophistication. In June 1052, Ermengol Guillem granted the castle of Malla to the canons of Vic; his father, Guillem de Mediona, had left the castle to him in his testament. The next week, the bishop granted the castle to Ermengol Ermemir in a *pactum scripturae*. While Ermengol Guillem was still alive, Ermengol Ermemir was to hold the castle from him. Although the initial grant did not refer to any reserved rights for Ermengol Guillem, they clearly existed. Furthermore, after Ermengol Guillem's death, Ermengol Ermemir was to hold the castle "according the *convenientia* between you"

---

[136] RBI 224 (26 March 1058).
[137] LA 4:55* (16 May 1058); RBI 239*, 240* (1 July 1058); Carreras y Candi, "Lo Montjuïch," 239, 357–58.

and "as a fief under our patronage," that is, according to the terms set out in an agreement between the two Ermengols *and* under the tutelage of the bishop. This arrangement was to apply to Ermengol's wife and his children, but everything would revert to the bishop after the second generation. In addition, the bishop reserved the right of residence (*statica*) in the castle whenever he wished it.[138] The *convenientia* to which the bishop's document referred has survived; it was dated the day before and was subscribed by the bishop. In the case of the castle of Malla, then, the bishop dealt directly with an individual two steps below him in a hierarchy. This was a *convenientia* concerning an episcopal castle, rather than one to which the bishop was a principal party. The same was true of two transactions from the next two years: an agreement, which did not mention episcopal overlordship, among various guardians of the castle of L'Aguilar, and a *comenda*, carried out with the "counsel and assent" of the bishop, concerning the castle of Voltregà.[139]

The first *convenientia* entered into by a bishop of Vic is, at the same time, the first episcopal document to mention military service owed to the bishop with respect to a castle. It is an agreement between Bishop Guillem and Ponç Guerau I, viscount of Girona. Ponç had already been party to a number of oaths and conventions involving castles, including some with the count of Barcelona, so he may have influenced the use of this particular form by the bishop. The document itself does appear, however, to have been a product of the episcopal chancery.[140] The agreement was not a *comenda*-convention (a grant of a castle against military service) but rather a grant of lands held by the bishop to a son of the viscount. In return for this grant, the bishop secured his rights in the castle of Vilagelans (*introitus et exitus, guerra et pax*), as well as a promise of military service from the viscount (*hostes, cavalcadas, seguimentum, adiutorium*), including twenty horsemen if the viscount could not serve in person.[141]

Another step toward the classic regime was taken in a series of agreements in 1063x64 involving the bishop's personal castles, among them Balsareny and Gaià. The *Liber feudorum maior* of the counts of Barcelona includes a *convenientia* and an oath between Ramon Berenguer I of Barcelona and the brothers Bernat and Mir Riculf for Balsareny and Gaià. The convention mentions the bishop three times. First, the count granted as a fief the *honores* associated with the castles, as well as "the

---

[138] RBI 124*; *LFM* 441 ("secundum convenienciam que inter vos facta est . . . per fevum sub nostro patrocinio"); ACV 9/ii/50. For the dating of these documents, see Kosto, "Agreements," 347 n. 103.   [139] ACV 6/1012; AME 9/24 ("consilio et assensu").

[140] AME 6/39. The scribe, Benet, drafted at least two other documents (ACV 6/1833, 6/2183). On Ponç Guerau I, and his successors who renewed this agreement, see Jaume Coll i Castanyer, "Els vescomtes de Girona," *Annals de l'Institut d'estudis gironins* 30 (1988–89), 56–83.

[141] For episcopal rights to Vilagelans see ACV 6/816*.

honor of Oristà after the death of Bishop Guillem." Second, if the bishop was participating in the comital host, the brothers were to supply their military service of fifty horsemen directly to him, rather than to the counts. Third, after the death of the bishop, the brothers were to have changes in *castlans* approved by the count. The bishop was also cited in an oath of the castellan of Gaià to the count; interestingly, this oath seems to have been intended to apply only *after* the death of the bishop.[142] A document dated four days after the comital *convenientia* clarifies the bishop's involvement in this agreement. In it the bishop commended to the same Bernat and Mir Riculf the castles of Balsareny and Gaià, granting them the fiefs associated with those castles as well as the *honores* of Cornet and Oristà. The brothers promised to serve in the host and cavalcade with fifty horsemen, a mechanism was established for settling disputes between the brothers and their knights, and the brothers were warned not to make personnel changes without the bishop's permission. Other familiar military rights were noted (*staticas, intrare et exire, guerram facere, potestas*), although these were said to be due to the brothers rather than to the bishop.[143] No provisions were made for relations with the bishop's successors, and the castles of Balsareny and Gaià disappeared after this date from the episcopal lists. These facts, coupled with the unusual clauses from the comital documents above, suggest the following scenario. Guillem was acting as lord of Balsareny as an individual, not in his capacity as bishop. The count reached an agreement with the bishop to keep the castle in comital hands, rather than letting it pass into the control of the see of Vic. Guillem would remain lord while he lived, but in the meantime his *castlans* would establish links with the count, links that would become primary after the bishop's death. Thus although this was a full-fledged *comenda*-convention involving a bishop of Vic, it was for a castle that did not belong to the see.[144]

Comenda-conventions for true episcopal castles appear in the documentation in 1065–66. The first example was rather tentative. It recorded a complicated agreement involving Bishop Guillem, Berenguer Sunifred (Guillem's successor as bishop), and Hug Dalmau de Cervera, in which the bishop and Berenguer partitioned the lordship over the frontier castles

[142] RBI 296★ ("simul cum ipso honore de Oristan post mortem Guilelmi episcopi"), sd 137★, sd 138★. The first is dated 5 July 1063; in a fourth document, dated the same day and known only from a register entry (*LFM* 178, *recte* a. 1063), the count pledged to Mir Riculf one-quarter of the tithes of a church "pro eo quod episcopus Ausonensis habebat in dictis castris de Balceren et de Gaiano et in honore de Oristano."   [143] AME 6/63.
[144] See also RBI 210★, 211★ (above, p. 173), in which the bishop was given control of the pledged castle of Colltort; here, too, he was acting as an independent lord, rather than in his capacity as bishop.

of Aguilar and Llavinera.[145] Berenguer granted Aguilar to Hug, on the condition that he commend himself to, swear fidelity to, and provide the usual military services to Berenguer *and* to the bishop. Hug was not the last link in the chain of command here, as he was given permission to appoint a *castellanus* if necessary. Hug also accepted the bishop and Berenguer as his lords for the castle of Llavinera, although the episcopal rights in this castle seem to have been in dispute, and ultimate possession remained to Hug's family rather than to the see.[146] The language of the second example, a *convenientia* of 1066 between Guillem and Ponç Guerau I, viscount of Girona, was entirely classic. The bishop commended the castle of S'Avellana to the viscount and granted him a fief. The viscount, in turn, promised *potestas*, *intrare et exire*, *guerra et pax*, and that if he, his wife, and his children should die, the *castellani* would grant *potestas* to the bishop. The agreement was extended for one generation on the viscount's side, although it did not mention the bishop's successors.[147]

The first written oaths of fidelity to the bishops of Vic since Ennec Bonfill's promise of 987 date from the last decade of Guillem's tenure. Two brief oaths, without their corresponding conventions, named Bishop Guillem as the recipient: an oath of Sicarda for the castle of Miralles, and a general oath from her husband, Alemany Hug de Cervelló, also perhaps for Miralles.[148] The single-sheet original containing the agreement over Aguilar and Llavinera, just mentioned, includes a more complete oath written after the subscriptions. This oath was sworn both to the bishop and to Berenguer Sunifred; it did not name the castles, and the oath was made reserving fidelity to the counts of Barcelona and one other individual.

Overall, the network of episcopal castles expanded under Guillem de Balsareny. On three occasions, however, the bishop alienated episcopal castles. The first such transaction was the sale of the frontier castle of Copons to the count of Barcelona for 50 ounces of gold in 1065.[149] There followed sometime before 1067 the exchange of the castles of Montfalcó and Veciana for half of the tithes of Manresa, again with the count of Barcelona.[150] Finally in 1067, after a dispute over the castle of Malla, the

---

[145] This is different from L'Aguilar, granted by Guillem de Mediona in the 1030s.

[146] AME 8/107 (incomplete version at ACV 6/2219): "accepimus et aprehendimus ipsum kastrum de Lavinera . . . per ipsum episcopum et per prefatum Berengarium."

[147] AME 6/47=6/43.

[148] RBII 43.2*, 43.3* (cf. RBII 43.1*=ACV 9/ii/74); Freedman, *Vic*, 194 (n. 10). Alemany Hug de Cervelló was the son of Hug de Cervelló, and thus the grandson of Ennec Bonfill, guardian of the castle for the bishop in 987. Hug granted his rights in Miralles to Alemany in 1018 (Benet, *Gurb-Queralt*, 64, citing *LBSC* 7).   [149] RBI 325*.

[150] Moncada, *Episcopologio*, 1:308–9, who notes that the castles had been granted to the church by the bishop's brother, Bernat Guifré, in his testament.

bishop sold a half interest in the site to the count for 40 ounces of gold.[151] The first two of these sales, which coincided with the wave of comital purchases of castles in the 1060s, can be interpreted as a loss of episcopal interest in maintaining a presence on the frontier. Indeed, the only surviving transactions concerning a castle beyond the Llobregat from Guillem's reign are the oaths of the Cervelló for Miralles. Furthermore, the bishop may have unwittingly lost control over frontier castles in which the see had acquired rights; two transactions during Guillem's pontificate involving Tous and Montbui made no reference to episcopal lordship.[152] This change in priorities may be related to the fact that the frontier had, by that time, moved beyond the Anoia and Segarra regions where most of the episcopal castles were located. Nevertheless, Guillem's successor did not adhere to this policy.

One of Bishop Guillem's last acts was to accept the donation of the castle of Quer from his soon-to-be successor Berenguer Sunifred upon his entry into the cathedral community.[153] It took a bishop from a castellan family, as well as dealings with the count of Barcelona and the viscount of Girona, gradually to introduce the *convenientia* into the episcopal castle-holding regime at Vic. Once implanted, it stayed. The new bishop, again from a powerful castellan family, would prove much more comfortable than his predecessor with the mechanics of oaths and conventions.

As in Vic and Barcelona, the turning point for the diocese of Urgell was the midcentury episcopacy of a particularly powerful and well-connected lord-bishop, Guillem Guifré (1041–75). For the first time in a century, the bishop of Urgell was the son not of a viscount, but of a count, Guifré II of Cerdanya. Guillem's journey to the *cathedra* was facilitated by a payment of 100,000 *solidi* to the dowager countess of Urgell, Constança, by his brother, Guifred, archbishop of Narbonne.[154] Guillem's brother, Ramon Guifré, was count of Cerdanya for much of his tenure, another brother was bishop of Elna, and his half-brothers were count of Berga and bishop of Girona. Given the length of his pontificate, the dozen castles that first appear in the documents during his tenure do not represent a particularly rapid increase in number. Nor do the locations of the castles with which he dealt reflect a change in the geographical focus of

---

[151] RBI 369*, 370*, 372*. The history of the castle given in RBI 369* does not correspond to the transactions of fifteen years earlier (above, pp. 195–96); either one of the sets of documents is forged, or there are two castles involved.   [152] ACB 1-4-211 (Montbui); AME 15/41 (Tous).

[153] Freedman, *Vic*, 107 and n. 39; *Els castells*, 4:895.

[154] *HGL* 5:251. The archbishop himself had been the beneficiary of an identical simoniacal act in 1019. See Abadal, *L'abat Oliba*, 120–22; Bonnassie, *La Catalogne*, 2:550.

the see's interests; most were located in regions where there was already an episcopal presence, in the areas surrounding Guissona and Solsona, or at the edge of the plain of Lleida. It was during the period of his rule, however, that the mechanisms of episcopal castle holding became regular and patent.

This is evident in the case of La Clua, the first castle a mentioned in documents from this period. In 1042, Amaltruda and her three sons granted the castle of La Clua to the canons of Urgell. Shortly thereafter (April 1045), the canons, along with the bishop, granted the castle back to the donors for life. Like the castle of Figuerola in an earlier era, La Clua was to be held against the payment of a yearly *receptum*, in this case four pigs, a cow, a *muig* of bread, and another *muig* of wine. In addition, however, the agreement stated that after the death of Amaltruda or one of her sons, the successor to the castle was to make the *castlans* (*castellani*) of the castle swear fidelity to the see. This is the earliest mention of *castlans* at an episcopal castle. Two years later (October 1047), the bishop and canons entered into a *convenientia* with Amaltruda concerning additional terms. Amaltruda promised that "the *castlà* or *castlans* who hold or will hold the castle of La Clua shall serve in the host and cavalcade with all the horsemen (*cavallarii*) that they have in the said *honor* . . . in the host they shall camp with the bishop." This is the first explicit mention of specific military service due to a bishop of Urgell. Amaltruda also acknowledged the canons' rights to one-third of the demesne.[155]

Guillem Guifré and the canons entered into several other agreements of this type. Cornellana, purchased by Sant Ermengol and granted to the see in his testament, was the subject of two *convenientiae* of 1050 that detailed for the first time the terms on which that castle was held. In one, the archdeacon Guillem promised the bishop not to replace the *castlà* without permission. In the other, Pere Udalard, presumably the *castlà*, promised host, cavalcade, and court service to the bishop, and that he would not accept any lord (*senior*) other than the archdeacon Guillem. Pere also swore an oath of fidelity to the bishop, the archdeacon, and the canons.[156] The castle of Solsona, acquired in an exchange with Ermengol III of Urgell in 1056, was already in 1057 the subject of a revised *convenientia* that described the division of revenues as well as the military obligations of the *castlà*, Eicard, and an intermediate lord, Pere Mir. The agreement specified, among other things, that the horsemen from Solsona under Pere's command were to camp with the bishop in the host,

---

[155] DACU 557, 584; ACU 384* ("ipso castellano vel castellanos qui tenent vel tenuerint ipso castro de ipsa Clusa faciant hostes et kavalcadas cum cunctos cavallarios que abuerint de predicta honore et in ostes albergent cum predicto episcopo"). See also ACU 375*, a *convenientia* concerning a loan for which the castle served as a pledge.   [156] ACU 399a*, 399b*; DACU 894.

whether or not Pere did so.[157] In a *convenientia* of 1062, the bishop and Berenguer Ricard established the military services due from the episcopal castles of Alinyà and Odèn. It detailed how the forces from those castles were to be divided among the bishop and Arnau Mir de Tost, if Berenguer Ricard were to come to an agreement with that lord in the future.[158] Five years later, the bishop and canons entered into a *convenientia* with Bernat Trasoari concerning the *potestas* of La Figuera, a castle that had just been granted to the see by Arnau Mir de Tost.[159]

Bishop Guillem Guifré also developed further the use of the written oath. In addition to the oath mentioned above for Cornellana, oaths survive for the castles of Llanera and Solsona. In these the bishop received promises of fidelity from men who also counted Arnau Mir de Tost and the count of Urgell as *seniores*.[160] He thus expanded his power base by merging his own networks of fidelity with those of other lords. The bishop also accepted oaths from Ramiro I of Aragón, Ermengol III of Urgell, and Guillem I Ramon of Cerdanya that included promises not to seize episcopal castles.[161] By the time of Bishop Guillem Guifré's death in 1075, conventions, oaths, *castlans*, *potestas*, host, and cavalcade were an established part of a growing regime of episcopal castle holding in Urgell.

Up to the mid-eleventh century, there is little evidence for episcopal connections to castles at Girona. Although the see held lands at La Bisbal and Sant Sadurní de l'Heura, there is no mention of fortifications at those sites. Conversely, sites for which castles are known, such as through the quitclaim of Ermessenda, reveal only shadowy links to the see. It was only under the episcopate of Berenguer Guifré (1051–93) that Girona began to establish various ties by means of conventions and oaths with the families in charge of its castles. If Berenguer's endeavors were less extensive than those of his episcopal colleagues, it is only because the resources with which he began were less substantial.

The earliest evidence for a castle at Sant Sadurní appears in 1052, when Amat Vives, nephew (*nepos*) of Ponç, the *precentor* of the cathedral, swore an oath to Bishop Berenguer.[162] Beyond the standard assurance of fidelity, Amat made several promises with respect to "my fortification (*forteda*) that I have at Sant Sadurní de *Salzed*." He would not knowingly harbor in that fortification enemies of the bishop or specific individuals named by the

---

[157] DACU 693, 694. In a *convenientia* of 1054, the count had pledged the village of Castellciutat that he would grant the castle of Solsona to the bishop (DACU 672).   [158] DACU 737.

[159] DACU 797, 798.   [160] DACU 892, 893. Cf. DACU 896.

[161] DACU 890, 891, 895. An oath of Ermengol IV (DACU 897) does not specifically mention the bishop's castles.

[162] *CCM* 111 [*CDSG* 260] ("meam fortedam quam habeo aput Sanctum Saturninum de Salzed"). For the relationship between Ponç and Amat Vives, see *VL* 12:28 [*CDSG* 300].

bishop. Furthermore, he would not deny the bishop entrance to the fortification and would grant *potestas* to him on demand. The first certain indication of a castle on the site of La Bisbal is a convention between Bishop Berenguer and Oliver Guillem from three decades later (1083). Oliver promised fidelity and aid to the bishop and undertook to guard the village and castle (*castellum*) of La Bisbal with his retainers (*mesnada*) six months of the year. As a guarantee, Oliver pledged his fief, consisting of the lands held by his father as well as additional lands granted to him by the bishop. The bishop increased the extent of Oliver's fief in a grant (*donum*) of 1085 in which the terms of the original agreement were repeated, this time with the particular six-month period specified. An undated oath of fidelity of an Oliver, son of Retruda, to Bishop Berenguer, which does not mention any specific properties, is probably related to this contract for castle-guard.[163]

Elsewhere, episcopal interest proved ephemeral or weak. In the case of Navata, well to the north of Girona, control over the castle was only a temporary accomplishment.[164] A series of four lords of Navata swore oaths to Bishop Berenguer Guifré: Adalbert, Bernat Adalbert, Bernat, and Guillem Bernat.[165] The first, third, and fourth of these swore purely general oaths, without mention of the castle. In 1072, however, Bernat Adalbert commended himself by *convenientia* and oath to Bishop Berenguer with respect to an *honor* being granted to his son. As part of Bernat's undertakings, he promised access to the castle of Navata, except against the count of Besalú.[166] At some point before the death of the bishop in 1093, however, a different Bernat swore an oath to the bishop on different terms. He promised to grant to the bishop the *potestas* of Navata on demand; no mention was made of the count of Besalú.[167] The castle seems at this point to have been more under the control of the bishop than of the count of Besalú. By 1099, however, the castle was once again linked to that count: a second Bernat Adalbert de Navata granted the castle to the count as an alod, swore fidelity, and promised to grant *potestas*.[168] Episcopal connections to Navata were purely due to the efforts

---

[163] *CCM* 152, 155, 156 [*CDSG* 387, 392, 433]. It is possible that the last document refers to a later Bishop Berenguer.

[164] Jaume Marquès i Casanovas and Lluís G. Constans i Serrats, *Navata* (s.l., [1985]), 79–88, provides a proposed genealogy.   [165] *CCM* 115, 139, 163, 167 [*CDSG* 425, 426, 428, 429].

[166] *CCM* 138, 139 [*CDSG* 343, 426].

[167] *CCM* 166 [*CDSG* 427]. Bernat is identified here as the son of the late "Em," probably a reference to Ermessenda, the wife of Bernat Adalbert (Marquès i Casanovas and Constans i Serrats, *Navata*, 83; Pelayo Negre Pastell, "La villa de Torroella de Montgrí y sus primitivos señores," *Anales del Instituto de estudios gerundenses* 4 [1949], 84–87). Marquès i Planagumà (*CCM* 163n) argues that the receipt of two oaths from the same individual is unlikely, but ignores the fact that one oath is general while the other is specifically for the castle.

[168] RBIII 60.1*, 60.2*. Bernat Adalbert is identified as the son of Adelaida; a Guillem, son of the late Adelaida, swore a general oath to Berenguer Guifré (*CCM* 167).

of Bishop Berenguer Guifré; after his death, the count of Besalú quickly regained control of the castle from the see.

In several situations, the episcopal involvement with a castle never extended beyond low-level engagements, such as the promise of entry or a simple undertaking not to injure the bishop or episcopal property from a site. Fidelity did not always lead to episcopal control over a castle. This was especially the case in the county of Empúries. For example, in an oath to Bishop Berenguer Guifré for the castles of Fonolleres and Canyà, Ponç Guillem promised to be the faithful man (*fidelis*) of the bishop, not to seize his property, and to aid him in defending his *honor*. With respect to the castles, he promised "intrare et exire et stare et guerreiare," that is, use of the castles rather than control over their disposition.[169] That control belonged to the counts of Empúries and eventually Rosselló.[170] Another series of oaths, to which it is difficult to assign precise dates, granted similar limited rights with respect to the castles of Toroella de Montgrí and Roca Maura. These included a pair of oaths, presumably contemporaneous, in which the bishop received permission to use the castles, except against the count of Empúries.[171]

The close of the eleventh century

Later bishops in the eleventh century built on the foundations established by these four great midcentury figures. In Urgell and Vic, there was some expansion, but generally these were years of consolidation. Bishops renewed preexisting relationships with castle guardians, and specified new obligations for sites held earlier without military service. The amount of evidence for this period is rather thin, as was the case with comital documentation.

From the tenure of Bishop Umbert of Barcelona (1069–85) there survives evidence for the consolidation of Guislabert's efforts at only one castle.

---

[169] *CCM* 168 [*CDSG* 441]. I am not convinced by Marquès i Planagumà's identifications here and at *CCM* 169.

[170] *CDSG* 265 (a. 1053), a *convenientia* of mutual aid between the brothers Pere and Guillem, involving a pledge of an eighth part of the castle of Fonolleres. The aid was limited against the count Ponç I Hug of Empúries (1040–78). *LFM* 698 (a. 1085), 700 (a. 1121), 704 (a. 1154): conventions between the counts of Empúries and Rosselló mentioning the two castles. ADG, Pia Almoina, Fonolleres 15 (a. 1123): a *convenientia* between Bernat and Guillem de Voltrera and Umbert and Guillem de La Tallada, in which the two pairs of brothers swore fidelity to each other for the portions of the castle held previously by Pere Bernat and Guillem Bernat, the brothers mentioned in *CDSG* 265; no mention is made of the bishop.

[171] *CCM* 245, 246 (dated by the editor to *c*. 1128) [*CDSG* 439, 435]; Negre Pastell, "La villa de Torroella de Montgrí," 87–89. In addition to the castles discussed above, the see received a grant of *turres* at Sords in 1075, though no later connections are evident (*CCM* 141, 143 [*CDSG* 351, 353]).

Two hostages presented themselves to Umbert to ensure that Pere Mir de Banyeres would do right to the bishop concerning his obligations: granting *potestas*, swearing fidelity, providing the service of the *castlans* in hosts and cavalcades, and serving the bishop in war and peace. The hostages indicate some tension in the relationship, but more significant for present purposes is the detailed listing of military obligations, which were entirely absent in the agreement of 1032.[172]

In Urgell, Bernat Guillem (1076–92) continued the tradition of high-born local bishops: he was the son of Guillem de Castellbò, viscount of Urgell, and Ermengarda, sister of Guillem, count of Pallars Sobirà. He continued, too, the military activity of his predecessors, accompanying Ermengol IV in a campaign against Calassanç, even while attempting to demilitarize the canons of the cathedral.[173] Only a few castle-holding conventions and oaths have survived from his episcopacy.[174] This is not an indication, however, that the bishop or canons were lax in maintaining their rights in castles that they already possessed. In 1075x77, they successfully defended episcopal claims to the castle of Coscó. In 1079x80, they accepted a grant of the castle of Castellet, confirming Arnau Mir de Tost's acknowledgment of episcopal rights made a generation earlier. In 1086 and 1090, the canons obtained recognition of episcopal rights in La Clua in the testaments of the original donors.[175] Their most significant action came in 1080, when Ermengol IV requested that the canons grant him temporary *potestas* of all their castles, as an example to the other *proceres* of the county; the canons assented with the condition that he confirm their exclusive rights in the castles and renounce any future claim to them. They thus transformed a potentially dangerous alienation of rights into an opportunity to strengthen their hold on episcopal castles.[176]

A similar trend, on an appropriately reduced scale, may be seen in Girona under Bernat Umbert (1093–1111). An episcopal *convenientia* of 1097 with Oliver Guillem renewed almost word for word the grant of La Bisbal from 1083.[177] He received an oath of fidelity for Sant Sadurní from the son of the previous holder; the fortification seems to have been expanded in the intervening years. Berenguer Amat's oath to Bishop

---

[172] LA 4:333. In the same agreement, the bishop "returned" ("reddat") the *castrum* of La Granada to Pere Mir, though no terms are specified.
[173] DACU 1079, cit. Ignasi M. Puig i Ferreté, "L'ascendència pallaresa dels bisbes d'Urgell Bernat Guillem (1076–1092) i Guillem Arnau de Montferrer (1092–1095)," *Urgellia* 3 (1980), 186 n. 6; Cebrià Baraut, ed., "Els documents, dels anys 1076–1092, de l'Arxiu Capitular de La Seu d'Urgell," *Urgellia* 7 (1984–85), 22 and n. 32.
[174] DACU 983 (Sallent), 1059 (Perarrua), 1099 (Arcalís).
[175] DACU 918, 934 (cf. 596), 1031, 1076.   [176] DACU 940.
[177] CCM 177 [CDSG 471]; cf. above p. 202. Another general oath may be associated with this convention (CCM 178 [CDSG 444]).

Bernat was essentially the same as the oath his father had made – a promise of fidelity and *potestas* – but the emphasis was changed. The promise of *potestas* was now central. The negative aspects of fidelity, formerly limited to not harboring enemies of the bishop, were altered and expanded. Berenguer was not to seize the property of the cathedral, do anything to harm the interests of the cathedral, or hand the castle over to someone other than the bishop or his appointees. This change may reflect an increased fear on the part of the bishop of the power of his *castlans*.[178]

Girona also gained temporary control over the castle of Montpalau. In a *convenientia* between Bernat Umbert and the viscount Ponç Guerau I, the bishop commended that castle to the viscount and granted to him in fief "the comital demesne, just as Guillem Umbert held it from the hand of Count Berenguer."[179] The viscount promised to grant *potestas* to the bishop and to give the castle to the son of Guillem Umbert when ordered to do so.[180] This Guillem Umbert must be the son of the Umbert who was Ramon Berenguer I's *castlà* for Montpalau and Gironella.[181] Indeed in 1089, Berenguer Ramon II commended the castle and the protection of the son of Guillem Umbert to an Arnau Jofre and his wife, an arrangement apparently renewed in *c.* 1113.[182] But in that same year, Guillem Umbert was named in a convention between Ramon Berenguer III and the new viscount, Guerau Ponç II; he was commended to the viscount along with the castle of Montpalau.[183] It is not known what happened to Guillem Umbert in the intervening years, but it is clear that between the commendations of Montpalau by the counts of Barcelona in 1089 and 1113, it was the bishop of Girona who had control. This control may have been based in a legal interest: Montpalau was among the properties "returned" to the bishopric by the countess Ermessenda in the 1050s.[184] Nevertheless, after this episode the castle remained firmly in the hands of the counts of Barcelona and the viscounts of Girona.[185]

As for earlier periods, a more detailed analysis is possible for the diocese of Vic. The pontificate of Berenguer Sunifred de Lluçà (1076–99) is generally considered the high point of the power and influence of the see. Berenguer served as virtual regent for the count of Barcelona, Berenguer Ramon II, and acquired from the pope in 1091 the title of Archbishop of Tarragona. In the years following his rule, however, the

---

[178] *CDSG* 446.

[179] *CCM* 196: "ipsam dominicaturam comitalem sicut Guilielmus Umberti tenebat eam per manum Berengarii comitis."

[180] "quando episcopus sibi preceperit sicut idem episcopus habebat iam dictum castrum per eundem Uicecomitem." Does this suggest that the bishop held the castle from the viscount?

[181] RBI sd 52*; cf. BC, MS 729, 4:51r–v.   [182] BRII 62*; *LFM* 409 (rubric only).

[183] RBIII 171*.   [184] *CCM* 120 [*CDSG* 282].   [185] *LFM* 415 (*c.* 1196); PEI 66* (a. 1199).

church fell from these heights.[186] The fate of the episcopal castles of Vic followed this general trajectory. The first half of Berenguer's reign was the high point of the extension of Vic's network of castles; the decline was not gradual, as Freedman has argued, but came relatively rapidly after his attentions turned elsewhere. Berenguer established links to only a few additional castles, but was energetic in reasserting episcopal influence on the frontier. He renewed and defended episcopal rights while articulating the ties of the see to the newly influential secular lords.

The most significant work of Berenguer's tenure was his management of the relationships with the three most powerful families in the region: the viscounts of Cardona (Osona), the seneschals of the counts of Barcelona, and the Gurb-Queralt-Cervelló. In the long term, the agreements with these families led to a loss of episcopal power in the region; in the short term, though, they served to strengthen the stability of the network of episcopal castles. The most important shift in the structures of power in the region of Vic was the rise in influence of the seneschals of the count of Barcelona. The focus of this transformation was a group of castles to the north of the city of Vic: Orís, Manlleu, Voltregà, and Solterra. These had been under the control of Amat Elderic, believed to be the first seneschal of the counts of Barcelona, who may have received them from the countess Ermessenda. Their later appearance as property of the Montcada family has led to the view that they were part of the patrimony of the seneschalcy, but the date at which this patrimony crystallized is unknown. The bishops of Vic became involved with these castles toward the end of Amat's life, in the late 1050s. In a convention of 1058, Bishop Guillem appeared as a joint lord of Voltregà, and in 1060 he subscribed the document that made Ramon Mir de L'Aguda the guardian of the son of the late seneschal, Pere Amat; the agreement named the castles of Orís and Solterra as part of the *honor* over which the bishop was to have control.[187] Pere Amat did not accede to his father's position, and the family's power was severely limited. In 1083, however, Bishop Berenguer failed in his attempt to commend the castle of Voltregà to Guillem Bernat de Gurb (Queralt), Pere's father-in-law, who, because of the location of the castle of Gurb, was no doubt interested in consolidating his own control in the region north of the city. Pere Amat still had the clout to block the deal, at least temporarily, entering a convention of

---

[186] Freedman, *Vic*, 29–39.

[187] AME 9/24, RBI 253.1*; RBI 253.2* is the comital donation to Pere. On this complicated transition, see: Antoni Pladevall i Font, "Els senescals dels comtes de Barcelona durant el segle XI," *Anuario de estudios medievales* 3 (1966), 118–21; Shideler, *Montcadas*, 21–24, 29; Freedman, *Vic*, 72–73.

Foundations (the eleventh century)

his own with the bishop with regard to his remaining possessions.[188] At his death, his widow Guisla attempted to solidify her family's ties with the see, granting to the bishop *potestas* of Orís, for which she acknowledged episcopal overlordship; she similarly accepted his lordship for Voltregà.[189] But less than a year later, and with Guisla still alive, the bishop violated the deal, transferring the patrimony of the former seneschal to the new one, Guillem Ramon.

The bishop's relationship with the new seneschal had begun in 1082, when Berenguer granted various churches to Guillem Ramon, his brother Arbert, and their ally Mir Foget de Besora in return for military service.[190] Then, in 1088, the bishop commended to the trio the castles of Voltregà, Orís, and Solterra, to be held in service of the bishop. This agreement also contained an offer to grant to them the former viscomital castle of Vic, an action that would mark the beginning of the eclipse of episcopal power within the city in the face of that of the Montcadas.[191]

On the frontier, the bishop turned to the Cervelló lineage, extending their influence in the region from Miralles, held by the family from the bishops since the tenth century, to the castle of Tous, still held for the bishops by the family of *castlans* that was in place under Guillem de Mediona in the 1030s. This move seems to have been principally an attempt to combat the continued problems with the Queralt family in the region; the bishop promised Guerau Alemany a fief in any lands that he could recover from Guillem Bernat de Queralt and made him swear not to make a separate agreement with Guillem without the bishop's knowledge. The bishop was also concerned, however, with further development of the castle network, instructing Guerau to construct a new fortification at Revell.[192] Guerau swore an oath for Tous, Revell, and Miralles on the day the *convenientia* was drawn up.[193]

The most striking reflection of this renewal of interest in the diocese's western claims is a puzzling agreement concerning three frontier castles that had been sold earlier to the count of Barcelona: Copons, Montfalcó, and Veciana. It was a classic *comenda*-convention, by which the bishop

---

[188] AME 9/23, 9/20=9/19. Pladevall i Font, "Els senescals," 122; Benet, *Gurb-Queralt*, 115. Note that in this agreement Pere did not acknowledge that the castles were held of the bishop, and promised *potestas* of Orís or Manlleu only if the count should demand *potestas* of Voltregà.
[189] AME 9/21=9/15. At the bishop's death, the castle was to remain in the *potestas* of Guisla.
[190] AME 7/15.
[191] AME 9/12bis, 9/30, 9/31, all of which are copies, now missing. The register of this series indicates that 9/30 also contained oaths of the Montcadas to the bishops of Vic in 1191, 1224, and 1270. See Moncada, *Episcopologio*, 1:344–46. ACV 9/ii/87 is an undated general oath of Guillem Ramon (I) Seneschal, to the bishop.
[192] ACV 9/ii/73 (copies at 9/ii/71, 9/ii/72); Benet, *Gurb-Queralt*, 119–20. The document names a Pere Ramon, "qui modo est inde castellanus," who must be the son of the Ramon, son of Bernat, to whom Guillem left the castle in his testament. [193] ACV 9/ii/74=RBII 43.1*.

207

granted the castles to Guillem Ramon de Cervera in return for military service. The agreement did not mention the count's overlordship, nor did the original sales imply any continued episcopal rights. These rights may, of course, have existed; equally likely, however, is the possibility that the bishop took advantage of his own strength and the count's weakness to reassert episcopal claims.[194]

Bishop Berenguer strengthened these claims elsewhere through renewals of earlier arrangements. Thus in 1078, the viscounts of Cardona (Osona), now Ramon Folc I and Ermessenda, renewed their recognition of episcopal lordship over Calaf, last made in 1038. A comparison of the two agreements places the changed circumstances in relief. In the agreement of 1038, the viscounts simply agreed to hold the castle from the bishop against a yearly payment. In this new agreement, after acknowledging that they had accepted the castle from the hands of the bishop, they promised *potestas* of the castle and a full range of military services. Ramon Folc also swore an oath of fidelity for the castle.[195] In his testament, Ramon Folc left the castle to his wife and brother on condition that it be held from the see of Vic, and in 1087 the new viscount (Folc II, the future bishop of Barcelona) renewed the agreement once again.[196] In 1080 the bishop renewed his predecessor's agreements with the viscount of Girona for the castles of S'Avellana and Vilagelans, again with more specific details as to the conditions of military service.[197] In 1086, Ponç Hug de Cervera renewed the convention that his father had entered into with Bishop Guillem and Berenguer himself twenty years earlier concerning the castles of Aguilar and Llavinera.[198]

Aside from the castles associated with the seneschalcy, which in any case appear to have entered episcopal control before Berenguer's reign, the only significant addition to the episcopal network of castles made by Berenguer was Sentfores, to the southwest of the city. In 1088, Guislabert Mir de Sentfores acknowledged the lordship of the bishop, against a money-fief for three years and a promise of a *cavalleria* of land thereafter. This, too, may simply be the first documentary evidence for this link, as the convention seems to refer to the rights of Berenguer's predecessors.[199] It is noteworthy that with this grant, Berenguer's interest in castles came to a virtual halt. He continued to arrange for military service, though in exchange for grants of episcopal lands and ecclesiastical offices rather than

---

[194] AME 6/70.   [195] AME 13/54, 13/67bis.
[196] Moncada, *Episcopologio*, 1:340–41; ACV 31/xlii/85★=AME 13/57★.
[197] AME 6/44.   [198] ACV 6/1507. See above, pp. 197–98.
[199] AME 8/87: "predicta terra revertatur in potestatem Sancti Petri et eius episcopi salve voce quam in eodem castro habuerunt antecessores eius episcopi Sancti Petri."

for castles.[200] In his final act as bishop, his testament of a decade later, Berenguer reaffirmed his family's grant of Quer to the see, adding the castle of Torroella, each of which would become a focus of activity only in the next century.[201] These last-minute additions could not, in the greater scheme of things, reverse the tide. The first half of Berenguer's reign had marked the high point of episcopal power and control over castles; the archbishop's successors would preside over the progressive unraveling of the network he had woven.

Freedman's description of the second half of the eleventh century as a period of general decline in episcopal power over castles is misleading. Most of his examples of "lost" castles do not, in fact, provide evidence for such a decline. Copons, Montfalcó, and Veciana were alienated to the count of Barcelona, but a decade later the holder of those castles recognized the bishop as his lord. Malla was sold after a dispute, but that dispute shows that episcopal title to the castle was not as unencumbered as the donation and conventions of 1051x52 suggest. The bishop of Vic and abbot of Santa Maria de Ripoll claimed the castle *jointly* against Ermengol Guillem de Mediona. Furthermore, the claim was based not on Ermengol Guillem's donation to the cathedral in 1051, but on a testamentary grant of Adelaida, viscountess of Berga.[202] The bishop granted Orís, Voltregà, and Solterra to the seneschals in 1088, but this was not a sign of weakness. Whatever the see's earlier position with relation to those castles, the bishop had never before been in a position to grant them. During the pontificate of Guillem de Balsareny, they were subject to an undefined form of episcopal tutelage; under Berenguer Sunifred, they were, for however brief a time, episcopal castles.

The "quiet usurpations" described by Freedman do reflect the increased power of the lords of these castles, but this must be seen in the context of regional developments, as well as in the context of the history of Vic's holdings. Rights in castles were partitioned and more explicitly enumerated, while the guardians of the castles became much more visible in the documentation. This documentary *and* structural change does not necessarily reflect a loss of control or power. In the 1020s, the high point of Vic's involvement on the frontier, the episcopal castles had all been farmed out to Guillem de Mediona against a recognition payment; there may have been more to the agreements, but that is all that the documents

---

[200] E.g., ACV 9/ii/81=AME 5/13 (a. 1090); ACV, calaix 37, Liber dotationum antiquarum, fol. 2v (a. 1095); AME 4/47 (a. 1097). Earlier examples: AME 4/41 (a. 1078), 7/15 (a. 1082); ACV 9/ii/76 (a. 1084). See also ACV 9/ii/75*, 9/ii/82*.

[201] Moncada, *Episcopologio*, 1:380–81.

[202] Above, pp. 198–99. For Adelaida, see *LFM* 554; ACU 198*; *CSCV* 474; DACU 516; and Miret i Sans, "Los vescomtes," 154–55.

reveal. This delegation of power has not been interpreted as a sign of loss of control, but rather a reflection of Oliba's skill in managing the episcopal domain.

Later in the century, the system had changed. Ramon Berenguer I's genius was in manipulating the system to his advantage, using oaths, conventions, and a castle-holding network to reestablish his power on a new footing. This is precisely what the bishops of Vic did. Faced with a new system of organizing power, they integrated their holdings into it. Episcopal castles in the 1080s were in the hands of guardians, just as they had been in the 1020s; the bishop's rights, however, especially in terms of military power, were now set forth clearly in written agreements. The increasing number of conventions, therefore, was not a sign of weakness, but of more active administration, of an attempt to organize and manage new structures of power. These documents show the church at its height at the end of the eleventh century, not in the midst of a general decline.

The surviving *convenientiae* from Vic provide two measures of the strength of the episcopal network of castles: the number of castles involved in agreements and the content of those agreements.[203] None of the bishops before 1046 entered into agreements concerning more than six castles during his tenure, and the total number of castles for which there is written evidence from this early period is thirteen. Guillem de Balsareny, during the thirty years of his pontificate, engaged in transactions concerning thirteen castles; although he alienated a number of them, he also subjected several new sites to episcopal control. Berenguer, in the first fifteen years of his tenure, dealt with twenty castles without alienating a single one.[204] Never again would the diocese of Vic take such an interest in managing the sources of its military strength.

In making these agreements, Berenguer was careful to articulate his rights. The most important element now was not a simple recognition of episcopal overlordship; although this was sometimes explicitly stated, it was merely implicit in some of the agreements (how could a bishop commend a castle that was not his?). Nor were the rights of entry and general promises of defense that first appeared in Guillem's reign the key undertakings. The important promises, from the standpoint of the bishop's military lordship, were *potestas* – the promise to render control of the castle to the bishop on demand – and military service. In the (ultimately abortive) commendation of Voltregà to Guillem Bernat de Gurb (Queralt), for example, Guillem promised right of entry and *potestas* of

---

[203] The total number of conventions per episcopate is not a particularly good measure, given the relatively low total number of documents, the growth over time of the surviving documentation, and the frequent presence of more than one castle in a single agreement.

[204] See Table 4.1.

Table 4.2. *Services due in castle-holding agreements under Berenguer Sunifred*[#]

Date	Documents	*potestas*	Service	Entry	Fidelity
1078 Nov 18	AME 13/54, 13/67	x	x		x
1079 Sep 14	ACV 9/ii/71–73	x	x		x
1080 Jun 06	AME 6/44		x	x	
1080 Sep 03	AME 9/36, 9/59	x			
1083 Sep 16	AME 9/23	x		x	
1084 Jan 2	AME 9/19–20	x	x	x	
1087 Oct 29	AME 13/57*	x	x		
1088 Jan 25	AME 9/21, 9/15	x	x		
1088 Feb 27	ACV 9/ii/80	x	x	x	x
1088 May 26	AME 8/87	x		x	
1076x91	AME 6/70		x		x

Note:

[#] AME 9/12bis (copies at 9/30, 9/31), a commendation of Voltregà, Orís, and Solterra known only from register notices, has been omitted because the notices do not include the relevant details. For the purposes of the table, "fidelity" includes specific promises of fidelity as well as statements such as "sit suus homo."

Voltregà to the bishop, but he also promised right of entry, and *only* right of entry, to his own castle of Gurb. Of eleven agreements or sets of agreements concerning episcopal castles from the period 1076–90, nine included a promise of *potestas*, and eight contained a specific commitment to perform military service (host, cavalcade, etc.) (Table 4.2). One final index of episcopal control – though perhaps not a particularly reliable one – is the frequency of agreements concerning castles controlled by the see that did not acknowledge the bishop's lordship. There were a few of these, as seen above, under Oliba and Guillem. They would become much more common in the twelfth century.[205]

The early development of networks of castle holding in the four principal Catalan dioceses followed similar patterns and chronologies. Barcelona, Vic, and Urgell first became associated with castles in the tenth century, and their bishops took active roles in fighting and efforts at repopulation along the frontier. From the mid-eleventh century, the bishops became involved in the new regime of castle holding that was spreading throughout the region. They organized tenurial arrangements in complex hierarchical structures, and new documentary forms, particularly the *convenientia*, emerged to detail these arrangements. These

[205] For example, two *comenda*-conventions for the castle of Meda: ACA, Diversos, Varia 10 (Vilanova Roselló), leg. 1, doc. 5, nos. 2 (p. 2, a. 1139), 4 (pp. 3–4, a. 1153). See Freedman, *Vic*, 110–12, esp. Table 3 (which does not include these agreements).

developments even affected Girona, where evidence for episcopal castles before midcentury cannot be found. New structures were consolidated in each diocese during the long midcentury pontificates of powerful lord-bishops, all members of local aristocratic families and implicated in the high politics of the period. After the flurry of activity during the reigns of these bishops, the closing years of the eleventh century seem calm. There are some indications that the dioceses were consolidating their holdings, but as was the case with the comital evidence, the documentation for this period is relatively thin. After a convention concerning the castle of Ribes in 1060, for example, the next appearance of the castle among the records of the diocese of Barcelona is in 1130. Is this an indication of a crisis around the year 1100? Was the system of castle tenure adversely affected at all levels by discord at the top? The twelfth-century evidence sheds some light on these questions.

MONASTIC MILITARY LORDSHIP

Like the counts, lay aristocracy, and the major bishoprics, Catalan monasteries took part in the organization and spread of the network of castles in the eleventh and twelfth centuries. Only the houses of Santa Maria de Gerri, Sant Pere d'Àger, and Sant Cugat del Vallès have left a substantial documentation on this subject. These records show that while monasteries did have ties to castles and did employ written agreements in regulating those relationships, these activities were invariably local, limited, and focused more on revenue than on military service.

According to the historian of Santa Maria de Gerri, five castles were "directly dependent" on the monastery: Castell Salat, Bresca, Rocafort, Baén, and Cuberes.[206] The abbot also had at one point a place in the chain of command over two other castles, Montcortès and Peramea. All of these castles were local, within 8 km of the monastery. As was the case for some of the bishoprics, a papal confirmation attests to the monastery's rights. But this bull, granted in 1164 by Alexander III, lists only four castles (Castell Salat, Bresca, Rocafort, and Baén),[207] and only two conventions and no oaths survive to provide details about these rights. With the aid of other types of documents, however, it is possible to uncover the often tenuous links between the monastery and its castles in the eleventh century.

---

[206] *Gerri*, 1:457–67. What follows draws heavily on this work, though with a different emphasis.

[207] *Gerri* 153 [Paul Kehr, ed., *Papsturkunden in Spanien: Vorarbeiten zur Hispania pontificia*, vol. 1, *Katalanien*, 2 parts, Abhandlungen der Gesellschaft der Wissenschaften zu Göttingen, Philologisch-historische Klasse, n.F., 18:2 (Berlin, 1926), no. 110 (pp. 396–400); J-L 10997].

In a *convenientia* from before 1070, Count Artau I of Pallars Sobirà and the abbot Arnau of Gerri jointly commended the castle of Peramea.[208] In 1076, in a clause of a donation to the abbot of rights in the castle of Montcortès, the count granted that "they who hold the castles of Montcortès and Peramea and Bresca and Baén should be the men (*homines*) of the abbot by his hand and will."[209] These two rather ambiguous documents are the only ones to link the abbots of Gerri to Peramea and Montcortès.[210] Castell Salat is only attested in the twelfth-century documentation.[211] While the situation at Baén, Rocafort, and Cuberes is better documented, the monastery's hold on these castles was no more secure. Although the community had legitimate rights at Baén dating from the tenth century, it acquired the castle only in 1086x87, when it exacted quitclaims from the two owners with threats of excommunication and a forgery of an eighth-century grant. The castle was granted back as a fief to one of the owners, who promised *potestas* and services to the abbot.[212] Gerri also claimed control of the castle of Rocafort in the late eleventh century, this time on the basis of a genuine charter – or a better forgery.[213] Guillem Guitard de Vallferrera granted the castle back to the monastery and promptly set off on crusade, leaving orders with the guardian of the castle to grant *potestas* to the monastery if he had not returned in two years.[214] Although Gerri had received the castle of Cuberes from Artau I as a pious donation in 1050, the monastery received the castle once again, this time from Mir Arnau, to whom Artau II had pledged it. Mir's grant actually consisted of the 2,000 *mancusos* owed by the counts, but until it was repaid, Mir was to hold Cuberes from the abbot and grant *potestas* upon demand.[215]

In these few documents that have survived there is almost no reference to military service due to the abbot. There are two possible explanations for this. The first is that the castles themselves were not militarily significant. Although located in the heart of the zone of conflict between the counts of the two Pallars, none is mentioned in the documents

---

[208] *Gerri* 12 [*HGL* 5:351].

[209] *Gerri* 18: "et sint illi homines qui tenuerint ipsum castrum de Moncortes, et de Petramedia, et de Bresca, et de Baien, de abbate et sint per manu eius et voluntate omni tempore ab integrum." This is not, as Puig i Ferreté suggests, a grant of the castle of Montcortès; it only renews rights of the monastery in the castle that had been held under Count Artau's father.

[210] They appear to have come under the control of the Vallferrera lineage; see DACU 1324 (a. 1120). The only other notice of Bresca is *Gerri* 127 (a. 1139).   [211] *Gerri* 132, 159.

[212] *Gerri* 16, 17, 38, 41, I (fals). For the tenth-century rights, *Gerri*, 1:460 n. 1275; *Pallars i Ribagorça* 132.

[213] *Gerri* 1, 46, 62. In 1086, the monastery accepted a grant of lands at the castle from Ramon Guillem, presumably the castellan (*Gerri* 37).

[214] *Gerri* 63. *Gerri* 64 is an oath to Guillem Guitard for the castles of Rocafort and Arcalís.

[215] *Gerri* 8, 57.

describing that violence.[216] The second is that the abbots themselves were not militarily significant. The abbots' control over all of these castles appears to have been mediated through or held in conjunction with the counts. A comital grant lies at the origin of the monastery's interest in most of these castles, and the counts were involved in or assented to many of the transactions cited above. For a mention of host and cavalcade we must wait until 1176, when the castle of Cuberes was given as an alod, but "without the cavalcade" ("absque ipsa cavalgada"). The counts may have allowed the monastery to exploit the castle as a source of revenue, but not as a source of military strength.

The community at Sant Pere d'Àger enjoyed rights over a number of castles donated to it in the 1050s and 1060s by Arnau Mir de Tost.[217] Much of the documentation from this important center was destroyed during the 1930s, but enough has survived to give an idea of the connections of the community to the network of oaths and conventions in the central portion of the western frontier. Although Àger seems to have been more actively engaged in the management of castles than was Gerri, the extent of the community's involvement in military activity appears similarly limited.

Despite indications that the abbot of Àger was entering agreements concerning his castles from the 1050s,[218] the first surviving evidence dates from 1067. It is a *convenientia* between Arnau Mir de Tost and Ramon Arnau de Meià in which Arnau commended the castle of Malagastre to Ramon, but required that Ramon commend himself to the abbot of Àger, accept the castle from his hands, and promise to render *potestas*.[219] As was the case with the monastery of Gerri, Àger's interest here was mediated through a secular lord, and the agreement did not specify any military obligations. This situation may also be seen in three conventions concerning the castle of Estanya from the last two decades of the eleventh

---

[216] Bonnassie, *La Catalogne*, 2:612–18; above, pp. 138–41.

[217] The precise number is hard to determine. The key grants would appear to have been on 31 December 1059 (BC 4116: Corçà, Espadella, Cas, Montclús, Oroners, Estanya) and 4 April 1067 (BC 4085*: Llordà, Malagastre, Foradada, Cas, Régola, Corçà, Sant Llorenç d'Ares, and Estanya), with confirmations on 4 April 1065 (BC 4125*) and 4 April 1068 (BC 4316, fols. 7v–9r*). On Arnau, see Pedro Sanahuja, "Arnau Mir de Tost, caudillo de la Reconquista en tierras de Lérida," *Ilerda* I (1943), 11–27, 155–69; 2:1 (1944), 7–21; 2:2 (1944), 53–147; 4 (1946), 25–55; Sanahuja, *Historia de la villa de Àger* (Barcelona, 1961), *passim*; Philippe Araguas, "Les châteaux d'Arnau Mir de Tost: Formation d'un grand domaine féodal en Catalogne au milieu du XIᵉ siècle," in *Les pays de la Méditerranée occidentale au Moyen Âge*, Actes du 106ᵉ Congrès national des sociétés savantes, Section de philologie et d'histoire jusqu'à 1610, Perpignan, 1981 (Paris, 1983), 61–76; Francesc Fité i Llevot, *Reculls d'història de la Vall d'Àger*, vol. 1, *Período antic i medieval* (Àger, 1985), 85–173; Bonnassie, *La Catalogne*, 2:789–97.

[218] Fité i Llevot (*Reculls*, p. 149, no. 64) cites a convention of 10 June 1057 between the abbot of Àger and Atinard Mir, *castlà* of Corçà. See below, n. 223.   [219] BC 4145.

century. In the first, dated 1079, Guillem Ramon, abbot of Àger, commended the *castlà* of Estanya, Arnau Ató, to Bertran Borrell de Casserres;
in return Bertran promised to defend Àger's interests and he commended
himself to the abbot. The agreement was concluded in the presence of
Ponç Guerau I, viscount of Girona, the son-in-law of Arnau Mir de
Tost.[220] A second *convenientia* between the two, also concluded before the
viscount, followed more closely the language of a standard *comenda*-
convention. While as in the earlier agreement the abbot commended the
castlà to Bertran, he also commended the castle and granted a fief; Bertran
and his son Pere promised *potestas* and military services (host, cavalcade,
etc.).[221] A third *convenientia* concerning the castle, dated 1100, made no
reference to a secular lord, but it returned to the language of the convention of 1080: Abbot Pere Guillem of Àger commended the *castlà* Hug
Arnau to Arnau Mir de Casserres, with no mention of specific military
service.[222]

The remaining convention, from 1109, recorded abbot Pere's grant to
Galceran, son of Galceran Erimany, of the castles of Cas and Corçà.
Military arrangements are more apparent here, though still somewhat
poorly defined: the castle of Cas was granted with its *milites*, host and cavalcade were included in a list of rights granted *to* Galceran, and the *castlans* were required to do host and cavalcade service to the abbot if
Galceran could not. Galceran himself made no such promise, although
his service was implied. What is clear from this convention is that the
chain of command over these castles was growing longer. Galceran
received Cas "just as today Bernat Erall holds it, and Pere Tedball from
him." Bernat Erall was henceforth to hold the castle from Galceran, with
"Pere Tedball below him ('sub eo')." The fief of Corçà was granted "as
Atinard held it," and Atinard's grandson, Pere Mir, was to hold it from
Galceran. All of these subordinate individuals were identified as *castlans*
(*castellani*).[223]

Sant Cugat del Vallès also operated within the network of oaths and
fidelity established by the counts, bishops, and secular lords, without
becoming wholly enmeshed in it. The monastery played an active role in
the repopulation and refortification of the frontier in the years when that
frontier was still relatively close to Barcelona. As seen in chapter 1, from

---

[220] BC 4210.   [221] BC 4230.
[222] BC 4185. This Hug Arnau may the son of Arnau Ató, the *castlà* in 1079.
[223] BC 4100 (=4033): "sicut Bernardus Eralli hodie tenet eam, et Petrus Tetballi per eum . . .
Bernardus Eralli teneat et habeat ipsum [c]astrum et ipsum fevum per eum, et Petrus Tetballi sub
eo . . . Simili modo prephatus abas donat ad eundem Gaucerandum ipsum castrum de Corcano
per fevum cum medietate ipsius parrochie sicut Atinardus tenuit eam . . ." This Atinard is probably the same as the Atinard Mir who appears as *castlà* for Corçà in 1057 (above, n. 218).

the first few decades of the eleventh century the abbots of Sant Cugat, in some of the earliest *convenientiae*, adapted the form of the agrarian contract to grants for the construction of castles designed to encourage settlement in the area. But all of these early grants must be understood as attempts to maintain some control over frontier lords acting independently on what the monastery saw as its lands, rather than as examples of the monastery exercising military strength.[224] The grant of the *oppidum* of Santa Oliva to Isembert in 1011 was a recognition of work already accomplished.[225] A grant of Calders in 1017, made on the condition that the recipient construct a tower (*turris*), followed a *placitum* before the count of Barcelona in 1013. A second grant of Calders, a *carta donationis sive conventionis* of 1037, made for the purpose of "construction and building and populating," followed at least three more judicial proceedings. A *convenientia* of 1040, agreed to on the condition that the beneficiary "construct and build a castle" at Albinyana, echoed a dispute of 1011. These castles were grouped together in the Baix Penedès, but this pattern also holds outside this region. The abbot Andreu Sendred granted the castle of Clariana to *Maiamborgs* and her sons in 1057, but only after he had argued successfully before a comital *placitum* that *Maiamborgs's* late husband, Guerau Màger, had violated the terms on which he was supposed to have held the castle from the monastery. From 1060 on, information on Sant Cugat's castles becomes strangely scarce until the latter half of the twelfth century. The grant of Clariana was renewed in a convention of 1115, and the monastery granted charters *ad edificandum* at two additional sites, El Bruc in 1108 and Sant Vicenç in 1082.[226]

These sites were fortifications, and reference to military matters was not entirely absent. But only three agreements mentioned specific military service: at Calders in 1017, Bonet Bernat was to guard the castle, and at Albinyana in 1040 the knights (*milites*) of the castle were to serve the abbot in the host, as was the *castlà* of Clariana in 1057. Two oaths of fidelity are related not to a grant of a castle by Sant Cugat, but to a grant

---

[224] Abadal, *L'abat Oliba*, 169–75; Bonnassie, *La Catalogne*, 2:540–44; Josep Maria Salrach, "Formació, organització i defensa del domini de Sant Cugat en els segles X–XII," *Acta historica et archaeologica mediaevalia* 13 (1992), 135, 139, 149–50, 162–63. Aside from the sites discussed here, Salrach notes ties to the castles of Gelida and Masquefa, and the *torres* of Badorc, Capellades, and Monistrol.   [225] OR, Sant Cugat del Vallès 122*.

[226] Calders: *CPF* 14 [*CSCV* 464] (a. 1017); *CSCV* 452 (a. 1013); OR, Sant Cugat del Vallès 192* (a. 1037: "[ad] construendum et hedificandum atque ad populandum"); *CSCV* 527, 529; OR, Sant Cugat del Vallès 194* (*recte* a. 1036). Albinyana: *CPF* 21 [*CSCV* 553] ("castrum construas atque edifices"); *CSCV* 437. Clariana: *CSCV* 612; *CPF* 47 [*CSCV* 826]. El Bruc: OR, Sant Cugat del Vallès 393*. Sant Vicenç: OR, Sant Cugat del Vallès 340*. See also OR, Sant Cugat del Vallès 315* (a. 1069); Flórez et al., *España sagrada . . .*, vol. 42, app. 1, 2 (pp. 279–84, a. 1097); *CPF* 46 [*CSCV* 806] (a. 1109); *CSCV* 825 (a. 1114).

of a church *to* the monastery.[227] There are some indications that the military nature of the castles made the abbots nervous. In the agreement for Calders in 1017, Bonet Bernat was forbidden to use the castle as a base for military forays.[228] The abbots of Sant Cugat viewed castles as a source of economic, not military strength. The projection of force from castles controlled by the monastery of Sant Cugat was essential to the collection of revenues. The evidence shows, however, that the abbots were more concerned with the revenues than with control over this projection of force. A combination of the movement of the frontier well past its lands and the patronage and protection of the counts of Barcelona no doubt contributed to their ability to view the castles in this way. But as seen above, this stance was consistent with the policies of their counterparts at Santa Maria de Gerri and Sant Pere d'Àger.

Sant Cugat, Gerri, and Àger account for most of the surviving monastic *convenientiae* concerning castles. There were certainly other monastic castle-holding agreements that have not survived. Santa Maria de Solsona controlled at least fourteen castles of varying importance between 1088 and 1212, but this fact is known almost entirely from donations *to* the institution, rather than by documents attesting to the community's management of its domains.[229] Some of the few remaining monastic castle-holding conventions show that more typical military relationships might exist. A *convenientia* dated 1077 involving the abbot of Sant Feliu de Girona described in great detail the variations on service in the host and cavalcade due to the monastery and the distribution of lands to horsemen (*caballarii*), although the land granted was described only as a *terra*, rather than any type of fortification.[230] In general, however, monastic integration into developing network of castle tenure had economic goals.

The monasteries only appear tangential because the evidence from other sectors of society for the developing network of castle tenure is so strong. Ramon Berenguer I's efforts to impose a regime based on written agreements were successful only during his lifetime within his immediate

---

[227] Oaths sewn to ACA, Diversos, Varia 24 (Uriz), Pergamins, no. 10 (a. 1062). Additional oaths (cit. Salrach, "Formació," 149 n. 55, 162 nn. 115, 117): *CSCV* 599, 613, 717, 785, 1120.

[228] *CPF* 14 [*CSCV* 464]: "Et non facias de hoc quod tibi donamus aliquam hostem aut alium exequium tu aut posteritas tua aut alii qui ibi habitaverint, sed tantum custodiam et gardam facias vel faciant de ipso castro."

[229] Manuel Riu i Riu, "La canònica de Santa Maria de Solsona: Precedents medievals d'un bisbat modern," *Urgellia* 2 (1979), 232–36.

[230] RBII 21. See also DTavèrnoles 50 (Sant Sadurní de Tavèrnoles), cf. DTavèrnoles 49; RBI 265* (Sant Joan de les Abadesses); AME 12/15 (copies at 12/16, 12/37; Cervera). Cervera was a Hospitaller house; conventions and oaths are surprisingly rare among the extensive documentation surviving concerning the military orders.

sphere of influence; his sons failed to build on his progress. But neighboring counts began using the *convenientia* as well, whether vigorously as in Pallars, or only tentatively as elsewhere. The events surrounding the alliance with Besalú, alongside the change in the opening formula of comital agreements around 1058, suggest that the *convenientia* and new developments in castle tenure were part of a conscious program on the part of the count to use writing to articulate his power. Conventions were particularly useful for this task because they not only recorded transactions that had occurred in the past, they established the outlines of relationships for the future. It is not likely that the count, or others using this new form, had a well-conceived notion of how the *convenientiae* that their scribes were producing might be helpful in the future. Still, the fact that they were written was clearly important in articulating power and in creating blueprints for the future. It is by providing these norms that they served as a basis for a new order for society. It is with respect to these functions – the expression of societal norms and the expression of comital power – that the *convenientia* may be seen as replacing the *placitum*.

Linguistic and institutional points of contact are apparent between the system of *convenientiae* and the judicial system described in documents of the ninth and tenth centuries. But although conventions occasionally recorded settlements in a manner analogous to earlier records of judgment, they operated in a different way. The *placitum* was essentially a retrospective exercise; it drew upon documents and the memory of witnesses in an attempt to restore an earlier state of affairs, or at times to give a new state of affairs the appearance of an old one. The *convenientia*, in contrast, looked to the future. It established relationships between lords and men with respect to castles, relationships articulated in fine detail. It also established mechanisms to guarantee the stability of these relationships, or at least to make possible the defusing of conflicts arising out of them. Although a *convenientia* might refer back in time, it more commonly provided for the perpetuation of a relationship for future generations. By creating and describing stable relationships that were to last into the future, the *convenientia* in the eleventh century offered new structures to Catalan society to replace older ones, such as those represented by the tenth-century comital *placitum*. In the case of the counts, these structures were structures of power. Around 1058, the *convenientiae* of Ramon Berenguer I acquired a new, instrumental aspect, and he used them systematically to establish structures of power. While his immediate successors failed to maintain his level of activity, the structures remained.

Chapter 5

FORTUNES (THE TWELFTH CENTURY)

Ramon Berenguer I's organization of a network of castle tenure and military service around *convenientiae* spread widely throughout Catalonia. Lower levels of the lay aristocracy mimicked the count's actions and his words; similarly, the regime spread – in varying degrees – to neighboring counties, and to the ecclesiastical hierarchy, both secular and monastic. The system of *convenientiae* was not, however, simply a phenomenon of the second half of the eleventh century, for the agreements outlasted the original participants. Their descendants, whether biological or institutional, renewed the arrangements repeatedly, maintaining these structures of power and lordship into the twelfth century. An original exemplar of a *convenientia* that Dalmau Bernat de Peratallada entered into in 1062 for the castle of Begur stands as a symbol of this phenomenon: in 1114 Dalmau's son, also named Dalmau, subscribed a brief codicil to the text of the first *convenientia*, promising to keep the same agreement with Ramon Berenguer III.[1] Not all renewals, of course, were on precisely the same terms. The content of these agreements evolved slowly, in response to economic and political developments. As the twelfth century progressed, there were more and more disputes over agreements, and the *convenientia* lost the near monopoly it had enjoyed in the eleventh century as the written manifestation of structures of power. But overall, the coherence of the structures established in the eleventh century persists deep into the twelfth.

RENEWAL

Though the nicknames accorded by Catalan history to its early counts are often inscrutable, such is not the case with Ramon Berenguer III "el Gran" (1096–1131). His claim to greatness was his rapid expansion of the

---

[1] RBI 273.1*, 273.2*; ADG, Mitra, 23/80* is fourteenth-century copy.

territorial control of the counts of Barcelona. In the second decade of the twelfth century alone, he absorbed into his patrimony Cerdanya, Besalú, and Peralada, and he effected the union of the houses of Barcelona and Provence by his marriage to Douce. But before the count could accomplish all this, he had to order his affairs at home. The discord of the reigns of his father and uncle, Ramon Berenguer II and Berenguer Ramon II, had died down by the time he came of age, but the young count needed to establish his own power base. To do this, he turned to the tools used so effectively by his grandfather: *convenientia* and oath.

By the terms of the settlement of 1086, the four-year-old Ramon Berenguer shared the comital title with his uncle, and he subscribed documents of 1089 and 1093 as count (*comes*).[2] Not until 1097, though, the year Berenguer Ramon II vanishes from the historical record, does the name of the young count appear consistently in charters. Even then, for several years most of his acts recorded confirmations or attempts to raise money to support western campaigns.[3] The lone exception is a convention, now lost, between Ramon Berenguer III and Artau II of Pallars Sobirà establishing an alliance to seize the city of Tortosa.[4] From 1102 on, perhaps because of the fall of València, the count's attention turned inward. There is no evidence of serious internal conflicts, although the programmatic nature of the count's activity may indicate continued tensions.

Ramon Berenguer III first solidified relations with the viscounts of Girona. Ponç Guerau I swore an oath of fidelity for and promised *potestas* of the castles of Blanes, Argimon, and Cabrera sometime before 1106; he may also have sworn an oath to the young count for the castle of Rocabertí.[5] His son, Guerau Ponç, as viscount of Baix Urgell, was included in a *convenientia* by which Pedro Ansúrez, count of Valladolid, acting as tutor for the young Ermengol VI of Urgell, granted Ramon Berenguer a half interest in the castle of Balaguer in return for military aid. This agreement contained only a limited promise of fidelity, but

---

[2] Bofarull, *Los condes*, 2:140 (a. 1089); RBIII 20 (a. 1093).

[3] *CSCV* 765, 767, 769, 770, 777; Enrique Flórez et al., *España sagrada . . .*, 51 vols. (Madrid, 1747–1879), vol. 42, app. 1–2 (pp. 279–84); Bofarull, *Los condes*, 2:138 n. 2; *CCM* 181; *LBSC* 26; RBIII 67.

[4] Francisco Diago, *Historia de los victoriosíssimos antiguos condes de Barcelona . . .* (Barcelona, 1603; repr. Valencia, 1974), fols. 143r–44r (lib. 2, cap. 80). Cf. Sobrequés, *Els grans comtes*, 138; Ferran Soldevila, *Història de Catalunya*, 2nd ed. in 1 vol. (Barcelona, 1963), 138–39; Antoni Rovira i Virgili, *Història nacional de Catalunya*, 7 vols. (Barcelona, 1922–34), 4:10. Diago's summary clearly suggests the typical language of a *convenientia*: "Este es el concierto hecho entre Ramon Conde de Barcelona y Artal Conde de Pallas. Encomienda el Conde Ramon a Artal el Castillo . . ."

[5] RBIII sd 20★; Jaume Coll i Castanyer, "Els vescomtes de Girona," *Annals de l'Institut d'estudis gironins* 30 (1988–89), 64–65. Montpalau does not seem to have been included in this arrangement, *pace* Marquès i Planagumà (*CCM* 196). Cf. BRII 62★.

Guerau Ponç became more tightly bound to the count when he entered conventions with and swore an oath to him for various holdings of the viscounty of Girona in 1106.[6]

The count next turned to the viscount of Cardona (Osona), Bernat Amat. He renewed the grant of "the whole *honor* that your father Deusdé Bernat held and had as a fief from my grandfather, count Ramon Berenguer [I]" and entered a convention with the viscount in 1108; to these he added additional viscomital lands (held previously by Ramon Folc I, viscount from 1040 to 1086) in a convention of 1111.[7] The year before, he had concluded a *convenientia* and oath with Guislabert (II) Udalard, viscount of Barcelona, in which he commended to him the viscomital castle. This agreement does not seem to have been satisfactory, however, for in 1112 he commended rights in the viscounty by *convenientia* to Jordà de Sant Martí; the viscount Guislabert (II) Udalard subscribed this document.[8] In the brief period from 1106 to 1112, then, Ramon Berenguer III had secured written agreements from each of the viscounts of the central counties.

Each of these conventions renewed an earlier arrangement. The convention and oath of Guislabert Udalard repeats nearly word for word the convention and oath of his father to Ramon Berenguer I in 1063.[9] Although no convention has survived between Ramon Berenguer I and the various contemporary members of the Cardona family, Ramon Berenguer III's agreement with Bernat Amat cites "those *convenienciae* that existed between my father Deusdé and your grandfather, count Ramon, concerning the aforesaid *honor*" and "those movables that your grandfather promised to my grandfather Bernat for the castle-guard of Tamarit."[10] The only surviving convention between the viscounts of

---

[6] RBIII 97*, 98*; Coll i Castanyer, "Els vescomtes," 69. For Pedro Ansúrez, see Simon Barton, *The Aristocracy in Twelfth-Century León and Castile*, CSMLT, 4th ser., 34 (Cambridge, 1997), 116, 275–77.

[7] RBIII 114* ("totum ipsum honorem quem pater tuus Deusde Bernard tenebat et habebat per fevum avii mei Raimundi Berengarii comitis"); *LFM* 208, 210 (rubrics only). The conventions are known only from their rubrics, although the grant (RBIII 114*) does refer to "hoc donum superius scriptum atque convenienciam," and the dating clause reads "facta convenientia."

[8] RBIII 131*, 132* (a. 1110); 159 (a. 1112: "De castro vero Barchinonensi super portam merchatalem quod vocant Castellum Vetus, convenio ego prenominatus Iordanus vobis prescripto comiti et prefate comitisse dare et facere omnes convenientias et potestates de me et de castellanis ipsius castelli quas convenit et fecit olim vicecomes prefate civitatis Barchinone Raimundo Berengarii comiti et Almodi comitisse avis tuis sicut scriptum est in convenientiis quas prefatus vicecomes fecit illis et manu propria firmavit, et in sacramentalibus que illis fecit et iuravit"). See also RBIII sd 18*, an oath of Jordà to the count for the castles of Castellet, Olèrdola, Eramprunyà, and the viscomital castle.   [9] RBI 292*, sd 61*.

[10] RBIII 114*: "illas conveniencias que fuerunt inter iam dictum patrem meum Deusde et iam dictum avum tuum Raimundum comitem de predicto honore" and "illud mobile quod avus tuus convenit ad avum meum Bernard per ipsam guardam de Tamarit." RBI sd 132* seems to be the oath of a castellan to Ramon Berenguer I for the castles of the Cardona family.

Girona and Ramon Berenguer I is a specific agreement related to the settlement of a dispute, but there is a series of detailed oaths of fidelity from the viscounts, in which they promise to grant *potestas* of the castles of Argimon, Blanes, Cabrera, and other castles in the city of Girona.[11] The oath of Ponç Guerau I to Ramon Berenguer III for these same castles repeats the text of one of his own earlier oaths; the oath of Guerau Ponç II in 1106, while slightly different in form and wording, is practically identical in content.[12] These were not cases of the count simply renewing agreements when the viscounties changed hands (except for Guerau Ponç II in 1106): Guislabert had held his title since *c.* 1080, Bernat Amat since 1086, and Ponç Guerau I since *c.* 1050. Nor were these men new to the count's entourage; each of the older viscounts appears among the subscribers to Ramon Berenguer III's earliest documents.[13]

During these years between 1106 and 1112, Ramon Berenguer III also acquired written agreements from the heads of two powerful castellan lineages. Curiously, no conventions have survived, only oaths. Like the conventions with the various viscounts, however, these also renewed older arrangements.[14] In 1110, Guillem Ramon I and Dorca de Castellvell swore a joint oath promising to render *potestas* of the castles of Castell Vell, Castellví, Òdena, Pontons, Castellbisbal, and El Far to the count. This oath bears a close resemblance to the one of Geribert Guitard to Ramon Berenguer I for Castell Vell in 1062, for which there is a corresponding convention; an earlier convention survives for the castle of Pontons, as well.[15] Two oaths from Guerau Alemany III de Cervelló covering an extensive list of castles may also date to this period; they recall oaths and conventions for the various castles of Guerau's predecessors.[16] As in the case of the viscounts, these men were not new to the count's following.[17] One notable absence from these early oaths and conventions acquired by Ramon Berenguer is any representative of the Queralt lineage, since Bernat Guillem de Queralt was a key supporter of the rights of the young count both during his joint reign with Berenguer Ramon II and during his minor-

[11] RBI 268*; sd 51*, sd 174*, sd 158*, sd 154*, sd 206*, sd 46.
[12] RBI sd 206*; RBIII sd 20*, 98* (a. 1106).
[13] E.g., *CSCV* 765 (Bernat Amat), 769 (Guislabert Udalard), 777 (Ponç Guerau).
[14] The lone exception to this pattern in the early years of the reign is RBIII 86*, a general oath of Reambau, son of Ode, in 1104. I have been unable to identify this figure.
[15] RBIII 142*; RBI 280*, 376*, sd 122*.
[16] RBI sd 160*; RBIII sd 21*; probably before 1112, as they do not mention Douce. Cf. esp. RBI 287*, sd 117*, sd 208*, but also RBI 143*, 239*, 240*, 373*, 445*, sd 68*, sd 108*, sd 136*, etc.
[17] *CSCV* 767 (Guerau Alemany), 769 (Guillem Ramon, Dorca), 777 (Guillem Ramon, Dorca).

ity. Still, Berenguer Bernat de Queralt, his son, eventually swore an oath to the count for ten castles in 1121.[18]

These renewals of ties with the viscounts and the great families were not routine. In the first decade of the twelfth century, the count of Barcelona consciously set out to articulate his power over the great families through written agreements. In doing this, he explicitly reprised the activity of his grandfather by using the *convenientia* and the oath. Having secured the support of these local magnates and confirmed the stability of the structures that were the foundation of his power, Ramon Berenguer III could more confidently turn his attention to territorial expansion. His first objective was Besalú, whose count, Bernat II,[19] aging and without an heir or a wife, needed to arrange for the succession of his county. In 1107, Ramon Berenguer III betrothed his two-year-old daughter to Bernat. She was to receive as her dowry the county of Osona; in return, the count of Besalú granted all of his *honor* to the count of Barcelona, provided he were to die without a male heir. To complete the arrangement, the counts swore identical oaths of fidelity to each other. The end result of this agreement, surely foreseen by all involved, was the absorption of the county of Besalú into the patrimony of the counts of Barcelona at the death of Bernat II in 1111.[20]

Ramon Berenguer III immediately moved to secure his position in his new territory, just as he had in the home counties. On 8 June 1111, presumably just following the death of the count of Besalú, Bernat Guillem of Cerdanya quitclaimed to the count of Barcelona the castle of Besalú along with the widespread *honores* that the counts of Cerdanya had held from the counts of Besalú; at the same time, he swore fidelity and promised to grant *potestas* of the various castles under his control. In a *difinicio et conveniencia* of 1112, Bernat Adalbert de Navata quitclaimed the oven of Besalú and some family properties, in return for which he received as a fief some lands and a bailiwick; he became the "solid man" of the count, and promised him military and court service. The lords of Navata had been among the men of the counts of Besalú from the beginning of the eleventh century; Guillem Bernat de Navata headed a long list of jurors in a collective oath to Bernat II, and Bernat Adalbert himself

---

[18] RBIII 230*. See Benet, *Gurb-Queralt*, 135–44, 153–61; Antoni Pladevall i Font, "Els senescals dels comtes de Barcelona durant el segle XI," *Anuario de estudios medievales* 3 (1966), 124–26; Shideler, *Montcadas*, 88 and n. 2.

[19] See now Gaspar Feliu i Montfort, "Existí el comte Bernat III de Besalú?" *Acta historica et archaeologica mediaevalia* 19 (1998), 391–402.

[20] RBIII 103*, 104*, 105*, 106. Cf. Sobrequés, *Els grans comtes*, 146–48; Aurell, *Les noces du comte*, 342–43. Aurell ignores Ramon Berenguer's identical oath (RBIII 106) and thus invests Bernat's oath with too much significance.

had recently sworn an oath of fidelity to Bernat II for the castle of Navata.[21]

At the same time that Ramon Berenguer III was maneuvering to acquire Besalú, he was laying the groundwork for his annexation of Cerdanya. The relationship between the counties of Barcelona and Cerdanya had been close since the marriage of Sança, sister of Ramon Berenguer II, to Guillem I Ramon of Cerdanya in 1079, but Ramon Berenguer III's legal interest in the county derived from a reversionary clause in the testament (1102) of Guillem II Jordà. When the next count, Bernat Guillem, died without heirs in 1117, Ramon Berenguer III assumed the comital title.[22] Of sixteen oaths of fidelity to the new count preserved in the *Liber feudorum Cerritaniae*, seven are renewals of oaths made by the same individuals to Bernat Guillem, and four are from relatives of individuals who had sworn oaths to that count.[23] Only one of the remaining five oaths cannot be linked to an earlier oath to a count of Cerdanya, either Guillem II Jordà or Guillem I Ramon.[24] In only a few cases were the terms of an oath changed, and then only slightly.[25] Only one of the oaths allows for close dating, to 1118, but it is probable that the rest of these oaths date from the first years of Ramon Berenguer's control, as well. How comprehensive was this program of renewals in Cerdanya? Some indication is provided by the fact that few of the surviving oaths to Bernat Guillem or indeed to Guillem II Jordà do not have corresponding renewals under the reign of the count of Barcelona.[26]

---

[21] RBIII 141*, *LFM* 510 (a. 1111); RBIII 158* (a. 1112); *LFM* 500, RBIII 60.2* (*c.* 1099). See Jaume Marquès i Casanovas and Lluís G. Constans i Serrats, *Navata* (s.l., [1985]), 81–88 (although this contains numerous errors).

[22] *LFM* 695; Aurell, *Les noces du comte*, 344–45. Although it has been assumed that this result was not as "expected" as the Besalú succession, the terms of Guillem II Jordà's testament suggest otherwise. If Bernat Guillem, the younger brother and logical heir, were to die without heirs, the county was to revert first to the uncle, Enric, and then to Bernat II of Besalú, before the count of Barcelona. Bernat II's frailties were presumably apparent by 1102, and although Enric already had heirs, they were not included in the succession (which, in the event, they disputed). If Bernat Guillem were to die without heirs, then, Ramon Berenguer III was the most likely successor to the comital title.

[23] RBIII sd 23* (renews RBIII sd 37*); *LFM* 542 (540), 548 (547), 578 (577, rubrics only), 614 (613), 615 (612), 672 (670–71); *LFM* 673–74, 657, RBIII sd 17*.

[24] RBIII sd 27* (renews RBIII sd 33*); *LFM* 644 (642), 645 (643), 665 (664). The only oath without a precedent is from Ramon Guillem de Prullans for the castle of Talló (*LFM* 543), which had been granted to the count of Cerdanya by Viscount Folc II of Cardona (Osona), acting as the schismatic bishop of Urgell, along with the castle of Cardona around 1091 (BRII 73*; *LFM* 220=551, 221=553).

[25] The most notable change was in *LFM* 548, which removed two castles from and added another to the contents of a previous oath. This change was not lost on the rubricator of the *LFM*: "de hoc sacramentali exempta fuerunt duo castra, secundum quod in dictis sacramentalibus reperimus, Cohener, scilicet, ac Viver, et fuit, tamen, additum castrum de Muial."

[26] RBIII sd 36*; *LFM* 220=551, 221=553, 660, 663, 684. This may, of course, be an illusion created by the *LFM*: earlier oaths would only have been preserved if the rights were preserved. Note,

Only one of the documents relating to Ramon Berenguer III's activity in Cerdanya is a *convenientia*: an agreement between the count and Ponç Hug de Cervera, dated 1129. This document, too, is a renewal, of a convention between Ponç Hug's father and Guillem I Ramon of Cerdanya.[27]

Both oath and convention reveal that Ramon Berenguer III was no innovator. Records from almost every county show him renewing agreements on fifty-year-old terms. In the home counties, he renewed the agreements of his grandfather. In the acquired counties of Besalú and Cerdanya, he renewed agreements made by the independent counts. The count may have been *gran*, but he was also *conservador*. In general terms, this is not true of his son, for Ramon Berenguer IV (1131–62) is a pivotal figure in the history of medieval Catalonia. He married Petronilla of Aragón, bringing to the counts of Barcelona a royal crown, extensive lands, and greater influence on the Iberian Peninsula and throughout Europe. He conquered Lleida (1148), Tortosa, and Fraga (both 1149), and ushered both the Cistercians and the military orders into his lands. The monks of Santa Maria de Ripoll composed the *Gesta comitum Barcinonensium* for him, jurists of his court compiled the *Usatges de Barcelona*, and the administrators of his domain introduced new methods of accounting.[28] But through the lens of the *convenientia*, the period 1131–62 is a time of gradual transition, for the new count's reign began in a manner similar to his father's, with the renewal of earlier relationships as expressed in oaths and conventions.

To judge from the surviving evidence, he was not as systematic in this effort as his father had been, but a high percentage of the oaths and conventions from the first half of the reign renewed old ties rather than establishing new ones. Conventions with the viscounts of Barcelona Reverter (1139) and Guillem (1147) refer back to the terms of agreements with the viscounts Udalard (II) Bernat (1041–c. 1080) and Guislabert (II) Udalard (c. 1080–1126). The convention and oath of Guerau Alemany IV de Cervelló in 1145 follow closely the texts of an oath to Ramon Berenguer III and a *convenientia* from the reign of Ramon Berenguer I. As part of an agreement with Guillem de Sant Martí in which the count granted to him Beatriu de Montcada as his wife, the count received a general oath of fidelity, just as his predecessors had received oaths from earlier heads of the Sant Martí family. Other agreements have less obvious, though still

---

however, the number of oaths from the reigns of the eleventh-century counts that are included in the *LFM* even though no later oath has survived (e.g., RBI sd 193*; *LFM* 533, 411=536, 592, 686, 687 . . .). ²⁷ *LFM* 535 (cf. 534).

²⁸ Bisson, *Medieval Crown*, 31–35; *FA*, 1:23–77. The reign of Ramon Berenguer IV deserves a full study; for now, see Percy E. Schramm, "Ramon Berenguer IV," trans. Margarida Fontseré, in Enric Bagué, Joan Cabestany, and Percy E. Schramm, *Els primers comtes-reis*, 3rd ed., Història de Catalunya, Biografies catalanes, 4 (Barcelona, 1985), 1–53.

very real, precedents. A *comenda*-convention and oath in 1134 of Pere Ramon, viscount of Castellbò (Alt Urgell), for Sant Martí, Miralles, and Queralt, are the first such documents explicitly linking that family of viscounts to the counts of Barcelona. It is highly likely, however, that this was an existing relationship, for Ramon Berenguer III had received promises of *potestas* from the *castlans* of those three castles.[29]

Ramon Berenguer IV also renewed several of the oaths received by his father from guardians of castles in the county of Cerdanya, many of which were themselves renewals of oaths to the independent counts of Cerdanya. This process of renewal may have begun before Ramon Berenguer III's death in July of 1131. In 1130, Berenguer de Perapertusa swore an oath to the future Ramon Berenguer IV; in doing so, he renewed an oath of his predecessor, sworn in 1118.[30] Most of the other surviving renewals of oaths for castles in Cerdanya came in the fourth and fifth years of the new count's reign; the one oath for which no precedent exists, from Galceran de Sales for the castle of Ribes, was offered shortly thereafter.[31]

The new count was less comprehensive in his renewal of oaths in Cerdanya than his father had been. The same is true in other counties where Ramon Berenguer III had been fairly persistent in grounding his claims. Only two other oaths survive from the first half of the count's reign, both renewals. The first is an oath of Guillem Ramon II de Castellvell dated 1134 that renewed an oath by the same individual to the previous count in 1126. The later oath differs from the earlier only in the addition of one castle (Sant Vicenç) and explicit mention of the county of Cerdanya. Also in 1134, the count received the oath of Alphonse-Jourdain, count of Toulouse, renewing one made to his father at the time of a settlement between the two counts in 1125. This process of renewing oaths went both ways: in 1140, Ramon Berenguer IV swore an oath to Bishop Udalguer, specifying that their *convenientia* would not invalidate "the fidelities and oaths that my predecessors, the counts of Besalú and Cerdanya, made to yours and to the holy church of Elna."[32]

---

[29] Barcelona: RBIV 106* (a. 1139), 191* (a. 1147); cf. RBI 292*, sd 61*; RBIII 131*, 132*. Cervelló: RBIV 172*, 176* (cf. RBI 287*; RBIII sd 21*). Sant Martí: RBIV 50*, sd 28*; cf. BRII 61*, 73*; RBIII sd 18*; etc. Castellbò: *LFM* 616–17 (cf. *LFM* 614–15).

[30] *LFM* 666 (cf. *LFM* 665); another copy of this oath seems to have been added to the *LFM* at a later date (*LFM*, 2:368 n. 2). See also *LFM* 667.

[31] RBIV 40* (a. 1135), 41* (a. 1135), 122* (a. 1140); *LFM* 544 (a. 1134), 561 (a. 1135, rubric only), 646–47 (a. 1131x62). The oath of Galceran de Pinós for Miralles, Queralt, and Sant Martí (*LFM* 544) is not precisely a renewal, for Galceran had only recently acquired those castles; there was a long tradition of oaths from the Pinós family in the region, however (RBIII sd 17*, sd 35*; *LFM* 537, 539). See also *LFM* 617 (a. 1134), with convention at *LFM* 616.

[32] Castellvell: RBIII 284* (a. 1126); *LFM* 239 (a. 1134). The scribe of the earlier document may have been following closely the formulae of earlier oaths of the Castellvell to the counts, oaths composed before the acquisition of the county of Cerdanya. The scribe of *LFM* 239 caught this

Fortunes (the twelfth century)

The reign of Alfons I (1162–96), the first count of Barcelona to adopt the royal title, witnessed great changes in the forms and nature of comital documentation, as well as in comital conceptions of power. But Alfons, too, renewed oaths of fidelity for castles long under comital control. With the exception of one renewal from the time of his acquisition of the county of Rosselló, the oaths concern castles in or near Cerdanya.[33] The level of Alfons's activity in this area continued the gradual decline in renewal of these oaths, seen already in the reigns of his grandfather and father. Nevertheless, a number of his renewals concern castles for which Ramon Berenguer IV had not received an oath, but Ramon Berenguer III had – further evidence for the persistence of the structures embodied in oaths and conventions. Scribes modeled the oaths on the texts they renewed, with the addition of new phrases specific to changed situations. Most notably, the *castlans* of Sant Martí, Miralles, and Queralt, who held their castles from Ramon II, viscount of Castellbò (Alt Urgell), promised Alfons not to grant *potestas* "to anyone with whom you are on bad terms, not even the viscount, if you should be on bad terms with him."[34] This clause foreshadowed the trouble Alfons would have in the 1180s with Ramon's son, Arnau.[35] None of these renewals has a corresponding *convenientia*. The few oaths for which direct precedents cannot be found are almost all associated with earlier conventions and other transactions.

Like comital castle-holding agreements, episcopal *convenientiae* outlasted the individuals who first established the relationships. Bishops in all four dioceses renewed agreements in later generations, maintaining the structures first established in the eleventh century by repeating *convenientiae* and oaths. The various dioceses approached the project of renewal in different ways, and the precise nature of the relationships evolved over time. In the end, however, the structures persisted.

Ribes disappeared for a time from Barcelonese episcopal records – for seventy years after the episcopate of Guislabert – but in 1130, Bishop Oleguer granted the castle to Arnau de Ribes. Arnau was the son of Ramon, the youngest son of Guisla and Mir Geribert, the son to whom

---

omission only as an afterthought: "et post obitum tuum similiter illi cui Barchinonam dimiseris testamento vel verbis, per Deum et hec sancta quatuor Evangelia, *simul cum ipso comitatu Ceritanie cum omnibus pertinenciis suis*. Actum est hoc . . ." (emphasis added). Toulouse: *LFM* 896–97 (rubrics only; dates reversed). Elna: *NH* 21:37 ("Ita tamen ut propter supradictam convenientiam non pereant fidelitates et sacramenta quae antecessores mei Bisullunenses et Ceritanenses Comites fecerunt antecessoribus tuis et sanctae Elenensi Eclesiae").

[33] ALI extra. 2626*, 2615*=RBIV 41.2dup*; *LFM* 579 (rubric only), 618, 619, 620, 648, 658, 763.

[34] *LFM* 619: "non dabo potestatem inde ad ullum hominem viventem qui tecum male steterit, nec eciam vicecomiti si tecum male steterit"; cf. *LFM* 620.

[35] Thomas N. Bisson, ed., "The War of the Two Arnaus: A Memorial of the Broken Peace in Cerdanya (1188)," in *Miscel·lània en homenatge al P. Agustí Altisent* (Tarragona, 1991), 95–107.

Ermengarda left Ribes in her testament of 1030.[36] Her wishes were superseded at the time by Mir's actions, but a century later, it was Ramon's descendants who were in control. The grant echoed the terms of the agreement of 1041. The bishop granted both Ribes and Sitges to Arnau and a son, who was to be a member of the cathedral community; the grant was limited to the life of Arnau and his son, after which the castles were to revert to the see; Arnau promised not to change the *castlans* without permission and to make the *castlans* swear not to hand over *potestas* of the castle to the son until he had done homage and sworn fidelity.[37] Although no oath survives from Arnau to Oleguer, there is such an oath to his successor, Arnau Ermengol (1137–43), patterned on the oath made by Mir Geribert a century before.[38] The next bishop, Guillem de Torroja extracted a quitclaim and revised convention in 1144 from Arnau de Ribes for Ribes and Sitges; the date of the act suggests that it was associated in some way with the bishop's election. The agreement included the interesting provision that if Arnau left only a daughter as an heir, she would receive only one of the castles. It also contained, for the first time in this series of documents, a material guarantee: Arnau granted to the bishop one manse from each castle as pledges. Also for the first time, the *castlans* of both castles subscribed the documents. The oath corresponding to this convention has survived, as well.[39] Twenty-four years later, Guillem commended Ribes to Arnau's younger son Ramon.[40] Similar continuity of episcopal control is evident at the minor site of Mal Consell, where the economic nature of the see's interest is clear. Not mentioned in episcopal documentation since 1042, it was the subject of an agreement in 1197. In that year Bishop Ramon granted half of the *honor* of Mal Consell to Guillem de La Granada, who already held the first half. Guillem and his successors were to be the men of the bishop, but were not required to perform host and cavalcade for Mal Consell. Furthermore, the bishop granted Guillem free tenure of any castle he built on the land. Guillem also promised not to populate his new holdings with inhabitants of La Granada.[41]

The collapse of the episcopal castle network at Vic began, as described in the previous chapter, in the second half of the reign of Berenguer Sunifred, continuing through a two-to-three-year interregnum and into the failed pontificate of Guillem Berenguer. Ten of twenty castles under

---

[36] For this point of genealogy, see Francesch Carreras y Candi, "Lo Montjuích de Barcelona," *Memorias de la Real academia de buenas letras de Barcelona* 8 (1906), 366, and *contra*, José Maria Coll, "Los castillos de San Pedro de Ribas, La Geltrú, Sitges y Miralpeix," *Analecta sacra Tarraconensia* 32 (1959), 244.   [37] LA 4:380*; ACB 4–70–1* is a fourteenth-century copy.

[38] LA 4:384*. This oath is only for Ribes, not Ribes and Sitges.

[39] Convention: ACB 4–70–134*=LA 4:381*; ACB 4–70–134bis is a fourteenth-century copy. Oath: LA 4:385*.   [40] LA 4:386*.   [41] LA 4:366*.

episcopal control in Berenguer Sunifred's time never again appeared under episcopal control. Even here, however, continuity is evident. During the vacancies, the canons of the cathedral acted on their own. Thus in August 1099, before Guillem Berenguer's election, the canons entered into a convention with the *castlà* of Voltregà, in episcopal hands since at least the tenure of Guillem de Balsareny.[42] And in March 1100, a Bernat Dalmau *clericus* subscribed a convention with the *castlà* of the episcopal castle of L'Espelt, originally acquired under Bishop Borrell (1010–17); although the see was mentioned in passing, its bishops were not.[43] Arnau de Malla (1102–9) renewed agreements with the viscount of Cardona (Osona) for Calaf, with the viscount of Girona for Vilagelans, and with the *castlans* of Meda.[44] Ramon Jofre (1109–46) recorded transactions concerning Tous, Artés, Miralles, Vilagelans, L'Aguilar, Eures, Montlleó, and Pomar – all but the last two had been episcopal castles since the reign of Oliba. Pere de Redorta (1147–85) compiled a similar record.

Paul Freedman has detailed how in the twelfth century, episcopal interest in castles had an increasingly economic basis. Thus in a *convenientia* concerning Tous toward the end of the century, Ramon de Tous promised to provide the military service of *alberga* for forty horsemen and their horses, as well as four knights for thirty days of participation in the host. But the bishop also had a right to one day of carting service between Tous and Montbui, unfettered access to straw, grass, and wood, and the sole right to sell wine in the castle district between Easter and the first week of July, or until his wine ran out (the *banvin*). A *convenientia* for Artés from 1199 detailed the complicated terms under which the castellan, Guillem de Guàrdia, was to provide military service, but it lavished even more care on specifying the fiscal disposition of over fifty manses, named individually, that were to provide produce to the castellan.[45] The multiplication of divisible rights in castles allowed the bishops to maintain ties even to castles that had long been in the unfettered hands of powerful local families. From some of these lords, the twelfth-century bishops were able to extract pro forma oaths, varying little from the language of a century earlier, that would be subscribed with each new generation or each new bishop. This practice secured episcopal rights in

---

[42] AME 9/25=ACV, calaix 37, Liber dotationum, fol. 133r–v.

[43] ACV 6/1547: "Et si ambo fratres obierint . . . habeat ille cui Berengarius dimiserit de fratribus vel de propinquis suis in servicio Sancti Petri vel successorum Bernardi Dalmacii (!)."

[44] ACV 6/1814 (Calaf); AME 3/116 (Vilagelans), 6/7 (Meda). ACV 9/ii/94 is a general renewal of "illa conveniencia que facta est inter domnum Berengarium Ausonensem episcopum et Fulconem vicecomitem Cardonensem et Ermissindem vicecomitissam et Deusdedit Bernardi."

[45] ACV 6/1787=6/1788.2=ALI 486* (a. 1188); AME 10/6 (a. 1199); Freedman, *Vic*, 100–106; Jan Frederik Niermeyer, *Mediae Latinitatis lexicon minus*, ed. C. van de Kieft (Leiden, 1976; repr. 1993), s.v. *bannus*, 22.

these castles until the fourteenth, and in some cases the seventeenth century.

While Urgell continued to acquire castles after the tenure of Guillem Guifré, there is a dropoff in episcopal *convenientiae* in the decades surrounding the turn of the century. Under the bishops Sant Ot (1095–1122) and Pere Berenguer (1123–41), conventions appeared once again in the documentation. These included straightforward *comenda*-conventions, with commendation of a castle and the grant of an associated fief in return for promises of homage, *potestas*, and military service. Such agreements survive for castles that the diocese had possessed for many years, such as Sanaüja, Guissona, and Bordell.[46] Bishops also extended the chains of command over episcopal castles during this period. Thus Pere Ramon, who accepted the commendation of the castles of Sanaüja, Palou, and Guissona from Sant Ot in 1106, had commended those same castles to Pere Ponç on the previous day. Pere Ponç was only an intermediate lord, however, for Pere Ramon also commended to him the *castlans* of those castles. Their agreement recognized the bishop's ultimate lordship. In a grant of Alcorassa, Sant Ot commended Bernat Ecard to Bernat Berenguer along with the castle, but Bernat Ecard had *castellani* of his own under his command. In a few cases, rights in castles were transferred without reference to the see. Gavarra, granted to the canons by Guerau Ponç, viscount of Baix Urgell, in 1095, was the subject of a *convenientia* between the viscount and an intermediate lord in 1120x21. Bernat d'Alp received the commendation of several castles ultimately controlled by the see (Montferrer, Carcolze, Llordà) in a *convenientia* of 1128.[47]

The see continued the practice of closely managing its castles through written agreements – though no longer strictly *convenientiae* – and oaths.[48] These castle-holding conventions show that, in contrast to Barcelona, the see of Urgell in the second half of the twelfth century maintained a strong interest in castles as centers of military strength, rather than as simple sources of revenue. In an agreement with the bishop Bernat Sanç (1141–62) concerning the Valls d'Andorra, for example, Arnau de Caboet promised *seguimentum* along with the men of the region within specified boundaries whenever the bishop requested it; Arnau would supply the men with arms and provisions.[49] When the bishop and canons commended the castle of Terrassa to Arnau de Tost in 1161, the

[46] DACU 1239, 1347.
[47] DACU 1238, 1239 (a. 1106); 1300 (a. 1117); 1134 (a. 1095), 1327 (a. 1120x21); 1393 (a. 1128).
[48] E.g., DACU 1548, 1555, 1563, 1725, 1800; Charles Baudon de Mony, *Relations politiques des comtes de Foix avec la Catalogne jusqu'au commencement du XIV* siècle*, 2 vols. (Paris, 1896), no. 15 (2:22–24). Oaths: DACU 1520, 1562, 1713, 1742, 1868, 1888 . . .   [49] DACU 1544.

agreement allowed them to house episcopal forces in the castle "when we make war from that castle." If the conflict was not with Arnau's other lords, he was to fight with the bishop.[50] In the early 1160s, the bishop complained against the guardians of the castle of Torres that he had, on account of their negligence, lost that castle, which he had warned them time and again to protect.[51]

Girona, too, renewed its oaths and conventions concerning episcopal castles in the twelfth century, including those absent from the records for decades. The focus of the limited documentation on bailiffs and economic rights suggests that the bishops of Girona in that era, like their counterparts elsewhere, saw in their castles as much sources of revenue as sources of military strength.[52] No certain information about the continuation of arrangements at La Bisbal survives from the tenure of Bishop Berenguer Dalmau (1111–40). The only possible such notice is in a *convenientia* of 1139, by which the bishop granted to Arnau Jofre a fief, in return for which Arnau promised fidelity and military and other standard services (*ost, curtes, pleds, seguimens, cavalcades*). Although the document did not mention castle-guard explicitly, it was transcribed in the margin of the episcopal cartulary next to the two earlier conventions with Oliver Guillem for La Bisbal. An oath of an Arnau to Bishop Berenguer de Llers (1142–59), dated 1145, which included a promise of fidelity for the castle, may have been from a member of the next generation.[53] No contract for castle-guard survives from the episcopacies of the next two bishops, Guillem de Peratallada (1160–69) and Guillem de Monells (1169–75), although in 1166 a *saio*, Joan de Monells, swore fidelity for the castle. This oath did not address the defense and guard of the castle, but rather its revenues (*expleta, homines et feminae, census, usatici, consuetudini, mansi*). Finally, in 1180, the contract for castle-guard reemerges, but for the last time, in a convention between the new bishop, Ramon Orusall, and Oliver de Llorà. This convention did not include information about a grant of a fief in return for castle-guard. It described, in language very

---

[50] DACU 1555: "quando fecerimus guerram de ipso castro."

[51] DACU 1613: "Secundo fecit querimoniam contra B. Guilelmi et contra supranominatos qui locum suum tenent de castro suo de Torres quod perdidit culpa ipsius et castellanorum suorum. Episcopus namque ammonuit frequentissime illum et castellanos suos ut bene custodirent supradictum castellum."

[52] In addition to the cases of La Bisbal and Sant Sadurní, see the documentation for Juià: *CDSG* 405; *CCM* 158 [*CDSG* 431], 213, 214, 589.

[53] *CCM* 268 (a. 1139), 278 (a. 1145). The oath of 1145 was subscribed by both an Arnau and an Arnau Jofre. An Arnau Jofre subscribed the grant of Bishop Berenguer to Oliver Guillem in 1085 (*CCM* 155 [*CDSG* 392]), as well, although the sixty-year difference suggests that this was not the same individual. It is interesting to note, however, that part of the land included in that earlier grant was a manse "ubi Arsendis filia cuiusdam Mauri habitat"; Arsenda is the name of the wife of the Arnau making the oath in 1145.

similar (though not identical) to its eleventh-century analogues, the six-month period of guard with retainers and the placing of Oliver's fief in pledge. The last evidence before 1200 for the castle of La Bisbal occurs in an oath in 1181 of Guillem de Frigola to Bishop Ramon. This oath, however, is more closely related to the oath of the *saio* Joan de Monells than to the oaths of *castlans* in the eleventh century; it was associated with the appointment of Guillem as a bailiff.[54]

The situation is better documented at Sant Sadurní de l'Heura. When the eleventh-century guardian, Berenguer Amat, decided to leave for Jerusalem in 1102, he left the castle in the care of the cathedral. Bishop Bernat Umbert quickly commended it to the brothers Berenguer and Ramon Arnau d'Anglès, and Ramon's wife Adelaida. In this *convenientia* the bishop granted the castle on the condition that the holders return it on demand and not do any harm to, claim any exactions from, or use any force against anyone in the demesne retained by the cathedral. The beneficiaries also promised to grant *potestas* on demand to the bishop, offering all their holdings at Sant Sadurní as a guarantee. The convention referred back to a previous written oath, which has not survived. Despite this apparent change in control over the castle, however, it was still technically a possession of Berenguer Amat, who in 1121, after his return from the pilgrimage, granted it to the canons of Girona in his testament, adding the ambiguous statement that it should also be in the *potestas* of the count. In order to clarify this situation, two months later Bishop Berenguer Dalmau purchased a confirmation of the see's rights to the castle from the count of Barcelona.[55]

Once again in secure control of the castle, the bishop and canons renewed the agreements with the Anglès family, whom they had established as *castlans* two decades earlier, by entering a convention with Ramon Arnau and his son Ramon. As in the previous *comenda*, the bishop granted the castle on condition that the recipients return it on demand and that the holders not molest the inhabitants. This agreement, however, also contained the details of the fief (*castellania, fevum*) granted along with the castle and provided for the extension of the relationship into the next generation. Ramon and his son were not allowed to grant the castle or the fief to anyone not of their lineage, but likewise the bishop and his successors were not allowed to grant any part of the castle to someone not related to the holders. The agreement even specified where the holders were to live during periods when the bishop chose to exercise his right of residence at the castle. The oath for this agreement, dated the same day, repeated the terms of the earlier oath of Berenguer

---

[54] *CCM* 312 (a. 1166), 339 (a. 1180), 344 (a. 1181), 445 (a. 1229).
[55] ADG, Mitra, 17/95★ (a. 1102), 17/98★ (a. 1102), 17/79★ (a. 1121), 17/60★ (a. 1121).

Amat for the castle, adding only a clause extending the fidelity to all of the holdings of the cathedral. A third document from the same day recorded quitclaims and confirmations of other lands at Sant Sadurní, lands no doubt involved in the deal that established the family of Ramon Arnau as *castlans* of Sant Sadurní.[56]

At Sant Sadurní, then, the cathedral had control over the castle from the mid-eleventh century, as indicated by a series of promises of *potestas*. In the three-quarters of a century following the first mention of the castle, however, the manifestation of this control was transformed. In the eleventh century, administration of the castle involved the collection of promises from the immediate holders of the castle, who were chosen by the *precentores*. In the twelfth century, the diocese acquired a comital confirmation of its ultimate rights, removed the castle from the control of the *precentores*, and set up a local family as *castlans*. The Anglès were still guardians of the castle when it next appears in the episcopal documentation, in 1214.[57]

It is significant, though not particularly surprising, that counts and ecclesiastical institutions were able to keep in place structures of power over the course of a century. More striking is the persistence of these structures at lower levels. We can trace this continuity by returning to the sample of 150 lay commendations of castles discussed in chapter 4. It was noted that these private conventions appear very rapidly in the late 1060s and then increase in number up to 1100, even while similar agreements at the comital level declined; this trend continues, though less dramatically, to 1175.[58] Similarly, while in the late eleventh century scribes had already begun to experiment with the form of the comital convention – experimentation which continued, as will be seen below, in the twelfth – the standard *convenientia* itself remained throughout this period the preferred document for recording these relationships among the lay aristocracy.[59] Also striking is the fact that almost all of these private conventions that do employ the standard opening phrase use the balanced version "Hec est convenientia inter N. et N." Only a few (5, or 3 percent) echo the unbalanced formula seen in the documents of Ramon Berenguer I

---

[56] ADG, Mitra, 17/94*=17/72*=17/96a–b*, 17/96*=17/152*, 17/97* (all 7 January 1123).

[57] ADG, Mitra, 17/93*; Josep Maria Marquès i Planagumà, ed., "La senyoria eclesiàstica de Sant Sadurní de l'Heurà, fins al 1319," *Estudis sobre temes del Baix Empordà* 3 (1984), 78.

[58] This confirms the suggestion of Bisson ("Feudalism in Twelfth-Century Catalonia," in *Medieval France*, 155–57).

[59] Roughly one-quarter of the documents do not strictly follow the form "Hec est convenientia," with the percentage increasing gradually over time from 10 percent (two of twenty documents) in the period 1050–74 to 31 percent (eleven of thirty-five) in the period 1150–74. Thus in all periods the *convenientia* was used in at least two-thirds of cases.

after 1058.[60] Finally, the strict conceptual division between the commendation of a castle and the grant of lands and rights associated with that castle, seen to hold in the documentation before 1100, persists thereafter, present in 135 of the 150 agreements (77 percent).

These documents also show that, contrary to received opinion, most conventions did not involve the *castlà*, as that term has traditionally been understood, that is, the individual at the bottom of the chain of command with direct operational control over the castle.[61] Rather they tended to record relationships at the intermediate levels of the chain of command. It is true that the place in the hierarchy or status of any given individual is often difficult to determine. Terms of rank (*castellanus, miles, caballarius*) found in the documents are untrustworthy, for scribes applied them inconsistently.[62] Furthermore, individuals at all levels of the hierarchy performed the standard services (host, cavalcade, court, etc.). Other indicators of status, however, may be read with more confidence. Many agreements refer directly to third parties, often in the context of a subordinate party's promise to replace a *castellanus* only with the lord's permission. In these agreements it is clear that the subordinate party did not occupy the bottom of the chain of command.[63] A grant of right of lodging in the castle (*statica*) to the subordinate party also indicates his higher status; *castlans*, in contrast, were required to grant the right of lodging to a superior. Agreements with *castlans* might include an explicit promise of a period of castle-guard, whereas this was rare at higher levels. A lord's promise to provide equipment for service in the host may hint at the low status of the subordinate party, although these terms, too, might appear in agreements between members of the upper levels of a hierarchy.[64] With these criteria as guides, it is evident that most of the

---

[60] Joan Serra Vilaró, "Los señores de Portell, patria de San Ramón, descendientes de los vizcondes de Cardona," *Analecta sacra Tarraconensia* 29 (1956), 250–51; RBIII 92, 186, 261.1*; ACA, Cancelleria reial, Registres 24, fol. 109v.

[61] Pierre Bonnassie, "Les conventions féodales dans la Catalogne du XIᵉ siècle," *AM* 80 (1968), 536–37; Bisson, "Feudalism," 155.   [62] See above, pp. 88–89.

[63] ACB 1–4–342: "per se ipsum aut per unum de ipsis castellanis." OM 15:329: "Et si venerit castlano in obertura estableschel Guifredi Bonifilio ad laudamentum de Ugoni Dalmacii."

[64] ACB 1–1–888: "Convenit namque prefato Berengarii ad suprascriptus Raimundi ut faciat ei hostes et chavalchadas et sequios et curtes infra terram cum duabus chavallarios cum conducto illorum et ut donet Raimundus Berengarii ad prefatus Berengarii quatuor assinos ad hoste vel in hostes cum ea sarcina (i.e., baggage) que portare debent, idem saccos et utres et sogas. Et insuper donat Raimundus Berengarii ad prefatus Berengarii quatuor homines qui tangant ipsos assinos." ACB 1–5–446: "guardet ei predictum castrum sex menses quales ipse Raimundus Guilelmi (i.e., the lord) voluerit . . . et ipsas hostes faciat ipse Rodlandus cum suo conducto, et donet ei Raimundus Guilelmi tres asinos et tres homines." AME 15/18: "hostes ego vadam cum meo cibo, et tu dones michi asinos iiiiᵒʳ, et convenio tibi guarda de ipsum kastrum de ipso Brul quando tu non stabis in prefato castro." DPoblet 61: "et in ipsa oste ut Gomball menara Ponc ut liberet Gomball ad Ponc asinos IIᵒˢ cum duos omines, et doni quinta, et Gomball ut emendat ipsas perditas que perdiderit in suo servicio." Also BC 8995=10108; RBIII 92; OM 3:338; etc.

surviving conventions concern the intermediate layers of control over castles, not the lowest ones.

The proliferation of agreements at the middle level of chains of command indicates that the private commendation was not so much a matter of military service as it was one of structures of alliance, structures that transcended simple contracts of castle-guard. While some agreements did detail the nature of military obligations, many of these mid-level conventions simply listed the standard services. Furthermore, the zeal with which counts exacted promises of *potestas* in their own conventions is not apparent in this group. Only about 60 percent of the documents in the sample include such a clause. The detail in these documents focused rather on economic matters. How much land was granted, and how much was exempted from the grant? What rights were granted, and what was excluded? What income could be expected? How were these lands and rights to be administered? In the case of rights of justice (*placita*), for example, many conventions specified that the beneficiary of a grant could not hold pleas outside the presence of an official of his lord.[65] When Arnau Mir de Sant Martí and his son commended the castle of Eramprunyà to Ramon Mir in 1097, they granted to him rights to a third of the *placita*, but also one of their "better men" (*meliores homines*) to serve as a bailiff, presumably to protect their interest in the exploitation of revenues.[66]

The continued use of the convention to commend castles and the consistency of the institutions and formulae seen in these agreements, despite emphases that vary over time, offer indirect evidence of the stability of these structures. Internal references within the conventions demonstrate this in a more direct manner. Often these are explicit statements that the fief or *cavalleria* or portion of demesne granted was once held by a relative, often the father, of the beneficiary.[67] The language of a convention might also reveal that the commendation itself was a renewal. When Ramon Amat commended the castle of El Brull to Ramon Guillem in 1084, he granted in fief the *castellania*, that is, the assemblage of lands and rights associated with the castle, "just as I gave it to your father Guillem Guifré on the day when I commended to him the aforesaid castle." In

---

[65] Extra. 3449*: "et predictos placitos fiant \placitatos cum baiulo domini Raimundi comiti et baiulo Arbertus predicti si illos fierint volent ad placitos supradictos, et si predictus Petrus mandaverit/ suum servitium ad ipsum saioni de Kastro Vetulo et noluerit facere, distringat illum predictus Petrus ad suam guisam." Also OR, Santa Maria de Montalegre 75*; BC 8995=10108; RBIII 11; LA 4:405*; etc. [66] OR, Santa Maria de Montalegre 72*.

[67] ACV 9/ii/50: "dominicatura quam pater eius Guilelmus habuit in predictis alodiis." RBI 153: "dominicaturam quod ibidem tenebat Seniofredus de Rio Rubio avvi Bernardi." OR, Santa Maria de Montalegre 75*: "ipsam castellaniam quomodo Berengarius Sanla quondam pater eorum tenebat."

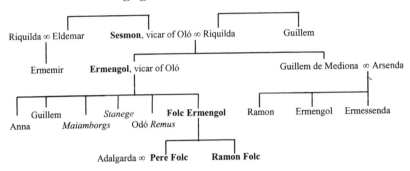

Figure 5.1. The vicars of Oló and their descendants

other cases, a relationship may be inferred from the names mentioned. When Berenguer Bertran and Ponç Bertran received a grant of "service of those men of Cabestany that Bertran Odó used to have," they were very likely accepting rights formerly enjoyed by their father.[68]

While two of the earliest commendations (1052, 1054) contain these internal indicators of continuity, the next to do so date from the 1080s; after that point they appear regularly. Agreements from the 1080s and 90s represent the renewals, one generation later, of relationships first established on a significant scale in the 1060s. In a few exceptional cases, continuity can be traced for more extended periods through the survival of a series of conventions concerning an individual castle. These allow the reconstruction of chains of command not just at one point in time, as was done in chapter 2 for the castle of Talarn held from the counts of Pallars Jussà,[69] but across the whole period.

The castle of Oló (Figure 5.2),[70] located 30 km to the southwest of Vic, was the subject of one of the earliest surviving private commendations. In 1058, Folc Ermengol commended the castle to Berenguer Llop, adding a grant that included two *cavalleriae*, two manses, a garden, a third of the *placita*, and other minor rights. In return, Berenguer promised Folc, his "better lord" (*melior senior*), to be his man (*homo*), perform fidelity, and grant *potestas* of the castle upon demand. Folc had a right to lodge in the castle whenever he wished; when he was not present, Berenguer was

---

[68] AME 15/28 ("sicut ego dedi ad patrem tuum Guilelmum Guiffredi quando ei comendavi predictum castellum"); BC 4233 ("servicium de ipsos omines de Caput Stagnum unde abebat Bertran Otoni").   [69] Above, pp. 86–88.

[70] Oló appears as a *castell termenat* early in the tenth century: *DVic* 153 (a. 930); *ACondal* 139 [*LFM* 447] (a. 957). The first notice of vicars at Oló is from later in that century (*DOliba* 108n; ACV 9/i/103★; *STCA* 129; see Bonnassie, *La Catalogne*, 1:270 n. 59, 332 n. 20, 2:562 n. 115). Guillem de Mediona would appear to be the younger brother of the vicar; Oló is not listed among the extensive possessions in his testament.

Lineage	ACB 1-4-332 (a. 1058)	RBIII 46* (a. 1097)	AEV, Perg. Estany 1* (a. 1106)	RBIII 205 (a. 1118)	ACB 1-5-433 (a. 1169)	ACB 1-5-425 (a. 1174)	see n. 78 (a. 1176)	see n. 78 (a. 1202)
Barcelona								Pere I
Gurb-Queralt		Bernat Guillem					Sibil·la Galceran de Sales	Berenguer III
Oló	Folc Ermengol	Pere Folc Ramon Folc	Pere Folc Adalgarda	Pere Folc	Pere	Pere	Pere	Pere
Olost		Bernat Guillem Guillem Bernat	Ramon Bernat (?)	Ramon Bernat	Ramon	Ramon		
Sentfores				Berenguer Guislabert	Ramon	Guillem		
(*castellanus*)	Berenguer Llop	Arbert		Arbert				

Figure 5.2. Chains of command for the castle of Oló (1058–1202)

responsible for its protection. Berenguer also promised to be Folc's "solid man" (*solidus*) against all his enemies, to perform the standard list of services (*ost, cavalcades, curtes, placitos, seguimentos*), and to provide horses and mules, presumably for military expeditions. The agreement established a thirty-day grace period for restitution following a violation.[71]

Who was this Folc Ermengol, and what rights did he hold in the castle? It is likely that he was the son of Ermengol, vicar of Oló, who died in 1023, and grandson of Sesmon, also vicar of Oló, who died in *c.* 1005.[72] This would seem to be a perfect example, in other words, of the "privatization" of the vicarial function: the lord of the castle of Oló in the mid-eleventh century was a descendant of the comital functionaries who controlled that castle in the tenth and early eleventh centuries. But privatization did not mean that Folc Ermengol was no longer tied to the count; he was an occasional member of the comital retinue, and a prominent figure in the county of Osona.[73] Nor did the castle itself entirely escape comital control, for at some point in the late eleventh century it came into the possession of the Gurb (Queralt) family, probably by means of a comital grant.[74] This last transaction did not result in the displacement of the former vicarial family, but merely their subordination to an intermediate lord.

The outcome may be seen from a second convention, dated 1097, in which Bernat Guillem de Gurb commended the castle to Pere Folc and his brother Ramon Folc, in all likelihood the sons of Folc Ermengol. The terms of this grant were less specific than those in the earlier agreement, but similar in substance. The chain of command over the castle of Oló also grew downward, for in the same grant of 1097, Bernat Guillem de Gurb commended to the brothers (Pere and Ramon Folc) Bernat Guillem d'Olost and his son Guillem Bernat. Then, in 1106, Pere Folc commended the castle to a Ramon Bernat, perhaps a member of the Olost family, along with "those fiefs that *castlans* (*castellani*) were accustomed to hold from the father of the aforesaid Pere." There were even more levels to this arrangement, however, for this Ramon Bernat himself had under his command *castlans* (*castellani*) and knights (*milites*).[75]

In 1118, a Ramon Bernat d'Olost commended the castle and a *castlà* named Arbert to Berenguer Guislabert de Sentfores, along with Arbert's

---

[71] ACB 1–4–332.

[72] *DOliba* 108n; ACV 9/i/103*; *STCA* 129. See the hypothetical genealogy in Figure 5.1.

[73] RBI 193*, 240*, 253.2*, 369*, 448*.

[74] Benet suggests that this was part of an alliance between the family and Ramon Berenguer II (*Gurb-Queralt*, 137). See also RBIII 230*, an oath sworn in 1121 by Berenguer Bernat de Queralt to Ramon Berenguer III for a group of castles including Oló.

[75] RBIII 46* (a. 1097); AEV, Pergamins de l'Estany 1* (a. 1106: "ipsos fevvos quos castellani soliti sunt tenere pro patre de supradicto Petro").

fief; this agreement was subscribed by Pere Folc.[76] Arbert, who also subscribed the agreement, was mentioned in the document of 1097 as a possible witness to the extent of the alods held by Folc Ermengol; he thus may have enjoyed a particularly long tenure as *castlà* at the site. In fact, the *castlà*'s fief was still remembered half a century later, in commendations by Ramon d'Olost to Ramon de Sentfores in 1169 and Guillem de Sentfores in 1174, as "the fief that the *castlà* Arbert held."[77] The upper levels of the chain of command persisted as well. Pere d'Oló, the descendant of the former vicarial family, subscribed each of these documents and recognized the overlordship of the Gurb family in 1176; the lords of Gurb continued to list the castle among their possessions, and required royal permission to pledge it in 1202.[78]

The terms of the convention of 1174 were not identical to those of the convention of 1058. Given the fact, however, that the agreements described relationships at two different levels of a hierarchy, their details were surprisingly similar. Ramon d'Olost commended the castle to Guillem de Sentfores and granted him a fief. Guillem was to have two months of lodging in the castle (recalling the right of Folc Ermengol to claim lodging from Berenguer Llop), and the *castlà* was to be his *solidus* for the holding. Guillem, in turn, was to be the man (*homo*) of Ramon, offer aid, fidelity, and *potestas* of the castle, and perform a list of services (*hostes, cavalcadas, curtes, placitos*); the *castlà* was responsible for military service to Ramon when Guillem was not present. Finally, Guillem could only replace the *castlà* with Ramon's permission. Except for an extension of the chain of command, which occurred quite early, little had changed over 117 years.

A similar series of conventions has survived concerning the castle of Òdena (fig. 5.3), located 75 km northwest of Barcelona.[79] The case of Òdena, too, begins with one of the earliest private *comenda*-conventions, from 1054.[80] This recorded the commendation of the castle by Guillem Bernat d'Òdena to Alemany Onofré. Alemany's father, Onofré Ermemir,

---

[76] RBIII 205 (a. 1118).

[77] ACB 1–5–433 (a. 1169), 1–5–425 (a. 1174: "ipsum fevum quod Arbertus castellanus tenuit").

[78] Benet, *Gurb-Queralt*, app. 26–27 (pp. 270–74, a. 1164); ACV 6/i/46 (a. 1176); Pere Bofill y Boix, "Lo castell de Gurb y la familia Gurb en lo segle XIIIᵉ," in *Congrés d'historia de la Corona d'Aragó dedicat al rey en Jaume I y a la seua época*, 2 vols., I Congrés d'història de la Corona d'Aragó, Barcelona, 1908 (Barcelona, 1909–13), 2:697 n. 2 (a. 1202); Benet, *Gurb-Queralt*, 174, 187.

[79] Earliest mention in 1000 (RBorrell 54 [cit. Bonnassie, *La Catalogne*, 1:123 n. 165]), although see Abadal, *L'abat Oliba*, 162.

[80] *Òdena* 10. An earlier *convenientia* concerning the castle, an agreement between the brothers Donús and Guillem Bernat from 1040, makes no mention of tenurial arrangements (*Òdena* 9). Òdena was one of the castles pledged by the countess Ermessenda to Berenguer Ramon I in 1023 (BRI 46★).

Lineage	Òdena 10 (a. 1054)	Òdena 17 (a. 1067)	Òdena 23 (a. 1081)	Òdena 28 (a. 1095)
Castellvell				
Òdena	Guillem I Bernat	Guillem I Bernat Ermengarda	Guillem I Bernat Ermengarda	Ramon I Guillem Ermengarda
Cervera		Guillem Ramon		——— (Guiller
(castellanus)	Onofré Ermemir Alemany Onofré	Alemany Onofré	Alemany Onofré	Umbert Aleman
(guard)	——— (Oliver Ermemir?) ———		Galceran Gombau	

Figure 5.3. Chains of command for the castle of Òdena (1054–1191)

appeared as a party to the agreement, as well, although many of the constitutive clauses did not refer to him; this suggests the existence of an earlier agreement between Guillem and Onofré. As in the early commendation of Oló, the lord commended the castle and granted the fief, here a *castellania*, along with one-third of the rights of justice. In return, Alemany promised to be Guillem's *solidus*, to aid him when necessary, and to disavow his fidelity to any other lords. Alemany and his father both promised service in the host and cavalcade.

In this case, too, the chain of command over the castle quickly became longer. In 1067, Guillem Bernat commended Òdena, along with the nearby castle of Rubinat, to Guillem Ramon de Cervera in return for his fidelity and service with seven knights in the host and cavalcade. He also granted to Guillem Ramon the *castellania* held by Alemany Onofré. In 1081, another layer appears, when Guillem Bernat and Alemany Onofré together commended the castle to Galceran Gombau in return for his becoming a *solidus*, service in the host and cavalcade, and guard service at the castle along with one knight. Galceran was not the first to serve under Alemany Onofré, however, for he was granted "that land in fief just as Oliver Ermemir held [it] from Alemany on the day that he died." In 1095, the sons of Guillem and Alemany, Ramon (I) Guillem d'Òdena and Umbert Alemany, renewed the convention for the castle in an agreement that repeated nearly word for word the convention of 1054. Two years later, these two commended the castle to the son of the previous castle guardian, Geribert Galceran; this agreement also repeated the language of the analogous convention from the previous generation. In the 1120s, the Castellvell family entered the chain of command. A convention of 1121 recorded the commendation of the castles of Òdena and Pontons by Guillem Ramon I de Castellvell to Ramon (I) Guillem

Òdena 29 (a. 1097)	RBIII 235 (a. 1121)	Òdena 33 (a. 1142)	Òdena 47 (a. 1187)	Òdena 51 (a. 1191)
	Guillem Ramon I			Arbert
amon I Guillem Ermengarda	Ramon I Guillem	Ramon Guillem I	Ramon II	Ramon II
)almau?) ———		Guerau de Jorba	Guerau de Jorba	Guillem I de Cardona Gueraua de Jorba
mbert Alemany		Ramon de Pujalt?		
eribert Gauceran				

d'Odena, along with grants of fiefs, *cavalleriae*, and demesne. Ramon Guillem owed in return aid, *potestas*, and various services.[81] The document was drawn up before Count Ramon Berenguer III, a fact that hints at his ultimate overlordship of the castle. This is confirmed by its presence in oaths of the Castellvell to the count of Barcelona in 1110, 1126, and 1134.[82]

The interest of the Cervera lineage in the castle of Òdena, though absent from the surviving documentation for over half a century, had not been extinguished.[83] In 1142, Ramon Guillem (I) d'Òdena commended the castle to Guerau de Jorba, brother of Guillem (II) de Cervera.[84] The transformed socioeconomic climate is reflected in the changes in the

---

[81] Òdena 17 (a. 1067), 23 (a. 1081: "donat ei ipsam terram per feuum sicut Oliuarius Ermemiri tenebat per iamdictum Alamannum ipso die quod obiit"), 28 (a. 1095), 29 (a. 1097); RBIII 235 (a. 1121). Òdena 23 provides one of the earliest references in Catalonia to a "dubbed" knight: "stet in iamdictum kastrum apud unum militem bene armatos et bene adobatos." See *GMLC*, s.v. *adobar*, and Eulalia Rodón Binué, *El lenguaje técnico del feudalismo en el siglo XI en Cataluña (contribución al estudio del latín medieval)*, Publicaciones de la Escuela de filología de Barcelona, Filología clásica, 16 (Barcelona, 1957), s.v. *adobatos*, both citing RBI 303★ (a. 1064). See also AAM, Sant Benet de Bages 165 (a. 1086: "que sia adobato cum kavallo et cum mulo et cum loricha"); RBIII 11 (a. 1092: "milites bene adobatos obtimos").

[82] RBIII 142★ (a. 1110), 284★ (a. 1126); *LFM* 239 (a. 1134, to Ramon Berenguer IV).

[83] After the convention of 1067, the Cervera lordship is mentioned only in the testament of Alemany Onofré (Òdena 25, a. 1085), who left his wife, children, and *honor* under the protection of "domno Guillelmo Reimundo, seniori meo, et domno Guillelmus Bernardus et Geirallus Alaman, seniores meos." Of course the Guillem Ramon here might be Guillem Ramon de Castellvell, not Guillem Ramon de Cervera. Guerau Alemany might be the lord of Cervelló, but there is no other documented connection between the castle of Òdena and that lineage.

[84] Genealogy can be established by the testament of Guillem (I) Dalmau de Cervera (*DPoblet* 82); see Agustí Altisent, "Seguint el rastre de Guerau de Jorba i el seu llinatge," *Aplec de treballs* (Centre d'estudis de la Conca de Barberà, Montblanc) 1 (1978), 33–83. Òdena also appears in the testament of Guillem III de Cervera in 1173 (*DPoblet* 457). The Ramon de Pujalt who subscribed the agreement of 1142 may represent a new *castlà* lineage, for the testament of Guillem (I) Dalmau de Cervera grants Òdena to Guerau de Jorba "tali modo ut Guilelmus Podioalti abeat per illum."

content of the grant, which included a variety of exactions and rights (*acaptes, forces, toltes, placitos, lexuis, exorchias, trobas*), but the essence of the transaction remained the same. Guerau promised to be Ramon's *solidus*, to grant *potestas* of the castle, and to provide aid and serve him in hosts and cavalcades, courts and pleas. This commendation was renewed in 1187, between Ramon (II) d'Òdena and Guerau de Jorba, and again in 1191 between Ramon (II) d'Òdena and Guillem, viscount of Cardona (Osona), who had married the granddaughter of Guerau de Jorba; Arbert de Castellvell subscribed this last agreement.[85] As at Oló, and as with comital, episcopal, and aristocratic holdings generally, the tenurial arrangements established by a mid-eleventh-century *convenientia* persisted well into the twelfth century.

CONFLICT

It was not, of course, that simple. At the same time that these arrangements for castle tenure and military service were being renewed generation after generation, there is increasing evidence for disputes over these relationships. These disputes appear in a variety of milieux. Around 1100, Guillem Umbert complained against Guadall Guillem before Ponç Guerau I, viscount of Girona, and the seneschal, Guillem Ramon (I), that he was violating a *convenientia* between their parents concerning the *turris* of Vilassar. First among the complaints that Guillem Ramon II de Castellvell brought against Ponç Pere de Banyeres before the court of Ramon Berenguer IV in 1143 was that Ponç Pere refused to recognize that he was Guillem's *homo solidus*, just as Ponç's father was the *homo solidus* of Guillem's father, and that Ponç had illegally taken on another lord. In 1160, the abbot of Sant Cugat del Vallès brought a sheaf of old parchments before the same venue, complaining against Ramon Pere de Banyeres with respect to the castle of Calders. In 1173, Ermengol VII of Urgell complained against Ramon de Peramola that the latter was unjustly denying him the *potestas* of the castle of Peramola; Ermengol claimed his rights in part on the basis of "a written *convenientia* and oath that Gombau, grandfather of Ramon de Peramola, made to his predecessor Ermengol, count of Urgell." And in 1181, the abbot of Sant Cugat went before another comital tribunal, defending the monastery's rights in the castle of Albinyana with *plurima instrumenta*.[86] These disputes are

---

[85] *Òdena* 47 (a. 1187), 51 (a. 1191).

[86] BC 10107 (c. 1100); RBIV 154* (a. 1143); *CSCV* 1031 [*DI* 4:114] (a. 1160); ALI 144 (a. 1175: "propter convenientiam scriptam et sacramentale que Gomballus avus Raimundi de Peramola fecerat predecessori suo Ermengaudo comiti Urgelli"; see Bisson, "Feudalism," 169 n. 95); *CSCV* 1134 (a. 1181).

evidence for tensions within the political, social, and economic structures defined by the *convenientia*. But these disputes are also further evidence for the existence of norms: norms that were challenged, norms that dissolved on occasion, but norms that were pervasive enough to persist over time. Often, as in some of the cases just cited, it is clear that the norms were able to persist because of the existence of written records. Though there are a few "private" cases, such as the dispute before the viscount of Girona in 1100, the rhythm of disputing in the twelfth century is best documented for the counts of Barcelona and for the various dioceses.

The fact that Ramon Berenguer I's sons failed to continue his efforts in the last decades of the eleventh century certainly caused problems for future counts. This is explicit in the settlement of a dispute between Ramon Berenguer III and Guillem (I) Dalmau de Cervera: "It is well known how recently there arose a dispute between Ramon Berenguer, count of Barcelona, and Guillem Dalmau concerning the excesses and novelties that the same Guillem unjustly engaged in at the castle of Cervera *after the death of the grandfather of the said count . . .*" Earlier in his reign, the count lost a dispute (*non minima altercacia*) with Ricard Guillem over the castle of Arraona in 1113 because he could not find the written oaths of the *castlans*.[87] Even successful renewals were the occasion of conflict, as shown by four settlements from the beginning of the reign of Ramon Berenguer IV. In 1134, the count received the quitclaim of the castle of Paracolls from Guillem de Salses, along with a promise of fidelity. Guillem, it would seem, had never come to terms with the succession of Ramon Berenguer III to the countship of Cerdanya. Bernat Berenguer de Perapertusa – perhaps the intermediate lord – had sworn an oath to Ramon Berenguer III for Paracolls and Montalban in 1118, but when his successor renewed the oath in 1130, Paracolls was left out. As compensation for his submission, Guillem received grants of minor fiefs in Cerdanya.[88] In 1136, Guillem Ramon (II) Seneschal and Ramon Berenguer IV resolved a dispute, the proximate cause of which was the seneschal's diversion of water away from the count's mills. That act may in turn have been a response to the count's disruption of the seneschal's marriage. One of the provisions of the settlement was that the seneschal should "perform to [the count] his fidelities and oaths that he ought to

---

[87] RBIII 309★ (a. 1129: "Satis est manifestum qualiter inter Raimundum Berengarii, Barchinonensem comitem, et Guilelmum Dalmacii aliquanto tempore querimonia acta est de superfluitatibus et novellitatibus quas idem Guilelmus in castro Cervarie *post obitum avi predicti comitis* iniuste fecerat"; emphasis added), 174★ (a. 1113). See also the records of the conflict between Ramon Berenguer III and his *vicarius* for Barcelona, Berenguer Ramon (RBIII 165★; *LFM* 383).
[88] *LFM* 692 (a. 1134), 665 (a. 1118), 666 (a. 1130).

perform to him"; these are recorded in a pair of documents, a *convenien-tia* and an oath, dated the same day as the settlement.[89] It has been argued that this agreement redefined the relationship between the count and Guillem Ramon, establishing that his patrimony was held of the count, and that this redefined status reflected Ramon Berenguer IV's "authoritarian views." These settlements, however, are perfectly in line with the efforts of the count's father and great-grandfather.[90]

The resolution in early March 1138 of a dispute between Ramon Berenguer IV and Ponç Hug I, count of Empúries, was likewise a renewal of an earlier situation, with differences in degree rather than in kind. The settlement, which lists various specific obligations incumbent upon Ponç Hug, draws upon a settlement of 1128 between that count and Ramon Berenguer III. A *convenientia* dated the same day contains the commendation of various castles, including Ceret and Molins, to Ponç Hug; soon thereafter, he swore an oath for the castles.[91] This convention was in turn a renewal of earlier commendations of those castles by Ramon Berenguer III to Ponç Hug in 1122 and 1130.[92] The settlement of 1138 was less onerous than the one imposed on the count by Ramon Berenguer III, but it maintained the relationship between the counts as it had existed.

Finally, in 1148, perhaps in order to gain an ally for his southern campaigns, the count settled a dispute with Ponç (II) de Cervera, viscount of

[89] RBIV 62* ("faciat ei suas fidelitates et sacramenta quas ei debet facere"), 63*, 64*, 65*; Shideler, *Montcadas*, 88–93; and above, p. 225. The witness list of the convention (RBIV 64*) is entirely different from the list on the settlement, although it is similar to the list on the instrument of divorce drawn up on the same day in connection with the settlement (RBIV 63*). According to the dating system proposed by Mundó (see above, p. xiii), the date of this settlement is in fact July 1135, *before* Ramon Berenguer IV's grant of Beatriu de Montcada and her lands to Guillem de Sant Martí (RBIV 50*) in October 1135. This is not impossible: the settlement documents make no mention of Guillem de Sant Martí; the divorce agreement describes what should happen *if* Beatriu remarries; and the grant to Guillem de Sant Martí refers to agreements between Guillem Ramon and Beatriu.
[90] The seneschal's convention with Ramon Berenguer III in 1126, at the time of his assumption of the protectorate over the patrimony of the viscounts of Bas (Besalú), promised *potestas* of the castles included in that patrimony, but the text also included, as was customary, a general promise of fidelity and service not limited to the castles in question (RBIII 281, 282*). The only things that distinguish the content of the agreements of 1126 and 1136 are the specific castles for which *potestas* is promised. Furthermore, many of the castles listed in the 1136 document had been subject to the *potestas* of the count's ancestors. Thus earlier counts had power both over the seneschal and the castles; the novelty was the explicit combination of the two. This is an important step, but it is not a radical departure from the program set in motion by Ramon Berenguer I.
[91] RBIV 80.1*, 80.2* (a. 1138); *LFM* 528 (a. 1138, rubric only); cf. RBIII 291*, 292*=241.4* (a. 1128). RBIII 291* and 292* are copied at ACG, Llibre Verd, 92r–94v.
[92] RBIII 241.1*; *LFM* 525 (rubric only). Two oaths corresponding to the grant of 1122 survive (RBIII 241.2*, 241.3*). RBIV sd 26*, an oath from Ponç Hug to a count Ramon Berenguer may correspond to the agreement of 1128; the future Ramon Berenguer IV appeared as a party to several agreements between his father and Ponç Hug.

Bas (Besalú). Ponç had abducted and married the count's sister, Almodis, perhaps as early as 1131. Ponç granted to the count the castle of Castellfollit, and in return the count commended the castle back to Ponç, receiving promises of fidelity and *potestas*.[93] Here, too, Ramon Berenguer IV was not expanding his power base; he was confirming it. Ponç's father, Ponç Hug de Cervera, had entered into a *convenientia* with Ramon Berenguer III for the castle of Castellfollit, among others, in 1129,[94] and Ramon Berenguer III granted the castle to his son in his testament.[95]

From 1150, Ramon Berenguer IV, and later his son, Alfons I, relied increasingly on formal judicial processes to redefine and reassert control over contested comital castles. Among the matters addressed in a series of great pleas from the 1150s were disputes over castle tenure and military service. Around 1151 the count complained against Galceran de Sales that he had "failed in his hosts and cavalcades and services," and that in particular he had failed to heed a comital call "in nomine de bataia" to an expedition against Lorca. The tribunal also judged that the count should control a castle illegally constructed by Galceran. At Lleida in 1157, the count complained against Pere de Puigverd that he had "seized from him his alod, that with much labor and at great expense he had recovered from the hands of the Saracens, namely the castles of Prenafeta and Pira . . ." Pere produced a *convenientia* and other documents showing that his family had rights in the castles dating back to the days of Ramon Berenguer I. The documents were found to be suspect. Among Pere's complaints against the count was that the count had failed to adhere to a *convenientia* promising each of the ten knights that Pere brought on the expedition to Lorca 30 *morabetins* per month. The count denied this, and stated that, in any case, as for his agreements with Pere concerning that expedition, he considered the matter settled.[96]

Alfons I's judicial assault on perceived violation of the order of castle tenure can be linked to a similar program of administrative reform, centered on the production of the *Liber feudorum maior* (*LFM*) and a reorganization of fiscal accounting. In 1178, a panel of arbitrators including the archbishop of Tarragona heard a dispute between the count-king and Berenguer de Fluvià concerning the castle of Forès, where the counts of Barcelona had claimed rights from the early eleventh century; the

---

[93] *LFM* 184–85 (rubrics only). See Aurell, *Les noces du comte*, 348–49, esp. 348 n. 2; Bofarull, *Los condes*, 2:169; Rovira i Virgili, *Història*, 4:98 n. 3. The precise chronology is mysterious.

[94] *LFM* 535.

[95] RBIII 316*: "et comitatum Cerritaniensem et Confluetensem, Berchitanensem cum omnibus sibi pertinentibus, et Castel Follit de Rivo Meritabili."

[96] RBIV sd 12* (*c.* 1151: "ei fallisset de suis ostibus et cavalcatis atque serviciis"), 305* (a. 1157: "auferebat ei suum alodium quod multo labore et magnis expensis recuperaverat de manibus sarracenorum").

settlement was embodied in a *convenientia* fixing rights and obligations.[97] In 1180, the count-king "alleged that the castles of Lluçà and Merlès were his, and sought the *potestas* of them from Pere." Pere (de Lluçà) countered that the castles were his alods and that he did not owe the count *potestas*, but the count produced documents "from his archive" ("de suo archivo producta") proving a connection dating back to the early eleventh century. The count won the judgment, and the comital vision of order was reestablished; Pere swore an oath for the castles to Ramon Berenguer IV's grandson, Pere I, in 1198.[98] It is noteworthy that Alfons's disputes over matters of castle tenure and military service extended into Aragón, as well, where the issues were very similar. In 1177, the count proceeded against Jimeno de Artosilla concerning the castle of Tubo. The count demanded *potestas*; Jimeno produced a document that stated that he was not to lose the castle unless for treason. The court clarified that he should grant *potestas*, but that that did not mean that he lost the castle.[99]

Twelfth-century disputes over episcopal castles are particularly well documented for the diocese of Barcelona. Soon after Guillem de Torroja's promotion to the archbishopric of Tarragona in 1171, the agreements addressed above between the see of Barcelona and the lineage of Ribes unraveled. In 1172, the see complained to the papal court – echoing its plea of 1002 – which sent letters to Arnau (II) and Ramon (II) de Ribes, ordering them to appear before the bishops of Tortosa and Zaragoza to have the matter resolved. The dispute was concluded in a general settlement of 1183 that also involved the castle of Banyeres.[100] As a result of the agreement, Bishop Bernat de Berga of Barcelona granted to Arnau de Ribes certain demesne lands and rights to revenues of justice, while retaining homage, fidelity, and *potestas* on demand. The major difference between this agreement and previous transactions concerning the castle is the removal of the façade of the life grant. Earlier grants of these castles had been for two generations, with detailed reversion clauses. Here the grant was made to Arnau and his heirs in perpetuity. This document also reveals for the first time a division between the rights of the bishop and those of the canons: rights in and revenues from Ribes belonged to the

---

[97] ALI 257★; cf. RBI 14★.
[98] ALI 302★ (a. 1180: "Dicebat enim dominus rex et allegabat quod castra de Luzano et de Merles sua erant et potestatem eorum a Petro predicto petebat"); PEI 43★ (a. 1198). Cf. BRI 36★, 46★; RBI sd 56★, extra. 2102★; *LFM* 505.
[99] ALI 224★ (mutilated; transcribed at ACA, Cancelleria reial, Registres 2, fols. 30v–31v★); cf. ALI 294★, extra. 3629★.
[100] LA 1:38★, 1:39★ (a. 1172); ACB 4–70–3★=LA 4:334★ (a. 1183); ACB 4–70–3bis is a transcription without date (see above, pp. 191–94). In 1177, the canons granted land at Ribes mentioning the lords of Ribes (LA 4:382★).

mensa episcopalis; those from Sitges pertained to the *mensa canonice*. Similarly, Arnau and his heirs were to be the men of the bishop with respect to Ribes and the men of the canons with respect to Sitges, although the bishop was to receive their oath for the latter castle "in the name of the canons" ("nomine canonice"). A separate oath for these castles has not survived, although the text of the oath that was to be sworn was included in the agreement. The disposition of another nearby castle was put off, as shown by an oath of Arnau and Ramon de Ribes to appear before and obey the judgment of the episcopal court with respect to the castle of La Geltrú.[101]

A few years before the dispute over Ribes, the see began the process of recovering the castle of Montmell, subject to the see since the late tenth century. Despite an episcopal presence in the area in the late 1070s,[102] *convenientiae* and other transactions in 1090, 1094, 1124, 1150, and 1151 detailing the castle-holding terms organized under the Banyeres lineage make no mention of episcopal overlordship.[103] The domination of this family over Montmell came to a halt in 1157. In that year Bernat de Montesquiu pledged the castle to Bishop Guillem for 100 *morabetins*, reserving the right of redemption to himself and his heirs; Ponç Pere de Banyeres was among the subscribers.[104] How the Montesquiu lineage acquired rights to Montmell is unknown,[105] but in 1181, Catalana, daughter of Bernat de Montesquiu, set in motion the return of Montmell into the hands of the see. In July, in a settlement that brought to a close an apparently long-running dispute, she quitclaimed the castle of Montmell to Bishop Bernat, against a payment of 500 *morabetins*. During the course of the dispute, the bishop had presented as proof of the see's rights the franchise charter of 974; Catalana was unable to produce proof that the see had ever granted the castle to her ancestors. On 19 November, Guisla de Banyeres quitclaimed the castle to the bishop, swearing fidelity to him for the castle and receiving a promise of a yearly payment of grain. Three days later, Berenguer de Santa Eulàlia and his wife granted to the bishop and the see "all of the acquisitions that we have made from Ponç Pere de Banyeres and his daughter, Guisla, or from

---

[101] LA 4:383*. This is the first appearance of the castle of La Geltrú in the documentation. Its origins are obscure; see José Coroleu, *Historia de Villanueva y Geltrú* (Vilanova i la Geltrú, 1878), 38.

[102] In 1078, Bishop Umbert granted the tower of Codony, within the territory of Montmell, to Guillem Ponç to be held from the see; Guillem's nephew was in possession a decade later (LA 4:421*, 4:422*; *CPF*, 1:678).

[103] LA 4:401*+4:402* (a. 1150), 4:404* (a. 1124?), 4:405* (a. 1124), 4:409* (a. 1151), 4:412* (a. 1094), 4:413* (a. 1090).   [104] LA 4:399*.

[105] In 1157 Bernat quitclaimed revenues from Montmell to Bishop Guillem (LA 4:398*). No members of the family were mentioned in a sale of 1173 by members of the *castlà* family of Montfar to the monastery of Santa Maria de Santes Creus of lands held "per fevum ipsius castri de Monte Macello" (LA 4:423*).

anyone else in the castle of Montmell." Berenguer and his wife retained the usufruct, and the bishop granted to them 200 *aiadins*. Guisla's father, who subscribed the original agreement, but neither of the documents in November, finally assented to the general settlement on 29 December, swearing an oath of fidelity to the bishop for the castle and promising to return it on demand.[106] The see managed to maintain these renewed rights in Montmell; in 1211, Bishop Pere de Sirac commended the castle to Guerau de Palamós, a member of a family that had been associated with the castle from the early twelfth century.[107]

The castle that gave its name to the Banyeres lineage also disappears from the written record for much of the twelfth century and when it reappears, the bishops are involved in litigation over it. A letter of Alexander III from 1172 shows that the lands of "the lady G." were under interdict because of her dispute with the see of Barcelona over the castle.[108] A judgment of the court of Alfons I dated 1178 recorded the complaint of the bishop against Guillem de Sant Martí and his wife Guisla (the lady G.) concerning the same castle. Just as he was to produce the franchise charter for Montmell in a dispute three years later, the bishop here produced the grant to Mir Llop Sanç in 1032. Guillem claimed that his wife's ancestors had made another agreement ("aliud placitum et alia conventio") with the see that superseded the one presented by the bishop. He was unable to produce it, however, and the court rendered judgment in the see's favor.[109] The matter was not settled completely until the agreement – discussed above – concerning Banyeres, Ribes, and Sitges. As part of that compromise, Guisla de Banyeres allowed the bishop to grant Banyeres to Arnau de Ribes after her death and also to set up a bailiff (*baiulus*) for the castle, now firmly back under episcopal control.[110]

The gap in documentation is not as extreme for Castellbisbal, where early-twelfth-century documentation indicates the development of an additional layer in the hierarchy of episcopal control.[111] Nevertheless, the see fell into conflict concerning this site, as well. Sometime between 1137 and 1160 the bishop complained of the abuses of Ramon Bremon de

---

[106] LA 4:394 (a. 974), 4:400* (26 July 1181), 4:403* (22 November 1181), 4:411* (19 November 1181), 4:414* (29 December). No year is given for the oath (LA 4:414*), but judging from the list of subscriptions, it is highly likely that it dates from 1181. The *aiadí* was a gold coin of Ibn 'Iyād of Murcia (1145–47); see Juan J. Rodríguez Lorente, *Numismática de la Murcia musulmana* (Madrid, 1984), 51–53, 57; and *FA*, 2:430, s.v. *mor(a)betinus*.

[107] LA 4:416* (a. 1211). Cf. 4:404* (c. 1124?), subscribed by Guerau de Palamós.

[108] LA 1:40*.

[109] LA 4:332*. He also produced as proof Mir Llop Sanç's testament (LA 4:328*).

[110] Above, pp. 246–47. Banyeres, like Sitges, was given to the canons rather than the bishop; problems at the site persisted into the thirteenth century (Sebastián Puig y Puig, *Episcopologio de la sede Barcinonense: Apuntes para la historia de la iglesia de Barcelona y de sus prelados*, Biblioteca histórica de la Biblioteca Balmes, ser. 1, 1 [Barcelona, 1929], 177). [111] LA 4:186*.

Castellbisbal. The *querimonia* included the charge that in selling the village of Sant Quintí, located within the territory of the castle, Ramon Bremon had alienated the rights of the bishop to the military service of the inhabitants of the village.[112] This Ramon Bremon must have been a subordinate of Guillem Ramon II de Castellvell, mentioned in the document. He, or perhaps his son, swore an oath in 1168 to Bishop Guillem, not of fidelity, but for payment of a debt; Guillem Ramon III de Castellvell subscribed this document.[113] As no mention was made of Ramon Bremon's responsibilities with respect to the castle, his exact role at this point is obscure. In 1177, however, Bernat de Castellbisbal and Bishop Bernat reached an accord over the abuses of the former at Castellbisbal. Here the representative of the Castellbisbal lineage acted independently; no member of the Castellvell line subscribed this document. In 1183, an Arbert *Biscoz* swore an oath to Bishop Bernat to rectify damages caused at Castellbisbal, again acting without the intervention of the Castellvell. In 1189, the bishop was himself a member of the Castellvell lineage and made an agreement directly with the inhabitants of Castellbisbal, without intermediaries.[114] By 1200, then, an independent lineage of castle guardians – the Castellbisbal – was in place below the Castellvell; despite the existence of two lineages with closer ties to the castle, however, the bishop remained the ultimate lord.

We have already noted changes in the regime of episcopal castle holding at Vic in the twelfth century: the reduced number of castles and the increasingly economic interest of the diocese in these sites. As at Barcelona, there was litigation. The losses around 1100 meant that the see had fewer castles to look after, but the increasingly complex nature of the division of rights in the castles that remained sustained constant conflict. The bishops of Vic had begun in the late eleventh century to turn to judicial processes in order to maintain the rights of the see in castles. Thus in a *querimonia* against Guillem Bernat de Queralt in 1080, Berenguer Sunifred complained that Guillem had usurped the castle of Meda, which his great uncle Bonfill had left to the see in 1007. As part of the settlement reached before the count of Barcelona, Guillem Bernat and his son, Bernat Guillem, recognized that they held the castle from the bishop, promising *potestas* and general aid (rather than specific military service).[115] Conflicts were not always resolved that easily, however. In 1088 the bishop and Deusdé Bernat settled a dispute over the castles

---

[112] LA 4:189*.   [113] LA 4:192*; *Els castells catalans*, 6 vols. in 7 parts (Barcelona, 1967–79), 2:34.
[114] LA 4:188* (a. 1177), 4:193* (a. 1183), 4:194* (a. 1189).
[115] Juan Luís de Moncada, *Episcopologio de Vich*, ed. Jaime Collell (vols. 1 and 2) and Luís B. Nadal (vol. 3), 3 vols., Biblioteca histórica de la Diócesis de Vich 1, 3 (vols. 1 and 2) (Vic, 1891–1904), 1:326–27; Benet, *Gurb-Queralt*, 112–13; AME 9/36=9/59. The version at AME 9/36 is subscribed by "Remundus comes."

of Montbui and Ocelló. In a *convenientia* between the two, Deusdé refused to acknowledge that the castles of Montbui and Ocelló were held of the bishop, but he did promise to grant *potestas*, to provide the military service of himself, his son, and the *castlans*, and to accept episcopal counsel in the appointment of new *castlans*. This result was not sufficient for the bishop, who soon thereafter had occasion to complain against Deusdé, "who seized the castle of Montbui from the same church . . . which ought to be the demesne of the bishop."[116]

This litigation became only more common in the twelfth century, mirroring an overall rise in disputes involving the diocese. Episcopal rights at Tous were the subject of a cause célèbre in 1174, when Bishop Pere de Redorta challenged the recalcitrant castellan, Ramon. The bishop produced documents proving his rights to an oath of fidelity from Ramon, as well as to lodging and other military and fiscal interests. Ramon swore his oath to the bishop three years later, but in 1183 the two were back before a tribunal, arguing the specifics of the bishop's fiscal rights and Ramon's military duties. The *convenientia* of 1188 (discussed above) settled matters, at least temporarily.[117] Bishop Pere also settled with Guillem de Lluçà concerning fiscal rights at Quer in 1167: "Let it be known to all, present and future, that Pere, bishop of Vic, and the canons of that see have struggled long with Guillem de Lluça concerning the demesne of the castle of Quer . . ." Nine years later, it was Bernat de Besora: "Let it be known to all, present and future, that Pere, bishop of Vic, and the canons of that see have struggled long with Bernat de Besora over half of the demesne of the castle of Quer . . ."[118] Disputes over Artés were similarly protracted: Pere's settlements with Guillem Ramon in 1151 and Berenguer de Pujalt in 1170 had to be renegotiated with Bishop Guillem de Tavertet in 1199.[119] Freedman has noted the element of compromise involved in all of this activity. The partitioning of economic rights in the castles allowed for negotiated settlements that offered both parties a degree of victory. Victory for the diocese in these years meant retaining ultimate control of the castle, in addition to whatever portion of the revenues it could claim.[120]

---

[116] ACV 9/ii/80 (a. 1088), 9/ii/90* (*post* a. 1091: "qui aufert eidem ecclesię castrum de Monteboio, cum omnibus que ad ipsum castrum pertinent, qui debet esse dominicum episcopi").

[117] ACV 6/1746 (a. 1174), 6/1757 (a. 1177), 6/1776=6/1924 (a. 1183), 6/1787=6/1788.2=ALI 486* (a. 1188); see Freedman, *Vic*, 102, 137–38.

[118] AME 13/19bis (a. 1167: "Pateat cunctis presentibus atque futuris Petrum Ausonensem episcopum et canonicos eiusdem sedis diutius contendisse cum Guilelmo de Luciano de dominicaturam castri de Cher"); AME 13/21 (=ACV 6/1756) (a. 1176: "Pateat cunctis presentibus atque futuris Petrum Ausonensem episcopum et canonicos eiusdem sedis diutius contendisse cum Bernardo de Besora pro medietate dominicature castri de Cher").

[119] AME 10/1 (a. 1151), 10/5=10/60 (a. 1170), 10/6 (a. 1199).

[120] Freedman, *Vic*, 102–5.

Quitclaims and records of judgment reveal that episcopal castles were the subject of disputes in the diocese of Urgell before the 1140s, but these were relatively infrequent and distributed among a number of castles.[121] Even the potential for conflict between bishop and chapter, hinted at during the tenure of Guillem Guifré, was kept under control; the bishops were invariably generous to the chapter during their tenures and in their testaments.[122] The cathedral continued its excellent relations, too, with the counts of the region, receiving grants of castles or rights in castles from Ermengols V and VI.[123] The beginning of the tenure of Bernat Sanç (1141–62) signaled a change. Ermengol VI, apparently unhappy with Bernat's election, imprisoned the bishop, an act that led the pope to excommunicate the count. In 1151, the archbishop of Tarragona deposed the bishop for alleged simony, and the bishop himself excommunicated the new count, Ermengol VII, in 1156x57.[124] At the same time, the diocese became embroiled in a series of disputes over its castles. While Bernat Sanç's successors Bernat Roger (1163–67) and Arnau de Preixens (1167–95) managed to avoid incarceration, the disputes over castles continued for the rest of the century.

One of the first documents in which Bernat Sanç appears as bishop recorded a dispute over the castle of Montferrer with Arnau de Montferrer. Faced with written evidence ("auctoritates quas ipsi mihi hostenderunt"), Arnau quitclaimed the castle and swore fidelity to the see.[125] In an earlier era, this might have been the end of the story; for the previous 100 years, disputes involving episcopal castles had tended to be isolated incidents. This conflict over Montferrer, on the other hand, continued. The see arrived at settlements concerning the castle with Pere Arnau III, viscount of Vilamur (Pallars), in 1160x61 and 1169, and with Pere Arnau IV in 1181; with Pere de Montferrer in 1168; with Sanç d'Alp

---

[121] DACU 804, 853, 918, 1205, 1378.

[122] See, for example, the clause added to the donation of the castle of La Clua to the canons in 1042 (DACU 557): "Semper mansura cautione, ut nulli episcopo nec presenti nec futuro sive cuiuscumque ordinis homini sit licitum iamdictum castellum alienare eo quod a predicta canonica tollat et in alterius potestatem transferat, nec sit licitum a canonicis episcopum acclamare et ad [honorem] prius episcopii succedere quam ipse qui vult fieri episcopus, tacto sacrosancto altari propria manu, confirmet iure iurando hoc esse canonice semper habendum sicut cetera, qualiter episcopi domnus Ermengaudus et Heriballus in scriptis suis constituerunt et excomunicaverunt." Pere Berenguer, for whom no testament survives, made at least three donations to the canons during his episcopacy (DACU 1428, 1455, 1476).

[123] DACU 1178, 1200, 1258, 1425 . . .

[124] These episodes are known almost entirely from papal correspondence: Paul Kehr, ed., *Papsturkunden in Spanien: Vorarbeiten zur Hispania pontificia*, vol. 1, *Katalanien*, 2 parts, Abhandlungen der Gesellschaft der Wissenschaften zu Göttingen, Philologisch-historische Klasse, n.F., 18:2 (Berlin, 1926), nos. 51, 59 [DACU 1509], 61, 62, 79 (pp. 319, 330–35, 362–63).

[125] DACU 1489.

in 1188; and with Arnau, viscount of Castellbò (Alt Urgell), in 1194 and 1199.[126] To put this in a larger context, only four of the transactions involving castles from the episcopacies of Sant Ot (1095–1122) and Pere Berenguer (1123–41) can be shown to be associated with a dispute.[127] For the episcopacies of Bernat Sanç, Bernat Roger, and Arnau de Preixens, the figure approaches thirty.[128]

Increased vigilance on the part of the bishops and canons in preserving the see's rights may have contributed to this growth in the number and frequency of disputes. Indeed both Bernat Sanç and Bernat Roger obtained papal confirmations of the see's properties, the first such documents since 1099.[129] But while in Barcelona twelfth-century disputes over castles seem to have been a result of lax enforcement of rights over many years, it is difficult to make that argument for Urgell. The see managed its castles very effectively during the late eleventh and early twelfth centuries. In contrast to the situation in Barcelona, few sites in Urgell disappear from the historical record for several generations. Another factor may have been more important. The records of settlements concerning episcopal castles catalog usurpations of economic rights and seizure of church property, but they also hint at a rise in the level of violence. The see's initial complaint against Arnau de Montferrer cited "invasion [of the property] of the holy see of Urgell, misdeeds, sacrileges, and even a certain homicide committed there." Other disputes concerned the destruction of castles, abuse of tenants, and other acts of violence; the bishop was not always the victim.[130] The attempt to insti-

---

[126] DACU 1556 (a. 1160x61), 1629 (a. 1168), 1632 (a. 1169), 1763 (a. 1181), 1834 (a. 1188), 1870 (a. 1194), 1900 (a. 1199). [127] DACU 1178, 1205/1206, 1378, 1433.

[128] Based on the reasonably accurate gauge of documents printed in DACU, the number of surviving documents per year in these two periods was nearly equal: 7.5 for the period 1095–1141; 7.2 for the period 1141–95.

[129] DACU 1523, 1599 [Kehr, ed., *Papsturkunden*, nos. 86, 116 (pp. 369–70, 410–12); J-L – , 11231]; see above, p. 178.

[130] DACU 1489: "Itterum episcopus predictus et canonici invasionem Sancte Urgellensis Sedis malefacta et sacrilegia etiam quedam homicidia et ibi perpetrata Arnallo clamabant." DACU 1664: "Item conquestus est episcopus quod R. proibebat, minando et multa mala ingerendo, homines suos et extraneos ad homines episcopi auferendo ne sua venire ad forum Sedis . . . Item conquestus est episcopus quod R. et homines sui destruxerant castrum de Terrassa." DACU 1682: "Secundo conquestus est episcopus quod Petrus . . . [forisfecerat Guilelmo de] Sanauga valens tria millia solidorum, et fecerat hoc cum hominibus Sanaugie de quibus verberaverat unum nomine Andream . . . Ad hoc respondit Petrus quod dampnum illud non erat tam magnum (!) . . . Tercio conquestus est episcopus, quod Petrus et sui homines fregerunt dominicaturam episcopi extrahendo inde exadas et guadengas, et ita excusserunt ibi quandam mulierem de sua guadenga quod membris confractis in brevi tempore mortua fuit." DACU 1834: "diffinimus et evacuamus . . . omnes querimonias quas a vobis (i.e., the bishop) habemus, videlicet de dirucione et destruccione castri Montisferrarii." DACU 1640: "Conquesta est pars filiorum de episcopo quod familia eius dischooperuerat domos illas de quibus placitabant et ligna combusserat." For the violence committed by Arnau, viscount of Castellbò (Alt Urgell), outside Urgell, see Bisson, ed., "The War of the Two Arnaus."

tute the Peace and Truce in the county of Urgell in 1187 may also be seen as evidence for the disorder of the period.[131]

As at Vic, the most common resolution of a dispute involved a compromise, like the initial agreement at Montferrer, that preserved the see's rights while maintaining a relationship with its adversary. Thus in 1154, after losing a judgment concerning the castle of Aguilar, the prior of Santa Maria d'Organyà "appealed to the mercy of the canons, that they might accept a quitclaim from him concerning that *honor*, and yet maintain him there while he lived." The canons assented and granted him tenure for life in return for a yearly measure of barley. They reached a similar accord with Mir Guillem de Puigverd in 1158 concerning rights in the castle of Montalé.[132] Following the quitclaim by Guerau Ponç III, viscount of Cabrera (Girona), of the castle of Gavarra in 1156x57, the bishop and canons commended the castle back to him, accepting promises of fidelity and *potestas*. Likewise, in 1178, the bishop and canons granted as a fief to Ramon de Tarroja the castle of Llenguaeixuta, which "he had seized from them unjustly and against their will." Ramon promised to surrender *potestas* of the castle and to make the *castlà* swear homage and fidelity to the see.[133]

Even Girona participated in the rising conflict over rights in castles in the twelfth century, though with a slightly different emphasis. Conventions and oaths reveal the emergence of division of labor concerning supervision of castles between military and fiscal representatives of the bishop, the castellans and the bailiffs. The task of the latter may in fact have been the more difficult; it certainly received the greater part of the bishops' attention. Bishops seem to have been more concerned with a secure claim to revenues and the presence on site of an administrative representative than with promises of *potestas* and military service. This preference may be seen in the history of conflicts over La Bisbal.[134]

The episcopal cartulary of Girona contains a series of quitclaims to the bishops of the renders (*taschas*) of La Bisbal, mostly by members of the Cruïlles lineage.[135] In the last two of these, the bishop had to purchase the quitclaim with a promise of a yearly payment of 50 *solidi*, first to

---

[131] Gener Gonzalvo i Bou, *La Pau i la Treva a Catalunya: Origen de les Corts Catalanes*, Curs d'història de Catalunya 11 (Barcelona, 1986), 56–58; Gonzalvo i Bou, ed., *Les constitucions de Pau i Treva de Catalunya (segles XI–XIII)*, Textos jurídics catalans, Lleis i costums, 2:3 (Barcelona, 1994), no. 16 (pp. 83–91).

[132] DACU 1521 (a. 1154: "misericordiam canonicis postulavit, ut diffinitionem ab eo de illo honore acciperent et ei saltim dum viveret conservarent"), 1540 (a. 1158). In 1161, Mir Guillem renounced all of his rights in return for a payment of 40 *solidi* (DACU 1557).

[133] DACU 1534 (a. 1156x57), 1736 (a. 1178: "iniuste et contra illorum voluntatem eis auferebat").

[134] In addition to the disputes over La Bisbal, the see engaged in a dispute in the 1170s over the castle of Lloret, pledged to it by Bernat de Palafolls (*VL* 13:41–42).

[135] CCM 234, 264, 281, 284.

Guislabert de Cruïlles, and then to Guislabert and his patron, Guerau Ponç III, viscount of Cabrera (Girona). These claims to revenues were part of more far-reaching claims on the part of the family, which pretended to the position of castellans of La Bisbal. Umbert de Cruïlles made the first of these claims, known from a document of 1136 that recorded sworn testimony in which Umbert and Alemany de Vall-llobrega attested to a *convenientia* between Bishop Berenguer Guifré and Guadall and Berenguer de Cruïlles.[136] According to their account, that document described an agreement by which Bishop Berenguer granted two parts of the *taschas* of La Bisbal, one in fief and the other as a pledge, until he could give the brothers a *cavalleria* of land. In return for this grant the brothers undertook to be the faithful men (*fideles*) of the bishop and to provide aid and one animal (*bestia*) for the host. It is not clear from their testimony whether or not the original document was presented at the dispute, and no other records survive attesting to this particular episode in the conflict.

The second of these quitclaims is known from the record of a judgment given in 1181. The plaintiff this time was Guislabert de Cruïlles, son of Umbert, who presented more inflated claims to Bishop Ramon Orusall.[137] He petitioned for the *castellania* of La Bisbal, claiming that his grandfather had held it and had passed it on to his father in his testament. Furthermore, he argued that the castle was held not from the bishop, but from the viscounts. The bishop's advocates argued against the evidence – witnesses and the testament – presented by Guislabert and added that, in any case, the castle pertained to the see by right of long-term possession.[138] Guislabert countered that episcopal possession of the castle had in fact been interrupted, during the pontificates of Berenguer de Llers (1142–59), Guillem de Peratallada (1160–69), and Guillem de Monells (1169–75), because of the introduction of a bailiff at the castle.[139] No one was surprised when the tribunal, composed of the judge Berenguer de Calonge and the *precentor* of the cathedral, acting on the advice of a papal legate, ruled in favor of the see. The claims of the Cruïlles family do not seem to have been raised again.

Like the counts of Barcelona, the Catalan dioceses frequently became involved in disputes over their castles as the twelfth century progressed, disputes with families by then firmly established as castellans or *castlans*. In Barcelona, and to some extent Girona, these disputes occurred after the castles in question had disappeared from the documentation for long

---

[136] ADG, Mitra 15/40*.   [137] *CCM* 343.
[138] "propter legitimam prescriptionem et longeuam posessionem."
[139] The earliest mention of a bailiff at La Bisbal is in 1166 (*CCM* 312).

periods – perhaps an indication of lack of attention to diocesan rights. At these two sees, the subject raised in the disputes tended to be revenues due from the castles rather than military service. An increased concern with revenue can also be seen in Vic and Urgell, but the bishops there – especially in Urgell – also maintained a strong military presence based on their episcopal castles. As the constant disputing in the twelfth century shows, these structures of episcopal lordship were also like their comital analogues in that they were imperfect, constantly challenged ideals of a sociopolitical order. Institutions and relationships evolved over time, of course, but the disputes were conducted within structures that had been established in the eleventh century and lasted intact well into the twelfth.

CHANGE

In the eleventh century, the development of networks of agreements, centered on castle tenure, but extending into other areas, was associated with the particular documentary form of the *convenientia*. Among the lay aristocracy, and to a certain extent in episcopal chanceries, this form remained standard. Comital documentation had already begun to change under Ramon Berenguer II and Berenguer Ramon II. Under the twelfth-century counts, while the *convenientia* continued to be used for a number of different transactions, it increasingly became confused with other diplomatic forms, and new types of documents developed to carry out its functions.

Ramon Berenguer III's efforts at renewal used the oath more often than the *convenientia*, but *convenientiae* concerning castle tenure during his reign did follow closely the form and language of their eleventh-century antecedents. In 1114 it was sufficient for Dalmau de Peratallada simply to add his subscription to a copy of a fifty-two-year-old *convenientia*.[140] In 1118 Guillem Jofre entered into a newly drawn-up *convenientia* that renewed a convention of his father Jofre Bastó with Ramon Berenguer I for the castles of Cervià and Púbol in 1065.[141] *Comenda*-conventions for some castles on the frontier, such as Corbins, Alcoletge, Castelldans, and Gebut, could not have such precedents, since they dealt with new territory. The only such new *convenientia* in the interior was for the castle of El Papiol in 1115. A convention between Ponç Hug I of Empúries and Ramon Berenguer III dealt with new castles (Ceret and Molins, formerly subject to the counts of Besalú and Empúries), but the accompanying

---

[140] RBI 273.1*, 273.2*; above, p. 219.
[141] LFM 487, 488 (rubric only); cf. RBI 321.1*, 321.2*. *LFM* 409 (rubric only) may be a renewal of BRII 62*.

oath renewed an oath that the count Ponç I Hug had sworn to Ramon Berenguer I. Following the dispute between the two counts in the 1120s, this *convenientia* for Ceret and Molins was renewed.[142]

It was more in the realm of treaties and settlements of disputes that scribes became creative. Ramon Berenguer III's agreement with Alphonse-Jourdain of Toulouse in 1125 was a simple *pax et concordia*, and his treaty with Ponç Hug I of Empúries began, "Hec est pacificacionis et concordie scriptura."[143] The settlement overseen in 1112 by Richard, archbishop of Narbonne, of the conflict between Ramon Berenguer III and Bernard Ato, viscount of Béziers, generated several new documentary forms. The principal record, a *carta de placito*, relates that the viscount was to become the man of the count and grant twelve castles to him as alods (*per alodem*); the count, in return, was to regrant the castles to Bernard Ato as a fief (*per fevum*). Bernard Ato's grant is recorded in the *carta de placito*, which refers to "the abovementioned settlement (*placitum*) and conventions (*convenientiae*)." Separate documents record Ramon Berenguer's grant in fief of the castles and quitclaim of the city of Carcassonne, Ramon Berenguer's oath *to* the viscount, the viscount's oath to Ramon Berenguer, and the viscount's recognition of homage and acceptance as a fief of the city of Carcassonne.[144]

Within Catalonia, too, notices of settlements might contain clauses usually found in conventions, such as promises of *potestas* or fidelity.[145] On the other hand, when a castle-holding relationship emerged from a settlement, it was not necessarily recorded in an oath and convention. The commendation, *not* in the form of a *convenientia*, of the castle of Tamarit in 1119 followed a dispute with the viscount of Cardona (Osona), which is described at the outset of the document. Similarly, the commendation of Montpalau to the viscount of Girona in 1113 is recorded in a "scriptura concordie et pacificationis."[146]

The changes of formula continued under Ramon Berenguer IV. As the twelfth century progresses, the term *convenientia* increasingly appears alongside *pactum, conventio, concordia, pax, amicitia, diffinitio, divisio,* and *concessio*, often in the same document, sometimes in the same phrase. The

---

[142] Corbins, Alcoletge, Castelldans, Gebut: RBIII 207*, 208*. El Papiol: RBIII 181*, sd 22*. Ceret, Molins: RBIII 241.1*, 241.2*, 241.3* (cf. RBI sd 127*; *LFM* 519); *LFM* 525 (rubric only).

[143] *LFM* 895 (a. 1125); RBIII 292*=241.4*, cf. 291*.

[144] RBIII sd 2.1*=RBI 392.2a*, RBIII sd 2.2*=RBI 392.2b*; *HGL* 5:443.1 ("supradictam placitum et convenientias"); *LFM* 844 [*HGL* 5:443.2].

[145] RBIII 165* ("Et convenit ipsis ut serviat eis et in hostes et in cavalcattis et in placita ubi ipsi mandaverint, et sit suus illorum contra cunctos homines vel feminas"), 309* ("Propter hoc quoque donum superius comprehensum, convenimus . . . ut simus tui homines et fideles, sicuti debent esse homines de suo bono seniori cui manibus se comendant, et serviamus tibi predictum fevum").

[146] RBIII 213dup* (a. 1119), 171* (a. 1113). Cf. RBIII 158* ("difinitio atque convenientia").

agreement by which the archbishop of Tarragona granted his rights in the city back to Ramon Berenguer IV in 1151 is referred to as a *pactum vel conveniencia*, as is the alliance sometime after 1157 of that count and Fernando II of León. The negotiations, also in 1151, with the Templars concerning the castle of Borja produced a *memoria*, also referred to as a *conveniencia*, with Teresa de Borja and a *firma concordia ac spontanea diffinicio* between the count and the military order. The scribe of the Treaty of Tudillén (1151) labeled his work a *vera pax et firma conveniencia ac perpetua concordia*.[147]

The same tendency is apparent in the renewal settlements from the early years of his reign. The quitclaim of the castle of Paracolls from Guillem de Salses was a *diffinicio et conveniencia*. The settlement in 1138 between Ramon Berenguer IV and Ponç Hug I of Empúries was recorded in a *spontanea pax et amicabilis concordia*, called a *convenientia* in the closing formulae.[148] These various documents not only blur the boundaries of standard documentary types, they introduce concepts alien to the eleventh-century *convenientia*: the grant in fief (*ad fevum*) of castles, as in a settlement of 1150 with Raimond Trencavel, viscount of Béziers;[149] the use of the *fief de reprise*, as in the precursor of that same settlement in 1112;[150] and the submission to comital protection, or *baiulia*, as in the case of the town of Peralada in 1132.[151] All of these mechanisms, and others, would become more common in the reign of Alfons I.

Under Ramon Berenguer III and Ramon Berenguer IV, a related transformation was underway with written oaths. The oaths of fidelity associated with *convenientiae* are usually individual oaths, or occasionally from a small group of individuals; these continued to accompany *convenientiae* in the twelfth century. A blank oath from the reign of Ramon Berenguer III, almost entirely in Latin and with a space left for the name of the juror, testifies to the routinization of this written tradition.[152]

---

[147] RBIV 243* (Tarragona); 236*, 249* (Templars); sd 9* (León); *LFM* 29 [*DI* 4:62] (Tudillén). See also ALI 387*, an *amicitia et concordia* in 1185 between Count Richard of Poitou and Alfons I; Richard Benjamin, "A Forty Years War: Toulouse and the Plantagenets, 1156–96," *Historical Research* 61 (1988), 270–85.

[148] *LFM* 692 (Paracolls); RBIV 80.1* (a. 1138). The settlement of 1128 on which the latter drew was a "pacificacionis et concordie scriptura" and "conveniencias" (RBIII 292*=241.4*).

[149] RBI 392.3* (a. 1150), renewing agreements of 1068 (RBI 392.1*) and 1112 (see following note). Cf. RBIV 238.1*, 238.2*; 301*, 311*, 324* (*LFM* 346 is apparently related); 275*.

[150] RBIII sd 2.1*=RBI 392.2a*, RBIII sd 2.2*=RBI 392.2b*; *HGL* 5:443. Other examples: RBIV 19* ("ipsum fevum comitale quod dominus prędicti castri per manum comitis solitus est habere"), 20*.

[151] RBIII 316*. Earlier examples: above, pp. 94–97; *CCM* 109. Rovira i Virgili (*Història*, 4:153) refers to a "secret pact" between Jofre III of Rosselló and the lord of Peralada, on the one hand, and Ramon Berenguer III, on the other, directed against the count of Empúries, presumably in the 1120s.   [152] RBIII extra. 2401*; below, p. 291.

There is an older tradition of oaths, however, which hearkens back to a Carolingian tradition of universal public fidelity. We noted earlier two collective oaths sworn to Ramon IV of Pallars Jussà (1047–98) in which the jurors swore as a community, but these are the only such examples from the eleventh century, and none has survived of an earlier date.[153] In the twelfth century, written collective oaths become more common and take on a very different appearance.

Sometime before 1120, Ramon Berenguer III was the recipient of the oath of approximately 500 townsmen of Carcassonne, who promised fidelity and aid against the viscount of Béziers.[154] More than ninety Provençal nobles swore an oath to the same count, probably in 1113 following Douce's donation of her rights in the county to her husband; this oath recorded the submission of representatives of many of the most important lineages of the region.[155] A similar list survives from 1147, when Ramon Berenguer IV made a tour of the region around Tarascon, accepting the submission of the local aristocracy.[156] Most oaths to this count, however, relate to his rule in Aragón, as in the cases of 35 barons (*barones*) of Ramiro II and the townsmen (*burgenses*) of Huesca, both in 1137, 400 Aragonese soon thereafter, and then 120 men at Canfranc in 1154.[157] While there may have been a history of collective submission, oath, or homage to the Aragonese king, no written record of these acts has survived. These first collective oaths from Aragón date from after the arrival on the scene of Ramon Berenguer IV. The collective form was new to Provence, as well, although that region possessed a tradition of

---

[153] RBI sd 183*, sd 185*. *LFM* 838 (rubric only), a group of oaths to Ramon Berenguer I and Almodis at the time of their acquisition of Carcassonne, may have been a single document rather than a collection. The lengthy rubric identifies 36 jurors individually, but the oaths took up 8 full folios of the original *LFM*.

[154] ALI 275.15*. Cheyette, "Sale," 860, suggests that this dates from 1120; Sobrequés, *Els grans comtes*, 144–45, puts it in 1105.

[155] *LFM* 878. The rubric reads "Sacramentale quod fecerunt homines Provintiae nobili dicto Raimundo, comiti Barcinonensi, *tempore quo eam adquisivit*" (emphasis added). The document appears in the *LFM* immediately following the donation of 13 January 1113 (*LFM* 877), but the beginning is missing. Jean-Pierre Poly, *La Provence et la société féodale (879–1166): Contribution à l'étude des structures dites féodales dans le Midi* (Paris, 1976), 326–29, offers a detailed analysis of the list of names, but his conclusions based on the absence of certain figures are undercut by his failure to recognize that the list is incomplete. The principal absentee was Pons de Fos, a supporter of the Toulousan party, who swore a separate oath for the castles of Fos and Hyères only after his castle fell to the Barcelonese forces in 1116 (*LFM* 879). The count received additional noble oaths, including one from Alphonse-Jourdain of Toulouse, at the time of his second campaign in 1123–26 (*LFM* 880, 881, 896 [rubric only]). See Poly, *La Provence*, 329, 333.

[156] *LFM* 882 (rubric only); Poly, *La Provence*, 338–39.

[157] RBIV 76* (Huesca), 86* (barons of Ramiro II), 268* (Canfranc), sd 27* (Aragonese). See Thomas N. Bisson, "A General Court of Aragon (Daroca, February 1228)," in *Medieval France*, 33; Antonio Ubieto Arteta, "Sobre demografía aragonesa del siglo XII," *Estudios de Edad Media de la Corona de Aragón* 7 (1962), 578–98.

written individual oaths; given the numbers of jurors involved, the collective oath may have been an administrative convenience.[158] The real innovation in both cases was the use of the oath by the count as a written expression of his power. Of the nineteen eleventh-century oaths from the county of Provence, only one was sworn to a count.

The first decade or so of the reign of Alfons I was a minority. Policies were set by men such as Guillem Ramon (II) Seneschal and the bishop of Barcelona, Guillem de Torroja. The networks of vicars and bailiffs set up in the reign of Ramon Berenguer IV and an increasingly organized chancery managed the day-to-day business of governance.[159] The change of reign, therefore, did not immediately precipitate changes in the forms and nature of documentation. But taken as a whole, the documents of Alfons I represent the greatest transformation in comital diplomatic since the years of Ramon Berenguer I, one which, in turn, reflects developments in the structure and organization of comital power. As for the *convenientia*, this period saw both further changes in its form and shifts in its areas of application.

The multiplication of written records, as complex negotiations led to the redaction of more than one document, contributed to the changes. This was not a new phenomenon. The *convenientia* of 1068 between Ramon Berenguer I and Raimond Bernard, viscount of Béziers, is closely linked with five additional charters, three of which were composed on the same day as the *convenientia*, and one the day before.[160] But by the twelfth century, the scale had changed. The alliance sealed in 1179 between Alfons I and Roger, viscount of Béziers, generated a dozen documents, including donations, *comenda*-conventions, oaths, and three treaty-conventions: a document in which the viscount confesses his error in joining Raimond V of Toulouse and promises to uphold the agreements (*convenienciae, pacciones*) that his father had entered into with Ramon Berenguer IV; a promise by Roger of aid to Alfons in the war against Raimond; and a counterpromise by Alfons to Roger.[161]

Treaties continued to develop, as well, perhaps under the influence of scribes from outside Catalonia-Aragón. Both documents recording the settlement of 1162 between the count of Barcelona and Frederick

---

[158] Poly, *La Provence*, 166 n. 204, identifies nineteen eleventh-century oaths from Provence. The one lineage for which a separate twelfth-century oath exists, the house of Fos (above, n. 155), had sworn an oath in the late eleventh century to the count of Toulouse (no. 18); see also Poly, *La Provence*, 151 n. 116.   [159] *FA*, 1:79–83.

[160] RBI 393*; RBI 392.1*; *LFM* 815, 816, 817; *HGL* 5:284.1; also *LFM* 840 (rubric only). See Cheyette, "Sale."

[161] RBI 392.4*; ALI 275.16*, 275.18*; *LFM* 855, 857, 858, 859, 860, 862 (rubric only), 863, 864, 865 (rubric only).

Barbarossa are apparently products of the imperial chancery. One seems closer to Catalan scribal tradition, beginning "Hec est concordia facta." The second, however, is a classic imperial privilege, with flourishes of imperial diplomatic, and not a hint of the language of the *convenientia*.[162] Of the two documents that make up the Treaty of Cazola of 1179 the one composed by Geraldo, "notary of the king of Castile" ("notarius rege Castelle"), begins "Hec est concordia et pactus et perpetua amicicia," while the other, composed by the Catalan Berenguer de Parets, begins "Hec est convenientia." Still, both of these scribes also use other terms to refer to the agreements, and there do not appear to be any consistent regional patterns in the application of various formulae.[163] Even individual scribes might alter their formulae: within the space of a year the Catalano-Aragonese royal scribe Joan de Berix labeled documents of similar content a *concordia condivisionis*, a *carta convencionum*, and a *scriptura conventionum*.[164]

The most significant shift in documentation under Alfons I, however, was the development of functional substitutes for the *convenientia*. From the time of Ramon Berenguer I, the *convenientia*, with its attendant oaths, was the principal document for recording and defining the relationship between the count and those with more immediate control over castles. From that time, as well, the form of the document was remarkably consistent: "Hec est convenientia." Under Ramon Berenguer III, the oath began to receive greater emphasis, but the substance of the agreements remained the same. In the second half of the twelfth century, however, new elements entered these transactions: homage, the castle as a fief, and comital protection. While these factors are present in the documentation of Ramon Berenguer III and Ramon Berenguer IV, it is under Alfons I that they became characteristic rather than anomalous. Scribes consequently departed from the traditional formula, sometimes retaining the term *convenientia*, but often avoiding any typological designation and beginning with a simple notification formula: "Let it be known to all . . ." ("Sit notum cunctis . . .").

Five conventions from December 1178 and January 1179, all of which address control over castles, illustrate these changes exceptionally well. Alfons's grant of the castle of Conesa to Ramon de Cervera was a traditional *comenda*-convention, maintaining the eleventh-century distinction

---

[162] *LFM* 901, 902 [Heinrich Appelt et al., eds., *Friderici I. Diplomata*, MGH Diplomata regum et imperatorum Germaniae 10, 5 vols. (Hanover, 1975–90), nos. 378, 382 (2:243–45, 248–51)]. See Josef Riedmann, *Die Beurkundung der Verträge Friedrich Barbarossas mit italienischen Städten: Studien zur diplomatischen Form von Vertragsurkunden im 12. Jahrhundert*, Österreichische Akademie der Wissenschaften, Philosophisch-historische Klasse, Sitzungsberichte, 291:3 (Vienna, 1973), 146–47.   [163] ALI 267*, 268*.   [164] ALI 585*, 594*, 597*; for Joan de Berix, *FA*, 1:243.

between commendation of the castle and donation of a fief associated with it; a grant to Guillem III de Cervera of the castles of Castelldans and Gebut, along with rights in Lleida and Cervera, employed the old formula, as well.[165] But in a grant to Berenguer de Fluvià of the castle of Forès, the castle has become part of the fief: "The lord-king commends to him the castle of Forès *and grants it to him as a fief, with its districts and the* castlà-*knights of that castle*, and grants to him as a fief the whole *honor*."[166] The same is true in grants of El Vilosell to Pere de Besora and Carboneras to Bertrán de San Esteban; in each of these, the term *comendare* is absent.[167] The language is similar in an undated *conveniencia et concordia* in which the count-king granted the castle of Mor to Guillem d'Anglesola.[168]

Transactions of this sort, in which the castle itself is part of the fief, are also found in documents that no longer necessarily carry the designation *convenientia*. Alfons's grant in 1171 of the castle of Montellà to the bishop of Urgell is a *comenda* ("Ego Ildefonsus . . . comendo tibi"),[169] but later documents refer exclusively to the count's donation, or a castellan's acceptance, of a castle as a fief ("Notum sit cunctis quod . . . recipimus et accipimus ad fevum"; "Notum sit cunctis quod . . . dono et comendo tibi ad fevum").[170] Furthermore, the comital grants are increasingly balanced by acts of homage, rather than the promises of fidelity or statements of homage ("sit suus homo": "he shall be his man") found in earlier documents. When Gaston, viscount of Béarn, accepted his lands from Alfons in 1187, the scribe wrote awkwardly: "Let it be known to all that this is the *conveniencia* and pact and recognition of lordship . . . and

---

[165] ALI 258*: "Comendat namque iamdictus dominus rex Raimundo de Cervaria castrum de Conesa . . . et donat ei per feudum sex pariliatas bovum." ALI 260*: "Comendat namque dominus rex supradictus Guilelmo supradicto castrum de Aiabut et donat ei ad feudum duas partes de omnibus expletis."

[166] ALI 257*: "Comendat ei dominus rex castrum de Fores \et donat illud ei in feudum/ *cum suis quadris et milites castlanos ipsius castri et donat ei ad fevum totum illum honorem*" (emphasis added). Note the superscript addition of the key phrase.

[167] ALI 367.2*: "Donat ei namque dominus rex castrum de Velosel cum omnibus terminis suis et donat et concedit ei medietatem decimi . . . Hec autem omnia donat ad fevum." ALI 261*: "Donat namque predictus dominus rex et auctorizat . . . ipsum castrum cum fortitudine . . . Et sic habeat Bertrandus ut superius dictum est predictum castrum per dominum regem."

[168] ALI extra. 2611 (=Extra. 3285): "donat et comendat predicto Guilelmo et suis in perpetuum castrum Dezmor et hoc omne etiam quod habet vel habere debet ibi ut habeant ipse et successores sui per dominum regem et posteros eius ad fevum et servicium eius."   [169] ALI 110*.

[170] ALI 545*, 640*. See also ALI 192* ("Donamus ad fevum . . . ipsum castrum de Montblanca et de ipsa Ripa"). LFM 632 [*Alfonso II* 563] (a. 1192), a grant by the count of the castle of Puigbalador to Ponç de Lillet, does not use the term *fevum*, nor does it begin with a notification formula: "In Dei nomine. Ego . . . dono, laudo, concedo et in perpetuum trado tibi . . . ut ipsum castrum tu et omnes successores tui habeatis, teneatis et possideatis perpetuo ad servicium et plenam fidelitatem meam et meorum" (see *FA*, 1:201). Cf. *LFM* 240 [*Alfonso II* 181] (a. 1174): "Hec autem castra . . . commendo et dono per fevum tibi."

of homage."[171] In these documents, too, while an early text maintains the language of commendation,[172] later texts drop the term.[173]

If the castle might now be granted as a fief, what was the source of the count's ability to grant that fief? In the traditional *comenda*-convention, while the counts were always careful to exact a promise of *potestas*, their relationship to the land and the castle was always left somewhat vague. The count, or some thoughtful person in his entourage, may have been thinking in terms of "public order," while the castle guardian may have simply been succumbing to superior force or to the realities of a particular political situation. The comital conception of this relationship may nevertheless be inferred from the distinction between *comendare* and *donare*. The castle was in theory the count's, and he granted in fief only the lands associated with the castle. The surviving documents show, however, that Alfons had a different relationship to at least some castles and land. Before a grant in fief, the count-king would receive a grant *from* the holder of the castle. The grant *to* the count-king would be unconditional; the count-king would regrant the castle only on terms. This is the *fief de reprise*, a few examples of which survive from Ramon Berenguer IV's reign. The count's scribes did not have a standard form for recording this type of transaction; the documents have an ad hoc feel to them, combining familiar elements in unfamiliar ways.

These procedures might still integrate the old *convenientia*. In 1178, Bernat de Les Piles and Berenguer Company granted to the count-king the castle of Torlanda, using the standard formula for a simple grant, or *donatio*: "de nostro iure in vestrum tradimus dominium et potestatem iam dicta omnia per alodium francum et liberum imperpetuum habendum et possidendum." Two days later, the count-king granted the castle back to the two by means of a *comenda*-convention and oath.[174] A similar trio (*donatio, convenientia,* oath) is found among the collection of documents associated with the defection of Roger of Béziers in 1179; by this means the count-king acquired control over the castles of Brusque, Sorgues, and Murasson.[175] The *convenientia* by which Alfons granted to Roger, and Roger accepted, Carcassonne, Razès, Minerve, and the Lauragais

---

[171] ALI 439*: "Notum sit cunctis quod hec est conveniencia et pactum et recognicio dominii . . . et hominii."

[172] *LFM* 894 [*Alfonso II* 218] (a. 1176): "Notum sit scire volentibus, quod dominus Ildefonsus . . . donat et comendat ad fevum Maiafredo . . . Qui Maiafredus facit domino regi inde hominium."

[173] ALI 557* (a. 1190): "Manifestum sit omnibus . . . dono, laudo atque concedo tibi . . . in feudum . . . Propter hanc vero donationem castri dicti . . . facio inde tibi hominium et fidelitatem." Similarly, ALI 554* (a. 1190): "Notum sit omnibus . . . accipimus castrum nostrum . . . Ego autem Ildefonsus . . . concedo et laudo vobis . . . ut ea similiter habeatis . . . ad fidelitatem et servicium meum." The number and extent of these grants of castles as fiefs is greater than is suggested by Bisson ("Feudalism," 170). [174] ALI 249*, 250*, 251*.

[175] *LFM* 863, 864, 865 (rubric only).

corresponds to an oath and a *donatio* of Minerve by Roger; a grant of Carcassonne, Razès, and the Lauragais may also have existed.[176] A similar mechanism was probably used to transfer to Alfons control of the viscounty of Nîmes.[177]

In many cases, however, scribes used entirely new forms. They recorded transactions in a single document, as in the grant to Alfons of the county and castle of Melgueil, and his regrant of those lands as a fief.[178] Alternatively, the scribe could draw up two separate documents: a sale and acceptance,[179] or a gift and acceptance.[180] At Illa, between 1168 and 1171, the count-king received a donation from one individual, and then granted the lands back in two separate acts to the donor and to a third party.[181] It is possible, too, that any of the simple grants in fief discussed above formed part of such a transaction.

Yet another means by which the count-king could establish control over a castle was by a grant of permission to build a fortification. The *LFM* contains five such grants.[182] The earliest of these, concerning land in Cerdanya, dates from 1166; the remainder are for lands in Rosselló (1175–83). In these the count-king gives license to build a *forcia* in a particular place. The grant is made on condition that the *forcia* be held from the count-king on terms ranging from service, homage, and fidelity to a promise not to let a wrong to the count-king committed from the place

---

[176] ALI 275.16*; *LFM* 855, 857; the grant is perhaps implicit in RBI 392.4*.

[177] *LFM* 867, 868 (rubrics only) suggest this: "Et primum, carta donationis . . . super civitate de Nemauso et super diversis et multis castris"; "Sequitur convenientia in qua idem dominus rex civitatem de Nemauso et castrum eidem Bernardo Atonis in feudum dedit et concessit . . . Sacramentale eiusdem Bernardi Atonis, vicecomitis, eidem domino regi pro observanda convenientia dicta factum." See also ALI 622 and 623*, a *donatio* and *convenientia* ("dono tibi . . . \in feudum/") concerning the castle of *Peraleu*; again, the key phrase is a superscript addition.

[178] *LFM* 870 [*Alfonso II* 134]: "dono, laudo et inter vivos transfero et in perpetuum concedo tibi, domino Ildefonso . . . Ideoque, ego Ildefonsus . . . recipiens hanc supradictam donacionem . . . dono, laudo et concedo in perpetuum ad feudum honoratum tibi." *LFM* 871 (rubric only) is an attendant oath. Also *LFM* 483 [*Alfonso II* 52] ("ego Miro de Ostoles . . . concedo atque dono tibi, Ildefonso regi . . . castrum de Rochacorba . . . Ipsum, vero, castrum de Rochacorba modo ad fevum a te, rege, domino meo, accipio"), 484 [*Alfonso II* 57] ("ego Berengarius de Rochacorba . . . donamus et in perpetuum tradimus tibi, Ildefonso . . . ipsum castrum de Rochacorba . . . Et ego iam dictus Ildefonsus . . . recipiens supradictum donum a te . . . comendo vobis supradictum castrum . . . ad feudum").

[179] ALI 277*, extra. 2625*. In this case, the sale is by the bishop of Urgell, while the acceptance is by his *castlà* ("mandato domini mei"). [180] ALI 388*, 546*.

[181] ALI 107*; *LFM* 679, 681 [*Alfonso II* 60], 682.

[182] ALI 31*; *LFM* 630 [*Alfonso II* 375], 631 [*Alfonso II* 376], 633 [*Alfonso II* 325] ("manuteneant et deffendant"), 661. The first was composed by Ponç d'Osor, the remainder by Bernat de Caldes. See also, e.g., ALI 30*, 458*; *Alfonso II* 91, 144, 291, 333 [*CPF* 166], 398 [*CPF* 175], 473; Jaime Caruana, "Itinerario de Alfonso II de Aragón," *Estudios de Edad Media de la Corona de Aragón* 7 (1962), 138 nn. 136–37, 167 n. 226, 250 n. 470; Bernard Alart, ed., *Priviléges et titres relatifs aux franchises, institutions et propriétés communales de Roussillon et de Cerdagne depuis le XIe siècle jusqu'à l'an 1660*, 1 vol. only (Perpignan, 1874), 52–53.

go unamended. In the one grant to an ecclesiastical institution, Sant Miquel de Cuixà, the count's bailiffs are to have license to "maintain and defend" the site; in the others, the licensees must promise to grant control (*potestas*) on demand. In a similar document, Guillem IV de Cervera promised homage and fidelity to the count-king, and that no evil would come to him "from the fortification that with your assent I am building in the castle district of Puiggròs." The document refers to "this . . . *conveniencia* with homage and oath."[183] These agreements reflect a renewal of the idea of a comital monopoly on castle building, partially seen in the *Usatges de Barcelona*.[184] They find substantive and diplomatic parallels in other types of royal licenses, all of which begin with a notification formula ("Notum sit . . .").[185]

The majority of the conventions from Alfons's last years record general promises. In a convention of 1189, only the count-king's undertakings are recorded: he will attempt to get Ramon de Cervera to do homage to the count of Urgell, and if he fails, will arrange for substitute homages or emendations.[186] In all the rest, however, both parties undertake to perform certain tasks or to act in a certain manner. Frequently, the count-king's half of the bargain is to provide "protection."[187] Thus when Gaucelmo de *Avarzone* promised in a "*convenientia* and pact" to split the proceeds of a certain debt with the count, Alfons accepted him "in my protection and security (*emparancia*) and defense" and promised to support him in his affairs.[188] In an agreement in 1188 with the countess of Urgell, Elvira de Lara, the count accepted her "homage" ("recipio te ad feminam"!) and promised to protect her and her marriage portion; in

---

183 ALI 562*: "de illa fortitudine sive forcia quam tuo assensu facio in meo castro de Podio Grosso . . . hec autem conveniencia cum hominio et sacramento."

184 Us. 93: "ET EX MAGNATIBVS uero . . . nullus presumat deincebs . . . castrum contra principem nouiter hedificare."

185 *Alfonso II* 144, a grant of permission to fortify a vill; ALI 340*, a grant of the license to purchase and export grain; ALI 602*, a grant of permission to operate a silver mine; ALI 458*, 553*, licenses to construct mills. These various licenses should be studied in the context of immunities; see Barbara H. Rosenwein, *Negotiating Space: Power, Restraint, and Privileges of Immunity in Early Medieval Europe* (Ithaca, 1999), e.g., 144–46.   186 ALI 523*.

187 See Freedman, *Origins*, 99–103. In addition to the documents cited below, see ALI 278*, 324*, 386*, 499*, 609, 686*, and Caruana, "Itinerario," 289. Alfons established a number of royal protectorates of monasteries and other ecclesiastical institutions (ALI 106*; *Alfonso II* 34, 124, 506; Charles Charronnet, ed., "Documents sur la chartreuse de Durbon," *Bibliothèque de l'École des chartes* 15 [1853–54], no. 4 [p. 442]; Caruana, "Itinerario," 180 n. 264; Alart, ed., *Priviléges*, 53) as well as of the military orders (*Alfonso II* 394, 491), and of individuals (OR, Sant Pere de Camprodon 38*). Grants of license and protection might be combined in a single document, as in grants to the abbeys of Sainte-Marie de La Grasse in 1179 (*Alfonso II* 291: "recipio sub mea speciali protectione et perpetua securitate . . . concedo etiam libere et absolute abbati et successoribus eius facere fortitudines et castra ubicumque voluerint in suo dominio") and Santa Maria d'Arles in 1188 (*Alfonso II* 473: "dono licentiam . . . quod possis facere et aedificare fortitudinem quam velis . . . Recipio autem sub protectione et defensione nostra predictum locum").

188 ALI 480*: "hanc convenienciam et pactum . . . in mea protectione et emparancia et defensione."

return, the countess promised her support and to attempt to influence her husband to promote the count-king's endeavors.[189]

These grants of protection also provided yet another means for the count-king to acquire control over land. In 1170, Marie of Béarn did homage to Alfons, in return for which he granted his protection of all her lands. Similarly, when in 1190 Jordán de Pina did homage for the castle of Grisén, Alfons received the castle into his "special protection and defense."[190] In 1167, Alfons promised to defend Udalguer de Millars and his castle in return for the donation of the castle and Udalguer's homage. A *convenientia* from 1174 records the grant of an alod outside the town of Elna to the count, the count's regrant of the land as a fief, and Alfons's promise of defense: "I receive all of the said alod into my protection (*garda*) and defense."[191] And in a *convenientia* between Alfons and the knights (*milites*) of the castle of Mor, Alfons granted his protection in return for their oaths of fidelity and homage.[192]

Alfons's scribes created a specialized form of document for the establishment of royal protectorates, several examples of which are preserved in the *LFM*.[193] Each involves the submission of property and/or individuals to the protection of the count-king, or acceptance by the king of the subject into his protection, in return for an annual payment. The subjects of the protection include, in addition to individuals, a mill, a manse, an alod, and an *honor*. The protection is designated by a variety of terms: *baiulia, proteccio, defensio, manutencia, imparancia, guarda*. The payments – in grain or, commonly, a "comital pig" (*porcum comitale*) – are called a *census* or *tasca*. In a few of the agreements, the count specifies that he will not alienate the property or the payment, or appoint an intermediate lord.

---

[189] ACV 6/1789: "ego semper te manuteneam omnesque res tuas speciali protectione et defenssione mea." Other balanced agreements: ALI 591*, 629*, 708* (a *conventio*). This revived a tenth-century practice; see Frederic Udina i Martorell, ed., "Versió canc[e]lleresca d'un document rossellonès del segle X, confirmat per Jaume I," in *Homenaje a Don José Maria Lacarra de Miguel en su jubilación del profesorado: Estudios medievales*, 5 vols. (Zaragoza, 1977), 1:87–95.

[190] ALI 81* (a. 1170), 559* (a. 1190: "sub speciali protectione et defenssione mea").

[191] *LFM* 794 (a. 1167), 795 (a. 1174: "recipio totum iam dictum alodium in mea garda ac deffensione"). See also ALI 107* (below, n. 194).

[192] ALI 231*. Other examples of protection: ALI 636*; *Alfonso II* 83, 142, 598 [*LBSC* 145, 163, 372]; Bisson, "Feudalism," 166 n. 75. *LFM* 804 is an example from the reign of Ramon Berenguer IV.

[193] ALI 35*, 264*, 357*, 690*; *LFM* 168 [*Alfonso II* 278], 512 (rubric only). See also ALI 276*, 278*, 504.2* (cit. Freedman, *Origins*, 99 n. 24). While rare examples can be found from the reigns of Ramon Berenguer III and Ramon Berenguer IV, the extension of the practice is a phenomenon of the reign of Alfons: ACV 6/366 (a. 1146: "Ego Iohannes de Lateranis et frater meus Berengarius mittimus nos in tuitione et defensione domini Raimundi Berengarii comitis et totum nostrum alodum . . . dabimus omnibus annis prenominato seniori nostro in nativitate Sancte Marie i porcum comitalem"); *LFM* 367 (a. 1154, rubric only), 804 (a. 1159); *Remences* 4 (a. 1132, cit. Freedman, *Origins*, 100 n. 28: "nos igitur supradicti Gaubertus scilicet et Raimundus atque Aimericus fratres eius mitimus tibi Raimundo iamdicto comiti Barchinonensi, nostram villam que vocatur Petralate in custodia et in baiulia tua et in defensione").

These documents record entry into the system of exploitation of the comital domain controlled by vicars and bailiffs, some of whom are mentioned by name in the documents as either the intended defenders of the subject, or the intended receivers of the payments.[194] These texts are very similar to documents issued by the count of Pallars Jussà in the eleventh century that were labeled *convenientiae*. The submission of the men of the castle of Mor in 1179 uses that term in reference to the agreement,[195] but generally these grants constitute a new diplomatic form. Like the grants of licenses, grants of protection begin with a notification formula.

Finally, Alfons's reign witnessed a further extension of the use of the written collective oath. The first such example was sworn by the inhabitants (*habitatores*) of Barcelona, shortly after the young count-king's accession; the text does not include names of individuals, nor is it subscribed. The remaining oaths are, like the few from earlier reigns, from outside the old Catalan counties. Two are associated with assemblies at which the young count was recognized, in Tortosa in 1163, and Zaragoza in 1164.[196] Later, Alfons demanded oaths from the men of the viscounts and counts of the Midi who submitted their lands to him in the 1170s and 80s: the *homines* of Perpinyà (1172); the *milites* of Roger of Béziers, as well as the *habitantes* of Nîmes, the *homines* of Carcassonne, and the *homines* of Limoux (1179); and perhaps the *homines* of Melgueil (1172).[197] A number of nobles of Béarn did homage alongside their viscountess, Marie, when that county passed into the control of Alfons, and the oaths of nine *milites* of Mor accompany their joint *convenientia* of submission to the count's protection. Shortly before his death Alfons received an oath as part of an agreement with the "consuls and all the men" of Arles; nine individuals swore on behalf of the count, while the number of consuls and men listed on the document surpasses 500.[198] Many more collective oaths of this sort may have been lost.[199]

---

194 ALI 35* (Bernat Bou), 690* (Berenguer Macip); *LFM* 168 (Pere Rossell); see *FA*, 1:261, 262, 272. ALI 107* is a commendation that includes a promise of royal protection, mentioning the bailiff Guillem de Santa Coloma (*FA*, 1:267).

195 *LFM* 168 [*Alfonso II* 278]: "penitus irrita sit dicta conveniencia et non tencamini nobis nec nostris de iam dicto censu."   196 ALI 5* (Barcelona), 6* (Tortosa), 20* (Zaragoza).

197 *LFM* 793 (Perpinyà), 862 (rubric only; Carcassonne and Limoux), 869 (Melgueil); ALI 275.18* (men of Roger of Béziers); Luc d'Achery, ed., *Spicilegium sive collectio veterum aliquot scriptorum qui in Galliae bibliothecis delituerant*, new ed., ed. Étienne Baluze, Edmond Martène, and Louis-François-Joseph de la Barre, 3 vols. (Paris, 1723), 3:543–44 (Nîmes: "faciat jurare idem B. Ato fidelitatem omnes habitantes in Nemauso & in Arenis, & in aliis omnibus supradictis castris"). ALI 275.17 lists additional oaths made "mandato expresso presentis domini mei Rodgerii." The dating of the oath of the men of Melgueil is problematic; see Thomas N. Bisson, "The Problem of Feudal Monarchy: Aragon, Catalonia, and France," in *Medieval France*, 246 and n. 32.

198 *Alfonso II* 629: "nos consules et omnes homines, tam maiores quam minores totius civitatis Arelatensis."

199 E.g., ALI 636*: "promitto me facturum quod magnates et milites predicti comitatus et terre, et in unaquaque villa centum de maioribus populi, iurent vobis et successoribus vestris fidelitatem."

From commendation to grant in fief, from fidelity to homage, the introduction of royal license and protection, large-scale use of the written collective oath . . . what is happening here? In the case of the fief, the count-king was participating in the more general spread of the fief as a means of tenure in his lands.[200] The practical differences for the count reflected by such changes in terminology are difficult to judge, though. In the five agreements from 1178 and 1179 discussed above, did Ramon and Guillem de Cervera hold their castles on substantially different terms from Berenguer de Fluvià, Pere de Besora, and Bertrán de San Esteban? It is difficult to say. As developments in the written expression of comital power, however, all of these developments are of a kind. Compared to the eleventh-century *convenientia*, these new documentary forms reflect a sense of increased distance between ruler and ruled, lord and subject. In eleventh-century conventions, small shifts in language – from "hec est convenientia que est facta inter" to "hec est convenientia que facio ego ad" – indicated the superiority of one party over the other, as did the inclusion in the document of the undertakings of only one of the parties. All of this was accomplished within the outwardly egalitarian form of the *convenientia*. As the twelfth century progressed, egalitarian forms became increasingly inappropriate. Thus the commendation, with its implication of service in office and shared goals, gave way to the stricter grant in fief. The oath of fidelity, with only an optional clause to indicate subordination ("sicut homo debet"), gave way to recognition of homage and other documents that highlighted subordination. In eleventh-century conventions, the responsibility to "defend and maintain" was incumbent upon both count and castellan; in the twelfth century, the count is the only one who protects and the one who grants permission.[201] This is the essence of the shift that takes place under Alfons I.

---

[200] Bisson, "Feudalism," 157–61.

[201] Alfons did not, of course, have a monopoly on protection, though the protection of the count-king (or perhaps of the military orders) was probably preferable to the extortion/protection practiced by other lords.

Chapter 6

WRITING AND POWER

The *convenientia* played a central role in the organization of Catalan society from the beginning of the eleventh century to the end of the twelfth, but its origins are to be found earlier and farther afield, in early medieval notarial traditions. The near total absence of documents from the Visigothic kingdom, however, precludes a demonstration of the direct influence of earlier traditions, whether indigenous or external, on the eleventh-century Catalan scribes who first composed *convenientiae*. The documentary context in which this form first appeared was particularly rich and, by the 1020s, increasingly fluid. Toward the end of the tenth century, the strict adherence of scribes to formulae, such as those found in the highly influential formulary of Santa Maria de Ripoll, began to break down. This development was perhaps connected to the disruption caused by the sack of Barcelona in 985, but whatever the precise reason for the change, scribes began to use new terms in standard types of documents and to create entirely new documentary types. Formally, the *convenientia* evolved from documents concerning conditional grants, the settlement of disputes, oaths of fidelity, and castle-holding agreements.

This understanding of the *development* of the *convenientia*, rather than simply the observation of its appearance, allows for a more sophisticated model of the connections between words written on parchment and the institutions that inspired those words. The *mutation documentaire* in Catalonia was not a simple stylistic development, but nor was it a mere reflection of institutional change: it was itself a part of that change. The development of the *convenientia* also shows that this change, while very real, was more drawn out than has been suggested. The earliest of signs of changes in judicial procedure date from the late tenth century, well before the minority of Berenguer Ramon I (*c.* 1018–22) where they are usually placed, and the system of vicars holding comital castles in this same period seems less than stable. The first surviving *convenientia*, a long and complex treaty between counts Ermengol II of Urgell and Berenguer Ramon I of Barcelona dating from *c.* 1021, is itself evidence for the pace of change. The level of detail recorded in the agreement and the sophistication of its technical vocabulary – it mentions commendation, homage, fidelity, and *potestas* – suggest that it should not be viewed as a true beginning, but rather as the product of forces already in effect for some time. It was out of this environment, with scribes turning to new formulae, litigants turning to new modes of dispute settlement, and lords restructuring the network of castle holding, that the *convenientia* emerged.

From this point on, the formula "hec est convenientia" quickly became standard and *convenientiae* began to address an ever wider variety of subjects. The *convenientia* appears as a highly flexible form, capable of organizing a wide range of political, social, and economic relationships. The majority of surviving *convenientiae* concern castle tenure: with them parties commended control of fortifications, pledged fidelity to superiors, and undertook to perform military service. The detailed nature of the documents permits a more precise knowledge of some of the feudo-vassalic institutions they describe, especially chains of command over castles, the duty of protection, and the requirement to grant control (*potestas*). Many agreements between great lords, though similar in form, transcended these simple grants of castles and lists of obligations; these shade in the twelfth century into "international" treaties. *Convenientiae* were also closely associated with the settlement of disputes; they reveal a highly complex and irregular system with considerable regional variation. At lower social levels, the *convenientia* served most often to structure the tenure and exploitation of land, through agrarian contracts, leases, grants in fief, and other conditional arrangements. Finally, parties at all levels turned to the *convenientia* to detail family settlements and to record simple promises.

Many of these agreements do not explicitly address the issue of how they were to be maintained. Others include merely spiritual threats, or brief statements that violation by either party of the agreement will render it void. Some, however, do describe complex ad hoc mechanisms for the settlement of disputes arising from the agreement itself. These may involve real and personal sureties, and intricate series of waiting periods for performance and default. Whatever the sureties, the maintenance of an agreement rested on mutual trust (though backed up by the threat of force), and this trust was often embodied in an accompanying oath. For agreements involving castle tenure, it was an oath of fidelity, but many written oaths are simply promises to keep specific *convenientiae*. Overlap between the *convenientia* and the written oath in some regions and periods shows that the oath was not a simple guarantee mechanism. In the end, it is the role of writing itself in the complex process of formation of the agreement that provides the most consistent source of guarantee.

From the time it first appeared on the scene, the *convenientia* was in a state of flux, both in its form and in its institutional role. Count Ramon Berenguer I began in the late 1050s to employ the *convenientia* in a systematic fashion to establish networks of castle holding. In doing so, he laid the foundations for structures of power that would persist in the region for over a century. Other counts followed suit, though the use to which the *convenientia* could be put depended on the relative power of the count and precedent local traditions. Scholars have interpreted the *convenientia*, and by extension the systems of castle tenure that it enshrined, as originally a tool of the aristocracy; Ramon Berenguer I is described as adopting the habits of those who threatened him to save his position. An analysis of *convenientiae* among the lay aristocracy, however, shows that it was they who adopted the habits of the count, at least in putting their agreements into written form. Bishops, too, used written agreements to structure networks of episcopal castles, though again patterns varied according to particular geographical and political circumstances. Nevertheless, in each of the four principal dioceses the establishment of networks of castle holding can be dated to the mid-eleventh-century reign of a powerful lord-bishop. Monasteries also cemented relationships with castle guardians by means of written agreements, though their interest was inevitably more local, limited, and focused on revenue rather than military service.

These systems of castle-holding *convenientiae* set up in the eleventh century persisted into the twelfth century; it is here that the effectiveness of the *convenientia* becomes apparent. The agreements outlasted the original participants, and their descendants, whether biological or institutional, renewed them repeatedly, extending structures of power into the twelfth century. Ramon Berenguer III reestablished ties dating from his grandfather's reign that had weakened during a period of civil war, and despite changed circumstances, Ramon Berenguer IV and Alfons I returned time and again to eleventh-century blueprints. Episcopal structures persisted as well, but it is the lay aristocracy that proved to be the most conservative in its adherence to the form and content of eleventh-century *convenientiae*. At the same time that these agreements were being renewed, disputes over them multiplied. While this reveals tensions within the structures defined by *convenientiae*, it is also further evidence for the persistence of those very structures. The content of the agreements evolved slowly over the course of the century, in response to economic and political developments, and the *convenientia* eventually lost the near monopoly it enjoyed in the eleventh century as the written manifestation of structures of power. But while the precise role of written agreements changed over time, the structures that the agreements defined were surprisingly stable. It is the very nature of the written agreement that allowed for this flexibility.

To ask why, within a society familiar with documentation, a new form for recording agreements appears assumes that the fact that these agreements were written down is in itself relevant. This is, admittedly, a difficult position to prove, in that our knowledge of *un*written agreements is poor. But older and more recent research has seen in medieval charters not simple records of transactions, but integral elements of the transactions themselves. The written nature of the *convenientia* is essential. This belief that documents matter does not require a *realist* approach; I do not assume that the relationships described in *convenientiae* existed in all cases, that the agreements, in other words, were always kept. But whether or not the relationships existed in fact, agreements articulated norms – norms that could be violated and still remain norms. *Convenientiae*, like other documents, served the practical function of constructing a memory of an action or decision (extension in time) that could be communicated at a distance (extension in space). But since the authority of the action or decision recorded was seldom absolute, dealing as it did with a contingent future, *convenientiae* can only be understood as establishing a vision of order. When considered en masse, they reveal the collective expectations of a society concerning political, economic, legal, and social structures. While individual agreements may be broken quickly, these collective expectations remain.

Thus in the *convenientia* the written word transcended its purely practical functions. The *convenientia* is far from an isolated case of this phenomenon. Other documentary forms fulfilled similarly complex roles. Charters recording the donation of the same piece of land to a monastery in several consecutive generations, for example, served symbolic as much as administrative ends. Documents as physical objects played important ritual roles not only in such transfers of land, but also in testamentary practice and the swearing of oaths.[1] In the case of the *convenientia*,

---

[1] Michael T. Clanchy, *From Memory to Written Record: England 1066–1307*, 2nd ed. (Oxford, 1993), 256–60; Emily Zack Tabuteau, *Transfers of Property in Eleventh-Century Norman Law* (Chapel Hill, 1988), 128, 130–31; Alain de Boüard, *Manuel de diplomatique française et pontificale*, vol. 2, *L'acte privé* (Paris, 1948), 115–17; Benito-Kosto-Taylor, "Approaches," 52; Brigitte Bedos-Rezak, "Diplomatic Sources and Medieval Documentary Practices: An Essay in Interpretive Methodology," in John van Engen, ed., *The Past and Future of Medieval Studies*, Notre Dame Conferences in Medieval Studies 4 (Notre Dame, 1994), 321–24; Chris Wickham, "Land

what stands out is its use in the exercise of power, whether in the case of an agrarian contract or of a treaty between lords. This interaction of power and the written word may be more easily understood if we examine the broader context of this connection in medieval Catalonia. It is easiest to trace in the court of the counts of Barcelona, in three particular cases: the general growth of literate administration, the development of the *Usatges de Barcelona*, and the creation of the *Liber feudorum maior* (*LFM*).

ADMINISTRATION

The counts of Barcelona had from the ninth century employed the technology of writing and not simply in response to the demands of ecclesiastical institutions. Records of judgment and transfers of land between the counts and laymen attest to this. Still, it is difficult to trace the earliest activity of a comital protobureaucracy, particularly because of the destruction of records at Barcelona at the time of al-Manṣūr's sack of the city in 985. Even after that date, a quantitative assessment of comital production of documents – as opposed to overall production – can only be highly impressionistic. Studies of the records relating to Guifré I (878–97) and Guifré II Borrell (897–911) mention fewer than 30 documents in 34 years; an incomplete collection of the acts of Alfons I (1162–96) contains more than 650 for the same period of time.[2] In these three centuries, the reign of Ramon Berenguer I was a watershed. His turn to the *convenientia* around 1060 in an attempt to keep castellans under control was only part of a secular growth in comital and noncomital production of documents. The earliest layers of the *Usatges de Barcelona* may represent another facet of Ramon Berenguer I's use of the written word.[3] But it was only in the twelfth century that the counts of Barcelona began to systematize a bureaucracy so as to take advantage of the technology of writing on a larger scale and in a more organized fashion.

footnote 1 (*cont.*)
  Disputes and Their Social Framework in Lombard-Carolingian Italy, 700–900," in Wendy Davies and Paul Fouracre, eds., *The Settlement of Disputes in Early Medieval Europe* (Cambridge, 1986), 117; Mayke de Jong, "Power and Humility in Carolingian Society: The Public Penance of Louis the Pious," *Early Medieval Europe* 1 (1992), 29–30.
2 Ferran Valls i Taberner, "Estudi sobre els documents del comte Guifré I de Barcelona," in *Homenatge a Antoni Rubió i Lluch: Miscel·lània d'estudis literaris, històrics i lingüístics*, 3 vols. (Barcelona, 1936), 1:11–31; Ramon d'Abadal i de Vinyals, "Un gran comte de Barcelona pretèrit: Guifre-Borrell (897–911)," *Cuadernos de arqueología e historia de la Ciudad de Barcelona* 5 (1964), 83–130; *Alfonso II*; Lawrence J. McCrank, "Documenting Reconquest and Reform: The Growth of Archives in the Medieval Crown of Aragon," *American Archivist* 56 (1993), 267–69, 271 (fig. 1), calculates document production for each count based on the number of parchments catalogued under each reign in the chronological series of the ACA, ignoring the fact that these contain a significant proportion of *non*comital documents.   3 Below, p. 278.

The scribes of early medieval Catalonia were monks and clergy. They were not a completely undifferentiated body, as hints survive of specialized competencies. Thus episcopal and monastic scribes attempted to follow the diplomatic of the papal court, while rural scribes employed a distinct subscription formula. Judges served as scribes inside and outside their own courts, and within the corps of judges there were some who specialized in probate procedure and in restricted geographical areas. The earliest indications of a comital writing office come from the first decades of the eleventh century: scribes identifying themselves as "of the count(ess)"; special titles for the head of the office (*pincerna, primiscrinius*); a copy of a donation to a monastery destined for the comital archive; the association of a comital scribe with the comital chapel. Yet these remain isolated notices, and the number of scribes involved is far too numerous to represent at this point a specialized, organized group.[4]

Ramon Berenguer III drew principally on clergy of the cathedral of Barcelona for his writing staff. In fact the comital writing office may have been the cathedral chancery itself. A chief scribe directed a fairly limited number of subordinates, complemented by a number of "occasional scribes": monks drafted documents destined for their own institutions; a number of deacons specialized in *convenientiae* and oaths of fidelity. Toward the end of the reign a scribe named Ponç entered comital service and continued his career as the principal scribe of Ramon Berenguer IV. Ponç drafted or subscribed 75 percent of the dated documents of that count preserved in the comital archive and presided over an increasingly limited number of comital scribes, who are identified as such and even exhibit areas of geographical or topical specialization. This period also saw the integration of the Catalan comital and Aragonese royal writing offices, though Catalan and Aragonese scribes and many scribal practices remained distinct for the remainder of the century. The increase in surviving documentation under Alfons I makes it possible to follow in detail the careers of his *notarii* and *scribae regis*, such as Ponç d'Osor (1163–90) and Bernat de Caldes (1167–88), and even to identify particular subordinate scribes who reported to them.[5] By the 1160s, a complex, organized comital bureaucracy was in place.

The greatest work of this new comital bureaucracy was the organization

---

[4] Bonnassie, *La Catalogne*, 1:169 and nn. 145–47; Josep Trenchs Òdena, "La escribanía de Ramón Berenguer III (1097–1131). Datos para su estudio," *Saitabi* 30 (1981), 12–16.

[5] Trenchs Òdena, "La escribanía," 16–24; Antoni M. Aragó Cabañas and Josep Trenchs Òdena, "Las escribanías reales catalano-aragonesas, de Ramón Berenguer IV a la minoría de Jaime I," *Revista de archivos, bibliotecas y museos* 80 (1977), 421–34; Trenchs Òdena, y escribanos de Alfonso II (1154–1196): Datos biográficos," *Saitabi* 28 (1978), 5–24; Trenchs Òdena, "Los escribanos de Ramón Berenguer IV: Nuevos datos," *Saitabi* 29 (1979), 5–19; *FA*, 1:235–50.

and reform of fiscal accounting.[6] In 1151, officials undertook a survey of rights and revenues in the comital domain. Other novel fiscal records survive from the next quarter century, such as lists of disbursements, memoranda of expenses, reviews of bailiffs' accounts, and records of accounting sessions with creditors. The procedures that these records reveal may have been traditional,[7] but the appearance of documents – especially of the survey of 1151 – at this point to reveal these procedures, coming as it does at the same time as the organization of the comital writing office, is significant in itself. Traditional accounting procedures underwent further reform in the period 1178–94, generating increasing revenue from the domains and allowing for the reduction of comital debt. More to the point, these reforms generated an increasing volume of new types of records, and a corps of fiscal specialists developed to complement the writing office. Administrators such as Bertran de Castellet and Ramon de Perella circulated in the comital retinue alongside Ponç the scribe and Bernat de Caldes; later Ramon de Caldes (Bernat's brother) and Guillem de Bassa developed careers as scribes specializing in fiscal records. Thomas Bisson writes that while in outlook the accounting procedures were more patrimonial and even archaic in Catalonia than in contemporary northern Europe, the "bureaucratic supervision . . . may reasonably be regarded [as] the most progressive aspect of Catalonian fiscal operations in the later twelfth century."[8]

The growth of this bureaucracy and the attendant multiplication of records necessitated advances in archival practice. Here, too, the indicators are few and far between, but they point to a burst of activity under Alfons I. In 1020, the countess Ermessenda had a copy made of a donation, perhaps destined for a comital archive. Ramon Berenguer III lost a dispute in 1113 because he could not find certain written oaths, lost through neglect. In 1178, Guillem de Bassa received a bundle of comital documents from a moneylender. Alfons I won his case against Pere de Lluçà in 1180 in part on the basis of oaths dating back to the beginning of the eleventh century produced from his archive (*archivum*). By 1186, the financial service was keeping records in registers: *libri computorum domini regis*. These, along with the *LFM*, foreshadowed the great series of over 6,000 volumes of royal registers, which begin under Jaume I (1213–76). Ramon de Caldes and Guillem de Bassa seem to have organized the loose single-sheet records, as well. Endorsements and annotations, still only imperfectly analyzed, offer clues to this process.[9]

[6] *FA*, 1:23–121.   [7] As Bisson suggests (*FA*, 1:24, 53).   [8] *FA*, 1:154–55.
[9] Bonnassie, *La Catalogne*, 1:169 n. 147; *FA*, 1:96–97, 100–101, 296–300; Robert I. Burns, *Diplomatarium of the Crusader Kingdom of Valencia: The Registered Charters of its Conqueror, Jaume I, 1257–1276*, vol. 1 (Introduction), *Society and Documentation in Crusader Valencia* (Princeton, 1985), 15–25, 48–57.

Administration, and particularly the use of the written word in administration, was not new in the eleventh and twelfth centuries, though many
accounts gloss over, devalue, or ignore entirely early medieval developments.[10] Early medieval papal administration is the best documented.
Under Gregory I (590–604) – and probably earlier – papal notaries
formed a coherent group, organized under the leadership of a *primicerius*.
The archives themselves are thought to date back to the pontificate of
Damasus I (366–84). Although only fragments of papal registers survive
from before the twelfth century, the practice of enregistration may have
already begun in the fourth century. Distinct legal, financial, and household offices and officers appear from the sixth century.[11] In the Frankish
kingdoms we can identify a series of *referendarii* in the service of the
Merovingian rulers; Gregory of Tours describes a Merovingian royal
archive at Chelles; and there is evidence that the Late Roman *gesta munic-
ipalia* continued in some places into the eighth century.[12] Detailed evidence, however, is found in these regions first and foremost in
Carolingian sources. The development of the Carolingian chancery may
be traced from its beginnings as the (nonroyal) chancery of Charles
Martel; over 1,000 charters of the first five Carolingian kings, alongside
the seventh-century *Formulary of Marculf* and the early-ninth-century
Formulae imperiales, allow a reconstruction of its organization, personnel,
and activities. A wide variety of agendas, minutes, memoranda, requisi-
tions, instructions, circulars, and orders complement the capitulary legislation and law codes that detail the judicial and fiscal activities of the
court, revealing a sophisticated, literate administrative culture.[13] Evidence

---

[10] E.g., Clanchy, *From Memory*.

[11] Thomas F. X. Noble, "Literacy and the Papal Government in Late Antiquity and the Early Middle
Ages," in Rosamond McKitterick, ed., *The Uses of Literacy in Early Medieval Europe* (Cambridge,
1990), 82–108; Noble, *The Republic of St. Peter: The Birth of the Papal State, 680–825* (Philadelphia,
1984), 212–55; Harry Bresslau, *Handbuch der Urkundenlehre für Deutschland und Italien*, 2nd ed., 2
vols. (Leipzig, 1912–31), 1:191–216.

[12] Bresslau, *Handbuch*, 1:359–69; Gregory of Tours, *Libri historiarum X*, ed. Bruno Krusch and
Wilhelm Levison, MGH Scriptores rerum Merovingicarum 1:1, 2nd ed. (Hanover, 1951; repr.
1965), X.19 (p. 512, lines 5–7); Ian Wood, "Administration, Law and Culture in Merovingian
Gaul," in McKitterick, ed., *The Uses of Literacy*, 63–67; Peter Classen, "Fortleben und Wandel
spätrömischen Urkundenwesens im frühen Mittelalter," in Classen, ed., *Recht und Schrift im
Mittelalter*, Vorträge und Forschungen 23 (Sigmaringen, 1977), 42–47.

[13] The classic study is François-Louis Ganshof, "Charlemagne et l'usage de l'écrit en matière administrative," *Le Moyen Âge* 57 (1951), 1–25. See now Rosamond McKitterick, *The Carolingians and
the Written Word* (Cambridge, 1989); McKitterick, *The Frankish Kingdoms under the Carolingians,
751–987* (London, 1983), 77–105; Janet L. Nelson, "Literacy in Carolingian Government," in
McKitterick, ed., *The Uses of Literacy*, 258–96; Karl Ferdinand Werner, "*Missus-marchio-comes*:
Entre l'administration centrale et l'administration locale de l'Empire carolingien," in Werner
Paravicini and Karl Ferdinand Werner, eds., *Histoire comparée de l'administration (IVᵉ–XVIIIᵉ siècles):
Actes du XIVᵉ colloque historique franco-allemand, Tours, 27 mars–1ᵉʳ avril 1977, organisé avec le Centre*

for the administrative activities of the Anglo-Saxon kings begins later; the reign of Alfred (871–99) is the normal starting point. This is likely a question of surviving evidence; the Felix who is described in *c. 850* as custodian of the king's letters was probably not the first such figure in Anglo-Saxon history.[14] Still, it is only from the late ninth century that historians can document complex systems of fiscal control, household management, and judicial organization, as well as the writing offices to support them.[15] Arguments about Anglo-Saxon administration are made with less confidence than in the papal and Carolingian cases as the surviving records do not offer detailed information concerning structures and personnel.[16] But if the details are vague, the vitality of an administration founded on the written word is undeniable.[17]

Given these early medieval foundations, the organization of a comital chancery, accounting procedures, and archival practice in Catalonia represents not novelty, but rather a new and distinct phase in a long-term evolution. In this respect, Catalonia was participating in wider European trends. The first English royal "chancellor" appears in 1069. Comital chancellors appear in Anjou around 1080, Champagne in 1101, Normandy between 1106 and 1135, and Flanders in 1136. The French *Trésor des chartes* traces its continuous history back to 1194, when Philip

footnote 13 (*cont.*)
> *d'études supérieures de la Renaissance par l'Institut historique allemand de Paris*, Beihefte der Francia 9 (Munich, 1980), 191–239; Mark Mersiowsky, "Regierungspraxis und Schriftlichkeit im Karolingerreich: Das Fallbeispiel der Mandate und Briefe," in Rudolf Schieffer, ed., *Schriftkultur und Reichsverwaltung unter den Karolingern: Referate des Kolloquiums der Nordrhein-westfälischen Akademie der Wissenschaften am 17./18. Februar 1994 in Bonn*, Abhandlungen der Nordrhein-westfälischen Akademie der Wissenschaften 97 (Opladen, 1996), 109–66.

14 Lupus of Ferrières, *Epistulae*, ed. Peter K. Marshall (Leipzig, 1984), no. 13 (p. 22, lines 2–3): "ex Felice didici, qui epistolarum uestrarum officio fungebatur."

15 Simon Keynes, "Royal Government and the Written Word in Late Anglo-Saxon England," in McKitterick, ed., *The Uses of Literacy*, 226–57; James Campbell, "Observations on English Government from the Tenth to the Twelfth Century," *Transactions of the Royal Historical Society*, 5th ser., 25 (1975), 39–54; H. R. Loyn, *The Governance of Anglo-Saxon England, 500–1087*, The Governance of England 1 (London, 1984), 94–171.

16 E.g., Keynes, "Royal Government," 256–57: "Needless to say (perhaps), such a degree of dependence on the written word presupposes the existence of a body of scribes in the king's service; for while kings might on occasion have relied on others to produce the written records of government, it is simply inconceivable that they could have done so as a matter of normal course. Little is known of the actual organization of the royal secretariat in the tenth and eleventh centuries, beyond the likelihood that it was a permanent office attached to the king's household, staffed by some laymen as well as by priests of the royal chapel, who accompanied the king on his peregrinations around the kingdom." See also Keynes, *The Diplomas of King Æthelred 'The Unready', 978–1016: A Study in Their Use as Historical Evidence*, CSMLT, 3rd ser., 13 (Cambridge, 1980).

17 For early medieval Iberia, see P. D. King, *Law and Society in the Visigothic Kingdom*, CSMLT, 3rd ser., 5 (Cambridge, 1972), 52–121; Roger Collins, "*Sicut lex Gothorum continet*: Law and Charters in Ninth- and Tenth-Century León and Catalonia," *English Historical Review* 100 (1985), 489–512; Collins, "Visigothic Law and Regional Custom in Disputes in Early Medieval Spain," in Davies and Fouracre, eds., *The Settlement of Disputes*, 85–104; Collins, "Literacy and the Laity in Early Mediaeval Spain," in McKitterick, ed., *The Uses of Literacy*, 117–18, 124–25, 129–30.

II Augustus of France famously lost the royal written records at Freteval, although there is evidence of organization of incoming correspondence as early as 1156. The output of the royal chanceries increased sharply under Philip Augustus (1179–1223) and Henry II of England (1154–89), as did the volume of papal correspondence under Alexander III (1159–81). The fiscal accounts and records of Catalonia find contemporary parallels in England's Domesday survey (1086), as well as in the pipe roll of 1130, which offers evidence for the early practices of the Exchequer. The *Constitutio domus regis* (1135x36) and *Dialogus de scaccario* (1177x79) offer additional details of administrative organization and procedure. The accounts of 1202–3 of Philip Augustus and the *Gros brief* of Flanders of 1187 represent parallel developments on the continent. The beginning of enregistration of outgoing royal correspondence also dates from this era. The series of English charter, close, and patent rolls start in the first years of the reign of King John (1199–1216), the fine and plea rolls a few years before. The first French royal registers appear from 1204, while a nearly continuous series of surviving papal registers begins with Innocent III (1198–1216).[18] As the papal case shows, the appearance of novelty is often a question of documentary survival; papal enregistration, as noted, probably dates back to the fourth century. Still, the survival is itself evidence of a change in practices, and along with an increased diversity and sophistication of administrative methods, it represents a distinct advance.

The contribution of all of these administrative tools to governance in this period is well known, if not completely understood. Documentation helped rulers centralize authority, defend rights, and maximize revenues – in short, exercise power. But an understanding of how the *convenientia* was able to act as "an agent for the structuring of society"[19] requires a still broader conception of the relationship between power and the written word in Catalonia than that suggested by analyses of the rise of bureaucratic government. The use of the written word by those in power could

---

[18] S. B. Chrimes, *An Introduction to the Administrative History of Mediaeval England*, Studies in Mediaeval History 7 (Oxford, 1952), 21–32, 51–64, 74–77; W. L. Warren, *The Governance of Norman and Angevin England, 1086–1272*, The Governance of England 2 (Stanford, 1987), 65–86, 95–169; John W. Baldwin, *The Government of Philip Augustus: Foundations of French Royal Power in the Middle Ages* (Berkeley, 1986), 147–50, 401–18, 420–22; Bedos-Rezak, "Diplomatic Sources," 325; Clanchy, *From Memory*, 58–61, 150–51; Bresslau, *Handbuch*, 1:216–48; Frank M. Bischoff, *Urkundenformate im Mittelalter: Größe, Format und Proportionen von Papsturkunden in Zeiten expandierender Schriftlichkeit (11.–13. Jahrhundert)*, Elementa diplomatica 5 (Marburg an der Lahn, 1996), 15–44, esp. graph at 16; Bryce Lyon and Adriaan E. Verhulst, *Medieval Finance: A Comparison of Financial Institutions in Northwestern Europe* (Providence, 1967); Thomas N. Bisson, "Les comptes des domaines au temps du Philippe Auguste: Essai comparatif," in *Medieval France*, 265–83. On numeracy, see Alexander Murray, *Reason and Society in the Middle Ages* (Oxford, 1978), 141–210.
[19] Bedos-Rezak, "Diplomatic Sources," 321.

not help but represent something more than an efficient technology. The written word and documents as a whole retained symbolic, representational value. They aided not just exercise of power, but also the expression of power.

THE *USATGES DE BARCELONA*

It is now generally acknowledged that the legal text known as the *Usatges de Barcelona* is not, as it claims to be, the work of Ramon Berenguer I. It is, rather, a compilation of compilations, the present form of which dates from the reign of Ramon Berenguer IV, more specifically, from the years around 1150.[20] Even after that date, however, the *Usatges* seem to have had little impact on contemporary practice.[21] There are disjunctions between the vocabulary of the code and the vocabulary of contemporary charters; in the *Usatges*, for example, the term *convenientia* refers to an association of knights; the agreement that the charters refer to as a *convenientia* is called in the code's single reference to it a *conventio*.[22] The judicial procedures described in the code, such as the ordeal and judicial duel, are rarely duplicated in practice.[23] The revived comital court of Ramon Berenguer IV seldom turned to the *Usatges* in its proceedings.[24] And the few apparent references to the code before the twelfth century concern well-established rules of castle tenure, embodied in scores of *convenientiae*.[25]

In the context of this short-term failure as a law code, the *Usatges* are better understood as a more sophisticated instrument of comital policy. First, the compiler of the *Usatges* presents them as the work of Ramon

---

[20] Josep Maria Pons i Guri, "El dret als segles VIII–XI," in *Symposium internacional*, 1:148–54; Frederic Udina i Martorell and Antoni M. Udina i Abelló, "Consideracions a l'entorn del nucli originari dels *Usatici Barchinonae*," in *La formació i expansió*, 87–92; Joan Bastardas i Parera, *Sobre la problemàtica dels Usatges de Barcelona* (Barcelona, 1977); Bonnassie, *La Catalogne*, 2:711–28.

[21] For a fuller treatment of this theme, see Adam J. Kosto, "The Failure of the *Usatges de Barcelona*" (forthcoming).

[22] Us. 36, 70. The Catalan version translates both of these terms as *covinença*.

[23] Us. 28; 1, 27, 45, 46, 53, 57, 106, 112, 113. Only six cases show that the procedure was actually carried out, rather than just proposed or threatened: *CSCV* 218 (a. 988); *VL* 8:31 (a. 1016); OR, Sant Cugat del Vallès 194* (a. 1036); Paris, Bibliothèque nationale, Collection Moreau, vol. 20, fols. 165–67* (a. 1044); *VL* 15:17 (a. 1080); DACU 1079 (a. 1091). See Bowman, "Law," 149–67; cf. Stephen D. White, "Proposing the Ordeal and Avoiding It: Strategy and Power in Western French Litigation," in Thomas N. Bisson, ed., *Cultures of Power: Lordship, Status, and Process in Twelfth-Century Europe* (Philadelphia, 1995), 90 and n. 5. Jeffrey Bowman kindly provided a transcription of the document from 1044.

[24] RBIV 154*, 237*, 242*, 300*, 304*, 305*, 333*, sd 11*, sd 12*, sd 13*; *DI* 4:114 [*CSCV* 1031]; see also Anscari M. Mundó, ed., "Fragment del *Libre jutge*, versió catalana antiga del *Liber iudiciorum*," *Estudis universitaris catalans* 26 (1984), 173–89.

[25] Cf. *contra*, Josep Maria Pons i Guri, "Documents sobre aplicació dels Usatges de Barcelona, anteriors al segle XIII," *Acta historica et archaeologica mediaevalia* 14–15 (1993–94), 39–46.

Berenguer I, when in fact they date from a century later, and as a code, when in fact they were never officially promulgated. Ramon Berenguer IV's court was thus able to create the illusion or effect of a code without putting his stamp on the text, perhaps to avoid negative repercussions. The inclusion of a list of magnates allegedly present at the promulgation of the *Usatges* under Ramon Berenguer I is instructive in this regard: it included the forebears of most of the great baronial families of the mid-twelfth century.[26] Law was good if it was old; by presenting a program as the work of the count's ancestors, the compiler insulated him from attacks. Second, the code includes elements that have been seen as part of the formulation of a "theory of the principate," including the declaration of the Peace within distinct territorial boundaries, a call for stable coinage, export controls on sales across the frontier, and the use of the Romanist appellation *princeps*. According to this theory, after his great conquests in the late 1140s at Almería, Tortosa, Lleida, and Fraga, a triumphant Ramon Berenguer IV set out to create a territorial principality, beginning a survey of his domains and reconstituting the comital court. The *Usatges* form part of this rethinking of comital power.[27]

From these perspectives, the *Usatges* appear less a legal text than a work of comital propaganda. As propaganda, however, they also failed – for more complex reasons. The novel, Romanist ideas lie side by side with regulations that seem perfectly compatible with contemporary customs of castle tenure and dispute settlement. It is possible to interpret these latter clauses to the advantage of the count: he had established himself at the apex of a network of castle holding, and regularization of various customs concerning castles could only enhance the prestige of his court. But while these traditional clauses may have been intended as an honest compilation of customs for use in the comital court, they may also have served as a facade behind which Ramon Berenguer IV and his advisors attempted to construct a new conception of territorial power. If the *Usatges* were a piece of comital propaganda, it is highly surprising to find that the Catalan barons, in the midst of their conflict in the 1170s and 80s with Alfons I, seem to have appealed to the code in attacking the Peace legislation proposed at Fondarella in 1173. At Girona in 1188, they forced

---

[26] Us. 4; see also Miquel Coll i Alentorn, "La llegenda d'Otger Cataló i els nou barons," *Estudis romànics* 1 (1947–48), 1–47.
[27] Us. 61, 64, 66, 69, 80, 93, 94, 95, 123. See Thomas N. Bisson, "The Rise of Catalonia: Identity, Power, and Ideology in a Twelfth-Century Society," in *Medieval France*, 139–40; Bisson, "Feudalism in Twelfth-Century Catalonia," in *Medieval France*, 164–65; Bisson, *Medieval Crown*, 34–35, 50–53. Bisson develops ideas first articulated in Ramon d'Abadal i de Vinyals, "Pedro el Ceremonioso y los comienzos de la decadencia política de Cataluña," prologue to Ramón Menéndez Pidal, ed., *Historia de España*, vol. 14, *España cristiana; Crisis de la Reconquista; Luchas civiles*, 2nd ed. (Madrid, 1966), xlviii–lvii.

Alfons to accept that his new enactments would in no way supersede the "written usage [the *Usatges*, it is assumed] concerning the granting of the *potestas* of castles."[28] This passage does not prove that the barons had in the past recognized the *Usatges* as a code of law; here, again, the only parts of the *Usatges* at issue are the traditional rules of castle tenure. But it does show how the barons were able to use the count's own propaganda against him. They seized on the conservative aspects of the code – not the regalian program that was the true comital interest – and made of them the central issue. Thus the *Usatges* became a pawn in the constitutional debates of the late twelfth century, and the count lost control of his own weapon.

Debates concerning the nature of the early medieval *leges* and Carolingian capitularies have expanded the possibilities for understanding a text such as the *Usatges*. The content of a legal source and its value as historical evidence – whether, for example, it is to be read as prescriptive or descriptive – are only starting points. The rationale behind its creation, the significance of its written nature, its relationship to the spoken word of the legislator and to unwritten customary law, its circulation and reception, its intended and actual use: these aspects are equally if not more important.[29] While the twelfth-century and Iberian context of the *Usatges* is different, questions concerning the practical and ideological roles and

---

[28] Gener Gonzalvo i Bou, ed., *Les constitucions de Pau i Treva de Catalunya (segles XI–XIII)*, Textos jurídics catalans, Lleis i costums, 2:3 (Barcelona, 1994), 17:20 (p. 99): "Item, volumus quod occasione huius institucionis in nullo derogetur Usatico scripto, scilicet, in dandis potestatibus castrorum a vassallis dominis suis, sive in restituendis ipsis vassallis vel omnibus aliis." Cf. nos. 15, 18 (pp. 74–82, 101–7).

[29] Important recent contributions include: Hermann Nehlsen, "Zur Aktualität und Effektivität germanischer Rechtsaufzeichnungen," in Classen, ed., *Recht und Schrift*, 449–502; Patrick Wormald, "*Lex scripta* and *verbum regis*: Legislation and Germanic Kingship, from Euric to Cnut," in P. H. Sawyer and I. N. Wood, eds., *Early Medieval Kingship* (Leeds, 1977), 105–38; Hanna Vollrath, "Gesetzgebung und Schriftlichkeit: Das Beispiel der angelsächsischen Gesetze," *Historisches Jahrbuch* 99 (1979), 28–54; Raymund Kottje, "Die Lex Baiuvariorum – das Recht der Baiern," in Hubert Mordek, ed., *Überlieferung und Geltung normativer Texte des frühen und hohen Mittelalters: Vier Vorträge, gehalten auf dem 35. Deutschen Historikertag 1984 in Berlin*, Quellen und Forschungen zum Recht im Mittelalter 4 (Sigmaringen, 1986), 9–23; Hubert Mordek, "Karolingische Kapitularien," in Mordek, ed., *Überlieferung*, 25–50; Mordek, "Kapitularien und Schriftlichkeit," in Schieffer, ed., *Schriftkultur und Reichsverwaltung*, 34–66; McKitterick, *The Carolingians*, 23–75; Wolfgang Sellert, "Aufzeichnung des Rechts und Gesetz," in Sellert, ed., *Das Gesetz in Spätantike und frühem Mittelalter: 4. Symposion der Kommission "Die Funktion des Gesetzes in Geschichte und Gegenwart,"* Abhandlungen der Akademie der Wissenschaften in Göttingen, Philologisch-historische Klasse, dritte Folge, 196 (Göttingen, 1992), 67–102. Wormald, who was developing the thesis of J. M. Wallace-Hadrill (*Early Germanic Kingship in England and on the Continent: The Ford Lectures Delivered in the University of Oxford in Hilary Term 1970* [Oxford, 1971], 36–37, 43–44), has restated and expanded his own position in *The Making of English Law: King Alfred to the Twelfth Century*, vol. 1, *Legislation and Its Limits* (Oxford, 1999), 29–108; see also Wormald, *Legal Culture in the Early Medieval West: Law as Text, Image and Experience* (London, 1999), xi–xv.

impact of such a text remain valid.[30] The argument for a practical inspiration for the *Usatges* is easy to make: they were produced in a sophisticated legal environment in which their provisions could have been applied as written law; there is limited evidence for attempts of various courts to do so in the twelfth century; and in the thirteenth century, this occurred regularly.[31] Because of the initial practical failure of the *Usatges*, however, it is their ideological aspect that comes to the fore in a twelfth-century context. Yet that ideological aspect is intimately bound up with their nature as a written text. Ramon Berenguer IV and Alfons I may have commissioned and appealed to the *Usatges* because that is what counts and kings were supposed to do, whether inspired by Visigothic or Roman models.[32] The fact that powerful lords did not bring disputes over fiefs to the court of Ramon Berenguer IV to be adjudicated on the basis of a written code might be interpreted as a reluctance to subscribe to that count's ideological program. Alfons I's barons did not appear regularly in his court, either, and the *Usatges* had an equally unimpressive practical record there. Nevertheless, his unruly barons made a point of appealing not to custom in general, but to the *written* custom of the *Usatges*, in an attempt to counter the count's use of the text for his own ends. In the second half of the twelfth century, even if the *Usatges* could be ignored in the courts, they could not be ignored as a written expression of comital power. The written word established the parameters of the debate.

THE *LIBER FEUDORUM MAIOR*

While the court of Ramon Berenguer IV produced the *Usatges de Barcelona*, the chief historical monument of Alfons I's reign is the great

---

[30] For comparative purposes in the twelfth century: Rudolf Schieffer, "Rechtstexte des Reformpapsttums und ihre zeitgenössische Resonanz," in Mordek, ed., *Überlieferung*, 51–69; Elmar Wadle, "Frühe deutsche Landfrieden," in Mordek, ed., *Überlieferung*, 71–92; Gerhard Dilcher, "Oralität, Verschriftlichung und Wandlungen der Normstruktur in den Stadtrechten des 12. und 13. Jahrhunderts," in Hagen Keller, Klaus Grubmüller, and Nikolaus Staubach, eds., *Pragmatische Schriftlichkeit im Mittelalter: Erscheinungsformen und Entwicklungsstufen (Akten des Internationalen Kolloquiums 17.–19. Mai 1989)*, Münstersche Mittelalter-Schriften 65 (Munich, 1992), 9–19. Even for the earlier period, the regions under Visigothic law may represent an exceptional case: see Nehlsen, "Zur Aktualität," 483–502; Wormald, *The Making of English Law*, 91; Collins, "Visigothic Law"; Collins, "*Sicut lex Gothorum continet*"; Collins, "Literacy and the Laity."
[31] For the application of the *Usatges* in the thirteenth century, see Guillermo Maria de Brocá, *Historia del derecho de Cataluña* . . ., 1 vol. only (Barcelona, 1918), 179–81; Josep Maria Pons i Guri, "Corpus iuris," in *Documents jurídics de la història de Catalunya*, 2nd ed. (Barcelona, 1992), 120–24.
[32] The Visigothic model is apparent from the references to the *Liber iudiciorum* in Us. 3: "Hoc enim fecit comes auctoritate Libri Iudicis qui dicit: 'Sane adiciendi leges, si iusta nouitas causarum exegerit, principalis eleccio licenciam habebit,' 'et potestatis regie discretione tractetur qualiter exortum negocium legibus inseratur,' et 'sola uero potestas regia erit in omnibus libera, qualemcunque iusserit in placitis inserere penam' (quoting Liber iudiciorum, II.1.13–14, II.5.8 [pp. 60–61, 109]). For Romanist inspiration, see above, p. 279.

cartulary of the counts of Barcelona, now known as the *Liber feudorum maior (LFM)*.[33] Initially compiled under the direction of Ramon de Caldes between 1178 and 1194, it originally contained transcriptions of 902 documents, principally from the eleventh and twelfth centuries. The documents were organized in geographical units and geographical or lineage-based subunits, and within those, in chronological order. The significance of the *LFM* transcends Alfons's reign, and not only because it preserves many of the comital *convenientiae* and oaths discussed in this study. Considered as a whole, it tells as much about the conceptions and organization of power in the late twelfth century as the documents that it contains do for earlier years. It also offers another example of the complex relationship between power and the written word.

Cartularies – organized collections of documents prepared by the individual or institution that possessed the documents – are not simply empty conduits for the documents they contain; they are historical artifacts in themselves. Study of the organization and production of a cartulary can offer evidence for its intended functions.[34] For the *LFM*, such clues are offered by the blank folios, which made up approximately half of the original work. Although they were used both for earlier documents not found during the initial organization of the work and for new documents deemed worthy of inclusion, they were principally intended for the latter use. The compilers left enough room for another 1,000 documents, and Ramon de Caldes was certainly aware of the scope, if not the exact number, of documents available. Thus the cartulary was not a finished work: the volumes were meant not only to provide a record of the past, but also to keep that record up to date. That the cartulary was quickly superseded as a record by a system of registers does not diminish the significance of that fact.

Ramon de Caldes, in his dedicatory preface, explained that the documents in the *LFM* were meant to fortify the position of the count-king in future legal disputes; the *Liber domini regis*, as he called it, was thus an

---

[33] ACA, Cancelleria reial, Registres 1. For a fuller development of the following theme, see Adam J. Kosto, "The *Liber feudorum maior* of the Counts of Barcelona: The Cartulary as an Expression of Power," *Journal of Medieval History* (forthcoming). Earlier treatments include: Anscari M. Mundó, "El pacte de Cazola del 1179 i el 'Liber feudorum maior': Notes paleogràfiques i diplomàtiques," in *Jaime I y su época: Comunicaciones*, 2 vols., X Congrés d'història de la Corona d'Aragó, Zaragoza, 1979 (Zaragoza, 1980–82), 1:119–29; Josep Maria Salrach, "El 'Liber feudorum maior' i els comptes fiscals de Ramon de Caldes," in *Documents jurídics*, 96–110; McCrank, "Documenting Reconquest and Reform," 281–90, 303–18; and below n. 39.

[34] Olivier Guyotjeannin, Laurent Morelle, and Michel Parisse, eds., *Les cartulaires: Actes de la table ronde organisée par l'École nationale des chartes et le G.D.R. 121 du C.N.R.S. (Paris, 5–7 décembre 1991)*, Mémoires et documents de l'École des chartes 39 (Paris, 1993); Patrick J. Geary, *Phantoms of Remembrance: Memory and Oblivion at the End of the First Millennium* (Princeton, 1994), 81–114.

administrative instrument of royal authority.[35] But the *LFM* was more than a simple instrument of power. If the individual conventions and oaths defined the powers of the count-king with respect to particular persons and castles, when considered as a whole, the *LFM*, like the *Usatges*, expresses a more abstract idea: traditional documents are put in the service of the new territorial conception of power.[36] The *LFM* is principally a Catalan document. The Aragonese charters that begin the cartulary are few in number (*LFM* 1–35), as are the records from trans-Pyrenean regions that fill the end of the cartulary (*LFM* 808–902); these latter regions had, moreover, been linked to the county of Barcelona since at least the reign of Ramon Berenguer III. The core of the *LFM* comprises sections relating to the central territories: Pallars Jussà first, the most recently acquired, followed by Urgell, Barcelona (including Osona and Girona), Besalú, Empúries, Cerdanya, and Rosselló. Not all of these had been formally annexed – Urgell and Empúries held out into the fourteenth century – though in a way that was precisely the point. The count-king was no longer first among equals; he was now claiming "pan-comital" authority.[37] As a retrospective record, however, the *LFM* was an awkward vehicle for expressing a new conception of authority. The court was slow to develop a language appropriate to the new situation, and the *LFM* offers evidence for this tension between old and new, mixing territorial and geographical references with references to lineage. The identification of sections by individual – for example, "Here begin the charters of Ramon de Papiol"[38] – reveals an older mindset that viewed comital power not in terms of territory, but in terms of relationships with lineages, defined in no small part by *convenientiae*.

The illuminations of the cartulary contribute a visual element to the expression of comital power while revealing these same ambiguities in its conception.[39] The surviving folios of the cartulary preserve seventy-nine

---

[35] *LFM* prologue: "ut, his instrumentis ad memoriam revocatis, unusquisque ius suum sortiatur, tum propter eternam magnarum rerum memoriam, ne inter vos et homines vestros, forte oblivionis occasione, aliqua questio vel discordia posset oriri." The preface is entitled "Prologus in libro domini regis"; a similar phrase – *libri (computorum) domini regis* – was employed in reference to contemporary fiscal registers (*FA*, 1:100–101, 118; Thomas N. Bisson, "Ramon de Caldes [*c.* 1135–1199]: Dean of Barcelona and King's Minister," in *Medieval France*, 196). Transcriptions dated 1233 and 1272 refer to the *LFM* as the *Registrum domini regis* (ADG, Mitra, 23/80.1★; RBIV 189.2a★). These designations stress the regalian nature of these records.

[36] "Feudal principles, applied to serve administrative . . . needs, remained subordinated to a conception of territorial sovereignty" (Bisson, "Feudalism," 163).

[37] Bisson, "The Rise of Catalonia," 152.

[38] *LFM* 349 (rubric): "Incipiunt cartae Raimundi de Papiol."

[39] M. Eugenia Ibarburu, "Los cartularios reales del Archivo de la Corona de Aragón," *Lambard: Estudis d'art medieval* 6 (1991–93), 197–210; Pedro Bohigas, *La ilustración y la decoración del libro manuscrito en Cataluña: Contribución al estudio de la historia de la miniatura catalana*, vol. 1, *Período románico* (Barcelona, 1960), 101–9.

illuminations in various stages of completion, datable to 1200x1220; although this is after the completion of the textual portion of the cartulary, it seems likely that the program of illustrations was determined at the time of the initial compilation. Many depict the ritual of homage, among the earliest such scenes in Europe.[40] Several appear in the cartulary next to charters describing promises of fidelity, grants of fiefs in return for fidelity, grants of fief *per manum*, and – in documents from the reign of Alfons I – homage (*hominium*).[41] These images reinforce visually the message of personal subordination inherent in the act of homage. The fact that all of the images do not depict homage to Alfons I does not dilute the cartulary's message of his power over individuals, for the constant repetition of the scene allows the abstraction of the idea of subordination from association with any particular lord; all lords represent in some sense the count-king.

The artistic program, however, like the organization of the cartulary, reflects more than one conception of comital and royal power. The standard image of the king in early illuminated cartularies is the isolated ruler, holding symbols of power, sitting on a throne.[42] The *LFM* contains some of these formal images, but the two principal illuminations of the *LFM* offer a contrast.[43] In the first, Ramon de Caldes sits just to the right of center, reading a document to the king, who is surrounded by his courtiers; a seated scribe works at a desk on the right. The image departs from the hierarchical composition common in other illuminated cartularies and in the scenes of homage in the *LFM* itself. It depicts the king not as superior, but as governor. The focal point of the composition is not the king, nor is it Ramon de Caldes, but it is the document that the administrator is holding and toward which both he and the king gesture. In the second image, a circular composition, the king and queen, gesturing toward one another, are surrounded by seven pairs of figures engaged in conversation, emerging from the border and arrayed radially above the

---

[40] *LFM*, plates 1:4, 7, 9, 11, 13, 15, 16, 17, 2:3, 4, 8, 10, 13, 14. See Jacques Le Goff, "The Symbolic Ritual of Vassalage," in Le Goff, *Time, Work, & Culture in the Middle Ages*, trans. Arthur Goldhammer (Chicago, 1980), 237–87; François Garnier, *Le langage de l'image au Moyen Âge*, 2 vols. (Paris, 1982–89), 1:208. On nave capital 30 of Notre-Dame de Vézelay (cit. Garnier, fig. 18), Isaac is shown feeling the hands of Jacob, covered with goatskin (Gen. 27.16, 22–23); Jacob's hands are held together between Isaac's hands. The cartulary of Tivoli, composed perhaps two decades before the *LFM*, contains an image of an oath of fidelity by a group of inhabitants of the town to the bishop; all members of the group are standing, while the bishop sits, but the front juror has his hands placed between those of the bishop (Luigi Bruzza, ed., *Regesto della chiesa di Tivoli*, Studi e documenti di storia e diritto [Rome, 1880], 6 and plate 4). Thomas Bisson initially brought this image to my attention.

[41] *LFM*, plates 1:4, 9, 11, 15, 17, 2:3, 8, 10 (docs. 19, 90, 106, 119, 403, 498, 630, 793).

[42] E.g., Fernando Galván Freile, *La decoración miniada en el Libro de las estampas de la catedral de León* (León, 1997), 62–70. Ezek. 1:26; Dan. 7:9; Rev. 4:2–11; etc. See Galienne Francastel, *Le droit au trône: Un problème de prééminence dans l'art chrétien d'Occident du IVe au XIIe siècle*, Collection le signe de l'art 9 (Paris, 1973).   [43] *LFM*, plates 1:1, 2:15.

central figures. The scene has been identified by some as Alfons I and Sancha of Castile presiding over their court, as they were prominent patrons of troubadour culture. This court scene finds echoes in other illuminated cartularies, but in scenes where attendants gesture toward the central figures. The gestures of this king and queen match those of the courtiers; they are as much members of the court as they are its focus. In content as well as composition, this image, too, rejects hierarchy.

While the attention devoted to contemporary Catalan cartularies marks them as more than simple copy-books, only the *Liber feudorum Cerritaniae* approaches the *LFM*.[44] The care taken to make the work a lavish production, its organization, and its artistic program allow the cartulary to transcend its administrative functions by expressing various conceptions of comital and royal power: the prince as territorial sovereign, as lord, as member of the court, or as administrator. That the precise message is not consistent is not overly troubling, for the same mixed messages are apparent in the *Usatges de Barcelona*. Text and image combine to communicate more than the mere content of the documents. Like the *Usatges* of the reign of Ramon Berenguer IV, the *LFM* should be seen as not only as a record or instrument of the count-king's power, but also as its expression. And as with the *convenientia* itself for Ramon Berenguer I and the new documentary forms developed under Alfons I, the means of this expression was the written word.

THE END OF THE *CONVENIENTIA*

The compilation of the *LFM* signaled the decline of the *convenientia*, which had been transformed at the Barcelonese court over the course of the twelfth century, and especially after 1150. The lay aristocracy continued to use *convenientiae* consistently into the 1170s, but the numbers of these documents decrease slowly thereafter. Ecclesiastical scribal practice was perhaps the most conservative, although even in episcopal and monastic documentation a turn away from the *convenientia* is noticeable in the last decades of the century. But decline did not mean disappearance. Examples of the *convenientia*, even in its classical form, can be found from 1196, the year of the death of Alfons I, and after.

The chancery of Pere I continued to use the formula "hec est convenientia" on occasion, as in a treaty between the count-king and Ermengol VIII of Urgell in 1200.[45] His scribes referred to several other agreements as *convenientiae* without using this formula.[46] Survivals may be cited from

---

[44] ACA, Cancelleria reial, Registres 4. See also above, n. 39. [45] OM 11:1903*.
[46] PEI 188* (a. 1204: "supradictam convenienciam attendamus"), 298* (a. 1208: "hanc convenientiam et compositionem").

outside the court, as well. In 1206, Pere de Claramunt commended by means of a *convenientia* a fortification to Guillem de Montbui in return for a promise of aid and fidelity.[47] In 1218, Bernat, prior of Santa Maria de Mur, and Ramon de *Tongui* concluded a *convenientia*, as did Guillem, provost of Santa Maria de l'Estany, and Bernat de Castellcir in 1228.[48]

Renewals of earlier documents encouraged the persistence of the form. When an episcopal scribe drew up a *convenientia* between Pere de Sirac, bishop of Barcelona, and Guerau de Palamós in 1211 concerning the castle of Montmell, he could look back on a series of *convenientiae* related to that castle.[49] Similarly, the *convenientia* by which Guillem de Tavertet, bishop of Vic, commended the castle of Artés to Guillem de Guàrdia in 1199 had clear precedents.[50] This latter document survives in transcriptions of 1227 and 1281, highlighting the fact that the constant recopying of documents also served to keep the form in circulation. The existence and use of cartularies, many compiled in precisely these years when the *convenientia* was dying out, would have had a similar effect.

Even when the form itself was not used, however, documents referred back to earlier *convenientiae*, perpetuating the use of the term for certain types of agreements. Thus the agreement in 1210 between Elvira de Lara and Pere I concerning the proposed marriage of their respective children Aurembiaix and Pere (the future Jaume I) included a clause preserving the validity of the *convenientiae* agreed between Ermengol VIII and Guillem, viscount of Cardona (Osona), a few years earlier.[51] In 1226, Roger Bernard, count of Foix and viscount of Castellbò (Alt Urgell), and his wife Ermessenda swore to Pere, bishop of Urgell, that they would observe the *convenientiae* agreed between Bernat de Vilamur, bishop of Urgell (1199–1203), and Arnau, viscount of Castellbò (Alt Urgell) (1185–1226), which agreements they had studied and fully understood.[52] In 1248, Ramon de Vernet claimed rights in the castle of Santa Oliva from the monastery of Sant Cugat del Vallès on the basis of a *convenientia* between Pere de Santa Oliva, and Pere and Bernat de Banyeres on 8 January 1174.[53]

The diffusion of the *Usatges* in the late twelfth and thirteenth centuries also played a role in maintaining the *convenientia* in scribal consciousness.[54] As noted above, the term *convenientia* appears only once in the text

[47] *Òdena* 59.
[48] BC, MS 150, no. 151 (fols. 109v–110r); MEV, MS 283, no. 127.3 (fol. 72r–v).
[49] LA 4:416*. See above, pp. 247–48.   [50] AME 10/6. Cf. AME 10/2; ACB 1–5–445.
[51] PEI 378*. See Aurell, *Les noces du comte*, 357–58.
[52] Joaquim Miret i Sans, *Investigación histórica sobre el vizcondado de Castellbó* (Barcelona, 1900), app. 18 (pp. 380–82): "in instrumentis super conuenienciis iamdictis confectis que quidem instrumenta sunt a nobis uisa deliberacione magna ad hibita et plenius intellecta."
[53] *CSCV* 1387. I have not been able to locate the earlier document.   [54] Above, n. 31.

of the code, in reference to an association of knights; an agreement between lord and man is referred to in the text as a *conventio*, which in the earliest Catalan version is rendered *covinença*. This is a slim foundation for linguistic influence, but the detailed description in the *Usatges* of the institutional framework in which the *convenientia* flourished certainly helped to perpetuate an awareness of it. The same may be said of the influential explication of these institutions in the *Commemoracions* of Pere Albert.[55] Ironically, the code, which as argued above had only limited impact for much of the twelfth century, enjoyed greater success after the *convenientia* began to decline. On the one hand, the code as a whole or individual *usatges* were imposed on municipalities and territories acquired by the count-kings. On the other, from Alfons I's first attempts to create an administrative peace at Fondarella in 1173, the *Usatges* became a focal point of the conflicts between the count-kings and the barons, developing quickly into a Catalonian national law. This status was confirmed by decrees of Jaume I in 1243, 1251, and 1276 establishing the *Usatges* as the all-but-exclusive norm for the functioning of comital-royal courts.

Despite these elements of continuity, the Catalan social order began in the late twelfth century to move away from the organization in which the *convenientia* had played a prominent role.[56] Networks of individual agreements were replaced by different types of power structures. Towns grew not only in size, but in political importance. The small, powerful patrician group that arose in Barcelona between 1140 and 1220 had a significant impact on comital policy.[57] The townsmen of Vic failed to establish a consular organization in the 1180s, but Pere I granted this right freely in the next decade.[58] Towns sent representatives to assemblies from the beginning of the reign of Jaume I. The efforts of Alfons I to establish a territorial government for Catalonia, beginning with the Peace of Fondarella in 1173, sparked a series of constitutional developments that would lead to the formation of the Corts in the course of the thirteenth century. Already in 1188–92, a baronial opposition had developed to protest these changes; the barons managed then to disrupt partially Alfons's program, but their success was only temporary. These changes

---

[55] Josep Rovira i Ermengol, ed., *Usatges de Barcelona i Commemoracions de Pere Albert*, Els nostres clàssics, Col·lecció A, 43–44 (Barcelona, 1933), Commemoracions, 6, 14 (pp. 145, 152–54): "les covinences," "covinença." See Tomas de Montagut Estragués, "La recepción del derecho feudal común en Cataluña (Notas para su estudio)," in Manuel Sánchez Martínez, ed., *Estudios sobre renta, fiscalidad y finanzas en la Cataluña bajomedieval*, Anuario de estudios medievales, Anejo 27 (Barcelona, 1993), 160.

[56] See, generally, Bisson, *Medieval Crown*, 40–56, 72–82.

[57] Bensch, *Barcelona*, esp. 170–233.

[58] Paul H. Freedman, "An Unsuccessful Attempt at Urban Organization in Twelfth-Century Catalonia," *Speculum* 54 (1979), 479–91; see also Philip Daileader, "The Vanishing Consulates of Catalonia," *Speculum* 74 (1999), 65–94.

institutionalized power in ways fundamentally different from the eleventh- and twelfth-century norms. The history of the thirteenth century is best studied not by an examination of networks of individual agreements, but of the activity of various interests: municipal, mercantile, royal, baronial, and clerical.

These large-scale trends made the *convenientia* obsolete, but it is possible to point to more specific causes of its decline. The most significant development was the renewal of Roman legal traditions prompted by the activities of the Italian schools.[59] It is impossible to assign a single date to the "reception" of the new Roman legal learning in Catalonia. While earlier documents echo texts and ideas of the *ius commune*, the *Usatges* themselves, in their compilation from *c.* 1150, are perhaps the first sign of significant influence, with their Romanist conception of princely power. Unquestionable references appear under Alfons I, in the 1170s, although many of the earliest are rejections of the new principles, rather than applications of them. A manuscript of the *Digest* was in the possession of the canons of the cathedral of Barcelona by 1188, as was the entire *Corpus* by the mid-1190s. Individual *usatges* datable to the reigns of Alfons I and Pere I draw on newly circulating Roman material, as do municipal custumals such as the one for Lleida of 1228. Despite popular and official objections to the new legal currents – seen, for example, in Jaume I's prohibitions – opponents of the trend were fighting a losing battle.

The key factor was not so much the new Roman legal currents themselves, but the rebirth of the public notariate and the Italianate practices that accompanied it. Under these influences, the language and formulae of documents underwent a transformation.[60] In the treaty of April 1176 between Alfons I and Raimond V of Toulouse, Alfons's scribe, Bernat de Caldes, called himself a *tabellio* and the document an *instrumentum*; this is

---

[59] Roman law itself, of course, never truly disappeared, making the language of "rediscovery" and "rebirth" somewhat misleading. Roman texts were transmitted in the *Codex Theodosianus* (a. 438) and its epitomes, notably the *Lex Romana Visigothorum* (a. 506); parts of the Justinianic *Corpus* were known in various versions; and Roman legal traditions influenced the legislation of the various successor kingdoms. See Jill Harries and Ian Wood, eds., *The Theodosian Code* (Ithaca, 1993); Ian Wood, "Roman Law in the Barbarian Kingdoms," in Alvar Ellegård and Gunilla Åkerström-Hougen, eds., *Rome and the North*, Studies in Mediterranean Archaeology and Literature 135 (Jonsered, 1996), 5–14; Wormald, *The Making of English Law*, 36–40, 56–58, 63–69, etc.; Clausdieter Schott, "Der Stand der Leges-Forschung," *Frühmittelalterliche Studien* 13 (1979), 43–46; Stephan Kuttner, "The Revival of Jurisprudence," in Robert L. Benson and Giles Constable, eds., *Renaissance and Renewal in the Twelfth Century* (Cambridge, Mass., 1982), 299–323. For what follows, see Pons i Guri, "Corpus iuris," esp. 118–21; Bisson, "Ramon de Caldes," 198 n. 70.

[60] José Bono, *Historia del derecho notarial español*, 1 vol. in 2 parts to date, Ars notariae hispanica 1 (Madrid, 1979–), 1.1:118–22, 292–329, 1.2:128–38; Félix Durán Cañameras, "Notas para la historia del notariado catalán," *Estudios históricos y documentos de los archivos de protocolos* 3 (1955), 73–87; Pons i Guri, "Corpus iuris," 118.

only the most striking evidence of a change, not the first.[61] The bishop of Vic had appointed a *scriptor publicus* for the town by 1155; in 1194, the canon Andreu was appointed *scriptor* of all of the charters of the town of Vic for life, and he subscribed as a *scriptor publicus* thereafter.[62] The *levita* Ermengol served as *publicus scriptor* of Girona perhaps as early as 1161, and certainly by 1179.[63] Alfons I established public notaries at Vilafranca del Penedès in 1188, Manresa in 1191, and Montblanc in 1194.[64] Pere I did the same for the monastery of Santa Maria de Santes Creus in 1211; Sant Cugat del Vallès could claim its own notary from 1218.[65] These notaries quickly imported a documentary typology, as well as new methods and principles for the conduct of transactions, in which the *convenientia* had no place.

The appearance and disappearance of the *convenientia* are linked to changes in the structures of Catalan society. Only during the eleventh and twelfth centuries, when these structures were defined primarily by networks of individual agreements, could the *convenientia* flourish. The content of these agreements varied, for social structures took many forms. This study has stressed networks of castle tenure; other research on this region has focused on marriage alliances and family structures.[66] In imperial lands, a different documentation reveals networks of high-level political groupings based on friendship treaties; elsewhere, gift giving cemented associative structures.[67] Parallel research on Catalonia might yield similar results. The particular contribution of Catalonia to

---

[61] *LFM* 899. This treaty was completed at Jarnègues, in Provence, an area that was well ahead of Catalonia in absorbing the new legal and notarial influences; Bernat de Caldes may have had some local assistance. See Jean-Pierre Poly, "Les légistes provençaux et la diffusion du droit romain dans le Midi," *Recueil de mémoires et travaux publié par la Société d'histoire des anciens pays de droit écrit* 9 (1974), 613–35; Marie-Louise Carlin, *La pénétration du droit romain dans les actes de la pratique provençale (XIᵉ–XIIIᵉ siècle)*, Bibliothèque d'histoire du droit et droit romain 11 (Paris, 1967), 41–49; Martin Aurell, "Le personnel politique catalan et aragonais d'Alphonse Iᵉʳ en Provence (1166–1196)," *AM* 93 (1981), 127–31.

[62] ACV 6/i/55 (a. 1194); Bono, *Historia*, 1.1:316 n. 53.

[63] CCM 306 (a. 1161); ADG, Pia Almoina, Fornells 16* (a. 1179).

[64] ALI 503* (a. 1188); Bono, *Historia*, 1.1:318, 1.2:129; Durán Cañameras, "Notas," 78–79.

[65] Antoni M. Aragó Cabañas, "L'escrivania pública de Santes Creus a l'època post-fundacional," in *I Col·loqui d'història del monaquisme català: Santes Creus, 1966*, 2 vols., Publicacions de l'Arxiu bibliogràfic de Santes Creus 24–25 (Santes Creus, 1967–69), 2:15–25; *CSCV* 1290 (a. 1218).

[66] Aurell, *Les noces du comte*; Ruiz-Domènec, *L'estructura feudal*.

[67] Gerd Althoff, *Verwandte, Freunde und Getreue: Zum politischen Stellenwert der Gruppenbindungen im früheren Mittelalter* (Darmstadt, 1990); Barbara H. Rosenwein, *Negotiating Space: Power, Restraint, and Privileges of Immunity in Early Medieval Europe* (Ithaca, 1999), 146–50. For earlier periods see Wolfgang Fritze, "Die fränkische Schwurfreundschaft der Merowingerzeit: Ihr Wesen und ihre politische Funktion," *Zeitschrift der Savigny-Stiftung für Rechtsgeschichte*, Germanistische Abteilung, 71 (1954), 74–125; Reinhard Schneider, *Brüdergemeine und Schwurfreundschaft: Der Auflösungsprozeß des Karlingerreiches im Spiegel der caritas-Terminologie in den Verträgen der karlingischen Teilkönige des 9. Jahrhunderts*, Historische Studien 388 (Lübeck, 1964).

this type of analysis of medieval societies is to highlight the role of the written word in the formation of such structures. The strength of the written tradition in Catalonia made this possible.

Possibility is not the same as necessity, however, and the question remains of why the participants in these agreements put them in a written form. *Convenientiae* might serve as proof in the course of a later dispute, but proof could cut both ways: the loss of a written record of an agreement could lead to its dissolution. Ramon Berenguer III learned this lesson when he had to absolve the guardians of the castle of Arraona from their oath and homage to him because he was unable to find the relevant *scripturae*.[68] If such *scripturae* had never existed, it might have been easier for the count to prevail. The reasons for the rise of these agreements in a *written* form are neither simple nor self-evident.

Appeals to a shift from oral to written culture cannot work in this context.[69] The 5,000 tenth-century documents that have survived in the archives are the surest indication that this was a society profoundly familiar with the written word. This familiarity was required by the Visigothic legal culture that still dominated the society. References to documents appear throughout the *Liber iudiciorum*, in titles concerning judicial procedures, testamentary practice, and transactions of many types. Book II, Title 5 (*De scripturis valituris et infirmandis ac defunctorum voluntatibus conscribendis*) and various titles of Book V (*De transactionibus*) were constantly cited in Catalan documents of practice.[70] Changes in legal culture in the late tenth and early eleventh centuries may have led to a temporary loss of respect for written proof in the context of the old legal procedures followed in the comital courts, but they did little to alter the status of the written word in the society as a whole. The scribe of a charter of sale of 1064 who wrote "The law orders that documents should be present in all matters" may have been blindly applying an ancient formula, but it was nonetheless true.[71]

Another attempt to describe a transformation in literacy in the eleventh century argues for a new *interaction* of the oral and the written: "oral discourse effectively began to function within a universe of communications governed by texts."[72] This argument, too, rests on the

---

[68] Above, pp. 148, 243.

[69] Despite the success and influence of Clanchy, *From Memory*, this work does not give enough weight to early medieval developments. See above, pp. 275–76, 280.

[70] See works cited above, p. 34.

[71] ACV 6/284: "Quia lex precipit ut in omnibus causis scripturę intercurrant." Cf. Bonnassie, *La Catalogne*, 1:22 n. 19, citing ACV 6/285; Michel Zimmermann, "Protocoles et préambules dans les documents catalans du Xᵉ au XIIᵉ siècle: Évolution diplomatique et signification spirituelle," *Mélanges de la Casa de Velázquez* 11 (1975), 52.

[72] Brian Stock, *The Implications of Literacy: Written Language and Models of Interpretation in the Eleventh and Twelfth Centuries* (Princeton, 1983), 3.

notion of a fundamentally oral tenth century, a description that does not apply to Catalonia, or elsewhere, for that matter. *Convenientiae* and associated documents do provide evidence for an interdependence of oral and written modes. An oath formula from the reign of Ramon Berenguer III, almost entirely in Latin and with a space left for the name of the juror, attests to the fact the that the oath quickly became as much a written as an oral act.[73] But this model of interaction of oral and written modes does little to explain the rapid proliferation of written agreements of all types in this period. Nor can their appearance be explained by a growth in "legal illiteracy." This model has been applied to the rise of new types of instruments in the fourth and fifth centuries, instruments that were unnecessary in the classical Roman law: "where the law was no longer understood, it had to be spelled out, illustrated, and explained."[74] Changes in the legal order in late-tenth- and early-eleventh-century Catalonia did not result from a loss of legal learning. The Barcelonese judges Orús, Ervigi Marc, Ponç Bonfill Marc, and Bonhom stand out among an increasingly professional corps of judges in the first half of the eleventh century, the last named as the compiler of the *Liber iudicum popularis*.[75] Ramon d'Abadal credited the judge Guifré with the creation of the episcopal castle-holding scheme at Vic in the 1020s, enshrined in new types of documents that foreshadowed the *convenientia*.[76] Changes in the judicial corps followed and were the result of, rather than a cause of, the decline of the comital *placitum*.[77] The new form of the *convenientia* developed because of the inadequacy of the old forms to meet the needs of a society undergoing structural transformations, not because people lost their ability to understand these old forms.

The problem with these models, all developed in non-Iberian contexts, is that they devalue or simply ignore the abundant early medieval evidence for the various uses of the technology of writing. The eleventh and twelfth centuries appear newly "literate" because ninth- and tenth-century societies are depicted as fundamentally oral. This is, in a way,

---

[73] RBIII extra. 2401*; above, p. 257.

[74] Stock, *The Implications of Literacy*, 42–49, quotation at 44.

[75] Bonnassie, *La Catalogne*, 1:187–92; Ferran Valls i Taberner, "El *Liber iudicum popularis* de Homobonus de Barcelona," *Anuario de historia del derecho español* 2 (1925), 200–212; Bowman, "Law," 100–117. See now for comparative purposes: François Bougard, *La justice dans le royaume d'Italie de la fin du VIIIe siècle au début du XIe siècle*, Bibliothèque des Écoles françaises d'Athènes et de Rome 291 (Rome, 1995); Davies and Fouracre, eds., *The Settlement of Disputes*; *La giustizia nell'alto medioevo (secoli V–VIII)*, 2 vols., Settimane di studio del Centro italiano di studi sull'alto medioevo 42 (Spoleto, 1995); *La giustizia nell'alto medioevo (secoli IX–XI)*, 2 vols., Settimane di studio del Centro italiano di studi sull'alto medioevo 44 (Spoleto, 1997).

[76] Above, p. 186.

[77] The evolution is traced in Nathaniel L. Taylor, "Judges in Barcelona in the Twelfth Century: The Decline of the Post-Visigothic Judiciary" (paper presented at the 114th annual meeting of the American Historical Association, Chicago, 8 January 2000).

parallel to the broader problem of the nature of the changes in medieval societies around the year 1000. The tenth century is poorly documented and even less well understood in many regions, making it easy to construct perfectly plausible characterizations of the period, which in turn are used to highlight the changes in or novelty of the eleventh century. As research into the early medieval period progresses, our understanding of the eleventh and twelfth centuries can only improve.[78] This study has attempted to say something about that broader transformation. *Convenientiae* reveal novel, flexible structures of socioeconomic and political power. But what precisely was new about them? With respect to castle tenure, for example, it was argued above that the novelty of the relationships centered on comital castles is unclear because of the opacity of the late-tenth-century evidence. What is new, however, in this case and in others, is the particular role of the written word in these relationships. Agreements were certainly not new; the *convenientia* certainly was. But the use of the written word in structuring power was not new either. Ninth- and tenth-century Catalonia, like many other early medieval European societies, knew the sophisticated use of written records in law and administration – and consequently in the formation and use of power. Thus what is new about a phenomenon such as the spread of the *convenientia* cannot simply be the use of the written word for these purposes. Here the Catalan case offers a model for a reevaluation of developments elsewhere in Europe. Research into the "uses of literacy" in the early medieval period has advanced beyond the simple question of whether or not the technology of writing was present in certain contexts to *how* it functioned.[79] The student of such issues in the eleventh and twelfth centuries risks being blinded by the false glare of apparent novelty. The fuller understanding now available of the early medieval evidence opens the eleventh and twelfth centuries for reevaluation in the absence of that glare. What emerges is not the revolution described by Michael Clanchy and Brian Stock, but something more subtle and potentially more important.

The rise of the written agreement in eleventh-century Catalonia is

---

[78] Particularly valuable in this respect are, e.g.: Matthew Innes, *State and Society in the Early Middle Ages: The Middle Rhine Valley, 400–1000*, CSMLT, 4th ser., 47 (Cambridge, 2000); Jane Martindale, "'His Special Friend'? The Settlement of Disputes and Political Power in the Kingdom of the French (Tenth to Mid-Twelfth Century)," *Transactions of the Royal Historical Society*, 6th ser., 5 (1995), 21–57, esp. 21–32; Gerd Althoff, *Amicitiae und pacta: Bündnis, Einung, Politik und Gebetsgedenken im beginnenden 10. Jahrhundert*, MGH Schriften 37 (Hanover, 1992).

[79] McKitterick, *The Carolingians*; McKitterick, ed., *The Uses of Literacy*; Julia M. H. Smith, "Oral and Written: Saints, Miracles, and Relics in Brittany, *c.* 850–1250," *Speculum* 65 (1990), 309–43; Matthew Innes, "Memory, Orality and Literacy in an Early Medieval Society," *Past & Present* 158 (1998), 3–36.

linked to changes in the role of the written word; to understand this the *convenientia* must be viewed not simply as a new form, but in its wider context. Ourliac suggested that an essential element of the *convenientia* was "the insertion into the contract of an uncertain limit, that is to say a time-factor ('facteur temps')."[80] This factor was not only essential, it was novel. The documentary types most common in Catalonia before the year 1000 – charters of sale, donation, and exchange – were records of complete transactions, as were most of the records of judgment. Testaments often contained conditions, but these were usually tied to specific acts or events: burial in a certain location, purchase of a liturgical item, the remarriage of a widow, the return of a relative from captivity.[81] Pledges were conditional agreements, too, but these had definite limits; when the agreed term was reached, the pledge was redeemed or forfeited, and the document became a dead letter. The *convenientia*, however, imposed no limits. It described relationships that were meant to persist in time. It was a guide for the future rather than a record of the past. It was precisely because of this prospective character that the *convenientia* was able to create lasting structures.

There are other indications that in eleventh- and twelfth-century Catalonia, people began to identify newly prospective functions for the written word, functions that went beyond recording completed or limited transactions. The earliest examples of agrarian contracts in Catalonia date to the mid-tenth century, but they become common only in the course of the eleventh. Clauses in these agreements that limited the transactions to one or two lifetimes gave way to language that implied perpetuity.[82] The short-term pledge developed into an agreement for the extended exploitation of lands; the earliest such "open-ended pledge" for Barcelona dates from 1080.[83] Parties entered into speculative agreements, granting or deciding the terms of tenure for lands not yet acquired. The "first" *convenientia* of *c.* 1021 includes two such clauses: Ermengol II's provision of sureties until he was in a position to grant to Berenguer Ramon I certain castles, and Berenguer's promise to grant to Ermengol certain lands once he had control of the county of Girona. This foreshadowed the prospective divisions of the Iberian Peninsula made by various leaders of the *Reconquista*.[84] Records that in the tenth and early eleventh centuries contained simple inventories of lands (*breves*) evolved into lists of

---

[80] Ourliac, "La *convenientia*," 248. Stephen Weinberger, "Precarial Grants: Approaches of the Clergy and Lay Aristocracy to Landholding and Time," *Journal of Medieval History* 11 (1985), 163–69, raises the issue of time in a different way.

[81] *STCA*, pp. 128–30; Nathaniel L. Taylor, "The Will and Society in Medieval Catalonia and Languedoc, 800–1200" (Ph.D. diss., Harvard University, 1995), e.g., 248–56.

[82] See above, p. 108.   [83] Bensch, *Barcelona*, 113–14.

[84] BRI extra. 2001*. See also *Alfonso II* 104, 255; and above, pp. 98–99.

fixed annual rents, and then into more complex summaries of the inter-relationship between lands held and a wider range of obligations due (*cap-breus*).[85] The transformation is reflected strikingly on a single piece of parchment from the church of Sant Pere de Vilamajor. One side, com-posed around 950, consists of a simple list of donations of property to the church at the time of its consecration, drawn up fifteen to twenty years after the fact, perhaps to replace a lost act of dedication. On the other side, datable to *c.* 1060, is a list of rents due to the church from the holders of those properties.[86] This change reveals both a new interest in Catalonia in fiscal management and a documentary development from simple record to tool of administration.

The shift in literacy was not one from memory to written record, but from memory to imagination, from the use of writing to reconstruct the past to the use of writing to construct the future. Was this part of a rethinking of time itself? A reassessment following the destruction of Barcelona in 985, or even the relatively uneventful passing of the millen-nium(s)?[87] The answer will be found with closer study of the full range of charter evidence from this region. But the acceptance of new uses of the written word clearly allowed for a functional change in the documen-tation just when transformations in Catalan society promoted the impor-tance of individual agreements. These changes explain the appearance of the *convenientia* in Catalonia in the eleventh century. It permitted and indeed facilitated the creation of structures for Catalan society, structures meant to last, in the words of the oath, *de ista ora in antea*.

---

[85] Pere Benito i Monclús, "'Hoc est breve . . .': L'emergència del costum i els orígens de la pràctica de capbrevació (segles XI–XIII)," in Sánchez Martínez, ed., *Estudios sobre renta,* 3–27. Robert F. Berkhofer, "Inventaires de biens et proto-comptabilités dans le nord de la France (XIᵉ–début du XIIᵉ siècle)," *Bibliothèque de l'École des chartes* 155 (1997), 339–49, traces a similar evolution in northern France. Both form part of a longer and more complicated European story: Robert Fossier, *Polyptyques et censiers,* Typologie des sources du Moyen Âge occidental 28 (Turnhout, 1978), 22–50; John Percival, "The Precursors of Domesday: Roman and Carolingian Land Registers," in Peter Sawyer, ed., *Domesday Book: A Reassessment* (London, 1985), 5–27; R. H. C. Davis, "Domesday Book: Continental Parallels," in J. C. Holt, ed., *Domesday Studies: Papers Read at the Novocentenary Conference of the Royal Historical Society and the Institute of British Geographers, Winchester, 1986* (Woodbridge, 1987), 15–39.

[86] Anscari M. Mundó, "Domains and Rights of Sant Pere de Vilamajor (Catalonia): A Polyptych of *c.* 950 and *c.* 1060," *Speculum* 49 (1974), 238–57. A very early list of rents associated with the act of dedication of the cathedral of Urgell in 839 has survived, but the next such documents date from the middle of the eleventh century. See Cebrià Baraut, ed., "Les actes de consagracions d'es-glésies del bisbat d'Urgell (segles IX–XII)," *Urgellia* 1 (1978), no. 3 (pp. 54–57); Benito i Monclús, "'Hoc est breve . . .'"; Bonnassie, *La Catalogne,* 2:243 n. 109.

[87] Michel Zimmermann, "La prise de Barcelone par Al-Mansûr et la naissance de l'historiographie catalane," *Annales de Bretagne et des pays de l'Ouest* 87 (1980), 191–218. Richard Landes offers a spirited rehabilitation of the relevance of the millennium in *Relics, Apocalypse, and the Deceits of History: Ademar of Chabannes, 989–1034,* Harvard Historical Studies 117 (Cambridge, Mass., 1995), esp. 285–327.

TABLE OF PUBLISHED DOCUMENTS

AAM (MONTSERRAT, ARXIU DE L'ABADIA DE MONTSERRAT)

SANT CUGAT DEL VALLÈS

32	*CSCV* 150
66	*CSCV* 438

ACA (BARCELONA, ARXIU DE LA CORONA D'ARAGÓ)

[#=document is a copy transcribed *from* the *LFM*]

Cancelleria reial, Registres 2, fols. 30v–31v (=ALI 224★)	*Alfonso II* 238

RBORRELL (RAMON BORRELL)

78	*NH* 15:2167
106	Sans i Travé, ed., *Barberà*, no. 2 (pp. 69–70)
119	*LFM* 141

BRI (BERENGUER RAMON I)

36	*LFM* 497
41	Benet, *Gurb-Queralt*, app. 6 (pp. 245–46)
41bis	Benet, *Gurb-Queralt*, app. 7 (pp. 246–47)
46	*LFM* 223
120	*LFM* 584
121	*LFM* 1
	Ubieto Arteta, "Estudios," app. 6 (p. 229)
extra. 2001	*LFM* 157
	Zimmermann, ed., *Les sociétés*, 175–86

RBI (RAMON BERENGUER I)

14	*LFM* 257
94	*LFM* 353
100	*LFM* 432
101	*LFM* 433
124	*LFM* 440
143	*LFM* 278
149	*LFM* 251
154	Constans i Serrats, ed., *Banyoles*, no. 72 (2:21–25)
162	*LFM* 398
168	*LFM* 124
171	*LFM* 126
173	*LFM* 125
174	Pladevall i Font, "Els senescals," no. 1 (p. 127)
182	Botet i Sisó, *Les monedes*, app. 4 (1:200)
191	*LFM* 60
193	*LFM* 489
206 [presently missing]	*LFM* 214
208	*LFM* 63
210	*NH* 15:2195
211	*NH* 15:2196
214	Pladevall i Font, "Els senescals," no. 2 (p. 128)
217	Coy y Cotonat, *Sort*, 227
218	*LFM* 171
219	*LFM* 324
228	Botet i Sisó, *Les monedes*, app. 5 (1:201)
230	*LFM* 148
239	*LFM* 296
	Carreras y Candi, "Lo Montjuích," app. 26 (pp. 419–21)
240	*LFM* 295
253.1	*LFM* 419
253.2	*LFM* 420
265	*NH* 15:2197
266	*LFM* 173
268	*LFM* 403
273.1 (=ADG, Mitra 23/80.1★)	*LFM* 472.1
273.2 (=ADG, Mitra 23/80.2★)	*LFM* 472.2
279	*LFM* 310
280	*LFM* 227
287	*LFM* 288
292	*LFM* 337
296	*LFM* 175
299	*LFM* 149
303	*LFM* 471

306	*LFM* 47
316	*LFM* 392
320	*LFM* 451
321.1	*LFM* 485
321.2	*LFM* 486
325	*LFM* 279
331	*LFM* 421
354	*LFM* 111
361	Botet i Sisó, *Les monedes*, app. 6 (1:201–2)
369	*LFM* 442
370	*LFM* 443
372	*LFM* 444
373	*LFM* 282
376	*LFM* 232
386	*LFM* 234
392.1	*LFM* 839
392.2a (=RBIII sd 2.1★)	*LFM* 843
392.2b (=RBIII sd 2.2★)	*LFM* 845
392.3	*LFM* 852
392.4	*LFM* 854
393	*LFM* 818
419	*LFM* 174
428	*LFM* 100
434	*FA* 139
443	*LFM* 364
445	*LFM* 275
448	*LFM* 265
449	Bonnassie, "Les conventions," no. 2 (pp. 547–50)
sd 2	*LFM* 147
sd 12	*LFM* 146
sd 14	Bonnassie, "Les conventions," no. 3 (p. 550)
sd 15	*LFM* 113
sd 16	*LFM* 88
sd 17	*LFM* 50
sd 19	*LFM* 48
sd 21	*LFM* 112
sd 22	*LFM* 80
sd 23	*LFM* 110
sd 25	*LFM* 106
sd 27	*LFM* 135
sd 28	*LFM* 133
sd 30 (=Extra. 4744.3)	*LFM* 586
sd 31	Constans i Serrats, ed., *Banyoles*, no. 77 (2:33–34)
sd 38	Carreras y Candi, "Lo Montjuích," app. 19 (pp. 403–13)
sd 39	*DOliba* 154

42.1	*LFM* 72
42.2	*LFM* 74
42.3	*LFM* 75
42.4	*LFM* 73
43.1 (=ACV 9/ii/74)	*LFM* 269
43.2	*LFM* 270
43.3	*LFM* 271
44	*LFM* 119
48	Bofarull, *Los condes*, 2:114–15
55	*LFM* 76
67	*LFM* 425
72	*LFM* 564
73	*LFM* 303
	Carreras y Candi, "Lo Montjuích," app. 30 (pp. 426–27)
77	*LFM* 562
78	*LFM* 565
79	*LFM* 655
83	*LFM* 582

BRII (BERENGUER RAMON II)

17	*LFM* 66
25	*LFM* 98
33	*LFM* 498
	NH 15:2203
34	Benet, *Gurb-Queralt*, app. 16 (pp. 258–59)
35	Benet, *Gurb-Queralt*, app. 17 (p. 259)
42	*NH* 15:2205
43	*LFM* 104
52	*LFM* 566
54	*LFM* 62, 67
59	Benet, *Gurb-Queralt*, app. 18 (pp. 260–61)
61	*LFM* 302
62	*LFM* 385
67	*LFM* 71
70	*LFM* 502
	NH 15:2207
73	*LFM* 219, 552

RBIII (RAMON BERENGUER III)

26 (=Extra. 3293)	*LFM* 51
27	*LFM* 49
46	Benet, *Gurb-Queralt*, app. 22 (pp. 266–67)
49	*LFM* 103
60.1	*LFM* 503
	NH 15:2213.1

sd 17	*LFM* 541
sd 18	*LFM* 304
sd 20	*LFM* 406
sd 21	*LFM* 292
sd 22	*LFM* 350
sd 23	*LFM* 560
sd 24	*LFM* 460
sd 25	*LFM* 461
sd 27	*LFM* 569
sd 33	*LFM* 567
sd 35	*LFM* 538
sd 36	*LFM* 685
sd 37	*LFM* 559
sd 40	*LFM* 91
sd 44	*LFM* 37
extra. 2401 [presently missing]	Trenchs Òdena, "La escribanía," 36
	trans. Kagay, trans., *Usatges*, 120
extra. 3601.1	*LFM* 90#

RBIV (RAMON BERENGUER IV)

15	*DI* 4:3
	LFM 529
19	*DI* 4:4
	Constans i Serrats, ed., *Banyoles*, no. 138
	(2:133–34)
20	*DI* 4:5
40	*DI* 4:7
	LFM 549
41	*DI* 4:8.1
	LFM 570
41.2dup (=ALI extra. 2615★)	*DI* 4:8.2
50	*DI* 4:16
	LFM 305
62	*DI* 4:17
	LFM 459
63	*DI* 4:18
	LFM 307
64	*DI* 4:19
	LFM 457
65	*DI* 4:15
	LFM 458
66	*DI* 4:20
73	*DI* 4:22 (cf. [Germain, ed.,] *Liber instrumentorum*,
	no. 152 [pp. 284–85])
76	*DI* 4:25
80.1	*DI* 4:23.1
	LFM 526

Table of published documents

PEI (PERE I)

43	*LFM* 226
66	*LFM* 416
188	*DI* 8:35
298	*DI* 8:38
378	Valls i Taberner, "Els orígens," 66–68

EXTRA. (EXTRAINVENTARI)

3252	*LFM* 108
3293	*see* RBIII 26★
3300	Miret i Sans, ed., "Pro sermone plebeico," 106–107
3449	Garí, "Castellvell," app. 30 (pp. 546–47)
4744.3	*see* RBI sd 30★

OM (ORDES MILITARS)

11:1903	Miret i Sans, *Castellbó*, app. 17 (pp. 378–80)

OR (ORDES RELIGIOSOS)

Sant Cugat del Vallès 83	*CSCV* 317
Sant Cugat del Vallès 86	*CSCV* 343
Sant Cugat del Vallès 92	*CSCV* 371
Sant Cugat del Vallès 122	*CSCV* 449
	CPF 11
Sant Cugat del Vallès 192	*CSCV* 544
	CPF 19
Sant Cugat del Vallès 194	*CSCV* 545
Sant Cugat del Vallès 232	*CSCV* 571
Sant Cugat del Vallès 314	*CSCV* 666
Sant Cugat del Vallès 315	*CSCV* 668
Sant Cugat del Vallès 340	*CSCV* 707
	CPF 37
Sant Cugat del Vallès 393	*CSCV* 665
Sant Cugat del Vallès 477	*CSCV* 926
Santa Cecília de Montserrat 54	Altés i Aguiló, ed., "Montserrat," no. 183 (37 [1995], 372–73)
Santa Cecília de Montserrat 59	Altés i Aguiló, ed., "Montserrat," no. 195 (37 [1995], 384–85)
Santa Maria de Montalegre 48a	Pérez i Gómez, ed., *Montalegre*, no. 51 (pp. 79–80)
Santa Maria de Montalegre 72	Pérez i Gómez, ed., *Montalegre*, no. 77 (pp. 108–9)
Santa Maria de Montalegre 75	Pérez i Gómez, ed., *Montalegre*, no. 80 (pp. 111–12)
Santa Maria de Montalegre 79	Pérez i Gómez, ed., *Montalegre*, no. 84 (pp. 117–18)

Table of published documents

Santa Maria de Montalegre 84	Pérez i Gómez, ed., *Montalegre*, no. 89 (p. 123)
Sant Llorenç del Munt 62	Schwab and Miret i Sans, eds., "Le plus ancien document," 231–33
	Puig i Ustrell, ed., *Sant Llorenç*, no. 138 (2:807–9)
Sant Llorenç del Munt 229	Puig i Ustrell, ed., *Sant Llorenç*, no. 491 (3:1310–11)
Sant Pere de Camprodon 38	reg. Sevillano Colom, *Inventario*, no. 38 (1:79)

ACB (BARCELONA, ARXIU CAPITULAR DE LA SANTA ESGLÉSIA CATEDRAL BASÍLICA DE BARCELONA)

1–1–2179	see LA 4:197*
1–2–134	Diago, *Historia*, fols. 92r–93r (lib. 2, c. 31)
1–2–1416	see LA 1:277*
1–2–1281	see LA 1:611*
1–5–463	see LA 4:274*
4–70–1 (=LA 4:380*)	reg. Baucells i Reig, *El Garraf*, Sitges, no. 4 (p. 45)
4–70–3 (=LA 4:334*)	reg. Baucells i Reig, *El Garraf*, Sitges, no. 10 (p. 47)
4–70–134 (=LA 4:381*)	reg. Baucells i Reig, *El Garraf*, Sitges, no. 6 (p. 46)
4–70–411 (=LA 4:377*)	reg. Baucells i Reig, *El Garraf*, Sitges, no. 2 (p. 45)
4–70–413a (=LA 4:371*)	reg. Baucells i Reig, *El Garraf*, Sitges, no. 1 (p. 44)
4–70–413b (=LA 4:372*)	reg. Baucells i Reig, *El Garraf*, Sitges, no. 1 (p. 44)

LA (LIBRI ANTIQUITATUM)

[Mas=reg. Mas, ed., *Rúbrica dels Libri antiquitatum*]

1:32	Mas 1929
	VL 17:52
	reg. J-L 11624
1:33	Mas 2007
	Fita, ed., "Areñs de Mar," 325–27
	reg. J-L 12720
1:38	Kehr, ed., *Papsturkunden*, no. 148 (pp. 442–43)
1:39	Mas 2730
	Kehr, ed., *Papsturkunden*, no. 149 (pp. 443–44)
1:40	Mas 2721
	Kehr, ed., *Papsturkunden*, no. 150 (pp. 444–45)
1:46	Mas 148
	DBarcelona 199
	Puig y Puig, *Episcopologio*, app. 26 (pp. 365–67)
1:105	Mas 2753
1:277 (=ACB 1–2–1416)	Mas 263
1:289	Mas 955

3:220	Mas 235
3:221	Mas 866
3:222	Mas 867
4:1 (cf. LA 4:6★)	Mas 2710
4:6 (cf. LA 4:1★)	Mas 2709
4:55	Mas 741
	Carreras y Candi, "Lo Montjuích," app. 23 (pp. 415–16)
4:58	Mas 534
4:150	Mas 149
	DBarcelona 265
	STCA 44
4:186	Mas 1259
4:188	Mas 2021
4:189	Mas 2696
	Els castells, 2:44 n. 25
4:192	Mas 1919
4:193	Mas 2130
4:194	Mas 2207
4:197 (=ACB 1–1–2179)	Mas 1161
4:271	Mas 1688
4:274 (=ACB 1–5–463)	Mas 1516
4:279	Mas 364
4:308	Mas 1329
4:328	Mas 671
4:329	Mas 458
4:332	Mas 2017
	Alfonso II 230
4:334 (=ACB 4–70–3★)	Mas 2134
4:355	Mas 240
	Puig y Puig, Episcopologio, app. 27 (pp. 367–68)
4:356	Mas 15
	DBarcelona 45
4:362	Mas 547
4:363	Mas 548
4:364	Mas 549
4:365	Mas 545
4:366	Mas 2275
4:367	Mas 515
	Carreras y Candi, "Lo Montjuích," app. 12 (pp. 393–94)
4:368	Mas 106
	CPF 10
	DBarcelona 205
	Zimmermann, ed., Les sociétés, pp. 198–201
	Carreras y Candi, "Lo Montjuích," app. 1 (pp. 367–68)

4:369	Mas 772
	Carreras y Candi, "Lo Montjuích," app. 29 (pp. 425–26)
4:370	Mas 754
4:371 (=ACB 4–70–413a★)	Mas 2664
	Carreras y Candi, "Lo Montjuích," app. 21 (pp. 413–14)
4:372 (=ACB 4–70–413b★)	Mas 531
	Carreras y Candi, "Lo Montjuích," app. 22 (pp. 414–15)
4:373	Mas 532
	Carreras y Candi, "Lo Montjuích," app. 20 (p. 413)
4:374	Mas 338
4:375	Mas 449
	Carreras y Candi, "Lo Montjuích," app. 9 (pp. 381–83)
4:376	Mas 817
4:377 (=ACB 4–70–411★)	Mas 530
	Carreras y Candi, "Lo Montjuích," app. 17 (pp. 399–400)
4:378	Mas 729
	Carreras y Candi, "Lo Montjuích," app. 24 (pp. 416–17)
	CPF 27
4:379	Mas 771
	Carreras y Candi, "Lo Montjuích," app. 28 (pp. 422–25)
4:380 (=ACB 4–70–1★)	Mas 1387
4:381 (=ACB 4–70–134★)	Mas 1569
4:382	Mas 2034
4:383	Mas 2135
4:384	Mas 1523
4:385	Mas 1570
4:386	Mas 1908
4:387	Mas 2660
	Kehr, ed., *Papsturkunden*, no. 2 (pp. 245–46)
	Carreras y Candi, "Lo Montjuích," app. 2 (pp. 369–70)
	Fita, ed., "Bula inédita," 248–49
4:391	Mas 2774
4:394	Mas 51
	CPF 7
	DBarcelona 108
4:398	Mas 1769
4:399	Mas 1781

ACG (GIRONA, ARXIU CAPITULAR DE GIRONA)

ACU (LA SEU D'URGELL, ARXIU CAPITULAR D'URGELL)

Table of published documents

[Marquès=reg. Marquès i Planagumà, *Pergamins*]
["La senyoria"=Marquès i Planagumà, ed., "La senyoria"]

Mitra, 2/206	Marquès 53
Mitra, 15/40	Marquès 40
Mitra, 17/60	Marquès 31
Mitra, 17/72 (=Mitra, 17/94★, 17/96a–b★)	Marquès 35 (cf. *CCM* 230) "La senyoria," app. 14
Mitra, 17/79	Marquès 30 "La senyoria," app. 12
Mitra, 17/93	Marquès 98
Mitra, 17/94 (=Mitra, 17/72★, 17/96a–b★)	Marquès 35 "La senyoria," app. 14 *CCM* 230
Mitra, 17/95	Marquès 23 "La senyoria," app. 9–10
Mitra, 17/96 (=Mitra, 17/152★)	Marquès 33 "La senyoria," app. 15 *CCM* 231
Mitra, 17/96a–b (=Mitra, 17/72★, 17/94★)	Marquès 35 "La senyoria," app. 14
Mitra, 17/97	Marquès 34 "La senyoria," app. 13
Mitra, 17/98	Marquès 24 "La senyoria," app. 11 Marquès i Planagumà, ed., "El cartulari," no. 99 (pp. 285–86) Grahit, ed., "El Llibre vert," no. 7 (pp. 169–70)
Mitra, 17/112	Marquès 36 "La senyoria," app. 16
Mitra, 17/152 (=Mitra, 17/96★)	Marquès 33 (cf. *CCM* 231) "La senyoria," app. 15
Mitra, 23/80.1	Marquès 13 reg. *CDSG* 287 *see* RBI 273.1★
Mitra, 23/80.2	Marquès 13 reg. *CDSG* 287 *see* RBI 273.2★
Pia Almoina, Fornells 16	Pruenca i Bayona, ed., *Amer*, no. 38 (pp. 74–76)

Table of published documents

ADPO (PERPIGNAN, ARCHIVES DÉPARTEMENTALES DES PYRÉNÉES-ORIENTALES)

B4, 74   Alart, ed., *Cartulaire*, no. 56 (pp. 83–86)

AEV (VIC, ARXIU EPISCOPAL DE VIC)

Pergamins de l'Estany 1   reg. Rocafiguera, "Documents," no. 1 (p. 128)

ACV (ARXIU CAPITULAR DE VIC)

6/180	*DVic* 631
	STCA 51
6/238	*DVic* 529
6/816	*STCA* 90
6/843	*STCA* 122
6/1249	*DVic* 277
6/1390	*see* ACV 9/ii/34★
6/1787 (=ACV 6/1788.2)	*see* ALI 486★
6/1788.2 (=ACV 6/1787)	*see* ALI 486★
9/i/96	*VL* 6:22
9/i/103	*DVic* 543
	STCA 34
9/ii/15	*STCA* 71
9/ii/16	*CPF* 12
9/ii/18	*STCA* 81
9/ii/19	*CPF* 13
9/ii/28	*VL* 6:23
9/ii/29	*DOliba* 69
9/ii/30	*DOliba* 78
9/ii/32	*DOliba* 95
	Benet, *Gurb-Queralt*, app. 8 (pp. 247–49)
9/ii/34 (=ACV 6/1390)	*DOliba* 99
	VL 6:27
9/ii/35	*DOliba* 108
9/ii/38 (=ACV 9/ii/39★)	*DOliba* 138
9/ii/39 (=ACV 9/ii/38★)	*DOliba* 138
9/ii/41	*DOliba* 105
	VL 6:25
9/ii/44	*DOliba* 128
9/ii/74	*see* RBII 43.1★
9/ii/75	*VL* 6:39.1
9/ii/82	*VL* 6:39.2
9/ii/90	*VL* 6:37
31/xlii/85 (=AME 13:57★)	Botet i Sisó, *Les monedes*, app. 18 (1:215–17)

Table of published documents

AME (ARXIU DE LA MENSA EPISCOPAL)

6/72	*DVic* 531
8/108	*DOliba* 115
8/114	*DOliba* 77
13/52	*DOliba* 113
13/53	*DOliba* 130
13/56	*DOliba* 131
13/57 (=ACV 31/xlii/85★)	Botet i Sisó, *Les monedes*, app. 18 (1:215–17)

BC (BARCELONA, BIBLIOTECA DE CATALUNYA)

2128	Bonnassie, ed., "Un contrat agraire," 449–50
3957	Miret i Sans, ed., "Documents," 16–17 [partial ed.]
	Miret i Sans, ed., "Los noms personals," no. 140 (p. 537) [partial ed.]
4085	Sanahuja, *Historia*, app. 23 (pp. 337–38)
4118	Corredera Gutierrez, *Ager*, app. 4 (pp. 224–27)
4125	Sanahuja, *Historia*, app. 20 (pp. 332–33) [partial ed.]
4143	Corredera Gutierrez, *Ager*, app. 3 (pp. 222–24)
4316, fols. 7v–9r	*MH* 270.1
	VL 9:16
4561	Corredera Gutierrez, *Ager*, app. 7 (pp. 228–30)
MS 941, fol. 482	Corredera Gutierrez, *Ager*, app. 8 (pp. 230–31)

PARIS, ARCHIVES NATIONALES

J. 307 (Toulouse IV), 48	Teulet et al., eds., *Layettes*, no. 12 (1:14–15)

PARIS, BIBLIOTHÈQUE NATIONALE

Collection Moreau, vol. 20, fols. 165–67	*MH* 222 [partial ed.]

WORKS CITED

I. ARCHIVAL SOURCES AND MANUSCRIPTS

BARCELONA

Arxiu de la Corona d'Aragó

Cancelleria reial
  Pergamins
    Ramon Borrell
    Berenguer Ramon I
    Ramon Berenguer I
    Ramon Berenguer II
    Berenguer Ramon II
    Ramon Berenguer III
    Ramon Berenguer IV
    Alfons I
    Pere I
    Extrainventari
  Cartes reials
    Papers per incorporar
      Caixa 1
  Volums
    Registres
      1 ("Liber feudorum maior")
      2 ("Liber testamentorum . . .")
      4 ("Liber feudorum Cerritaniae")
      24 (Diversorum)
Ordes Militars
  Pergamins
    Armari 1 (Barcelona)
    Armari 2 (Susterris)
    Armari 3 (Cervera)
    Armari 5 (Granyena)
    Armari 11 (Gardeny)
    Armari 15 (Espluga de Francolí)

Armari 17 (Vilafranca)
Armari 23 (Comunes)
Volums
   179 (Cartulari de Gardeny, *olim* Armari 11, vol. 1)
Ordes Religiosos (Monacals)
   Pergamins
      Sant Benet de Bages
      Sant Cugat del Vallès
      Sant Llorenç del Munt
      Sant Pere de Camprodon
      Santa Cecília de Montserrat
      Santa Maria de Montalegre
      sense procedència
Diversos
   Varia
      10 (Vilanova Roselló)
         Lligal 1
      24 (Uriz)
         Pergamins

Arxiu Capitular de la Santa Església Catedral Basílica de Barcelona

Pergamins
   1–1 (Diversorum A)
   1–2 (Diversorum B)
   1–4 (Diversorum C-b)
   1–5 (Diversorum C-c)
   4–70 (Pia Almoina, Sitges)
Libri antiquitatum

Biblioteca de Catalunya, Unitat bibliogràfica, Secció de manuscrits

Manuscrits
   MS 150 (Joseph Martí, "Recopliacion y resumen de los instrumentos y papeles
      que se hallan reconditos en el archivo de la iglesia collegiata de Mur")
   MS 729 (Jaume Pasqual, "Sacra Cathaloniae antiquitatis monumenta," 11 vols.)
   MS 941 (Jaume Caresmar, "Compendi de tots els instruments antichs y
      moderns que es troban en l'arxiu de la molt insigne iglesia colegia de San
      Pere de Ager")
Arxiu Històric
Pergamins

GIRONA

Arxiu Capitular de Girona

Pergamins
Llibre Verd

Works cited

Arxiu Diocesà de Girona

Mitra
  Pergamins
    Calaixos 2, 15, 17, 23
Pia Almoina
  Pergamins
    Cassa de la Selva
    Fornells
    Fonolleres
    Girona "subratllat" 1 (Testaments)

LA SEU D'URGELL

Arxiu Capitular d'Urgell

Pergamins
Liber dotaliorum ecclesie Urgellensis

MONTSERRAT

Arxiu de l'Abadia de Montserrat

Pergamins
  Sant Benet de Bages
  Sant Cugat del Vallès

MONTPELLIER

Société archéologique de Montpellier

MS 10 (consulted on microfilm at the Archives départementales de l'Hérault)

PARIS

Archives nationales

Série J
  307 (Toulouse IV)

Bibliothèque nationale

Collection Moreau
  vol. 20

PERPIGNAN

Archives départementales des Pyrénées-Orientales

Série B
  4

Works cited

Arxiu Episcopal de Vic

Pergamins de l'Estany
Arxiu Capitular de Vic
  Calaix 6
    Pergamins
    vol. 1 (Episcopologi I)
  Calaix 9
    vol. 1 (Episcopologi I)
    vol. 2 (Episcopologi II)
  Calaix 31
    vol. 42 (Jaume Ripoll, "Collección de instrumentos para la història del territorio de Urgel . . .")
  Calaix 37
    Liber dotationum antiquarum
Arxiu de la Mensa Episcopal
  Llibres de pergamins 3–10, 12–13, 15
Museu Episcopal de Vic
  MS 283 (Cartulari de Santa Maria de l'Estany)

II. PRINTED SOURCES

Abadal i de Vinyals, Ramon d'. *L'abat Oliba, bisbe de Vic, i la seva època*. 3rd ed. Barcelona, 1962. Reprinted as "L'abat Oliba i la seva època" in Abadal i de Vinyals, *Dels Visigots als Catalans*, 2:141–277.
"Com neix i com creix un gran monestir pirinenc abans de l'any mil: Eixalada-Cuixà." *Analecta Montserratensia* 8 (1954–55), 125–337. Reprinted (pp. 125–238, without documentary appendix) in Abadal i de Vinyals, *Dels Visigots als Catalans*, 1:377–484.
Dels Visigots als Catalans. Ed. Jaume Sobrequés i Callicó. 3rd ed. 2 vols. Col·lecció estudis i documents 13–14. Barcelona, 1986.
"Un gran comte de Barcelona preterit: Guifre-Borrell (897–911)." *Cuadernos de arqueologia e historia de la Ciudad de Barcelona* 5 (1964), 83–130. Also appeared in *Miscellanea Barcinonensia* 3, no. 8 (1964), 49–90. Reprinted in Abadal i de Vinyals, *Dels Visigots als Catalans*, 1:323–62.
"Origen i procés de consolidació de la seu ribagorçana de Roda." Trans. Gaspar Feliu i Montfort in Abadal i de Vinyals, *Dels Visigots als Catalans*, 2:57–139. Pp. 57–112 originally appeared as "Origen y proceso de consolidación de la sede ribagorzana de Roda," *Estudios de Edad Media de la Corona de Aragón* 5 (1952), 7–82; pp. 112–39 originally appeared (in Catalan) in Abadal i de Vinyals, ed., *Pallars i Ribagorça*, pp. 193–224.
"Pedro el Ceremonioso y los comienzos de la decadencia política de Cataluña." In Ramón Menéndez Pidal, ed., *Historia de España*, vol. 14, *España cristiana; Crisis de la Reconquista; Luchas civiles*, 2nd ed. (Madrid, 1966), ix–cciii (prologue).
Els primers comtes catalans. Història de Catalunya, Biografies catalanes, 1. [3rd ed.] Barcelona, [1980].

Works cited

"La reconquesta d'una regió interior de Catalunya: La Plana de Vic." In Abadal i de Vinyals, *Dels Visigots als Catalans*, 1:309–21.

Abadal i de Vinyals, Ramon d', ed. *Els comtats de Pallars i Ribagorça*. Vol. 3 of *Catalunya carolíngia*. 2 parts. Memòries de la Secció històrico-arqueològica 14–15. Barcelona, 1955.

Els diplomes carolingis a Catalunya. Vol. 2 of *Catalunya carolíngia*. 2 parts. Memòries de la Secció històrico-arqueològica 2. Barcelona, 1926–52.

Achery, Luc d', ed. *Spicilegium sive collectio veterum aliquot scriptorum qui in Galliae bibliothecis deliterant*. New ed., ed. Étienne Baluze, Edmond Martène, and Louis-François-Joseph de la Barre. 3 vols. Paris, 1723.

Alart, Bernard, ed. *Cartulaire roussillonnais*. Perpignan, 1880.

Priviléges et titres relatifs aux franchises, institutions et propriétés communales de Roussillon et de Cerdagne depuis le XIe siècle jusqu'à l'an 1660. 1 vol. only. Perpignan, 1874.

Altés i Aguiló, Francesc Xavier, ed. "El diplomatari del monestir de Santa Cecília de Montserrat." *Studia monastica* 36 (1994), 223–302; 37 (1995), 301–94; 38 (1996), 291–400.

Althoff, Gerd. *Amicitiae und pacta: Bündnis, Einung, Politik und Gebetsgedenken im beginnenden 10. Jahrhundert*. MGH Schriften 37. Hanover, 1992.

Spielregeln der Politik im Mittelalter: Kommunikation in Frieden und Fehde. Darmstadt, 1997.

Verwandte, Freunde und Getreue: Zum politischen Stellenwert der Gruppenbindungen im früheren Mittelalter. Darmstadt, 1990.

Altisent, Agustí. "Seguint el rastre de Guerau de Jorba i el seu llinatge." *Aplec de treballs* (Centre d'estudis de la Conca de Barberà, Montblanc) 1 (1978), 33–83.

Altisent, Agustí, ed. *Diplomatari de Santa Maria de Poblet*. 1 vol. to date. Col·lecció fonts i estudis 2. Barcelona, 1993–.

Alturo i Perucho, Jesús, ed. *L'arxiu antic de Santa Anna de Barcelona del 942 al 1200 (Aproximació històrico-lingüística)*. 3 vols. Col·lecció textos i documents 8–10. Barcelona, 1985.

Diplomatari de Polinyà del Vallès: Aproximació a la història d'un poble del segle X al XII. Faventia, Monografies, [2]. Bellaterra, 1985.

Álvarez Márquez, María del Carmen, ed. *La baronia de la Conca d'Òdena*. Col·lecció textos i documents 25. Barcelona, 1990.

Amargier, Paul. "Un épisode de justice à la Cadière (Var) à la fin du Xe siècle." *Provence historique* 28 (1978), 295–304.

Andenna, Giancarlo. "La signoria ecclesiastica nell'Italia settentrionale." In *Chiesa e mondo feudale nei secoli X–XII: Atti della dodicesima Settimana internazionale di studio Mendola, 24–28 agosto 1992*, Miscellanea del Centro di studi medioevali 14, Scienze storiche 59 (Milan, 1995), 111–47.

Appelt, Heinrich, et al., eds. *Friderici I. Diplomata*. MGH Diplomata regum et imperatorum Germaniae 10. 5 vols. Hanover, 1975–90.

Aragó Cabañas, Antoni M. "L'escrivania pública de Santes Creus a l'època post-fundacional." In *I Col·loqui d'història del monaquisme català: Santes Creus, 1966*, 2 vols., Publicacions de l'Arxiu bibliogràfic de Santes Creus 24–25 (Santes Creus, 1967–69), 2:15–25.

Aragó Cabañas, Antoni M., and Josep Trenchs Òdena. "Las escribanías reales catalano-aragonesas, de Ramón Berenguer IV a la minoría de Jaime I." *Revista de archivos, bibliotecas y museos* 80 (1977), 421–42.

Works cited

Araguas, Philippe. "Les châteaux d'Arnau Mir de Tost: Formation d'un grand domaine féodal en Catalogne au milieu du XIe siècle." In *Les pays de la Méditerranée occidentale au Moyen Âge*, Actes du 106e Congrès national des sociétés savantes, Section de philologie et d'histoire jusqu'à 1610, Perpignan, 1981 (Paris, 1983), 61–76.

Aurell, Martin. "La chevalerie urbaine en Occitanie (fin X^e–début XIIIe siècle)." In *Les élites urbaines au Moyen Âge: XXVIIe Congrès de la S.H.M.E.S. (Rome, mai 1996)*, Collection de l'École française de Rome 238, Publications de la Sorbonne, Série histoire ancienne et médiévale, 46 (Rome and Paris, 1997), 71–118.

"La détérioration du statut de la femme aristocratique en Provence (X^e–XIIIe siècles)," *Le Moyen Âge* 91 (1985), 5–32.

"Du nouveau sur les comtesses catalanes (IXe–XIIe siècles)." *Annales du Midi* 109 (1997), 357–80.

Les noces du comte: Mariage et pouvoir en Catalogne (785–1213). Publications de la Sorbonne, Série histoire ancienne et médiévale, 32. Paris, 1995.

"Le personnel politique catalan et aragonais d'Alphonse Ier en Provence (1166–1196)." *Annales du Midi* 93 (1981), 121–39.

Bach, Antoni, ed. *Col·lecció diplomàtica del monestir de Santa Maria de Solsona: El Penedès i altres llocs del comtat de Barcelona (segles X–XV)*. Col·lecció fonts i estudis, Sèrie fonts, 1. Barcelona, 1987.

"Els documents del priorat de Santa Maria de Gualter de l'Arxiu Episcopal de Solsona (segles XI–XIII)." *Urgellia* 8 (1986–87), 211–69.

Badia i Margarit, Antoni M. *La formació de la llengua catalana: Assaig d'interpretació històrica*. 2nd ed. Barcelona, 1981.

Balari Jovany, José. *Orígenes históricos de Cataluña*. 2nd ed. 3 vols. Biblioteca filológica-histórica 10–11bis. Sant Cugat del Vallès, 1964.

Baldwin, John W. *The Government of Philip Augustus: Foundations of French Royal Power in the Middle Ages*. Berkeley, 1986.

Banniard, Michel. "Language and Communication in Carolingian Europe." In McKitterick, ed., *New Cambridge Medieval History*, 695–708.

Viva voce: Communication écrite et communication orale du IVe au IXe siècle en Occident latin. Collection des études augustiniennes, Série Moyen-Âge et temps modernes, 25. Paris, 1992.

Baraut, Cebrià. "La data de l'acta de consagració de la catedral carolíngia de La Seu d'Urgell." *Urgellia* 7 (1984–85), 515–29.

Baraut, Cebrià, ed. *Les actes de consagracions d'esglésies de l'antic bisbat d'Urgell (segles IX–XII)*. La Seu d'Urgell, 1986.

"Les actes de consagracions d'esglésies del bisbat d'Urgell (segles IX–XII)." *Urgellia* 1 (1978), 11–182. Reprinted (with additional texts and different numeration) in Baraut, ed., *Les actes de consagracions*.

"Diplomatari del monestir de Sant Sadurní de Tavèrnoles (segles IX–XIII)." *Urgellia* 12 (1994–95), 7–414.

"Els documents, dels anys 981–1010, de l'Arxiu Capitular de La Seu d'Urgell." *Urgellia* 3 (1980), 7–166.

"Els documents, dels anys 1010–1035, de l'Arxiu Capitular de La Seu d'Urgell." *Urgellia* 4 (1981), 7–186.

"Els documents, dels anys 1036–1050, de l'Arxiu Capitular de La Seu d'Urgell." *Urgellia* 5 (1982), 7–158.

Works cited

"Els documents, dels anys 1051–1075, de l'Arxiu Capitular de La Seu d'Urgell." *Urgellia* 6 (1983), 7–243.

"Els documents, dels anys 1076–1092, de l'Arxiu Capitular de La Seu d'Urgell." *Urgellia* 7 (1984–85), 7–218.

"Els documents, dels anys 1093–1100, de l'Arxiu Capitular de La Seu d'Urgell." *Urgellia* 8 (1986–87), 7–149.

"Els documents, dels anys 1101–1150, de l'Arxiu Capitular de La Seu d'Urgell." *Urgellia* 9 (1988–89), 7–312. With "Índexs dels documents de l'Arxiu Capitular de La Seu d'Urgell, publicats en els volums IV–VIII d'*Urgellia*," at 403–570.

"Els documents, dels anys 1151–1190, de l'Arxiu Capitular de La Seu d'Urgell." *Urgellia* 10 (1990–91), 7–349. With "Índexs dels documents de l'Arxiu Capitular de La Seu d'Urgell, publicats en els volums IX–X d'*Urgellia*," at 473–625.

"Els documents, dels anys 1191–1200, de l'Arxiu Capitular de La Seu d'Urgell." *Urgellia* 11 (1992–93), 7–160.

"Els documents, dels segles IX i X, conservats a l'Arxiu Capitular de La Seu d'Urgell." *Urgellia* 2 (1979), 7–145.

"Set actes més de consagracions d'esglésies del bisbat d'Urgell (segles XI–XII)." *Urgellia* 2 (1979), 481–88. Reprinted (with additional texts and different numeration) in Baraut, ed., *Les actes de consagracions*.

Barbero, Abilio, and Marcelo Vigil. *La formación del feudalismo en la Península Ibérica.* 2nd ed. Barcelona, 1979.

Barceló, Miquel, and Pierre Toubert, eds. *L'incastellamento: Actes des rencontres de Gérone (26–27 novembre 1992) et de Rome (5–7 mai 1994).* Collection de l'École française de Rome 241. Rome, 1998.

Barral i Altet, Xavier, et al., eds. *Catalunya i França meridional a l'entorn de l'any mil / La Catalogne et la France méridionale autour de l'an mil: Colloque international [C].N.R.S. / Generalitat de Catalunya: Hugues Capet 987–1987. La France de l'an mil: Barcelona, 2–5 juliol 1987.* Col·lecció actes de congressos 2. Barcelona, 1991.

Barthélemy, Dominique. *Les deux âges de la seigneurie banale: Pouvoir et société dans la terre des sires de Coucy (milieu XIe–milieu XIIIe siècle).* Publications de la Sorbonne, Série histoire ancienne et médiévale, 12. Paris, 1984.

"Encore le débat sur l'an mil!" *Revue historique de droit français et étranger* 73 (1995), 349–60.

La mutation de l'an mil a-t-elle eu lieu?: Servage et chevalerie dans la France des Xe et XIe siècles. Paris, 1997.

"La mutation féodale a-t-elle eu lieu? (Note critique)." *Annales: Économies, sociétés, civilisations* 47 (1992), 767–77. Reprinted as "Une note critique" in Barthélemy, *La mutation de l'an mil*, 13–28.

La société dans le comté de Vendôme de l'an mil au XIVe siècle. Paris, 1993.

Barthélemy, Dominique, Stephen D. White, Timothy Reuter, Chris Wickham, and Thomas N. Bisson. "Debate: The 'Feudal Revolution.'" *Past & Present* 152 (1996), 196–223; 155 (1997), 177–225.

Bartlett, Robert. *The Making of Europe: Conquest, Colonization and Cultural Change, 950–1350.* Princeton, 1993.

Barton, Simon. *The Aristocracy in Twelfth-Century León and Castile.* Cambridge Studies in Medieval Life and Thought, 4th ser., 34. Cambridge, 1997.

Bassols de Climent, M., et al., eds. *Glossarium mediae latinitatis Cataloniae: Voces latinas y romances documentadas en fuentes catalanas del año 800 al 1100.* 1 vol. to date. Barcelona, 1960–.

Bastardas i Parera, Joan. *Sobre la problemàtica dels Usatges de Barcelona.* Barcelona, 1977.

Bastardas i Parera, Joan, ed. "Dos judicis antics (s. IX i XI): La pràctica judicial en el període de la formació nacional de Catalunya." In *Documents jurídics*, 23–30.

  Usatges de Barcelona: El codi a mitjan segle XII . . . 2nd ed. Col·lecció textos i documents 6. Barcelona, 1991.

Baucells i Reig, Josep. *El Garraf i la Pia Almoina de la seu de Barcelona: Catàleg del fons en pergamí de l'Arxiu Capitular de la Catedral de Barcelona.* Col·lecció catàlegs-inventaris d'arxius eclesiàstics de Catalunya 5. Catàleg de l'Arxiu Capitular de la Catedral de Barcelona 4. Barcelona, 1990.

Baudon de Mony, Charles. *Relations politiques des comtes de Foix avec la Catalogne jusqu'au commencement du XIVe siècle.* 2 vols. Paris, 1896.

Bautier, Robert-Henri. "Normalisation internationale des méthodes de publication des documents latins du Moyen Âge (2e édition)." *Bulletin philologique et historique (jusqu'à 1610) du Comité des travaux historiques et scientifiques: Année 1976* (1978), 9–54.

Becher, Matthias. *Eid und Herrschaft: Untersuchungen zum Herrscherethos Karls des Großen.* Vorträge und Forschungen, Sonderband 39. Sigmaringen, 1993.

Bedos-Rezak, Brigitte. "Diplomatic Sources and Medieval Documentary Practices: An Essay in Interpretive Methodology." In John van Engen, ed., *The Past and Future of Medieval Studies*, Notre Dame Conferences in Medieval Studies 4 (Notre Dame, 1994), 313–43.

Beech, George T. "The Lord/Dependant (Vassal) Relationship: A Case Study from Aquitaine c. 1030." *Journal of Medieval History* 24 (1998), 1–30.

Beech, George T., Yves Chauvin, and Georges Pon, eds. *Le Conventum (vers 1030): Un précurseur aquitain des premières épopées.* Publications romanes et françaises 212. Geneva, 1995.

Benet i Clarà, Albert. *La família Gurb-Queralt (956–1276). Senyors de Sallent, Oló, Avinyó, Gurb, Manlleu, Voltregà, Queralt i Santa Coloma de Queralt.* Sallent, 1993.

Benito i Monclús, Pere. "Clergues 'feudataris.' La disgregació del patrimoni de la seu de Barcelona i els orígens del sistema beneficial (1091–1157)." *Anuario de estudios medievales* 29 (1999), 105–19.

  "'Hoc est breve . . .': L'emergència del costum i els orígens de la pràctica de capbrevació (segles XI–XIII)." In Sánchez Martínez, ed., *Estudios sobre renta*, 3–27.

  "Senyoria de la terra i tinença pagesa: Estudi sobre les relacions contractuals agràries al comtat de Barcelona des de la fi dels sistemes d'explotació dominical als orígens de l'emfiteusi (segles XI–XIII)." Tesi de doctorat, Universitat de Barcelona, 2000.

Benito i Monclús, Pere, Adam J. Kosto, and Nathaniel L. Taylor. "Three Typological Approaches to Catalonian Archival Evidence, 10–12 Centuries." *Anuario de estudios medievales* 26 (1996), 43–88.

Benjamin, Richard. "A Forty Years War: Toulouse and the Plantagenets, 1156–96." *Historical Research* 61 (1988), 270–85.

Bensch, Stephen P. *Barcelona and its Rulers, 1096–1291.* Cambridge Studies in Medieval Life and Thought, 4th ser., 26. Cambridge, 1995.

Berkhofer, Robert F. "Inventaires de biens et proto-comptabilités dans le nord de la

Works cited

France (XIᵉ–début du XIIᵉ siècle)." *Bibliothèque de l'École des chartes* 155 (1997), 339–49.

Berman, Constance Hoffman. *Medieval Agriculture, the Southern French Countryside, and the Early Cistercians: A Study of Forty-Three Monasteries.* Transactions of the American Philosophical Society 76:5. Philadelphia, 1986.

Bischoff, Frank M. *Urkundenformate im Mittelalter: Größe, Format und Proportionen von Papsturkunden in Zeiten expandierender Schriftlichkeit (11.–13. Jahrhundert).* Elementa diplomatica 5. Marburg an der Lahn, 1996.

Bisson, Thomas N. "Les comptes des domaines au temps du Philippe-Auguste: Essai comparatif." In Bisson, *Medieval France,* 265–83. Originally appeared in Robert-Henri Bautier, ed., *La France de Philippe Auguste: Le temps des mutations: Actes du colloque international organisé par le C.N.R.S. (Paris, 29 septembre–4 octobre 1980),* Colloques internationaux du Centre national de la recherche scientifique 602 (Paris, 1982), 521–38.

"Feudalism in Twelfth-Century Catalonia." In Bisson, *Medieval France,* 153–78. Originally appeared (without documentary appendix) in *Structures féodales,* 173–92.

"The 'Feudal Revolution.'" *Past & Present* 142 (1994), 6–42.

"A General Court of Aragon (Daroca, February 1228)." In Bisson, *Medieval France,* 31–48. Originally appeared in *English Historical Review* 92 (1977), 107–24.

The Medieval Crown of Aragon: A Short History. Oxford, 1986.

Medieval France and Her Pyrenean Neighbours: Studies in Early Institutional History. Studies Presented to the International Commission for the History of Representative and Parliamentary Institutions 70. London, 1989.

"The Problem of Feudal Monarchy: Aragon, Catalonia, and France." In Bisson, *Medieval France,* 237–55. Originally appeared in *Speculum* 53 (1978), 460–78.

"Ramon de Caldes (*c.* 1135–1199): Dean of Barcelona and King's Minister." In Bisson, *Medieval France,* 187–98. Originally appeared in Kenneth Pennington and Robert Somerville, eds., *Law, Church, and Society: Essays in Honor of Stephan Kuttner* (Philadelphia, 1977), 281–92.

"The Rise of Catalonia: Identity, Power, and Ideology in a Twelfth-Century Society." In Bisson, *Medieval France,* 125–52. Originally published as "L'essor de la Catalogne: Identité, pouvoir et idéologie dans une société du XIIᵉ siècle," *Annales: Économies, sociétés, civilisations* 39 (1984), 454–79.

Tormented Voices: Power, Crisis, and Humanity in Rural Catalonia, 1140–1200. Cambridge, Mass., 1998.

"Unheroed Pasts: History and Commemoration in South Frankland before the Albigensian Crusades." *Speculum* 65 (1990), 281–308.

Bisson, Thomas N., ed. *Cultures of Power: Lordship, Status, and Process in Twelfth-Century Europe.* Philadelphia, 1995.

Fiscal Accounts of Catalonia under the Early Count-Kings (1151–1213). 2 vols. Berkeley, 1984.

"The War of the Two Arnaus: A Memorial of the Broken Peace in Cerdanya (1188)." In *Miscel·lània en homenatge al P. Agustí Altisent* (Tarragona, 1991), 95–107.

Blaise, Albert. *Dictionnaire latin-français des auteurs chrétiens.* Turnhout, 1954.

Bloch, Marc. "Pour une histoire comparée des sociétés européennes." *Revue de synthèse historique* 46 (1928), 15–50. Trans. as "A Contribution towards a

Comparative History of European Societies," in Bloch, *Land and Work in Medieval Europe: Selected Papers by Marc Bloch*, trans. J. E. Anderson (Berkeley, 1967), 44–81.

Bofarull y Mascaró, Próspero de. *Los condes de Barcelona vindicados* . . . 2 vols. Barcelona, 1836; repr. 1988.

Bofarull y Mascaró, Próspero de, et al., eds. *Colección de documentos inéditos del Archivo general de la Corona de Aragón.* 50 vols. to date. Barcelona, 1847–.

Bofill y Boix, Pere. "Lo castell de Gurb y la familia Gurb en lo segle XIIIè." In *Congrés d'historia de la Corona d'Aragó dedicat al rey en Jaume I y a la seua época*, 2 vols., I Congrés d'història de la Corona d'Aragó, Barcelona, 1908 (Barcelona, 1909–13), 2:695–743.

Bohigas, Pedro. *La ilustración y la decoración del libro manuscrito en Cataluña: Contribución al estudio de la historia de la miniatura catalana.* Vol. 1, *Período románico.* Barcelona, 1960.

Bonnassie, Pierre. *La Catalogne du milieu du Xᵉ à la fin du XIᵉ siècle: Croissance et mutations d'une société.* 2 vols. Publications de l'Université de Toulouse–Le Mirail, ser. A, 23, 29. Toulouse, 1975–76.

"Les conventions féodales dans la Catalogne du XIᵉ siècle," *Annales du Midi* 80 (1968), 529–50. Reprinted in *Les structures sociales*, 187–208. Trans. as "Feudal Conventions in Eleventh-Century Catalonia," in Bonnassie, *From Slavery to Feudalism*, 170–94.

"Du Rhône à la Galice: Genèse et modalités du régime féodal." In *Structures féodales*, 17–44. Trans. as "From the Rhône to Galicia: Origins and Modalities of the Feudal Order," in Bonnassie, *From Slavery to Feudalism*, 104–31.

From Slavery to Feudalism in South-Western Europe. Trans. Jean Birrell. Cambridge, 1991.

Bonnassie, Pierre, ed. "Un contrat agraire inédit du monastère de Sant Cugat (28 août 1040)." *Anuario de estudios medievales* 3 (1966), 441–50.

Bono, José. *Historia del derecho notarial español.* 1 vol. in 2 parts to date. Ars notariae hispanica 1. Madrid, 1979–.

Boretius, Alfred, and Victor Krause, eds. *Capitularia regum Francorum.* 2 vols. MGH Legum sectio II, 1–2. Hanover, 1883–97; repr. 1960.

Borgolte, Michael. *Geschichte der Grafschaften Alemanniens in fränkischer Zeit.* Vorträge und Forschungen, Sonderband 31. Sigmaringen, 1984.

Botet i Sisó, Joaquim. *Les monedes catalanes: Estudi y descripció de les monedes carolingies, comtals, senyorials, reyals y locals propies de Catalunya.* 3 vols. Barcelona, 1908–11.

Boüard, Alain de. *Manuel de diplomatique française et pontificale.* Vol. 2, *L'acte privé.* Paris, 1948.

Bougard, François. *La justice dans le royaume d'Italie de la fin du VIIIᵉ siècle au début du XIᵉ siècle.* Bibliothèque des Écoles françaises d'Athènes et de Rome 291. Rome, 1995.

Boutruche, Robert. *Seigneurie et féodalité.* Vol. 2, *L'apogée (XIᵉ–XIIIᵉ siècles).* Paris, 1970.

Bowman, Alan K., and Greg Woolf, eds. *Literacy and Power in the Ancient World.* Cambridge, 1994.

Bowman, Jeffrey A. "Do Neo-Romans Curse? Law, Land, and Ritual in the Midi (900–1100)." *Viator* 28 (1997), 1–32.

"Law, Conflict, and Community around the Year 1000: The Settlement of

Works cited

Disputes in the Province of Narbonne, 985–1060." Ph.D. diss., Yale University, 1997.

Bresslau, Harry. *Handbuch der Urkundenlehre für Deutschland und Italien.* 2nd ed. 2 vols. Leipzig, 1912–31.

Brocá, Guillermo Maria de. *Historia del derecho de Cataluña . . .* 1 vol. only. Barcelona, 1918.

Brown, Elizabeth A. R. "The Tyranny of a Construct: Feudalism and Historians of Medieval Europe." *American Historical Review* 79 (1974), 1063–88.

Bruguera, Jordi, and Joan Coromines, eds. *Homilies d'Organyà: Edició facsímil del manuscrit núm. 289 de la Biblioteca de Catalunya.* Llibres del mil·lenari 1. Barcelona, 1989.

Brunel, Clovis. "Les premiers exemples de l'emploi du Provençal dans les chartes." *Romania* 48 (1922), 335–64.

Brunel, Clovis, ed. *Les plus anciennes chartes en langue provençale: Recueil des pièces originales antérieures au XIIIe siècle, publiées avec une étude morphologique.* 2 vols. Paris, 1926–52.

Bruzza, Luigi, ed. *Regesto della chiesa di Tivoli.* Studi e documenti di storia e diritto. Rome, 1880.

Buc, Philippe. "Ritual and Interpretation: The Early Medieval Case." *Early Medieval Europe* (forthcoming).

Burns, Robert I., ed. *Diplomatarium of the Crusader Kingdom of Valencia: The Registered Charters of its Conqueror, Jaume I, 1257–1276.* Vol. 1 (Introduction), *Society and Documentation in Crusader Valencia.* Princeton, 1985.

Büschgens, Andrea. *Die politischen Verträge Alfons' VIII. von Kastilien (1158–1214) mit Aragón-Katalonien und Navarra: Diplomatische Strategien und Konfliktlösung im mittelalterlichen Spanien.* Europäische Hochschulschriften, Reihe III, Geschichte und ihre Hilfswissenschaften, 678. Frankfurt am Main, 1995.

Calasso, Francesco. *La "convenientia": Contributo alla storia del contratto in Italia durante l'alto medio evo.* Biblioteca della Rivista di storia del diritto italiano 9. Bologna, 1932.

Calmette, Joseph, ed. "Un jugement original de Wifred le Velu pour l'abbaye d'Amer." *Bibliothèque de l'École des chartes* 67 (1906), 60–69.

Campbell, James. "Observations on English Government from the Tenth to the Twelfth Century." *Transactions of the Royal Historical Society,* 5th ser., 25 (1975), 39–54. Reprinted in Campbell, *Essays in Anglo-Saxon History* (London, 1986), 155–70.

Canellas López, Ángel. *Diplomática hispano-visigoda.* Publicaciones de la Institución "Fernando el Católico" 730. Zaragoza, 1979.

Carlin, Marie-Louise. *La pénétration du droit romain dans les actes de la pratique provençale (XIe–XIIIe siècle).* Bibliothèque d'histoire du droit et droit romain 11. Paris, 1967.

Carreras y Candi, Francesch. "Lo Montjuích de Barcelona." *Memorias de la Real academia de buenas letras de Barcelona* 8 (1906), 195–450.

Notes sobre los origens de la enfiteusis en lo territori de Barcelona. Barcelona, 1910.

Caruana, Jaime. "Itinerario de Alfonso II de Aragón." *Estudios de Edad Media de la Corona de Aragón* 7 (1962), 73–298.

Els castells catalans. 6 vols. in 7 parts. Barcelona, 1967–79.

Catalunya romànica. 27 vols. Barcelona, 1984–98.

Catel, Guillaume de. *Mémoires de l'histoire du Languedoc . . .* Toulouse, 1633.

Works cited

Charronnet, Charles, ed. "Documents sur la chartreuse de Durbon." *Bibliothèque de l'École des chartes* 15 (1853–54), 435–43.

Cheyette, Fredric L. "The Invention of the State." In Bede Karl Lackner and Kenneth Roy Philp, eds., *Essays on Medieval Civilization*, The Walter Prescott Webb Memorial Lectures 12 (Austin, 1978), 143–78.

"The 'Sale' of Carcassonne to the Counts of Barcelona (1067–1070) and the Rise of the Trencavels." *Speculum* 63 (1988), 826–64.

"Women, Poets, and Politics in Occitania." In Theodore Evergates, ed., *Aristocratic Women in Medieval France* (Philadelphia, 1999), 138–77.

Chrimes, S. B. *An Introduction to the Administrative History of Mediaeval England.* Studies in Mediaeval History 7. Oxford, 1952.

Clanchy, Michael T. *From Memory to Written Record: England, 1066–1307.* 2nd ed. Oxford, 1993.

Classen, Peter. "Fortleben und Wandel spätrömischen Urkundenwesens im frühen Mittelalter." In Classen, ed., *Recht und Schrift im Mittelalter*, 13–54.

Classen, Peter, ed. *Recht und Schrift im Mittelalter.* Vorträge und Forschungen 23. Sigmaringen, 1977.

Coll, José Maria. "Los castillos de San Pedro de Ribas, La Geltrú, Sitges y Miralpeix." *Analecta sacra Tarraconensia* 32 (1959), 237–53.

Coll i Alentorn, Miquel. "La llegenda d'Otger Cataló i els nou barons." *Estudis romànics* 1 (1947–48), 1–47. Reprinted in Coll i Alentorn, *Obres*, vol. 4, *Llegendari*, Textos i estudis de cultura catalana 30 (Barcelona, 1993), 7–50.

Coll i Castanyer, Jaume. "Els vescomtes de Girona." *Annals de l'Institut d'estudis gironins* 30 (1988–89), 39–98.

Collins, Roger. *Early Medieval Spain: Unity in Diversity, 400–1000.* 2nd ed. New York, 1995.

Law, Culture and Regionalism in Early Medieval Spain. [Aldershot], 1992.

"Literacy and the Laity in Early Mediaeval Spain." In McKitterick, ed., *The Uses of Literacy*, 109–33. Reprinted in Collins, *Law, Culture and Regionalism*, XV.

"*Sicut lex Gothorum continet*: Law and Charters in Ninth- and Tenth-Century León and Catalonia." *English Historical Review* 100 (1985), 489–512. Reprinted in Collins, *Law, Culture and Regionalism*, V.

"Visigothic Law and Regional Custom in Disputes in Early Medieval Spain." In Davies and Fouracre, eds., *The Settlement of Disputes*, 85–104. Reprinted (with documentary appendix, pp. 252–57) in Collins, *Law, Culture and Regionalism*, VI.

Constans i Serrats, Lluís G., ed. *Diplomatari de Banyoles.* 6 vols. Banyoles, 1985–93.

Constant, André. "Châteaux et peuplement dans le massif des Albères et ses marges du IXe siècle au début du XIe siècle." *Annales du Midi* 109 (1997), 443–66.

Contreni, John J. "The Carolingian Renaissance: Education and Literary Culture." In McKitterick, ed., *New Cambridge Medieval History*, 709–57.

Coroleu, José. *Historia de Villanueva y Geltrú.* Vilanova i la Geltrú, 1878.

Coromines, Joan, ed. *Diccionari etimològic i complementari de la llengua catalana.* 9 vols. Barcelona, 1980–91.

Onomasticon Cataloniae: Els noms de lloc i noms de persona de totes les terres de llengua catalana. 8 vols. Barcelona, 1989–97.

Corredera Gutierrez, Eduardo. *El archivo de Ager y Caresmar.* Balaguer, 1978.

Coulson, Charles. "The French Matrix of the Castle-Provisions of the Chester-Leicester *conventio*." *Anglo-Norman Studies* 17 (1994), 65–86.

Works cited

Coy y Cotonat, Agustín. *Sort y comarca Noguera-Pallaresa.* Barcelona, 1906.

Crouch, David. "A Norman 'conventio' and Bonds of Lordship in the Middle Ages." In George Garnett and John Hudson, eds., *Law and Government in Medieval England and Normandy: Essays in Honour of Sir James Holt* (Cambridge, 1994), 299–324.

Cuadrada, Coral. *El Maresme medieval: Les jurisdiccions baronals de Mataró i Sant Vicenç/Vilassar (hàbitat, economia i societat, segles X–XIV).* Mataró, 1988.

Daileader, Philip. *True Citizens: Violence, Memory, and Identity in the Medieval Community of Perpignan, 1162–1397.* The Medieval Mediterranean 25. Leiden, 2000.

"The Vanishing Consulates of Catalonia." *Speculum* 74 (1999), 65–94.

Dameron, George W. *Episcopal Power and Florentine Society, 1000–1320.* Harvard Historical Studies 107. Cambridge, Mass., 1991.

Davies, Wendy, and Paul Fouracre, eds. *The Settlement of Disputes in Early Medieval Europe.* Cambridge, 1986.

Davis, R. H. C. "Domesday Book: Continental Parallels." In J. C. Holt, ed., *Domesday Studies: Papers Read at the Novocentenary Conference of the Royal Historical Society and the Institute of British Geographers, Winchester, 1986* (Woodbridge, 1987), 15–39. Reprinted (with a postscript) in Davis, *From Alfred the Great to Stephen* (London, 1991), 141–65.

Débax, Hélène. "Le cartulaire des Trencavel (*Liber instrumentorum vicecomitalium*)." In Guyotjeannin, Morelle, and Parisse, eds., *Les cartulaires,* 291–99.

Debord, André. *La société laïque dans les pays de la Charente X^e–XIIe s.* Paris, 1984.

De Jong, Mayke. "Power and Humility in Carolingian Society: The Public Penance of Louis the Pious." *Early Medieval Europe* 1 (1992), 29–52.

Deswarte, Thomas. "Rome et la spécificité catalane. La papauté et ses relations avec la Catalogne et Narbonne (850–1030)." *Revue historique* 294 (1995), 3–43.

Diago, Francisco. *Historia de los victoriosíssimos antiguos condes de Barcelona . . .* Barcelona, 1603; repr. Valencia, 1974.

Dilcher, Gerhard. "Oralität, Verschriftlichung und Wandlungen der Normstruktur in den Stadtrechten des 12. und 13. Jahrhunderts." In Hagen Keller, Klaus Grubmüller, and Nikolaus Staubach, eds., *Pragmatische Schriftlichkeit im Mittelalter: Erscheinungsformen und Entwicklungsstufen (Akten des Internationalen Kolloquiums 17.–19. Mai 1989),* Münstersche Mittelalter-Schriften 65 (Munich, 1992), 9–19.

Documents jurídics de la història de Catalunya. 2nd ed. Barcelona, 1992.

Dopsch, Heinz. "Burgenbau und Burgenpolitik des Erzstiftes Salzburg im Mittelalter." In Hans Patze, ed., *Die Burgen im deutschen Sprachraum: Ihre rechts- und verfassungsgeschichtliche Bedeutung,* 2 vols., Vorträge und Forschungen 19 (Sigmaringen, 1976), 2:387–417.

Duby, Georges. "Recherches sur l'évolution des institutions judiciaires pendant le Xe et le XIe siècle dans le sud de la Bourgogne." *Le Moyen Âge* 52 (1946), 149–94; 53 (1947), 15–38. Trans. as "The Evolution of Judicial Institutions: Burgundy in the Tenth and Eleventh Centuries," in Duby, *The Chivalrous Society,* trans. Cynthia Postan (Berkeley, 1977), 15–58.

La société aux XIe et XIIe siècles dans la région mâconnaise. 2nd ed. Paris, 1971; repr. 1988.

Du Cange, Charles du Fresne, sieur. *Glossarium mediae et infimae latinitatis.* Ed. Léopold Favre. 10 vols. Niort, 1883–87.

Works cited

Dufour, Jean. "Obédience respective des Carolingiens et des Capétiens (fin Xe siècle–début XIe siècle)." In Barral i Altet et al., eds., *Catalunya i França*, 21–44.

Dunbabin, Jean. *France in the Making, 843–1180*. Oxford, 1985.

Durán Cañameras, Félix. "Notas para la historia del notariado catalán." *Estudios históricos y documentos de los archivos de protocolos* 3 (1955), 71–207.

Duursma, Jorri. *Fragmentation and the International Relations of Micro-States: Self-Determination and Statehood*. Cambridge Studies in International and Comparative Law 2. Cambridge, 1996.

Emiliano, António. "Latin or Romance? Graphemic Variation and Scripto-linguistic Change in Medieval Spain." In Wright, ed., *Latin and the Romance Languages*, 233–47.

Engels, Odilo. "Die weltliche Herrschaft des Bischofs von Ausona-Vich (889–1315)." *Gesammelte Aufsätze zur Kulturgeschichte Spaniens* 24 (1968), 1–40.

Fàbrega i Grau, Àngel, ed. *Diplomatari de la Catedral de Barcelona: Documents dels anys 844–1260*. 1 vol. to date. Fonts documentals 1. Barcelona, 1995–.

Feliu i Montfort, Gaspar. "Existí el comte Bernat III de Besalú?" *Acta historica et archaeologica mediaevalia* 19 (1998), 391–402.

"Els inicis del domini territorial de la seu de Barcelona." *Cuadernos de historia económica de Cataluña* 14 (1976), 45–61.

"El patrimoni de la seu de Barcelona durant el pontificat del Bisbe Aeci (995–1010)." *Estudis universitaris catalans* 30 (1994), 51–68.

"Sant Joan de les Abadesses: Algunes precisions sobre l'acta judicial del 913 i el poblament de la vall." In *Homenatge a la memòria del Prof. Dr. Emilio Sáez: Aplec d'estudis dels seus deixebles i col·laboradors* (Barcelona, 1989), 421–34.

"Societat i economia." In *Symposium internacional*, 1:81–115.

Fichtenau, Heinrich. "'Politische' Datierungen des frühen Mittelalters." In Herwig Wolfram and Anton Scharer, eds., *Intitulatio*, 3 vols., Mitteilungen des Instituts für österreichische Geschichtsforschung, Ergänzungsband 21, 24, 29 (Graz, 1967–88), 2:453–548.

Fita, Fidel, ed. "Arenys de Mar, Provincia de Barcelona: Datos inéditos anteriores al siglo XIII." *Boletín de la Real academia de la historia* 6 (1885), 317–36.

"Barcelona en 1079: Su castillo de puerto y su aljama hebrea: Documento inédito." *Boletín de la Real academia de la historia* 43 (1903), 361–68.

"Bula inédita de Silvestre II." *Boletín de la Real academia de la historia* 18 (1891), 247–49.

"Destrucción de Barcelona por Almanzor, 6 julio 985." *Boletín de la Real academia de la historia* 7 (1885), 189–92.

Fité i Llevot, Francesc. *Reculls d'història de la Vall d'Àger*. Vol. 1, *Període antic i medieval*. Àger, 1985.

Flórez, Enrique, et al., *España sagrada . . .* 51 vols. Madrid, 1747–1879.

Font Rius, José Maria. "Les modes de détention de châteaux dans la 'vielle Catalogne' et ses marches extérieures du début du IXe au début du XIe siècle." *Annales du Midi* 80 (1968), 405–14. Reprinted in *Les structures sociales*, 63–72.

Font Rius, José Maria, ed. *Cartas de población y franquicia de Cataluña*. 2 vols. in 3 parts. Consejo superior de investigaciones científicas, Escuela de estudios medievales, Textos, 36, Publicaciones de la Sección de Barcelona, 17 (vol. 1). Anuario de estudios medievales, Anejo 12 (vol. 2). Barcelona, 1969–83.

Fossier, Robert. *Enfance de l'Europe, X^e–XIIe siècles: Aspects économiques et sociaux*. 2nd ed. 2 vols. Nouvelle Clio 17, 17bis. Paris, 1989.

Works cited

Polyptyques et censiers. Typologie des sources du Moyen Âge occidental 28. Turnhout, 1978.

Francastel, Galienne. *Le droit au trône: Un problème de prééminence dans l'art chrétien d'Occident du IVe au XIIe siècle.* Collection le signe de l'art 9. Paris, 1973.

Freedman, Paul H. *The Diocese of Vic: Tradition and Regeneration in Medieval Catalonia.* New Brunswick, N.J., 1983.

——. *The Origins of Peasant Servitude in Medieval Catalonia.* Cambridge, 1991.

——. "Symbolic Implications of the Events of 985–988." In *Symposium internacional,* 1:117–29.

——. "An Unsuccessful Attempt at Urban Organization in Twelfth-Century Catalonia." *Speculum* 54 (1979), 479–91. Reprinted in Freedman, *Church, Law and Society in Catalonia, 900–1500* (Aldershot, 1994), VIII.

Fritze, Wolfgang. "Die fränkische Schwurfreundschaft der Merowingerzeit: Ihr Wesen und ihre politische Funktion." *Zeitschrift der Savigny-Stiftung für Rechtsgeschichte,* Germanistische Abteilung, 71 (1954), 74–125.

Galbert of Bruges. *De multro, traditione, et occisione gloriosi Karoli comitis Flandriarum.* Ed. Jeff Rider. Corpus christianorum, Continuatio mediaevalis, 131. Turnhout, 1994.

Galtier Martí, Fernando. *Ribagorza, condado independiente: Desde los origines hasta 1025.* Zaragoza, 1981.

Galván Freile, Fernando. *La decoración miniada en el Libro de las estampas de la catedral de León.* León, 1997.

Ganshof, François-Louis. "Charlemagne et l'usage de l'écrit en matière administrative." *Le Moyen Âge* 57 (1951), 1–25. Trans. as "The Use of the Written Word in Charlemagne's Administration," in Ganshof, *The Carolingians and the Frankish Monarchy: Studies in Frankish History,* trans. Janet Sondheimer (Ithaca, 1971), 125–42.

García, Arcadio. "La 'commenda' de castillos en el siglo XI." *Ausa* 3 (1958–60), 321–28.

García López, Yolanda. *Estudios críticos y literarios de la "Lex Wisigothorum."* Memorias del Seminario de historia antigua 5. Alcalá de Henares, 1996.

García Villada, Zacarías. *Paleografía española . . .* 2 vols. Publicaciones de la Revista de filología española 6. Madrid, 1923.

Garí, Blanca. "El linaje de los Castellvell en los siglos XI y XII: Un análisis prosopográfico de sus estructuras familiares y de su organización social (*c.* 938–*c.* 1226)." Tesi de doctorat, Universitat Autònoma de Barcelona, 1983.

Garnier, François. *Le langage de l'image au Moyen Âge.* 2 vols. Paris, 1982–89.

Geary, Patrick J. "Extra-judicial Means of Conflict Resolution." In *La giustizia nell'alto medioevo (secoli V–VIII),* 1:569–601.

——. *Phantoms of Remembrance: Memory and Oblivion at the End of the First Millennium.* Princeton, 1994.

——. "Vivre en conflit dans une France sans état: Typologie des mécanismes de règlement des conflits (1050–1200)." *Annales: Économies, sociétés, civilisations* 41 (1986), 1107–33. Trans. as "Living with Conflicts in Stateless France: A Typology of Conflict Management Mechanisms, 1050–1200," in Geary, *Living with the Dead in the Middle Ages* (Ithaca, 1994), 125–60.

Gerbert of Reims. *Die Briefsammlung Gerberts von Reims.* Ed. Fritz Weigle. MGH Die Briefe der deutschen Kaiserzeit 2. Weimar, 1966.

Works cited

[Germain, A., ed.] *Liber instrumentorum memorialium: Cartulaire des Guillems de Montpellier.* Montpellier, 1884–86.

Gigot, Jean-Gabriel, ed. "Les plus anciens documents d'archives des Pyrénées-Orientales (865–989)." *Bulletin philologique et historique (jusqu'à 1610) du Comité des travaux historiques et scientifiques: Année 1962* (1965), 359–99.

Gilissen, John. "Esquisse d'une histoire comparée des sûretés personnelles: Essai de synthèse général." In *Les sûretés personnelles,* 3 vols., Recueils de la Société Jean Bodin pour l'histoire comparative des institutions 28–30 (Brussels, 1969–74), 1:5–127.

Giry, Arthur. *Manuel de diplomatique.* New ed. Paris, 1925.

La giustizia nell'alto medioevo (secoli V–VIII). 2 vols. Settimane di studio del Centro italiano di studi sull'alto medioevo 42. Spoleto, 1995.

La giustizia nell'alto medioevo (secoli IX–XI). 2 vols. Settimane di studio del Centro italiano di studi sull'alto medioevo 44. Spoleto, 1997.

Goetz, Hans-Werner. *Moderne Mediävistik: Stand und Perspektiven der Mittelalterforschung.* Darmstadt, 1999.

Golobardes Vila, Miquel. *Els remences dins el quadre de la pagesia catalana fins el segle XV.* 2 vols. Peralada, 1970–73.

Goñi Gaztambide, José. *Historia de los obispos de Pamplona.* Vol. 1, *Siglos IV–XIII.* Pamplona, 1979.

González, Julio. *Alfonso IX.* 2 vols. Madrid, 1944.

El Reino de Castilla en la época de Alfonso VIII. 3 vols. Consejo superior de investigaciones científicas, Escuela de estudios medievales, Textos, 25–27. Madrid, 1960.

Gonzalvo i Bou, Gener. *La Pau i la Treva a Catalunya: Origen de les Corts Catalanes.* Curs d'història de Catalunya 11. Barcelona, 1986.

Gonzalvo i Bou, Gener, ed. *Les constitucions de Pau i Treva de Catalunya (segles XI–XIII).* Textos jurídics catalans, Lleis i costums, 2:3. Barcelona, 1994.

Grahit, Emilio, ed. "El Llibre vert del Cabildo de la Catedral de Gerona." *Revista histórica* 4 (1877), 118–19, 165–73, 365–75.

Gramain, Monique. "*Castrum*, structures féodales et peuplement en Biterrois au XIe siècle." In *Structures féodales,* 119–33.

Grand, Roger. *Le contrat de complant depuis les origines jusqu'à nos jours.* Paris, 1917.

Grassotti, Hilda. *Las instituciones feudo-vasalláticas en León y Castilla.* 2 vols. Pubblicazioni del Centro italiano di studi sull'alto medioevo 4. Spoleto, 1969.

Miscelanea de estudios sobre instituciones castellano-leonesas. Bilbao, 1978.

Grassotti, Hilda, ed. "Una 'convenientia' prestimonial entre un arzobispo y el emperador." *Cuadernos de historia de España* 51–52 (1970), 5–23. Reprinted in Grassotti, *Miscelanea,* 373–89.

"Homenaje de García Ramírez a Alfonso VII: Dos documentos inéditos." *Cuadernos de historia de España* 37–38 (1963), 318–29. Reprinted in Grassotti, *Miscelanea,* 311–22.

"Sobre una concesión de Alfonso VII a la iglesia salmantina." *Cuadernos de historia de España* 49–50 (1969), 323–48. Reprinted in Grassotti, *Miscelanea,* 351–72.

Grat, Félix, et al., eds. *Recueil des actes de Louis II le Bègue, Louis III et Carloman II, rois de France (877–884).* Paris, 1978.

Gregory of Tours. *Libri historiarum X.* Ed. Bruno Krusch and Wilhelm Levison. MGH Scriptores rerum Merovingicarum 1:1. 2nd ed. Hanover, 1951; repr. 1965.

Works cited

Guillot, Olivier. *Le comte d'Anjou et son entourage au XIe siècle*. 2 vols. Paris, 1972.

Guyotjeannin, Olivier. *Episcopus et comes: Affirmation et déclin de la seigneurie épiscopale au nord du royaume de France (Beauvais-Noyon, X^e–début XIIIe siècle)*. Mémoires et documents publiés par la Société de l'École des chartes 30. Geneva, 1987.

"Recherches sur le développement de la seigneurie épiscopale du nord du royaume de France (Xème–début XIIIème s.): Les exemples de Beauvais et Noyon." 2 vols. Thèse de 3e cycle, Paris IV, 1981.

Guyotjeannin, Olivier, Laurent Morelle, and Michel Parisse, eds. *Les cartulaires: Actes de la table ronde organisée par l'École nationale des chartes et le G.D.R. 121 du C.N.R.S. (Paris, 5–7 décembre 1991)*. Mémoires et documents de l'École des chartes 39. Paris, 1993.

Hallam, Elizabeth M. *Capetian France, 987–1328*. London, 1980.

Harries, Jill, and Ian Wood, eds. *The Theodosian Code*. Ithaca, 1993.

Head, Thomas, and Richard Landes, eds. *The Peace of God: Social Violence and Religious Response in France around the Year 1000*. Ithaca, 1992.

Herman, József, ed. *La transizione dal latino alle lingue romanze: Atti della Tavola rotonda di linguistica storica, Università Ca' Foscari di Venezia, 14–15 giugno 1996*. Tübingen, 1998.

Hibbitts, Bernard J. "'Coming to Our Senses': Communication and Legal Expression in Performance Cultures." *Emory Law Journal* 41 (1992), 873–960.

Hierro, Ernest Marcos. *Die byzantinisch-katalanischen Beziehungen im 12. und 13. Jahrhundert unter besonderer Berücksichtigung der Chronik Jakobs I. von Katalonien-Aragon*. Miscellanea Byzantina Monacensia 37. Munich, 1996.

Hinojosa, Eduardo de. *El régimen señorial y la cuestión agraria en Cataluña durante la Edad Media*. Madrid, 1905.

Ibarburu, M. Eugenia. "Los cartularios reales del Archivo de la Corona de Aragón." *Lambard: Estudis d'art medieval* 6 (1991–93), 197–210.

Iglesia Ferreirós, Aquilino. "La creación del derecho en Cataluña." *Anuario de historia del derecho español* 47 (1977), 99–423.

La prenda contractual: Desde sus orígenes hasta la recepción del Derecho Común. Las garantías reales en el derecho histórico español 1:1. Monografias de la Universidad de Santiago de Compostela 38. Santiago de Compostela, 1977.

Innes, Matthew. "Memory, Orality and Literacy in an Early Medieval Society." *Past & Present* 158 (1998), 3–36.

State and Society in the Early Middle Ages: The Middle Rhine Valley, 400–1000. Cambridge Studies in Medieval Life and Thought, 4th ser., 47. Cambridge, 2000.

Isidore of Seville. *Etymologiarum sive originum libri XX*. Ed. W. M. Lindsay. 2 vols. Oxford, 1911.

Jaeger, C. Stephen. *The Origins of Courtliness: Civilizing Trends and the Formation of Courtly Ideals, 939–1210*. Philadelphia, 1985.

Jaffé, Philipp, ed. *Regesta pontificum Romanorum ab condita ecclesia ad annum post Christum natum MCXCVIII*. 2nd ed., ed. Wilhelm Wattenbach, Samuel Loewenfeld et al. 2 vols. Leipzig, 1885–88; repr. Graz, 1956.

Junyent i Subirà, Eduard, ed. *Diplomatari de la Catedral de Vic, segles IX–X*. Sèrie documents 1. Vic, 1980–96.

Diplomatari i escrits literaris de l'abat i bisbe Oliba. Ed. Anscari M. Mundó. Memòries de la Secció històrico-arqueològica 44. Barcelona, 1992.

Kagay, Donald J., trans. *The Usatges of Barcelona: The Fundamental Law of Catalonia.* Philadelphia, 1995.

Katsura, Hideyuki. "Serments, hommages et fiefs dans la seigneurie des Guilhem de Montpellier (fin XIᵉ–début XIIIᵉ siècle)." *Annales du Midi* 104 (1992), 141–61.

Kehr, Paul. *Das Papsttum und der katalanische Prinzipat bis zur Vereinigung mit Aragon.* Abhandlungen der preussischen Akademie der Wissenschaften, Jahrgang 1926, Philosophisch-historische Klasse, no. 1. Berlin, 1926. Trans. Ramon d'Abadal i de Vinyals as "El papat i el Principat de Catalunya fins a la unió amb Aragó," *Estudis universitaris catalans* 12 (1927), 321–47; 13 (1928), 1–12, 289–323; 14 (1929), 14–32, 213–26; 15 (1930), 1–20.

Kehr, Paul, ed. *Papsturkunden in Spanien: Vorarbeiten zur Hispania pontificia.* Vol. 1, *Katalanien.* 2 parts. Abhandlungen der Gesellschaft der Wissenschaften zu Göttingen, Philologisch-historische Klasse, n.F., 18:2. Berlin, 1926.

Keynes, Simon. *The Diplomas of King Æthelred 'The Unready', 978–1016: A Study in Their Use as Historical Evidence.* Cambridge Studies in Medieval Life and Thought, 3rd ser., 13. Cambridge, 1980.

"Royal Government and the Written Word in Late Anglo-Saxon England." In McKitterick, ed., *The Uses of Literacy,* 226–57.

Kienast, Walther. *Studien über die französischen Volkstämme des Frühmittelalters.* Pariser historische Studien 7. Stuttgart, 1968. Pp. 151–70 (chapter 3, "Das Fortleben des gotischen Rechtes in Südfrankreich und Katalonien") trans. José Maria Font Rius as "La pervivencia del derecho godo en el sur de Francia y Cataluña," *Boletín de la Real academia de buenas letras de Barcelona* 35 (1973–74), 265–95. An earlier German version of this chapter appeared in *Album J. Balon* (Namur, 1968), 97–115.

King, Edmund. "Dispute Settlement in Anglo-Norman England." *Anglo-Norman Studies* 14 (1991), 115–30.

King, P. D. *Law and Society in the Visigothic Kingdom.* Cambridge Studies in Medieval Life and Thought, 3rd ser., 5. Cambridge, 1972.

Kolmer, Lothar. *Promissorische Eide im Mittelalter.* Regensburger historische Forschungen 12. Kallmünz, 1989.

Kosto, Adam J. "The *convenientiae* of the Catalan Counts in the Eleventh Century: A Diplomatic and Historical Analysis." *Acta historica et archaeologica mediaevalia* 19 (1998), 191–228.

"The *convenientia* in the Early Middle Ages." *Mediaeval Studies* 60 (1998), 1–54.

"The Failure of the *Ustages de Barcelona*" (forthcoming).

"The *Liber feudorum maior* of the Counts of Barcelona: The Cartulary as an Expression of Power." *Journal of Medieval History* (forthcoming).

"Making and Keeping Agreements in Medieval Catalonia, 1000–1200." Ph.D. diss., Harvard University, 1996.

"Oliba, Peacemaker." In Ollich i Castanyer, ed., *Gerbert d'Orlhac,* 135–49.

Kottje, Raymund. "Die Lex Baiuvariorum – das Recht der Baiern." In Mordek, ed., *Überlieferung,* 9–23.

Koziol, Geoffrey. *Begging Pardon and Favor: Ritual and Political Order in Early Medieval France.* Ithaca, 1992.

Krueger, Paul, ed. *Corpus iuris civilis.* Vol. 2, *Codex Iustinianus.* 11th ed. Berlin, 1954.

Kuttner, Stephan. "The Revival of Jurisprudence." In Robert L. Benson and Giles Constable, eds., *Renaissance and Renewal in the Twelfth Century* (Cambridge,

Mass., 1982), 299–323. Reprinted in Kuttner, *Studies in the History of Medieval Canon Law* (Aldershot, 1990), III.

Lacarra, José María. "Aspectos económicos de la sumisión de los reinos de taifas (1010–1102)." In *Homenaje a Jaime Vicens Vives*, 2 vols. (Barcelona, 1965–67), 1:255–77. Reprinted in Lacarra, *Colonización, parias, repoblación y otros estudios* (Zaragoza, 1981), 41–76.

Lalinde Abadía, Jesús. *La jurisdicción real inferior en Cataluña ("Corts, veguers, batlles")*. Publicaciones del Seminario de arqueología e historia de la ciudad 14, Estudios, 1. Barcelona, 1966.

"Los pactos matrimoniales catalanes (Esquema histórico)." *Anuario de historia del derecho español* 33 (1963), 133–266.

Landes, Richard. *Relics, Apocalypse, and the Deceits of History: Ademar of Chabannes, 989–1034*. Harvard Historical Studies 117. Cambridge, Mass., 1995.

Lange, Wolf-Dieter. *Philologische Studien zur Latinität westhispanischer Privaturkunden des 9.–12. Jahrhunderts*. Mittellateinische Studien und Texte 3. Leiden, 1966.

Lauranson-Rosaz, Christian. *L'Auvergne et ses marges (Velay, Gévaudan) du VIIIᵉ au XIᵉ siècle: La fin du monde antique?* Le Puy-en-Velay, 1987.

"Les mauvaises coutumes d'Auvergne (fin Xᵉ–XIᵉ siècle)." *Annales du Midi* 102 (1990), 557–86.

Le Goff, Jacques. "The Symbolic Ritual of Vassalage." In Le Goff, *Time, Work, & Culture in the Middle Ages*, trans. Arthur Goldhammer (Chicago, 1980), 237–87. Translation of "Le rituel symbolique de la vassalité," in Le Goff, *Pour un autre Moyen Âge: Temps, travail et culture en Occident: 18 essais* (Paris, 1977), 349–420. Originally published as "Les gestes symboliques dans la vie sociale: Les gestes de la vassalité," in *Simboli i simbologia nell'alto medioevo*, 2 vols., Settimane di studio del Centro italiano di studi sull'alto medioevo 23 (Spoleto, 1976), 2:679–779.

Levison, Wilhelm, ed. "Iudicium in tyrannorum perfidia promulgatum." In Bruno Krusch and Wilhelm Levison, eds., *Passiones vitaeque sanctorum aevi Merovingici*, MGH Scriptores rerum Merovingicarum 5 (Hanover, 1910; repr. 1979), 529–35.

Little, Lester K. *Benedictine Maledictions: Liturgical Cursing in Romanesque France*. Ithaca, 1993.

Llopis Bofill, Joan. *Ensaig històrich sobre la vila de Sitges*. Barcelona, 1891.

Loyn, H. R. *The Governance of Anglo-Saxon England, 500–1087*. The Governance of England 1. London, 1984.

Lupus of Ferrières. *Epistulae*. Ed. Peter K. Marshall. Leipzig, 1984.

Lyon, Bryce. *From Fief to Indenture: The Transition from Feudal to Non-feudal Contract in Western Europe*. Harvard Historical Studies 68. Cambridge, Mass., 1957.

Lyon, Bryce, and Adriaan E. Verhulst. *Medieval Finance: A Comparison of Financial Institutions in Northwestern Europe*. Providence, 1967. Also published as Rijksuniversiteit te Gent, Werken uitgegeven door de Faculteit van de letteren en wijsbegeerte, 143 (Bruges, 1967).

Magdalino, Paul. *The Empire of Manuel I Komnenos, 1143–1180*. Cambridge, 1993.

Magnou-Nortier, Élisabeth. Comments. In Discussion of Magnou-Nortier, "Fidélité et féodalité," *Annales du Midi* 80 (1968), 477–84, at 477–82, 484. Reprinted in *Les structures sociales*, 135–42, at 135–40, 142.

"Convenientia." In *Lexikon des Mittelalters*, 10 vols. (Munich, 1977–99), 3:206–7.

"Fidélité et féodalité méridionales d'après les serments de fidélité (Xᵉ–début XIIᵉ

Works cited

siècle). *Annales du Midi* 80 (1968), 457–77. Reprinted in *Les structures sociales*, 115–35.

Foi et fidélité: Recherches sur l'évolution des liens personnels chez les Francs du VIIᵉ au IXᵉ siècle. Publications de l'Université de Toulouse–Le Mirail, ser. A, 28. Toulouse, 1976.

"La foi et les *convenientiae*: Enquête lexicographique et interprétation sociale." In Danielle Buschinger, ed., *Littérature et société au Moyen Âge: Actes du colloque des 5 et 6 mai 1978* ([Amiens], 1978), 249–62.

"Les mauvaises coutumes en Auvergne, Bourgogne méridionale, Languedoc et Provence au XIᵉ siècle: Un moyen d'analyse sociale." In *Structures féodales*, 135–72.

La société laïque et l'Église dans la province ecclésiastique de Narbonne (zone cispyrénéenne) de la fin du VIIIᵉ à la fin du XIᵉ siècle. Publications de l'Université de Toulouse–Le Mirail, ser. A, 20. Toulouse, 1974.

"La terre, la rente et le pouvoir dans les pays de Languedoc pendant le Haut Moyen Âge." *Francia* 9 (1981), 79–115; 10 (1982), 21–66; 12 (1984), 53–118.

Magnou-Nortier, Élisabeth, and Anne-Marie Magnou, eds. *Recueil des chartes de l'abbaye de La Grasse.* Vol. 1, *779–1119.* Collection de documents inédits sur l'histoire de France, Section d'histoire médiévale et de philologie, Série in-8°, 24. Paris, 1996.

Malafosse, Jehan de. "Contribution à l'étude du crédit dans le Midi aux Xᵉ et XIᵉ siècles: Les sûretés réelles." *Annales du Midi* 63 (1951), 105–48.

Malkiel, Yakov. *Development of the Latin Suffixes -antia and -entia in the Romance Languages, with Special Regard to Ibero-Romance.* University of California Publications in Linguistics 1:4 (pp. 41–188). Berkeley, 1945.

Malpica, A., and T. Quesada, eds. *Los orígenes del feudalismo en el mundo mediterráneo.* 2nd ed. Granada, 1998.

Marca, Pierre de. *Marca Hispanica, sive limes Hispanicus . . .* Paris, 1688; repr. Barcelona, 1998.

Marquès i Casanovas, Jaume. "Sobre los antiguos judíos de Gerona." *Sefarad* 23 (1963), 22–35.

Marquès i Casanovas, Jaume, and Lluís G. Constans i Serrats. *Navata.* s.l., [1985].

Marquès i Planagumà, Josep Maria. *Pergamins de la Mitra (891–1687): Arxiu Diocesà de Girona.* Col·lecció de monografies de l'Institut d'estudis gironins 10. Girona, 1984.

Marquès i Planagumà, Josep Maria, ed. *El cartoral de Santa Maria de Roses (segles X–XIII).* Memòries de la Secció històrico-arqueològica 37. Barcelona, 1986.

Cartoral, dit de Carlemany, del bisbe de Girona (s. IX–XIV). 2 vols. Col·lecció diplomataris 1–2. Barcelona, 1993.

"El cartulari 'De rubricis coloratis' de Pere de Rocaberti, bisbe de Girona (1318–1324)." Tesi de llicenciatura, Universitat Autònoma de Barcelona, 1981.

"La senyoria eclesiàstica de Sant Sadurní de l'Heurà, fins al 1319." *Estudis sobre temes del Baix Empordà* 3 (1984), 71–106.

Martí Castelló, Ramon. "Els inicis de l'organització feudal de la producció al bisbat de Girona (Col·lecció diplomàtica de la seu, anys 817–1100)." 3 vols. Tesi de doctorat, Universitat Autònoma de Barcelona, 1988.

Martí Castelló, Ramon, ed. *Col·lecció diplomàtica de la seu de Girona (817–1100).* Col·lecció diplomataris 13. Barcelona, 1997.

Martindale, Jane. "Dispute, Settlement and Orality in the *Conventum inter Guillelmum*

Works cited

Aquitanorum comitem et Hugonem Chiliarchum: A Postscript to the Edition of 1969." In Martindale, *Status, Authority and Regional Power*, VIII (pp. 1–36).

"'His Special Friend'? The Settlement of Disputes and Political Power in the Kingdom of the French (Tenth to Mid-Twelfth Century)." *Transactions of the Royal Historical Society*, 6th ser., 5 (1995), 21–57.

"An Introduction to the *Conventum inter Guillelmum Aquitanorum comitem et Hugonem Chiliarchum*, 1969." In Martindale, *Status, Authority and Regional Power*, VIIa.

Status, Authority and Regional Power: Aquitaine and France, 9th to 12th Centuries. Aldershot, 1997.

Martindale, Jane, ed. "*Conventum inter Guillelmum Aquitanorum comitem et Hugonem Chiliarchum.*" In Martindale, *Status, Authority and Regional Power*, VIIb. Originally appeared (Latin text only) in *English Historical Review* 84 (1969), 528–48.

Martínez i Teixidó, Lydia. *Les famílies nobles del Pallars en els segles XI i XII.* Estudis 3. Lleida, 1991.

Mas, Joseph, ed. *Rúbrica dels Libri antiquitatum de la Sèu de Barcelona.* 4 vols. Notes històriques del bisbat de Barcelona 9–12. Barcelona, 1914–15.

Mas Martinez, José. "Las conveniencias condales de Ramon Berenguer I, 1040–1076." Tesi de llicenciatura, Universitat Autònoma de Barcelona, 1983.

Masnou, Josep M. "L'escola de la catedral de Vic al segle XI." In Ollich i Castanyer, ed., *Gerbert d'Orlhac*, 621–34.

Matzinger-Pfister, Regula. *Paarformel, Synonymik und zweisprachiges Wortpaar: Zur mehrgliedrigen Ausdrucksweise der mittelalterlichen Urkundensprache.* Rechtshistorische Arbeiten 9. Zurich, 1972.

McCormick, Michael. *Eternal Victory: Triumphal Rulership in Late Antiquity, Byzantium, and the Early Medieval West.* Cambridge, 1987.

McCrank, Lawrence J. "Documenting Reconquest and Reform: The Growth of Archives in the Medieval Crown of Aragon." *American Archivist* 56 (1993), 256–318. Reprinted in McCrank, *Medieval Frontier History in New Catalonia* (Aldershot, 1996), I.

"Restauración canónica e intento de reconquista de la sede Tarraconense, 1076–1108." *Cuadernos de historia de España* 61–62 (1977), 145–245.

"Restoration and Reconquest in Medieval Catalonia: The Church and Principality of Tarragona, 971–1177." Ph.D. diss., University of Virginia, 1974.

McKitterick, Rosamond. *The Carolingians and the Written Word.* Cambridge, 1989.

The Frankish Kingdoms under the Carolingians, 751–987. London, 1983.

"Introduction: Sources and Interpretation." In McKitterick, ed., *New Cambridge Medieval History*, 3–17.

"Latin and Romance: An Historian's Perspective." In Wright, ed., *Latin and the Romance Languages*, 130–45. Reprinted in McKitterick, *The Frankish Kings and Culture in the Early Middle Ages* (Aldershot, 1995), IX.

McKitterick, Rosamond, ed. *The New Cambridge Medieval History.* Vol. 2., *c. 700–c. 900.* Cambridge, 1995.

The Uses of Literacy in Early Medieval Europe. Cambridge, 1990.

Menéndez Pidal, Ramón, ed. *Poema de mio Cid.* 6th ed. Clásicos castellanos 24. Madrid, 1951.

Mersiowsky, Mark. "Regierungspraxis und Schriftlichkeit im Karolingerreich: Das Fallbeispiel der Mandate und Briefe." In Schieffer, ed., *Schriftkultur*, 109–66.

335

Miquel Rosell, Francisco, ed. *Liber feudorum maior: Cartulario real que se conserva en el Archivo de la Corona de Aragón*. 2 vols. Textos y estudios de la Corona de Aragón [1–]2. Barcelona, 1945[–47].

Miret i Sans, Joaquim. *Investigación histórica sobre el vizcondado de Castellbó*. Barcelona, 1900.

"Los vescomtes de Cerdanya, Conflent y Bergadà." *Memorias de la Real academia de buenas letras de Barcelona* 7 (1901), 117–75.

Miret i Sans, Joaquim, ed. "Documents en langue catalane (haute vallée du Sègre, XIe–XIIe siècles)." *Revue hispanique* 19 (1908), 6–19.

"Los noms personals y geogràfichs de la encontrada d'Organyà en los segles X^è y XI^è." *Boletín de la Real academia de buenas letras de Barcelona* 8 (1915–16), 414–44, 522–46.

"Pro sermone plebeico." *Boletín de la Real academia de buenas letras de Barcelona* 7 (1913–14), 30–41, 101–15, 163–85, 229–51, 275–80.

Mitteis, Heinrich. *Lehnrecht und Staatsgewalt: Untersuchungen zur mittelalterlichen Verfassungsgeschichte*. Weimar, 1933.

Molina, Luis, ed. "Las campañas de Almanzor a la luz de un nuevo texto." *Al-Qantara* 2 (1981), 209–63.

Moncada, Juan Luís de. *Episcopologio de Vich*. Ed. Jaime Collell (vols. 1 and 2) and Luís B. Nadal (vol. 3). 3 vols. Biblioteca histórica de la Diócesis de Vich 1, 3 (vols. 1 and 2). Vic, 1891–1904.

Monsalvatge y Fossas, Francisco. *Noticias históricas*. 26 vols. Olot, 1889–1919.

Montagut Estragués, Tomas de. "La recepción del derecho feudal común en Cataluña (Notas para su estudio)." In Sánchez Martínez, ed., *Estudios sobre renta*, 153–75.

Mordek, Hubert. "Kapitularien und Schriftlichkeit." In Schieffer, ed., *Schriftkultur*, 34–66.

"Karolingische Kapitularien." In Mordek, ed., *Überlieferung*, 25–50.

Mordek, Hubert, ed. *Überlieferung und Geltung normativer Texte des frühen und hohen Mittelalters: Vier Vorträge, gehalten auf dem 35. Deutschen Historikertag 1984 in Berlin*. Quellen und Forschungen zum Recht im Mittelalter 4. Sigmaringen, 1986.

Mundó, Anscari M. "El concili de Tarragona de 1180: Dels anys dels reis francs als de l'Encarnació." *Analecta sacra Tarraconensia* 67:1 (1994), xxiii–xliii.

"La datació de documents pel rei Robert (996–1031) a Catalunya." *Anuario de estudios medievales* 4 (1967), 13–34.

"Moissac, Cluny et les mouvements monastiques de l'Est des Pyrénées du Xe au XIIe siècle." *Annales du Midi* 75 (1963), 551–70. Trans. as "Monastic Movements in the East Pyrenees," in Noreen Hunt, ed., *Cluniac Monasticism in the Central Middle Ages* (Hamden, Conn., 1971), 98–122.

"La mort del comte Ramon Borrell de Barcelona i els bisbes de Vic Borrell i Oliba." *Estudis d'història medieval* 1 (1969), 3–15. Reprinted in Mundó, *Obres completes*, 333–45.

Obres completes. Vol. 1, *Catalunya* 1: *De la romanitat a la sobirania*. Textos i estudis de cultura catalana 66. Barcelona, 1998.

"El pacte de Cazola del 1179 i el 'Liber feudorum maior': Notes paleogràfiques i diplomàtiques." In *Jaime I y su época: Comunicaciones*, 2 vols., X Congrés d'història de la Corona d'Aragó, Zaragoza, 1979 (Zaragoza, 1980–82), 1:119–29.

Mundó, Anscari M., ed. "Domains and Rights of Sant Pere de Vilamajor (Catalonia): A Polyptych of *c.* 950 and *c.* 1060." Trans. Thomas N. Bisson.

Speculum 49 (1974), 238–57. Originally appeared as "El políptic dels béns i censos de Sant Pere de Vilamajor (*c.* 950 i *c.* 1060)," *Circular* (Archivo histórico y Museo Fidel Fita, Arenys de Mar) 9 (1961), 48–67. Reedited in Pierre Vilar, ed., *Història de Catalunya,* 8 vols. (Barcelona, 1987–90), 8:54–74. Reprinted in Mundó, *Obres completes,* 101–27.

"Fragment del *Libre jutge,* versió catalana antiga del *Liber iudiciorum.*" *Estudis universitaris catalans* 26 (1984), 155–93.

Murray, Alexander. *Reason and Society in the Middle Ages.* Oxford, 1978.

Negre Pastell, Pelayo. "La villa de Torroella de Montgrí y sus primitivos señores." *Anales del Instituto de estudios gerundenses* 4 (1949), 78–128.

Nehlsen, Hermann. "Zur Aktualität und Effektivität germanischer Rechtsaufzeichnungen." In Classen, ed., *Recht und Schrift im Mittelalter,* 449–502.

Nelson, Janet L. "Literacy in Carolingian Government." In McKitterick, ed., *The Uses of Literacy,* 258–96. Reprinted in Nelson, *The Frankish World: 750–900* (London, 1996), 1–36.

Politics and Ritual in Early Medieval Europe. London, 1986.

"Public *Histories* and Private History in the Work of Nithard." *Speculum* 60 (1985), 251–93. Reprinted (with appendices) in Nelson, *Politics and Ritual,* 195–237.

Niermeyer, Jan Frederik. *Mediae Latinitatis lexicon minus.* Ed. C. van de Kieft. Leiden, 1976; repr. 1993.

Noble, Thomas F. X. "Literacy and the Papal Government in Late Antiquity and the Early Middle Ages." In McKitterick, ed., *The Uses of Literacy,* 82–108.

The Republic of St. Peter: The Birth of the Papal State, 680–825. Philadelphia, 1984.

Noguera de Guzmán, Raimundo. "El precario y la 'precaria' (Notas para la historia de la enfiteusis)." *Estudios históricos y documentos de los archivos de protocolos* 2 (1950), 151–274.

Oliver Asín, Jaime. "En torno a los orígenes de Castilla: Su toponimia en relación con los árabes y los beréberes." *Al-Andalus* 38 (1973), 319–91. Published separately (Madrid, 1975).

Ollich i Castanyer, Imma, ed. *Actes del Congrés internacional Gerbert d'Orlhac i el seu temps: Catalunya i Europa a la fi del 1r mil·lenni: Vic-Ripoll, 10–13 de novembre de 1999.* Documents 31. Vic, 1999.

Ors, Alvaro d'. *La era hispánica.* Mundo antiguo 1. Pamplona, 1962.

Ostos Salcedo, Pilar, ed. "Documentación del Vizcondado de Vilamur en el Archivo Ducal de Medinaceli (1126–1301). Estudio diplomático y edición." *Historia. Instituciones. Documentos* 8 (1981), 267–384.

Ourliac, Paul. Comments. In Discussion of Bonnassie, "Les conventions féodales," *Annales du Midi* 80 (1968), 551–61, at 555–56, 559. Reprinted in *Les structures sociales,* 209–19, at 213–14, 217.

"La *convenientia.*" In Ourliac, *Études d'histoire du droit médiéval* (Paris, 1979), 243–52. Originally appeared in *Études d'histoire du droit privé offertes à Pierre Petot* (Paris, 1959), 413–22.

"Juges et justiciables au XIe siècle: Les *boni homines.*" *Recueil de mémoires et travaux publié par la Société d'histoire du droit et des institutions des anciens pays de droit écrit* 16 (1994), 17–33.

"La tradition romaine dans les actes toulousains des Xe et XIe siècles." *Revue historique de droit français et étranger* 60 (1982), 577–88. Reprinted in Ourliac, *Les pays de Garonne vers l'an mil: La société et le droit: Recueil d'études* (Toulouse, 1993), 65–77.

"Troubadours et juristes." In Ourliac, *Études d'histoire du droit médiéval* (Paris, 1979), 273–301. Originally published in *Cahiers de civilisation médiévale* 8 (1965), 159–77.

Ourliac, Paul, and Jehan de Malafosse. *Histoire du droit privé*. 2nd ed. 2 vols. Paris, 1969–71.

Paoli, Cesare. *Diplomatica*. New ed., ed. G. C. Bascapè. Manuali di filologia e storia, 1st ser., 1. Florence, 1942; repr. 1969.

Parisse, Michel, and Jacqueline Leuridan, eds. *Atlas de la France de l'an mil: État de nos connaissances*. Paris, 1994.

Pensado, Carmen. "How Was Leonese Vulgar Latin Read?" In Wright, ed., *Latin and the Romance Languages*, 190–204.

Percival, John. "The Precursors of Domesday: Roman and Carolingian Land Registers." In Peter Sawyer, ed., *Domesday Book: A Reassessment* (London, 1985), 5–27.

Pérez i Gómez, Xavier, ed. *Diplomatari de la cartoixa de Montalegre (segles X–XII)*. Col·lecció diplomataris 14. Barcelona, 1998.

Pérez González, Maurilio. *El latín de la cancillería castellana (1158–1214)*. Acta Salmanticensia, Filosofía y letras, 163. Salamanca, 1985.

Pfister, Max. "Die Anfänge der altprovenzalischen Schriftsprache." *Zeitschrift für romanische Philologie* 86 (1970), 305–23.

Pladevall i Font, Antoni. "Els senescals dels comtes de Barcelona durant el segle XI." *Anuario de estudios medievales* 3 (1966), 111–30.

Poly, Jean-Pierre. "Les légistes provençaux et la diffusion du droit romain dans le Midi." *Recueil de mémoires et travaux publié par la Société d'histoire du droit et des institutions des anciens pays de droit écrit* 9 (1974), 613–35.

La Provence et la société féodale (879–1166): Contribution à l'étude des structures dites féodales dans le Midi. Paris, 1976.

Poly, Jean-Pierre, and Eric Bournazel. *La mutation féodale: X^e–XIIe siècle*. 2nd ed. Nouvelle Clio 16. Paris, 1991. Trans. from the 1st French ed. (1980) as *The Feudal Transformation: 900–1200*, trans. Caroline Higgett (New York, 1991).

"Post scriptum." *Revue historique de droit français et étranger* 73 (1995), 361–62.

"Que faut-il préférer au 'mutationnisme'? ou le problème du changement social." *Revue historique de droit français et étranger* 72 (1994), 401–12.

Pons i Guri, Josep Maria. "Corpus iuris." In *Documents jurídics*, 111–34.

"Documents sobre aplicació dels Usatges de Barcelona, anteriors al segle XIII." *Acta historica et archaeologica mediaevalia* 14–15 (1993–94), 39–46.

"El dret als segles VIII–XI." In *Symposium internacional*, 1:131–59.

Portella i Comas, Jaume, ed. *La formació i expansió del feudalisme català: Actes del col·loqui organitzat pel Col·legi universitari de Girona (8–11 de gener de 1985): Homenatge a Santiago Sobrequés i Vidal*. Estudi general 5–6 (1985–86). Girona, [1986].

Powers, James F. *A Society Organized for War: The Iberian Municipal Militias in the Central Middle Ages, 1000–1284*. Berkeley, 1988.

Pruenca i Bayona, Esteve, ed. *Diplomatari de Santa Maria d'Amer*. Ed. Josep M. Marquès. Col·lecció diplomataris 7. Barcelona, 1995.

Puig i Ferreté, Ignasi M. "L'ascendència pallaresa dels bisbes d'Urgell Bernat Guillem (1076–1092) i Guillem Arnau de Montferrer (1092–1095)." *Urgellia* 3 (1980), 185–93.

El monestir de Santa Maria de Gerri (segles XI–XV). 2 vols. Memòries de la Secció històrico–arqueològica 42. Barcelona, 1991.

Puig i Ferreté, Ignasi M, ed. *El cartoral de Santa Maria de Lavaix: El monestir durant els segles XI–XIII.* La Seu d'Urgell, 1984.

Puig i Ustrell, Pere. *Els pergamins documentals: Naturalesa, tractament arxivístic i contingut diplomàtic.* Col·lecció normativa arxivística 3. Barcelona, 1995.

Puig i Ustrell, Pere, ed. *El monestir de Sant Llorenç del Munt sobre Terrassa: Diplomatari dels segles X i XI.* 3 vols. Col·lecció diplomataris 8–10. Barcelona, 1995.

Puig y Puig, Sebastián. *Episcopologio de la sede Barcinonense: Apuntes para la historia de la iglesia de Barcelona y de sus prelados.* Biblioteca histórica de la Biblioteca Balmes, ser. 1, 1. Barcelona, 1929.

Pujades, Gerónimo. *Crónica universal del principado de Cataluña.* 8 vols. Barcelona, 1829–32.

al-Rāzī, 'Īsà ibn Aḥmad. *Anales palatinos del califa de Córdoba al-Ḥakam II, por 'Īsā ibn Aḥmad al-Rāzī (360–364 H. = 971–975 J. C.).* Trans. Emilio García Gómez. Madrid, 1967.

Reilly, Bernard F., ed. *Santiago, Saint-Denis, and Saint Peter: The Reception of the Roman Liturgy in León-Castile in 1080.* New York, 1985.

Reynolds, Susan. *Fiefs and Vassals: The Medieval Evidence Reinterpreted.* Oxford, 1994.

Kingdoms and Communities in Western Europe, 900–1300. 2nd ed. Oxford, 1997.

Richter, Michael. *Studies in Medieval Language and Culture.* Dublin, 1995.

Riedmann, Josef. *Die Beurkundung der Verträge Friedrich Barbarossas mit italienischen Städten: Studien zur diplomatischen Form von Vertragsurkunden im 12. Jahrhundert.* Österreichische Akademie der Wissenschaften, Philosophisch-historische Klasse, Sitzungsberichte, 291:3. Vienna, 1973.

Riu i Riu, Manuel. "A propósito del feudalismo todavía." In *Estudios en homenaje a Don Claudio Sánchez Albornoz en sus 90 años,* 6 vols. to date (Buenos Aires, 1983–), 2:65–82.

"La canònica de Santa Maria de Solsona: Precedents medievals d'un bisbat modern." *Urgellia* 2 (1979), 211–56.

"Castells i fortificacions menors: Llurs orígens, paper, distribució i formes de possessió." In Barral i Altet et al., eds., *Catalunya i França,* 248–60.

Rius Serra, José. "*Reparatio scripturae.*" *Anuario de historia del derecho español* 5 (1928), 246–53. Reprinted in Rius Serra, *Miscelánea Mons. José Rius Serra,* 2 vols., Biblioteca filológica-histórica [14–]15 (Sant Cugat del Vallès, 1965), 1:119–26.

Rius Serra, José, ed. *Cartulario de "Sant Cugat" del Vallés.* 3 vols. Textos y estudios de la Corona de Aragón [3–]5. Barcelona, 1945–47.

Rocafiguera, Francesc de. "Documents del monestir de l'Estany existents a l'Arxiu Episcopal de Vic (1106–1498)." *Studia Vicensia* 1 (1989). 127–36.

Rodón Binué, Eulalia. *El lenguaje técnico del feudalismo en el siglo XI en Cataluña (contribución al estudio del latín medieval).* Publicaciones de la Escuela de filología de Barcelona, Filología clásica, 16. Barcelona, 1957.

Rodríguez Lorente, Juan J. *Numismática de la Murcia musulmana.* Madrid, 1984.

Rosenwein, Barbara H. *Negotiating Space: Power, Restraint, and Privileges of Immunity in Early Medieval Europe.* Ithaca, 1999.

To Be the Neighbor of Saint Peter: The Social Meaning of Cluny's Property, 909–1049. Ithaca, 1989.

Rouche, Michel. "Les survivances antiques dans trois cartulaires du Sud-Ouest de la France aux Xe et XIe siècles." *Cahiers de civilisation médiévale* 23 (1980), 93–108.

Roura, Gabriel, ed. "Un diploma desconegut del rei Odó a favor del seu fidel Wicfrid (888–898)." In Portella i Comas, ed., *La formació i expansió*, 65–75.

Rovira i Ermengol, Josep, ed. *Usatges de Barcelona i Commemoracions de Pere Albert.* Els nostres clàssics, Col·lecció A, 43–44. Barcelona, 1933.

Rovira i Virgili, Antoni. *Història nacional de Catalunya.* 7 vols. Barcelona, 1922–34.

Ruggieri, Ruggero M., ed. *Testi antichi romanzi.* 2 vols. Testi e manuali 29–30. Modena, 1949.

Ruiz-Domènec, José Enrique. *L'estructura feudal: Sistema de parentiu i teoria de l'aliança en la societat catalana (c. 980–c. 1220).* Barcelona, 1985.

Sabatini, Francesco. "Dalla 'scripta latina rustica' alle 'scriptae' romanze." *Studi medievali*, 3rd ser., 9 (1968), 320–58.

Sahlins, Peter. *Boundaries: The Making of France and Spain in the Pyrenees.* Berkeley, 1989.

Sainte-Marthe, Denis de, and Barthélemy Hauréau, eds. *Gallia christiana in provincias ecclesiasticas distributa.* 16 vols. Paris, 1715–1865.

Salrach, Josep Maria. "Entre l'estat antic i el feudal. Mutacions socials i dinàmica político-militar a l'Occident carolingi i als comtats catalans." In *Symposium internacional*, 1:191–252.

——— "Les féodalités méridionales: Des Alpes à la Galice." In Eric Bournazel and Jean-Pierre Poly, eds., *Les féodalités* (Paris, 1998), 313–88.

——— "Formació, organització i defensa del domini de Sant Cugat en els segles X–XII." *Acta historica et archaeologica mediaevalia* 13 (1992), 127–73.

——— "El 'Liber feudorum maior' i els comptes fiscals de Ramon de Caldes." In *Documents jurídics*, 85–110.

——— *El procés de formació nacional de Catalunya (segles VIII–IX).* 2 vols. Barcelona, 1978.

Sanahuja, Pedro. "Arnau Mir de Tost, caudillo de la Reconquista en tierras de Lérida." *Ilerda* 1 (1943), 11–27, 155–69; 2:1 (1944), 7–21; 2:2 (1944), 53–147; 4 (1946), 25–55.

——— *Historia de la villa de Ager.* Barcelona, 1961.

Sánchez Casabón, Ana Isabel, ed. *Alfonso II Rey de Aragón, Conde de Barcelona y Marqués de Provenza. Documentos (1162–1196).* Fuentas históricas aragonesas 23. Publicaciones de la Institución "Fernando el Católico" 1691. Zaragoza, 1995.

Sánchez Martínez, Manuel. "La expedición de Al-Manṣūr contra Barcelona en el 985 según las fuentes árabes." In Barral i Altet et al., eds., *Catalunya i França*, 293–301.

Sánchez Martínez, Manuel, ed. *Estudios sobre renta, fiscalidad y finanzas en la Cataluña bajomedieval.* Anuario de estudios medievales, Anejo 27. Barcelona, 1993.

Sangés, Domènec, ed. "Recull de documents del segle XI referents a Guissona i la seva plana." *Urgellia* 3 (1980), 195–305.

Sans i Travé, Josep Maria, ed. *Col·lecció diplomàtica de la casa del Temple de Barberà (945–1212).* Textos jurídics catalans, Documents, 1. Barcelona, 1997.

Schieffer, Rudolf. "Rechtstexte des Reformpapsttums und ihre zeitgenössische Resonanz." In Mordek, ed., *Überlieferung*, 51–69.

Schieffer, Rudolf, ed. *Schriftkultur und Reichsverwaltung unter den Karolingern: Referate des Kolloquiums der Nordrhein-westfälischen Akademie der Wissenschaften am 17./18. Februar 1994 in Bonn.* Abhandlungen der Nordrhein-westfälischen Akademie der Wissenschaften 97. Opladen, 1996.

Schmidt-Wiegand, Ruth. "Eid und Gelöbnis, Formel und Formular im mittelalterlichen Recht." In Classen, ed., *Recht und Schrift im Mittelalter*, 55–90.

Works cited

Schmitt, Jean-Claude. *La raison des gestes dans l'Occident médiéval*. Paris, 1990.

Schneider, Reinhard. *Brüdergemeine und Schwurfreundschaft: Der Auflösungsprozeß des Karlingerreiches im Spiegel der caritas-Terminologie in den Verträgen der karlingischen Teilkönige des 9. Jahrhunderts*. Historische Studien 388. Lübeck, 1964.

Schott, Clausdieter. "Der Stand der Leges-Forschung." *Frühmittelalterliche Studien* 13 (1979), 29–55.

Schwab, Moïse, and Joachim Miret i Sans, eds. "Le plus ancien document à présent connu des juifs catalans." *Boletín de la Real academia de buenas letras de Barcelona* 8 (1915–16), 229–33.

Schramm, Percy E. "Ramon Berenguer IV." Trans. Margarida Fontseré. In Enric Bagué, Joan Cabestany, and Percy E. Schramm, *Els primers comtes-reis*, 3rd ed., Història de Catalunya, Biografies catalanes, 4 (Barcelona, 1985), 1–53. Originally appeared as "Die Entstehung eines Doppelreiches: Die Vereinigung von Aragon und Barcelona durch Ramón Berenguer IV. (1137–62)," in Hellmut Kretzschmar, ed., *Vom Mittelalter zur Neuzeit: Zum 65. Geburtstag von Heinrich Sproemberg*, Forschungen zur mittelalterlichen Geschichte 1 (Berlin, 1956), 19–50.

Sellert, Wolfgang. "Aufzeichnung des Rechts und Gesetz." In Sellert, ed., *Das Gesetz in Spätantike und frühem Mittelalter: 4. Symposion der Kommission "Die Funktion des Gesetzes in Geschichte und Gegenwart,"* Abhandlungen der Akademie der Wissenschaften in Göttingen, Philologisch-historische Klasse, dritte Folge, 196 (Göttingen, 1992), 67–102.

Serra Vilaró, Joan. "Los señores de Portell, patria de San Ramón, descendientes de los vizcondes de Cardona." *Analecta sacra Tarraconensia* 29 (1956), 209–72; 30 (1957), 97–152.

Serrano y Sanz, Manuel. *Noticias y documentos históricos del condado de Ribagorza hasta la muerte de Sancho Garcés III (año 1035)*. Madrid, 1912.

Sevillano Colom, Francisco. *Inventario de pergaminos medievales de monasterios gerundenses*. 1 vol. only. Madrid, 1953.

Shideler, John C. *A Medieval Catalan Noble Family: The Montcadas, 1000–1230*. Publications of the UCLA Center for Medieval and Renaissance Studies 20. Berkeley, 1983.

Sitjes i Molins, X., and Antoni Pladevall i Font. "El castell bisbal d'Artés." *Ausa* 8 (1975–79), 334–47.

Smith, Julia M. H. "*Fines imperii*: The Marches." In McKitterick, ed., *New Cambridge Medieval History*, 169–89.

——— "Oral and Written: Saints, Miracles, and Relics in Brittany, c. 850–1250." *Speculum* 65 (1990), 309–43.

——— *Province and Empire: Brittany and the Carolingians*. Cambridge Studies in Medieval Life and Thought, 4th ser., 18. Cambridge, 1992.

Sobrequés, Santiago. *Els barons de Catalunya*. 4th ed. Història de Catalunya, Biografies catalanes, 3. Barcelona, 1989.

——— *Els grans comtes de Barcelona*. 4th ed. Història de Catalunya, Biografies catalanes, 2. Barcelona, 1985.

Soldevila, Ferran. *Història de Catalunya*. 2nd ed. in 1 vol. Barcelona, 1963.

Soler García, Josefina, ed. "El cartulario de Tavernoles." *Boletín de la Sociedad castellonense de cultura* 36 (1960), 196–216, 248–79; 37 (1961), 65–80, 149–206; 38

(1962), 110–26, 218–38, 319–46, 428–42. Published separately, with additional material: Libros raros y curiosos 14 (Castellón de la Plana, 1961).

Stenton, Frank M. *The First Century of English Feudalism, 1066–1166.* 2nd ed. Oxford, 1961.

Stenton, Frank M., ed. *Transcripts of Charters Relating to the Gilbertine Houses of Sixle, Ormsby, Catley, Bullington, and Alvingham.* Publications of the Lincoln Record Society 18. Horncastle, 1922.

Stock, Brian. *The Implications of Literacy: Written Language and Models of Interpretation in the Eleventh and Twelfth Centuries.* Princeton, 1983.

Straka, Georges, ed. *Les anciens textes romans non littéraires: Leur apport à la connaissance de la langue au Moyen Âge: Colloque international organisé par le Centre de philologie et de littératures romanes de l'Université de Strasbourg du 30 janvier au 4 février 1961.* Actes et colloques 1. Paris, 1963.

Structures féodales et féodalisme dans l'Occident méditerranéen (X^e–XIIIe siècles): Bilan et perspectives de recherches: École française de Rome, 10–13 octobre 1978. Colloques internationaux du Centre national de la recherche scientifique 588. Paris, 1980. Also published as Collection de l'École française de Rome 44 (Rome, 1980).

Les structures sociales de l'Aquitaine, du Languedoc et de l'Espagne au premier âge féodal: Toulouse 28–31 mars 1968. Paris, 1969.

Studtmann, Joachim. "Die Pönformel der mittelalterlichen Urkunden." *Archiv für Urkundenforschung* 12 (1932), 251–374.

Symposium internacional sobre els orígens de Catalunya (segles VIII–XI). 2 vols. Barcelona, 1991–92. Also published as *Memorias de la Real academia de buenas letras de Barcelona* 23–24 (1991).

Tabuteau, Emily Zack. *Transfers of Property in Eleventh-Century Norman Law.* Chapel Hill, 1988.

Taylor, Nathaniel L. "Judges in Barcelona in the Twelfth Century: The Decline of the Post-Visigothic Judiciary." Paper presented at the 114th annual meeting of the American Historical Association, Chicago, 8 January 2000.

"The Will and Society in Medieval Catalonia and Languedoc, 800–1200." Ph.D. diss., Harvard University, 1995.

Teulet, Alexandre, et al., eds. *Layettes du Trésor des chartes.* 5 vols. Paris, 1863–1909.

Thesaurus linguae latinae. Leipzig, 1900–.

To Figueras, Lluís. "Le mas catalan du XIIe s.: Genèse et évolution d'une structure d'encadrement et d'asservissement de la paysannerie." *Cahiers de civilisation médiévale* 36 (1993), 151–77.

El monestir de Santa Maria de Cervià i la pagesia: Una anàlisi local del canvi feudal: Diplomatari segles X–XII. Publicacions de la Fundació Salvador Vives Casajuana 110. Barcelona, 1991.

Toubert, Pierre. "Les féodalités méditerranéennes: Un problème d'histoire comparée." In *Structures féodales,* 1–13.

Les structures du Latium médiéval: Le Latium méridional et la Sabine du IXe siècle à la fin du XIIe siècle. 2 vols. Bibliothèque des Écoles françaises d'Athènes et de Rome 221. Rome, 1973.

Trenchs Òdena, Josep. "La escribanía de Ramón Berenguer III (1097–1131). Datos para su estudio." *Saitabi* 30 (1981), 11–36.

"Los escribanos de Ramón Berenguer IV: Nuevos datos." *Saitabi* 29 (1979), 5–20.

Works cited

"Notarios y escribanos de Alfonso II (1154–1196): Datos biográficos." *Saitabi* 28 (1978), 5–24.

Ubieto Arteta, Antonio. "Estudios en torno a la división del reino por Sancho el Mayor de Navarra." *Príncipe de Viana* 21 (1960), 5–56, 163–236.

"Sobre demografía aragonesa del siglo XII." *Estudios de Edad Media de la Corona de Aragón* 7 (1962), 578–98.

Ubieto Arteta, Antonio, ed. *Cartulario de San Juan de la Peña.* 2 vols. Textos medievales 6, 9. Valencia, 1962–63.

Udina i Abelló, Antoni M. "L'administració de justícia en els comtats pirinencs (segles IX–XII)." In *Miscel·lània homenatge a Josep Lladonosa* (Lleida, 1992), 129–45.

La successió testada a la Catalunya altomedieval. Col·lecció textos i documents 5. Barcelona, 1984.

Udina i Martorell, Frederic. *El nom de Catalunya.* Barcelona, 1961.

Udina i Martorell, Frederic, ed. *El archivo condal de Barcelona: Estudio crítico de sus fondos.* Consejo superior de investigaciones científicas, Escuela de estudios medievales, Textos, 18, Publicaciones de la Sección de Barcelona, 15. Barcelona, 1951.

El "Llibre Blanch" de Santas Creus (Cartulario del siglo XII). Textos y estudios de la Corona de Aragón 9. Barcelona, 1947.

"Versió canc[e]lleresca d'un document rossellonès del segle X, confirmat per Jaume I." In *Homenaje a Don José Maria Lacarra de Miguel en su jubilación del profesorado: Estudios medievales,* 5 vols. (Zaragoza, 1977), 1:87–95.

Udina i Martorell, Frederic, and Antoni M. Udina i Abelló. "Consideracions a l'entorn del nucli originari dels *Usatici Barchinonae.*" In Portella i Comas, ed., *La formació i expansió,* 87–104.

Uytfanghe, Marc van. "Histoire du Latin, protohistoire des langues romanes et histoire de la communication: A propos d'un recueil d'études, et avec quelques observations préliminaires sur le débat intellectuel entre pensée structurale et pensée historique." *Francia* 11 (1983), 579–613.

Valls i Taberner, Ferran. "Estudi sobre els documents del comte Guifré I de Barcelona." In *Homenatge a Antoni Rubió i Lluch: Miscel·lània d'estudis literaris, històrics i lingüístics,* 3 vols. (Barcelona, 1936), 1:11–31. Reprinted in Valls i Taberner, *Obras selectas,* 4:47–70.

"El *Liber iudicum popularis* de Homobonus de Barcelona." *Anuario de historia del derecho español* 2 (1925), 200–212. Reprinted in Valls i Taberner, *Obras selectas,* 2:235–46.

Obras selectas. 4 vols. in 6 parts. Madrid, 1952–61.

"Els orígens dels comtats de Pallars i Ribagorça." *Estudis universitaris catalans* 9 (1915–16), 1–101. Partial reprint (of pp. 40–101) as "Els comtats de Pallars i Ribagorça a partir del segle XI," in Valls i Taberner, *Obras selectas,* 4:125–205.

"La primera dinastia vescomtal de Cardona." *Estudis universitaris catalans* 16 (1931), 112–36. Reprinted (without documents) in Valls i Taberner, *Obras selectas,* 4:207–15.

Viader, Roland. "Remarques sur la tenure et le statut des tenanciers dans la Catalogne du XIe au XIIIe siècle." *Annales du Midi* 107 (1995), 149–65.

Vic, Claude de, and Joseph Vaissette. *Histoire générale de Languedoc avec des notes et les pièces justificatives.* New ed. (Privat). 16 vols. Toulouse, 1872–1904.

Vielliard, Françoise. "Les langues vulgaires dans les cartulaires français du Moyen Âge." In Guyotjeannin, Morelle, and Parisse, eds., *Les cartulaires,* 137–50.

Works cited

Villanueva, Jaime. *Viage literario a las iglesias de España*. 22 vols. Madrid, 1803–52.

Virgili, Antoni. "Conquesta, colonització i feudalització de Tortosa (segle XII), segons el cartulari de la catedral." In Portella i Comas, ed., *La formació i expansió*, 275–89.

Vollrath, Hanna. "Gesetzgebung und Schriftlichkeit: Das Beispiel der angelsächsischen Gesetze." *Historisches Jahrbuch* 99 (1979), 28–54.

Wadle, Elmar. "Frühe deutsche Landfrieden." In Mordek, ed., *Überlieferung*, 71–92.

Wallace-Hadrill, J. M. *Early Germanic Kingship in England and on the Continent: The Ford Lectures Delivered in the University of Oxford in Hilary Term 1970*. Oxford, 1971.

Walsh, Thomas J. "Spelling Lapses in Early Medieval Latin Documents and the Reconstruction of Primitive Romance Phonology." In Wright, ed., *Latin and the Romance Languages*, 205–18.

Warren, W. L. *The Governance of Norman and Angevin England, 1086–1272*. The Governance of England 2. Stanford, 1987.

Weinberger, Stephen. "Les conflits entre clercs et laïcs dans la Provence du XIe siècle." *Annales du Midi* 92 (1980), 269–79.

"Cours judiciaires, justice et responsabilité sociale dans la Provence médiévale: IXe–XIe siècle." *Revue historique* 267 (1982), 273–88.

"Precarial Grants: Approaches of the Clergy and Lay Aristocracy to Landholding and Time." *Journal of Medieval History* 11 (1985), 163–69.

Weiß, Stefan. *Die Urkunden der päpstlichen Legaten von Leo IX. bis Coelestin III. (1049–1198)*. Forschungen zur Kaiser- und Papstgeschichte des Mittelalters 13. Cologne, 1995.

Werner, Karl Ferdinand. "*Missus-marchio-comes*: Entre l'administration centrale et l'administration locale de l'Empire carolingien." In Werner Paravicini and Karl Ferdinand Werner, eds., *Histoire comparée de l'administration (IVe–XVIIIe siècles): Actes du XIVe colloque historique franco-allemand, Tours, 27 mars–1er avril 1977, organisé avec le Centre d'études supérieures de la Renaissance par l'Institut historique allemand de Paris*, Beihefte der Francia 9 (Munich, 1980), 191–239. Reprinted in Werner, *Vom Frankenreich zur Entfaltung Deutschlands und Frankreichs: Ursprünge-Strukturen-Beziehungen: Ausgewählte Beiträge: Festgabe zu seinem sechzigsten Geburtstag* (Sigmaringen, 1984), 108–56.

White, Stephen D. "Proposing the Ordeal and Avoiding It: Strategy and Power in Western French Litigation." In Bisson, ed., *Cultures of Power*, 89–123.

Wickham, Chris. "Land Disputes and Their Social Framework in Lombard-Carolingian Italy, 700–900." In Davies and Fouracre, eds., *The Settlement of Disputes*, 105–24. Reprinted (with additional notes) in Wickham, *Studies in Italian and European Social History, 400–1200* (London, 1994), 229–56.

Wood, Ian. "Administration, Law and Culture in Merovingian Gaul." In McKitterick, ed., *The Uses of Literacy*, 63–81.

"Roman Law in the Barbarian Kingdoms." In Alvar Ellegård and Gunilla Åkerström-Hougen, eds., *Rome and the North*, Studies in Mediterranean Archaeology and Literature 135 (Jonsered, 1996), 5–14.

Wormald, Patrick. *Legal Culture in the Early Medieval West: Law as Text, Image and Experience*. London, 1999.

"*Lex scripta* and *verbum regis*: Legislation and Germanic Kingship, from Euric to Cnut." In P. H. Sawyer and I. N. Wood, eds., *Early Medieval Kingship* (Leeds,

1977), 105–38. Reprinted (with addenda) in Wormald, *Legal Culture in the Early Medieval West*, 1–44.

The Making of English Law: King Alfred to the Twelfth Century. Vol. 1, *Legislation and Its Limits*. Oxford, 1999.

Wright, Roger. *Early Ibero-Romance: Twenty-one Studies on Language and Texts from the Iberian Peninsula between the Roman Empire and the Thirteenth Century*. Estudios lingüísticos 5. Newark, Del., 1994.

Late Latin and Early Romance in Spain and Carolingian France. ARCA Classical and Medieval Texts, Papers and Monographs 8. Liverpool, 1982.

Wright, Roger, ed. *Latin and the Romance Languages in the Early Middle Ages*. London, 1991.

Zeumer, Karl, ed. "Formulae Visigothicae." In Zeumer, ed., *Formulae Merowingici et Karolini aevi*, MGH Legum sectio V (Hanover, 1886; repr. 1963), 572–95.

"Liber iudiciorum sive Lex Visigothorum." In Zeumer, ed., *Leges Visigothorum*, MGH Legum sectio I (Hanover, 1902; repr. 1973), 33–456.

Zimmermann, Michel. "Aux origines de la Catalogne féodale: Les serments non-datés du règne de Ramon Berenguer Ier." In Portella i Comas, ed., *La formació i expansió*, 109–51.

"La datation des documents catalans du IXe au XIIe siècle: Un itinéraire politique." *Annales du Midi* 93 (1981), 345–75.

"'Et je t'empouvoirrai' (Potestativum te farei): A propos des relations entre fidélité et pouvoir en Catalogne au XIe siècle." *Médiévales* 10 (1986), 17–36.

"Glose, tautologie ou inventaire? L'énumération descriptive dans la documentation catalane du Xème au XIIème siècle." *Cahiers de linguistique hispanique médiévale* 14–15 (1989–90), 309–38.

"Naissance d'une principauté: Barcelone et les autres comtés catalans aux alentours de l'an Mil." In Barral i Altet et al., eds., *Catalunya i França*, 111–35.

"La prise de Barcelone par Al-Mansûr et la naissance de l'historiographie catalane." *Annales de Bretagne et des pays de l'Ouest* 87 (1980), 191–218.

"Protocoles et préambules dans les documents catalans du Xe au XIIe siècle: Évolution diplomatique et signification spirituelle." *Mélanges de la Casa de Velázquez* 10 (1974), 41–76; 11 (1975), 51–79.

"L'usage du droit wisigothique en Catalogne du IXe au XIIe siècle: Approches d'une signification culturelle." *Mélanges de la Casa de Velázquez* 9 (1973), 233–81.

"Le vocabulaire latin de malédiction du IXe au XIIe siècle: Construction d'un discours eschatologique." *Atalaya: Revue française d'études médiévales hispaniques* 5 (1994), 37–55.

Zimmermann, Michel, ed. "Un formulaire du Xème siècle conservé à Ripoll." *Faventia* 4:2 (1982), 25–86.

Les marches méridionales du royaume aux alentours de l'an mil: Inventaire typologique des sources documentaires: Colloque Hugues Capet 987–1987: La France de l'an mil (Nancy, 1987).

Les sociétés méridionales autour de l'an mil: Répertoire des sources et documents commentés (Paris, 1992).

INDEX OF NAMES

Personal names are indexed by given name rather than toponymic. Information about family relationships is provided only when necessary to aid identification in the text or to distinguish individuals with the same name in the index. Page numbers in *italics* indicate locations in the text where an individual is referred to without a name (e.g., only by office or relationship). Modern Catalan forms that differ from the Latin (see above, p. xiv) are given according to the following principles: *-us* or *-o* are omitted; the addition of accents, doubling of letters, and certain other orthographic changes (a/ai, e/i, c/t, c/s, c/ch, d/t, g/gu, ga/ia, gu/w, i/hi, i/y, ld/ll) are not noted; *-allus* or *-aldus* > *-au*; *-dis* > *-da*; *-mundus* > *-mon* ; *-uinus* > *-uí*. Thus, e.g.: *Adalaidis* > Adelaida; *Adalbertus* > Adalbert; *Arluuinus* > Arluí; *Arnallus* > Arnau; *Raimundus* > Ramon. In other cases, the most common Latin form is given in brackets after the first main entry. When no obvious modern equivalent exists, the name is given in *italics* as it appears in the source. Main entries for personal names (except for modern authors) are given in SMALL CAPS (with repetition indicated thus: ~), as are two-part subentries (with repetition indicated thus: ~ ~). Unidentified place names are given in *italics*. Cross-references in **bold** are to the subject index.

Abbreviations: a.=abbot/abbess; abp.=archbishop; ad.=archdeacon; bp.=bishop; b.=brother; c.=count(ess), county; d.=diocese; dép.=département (France); emp.=emperor; f.=son/daughter; h.=husband; k.=king, kingdom; m.=mother; mtns.=mountains; p.=father; pr.=prior, provost; prov.=province (Spain, Italy); r.=river; s.=sister; vc.=viscount(ess), viscounty; w.=wife

Catalan *comarcas*: ACA Alt Camp AEM Alt Empordà ANO Anoia APE Alt Penedès ARI Alta Ribagorça AUR Alt Urgell BAG Bages BAR Barcelonès BCI Baix Cinca BEB Baix Ebre BEM Baix Empordà BER Berguedà BLL Baix Llobregat BPE Baix Penedès BRI Baixa Ribagorça CBA Conca de Barberà CER Cerdanya CON Conflent FEN Fenolleda GAF Garraf GAR Garrigues GAX Garrotxa GIR Gironès LLI Llitera MAR Maresme NOG Noguera OSO Osona PJU Pallars Jussà PSO Pallars Sobirà PUR Pla d'Urgell RIP Ripollès ROS Rosselló SEL Selva SGA Segarra SGR Segrià SOL Solsonès TAR Tarragonès URG Urgell VAL Vallespir VOC Vallès Occidental VOR Vallès Oriental

Index of names

354

Index of names

ORUNDINA [*Aurundina*], 41
ORÚS [*Aurucius*], *judge*, 47, 291
Osona, *c.*, 5, 28, 31, 63, 73, 74, 145, 147, 162, 171, 223, 238, 283
Osona, *d. See* Vic, *d.*
Osona, *vc.* (from 1062 Cardona), viscounts of, 183, 185, 187. *See also* viscounts: Bermon; Bernat Amat; *Engúncia*; Ermessenda; Folc I, II; Guadall II; Guillem; Guisla; Ramon; Ramon Folc I, II
OT [*Odo*], Sant, bp. Urgell (1095–1122), 230, 252
OTGER [*Audegarius*], vc. Girona (*c.* 949–*c.* 968), 60n
Ourliac, Paul, 19–20, 23, 293

Palad, 83
Palau-sator (BEM), 190
Pallars, *c.*, 6n, 8, 13, 86, 89n, 94, 142, 143, 174, 218
Pallars, *vc.* (from *c.* 1149 Vilamur): viscounts of, 166. *See also* viscounts: Arnau Bernat; Pere Arnau III, IV
Pallars Jussà, *c.*, 16, 86, *90*, 91, 93, 94, 96, 140, 166–67, 168, 170, 213, 236, 283; counts of, 102, 236. *See also* counts: Arnau Mir; Arnau Ramon; Berenguer Ramon; Pere Ramon; Ramon III, IV; Valença
Pallars Sobirà, *c.*, 86, 140, 169, 213; counts of, 102. *See also* counts: Artau I, II, III; Guillem; Llúcia
Palomera, 179
Palou *de Sanaüja* (Torrefeta, SGA), 230
Pals (BEM), 190n
Papiol, El (BLL), 255
Paracolls (Campome, CON; dép. Pyrénées-Orientales), 243, 257
Passanant (CBA), 117
PEDRO [*Petrus*], bp. Zaragoza, *246*; ~ Ansúrez, *c.* Valladolid, 220; ~ Manrique de Lara, *c.*, 132–33
PELEGRÍN de Castillazuelo, 127
Penedès, *c.*, 145
Penedès, *region*, 104, 118, 180, 181, 182; Baix ~, 216
Peralada (orig. *Tolon*[e]; AEM), 189, 257, 265n
Peralada, *c.*, 142, 220. *See also* Empúries, *c.*
Peralada, *vc.* (from *c.* 1100 Rocabertí), 142. *See also* viscount: Jofre I
Peraleu, 263n
Peramea (Gerri de la Sal, PSO), 212–13
Peramola (AUR), 242
Perarrua (BRI), 204n
PERE [*Petrus*], 46; ~, bp. Barcelona (959–72), 181; ~, bp. Girona (1010–51), *30*, 55, 71n, *82n*, 94, 189, 190; ~ I, *c.* Barcelona, k.

Aragón (1196–1213), 2, 237, 246, 285–89; ~, f. Bertran Borrell de Casseres, 215; ~, f. Pere I (*see* Jaume I); ~, sacristan of Barcelona, 112; ~ (Sanaüja), 252n; ~ de Balenyà, 114; ~ de Banyeres, 286; ~ de Bellvís, 100; ~ de Berga, 103; ~ de Besora, 261, 267; ~ de Claramunt, 286; ~ de Lluçà, 246, 274; ~ de Montferrer, 251; ~ d'Oló, 237, 239; ~ de Puigverd, 100, 123n, 245; ~ de Puigverd, bp. Urgell (1204–30), 286; ~ de Redorta, bp. Vic (1147–85), 179, 229, 250, *289*; ~ de Santa Oliva, 286; ~ (I) de Sentmenat, 116, 124; ~ de Sirac, bp. Barcelona (1208–11), 248, 286; ~ Albert, 287; ~ Amat, *seneschal*, 79, 206–7; PERE ARNAU III, vc. Vilamur (Pallars), 251; ~ ~ IV, vc. Vilamur (Pallars), 251; ~ Berenguer, bp. Urgell (1123–41), 230, 251n, 252; ~ Bernat, br. Guillem Bernat, 117, 203n; ~ Bertran de Bell-lloc, 84, 132; ~ Folc, 236–39; ~ Geribert, 99–100; PERE GUILLEM, 115; ~ ~, a. Sant Pere d'Àger (1091–1110), 215; ~ ~, ad. Urgell, *106*; ~ Guislabert, 72; PERE MIR, grandson of Atinard, 215; ~ ~, *hostage*, 129; ~ ~ (Ponts), 72; ~ ~ (Solsona), 200–201; ~ ~ de Banyeres, p. Ponç Pere de Banyeres, 204, 235n, *242*; ~ Poc [*Paucus*], 128; PERE PONÇ, 230; ~ ~, br. Gombau, Guillem, 117; PERE RAMON, 230; ~ ~, *c.* Pallars Jussà (1098–1112), 93n, 96, 126; ~ ~, f. Ramon, 207n; ~ ~, vc. Castellbò (Alt Urgell) (1114–50), 226; ~ ~ (I) d'Erill, 139–40; ~ Rossell, 266n; ~ Tedball, 215; ~ Udalard, 200
Perpinyà (ROS), 266
PETRONILLA, c. Barcelona (w. Ramon Berenguer IV), 8, 225
PHILIP II Augustus, k. France (1179–1223), 276–77
Piera (orig. Fontanet; ANO), 40, 191n
PIERRE [*Petrus*], vc. Minerve, 148
PIETRO [*Petrus*] Uresol, doge of Venice (991–1008), 4
Pinós, *lineage* (<~ de Solsonès, SOL), 226n
Pinyana (ACA), 162
Pira (CBA), 245
Poitou, *c. See* count: Richard
Pomar (Sant Antolí i Vilanova, SGA), 179, 229
PONÇ [*Poncius*], a. Sant Sadurní de Tavèrnoles (*c.* 1031–*c.* 1055), 71; ~, a. Santa Maria d'Alaó (1150–71), *106*; ~ I Hug, c. Empúries (1040–78), *98*, 173, 203n, 256; ~, f. Ponç de Santa Fe, 129; ~, *precentor* of Girona, 201; ~, *scribe*, 273, 274; ~ III, vc. Cabrera (Girona) (1161–*c.* 1199), 129; ~ (I) de Cervera, vc. Bas (Besalú) (1127–*c.* 1130), 117; ~ (II) de Cervera, vc. Bas (Besalú) (*c.* 1145–53×55),

356

Index of names

Index of names

SUBJECT INDEX

For many commonly occurring subjects (*convenientia*, castles, oath, etc.), only general statements are indexed here, rather than every specific instance.

Cambridge Studies in Medieval Life and Thought
Fourth series

Titles in series

★ *Also published as a paperback*